The Art of the Critic

The Art of the Critic

Literary Theory and Criticism from the Greeks to the Present

Volume 8
Early Twentieth Century

EDITED WITH AN INTRODUCTION BY

HAROLD BLOOM

Sterling Professor of the Humanities, Yale University

1989
CHELSEA HOUSE PUBLISHERS
NEW YORK   PHILADELPHIA

Project Editor: S. T. Joshi
Editorial Coordinator: Karyn Gullen Browne
Copy Chief: Richard Fumosa
Editorial Staff: Neal Dolan, Jacques Denis
Design: Susan Lusk

Printed and bound in the United States of America.

Library of Congress Cataloging in Publication Data
Main entry under title:

The Art of the Critic.

    Includes bibliographies and Index.
    Contents: v. 1. Classical and medieval—   —v. 7. Later nineteenth century.—
v. 8. Early twentieth century.
    1. Criticism—Collected works. 2. Literature—
Philosophy—Collected works. I. Bloom, Harold.
PN86.A77 1985   809   84–15547
ISBN 0-87754–493–X (set)
     0-87754–501–4 (v. 8)

Contents

Index and Glossary are contained in Volume 11.

Freud and Valéry: The Literary Mind of the Early Twentieth Century

Harold Bloom

1

SIGMUND FREUD began his characteristic work in 1886, when he opened a private practice, in Vienna, for the treatment of hysteria. A decade later, just before his fortieth birthday, he began to use his personal term, "psychoanalysis," to describe his mode of therapy. Psychoanalysis still survives among us, as an isolated and disputable therapy, a particular variety of psychiatry. As such, though international in scope, it can be said to have become a small sub-branch, almost a sect, within American psychiatric medicine. Freud hated the notion that his legatees would be part of the American medical profession, since he cordially disliked both the United States and most doctors of medicine. His preference in disciples would have continued to be European intellectuals, lay analysts with broad cultural interests who could have applied the Freudian theory of the mind to every sort of cultural or social question. In some sense, Hitler destroyed Freud's world, and with it such hopes.

"Science" was Freud's prime value-term, and until his death, in 1939, he continued to insist that in psychoanalysis he had invented a science, akin to biology, and capable of contributing something to biology. Karl Kraus, the witty Viennese polemicist who was Freud's contemporary, made the famous observation that "psychoanalysis is itself that mental illness of which it purports to be the cure." This continues to be funny, and appears to be even truer now than when Kraus first said it. Psychoanalysis, according to Freud himself, employs as its chief instrument of therapy the "analytical transference," called by Freud an "artificial illness" or "false connection." Inducing a "transference neurosis" in the patient, psychoanalysis supposedly heals an authentic neurosis in the course of clearing up the artificial one. The transference is the relationship between analyst and patient, in which the analyst takes the place of the patient's parents or lovers. If Kraus was correct, then psychoanalysis in 1988 could be called a kind of universal transference neurosis, an artificial illness in which Freud is everyone's analyst, everyone's surrogate for parents and lovers.

What makes this not the full truth is the largest paradox about Freud and his work. Intended theoretically as science, and pragmatically as therapy, psychoanalysis has become something very different, and perhaps always was quite different from what Freud said he wanted it to be. A science presumably is more than a descriptive discipline, supposedly is capable of verification, and perhaps need not depend upon metaphors in its pursuit of reality. Yet all Freud's copious writing is intensely metaphorical, very little of it is verifiable, and much of it is devoted to what cannot be described.

Ludwig Wittgenstein dismissed psychoanalysis as "a powerful mythology," indeed as a mere "speculation" rather than a theory. Essentially, Wittgenstein was correct, and yet we would be unwise to emulate him in this dismissal. Freud was one of the greatest Western speculators, and was certainly the most suggestive mythmaker of the last century. Asserting that his new science was firmly founded on evidence, on practice and observation, Freud nevertheless imagined a new map of the mind, or else he discovered remarkable ways of mythologizing a Western map of the mind that had been developing for some centuries. Seeing himself as making a third with Copernicus and Darwin, Freud actually may have made a fourth in the sequence of Plato, Montaigne, and Shakespeare. The neurologist who sought a dynamic psychology seems today to have been a speculative moralist and a mythologizing dramatist of the inner life.

Freud would have rejected any classification that made his work more important as literature than as science, or even one that saw an intersection in him of such curves of importance. His stubborn insistence upon the truth made him proudly reductive, and yet he knew that his principal theories were closer to myths and metaphors than to the traditional empirical facts and observations that passed for the Western science of psychology. In his final, unfinished book, *An Outline of Psychoanalysis*, he cheerfully declared that his theory of the drives or instincts was, so to speak, his own mythology, since drives were magnificent conceptions, surpassing mere definiteness.

It may be that Freud's importance to our culture continues to increase almost in direct proportion to the waning of psychoanalysis as a therapy. His conceptions are so magnificent in their indefiniteness that they have begun to merge with our culture, and indeed now form the only Western mythology that contemporary intellectuals have in common. As with every true mythology, a diffused version of psychoanalysis has become a common possession of most people in middle-class Western society, who may not be particularly intellectual, and doubtless are not always aware that psychoanalysis has provided the psychology in which they can believe, without continual reflection or conscious effort. What anyone finds possible to believe, without self-questioning, is necessarily myth, whether or not it also purports to be religion

Few recent writers on Freud would agree with much that I am saying, and no psychoanalysts would, but Freud is the most persuasive of modern discursive writers, and he is difficult to resist when he is read deeply. He is a powerful rhetorician, a subtle ironist, and probably the most fascinating of all really tendentious writers in the Western intellectual tradition. His general theory of the mind not only has the speculative force of a great metaphysician, like Plato, but it also has the personal moral urgency of the greatest of essayists, Montaigne, and an astonishingly Shakespearean eloquence as well. More than the Freudian eloquence, and the Freudian sense of drama, is Shakespearean. The more deeply I read Freud, the more I learn to see the Shakespearean representation of human personality and motivation emerging, but emerging in a codified and rationalized form. Perhaps we need a Shakespearean interpretation of Freud rather more than we need further Freudian interpretations of Shakespeare.

Freud wished us to believe that psychoanalysis was a method of interpretation, but it is more an interpretation than it is a method. What that interpretation is has been much disputed by Freud's best exegetes, and evidently always will be disputed. If one of the marks of major literature is its uncanny ability to evoke endlessly diverse readings, then Freud matches nearly any difficult and original writer who has informed our culture in ways that are inescapable. Setting aside versions of Freud that seem to me fantastic, however fashionable (they are mostly French, or French-inspired), the principal schools of interpretation of Freud (as opposed to Freudian interpretations, or interpretations purporting to be Freudian) would include those grounded in: history; social psychology—Marxist or otherwise—; sociology; philosophy—whether analytical or idealist—; humanism, whether secular or religious; socio-biology; and lastly, literary criticism, of whatever variety. I will give an instance of each of these, but only briefly, and will then sum up the tribute that all these approaches necessarily make to Freud's mythologizing power.

Like Carl E. Schorske's *Fin-de-siècle Vienna: Politics and Culture* (1980), which related the image of parricide in Freud's *Interpretation of Dreams* (1900) to contemporary Viennese politics and culture, William J. McGrath's recent *Freud's Discovery of Psychoanalysis: The Politics of Hysteria* traces the Freudian emphasis upon fantasy to political considerations. Frustrated by a political reality that drove Jewish intellectuals into neurotic compulsiveness, Freud (on this interpretation) opted for a counterpolitical drive into the fantasy-dominated cosmos of early childhood. McGrath can thus conclude that: "Freud's interpretation represented a wish-fulfillment no less than the dream itself—the wish to free himself from the power of politics."

In the very different interpretation of the late Herbert Marcuse, political philosopher and social psychologist, Freud ultimately expressed "the accumulated guilt of mankind against its victims," a guilt that darkened, for Freud and for us, "the prospect of a civilization without repression." This is again very different from the interpretative vision of the sociologist Philip Rieff, whose Freud "restored to science its ethical verve," and who wisely remarked that Freud's "moralizing is of the sort peculiar to our age, most effective when executed with a bad conscience."

The most impressive interpreter of Freud to emerge from analytical philosophy, Richard Wollheim, shrewdly wrote that Freud's work "was a research into the deafness of the mind," a research undertaken by a rational pessimist who believed that finally reason would prevail, but refused to prophesy when or how that might come about. Paul Ricoeur, idealist philosopher and religious humanist, insisted that Freud saw religion as "more an art of bearing the hardships of life than an indefinite exorcism of the paternal accusation." That is subtly different from the judgment of Lionel Trilling, literary critic and secular humanist, who wrote that "Freud, in insisting upon the essential immitigability of the human condition as determined by the nature of the mind, had the intention of sustaining the authenticity of human existence that formerly had been ratified by God."

The socio-biological interpretation of Freud, widely divergent from all I have cited, received its strong statement in Frank J. Sulloway's *Freud, Biologist of the Mind* (1979). Following the Harvard socio-biologist Edward O. Wilson, Sulloway argued that: "Perhaps no one synthesized the biological assumptions of his scientific generation more boldly than did Freud." Sulloway's Freud is thus "a crypto-biologist even in his lifetime," someone who could not get beyond his historical debt to nineteenth-century biology.

A very different interpretation of Freud, my own, would begin with a literary critic's realization that Freud's relation to his nineteenth-century scientific precursors is precisely similar to that of later Romantic poets to their forerunners. What Sulloway sees as a reliance upon biology becomes instead Freud's overcoming of his own anxieties of influence, and psychoanalysis is thus revealed as a triumphantly strong and deliberate misreading of nineteenth-century biology.

All of these interpretations—McGrath's, Marcuse's, Rieff's, Wollheim's, Ricoeur's, Trilling's, Sulloway's, my own—bear both voluntary and involuntary witness to Freud's uncanny mythological power. McGrath underestimates Freud's analytical ability to apprehend the possible causes for any theorist's fixation upon the human tendency to fantasize, including Freud's own, so that McGrath is not so much mistaken as he is less comprehensive than Freud. Marcuse's moving sense of guilt is not shared by Freud, who seems to me closer to Rieff's irony that moralizing, in our age, is most effective when done with a bad conscience, yet Freud can contain both Marcuse and Rieff equally well. Doubtless, Freud would have approved Wollheim's emphasis upon the disenchantments of reason, but I suspect that Freud invariably was perfectly happy to make surmises upon the basis of little or no evidence, which is highly contrary to Wollheim's expectations of Freud.

I suspect also that Freud contains both Ricoeur's and Trilling's views of religion, since the Freudian reality principle is ultimately a taking into account all the conditions imposed upon us by nature, which means coming to terms with the necessity of dying. The Freudian severity thus could accept religion as an art of bearing the hardships of life while also refusing every aspect of religion except its tragic sense. Sulloway's sense of Freud's bondage to his immediate scientific tradition, and my opposing sense that Freud's originality stemmed from his aggression and ambition in his agon with biology, can both find sanction in differing aspects of Freud's understanding of the ambivalent relations between human generations.

We are left, I think, with the clash of interpretations, and with Freud's cultural strength, as great in its way as the force of Plato, Montaigne, and Shakespeare. No twentieth-century writer—not even Proust or Joyce or Kafka—rivals Freud's position as the central imagination of our age. We turn to Freud when we wish to read someone absolutely relevant on any matter that torments or concerns us: love, jealousy, envy, masochism, cruelty, possessiveness, fetishism, curiosity, humor, or what we will. Like Plato, Montaigne, Shakespeare, Freud is endlessly suggestive, and brimming with insight on all these matters and more, always much more. Does it matter that Freud's scientific "explanation" of these crucial subjects nearly always fails to distinguish between a reason and a cause, as Wittgenstein accurately complained? We do not care when Montaigne confuses reasons and causes, and I suspect that Wittgenstein knew that Freud was hardly damaged by such a confusion either. Myth confounds reasons and causes, and achieves its power to affect us partly by way of such amalgamations.

Freud's cultural pervasiveness seems to me ultimately to stem from his unique powers of contamination. If you dispute Freud, he contaminates you anyway, and his interpretations insinuate themselves into your consciousness. Montaigne and Shakespeare wrote in the intellectually generous time of the Renaissance, when contamination was a more joyous phenomenon in intellectual relationships than it is now. Freud has contaminated every twentieth-century intellectual discipline, and this in a time when each discipline fights desperately for its own ground. "Great havoc makes he among our originalities," Emerson ruefully observed of Plato, and Emerson came near to saying the same of Montaigne and of Shakespeare. We must say of Freud: after him there is only commentary. I conclude by returning to Emerson on Plato in *Representative Men,* because what Emerson says of Plato there seems to me true of Freud also:

> There never was such range of speculation. Out of Plato come all things that are still written and debated among men of thought. Great havoc makes he among our originalities. We have reached the mountain from which all these drift boulders were detached . . .

2

In the Preface to his *Leonardo Poe Mallarmé,* Valéry calls these precursors "three masters of the art of abstraction." "Man fabricates by abstraction" is a famous Valérian formula, reminding us that this sense of abstraction is Latin: "withdrawn, taken out from, removed." "It Must Be Abstract," the first part of Stevens' *Notes toward a Supreme Fiction,* moves in the atmosphere of an American version of Valéry's insight, but the American is Walt Whitman and not Edgar Poe:

> The weather and the giant of the weather,
> Say the weather, the mere weather, the mere air:
> An abstraction blooded, as a man by thought.

Valéry fabricates by withdrawing from a stale reality, which he refuses to associate with the imaginings of his masters. These "enchanted, dominated me, and—as was only fitting—tormented me as well; the beautiful is that which fills us with despair." Had Valéry spoken of pain, rather than despair, he would have been more Nietzschean. The genealogy of imagination is not truly Valéry's subject. Despair is not a staleness in reality, or an absence of it; it is the overwhelming presence of reality, of the reality-principle, or the necessity of death-in-life, or simply of dying. Valéry's beautiful *Palme* concludes with a metaphor that seems central to all of his poetry:

> *Pareille a celui qui pense*
> *Et dont l'âme se depense*
> *A s'accoutre de ses dons!*

The palm is the image of a mind so rich in thinking that the gifts of its own soul augment it constantly. That may be one of the origins of Stevens' death-poem, "Of Mere Being," but Valéry's palm is less pure and less flickering than Stevens' final emblem. The two poets and poetic thinkers do not much resemble one another, despite Stevens' yearning regard for Valéry. Perhaps the largest difference is in the attitudes towards precursors. Valéry is lucid and candid, and confronts Mallarmé. Stevens insists that he does not read Whitman, condemns Whitman for his tramp *persona,* and yet he cannot cease revising Whitman's poems in his own poems. But then that is how Whitman came to discuss his relation to Ralph Waldo Emerson, so clearly they order these matters differently in America.

In a meditation of 1919 on "The Intellectual Crisis," Valéry memorably depicted the European Hamlet staring at millions of ghosts:

> But he is an intellectual Hamlet. He meditates on the life and death of truths. For phantoms he has all the subjects of our controversies; for regrets he has all our titles to glory; he bows under the weight of discoveries and learning, unable to renounce and unable to resume this limitless activity. He reflects on the boredom of recommencing the past, on the folly of always striving to be original. He wavers between one abyss and the other, for two dangers still threaten the world: order and disorder.

This retains its force nearly seventy years later, just as it would baffle us if its subject were the American Hamlet. Valéry's fear was that Europe might "become *what she is in reality*: that is, a little cape of the Asiatic continent." The fear was prophetic, though the prophecy fortunately is not yet wholly fulfilled. When Valéry writes in this mode, he is principally of interest to editorial writers and newspaper columnists of the weightier variety. Yet his concern for European culture, perhaps a touch too custodial, is a crucial element in all his prose writing. Meditating upon Descartes, the archetypal French intellect, Valéry states the law of his own nature: "Descartes is, above all, a man of intentional action." Consciousness was for Valéry an intentional adventure, and this sense of deliberate quest in the cultivation of consciousness is partly what makes Valéry a central figure of the Western literary intellect.

The Art of the Critic

George Bernard Shaw

1856–1950

George Bernard Shaw was born into a Protestant family in Dublin on July 26, 1856. At an early age he was exposed to music by George John Vandeleur Lee, an unusual musician who lived with the Shaws during the 1860s and early 1870s as the third partner in a loveless marriage. A Catholic, Lee may have been responsible for Mrs. Shaw's lack of Protestant fervor and George's brief attendance at a Dublin Catholic school. At age sixteen Shaw began working in a land agent's office as a rent collector. When Lee moved to London in 1875 Shaw's mother and two sisters followed him, forsaking George's father forever. A few years later the young Shaw left Dublin to join his mother in London.

Shaw worked several years for the Edison Telephone Company and spent much of his free time reading. In 1882 he became a Socialist and eagerly read the works of Marx. He also became a vegetarian during these early years in London as he tried to find his literary voice. During the mid-1880s Shaw began to associate with the newly founded Fabian Society, a middle-class Socialist group for which he was a prolific pamphleteer and frequent orator. Shaw later helped found the Labour Party and maintained a lifelong interest in progressive politics. During these late Victorian years he also worked as a journalist, first as an art critic and later as a music and theatre critic. Shaw's music pieces were highly regarded and are still read today, especially *The Perfect Wagnerite* (1898). His theatre criticism tended to praise the new realistic works of playwrights like Ibsen. Shaw wrote the first English book on his Norwegian counterpart, *The Quintessence of Ibsenism* (1891).

Shaw's own career as a writer began in the 1870s soon after his arrival in London. He wrote several unsuccessful novels, most of which were not published until much later in his career. Perhaps the best of his early works, *Cashel Byron's Profession* (1882), deals with one of Shaw's favorite subjects, boxing. As a failed fiction writer Shaw began work on a dramatic collaboration with William Archer in 1884. Although the project was soon abandoned, eight years later Shaw revived their effort and presented his first play, *Widowers' Houses* (1892). A play of economic metaphors and Socialist philosophy, it was followed by *The Philanderer, Mrs. Warren's Profession,* and *Arms and the Man.* Although because of stage censorship

3

The Philanderer and *Mrs. Warren's Profession* were not performed until ten years later, by 1895 Shaw had become a major force in the British theatre.

After several affairs with married and divorced women, he married Charlotte Payne-Townshend in 1898. Of Irish stock, she had nursed Shaw during a brief illness. Although they were married for forty-five years, their union lacked passion. Shaw liked to think of himself as a philanderer and he often engaged in flirtatious epistolary relationships. One of his long-standing admirers, Mrs. Stella Patrick, served as the model for Eliza Doolittle in *Pygmalion*.

By 1914 Shaw had written several more masterpieces, including *Man and Superman, Major Barbara, Pygmalion*, and *Caesar and Cleopatra;* during the war he wrote a memorable pamphlet, *Common Sense about War* (1914), which is reminiscent of Swift's prose. Shaw's next major effort was *Heartbreak House*, a highly acclaimed play first performed in 1920. Following the canonization of Joan of Arc in 1920 Shaw began work on an earlier idea for a play. The result was *Saint Joan* (1923), which contributed greatly to his winning the Nobel Prize for Literature in 1925. Although Shaw accepted the award, the prize money was used to translate Swedish works, especially Strindberg's plays, into English.

Shaw's wife died in 1943 and he retired to his country home at Ayot St. Lawrence, Hertfordshire. He continued to write into his nineties. In 1938 he won the Academy Award for Best Screenplay for the movie version of *Pygmalion*. He died at the age of ninety-four, on November 2, 1950, at his Hertfordshire home. The curious terms of his will directed his estate's trustees to publish all his works under the name Bernard Shaw. He also requested that most of his vast wealth be used in an effort to reform English spelling by use of a forty-letter phonetic alphabet. His main beneficiaries, several British and Irish cultural organizations, successfully contested this clause and now receive the majority of the income from Shaw's estate.

Much of Shaw's best criticism is embodied in the sometimes extensive prefaces to his plays, especially those for *Man and Superman* and *Heartbreak House*. In an early paper, "The Sanity of Art" (1895), Shaw defends modern literature and music from the attacks of Max Nordau in his famous treatise, *Degeneration* (1895), which accused Ruskin, the Pre-Raphaelites, Wagner, and other artists of ushering in a period of morbidity and decadence.

THE SANITY OF ART

Impressionism

When I was engaged chiefly in the criticism of pictures, the Impressionist movement was struggling for life in London; and I supported it vigorously because, being the outcome of heightened attention and quickened consciousness on the part of its disciples, it was evidently destined to improve pictures greatly by substituting a natural, observant, real style for a conventional, taken-for-granted, ideal one. The result has entirely justified my choice of sides. I can remember when Whistler, bent on forcing the public to observe the qualities he was introducing into pictorial work, had to exhibit a fine drawing of a girl with the head deliberately crossed out with a few rough pencil strokes, knowing perfectly well that if he left a woman's face discernible the British philistine would simply look to see whether she was a pretty girl or not, or whether she represented some of his pet characters in fiction, and pass on without having seen any of the qualities of artistic execution which made the drawing valuable. But it was easier for the critics to resent the obliteration of the face as an insolent eccentricity, and to shew their own good manners by writing of Mr Whistler as Jimmy, than to think out what he meant. It took several years of 'propaganda by deed' before the qualities which the Impressionists insisted on came to be looked for as matters of course in pictures; so that at last the keen picture-gallery frequenter, when he came face to face with Bouguereau's 'Girl in a Cornfield,' could no longer accept it as a window-glimpse of nature, because he saw at once that the girl is really standing in a studio with what the house agents call a good north light, and that the cornfield is a conventional sham. This advance in the education of our art fanciers was effected by persistently exhibiting pictures which, like Whistler's girl with her head scratched out, were propagandist samples of workmanship rather than complete works of art. But the moment Whistler and his party forced the dealers and the societies of painters to exhibit these studies, and, by doing so, to accustom the public to tolerate what appeared to it at first to be absurdities, the door was necessarily opened to real absurdities. Artists of doubtful or incomplete vocation find it difficult to draw or paint well; but it is easy for them to smudge paper or canvas so as to suggest a picture just as the stains on an old ceiling or the dark spots in a glowing coal-fire do. Plenty of rubbish of this kind was produced, exhibited and tolerated at the time when people could not see the difference between any daub in which there were aniline shadows and a landscape by Monet. Not that they thought the daub as good as the Monet: they thought the Monet as ridiculous as the daub; but they were afraid to say so, because they had discovered that people who were good judges did not think Monet ridiculous.

Then, beside the mere impostors, there were certain unaffected and conscientious painters who produced abnormal pictures because they saw abnormally. My own sight happened to be 'normal' in the oculist's sense; that is, I saw things with the naked eye as most people can only be made to see them by the aid of spectacles. Once I had a discussion with an artist who was shewing me a clever picture of his in which the parted lips in a pretty woman's face revealed what seemed to me like a mouthful of virgin snow. The painter lectured me for not consulting my eyes instead of my knowledge of facts. 'You don't see the divisions in a set of teeth when you look at a person's mouth,' he said, 'all you see is a strip of white, or yellow, or pearl, as the case may be. But because you know, as a matter of anatomic fact, that there are divisions there, you want to have them represented by strokes in a drawing. That is just like you art critics, etc., etc.' I do not think he believed me when I told him that when I looked at a row of teeth, I saw, not only the divisions between them, but their exact shape, both in contour and in modelling, just as well as I saw their general color. Some of the most able of the Impressionists evidently did not see forms as definitely as they appreciated color relationship; and, since there is always a great deal of imitation in the arts, we soon had young painters with perfectly good sight looking at landscapes or at their models with their eyes half closed and a little asquint, until what they saw looked to them like one of their favorite master's pictures.

Further, the Impressionist movement led to a busy study of the atmosphere, conventionally supposed to be invisible, but seldom really completely so, and of what were called values: that is, the relation of light and dark between the various objects depicted, on the correctness of which relation truth of effect largely depends. This, though very difficult in full outdoor light with the various colors brilliantly visible, was comparatively easy in gloomy rooms where the absence of light reduced all colors to masses of brown or grey of varying depth. Whistler's portrait of Sarasate, a masterpiece in its way, would look like a study in monochrome if hung beside a portrait by Holbein; and the little bouquets of color with which he sometimes decorates his female sitters, exquisite as the best of them are, have the character of enamel, of mosaic, of jewellery, never of primitive nature. His disciples could paint dark interiors, or figures placed apparently in coal cellars, with admirable truth and delicacy of values whilst they were still helplessly unable to represent a green tree or a blue sky, much less paint an interior with the light and local color as clear as they are in the works of Peter de Hooghe. Naturally the public eye, with its utilitarian familiarity with local color, and its Philistine insensibility to values and atmosphere, did not at first see what the Impressionists were driving at, and dismissed them as mere perverse, notoriety-hunting cranks.

Here, then, you had a movement wholly beneficial and progressive, and in no sense insane or decadent. Nevertheless it led to the public exhibition of daubs which even the authors themselves would never have presumed to offer for exhibition before; it betrayed aberrations of vision in painters who, on the old academic lines, would have hidden their defects by drawing objects (teeth for instance) as they knew them to exist, and not as they saw them; it set clear-sighted students practising optical distortion, so as to see things myopically and astigmatically; and it substituted canvases which looked like enlargements of under-exposed photographs for the familiar portraits of masters of the hounds in cheerfully unmistakable pink coats, mounted on bright chestnut horses. All of which, and much else, to a man who looked on without any sense of the deficiencies in conventional painting, necessarily suggested that the Impressionists and their contemporaries were much less sane than their fathers.

Wagnerism

Again, my duties as a musical critic compelled me to ascertain very carefully the exact bearings of the controversy which has raged round Wagner's music-dramas since the middle of the century. When you and I last met, we were basking in the sun between the acts of *Parsifal* at Bayreuth; but experience has taught me that an American may appear at Bayreuth without being necessarily fonder than most men of a technical discussion on music. Let me therefore put the case to you in a mercifully intelligible way. Music is like drawing, in that it can be purely decorative, or purely dramatic, or anything between the two. A draughtsman may be a pattern-designer like William Morris, or he may be a delineator of life and character, like Ford Madox Brown. Or he may come between these two extremes, and treat scenes of life and character in a decorative way, like Walter Crane or Burne-Jones: both of them consummate pattern-designers, whose subject-pictures and illustrations are also fundamentally figure-patterns, prettier than Madox Brown's, but much less convincingly alive. Do you realize that in music we have these same alternative applications of the art to drama and decoration? You can compose a graceful, symmetrical sound-pattern that exists solely for the sake of its own grace and symmetry. Or you can compose music to heighten the expression of human emotion; and such music will be intensely affecting in the presence of that emotion and utter nonsense apart from it. For examples of pure pattern-designing in music I should have to go back to the old music of the thirteenth, fourteenth, and fifteenth centuries, before the operatic movement gained the upper hand; but I am afraid my assertions that much of this music is very beautiful, and hugely superior to the stuff our music publishers turn out today, would not be believed in America; for when I hinted at something of the kind lately in the American Musical Courier, and pointed out also the beauty of the instruments for which this old music was written (viols, virginals and so on), one of your leading musical critics rebuked me with an expatiation on the superiority (meaning apparently the greater loudness) of the modern concert grand pianoforte, and contemptuously ordered the Middle Ages out from the majestic presence of the nineteenth century.[1] You must take my word for it that in England alone a long line of composers, from Henry VIII to Lawes and Purcell, have left us quantities of instrumental music which was neither dramatic music nor descriptive music, but was designed to affect the hearer solely by its beauty of sound and grace and ingenuity of pattern. This is the art which Wagner called absolute music. It is represented today by the formal sonata and symphony; and we are coming back to it in something like its old integrity by a post-Wagnerian reaction led by that greatly gifted absolute musician and hopelessly commonplace and tedious homilist, Johannes Brahms.

To understand the present muddle, you must know that modern dramatic music did not appear as an independent branch of musical art, but as an adulteration of decorative music. The first modern dramatic composers accepted as binding on them the rules of good pattern-designing in sound; and this absurdity was made to appear practicable by the fact that Mozart had such an extraordinary command of his art that his operas contain numbers which, though they seem to follow that dramatic play of emotion and character without reference to any other consideration whatever, are seen, on examining them from the point of view of the absolute musician, to be symmetrical sound-patterns. But these *tours de force* were no real justification for imposing the laws of pattern-designing on other dramatic musicians; and even Mozart himself broke away from them in all directions, and was violently attacked by his contemporaries for doing so, the accusations levelled at him (absence of melody, illegitimate and discordant harmonic progressions and monstrous abuse of the orchestra) being exactly those with which the opponents of Wagner so often pester ourselves. Wagner, whose leading lay characteristic was his enormous common-sense, completed the emancipation of the dramatic musician from these laws of pattern-designing; and we now have operas, and very good ones too, written by composers like Bruneau, who are not musicians in the old sense at all: that is, they are not pattern-designers; they do not compose music apart from drama; and when they have to furnish their operas with dances, instrumental intermezzos or the like, they either take themes from the dramatic part of their operas and rhapsodize on them, or else they turn out some perfectly simple song or dance tune, at the cheapness of which Haydn would have laughed, and give it an air of momentousness by orchestral and harmonic fineries.

If I add now that music in the academic, professorial, Conservative, respectable sense always means decorative music, and that students are taught that the laws of pattern-designing are binding on all musicians, and that violations of them are absolutely 'wrong'; and if I mention incidentally that these laws are themselves confused by the survivals from a still older tradition based on the Church art, technically very highly specialized, of writing perfectly smooth and beautiful vocal harmony for unaccompanied voices, worthy to be sung by angelic doctors round the throne of God (this was Palestrina's art), you will understand why all the professional musicians who could not see beyond the routine they were taught, and all the men and women (and there are many of them) who have little or no sense of drama, but a very keen sense of beauty of sound and prettiness of pattern in music, regarded Wagner as a madman who was reducing music to chaos, perversely introducing ugly and brutal sounds into a region where beauty and grace had reigned alone, and substituting an incoherent, aimless, formless, endless meandering for the old familiar symmetrical tunes like Pop Goes the Weasel, in which the second and third lines repeat, or nearly repeat, the pattern of the first and second; so that anyone can remember and treasure them like nursery rhymes. It was the unprofessional, 'unmusical' public which caught the dramatic clue, and saw order and power, strength and sanity, in the supposed Wagner chaos; and now, his battle being won and overwon, the professors, to avert the ridicule of their pupils, are compelled to explain (quite truly) that Wagner's technical procedure in music is almost pedantically logical and grammatical; that the Lohengrin and Tristan preludes are masterpieces of the form proper to their aim; and that his disregard of 'false relations', and his free use of the most extreme discords without 'preparation', are straight and sensible instances of that natural development of harmony which has proceeded continuously from the days when common six-four chords were considered 'wrong', and such free use of unprepared dominant sevenths and minor ninths as had become common in Mozart's time would have seemed the maddest cacophony.[2]

The dramatic development also touched purely instrumental music. Liszt tried hard to extricate himself from pianoforte arabesques, and become a tone poet like his friend Wagner. He wanted his symphonic poems to express emotions and their development. And he defined the emotion by connecting it with some known story, poem or even picture: Mazeppa, Victor Hugo's *Les Préludes*, Kaulbach's *Die Hunnenschlacht*, or the like. But the moment you try to make an instrumental composition follow a story, you are forced to abandon the decorative pattern forms, since all patterns consist of some form which is repeated over and over again, and which generally consists in itself of a repetition of two similar halves. For example, if you take a playing-card (say the five of diamonds) as a simple example of a pattern, you find not only that the diamond figure is repeated five times, but that each side of each pip is a reversed duplicate of the other. Now, the established form for a symphony is essentially a pattern form involving just such symmetrical repetitions; and, since a story does not repeat itself, but pursues a continuous chain of fresh incident and correspondingly varied emotions, Liszt had either to find a new musical form for his musical poems, or else face the intolerable anomalies and absurdities which spoil the many attempts made by Mendelssohn, Raff and others, to handcuff the old form to the new matter. Consequently he invented the symphonic poem, a perfectly simple and fitting commonsense form for his purpose, and one which makes *Les Préludes* much plainer sailing for the ordinary hearer than Mendelssohn's Melusine overture or Raff's Lenore or Im Walde symphonies, in both of which the formal repetitions would stamp Raff as a madman if we did not know that they were mere superstitions, which he had not the strength of mind to shake off as Liszt did. But still, to the people who would not read Liszt's explanations and cared nothing for his purpose, who had no taste for symphonic poetry, and consequently insisted on judging the symphonic poems as sound-patterns, Liszt must needs appear, like Wagner, a perverse egotist with something fundamentally disordered in his intellect; in short, a lunatic.

The sequel was the same as in the Impressionist movement. Wagner, Berlioz, and Liszt, in securing tolerance for their own works, secured it for what sounded to many people absurd; and this tolerance necessarily extended to a great deal of stuff which was really absurd, but which the secretly bewildered critics dared not denounce, lest it, too, should turn out to be great, like the music of Wagner, over which they had made the most ludicrous exhibition of their incompetence. Even at such stupidly conservative concerts as those of the London Philharmonic Society I have seen ultra-modern composers, supposed to be representatives of the Wagnerian movement, conducting pretentious rubbish in no essential superior to Jullien's British Army Quadrilles. And then, of course, there are the young imitators, who are corrupted by the desire to make their harmonies sound like those of the masters whose purposes and principles of work they are too young to understand, and who fall between the old forms and the new into simple incoherence.

Here, again, you see, you have a progressive, intelligent, wholesome and thoroughly sane movement in art, producing plenty of evidence to prove the case of any clever man who does not understand music, but who has a theory which involves the proposition that all the leaders of the art movements of our time are degenerate and, consequently, retrogressive lunatics.

Ibsenism

There is no need for me to go at any great length into the grounds on which any development in our moral views must at first appear insane and blasphemous to people who are satisfied, or more than satisfied, with the current morality. Perhaps you remember the opening chapters of my *Quintessence of Ibsenism,* in which I shewed why the London press, now abjectly polite to Ibsen, received him four years ago with a shriek of horror. Every step in morals is made by challenging the validity of the existing conception of perfect propriety of conduct; and when a man does that, he must look out for a very different reception from the painter who has ventured to paint a shadow brilliant lilac, or the composer who ends his symphony with an unresolved discord. Heterodoxy in art is at worst rated as eccentricity or folly: heterodoxy in morals is at once rated as scoundrelism, and, what is worse, propagandist scoundrelism, which must, if successful, undermine society and brings us back to barbarism after a period of decadence like that which brought imperialist Rome to its downfall. Your function as a philosophic Anarchist in American society is to combat the attempts that are constantly being made to arrest development by using the force of the State to suppress all departures from those habits of the majority which it pretentiously calls its morals. You must find the modern democratic voter a very troublesome person, chicken-heartedly diffident as to the value of his opinions on the technics of art or science, about which he can learn all that there is to be known, but cocksure about right and wrong in morals, politics and religion, about which he can at best only guess at the depth and danger of his ignorance. Happily, this cocksureness is not confined to the Conservatives. Shelley was as cocksure as the dons who expelled him from Oxford. It is true that the revolutionist of twenty-five, who sees nothing for it but a clean sweep of all our institutions, finds himself, at forty, accepting and even clinging to them on condition of a few reforms to bring them up to date. But he does not wait patiently for this reconciliation. He expresses his (or her) early dissatisfaction with the wisdom of his elders loudly and irreverently, and formulates his heresy as a faith. He demands the abolition of marriage, of the State, of the Church; he preaches the divinity of love and the heroism of the man who believes in himself and dares do the thing he wills; he contemns the slavery to duty and discipline which has left so many soured old people with nothing but envious regrets for a virtuous youth. He recognizes his gospel in such utterances as that quoted by Nordau from Brandes: 'To obey one's senses is to have character. He who allows himself to be guided by his passions has individuality.' For my part, I am not at all afraid of this doctrine, either in Brandes's form or in the older form: 'He that is unjust, let him be unjust still; and he which is filthy, let him be filthy still; and he that is righteous, let him be righteous still; and he that is holy, let him be holy still.' But Nordau expresses his horror of Brandes with all the epithets he can command: 'debauchery, dissoluteness, depravity disguised as modernity, bestial instincts, *maître de plaisir,* egomaniacal Anarchist', and such sentences as the following:

> It is comprehensible that an educator who turns the schoolroom into a tavern and a brothel should have success and a crowd of followers. He certainly runs the risk of being slain by the parents if they come to know what he is teaching their children; but the pupils will hardly complain and will be eager to attend the lessons of so agreeable a teacher. This is the explanation of the influence Brandes gained over the youth of his country, such as his writings, with their emptiness of thought and unending tattle, would certainly never have procured for him.

To appreciate this spluttering, you must know that it is immediately followed by an attack on Ibsen for the weakness of 'obsession by the doctrine of original sin'. Yet what would the passage I have just quoted be without the doctrine of original sin as a postulate? If 'the heart of man is deceitful above all things, and desperately wicked', then, truly, the man who allows himself to be guided by his passions must needs be a scoundrel; and his teacher might well be slain by his parents. But how if the youth thrown helpless on his passions found that honesty, that self-respect, that hatred of cruelty and injustice, that the desire for soundness and health and efficiency, were master passions; nay, that their excess is so dangerous to youth that it is part of the wisdom of age to say to the young: 'Be not righteous overmuch: why shouldst thou destroy thyself?' I am sure, my dear Tucker, your friends have paraphrased that in vernacular American often enough in remonstrating with you for your Anarchism, which defies not only God, but even the wisdom of the United States Congress. On the other hand, the people who profess to renounce and abjure their own passions, and ostentatiously regulate their conduct by the most convenient interpretation of what the Bible means, or, worse still, by their ability to find reasons for it (as if there were not excellent reasons to be found for every conceivable course of conduct, from dynamiting and vivisection to martyrdom), seldom need a warning against being righteous overmuch, their attention, indeed, often needing a rather pressing jog in the opposite direction.

Passion is the steam in the engine of all religious and moral systems. In so far as it is malevolent, the religious are malevolent too, and insist on human sacrifices, on hell, wrath, and vengeance. You cannot read Browning's *Caliban upon Setebos* (Natural Theology in The Island) without admitting that all our religions have been made as Caliban made his, and that the difference between Caliban and Prospero is not that Prospero has killed passion in himself whilst Caliban has yielded to it, but that Prospero is mastered by holier passions than Caliban's. Abstract principles of conduct break down in practice because kindness and truth and justice are not duties founded on abstract principles external to man, but human passions, which have, in their time, conflicted with higher passions as well as with lower ones. If a young woman, in a mood of strong reaction against the preaching of duty and self-sacrifice and the rest of it, were to tell me that she was determined not to murder her own instincts and throw away her life in obedience to a mouthful of empty phrases, I should say to her 'By all means do as you propose. Try how wicked you can be: it is precisely the same experiment as trying how good you can be. At worst you will only find out the sort of person you really are. At best you will find that your passions, if you really and honestly let them all loose impartially, will discipline you with a severity which your conventional friends, abandoning themselves to the mechanical routine of fashion, could not stand for a day.' As a matter of fact, we have seen over and over again this comedy of the 'emancipated' young enthusiast flinging duty and religion, convention and parental authority, to the winds, only to find herself, for the first time in her life, plunged into duties, responsibilities, and sacrifices from which she is often glad to retreat, after a few years' wearing down of her enthusiasm, into the comparatively loose life of an ordinary respectable woman of fashion.

Why Law Is Indispensable

The truth is, laws, religions, creeds and systems of ethics, instead of making society better than its best unit, make it worse than its average unit, because they are never up to date. You will ask me: 'Why have them at all?' I will tell you. They are made necessary, though we all secretly detest them, by the fact that the number of people who can think out a line of conduct for themselves even on one point is very small, and the number who can afford the time for it still smaller. Nobody can afford the time to do it on all points. The professional thinker may on occasion make his own morality and philosophy as the cobbler may make his own boots; but the ordinary man of business must buy at the shop, so to speak, and put up with what he finds on sale there, whether it exactly suits him or not, because he can neither make a morality for himself nor do without one. This typewriter with which I am writing is the best I can get; but it is by no means a perfect instrument; and I have not the

smallest doubt that in fifty years' time authors will wonder how men could
have put up with so clumsy a contrivance. When a better one is invented I shall
buy it; until then, not being myself an inventor, I must make the best of it, just
as my Protestant and Roman Catholic and Agnostic friends make the best of
their imperfect creeds and systems. Oh, Father Tucker, worshipper of Liberty,
where shall we find a land where the thinking and moralizing can be done
without division of labor?

Besides, what have deep thinking and moralizing to do with the most
necessary and least questionable side of law? Just consider how much we need
law in matters which have absolutely no moral bearing at all. Is there anything
more aggravating than to be told, when you are socially promoted, and are not
quite sure how to behave yourself in the circles you enter for the first time, that
good manners are merely a matter of good sense, and that rank is but the
guinea's stamp: the man's the gowd for a' that? Imagine taking the field with
an army which knew nothing except that the soldier's duty is to defend his
country bravely, and think, not of his own safety, nor of home and beauty, but
of ENGLAND! Or of leaving the traffic of Piccadilly or Broadway to proceed on the
understanding that every driver should keep to that side of the road which
seemed to him to promote the greatest happiness of the greatest number! Or of
stage-managing *Hamlet* by assuring the Ghost that whether he entered from
the right or the left could make no difference to the greatness of Shakespear's
play, and that all he need concern himself about was holding the mirror up to
nature! Law is never so necessary as when it has no ethical significance
whatever, and is pure law for the sake of law. The law that compels me to keep
to the left when driving along Oxford Street is ethically senseless, as is shewn
by the fact that keeping to the right answers equally well in Paris; and it
certainly destroys my freedom to choose my side; but by enabling me to count
on everyone else keeping to the left also, thus making traffic possible and safe,
it enlarges my life and sets my mind free for nobler issues. Most laws, in short,
are not the expression of the ethical verdicts of the community, but pure
etiquet and nothing else. What they do express is the fact that over most of the
field of social life there are wide limits within which it does not matter what
people do, though it matters enormously whether under given circumstances
you can depend on their all doing the same thing. The wasp, who can be
depended on absolutely to sting you if you squeeze him, is less of a nuisance
than the man who tries to do business with you not according to the customs
of business, but according to the Sermon on the Mount, or than the lady who
dines with you and refuses, on republican and dietetic principles, to allow
precedence to a duchess or to partake of food which contains uric acid. The
ordinary man cannot get through the world without being told what to do at
every turn, and basing such calculations as he is capable of on the assumption
that everyone else will calculate on the same assumptions. Even your man of
genius accepts a hundred rules for every one he challenges; and you may lodge
in the same house with an Anarchist for ten years without noticing anything
exceptional about him. Martin Luther, the priest, horrified the greater half of
Christendom by marrying a nun, yet was a submissive conformist in countless

ways, living orderly as a husband and father, wearing what his bootmaker and tailor made for him, and dwelling in what the builder built for him, although he would have died rather than take his Church from the Pope. And when he got a Church made by himself to his liking, generations of men calling themselves Lutherans took that Church from him just as unquestioningly as he took the fashion of his clothes from his tailor. As the race evolves, many a convention which recommends itself by its obvious utility to everyone passes into an automatic habit, like breathing. Doubtless also an improvement in our nerves and judgment may enlarge the list of emergencies which individuals may be trusted to deal with on the spur of the moment without reference to regulations; but a ready-made code of conduct for general use will always be needed as a matter of overwhelming convenience by all members of communities.

The continual danger to liberty created by law arises, not from the encroachments of Governments, which are always regarded with suspicion, but from the immense utility and consequent popularity of law, and the terrifying danger and obvious inconvenience of anarchy; so that even pirates appoint and obey a captain. Law soon acquires such a good character that people will believe no evil of it; and at this point it becomes possible for priests and rulers to commit the most pernicious crimes in the name of law and order. Creeds and laws come to be regarded as applications to human conduct of eternal and immutable principles of good and evil; and breakers of the law are abhorred as sacrilegious scoundrels to whom nothing is sacred. Now this, I need not tell you, is a very serious error. No law is so independent of circumstances that the time never comes for breaking it, changing it, scrapping it as obsolete, and even making its observance a crime. In a developing civilization nothing can make laws tolerable unless their changes and modifications are kept as closely as possible on the heels of the changes and modifications in social conditions which development involves. Also there is a bad side to the very convenience of law. It deadens the conscience of individuals by relieving them of the ethical responsibility of their own actions. When this relief is made as complete as possible, it reduces a man to a condition in which his very virtues are contemptible. Military discipline, for example, aims at destroying the individuality and initiative of the soldier whilst increasing his mechanical efficiency, until he is simply a weapon with the power of hearing and obeying orders. In him you have legality, duty, obedience, self-denial, submission to external authority, carried as far as it can be carried; and the result is that in England, where military service is voluntary, the common soldier is less respected than any other serviceable worker in the community. The police constable, who is a civilian and has to use his own judgment and act on his own responsibility in innumerable petty emergencies, is by comparison a popular and esteemed citizen. The Roman Catholic peasant who consults his parish priest instead of his conscience, and submits wholly to the authority of his Church, is mastered and governed either by statesmen and cardinals who despise his superstition, or by Protestants who are at least allowed to persuade themselves that they have arrived at their religious opinions through the exercise of their private judgment. The moral evolution of the social individual is from submission and obedience as economizers of effort and responsibility, and safeguards against panic and incontinence, to wilfulness and self-assertion made safe by reason and self-control, just as plainly as his physical growth leads from the perambulator and the nurse's apron-string to the power of walking alone, and from the tutelage of the boy to the responsibility of the man. But it is useless for impatient spirits (you and I, for instance) to call on people to walk before they can stand. Without high gifts of reason and self-control, that is, without strong common-sense, no man dares yet trust himself out of the school of authority. What he does is to claim gradual relaxations of the discipline, so as to have as much liberty as he thinks is good for him, and as much government as he thinks he needs to keep him straight. If he goes too fast he soon finds himself asking helplessly 'What ought I to do?' and so, after running to the doctor, the lawyer, the expert, the old friend and all the other quacks for advice, he runs back to the law again to save him from all these and from himself. The law may be wrong; but anyhow it spares him the responsibility of choosing, and will either punish those who make him look ridiculous by exposing its folly, or, when the constitution is too democratic for this, at least guarantee that the majority is on his side.

Protestant Anarchism

We see this in the history of British-American Christianity. Man, as the hero of that history, starts by accepting as binding on him the revelation of God's will as interpreted by the Church. Finding his confidence, or rather his intellectual laziness, grossly abused by the Church, he claims a right to exercise his own judgment, which the Reformed Church, competing with the Unreformed for clients, grants him on condition that he arrive at the same conclusions as itself. Later on he violates this condition in certain particulars, and dissents, flying to America in the Mayflower from the prison of Conformity, but promptly building a new jail, suited to the needs of his sect, in his adopted country. In all these mutinies he finds excellent arguments to prove that he is exchanging a false authority for *the* true one, never daring even to think of brazenly admitting that what he is really doing is substituting his own will, bit by bit, for what he calls the will of God or the laws of Nature. These arguments so accustom the world to submit authority to the test of discussion that he is at last emboldened to claim the right to do anything he can find good arguments for, even to the extent of questioning the scientific accuracy of the Book of Genesis, and the validity of the popular conception of God as an omniscient, omnipotent and frightfully jealous and vindictive old gentleman sitting on a throne above the clouds. This seems a giant stride towards emancipation; but it leaves our hero, as Rationalist and Materialist, regarding Reason as a creative dynamic motor, independent of and superior to his erring passions, at which point it is easy for the churches to suggest that if Reason is to decide the matter, perhaps the conclusions of an Ecumenical Council of learned and skilled churchmen might be more trustworthy than the first crop of cheap syllogisms excogitated by a handful of raw Rationalistists in their sects of 'Freethinkers' and 'Secularists' and 'Positivists' or 'Don't Knowists' (Agnostics).

Yet it was not the churches but that very freethinking philosopher Schopenhauer who re-established the old theological doctrine that reason is no motive power; that the true motive power in the world is will (otherwise Life); and that the setting-up of reason above will is a damnable error. But the theologians could not open their arms to Schopenhauer, because he led gloomily disposed thinkers into the Rationalist-Mercantilist error of valuing life according to its individual profits in pleasure, with its idiotic pessimist conclusion that life is not worth living, and that the will which urges us to live in spite of this is necessarily a malign torturer, or at least a bad hand at business, the desirable end of all things being the cessation of the will and the consequent setting of life's sun 'into the blind cave of eternal night'. Further, the will of the theologians was the will of a God standing outside man and in authority above him, whereas the Schopenhauerian will is a purely secular force of nature, attaining various degrees of organization, here as a jelly-fish, there as a cabbage, more complexly as an ape or a tiger, and attaining its highest (and sometimes most mischievous) form so far in the human being. As to the Rationalists, they approved of Schopenhauer's secularism and pessimism, but of course could not stomach his metaphysical method nor his dethronement of reason by will. Accordingly, his turn for popularity did not come until after Darwin's, and then mostly through the influence of two great artists, Richard Wagner and Ibsen, whose *Tristan and Isolde,* and *Emperor or Galilean,* shew that Schopenhauer was a true pioneer in the forward march of the human spirit. We can now, as soon as we are strong-minded enough, drop the pessimism, the rationalism, the supernatural theology, and all the other subterfuges to which we cling because we are afraid to look life straight in the face and see in it, not the fulfilment of a moral law or of the deductions of reason, but the satisfaction of a passion in us of which we can give no rational account whatever.

It is natural for man to shrink from the terrible responsibility thrown on him by this inexorable fact. All his stock excuses vanish before it: 'The woman tempted me', 'The serpent tempted me', 'I was not myself at the time', 'I meant well', 'My passion got the better of my reason', 'It was my duty to do it', 'The Bible says that we should do it', 'Everybody does it', and so on. Nothing is left but the frank avowal: 'I did it because I am built that way'. Every man hates to say that. He wants to believe that his generous actions are characteristic of him, and that his meannesses are aberrations or concessions to the force of circumstances. Our murderers, with the assistance of the jail chaplain, square accounts with the devil and with God, never with themselves. The convict gives every reason for his having stolen something except the reason that he is a thief. Cruel people flog their children for their children's good, or offer the information that a guinea-pig expires under atrocious torture as an affectionate contribution to science. Lynched negroes are riddled by dozens of superfluous bullets, every one of which is offered as the expression of a sense of outraged justice and chastity in the scamp and libertine who fires it. And such is the desire of men to keep one another in countenance that they positively demand such excuses from one another as a matter of public decency. An uncle of mine, who made it a rule to offer tramps a job when they begged from him, naturally very soon became familiar with every excuse that human ingenuity can invent for not working. But he lost his temper only once; and that was with a tramp who frankly replied that he was too lazy. This my uncle described with disgust as 'cynicism'. And yet our family arms bear the motto, in Latin, 'Know thyself'.

As you know, the true trend of this movement has been mistaken by many of its supporters as well as by its opponents. The ingrained habit of thinking of the propensities of which we are ashamed as 'our passions', and our shame of them and our propensities to noble conduct as a negative and inhibitory department called generally our conscience, leads us to conclude that to accept the guidance of our passions is to plunge recklessly into the insupportable tedium of what is called a life of pleasure. Reactionists against the almost equally insupportable slavery of what is called a life of duty are nevertheless willing to venture on these terms. The revolted daughter, exasperated at being systematically lied to by her parents on every subject of vital importance to an eager and intensely curious young student of life, allies herself with really vicious people and with humorists who like to shock the pious with gay paradoxes, in claiming an impossible licence in personal conduct. No great harm is done beyond the inevitable and temporary excesses produced by all reactions; for, as I have said, the would-be wicked ones find, when they come to the point, that the indispensable qualification for a wicked life is not freedom but wickedness. But the misunderstanding supports the clamor of the opponents of the newest opinions, who naturally shriek as Nordau shrieks in the passages about Brandes, quoted above. Thus you have here again a movement which is thoroughly beneficial and progressive presenting a hideous appearance of moral corruption and decay, not only to our old-fashioned religious folk, but to our comparatively modern scientific Rationalists as well. And here again, because the press and the gossips have found out that this apparent corruption and decay is considered the right thing in some influential quarters, and must be spoken of with respect, and patronized and published and sold and read, we have a certain number of pitiful imitators taking advantage of their tolerance to bring out really silly and vicious stuff, which the reviewers are afraid to expose, lest it, too, should turn out to be the correct thing.

Nordau's Book

After this long preamble, you will have no difficulty in understanding the sort of book Nordau has written. Imagine a huge volume, stuffed with the most slashing of the criticisms which were hurled at the Impressionists, the Tone Poets, and the philosophers and dramatists of the Schopenhauerian revival, before these movements had reached the point at which it began to require some real courage to attack them. Imagine a rehash not only of the newspaper criticisms of this period, but of all its little parasitic paragraphs of small-talk and scandal, from the long-forgotten jibes against Oscar Wilde's momentary attempt to bring knee-breeches into fashion years ago, to the latest scurrilities about 'the New Woman'. Imagine the general staleness and occasional putrescence of this mess disguised by a dressing of the terminology invented by Krafft-Ebing, Lombroso, and all the latest specialists in madness and crime, to describe the artistic faculties and propensities as they operate in the insane. Imagine all this done by a man who is a vigorous and capable journalist, shrewd enough to see that there is a good opening for a big reactionary book as a relief to the Wagner and Ibsen booms, bold enough to let himself go without respect to persons or reputations, lucky enough to be a stronger, clearer-headed man than ninety-nine out of a hundred of his critics, besides having a keener interest in science: a born theorist, reasoner and busybody; therefore able, without insight, or even any very remarkable intensive industry (he is, like most Germans, *ex*tensively industrious to an appalling degree), to produce a book which has made a very considerable impression on the artistic ignorance of Europe and America. For he says a thing as if he meant it; he holds superficial ideas obstinately, and sees them clearly; and his mind works so impetuously that it is a pleasure to watch it—for a while. All the same, he is the dupe of a theory which would hardly impose even on the gamblers who have a system or martingale founded on a solid rock of algebra, by which they can infallibly break the bank at Monte Carlo. 'Psychiatry' takes the place of algebra in Nordau's martingale.

This theory of his is, at bottom, nothing but the familiar delusion of the used-up man that the world is going to the dogs. But Nordau is too clever to be driven back on ready-made mistakes—he makes them for himself in his own way. He appeals to the prodigious extension of the quantity of business a single man can transact through the modern machinery of social intercourse: the railway, the telegraph and telephone, the post and so forth. He gives appalling statistics of the increase of railway mileage and shipping, of the number of letters written per head of the population,[3] of the newspapers which tell us things (mostly lies) of which we used to know nothing. 'In the last fifty years,' he says, 'the population of Europe has not doubled, whereas the sum of its labors has increased tenfold; in part, even fifty-fold. Every civilized man furnishes, at the present time, from five to twenty-five times as much work as was demanded of him half a century ago.'[4] Then follow more statistics of 'the constant increase of crime, madness and suicide', of increases in the mortality from diseases of the nerves and heart, of increased consumption of stimulants, of new nervous diseases like 'railway spine and railway brain', with the general moral that we are all suffering from exhaustion, and that symptoms of degeneracy are visible in all directions, culminating at various points in Wagner's music, Ibsen's dramas, Manet's pictures, Tolstoy's novels, Whitman's poetry, Dr Jaeger's woollen clothing, vegetarianism, scepticism as to vivisection and vaccination, Anarchism and Humanitarianism, and, in short, everything that Dr Nordau does not happen to approve of.

You will at once see that such a case, if well got up and argued, is worth hearing, even though its advocate has no chance of a verdict, because it is sure to bring out a certain number of interesting and important facts. It is, I take it, quite true that with our railways and our postal services many of us are for the moment very like a pedestrian converted to bicycling, who, instead of using his machine to go twenty miles with less labor than he used to walk seven, proceeds to do a hundred miles instead, with the result that the 'labor-saving' contrivance acts as a means of working its user to exhaustion. It is also true that, under our existing industrial system, machinery in industrial processes is regarded solely as a means of extracting a larger product from the unremitted toil of the actual wage-worker. And I do not think any person who is in touch with the artistic professions will deny that they are recruited largely by persons who become actors, or painters, or journalists and authors because they are incapable of steady work and regular habits, or that the attraction which the patrons of the stage, music, and literature find in their favorite arts has often little or nothing to do with the need which nerves great artists to the heavy travail of creation. The claim of art to our respect must stand or fall with the validity of its pretension to cultivate and refine our senses and faculties until seeing, hearing, feeling, smelling and tasting become highly conscious and critical acts with us, protesting vehemently against ugliness, noise, discordant speech, frowzy clothing and re-breathed air, and taking keen interest and pleasure in beauty, in music and in nature, besides making us insist, as necessary for comfort and decency, on clean, wholesome, handsome fabrics to wear and utensils of fine material and elegant workmanship to handle. Further, art should refine our sense of character and conduct, of justice and sympathy, greatly heightening our self-knowledge, self-control, precision of action, and considerateness, and making us intolerant of baseness, cruelty, injustice and intellectual superficiality or vulgarity. The worthy artist or craftsman is he who serves the physical and moral senses by feeding them with pictures, musical compositions, pleasant houses and gardens, good clothes and fine implements, poems, fictions, essays and dramas which call the heightened senses and ennobled faculties into pleasurable activity. The great artist is he who goes a step beyond the demand, and, by supplying works of a higher beauty and a higher interest than have yet been perceived, succeeds after a brief struggle with its strangeness, in adding this fresh extension of sense to the heritage of the race. This is why we value art; this is why we feel that the iconoclast and the Philistine are attacking something made holier, by solid usefulness, than their own theories of purity and practicality; this is why art has won the privileges of religion; so that London shopkeepers who would fiercely resent a compulsory church rate, who do not know 'Yankee Doodle' from Luther's hymn, and who are more interested in photographs of the latest celebrities than in the Velasquez portraits in the National Gallery, tamely allow the London County Council to spend their money on bands, on municipal art inspectors and on plaster casts from the antique.

But the business of responding to the demand for the gratification of the senses has many grades. The confectioner who makes unwholesome sweets, the bull-fighter, the women whose advertisements in the American papers are so astounding to English people, are examples ready to hand to shew what the art and trade of pleasing may be, not at its lowest, but at the lowest that we can speak of without intolerable shame. We have dramatists who write their lines in such a way as to enable low comedians of a certain class to give them an indecorous turn; we have painters who aim no higher than Giulio Romano did when he decorated the Palazzo Te in Mantua; we have poets who have nothing to versify but the commonplaces of amorous infatuation; and, worse than all the rest put together, we have journalists who openly profess that it is their duty to 'reflect' what they believe to be the ignorance and prejudice of their readers, instead of leading and enlightening them to the best of their ability; an excuse for cowardice and time-serving which is also becoming well worn in political circles as 'the duty of a democratic statesman'. In short, the artist can be a prostitute, a pander and a flatterer more easily, as far as external pressure goes, than a faithful servant of the community, much less the founder of a school or the father of a church. Even an artist who is doing the best he can may be doing a very low class of work; for instance, many performers at the rougher music-halls, who get their living by singing coarse songs in the rowdiest possible way, do so to the utmost of their ability in that direction in the most conscientious spirit of earning their money honestly and being a credit to their profession. And the exaltation of the greatest artists is not continuous: you cannot defend every line of Shakespear or every stroke of Titian. Since the artist is a man and his patron a man, all human moods and grades of development are reflected in art; consequently the iconoclast's or the Philistine's indictments of art have as many counts as the misanthrope's indictment of humanity. And this is the Achilles heel of art at which Nordau has struck. He has piled the iconoclast on the Philistine, the Philistine on the misanthrope, in order to make out his case.

Echolalia

Let me describe to you one or two of his artifices as a special pleader making the most of the eddies at the sides of the stream of progress. Take as a first specimen the old and effective trick of pointing out, as 'stigmata of degeneration' in the person he is abusing, features which are common to the whole human race. The drawing-room palmist astonishes ladies by telling them 'secrets' about themselves which are nothing but the inevitable experiences of ninety-nine people out of every hundred, though each individual is vain enough to suppose that they are peculiar to herself. Nordau turns the trick inside out by trusting to the fact that people are in the habit of assuming that uniformity and symmetry are laws of nature: for example, that every normal person's face is precisely symmetrical, that all persons have the same number of bones in their bodies, and so on. He takes advantage of this popular error to claim asymmetry as a stigma of degeneration. As a matter of fact, perfect symmetry or uniformity does not exist in nature. My two profiles, when photographed, are hardly recognizable as belonging to the same person by those who do not know me; so that the camera would prove me an utter degenerate if my case were exceptional. Probably, however, you would not object to testify that my face is as symmetrical as faces are ordinarily made. Another unfailing trick is the common one of having two names for the same thing, one abusive, the other complimentary, for use according to circumstances. You know how it is done: 'We trust the Government will be firm' in one paper and 'We hope the obstinate elements in the Cabinet will take warning in time' in another. The powers of Empires armed to the teeth to impose their will by fire and sword on weaker communities are called simply Sanctions. Repudiations of national debts are called stabilizations of the currency. The following is a typical specimen of Nordau's use of this device. First, let me explain that when a man with a turn for rhyming goes mad, he repeats rhymes as if he were quoting a rhyming dictionary. You say 'Come' to him, and he starts away with 'Dumb, plum, sum, rum, numb, gum' and so on. This the doctors call echolalia. Dickens gives a specimen of it in *Great Expectations,* where Mr Jaggers's Jewish client expresses his rapture of admiration for the lawyer by exclaiming, 'Oh, Jaggerth, Jaggerth, Jaggerth! all otherth ith Cag-Maggerth: give me Jaggerth!' There are some well-known verses by Swinburne, beginning, 'If love were what the rose is', which, rhyming and tripping along very prettily, express a sentiment without making any intelligible statement whatsoever; and we have plenty of nonsensically inconsequent nursery rhymes, like 'Ba, Ba, Black Sheep', or 'Old Daddy Long Legs', which please sane children just as Mr Swinburne's verses please sane adults, simply as funny or pretty little word-patterns. People do not write such things for the sake of conveying information, but for the sake of amusing and pleasing, just as people do not eat strawberries and cream to nourish their bones and muscles, but to enjoy the taste of a toothsome dish. A lunatic may plead that he eats kitchen soap and tin tacks on the same ground; and as far as I can see the lunatic would completely shut up Nordau by this answer; for Nordau is absurd enough, in the case of rhyming, to claim that every rhyme made for its own sake, as proved by the fact that it does not convey an intelligible statement of fact of any kind, convicts the rhymer of echolalia. He can thus convict any poet whom he dislikes of being a degenerate by simply picking out a rhyme which exists for its own sake, or a pun, or what is called a burden in a ballad, and claiming them as symptoms of echolalia, supporting this diagnosis by carefully examining the poem for contradictions and inconsistencies as to time, place, description, or the like. It will occur to you probably that by this means he must bring out Shakespear as the champion instance of poetic degeneracy, since Shakespear was an incorrigible punster; delighted in burdens (for instance, 'With hey, ho, the wind and the rain,' which exactly fulfills all the conditions accepted by Nordau as symptomatic of insanity in Rossetti's case); and rhymed for the sake of rhyming in a quite childish fashion; whilst, as to contradictions and inconsistencies, *A Midsummer Night's Dream,* as to which Shakespear never made up his mind whether the action covered a week or a single night, is only one of a dozen instances of his slips.

But no: Shakespear, not being a nineteenth-century poet, would have spoiled the case for modern degeneration by shewing that its symptoms existed before the telegraph and the railway were dreamt of; and besides, Nordau likes Shakespear, just as he likes Goethe, and holds him up as a model of sanity in contrast to the nineteenth-century poets. Thus Wagner is a degenerate because he made puns; and Shakespear, who made worse ones, is a great poet. Swinburne, with his 'unmeaning' refrains of 'Small red leaves in the mill water' and 'Apples of gold for the King's daughter' is a diseased madman; but Shakespear, with his 'In spring time, the only merry ring time, when birds do sing hey ding a ding ding' (if this is not the worst case of echolalia in the world, what *is* echolalia?), is a sober master mind. Rossetti, with his Blessed Damozel leaning out from the gold bar of heaven; weeping though she is in paradise, which is a happy place; describing the dead in one line as 'dressed in white' and in another as 'mounting like thin flames'; and calculating days and years quite otherwise than commercial almanacks do, is that dangerous and cranky thing, a mystic; whilst Goethe (the author of the second part of *Faust,* if you please) is a hard-headed, accurate, sound, scientific poet. As to the list of inconsistencies of which poor Ibsen is convicted, it is too long to be dealt with in detail. But I assure you I am not doing Nordau less than justice when I say that if he had accused Shakespear of inconsistency on the ground that Othello is represented in the first act as loving his wife, and in the last as strangling her, the demonstration would have left you with more respect for his good sense than his pages on Ibsen, the folly of which goes beyond all patience.[5]

When Nordau deals with painting and music, he is less irritating, because he errs through ignorance, and ignorance, too, of a sort that is now perfectly well recognized and understood. We all know what the old-fashioned critic of literature and science who cultivated his detective logic without ever dreaming of cultivating his eyes and ears, can be relied upon to say when painters and composers are under discussion. Nordau gives himself away with laughable punctuality. He celebrates 'the most glorious period of the Renaissance' and 'the rosy dawn of the new thought' with all the gravity of the older editions of Murray's *Guides to Italy.* He tells us that 'to copy Cimabue and Giotto is comparatively easy: to imitate Raphael it is necessary to be able to draw and paint to perfection.' He lumps Fra Angelico with Giotto and Cimabue, as if they represented the same stage in the development of technical execution, and Pollaiuolo with Ghirlandaio. 'Here,' he says, speaking of the great Florentine painters, from Giotto to Masaccio, 'were paintings bad in drawing, faded or smoked, their coloring either originally feeble or impaired by the action of centuries, pictures *executed with the awkwardness of a learner* . . . easy of imitation, since, in painting pictures in the style of the early masters, faulty drawing, deficient sense of color, and *general artistic incapacity,* are so many advantages.' To make any comment on these howlers would be to hit a man when he is down. Poor Nordau offers them as a demonstration that Ruskin, who gave this sort of ignorant nonsense its death-blow in England, was a delirious mystic. Also that Millais and Holman Hunt, in the days of the pre-Raphaelite brotherhood, strove to acquire the qualities of the early

Florentine masters because the Florentine easel pictures were so much easier to imitate than those of the apprentices in Raphael's Roman fresco factory.

In music we find Nordau equally content with the theories as to how music is composed which were current among literary men fifty years ago. He tells us of 'the severe discipline and fixed rules of the theory of composition, which gave a grammar to the musical babbling of primeval times, and made of it a worthy medium for the expression of the emotions of civilized men', and describes Wagner as breaking these fixed rules and rebelling against this severe discipline because he was 'an inattentive mystic, abandoned to amorphous dreams'. This notion that there are certain rules, derived from a science of counterpoint, by the application of which pieces of music can be constructed just as an equilateral triangle can be constructed on a given straight line by anyone who has mastered Euclid's first proposition, is highly characteristic of the generation of blind and deaf critics to which Nordau belongs. It is evident that if there were fixed rules by which Wagner or anyone else could have composed good music, there could have been no more severe discipline in the work of composition than in the work of arranging a list of names in alphabetical order. The severity of artistic discipline is produced by the fact that in creative art no ready-made rules can help you. There is nothing to guide you to the right expression for your thought except your own sense of beauty and fitness; and, as you advance upon those who went before you, that sense of beauty and fitness is necessarily often in conflict, not with fixed rules, because there are no rules, but with precedents, which are what Nordau means by fixed rules, as far as he knows what he is talking about enough to mean anything at all. If Wagner had composed the prelude to *Das Rheingold* with a half close at the end of the eighth bar and a full close at the end of the sixteenth, he would undoubtedly have followed the precedent of Mozart and other great composers, and complied with the requirements of Messrs Hanslick, Nordau and Company. Only, as it happened, that was not what he wanted to do. His purpose was to produce a tone picture of the mighty flood in the depths of the Rhine; and, as the poetic imagination does not conceive the Rhine as stopping at every eight feet to take off its hat to the author of *Degeneration,* the closes and half closes are omitted, and Nordau, huffed at being passed by as if he were a person of no consequence, complains that the composer is 'an inattentive mystic, abandoned to amorphous dreams'. But, even if Wagner's descriptive purpose is left out of the question, Nordau's general criticism of him is an ignorant one; for the truth is that Wagner, like most artists who have great intellectual power, was dominated in the technical work of his gigantic scores by so strong a regard for system, order, logic, symmetry and syntax, that when in the course of time his melody and harmony become perfectly familiar to us, he will be ranked with Handel as a composer whose extreme regularity of procedure must make his work appear drily mechanical to those who cannot catch its dramatic inspiration. In this very fluminous *Rheingold* prelude which I have cited there is a four-bar rhythm of Mozartian symmetry which may yet serve as the text of such a reproach. If Nordau had said: 'This fellow, whom you all imagine to be the creator of a new heaven and a new earth in music out of a chaos of poetic emotion, is really an arrant pedant and formalist,' I should have pricked up my ears and listened to him with some curiosity, knowing how good a case a really keen technical critic could make out for that view. As it is, I have only to expose him as having picked up a vulgar error under the influence of a vulgar literary superstition. For the rest, you will hardly need any prompting of mine to appreciate the absurdity of dismissing as 'inattentive' the Paris journalist, the Dresden conductor, the designer and founder of the Bayreuth enterprise, the humorous and practical author of *On Conducting*, and the man who scored and stage-managed the four evenings of *The Niblung's Ring*. I purposely leave out the composer, the poet, the philosopher, the reformer, since Nordau cannot be compelled to admit that Wagner's eminence in these departments was real. Striking them all out accordingly, there remain the indisputable objective facts of Wagner's practical professional ability and organizing power to put Nordau's diagnosis of Wagner as an amorphous, inattentive person out of the question. If Nordau had one hundreth part of the truly terrific power of attention which Wagner must have maintained all his life almost as easily as a common man breathes, he would not now be so deplorable an example of the truth of his own saying that the power of attention may be taken as the measure of mental strength.

Nordau's trick of calling rhyme echolalia when he happens not to like the rhymer is reapplied in the case of authorship, which he calls graphomania when he happens not to like the author. He insists that Wagner, who was a voluminous author as well as a composer, was a graphomaniac; and his proof is that in his books we find 'the restless reptition of one and the same strain of thought . . . *Opera and Drama, Judaism in Music, Religion and the State, Art and Religion,* and the *Vocation of Opera* are nothing more than the amplification of single passages in *The Art-Work of the Future*'. This is a capital example of Nordau's limited power of attention. The moment that limited power is concentrated on his theory of degeneration, he loses sight of everything else, and drives his one borrowed horse into every obstacle on the road. To those of us who can attend to more than one thing at a time, there is no observation more familiar and more frequently confirmed than that this growth of pregnant single sentences into whole books which Nordau discovers in Wagner, balanced as it always is by the contraction of whole boyish chapters into single epigrams, is the process by which all great writers, speakers, artists and thinkers elaborate their life-work. Let me take a writer after Nordau's own heart, a shrewd Yorkshireman, one whom he quotes as a trustworthy example of what he calls 'the clear, mentally sane author, who, feeling himself impelled to say something, once for all expresses himself as distinctly and impressively as it is possible for him to do, and has done with it', namely, Dr Henry Maudsley. Dr Maudsley is a clever and cultivated specialist in insanity, who has written several interesting books, consisting of repetitions, amplifications and historical illustrations of the same idea, which is, if I may put it rather more bluntly than the urbane author, nothing less than the identification of religious with sexual ecstasy. And the upshot of it is the conventional scientific pessimism, from which Dr Maudsley never gets away; so that his last book repeats his first book, instead of leaving it far behind, as Wagner's *State and Religion* leaves his *Art and Revolution* behind. But now that I have prepared the way by quoting Dr Maudsley, why should I not ask Max Nordau himself to step before the looking-glass and tell us frankly whether, even in the ranks of his 'psychiatrists' and lunacy doctors, he can pick out a crank more hopelessly obsessed with one idea than himself? If you want an example of echolalia, can you find a more shocking one than this gentleman who, when you say 'mania', immediately begins to gabble Egomania, Graphomania, Megalomania, Onomatomania, Pyromania, Kleptomania, Dipsomania, Erotamania, Arithmomania, Oniomania, and is started off by the termination 'phobia' with a string of Agoraphobia, Claustrophobia, Rupophobia, Iophobia, Nosophobia, Aichmophobia, Belenophobia, Cremnophobia, and Trichophobia? After which he suddenly observes, 'This is simply philologico-medical trifling,' a remark which looks like returning sanity until he follows it up by clasping his temples in the true bedlamite manner, and complaining that 'psychiatry is being stuffed with useless and disturbing designations', whereas, if the psychiatrists would only listen to him, they would see that there is only one phobia and one mania, namely, degeneracy. That is, the philologico-medical triflers are not crazy enough for him. He is so utterly mad on the subject of degeneration that he finds the symptoms of it in the loftiest geniuses as plainly as in the lowest jailbirds, the exceptions being himself, Lombroso, Krafft-Ebing, Dr Maudsley, Goethe, Shakespear, and Beethoven. Perhaps he would have dwelt on a case so convenient in many ways for his theory as Coleridge but that it would spoil the connection between degeneration and 'railway spine'. If a man's senses are acute, he is degenerate, hyperaesthesia having been observed in asylums. If they are dull, he is degenerate, anaesthesia being the stigma of the craziness which made old women confess to witchcraft. If he is particular as to what he wears, he is degenerate: silk dressing-gowns and knee-breeches are grave symptoms and woollen shirts conclusive. If he is negligent in these matters, clearly he is inattentive, and therefore degenerate. If he drinks, he is neurotic: if he is a vegetarian and teetotaller, let him be locked up at once. If he lives an evil life, that fact condemns him without further words; if, on the other hand, his conduct is irreproachable, he is a wretched 'mattoid', incapable of the will and courage to realize his vicious propensities in action. If he writes verse, he is afflicted with echolalia; if he writes prose, he is a graphomaniac; if in his books he is tenacious of his ideas, he is obsessed; if not, he is 'amorphous' and 'inattentive'. Wagner, as we have seen, contrived to be both obsessed and inattentive, as might be expected from one who was 'himself alone charged with a greater abundance of degeneration than all the other degenerates put together'. And so on and so forth.

There is, however, one sort of mental weakness, common among men who take to science, as so many people take to art, without the necessary brain power, which Nordau, with amusing unconsciousness of himself, has omitted. I mean the weakness of a man who, when his theory works out into a flagrant contradiction of the facts, concludes 'So much the worse for the facts: let them be altered', instead of 'So much the worse for my theory'. What in the name of common-sense is the value of a theory which identifies Ibsen, Wagner, Tolstoy, Ruskin and Victor Hugo with the refuse of our prisons and lunatic asylums? What is to be said of the state of mind of an inveterate pamphleteer and journalist who, instead of accepting that identification as a *reductio ad absurdum* of the theory, desperately sets to work to prove it by pointing out that there are numerous resemblances; that they all have heads and bodies, appetites, aberrations, whims, weaknesses, asymmetrical features, erotic impulses, fallible judgments, and the like common properties, not merely of all human beings, but all vertebrate organisms. Take Nordau's own list: 'vague and incoherent thought, the tyranny of the association of ideas, the presence of obsessions, erotic excitability, religious enthusiasm, feebleness of perception, will, memory and judgment, as well as inattention and instability'. Is there a single man capable of understanding these terms who will not plead guilty to some experience of all of them, especially when he is accused vaguely and unscientifically, without any statement of the subject, or the moment, or the circumstances to which the accusation refers, or any attempt to fix a standard of sanity? I could prove Nordau to be an elephant on more evidence than he has brought to prove that our greatest men are degenerate lunatics. The papers in which Swift, having predicted the death of the sham prophet Bickerstaff on a certain date, did, after that date, immediately prove that he was dead, are much more closely and fairly reasoned than any of Nordau's chapters. And Swift, though he afterwards died in a madhouse, was too sane to be the dupe of his own logic. At that rate, where will Nordau die? Probably in a highly respectable suburban villa.

Nordau's most likeable point is the freedom and boldness with which he expresses himself. Speaking of Peladan (of whose works I know nothing), he says, whilst holding him up as a typical degenerate of the mystical variety: 'His moral idea is high and noble. He pursues with ardent hatred all that is base and vulgar, every form of egoism, falsehood and thirst for pleasure; and his characters are thoroughly aristocratic souls, whose thoughts are concerned only with the worthiest, if somewhat exclusively artistic, interests of society.' On the other hand, Maeterlinck is a 'poor devil of an idiot'; Mr W. D. O'Connor, for describing Whitman as 'the good grey poet', is politely introduced as 'an American driveller'; Nietzsche 'belongs, body and soul, to the flock of the mangy sheep'; Ibsen is 'a malignant, anti-social simpleton'; and so on. Only occasionally is he Pharisaical in his tone, as, for instance, when he becomes virtuously indignant over Wagner's dramas, and plays to Mrs Grundy by exclaiming ironically, 'How unperverted must wives and readers be, when they are in a state of mind to witness these pieces without blushing crimson and sinking into the earth for shame!' This, to do him justice, is only an exceptional lapse: a far more characteristic comment of his on Wagner's love-scenes is 'The lovers in his pieces behave like tom cats gone mad, rolling in contortions and convulsions over a foot of valerian.' And he is not always on the side of the police, so to speak; for he is as careless of the feelings of the 'beer-drinking' German *bourgeoisie* as of those of the aesthetes. Thus, though

on one page he is pointing out that socialism and all other forms of discontent
with the existing social order are 'stigmata of degeneration', on the next he is
talking pure Karl Marx. For example, taking the two sides in their order:

> Ibsen's egomania assumes the form of Anarchism. He is in a state of
> constant revolt against all that exists . . . The psychological roots of his
> anti-social impulses are well known. They are the degenerate's inca-
> pacity for self-adaptation, and the resultant discomfort in the midst of
> circumstances to which, in consequence of his organic deficiencies,
> he cannot accommodate himself. 'The criminal,' says Lombroso,
> 'through his neurotic and impulsive nature, and his hatred of the
> institutions which have punished or imprisoned him, is a perpetual
> latent political rebel, who finds in insurrection the means, not only of
> satisfying his passions, but of even having them countenanced for the
> first time by a numerous public.'
>
> Wagner is a declared Anarchist . . . He betrays that mental condition
> which the degenerate shares with enlightened reformers, born crim-
> inals with the martyrs of human progress, namely, deep, devouring
> discontent with existing facts . . . He would like to crush 'political and
> criminal civilization,' as he calls it.

Now for Nordau speaking for himself:

> Is it not the duty of intelligent philanthropy and justice, without
> destroying civilization, to adopt a better system of economy and
> transform the artisan from a factory convict, condemned to misery and
> ill-health, into a free producer of wealth, who enjoys the fruits of his
> labor himself, and works no more than is compatible with his health
> and his claims on life?
>
> Every gift that a man receives from some other man without work,
> without reciprocal service, is an alms, and as such is deeply immoral.
>
> Not in the impossible 'return to nature' lies healing for human
> misery, but in the reasonable organization of our struggle with
> nature—I might say, in universal and obligatory service against it,
> from which only the crippled should be exempted.
>
> In England it was Tolstoy's sexual morality that excited the greatest
> interest; for in that country economic reasons condemn a formidable
> number of girls, particularly of the educated classes, to forgo marriage;
> and, from a theory which honored chastity as the highest dignity and
> noblest human destiny, and branded marriage with gloomy wrath as
> abominable depravity, these poor creatures would naturally derive rich
> consolation for their lonely, empty lives and their cruel exclusion from
> the possibility of fulfilling their natural calling.

So it appears that Nordau, too, shares 'the degenerate's incapacity for
self-adaptation, and the resultant discomfort in the midst of circumstances to
which, in consequence of his organic deficiencies, he cannot accommodate

himself'. Is he not, indeed, the author of *Conventional Lies of Civilization*? But
he has his usual easy way out of the dilemma. If Ibsen and Wagner are
dissatisfied with the world, that is because the world is too good for them; but,
if Max Nordau is dissatisfied, it is because Max is too good for the world. His
modesty does not permit him to draw the distinction in these exact terms. Here
is his statement of it:

> Discontent shews itself otherwise in the degenerate than in reform-
> ers. The latter grow angry over real evils only and make rational
> proposals for their remedy which are in advance of the time these
> remedies may presuppose a better and wiser humanity than actually
> exists, but at least they are capable of being defended on reasonable
> grounds. The degenerate, on the other hand, selects among the
> arrangements of civilization such as are either immaterial or distinctly
> suitable, in order to rebel against them. His fury has either ridiculously
> insignificant aims, or simply beats the air. He either gives no earnest
> thought to improvement, or hatches astoundingly mad projects for
> making the world happy. His fundamental frame of mind is persistent
> rage against everything and everyone, which he displays in venomous
> phrases, savage threats, and the destructive mania of wild beasts.
> *Wagner is a good specimen of this species*.

Wagner was named because the passage occurs in the almost incredibly
foolish chapter which is headed with his name. In another chapter it might
have been Ibsen, or Tolstoy, or Ruskin, or William Morris, or any other
eminent artist who shares Nordau's objection, and yours and mine, to our
existing social arrangements. In the face of this, it is really impossible to deny
oneself the fun of asking Nordau, with all possible good humor, who he is and
what he is, that he should rail in this fashion at great men. Wagner was
discontented with the condition of musical art in Europe. In essay after essay
he pointed out with the most laborious exactitude what it was he complained
of, and how it might be remedied. He not only shewed, in the teeth of the most
envenomed opposition from all the dunderheads, pedants and vested interests
in Europe, what the musical drama ought to be as a work of art, but how
theatres for its proper performance should be managed—nay, how they should
be built, down to the arrangement of the seats and the position of the
instruments in the orchestra. And he not only shewed this on paper, but he
successfully composed the music dramas, built a model theatre, gave the
model performances, *did* the impossible; so that there is now nobody left, not
even Hanslick, who cares to stultify himself by repeating the old anti-Wagner
cry of craziness and Impossibilism—nobody, save only Max Nordau, who, like
a true journalist, is fact-proof. William Morris objected to the abominable
ugliness of early Victorian decoration and furniture, to the rhymed rhetoric
which did duty for poetry from the Renaissance to the nineteenth century, to
kamptulicon-stained glass, and, later on, to the shiny commercial gentility of
typography according to the American ideal, spread through England by

Harper's Magazine and *The Century*. Well, did he sit down, as Nordau suggests, to rail helplessly at the men who were at all events getting the work of the world done, however inartistically? Not a bit of it: he designed and manufactured the decorations he wanted, and furnished and decorated houses with them; he put into public halls and churches tapestries and picture-windows which cultivated people now travel to see as they travel to see first-rate fifteenth-century work in that kind; the books from his Kelmscott Press, printed with type designed by his own hand, are pounced on by collectors like the treasures of our national museums: all this work, remember, involving the successful conduction of a large business establishment and factory, and being relieved by the incidental production of a series of poems and prose romances which placed their author in the position of the greatest living English poet. Now let me repeat the terms in which Nordau describes this kind of activity. 'Ridiculously insignificant aims—beating the air—no earnest thought to improvement—astoundingly mad projects for making the world happy—persistent rage against everything and everyone, displayed in venomous phrases, savage threats and destructive mania of wild beasts.' Is there not something deliciously ironical in the ease with which a splenetic pamphleteer, with nothing to shew for himself except a bookful of blunders tacked on to a mock scientific theory picked up at second hand from a few lunacy doctors with a literary turn, should be able to create a European scandal by declaring that the greatest creative artists of the century are barren and hysterical madmen? I do not know what the American critics have said about Nordau; but here the tone has been that there is much in what he says, and that he is evidently an authority on the subjects with which he deals. And yet I assure you, on my credit as a man who lives by art criticism, that from his preliminary description of a Morris design as one 'on which strange birds flit among crazily ramping branches, and blowzy flowers coquet with vain butterflies' (which is about as sensible as a description of the Norman chapel in the Tower of London as a characteristic specimen of Baroque architecture would be) to his coupling of Cimabue and Fra Angelico as primitive Florentine masters—from his unashamed bounce about 'the conscientious observance of the laws of counterpoint' by Beethoven and other masters celebrated for breaking them to his unlucky shot about 'a pedal bass with correct harmonization' (a pedal bass happening to be the particular instance in which even the professor-made rules of 'correct harmonization' are suspended), Nordau exposes his sciolism time after time as an authority upon the fine arts. But his critics, being for the most part ignorant literary men like himself, with sharpened wits and neglected eyes and ears, have swallowed Cimabue and Ghirlandaio and the pedal bass like so many gulls. Here an Ibsen admirer may maintain that Ibsen is an exception to the degenerate theory and should be classed with Goethe; there a Wagnerite may plead that Wagner is entitled to the honors of Beethoven; elsewhere one may find a champion of Rossetti venturing cautiously to suggest a suspicion of the glaringly obvious fact that Nordau has read only the two or three popular ballads like 'The Blessed Damozel', 'Eden Bower', 'Sister Helen' and so on, which every smatterer reads, and that his knowledge of the mass of pictorial, dramatic, and decorative work turned out by Rossetti, Burne-Jones, Ford Madox Brown, William Morris and Holman Hunt, without a large knowledge and careful study of which no man can possibly speak with any critical authority of the pre-Raphaelite movement, is apparently limited to a glance at Holman Hunt's *Shadow of the Cross* or possibly an engraving thereof. But in the main he is received as a serious authority on his subjects; and that is why we two, without malice and solely as a matter of public duty, are compelled to take all this trouble to destroy him.

And now, my dear Tucker, I have told you as much about Nordau's book as it is worth. In a country where art was really known to the people, instead of being merely read about, it would not be necessary to spend three lines on such a work. But in England, where nothing but superstitious awe and self-mistrust prevents most men from thinking about art as Nordau boldly speaks about it; where to have a sense of art is to be one in a thousand, the other nine hundred and ninety-nine being either Philistine voluptuaries or Calvinistic anti-voluptuaries, it is useless to pretend that Nordau's errors will be self-evident. Already we have native writers, without half his cleverness or energy of expression, clumsily imitating his sham-scientific vivisection in their attacks on artists whose work they happen to dislike. Therefore, in riveting his book to the counter, I have used a nail long enough to go through a few pages by other people as well; and that must be my excuse for my disregard of the familiar editorial stigma of degeneracy which Nordau calls Agoraphobia, or Fear of Space.

NOTES

1. Perhaps by this time, however, Mr Arnold Dolmetsch has educated America in this matter, as he educated London and educated me.

2. As I spent the first twenty years of my life in Ireland I am, for the purposes of this survey of musical art, at least a century and a half old. I can remember the sensation given by the opening chord of Beethoven's youthful *Prometheus* overture. It sounded strangely strong and momentous, because the use of the third inversion of the chord of the dominant seventh without preparation was unexpected in those days. As to exploding undiminished chords of the ninth and thirteenth on the unsuspecting ear in the same way (everybody does it nowadays), one might as well have sat down on the keyboard and called it music. The very name of the thirteenth was inconceivable; a discreetly prepared and resolved suspension of 'four to three' was the only form in which that discord was known. I can remember, too, the indignation with which Macfarren, after correcting his pupils for unintentional consecutive fifths all his life, found himself expected to write an analytic program for the performance at a Philharmonic concert of an overture by a composer (Goetz) who actually wrote consecutive sevenths intentionally because he liked them.

However, I do not insert this note for the sake of my reminiscences, but because, since writing the text above, a composer of the first order (Richard Strauss) has become known in London, and has been attacked, just as Wagner was, by the very men who lived through the huge blunder of anti-Wagnerism. This cannot be accounted for by the superstitions of the age of decorative music. Every critic nowadays is thoroughly inured to descriptive and dramatic music which is not only as independent of the old decorative forms as Strauss's, but a good deal more so; for Strauss lives on the verge of a barcarolle and seldom resists a nursery tune for long. The hostility to him may be partly due to the fact that by his great achievement of rescuing music from the realm of tights and wigs and stage armor in which Wagner, with all his genius, dwelt to the last, and bringing it into direct contact with modern life, he was enabled in his Heldenleben to give an orchestral caricature of his critics which comes much closer home than Wagner's medievally disguised Beckmesser. But Strauss is denounced by men who are quite capable of laughing at themselves, who are sincere advocates of modern realism in other arts, and who are sufficiently good judges to know, for instance, that the greater popularity of Tchaikowsky is like the greater popularity of Rossini as compared with Beethoven nearly a century ago; that is, the vogue of a musical voluptuary, who, though very pleasant in his lighter vein, very strenuous in his energetic vein, and at least grandiose in his sublime vein, never attains, nor desires to attain, the elevation at which the great modern musicians from Bach to Strauss maintain themselves. Anti-Straussism is therefore accounted for neither by the old anti-Wagnerian confusion nor by the petulance of the critic who is beaten by his job.

I conclude that the disagreeable effect which an unaccustomed discord produces on people who cannot divine its resolution is to blame for most of the nonsense now written about Strauss. Strauss's technical procedure involves a profusion of such shocks. But the disagreeable effect will not last. There is no longer a single discord used by Wagner of which the resolution is not already as much a platitude as the resolution of the simple sevenths of Mozart and Meyerbeer. Strauss not only goes from discord to discord, leaving the implied resolutions to be inferred by people who never heard them before, but actually makes a feature of unresolved discords, just as Wagner made a feature of unprepared ones. Men who were reconciled quite late in life to compositions beginning with dominant thirteenths *fortissimo,* find themselves disquieted now by compositions ending with unresolved tonic sevenths.

I think this phase of protest will soon pass. I think so because I find myself able to follow Strauss's harmonic procedure; to divining the destination of his most discordant passing phrases (it is too late now to talk of mere 'passing notes'); and to tolerate his most off-hand ellipses and most unceremonious omissions of final concords, with enjoyment, though my musical endowment is none of the acutest. In twenty years the complaints about his music will be as unintelligible as the similar complaints about Handel, Mozart, Beethoven and Wagner in the past.

I must apologize for the technical jargon I have had to use in this note. Probably it is all obsolete by this time; but I know nothing newer. Stainer would have understood it thirty years ago. If nobody understands it today, my knowledge will seem all the more profound.

3. Perhaps I had better remark in passing that unless it were true—which it is not—that the length of the modern penny letter or halfpenny post-card is the same as that of the eighteenth-century letter, and that the number of persons who know how to read and write has not increased, there is no reason whatever to draw Nordau's conclusion from the postal statistics.

4. Here again we have a statement which means nothing unless it be compared with statistics as to the multiplication of the civilized man's power of production by machinery, which in some industries have multiplied a single man's output by

hundreds and in others by thousands whilst actually lightening his labor. As to crimes and disease, Nordau should state whether convictions under modern laws—for offences against the Joint Stock Company Acts, for instance—prove that we have degenerated since those Acts were passed, and whether the invention of new names for a dozen varieties of fever which were formerly counted as one single disease is any evidence of decaying health in the face of the increasing duration of life.

5. Perhaps I had better give one example. Nordau first quotes a couple of speeches from *An Enemy of the People* and *The Wild Duck:*

STOCKMANN: I love my native town so well that I had rather ruin it than see it flourishing on a lie. All men who live on lies must be exterminated like vermin. *(An Enemy of the People.)*

RELLING: Yes: I said illusion [lie]. For illusion, you know, is the stimulating principle. Rob the average man of his life illusion and you rob him of his happiness at the same time. *(The Wild Duck.)*

Nordau proceeds to comment as follows: 'Now, what is Ibsen's real opinion? Is a man to strive for truth or to swelter in deceit? Is Ibsen with Stockmann or with Relling? Ibsen owes us an answer to these questions or, rather, he replies to them affirmatively and negatively with equal ardor and equal poetic power.'

Sigmund Freud

1856–1939

Sigmund Freud was born in Freiburg, Moravia, on May 6, 1856. His parents were Galician Jews; Jakob Freud, his father, earned a passable living in the wool business until an unwise investment almost ruined him financially. Amalia Freud, Jakob's second wife, never completely mastered German, speaking her own brand of Galician Yiddish, interspersed with German, until her death. As a young boy Sigmund was brought up in a household beset with financial difficulties and astride two cultures, the German and the Jewish.

Freud's education at *Gymnasium* emphasized Latin and Greek authors as well as Goethe, Schiller, and Lessing, and laid the groundwork for the literary aspect of psychoanalysis. But the young Freud legitimized his nascent discipline of psychoanalysis as science in the positivist traditions of Wilhelm Wundt and Hermann Helmholtz. And, besides positivism, with its emphasis on the empirical approach, Freud stood squarely in the tradition of evolutionism from the very beginning. Darwin provided for him a theoretical model that complemented his rigorous empiricist training in chemistry, anatomy, and physiology.

Freud's first researches under Ernst von Brücke (a student of Helmholtz and an empiricist physiologist) and T. H. Meynert the neuranatomist were competent, if unremarkable when compared with his subsequent work. With the former's support, Freud obtained a fellowship in 1885 to study in Paris with the eminent neuropathologist Jean Martin Charcot. A year later he married Martha Bernays, with whom he eventually had six children, one of whom was the celebrated psychoanalyst Anna Freud.

At that time the study of hysteria was Charcot's primary interest. Previous to Charcot, few had paid attention to hysterical symptoms; until Joseph Breuer, no headway had been made in treatment. Freud became occupied with the etiology of hysteria following Charcot's first demonstrations. He improved the active treatment of this disorder after witnessing Breuer's discovery that hysterical symptoms could be at least temporarily alleviated by the "cathartic" method of allowing and encouraging the patient to recollect the emotions that led up to the attacks. With Breuer, back in Vienna, Freud published the results of those initial experimental treatments, *Studies on Hysteria* (1895), which relied heavily on hypnosis as a therapeutic technique to uncover repressed memories.

Freud's shift from the use of hypnosis to that of free-association in the early 1890s may be seen as the first crystallization of psychoanalytic technique. At the time Freud was intensely engaged in perfecting his theories and technique, concentrating upon the theme of the sexual etiology of hysteria in particular and neurotic manifestations in general. He was isolated from the medical community of Vienna in the most profound sense; his hopes of winning a much desired professorship dwindled in proportion to the rise of an anti-Semitic climate that was also deeply hostile to scientific innovation.

Freud soon turned his attention toward dreams as manifestations of the struggle between conscious and unconscious processes he had first observed in studying hysteria. *The Interpretation of Dreams* (1900) was, in Freud's own words, "scarcely reviewed in the technical journals." This study brought psychoanalysis into its own theoretically, and was equally indispensable in its practical and therapeutic implications. He asserted that all dreams derive from unconscious (though not necessarily sexual) wishes, that they are compromised formations that provide evidence of a distinction between latent and manifest content. Such ideas were wholly radical to those who had until then dismissed dreams as mere nonsense.

From symptomatology and dreams to the psychoanalytic exploration of the bases of culture and religion was but a small step, but a decisive one. Freud, like Emile Durkheim, sought to uncover the origins of cult and morality, but, unlike the French sociologist, he gave primacy to individual psychology rather than to the collective function. *Totem and Tabu* (1912), which first appeared as a series of articles in the journal *Imago,* represents Freud's first attempt at the psychology of religion, a subject that fascinated and occupied him as a result of his discussions with Carl Jung and his readings of the anthropologists Sir James George Frazer and Robertson Smith on totemism. The psychoanalytic examination of religion became a significant concern of Freud, one that he developed in *The Future of an Illusion* (1927) and most speculatively in his last work, the "novel" (Freud's designation) *Moses and Monotheism* (1939).

By 1930 Freud had received what he saw as justified, if belated, recognition for his efforts in the form of the Goethe Prize. As he grew older, psychoanalysis became an increasingly inevitable presence on the map of the European intellect. Figures such as André Breton, founder of Surrealism, and the Bloomsbury group in England began to encourage a Freudian aesthetics of literature. In France and England psychoanalysis enjoyed a primarily aesthetic interest; in America it began (during World War II, especially) to adapt itself to the medical psychiatric profession. On the whole, the influence of Freud is now most felt not as a scientific, but as a cultural phenomenon. Psychoanalytic theory has had profound implications for every humanistic discipline. It came to provide a kind of *lingua franca* for the educated West not long after Freud himself died.

Freud's last years were spent in exile in London. He responded to the growing Nazi threat with a kind of unhurried concern. His health had been steadily worsening; he worked well past his eightieth year with the chronic pain of an oral cancer, the result of a lifetime of cigar-smoking. He finally had to be persuaded to leave Vienna in 1938, with the assistance of the analyst Marie Bonaparte, who bribed the Nazis. Freud died on September 23, 1939.

THE RELATION OF THE POET TO DAY-DREAMING

We laymen have always wondered greatly—like the cardinal who put the question to Ariosto—how that strange being, the poet, comes by his material. What makes him able to carry us with him in such a way and to arouse emotions in us of which we thought ourselves perhaps not even capable? Our interest in the problem is only stimulated by the circumstance that if we ask poets themselves they give us no explanation of the matter, or at least no satisfactory explanation. The knowledge that not even the clearest insight into the factors conditioning the choice of imaginative material, or into the nature of the ability to fashion that material, will ever make writers of us does not in any way detract from our interest.

If we could only find some activity in ourselves, or in people like ourselves, which was in any way akin to the writing of imaginative works! If we could do so, then examination of it would give us a hope of obtaining some insight into the creative powers of imaginative writers. And indeed, there is some prospect of achieving this—writers themselves always try to lessen the distance between their kind and ordinary human beings; they so often assure us that every man is at heart a poet, and that the last poet will not die until the last human being does.

We ought surely to look in the child for the first traces of imaginative activity. The child's best loved and most absorbing occupation is play. Perhaps we may say that every child at play behaves like an imaginative writer, in that he creates a world of his own or, more truly, he rearranges the things of his world and orders it in a new way that pleases him better. It would be incorrect to think that he does not take this world seriously; on the contrary, he takes his play very seriously and expends a great deal of emotion on it. The opposite of play is not serious occupation but—reality. Notwithstanding the large affective cathexis of his play-world, the child distinguishes it perfectly from reality; only he likes to borrow the objects and circumstances that he imagines from the tangible and visible things of the real world. It is only this linking of it to reality that still distinguishes a child's "play" from "day-dreaming."

Now the writer does the same as the child at play; he creates a world of phantasy which he takes very seriously; that is, he invests it with a great deal of affect, while separating it sharply from reality. Language has preserved this relationship between children's play and poetic creation. It designates certain kinds of imaginative creation, concerned with tangible objects and capable of representation, as "plays"; the people who present them are called "players." The unreality of this poetical world of imagination, however, has very important consequences for literary technique; for many things which if they happen in real life could produce no pleasure can nevertheless give enjoyment in a play—many emotions which are essentially painful may become a source of enjoyment to the spectators and hearers of a poet's work.

There is another consideration relating to the contrast between reality and play on which we will dwell for a moment. Long after a child has grown up and stopped playing, after he has for decades attempted to grasp the realities of life with all seriousness, he may one day come to a state of mind in which the contrast between play and reality is again abrogated. The adult can remember with what intense seriousness he carried on his childish play; then by comparing his would-be serious occupations with his childhood's play, he manages to throw off the heavy burden of life and obtain the great pleasure of humour.

As they grow up, people cease to play, and appear to give up the pleasure they derived from play. But anyone who knows anything of the mental life of human beings is aware that hardly anything is more difficult to them than to give up a pleasure they have once tasted. Really we never can relinquish anything; we only exchange one thing for something else. When we appear to give something up, all we really do is to adopt a substitute. So when the human being grows up and ceases to play he only gives up the connection with real objects; instead of playing he then begins to create phantasy. He builds castles in the air and creates what are called day-dreams. I believe that the greater number of human beings create phantasies at times as long as they live. This is a fact which has been overlooked for a long time, and its importance has therefore not been properly appreciated.

The phantasies of human beings are less easy to observe than the play of children. Children do, it is true, play alone, or form with other children a closed world in their minds for the purposes of play; but a child does not conceal his play from adults, even though his playing is quite unconcerned with them. The adult, on the other hand, is ashamed of his day-dreams and conceals them from other people; he cherishes them as his most intimate possessions and as a rule he would rather confess all his misdeeds than tell his day-dreams. For this reason he may believe that he is the only person who makes up such phantasies, without having any idea that everybody else tells themselves stories of the same kind. Day-dreaming is a continuation of play, nevertheless, and the motives which lie behind these two activities contain a very good reason for this different behaviour in the child at play and in the day-dreaming adult.

The play of children is determined by their wishes—really by the child's *one* wish, which is to be grown-up, the wish that helps to "bring him up." He always plays at being grown-up; in play he imitates what is known to him of the lives of adults. Now he has no reason to conceal this wish. With the adult it is otherwise; on the one hand, he knows that he is expected not to play any longer or to day-dream, but to be making his way in a real world. On the other hand, some of the wishes from which his phantasies spring are such as have to be entirely hidden; therefore he is ashamed of his phantasies as being childish and as something prohibited.

If they are concealed with so much secretiveness, you will ask, how do we know so much about the human propensity to create phantasies? Now there is a certain class of human beings upon whom not a god, indeed, but a stern goddess—Necessity—has laid the task of giving an account of what they suffer and what they enjoy. These people are the neurotics; among other things they have to confess their phantasies to the physician to whom they go in the hope of recovering through mental treatment. This is our best source of knowledge, and we have later found good reason to suppose that our patients tell us about themselves nothing that we could not also hear from healthy people.

Let us try to learn some of the characteristics of day-dreaming. We can begin by saying that happy people never make phantasies, only unsatisfied ones. Unsatisfied wishes are the driving power behind phantasies; every separate phantasy contains the fulfilment of a wish, and improves on unsatisfactory reality. The impelling wishes vary according to the sex, character and circumstances of the creator; they may be easily divided, however, into two principal groups. Either they are ambitious wishes, serving to exalt the person creating them, or they are erotic. In young women erotic wishes dominate the phantasies almost exclusively, for their ambition is generally comprised in their erotic longings; in young men egoistic and ambitious wishes assert themselves plainly enough alongside their erotic desires. But we will not lay stress on the distinction between these two trends; we prefer to emphasize the fact that they are often united. In many altar-pieces the portrait of the donor is to be found in one corner of the picture; and in the greater number of ambitious day-dreams, too, we can discover a woman in some corner, for whom the dreamer performs all his heroic deeds and at whose feet all his triumphs are to be laid. Here you see we have strong enough motives for concealment; a well-brought-up woman is, indeed, credited with only a minimum of erotic desire, while a young man has to learn to suppress the overweening self-regard he acquires in the indulgent atmosphere surrounding his childhood, so that he may find his proper place in a society that is full of other persons making similar claims.

We must not imagine that the various products of this impulse towards phantasy, castles in the air or day-dreams, are stereotyped or unchangeable. On the contrary, they fit themselves into the changing impressions of life, alter with the vicissitudes of life; every deep new impression gives them what might be called a "date-stamp." The relation of phantasies to time is altogether of great importance. One may say that a phantasy at one and the same moment hovers between three periods of time—the three periods of our ideation. The activity of phantasy in the mind is linked up with some current impression, occasioned by some event in the present, which had the power to rouse an intense desire. From there it wanders back to the memory of an early experience, generally belonging to infancy, in which this wish was fulfilled. Then it creates for itself a situation which is to emerge in the future, representing the fulfilment of the wish—this is the day-dream or phantasy, which now carries in it traces both of the occasion which engendered it and of some past memory. So past, present and future are threaded, as it were, on the string of the wish that runs through them all.

A very ordinary example may serve to make my statement clearer. Take the case of a poor orphan lad, to whom you have given the address of some employer where he may perhaps get work. On the way there he falls into a day-dream suitable to the situation from which it springs. The content of the phantasy will be somewhat as follows: He is taken on and pleases his new employer, makes himself indispensable in the business, is taken into the family of the employer, and marries the charming daughter of the house. Then he comes to conduct the business, first as a partner, and then as successor to his father-in-law. In this way the dreamer regains what he had in his happy childhood, the protecting house, his loving parents and the first objects of his affection. You will see from such an example how the wish employs some event in the present to plan a future on the pattern of the past.

Much more could be said about phantasies, but I will only allude as briefly as possible to certain points. If phantasies become over-luxuriant and over-powerful, the necessary conditions for an outbreak of neurosis or psychosis are constituted; phantasies are also the first preliminary stage in the mind of the symptoms of illness of which our patients complain. A broad by-path here branches off into pathology.

I cannot pass over the relation of phantasies to dreams. Our nocturnal dreams are nothing but such phantasies, as we can make clear by interpreting them. Language, in its unrivalled wisdom, long ago decided the question of the essential nature of dreams by giving the name of "day-dreams" to the airy creations of phantasy. If the meaning of our dreams usually remains obscure in spite of this clue, it is because of the circumstance that at night wishes of which we are ashamed also become active in us, wishes which we have to hide from ourselves, which were consequently repressed and pushed back into the unconscious. Such repressed wishes and their derivatives can therefore achieve expression only when almost completely disguised. When scientific work had succeeded in elucidating the distortion in dreams, it was no longer difficult to recognize that nocturnal dreams are fulfilments of desires in exactly the same way as day-dreams are—those phantasies with which we are all so familiar.

So much for day-dreaming; now for the poet! Shall we dare really to compare an imaginative writer with "one who dreams in broad daylight," and his creations with day-dreams? Here, surely, a first distinction is forced upon us; we must distinguish between poets who, like the bygone creators of epics and tragedies, take over their material ready-made, and those who seem to create their material spontaneously. Let us keep to the latter, and let us also not choose for our comparison those writers who are most highly esteemed by critics. We will choose the less pretentious writers of romances, novels and stories, who are read all the same by the widest circles of men and women. There is one very marked characteristic in the productions of these writers which must strike us all: they all have a hero who is the centre of interest, for whom the author tries to win our sympathy by every possible means, and whom he places under the protection of a special providence. If at the end of one chapter the hero is left unconscious and bleeding from severe wounds, I am sure to find him at the beginning of the next being carefully tended and on the way to recovery; if the first volume ends in the hero being shipwrecked in a storm at sea, I am certain to hear at the beginning of the next of his hairbreadth escape—otherwise, indeed, the story could not continue. The feeling of security with which I follow the hero through his dangerous adventures is the same as that with which a real hero throws himself into the water to save a drowning man, or exposes himself to the fire of the enemy while storming a battery. It is this very feeling of being a hero which one of our best authors has well expressed in the famous phrase, *"Es kann dir nix g'schehen!"*[1] It seems to me, however, that this significant mark of invulnerability very clearly betrays—His Majesty the Ego, the hero of all day-dreams and all novels.

The same relationship is hinted at in yet other characteristics of these egocentric stories. When all the women in a novel invariably fall in love with the hero, this can hardly be looked upon as a description of reality, but it is easily understood as an essential constituent of a day-dream. The same thing holds good when the other people in the story are sharply divided into good and bad, with complete disregard of the manifold variety in the traits of real human beings; the "good" ones are those who help the ego in its character of hero, while the "bad" are his enemies and rivals.

We do not in any way fail to recognize that many imaginative productions have travelled far from the original naïve day-dream, but I cannot suppress the surmise that even the most extreme variations could be brought into relationship with this model by an uninterrupted series of transitions. It has struck me in many so-called psychological novels, too, that only one person—once again the hero—is described from within; the author dwells in his soul and looks upon the other people from outside. The psychological novel in general probably owes its peculiarities to the tendency of modern writers to split up their ego by self-observation into many component-egos, and in this way to personify the conflicting trends in their own mental life in many heroes. There are certain novels, which might be called "excentric," that seem to stand in marked contradiction to the typical day-dream; in these the person introduced as the hero plays the least active part of anyone, and seems instead to let the actions and sufferings of other people pass him by like a spectator. Many of the later novels of Zola belong to this class. But I must say that the psychological analysis of people who are not writers, and who deviate in many things from the so-called norm, has shown us analogous variations in their day-dreams in which the ego contents itself with the rôle of spectator.

If our comparison of the imaginative writer with the day-dreamer, and of poetic production with the day-dream, is to be of any value, it must show itself fruitful in some way or other. Let us try, for instance, to examine the works of writers in reference to the idea propounded above, the relation of the phantasy to the wish that runs through it and to the three periods of time; and with its help let us study the connection between the life of the writer and his productions. Hitherto it has not been known what preliminary ideas would constitute an approach to this problem; very often this relation has been regarded as much simpler than it is; but the insight gained from phantasies leads us to expect the following state of things. Some actual experience which made a strong impression on the writer had stirred up a memory of an earlier experience, generally belonging to childhood, which then arouses a wish that finds a fulfilment in the work in question, and in which elements of the recent event and the old memory should be discernible.

Do not be alarmed at the complexity of this formula; I myself expect that in reality it will prove itself to be too schematic, but that possibly it may contain a first means of approach to the true state of affairs. From some attempts I have made I think that this way of approaching works of the imagination might not be unfruitful. You will not forget that the stress laid on the writer's memories of his childhood, which perhaps seems so strange, is ultimately derived from the hypothesis that imaginative creation, like day-dreaming, is a continuation of and substitute for the play of childhood.

We will not neglect to refer also to that class of imaginative work which must be recognized not as spontaneous production, but as a re-fashioning of ready-made material. Here, too, the writer retains a certain amount of independence, which can express itself in the choice of material and in changes in the material chosen, which are often considerable. As far as it goes, this material is derived from the racial treasure-house of myths, legends and fairy-tales. The study of these creations of racial psychology is in no way complete, but it seems extremely probable that myths, for example, are distorted vestiges of the wish-phantasies of whole nations—the age-long dreams of young humanity.

You will say that, although writers came first in the title of this paper, I have told you far less about them than about phantasy. I am aware of that, and will try to excuse myself by pointing to the present state of our knowledge. I could only throw out suggestions and bring up interesting points which arise from the study of phantasies, and which pass beyond them to the problem of the choice of literary material. We have not touched on the other problem at all, *i.e.* what are the means which writers use to achieve those emotional reactions in us that are roused by their productions. But I would at least point out to you the path which leads from our discussion of day-dreams to the problems of the effect produced on us by imaginative works.

You will remember that we said the day-dreamer hid his phantasies carefully from other people because he had reason to be ashamed of them. I may now add that even if he were to communicate them to us, he would give us no pleasure by his disclosures. When we hear such phantasies they repel us, or at least leave us cold. But when a man of literary talent presents his plays, or relates what we take to be his personal day-dreams, we experience great pleasure arising probably from many sources. How the writer accomplishes this is his innermost secret; the essential *ars poetica* lies in the technique by which our feeling of repulsion is overcome, and this has certainly to do with those barriers erected between every individual being and all others. We can guess at two methods used in this technique. The writer softens the egotistical character of the day-dream by changes and disguises, and he bribes us by the offer of a purely formal, that is, aesthetic, pleasure in the presentation of his phantasies. The increment of pleasure which is offered us in order to release yet greater pleasure arising from deeper sources in the mind is called an "incitement premium" or technically, "fore-pleasure." I am of opinion that all the aesthetic pleasure we gain from the works of imaginative writers is of the same type as this "fore-pleasure," and that the true enjoyment of literature proceeds from the release of tensions in our minds. Perhaps much that brings about this result consists in the writer's putting us into a position in which we can enjoy our own day-dreams without reproach or shame. Here we reach a path leading into novel, interesting and complicated researches, but we also, at least for the present, arrive at the end of the present discussion.

NOTES

1. "Nothing can happen to me!"—Tr.

THE THEME OF THE THREE CASKETS

Two scenes from Shakespeare, one from a comedy and the other from a tragedy, have lately given me occasion for setting and solving a little problem.

The former scene is the suitors' choice between the three caskets in *The Merchant of Venice*. The fair and wise Portia, at her father's bidding, is bound to take for her husband only that one among her suitors who chooses the right casket from among the three before him. The three caskets are of gold, silver and lead: the right one is that containing her portrait. Two suitors have already withdrawn, unsuccessful: they have chosen gold and silver. Bassanio, the third, elects for the lead; he thereby wins the bride, whose affection was already his before the trial of fortune. Each of the suitors had given reasons for his choice in a speech in which he praised the metal he preferred, while depreciating the other two. The most difficult task thus fell to the share of the third fortunate suitor; what he finds to say in glorification of lead as against gold and silver is but little and has a forced ring about it. If in psychoanalytic practice we were confronted with such a speech, we should suspect concealed motives behind the unsatisfying argument.

Shakespeare did not invent this oracle of choosing a casket; he took it from a tale in the *Gesta Romanorum,* in which a girl undertakes the same choice to win the son of the Emperor.[1] Here too the third metal, the lead, is the bringer of fortune. It is not hard to guess that we have here an ancient theme, which requires to be interpreted and traced back to its origin. A preliminary conjecture about the meaning of this choice between gold, silver, and lead is soon confirmed by a statement from E. Stucken,[2] who has made a study of the same material in far-reaching connections. He says, "The identity of the three suitors of Portia is clear from their choice: the Prince of Morocco chooses the gold casket: he is the sun; the Prince of Arragon chooses the silver casket: he is the moon; Bassanio chooses the leaden casket: he is the star youth." In support of this explanation he cites an episode from the Esthonian folk-epic "Kalewipoeg," in which the three suitors appear undisguisedly as the sun, moon and star youths ("the eldest son of the Pole star") and the bride again falls to the lot of the third.

Thus our little problem leads to an astral myth. The only pity is that with this explanation we have not got to the end of the matter. The question goes further, for we do not share the belief of many investigators that myths were read off direct from the heavens; we are more inclined to judge with Otto Rank[3] that they were projected on to the heavens after having arisen quite otherwise under purely human conditions. Now our interest is in this human content.

Let us glance once more at our material. In the Esthonian epic, as in the tale from the *Gesta Romanorum,* the subject is the choice of a maiden among three suitors; in the scene from *The Merchant of Venice* apparently the subject is the same, but at the same time in this last something in the nature of an inversion of the idea makes its appearance: a man chooses between three— caskets. If we had to do with a dream, it would at once occur to us that caskets are also women, symbols of the essential thing in woman, and therefore of a woman herself, like boxes, large or small, baskets, and so on. If we let ourselves assume the same symbolic substitution in the story, then the casket scene in *The Merchant of Venice* really becomes the inversion we suspected. With one wave of the hand, such as usually only happens in fairy-tales, we have stripped the astral garment from our theme; and now we see that the subject is an idea from human life, a man's choice between three women.

This same content, however, is to be found in another scene of Shakespeare's, in one of his most powerfully moving dramas; this time not the choice of a bride, yet linked by many mysterious resemblances to the casket-choice in *The Merchant of Venice.* The old King Lear resolves to divide his kingdom while he yet lives among his three daughters, according to the love they each in turn express for him. The two elder ones, Goneril and Regan, exhaust themselves in asseverations and glorifications of their love for him, the third, Cordelia, refuses to join in these. He should have recognized the unassuming, speechless love of the third and rewarded it, but he misinterprets it, banishes Cordelia, and divides the kingdom between the other two, to his own and the general ruin. Is not this once more a scene of choosing between three women, of whom the youngest is the best, the supreme one?

There immediately occur to us other scenes from myth, folk-tale and literature, with the same situation as their content: the shepherd Paris has to choose between three goddesses, of whom he declares the third to be the fairest. Cinderella is another such youngest, and is preferred by the prince to the two elder sisters; Psyche in the tale of Apuleius is the youngest and fairest of three sisters; on the one hand, she becomes human and is revered as Aphrodite, on the other, she is treated by the goddess as Cinderella was treated by her stepmother and has to sort a heap of mixed seeds, which she accomplishes with the help of little creatures (doves for Cinderella, ants for Psyche).[4] Anyone who cared to look more closely into the material could undoubtedly discover other versions of the same idea in which the same essential features had been retained.

Let us content ourselves with Cordelia, Aphrodite, Cinderella and Psyche! The three women, of whom the third surpasses the other two, must surely be regarded as in some way alike if they are represented as sisters. It must not lead us astray if in *Lear* the three are the daughters of him who makes the choice; this means probably nothing more than that Lear has to be represented as an old man. An old man cannot very well choose between three women in any other way: thus they become his daughters.

But who are these three sisters and why must the choice fall on the third? If we could answer this question, we should be in possession of the solution we are seeking. We have once already availed ourselves of an application of psychoanalytic technique, in explaining the three caskets as symbolic of three women. If we have the courage to continue the process, we shall be setting foot on a path which leads us first to something unexpected and incomprehensible, but perhaps by a devious route to a goal.

It may strike us that this surpassing third one has in several instances certain peculiar qualities besides her beauty. They are qualities that seem to be tending towards some kind of unity; we certainly may not expect to find them equally well marked in every example. Cordelia masks her true self, becomes as unassuming as lead, she remains dumb, she "loves and is silent." Cinderella hides herself, so that she is not to be found. We may perhaps equate concealment and dumbness. These would of course be only two instances out of the five we have picked out. But there is an intimation of the same thing to be found, curiously enough, in two other cases. We have decided to compare Cordelia, with her obstinate refusal, to lead. In Bassanio's short speech during the choice of the caskets these are his words of the lead—properly speaking; without any connection:

> Thy paleness moves me more than eloquence
> ("Plainness," according to another reading)

Thus: Thy plainness moves me more than the blatant nature of the other two. Gold and silver are "loud"; lead is dumb, in effect like Cordelia, who "loves and is silent."[5]

In the ancient Greek tales of the Judgement of Paris, nothing is said of such a withholding of herself on the part of Aphrodite. Each of the three goddesses speaks to the youth and tries to win him by promises. But, curiously enough, in a quite modern handling of the same scene this characteristic of the third that has struck us makes its appearance again. In the libretto of Offenbach's *La Belle Hélène*, Paris, after telling of the solicitations of the other two goddesses, relates how Aphrodite bore herself in this contest for the prize of beauty:

> *La troisième, ah! la troisième!*
> *La troisième ne dit rien,*
> *Elle eut le prix tout de même. . . .*

If we decide to regard the peculiarities of our "third one" as concentrated in the "dumbness," then psychoanalysis has to say that dumbness is in dreams a familiar representation of death.[6]

More than ten years ago a highly intelligent man told me a dream which he wanted to look upon as proof of the telepathic nature of dreams. He saw an absent friend from whom he had received no news for a very long time, and reproached him warmly for his silence. The friend made no reply. It then proved that he had met his death by suicide about the time of the dream. Let us leave the problem of telepathy on one side: there seems to be no doubt that here the dumbness in the dream represents death. Concealment, disappearance from view, too, which the prince in the fairy-tale of Cinderella has to experience three times, is in dreams an unmistakable symbol of death; and no less so is a striking pallor, of which the paleness of the lead in one reading of Shakespeare's text reminds us.[7] The difficulty of translating these significations from the language of dreams into the mode of expression in the myth now occupying our attention is much lightened if we can show with any probability that dumbness must be interpreted as a sign of death in other productions that are not dreams.

I will single out at this point the ninth of Grimm's *Fairy Tales,* the one with the title "The Twelve Brothers." A king and a queen have twelve children, all boys. Thereupon the king says, "If the thirteenth child is a girl, the boys must die." In expectation of this birth he has twelve coffins made. The twelve sons flee with their mother's help into a secret wood, and swear death to every maiden they shall meet.

A girl-child is born, grows up, and learns one day from her mother that she had twelve brothers. She decides to seek them out, and finds the youngest in the wood; he recognizes her but wants to hide her on account of the brothers' oath. The sister says: "I will gladly die, if thereby I can save my twelve brothers." The brothers welcome her gladly, however, and she stays with them and looks after their house for them.

In a little garden near the house grow twelve lilies: the maiden plucks these to give one to each brother. At that moment the brothers are changed into ravens, and disappear, together with the house and garden. Ravens are spirit-birds, the killing of the twelve brothers by their sister is thus again represented by the plucking of the flowers, as at the beginning of the story by the coffins and the disappearance of the brothers. The maiden, who is once more ready to save her brothers from death, is now told that as a condition she is to be dumb for seven years, and not speak one single word. She submits to this test, by which she herself goes into danger, *i.e.* she herself dies for her brothers, as she promised before meeting with them. By remaining dumb she succeeds at last in delivering the ravens.

In the story of "The Six Swans" the brothers who are changed into birds are released in exactly the same way, *i.e.* restored to life by the dumbness of the sister. The maiden has taken the firm resolve to release her brothers, "an if it cost her life"; as the king's wife she again risks her own life because she will not relinquish her dumbness to defend herself against evil accusations.

Further proofs could undoubtedly be gathered from fairy-tales that dumbness is to be understood as representing death. If we follow these indications, then the third one of the sisters between whom the choice lies would be a dead woman. She may, however, be something else, namely, Death itself, the Goddess of Death. By virtue of a displacement that is not infrequent, the qualities that a deity imparts to men are ascribed to the deity himself. Such a displacement will astonish us least of all in relation to the Goddess of Death, since in modern thought and artistic representation, which would thus be anticipated in these stories, death itself is nothing but a dead man.

But if the third of the sisters is the Goddess of Death, we know the sisters. They are the Fates, the Moerae, the Parcae or the Norns, the third of whom is called Atropos, the inexorable.

II

Let us leave on one side for a while the task of inserting this new-found meaning into our myth, and let us hear what the mythologists have to say about the origin of and the part played by the Fates.[8]

The earliest Greek mythology only knows one Moera, personifying the inevitable doom (in Homer). The further development of this one Moera into a group of three sisters—goddesses—, less often two, probably came about in connection with other divine figures to which the Moerae are clearly related: the Graces and the Horae, the Hours.

The Hours are originally goddesses of the waters of the sky, dispensing rain and dew, and of the clouds from which rain falls; and since these clouds are conceived of as a kind of web it comes about that these goddesses are looked on as spinners, a character that then became attached to the Moerae. In the sun-favoured Mediterranean lands it is the rain on which the fertility of the soil depends, and thus the Hours become the goddesses of vegetation. The beauty of flowers and the abundance of fruit is their doing, and man endows them plentifully with charming and graceful traits. They become the divine representatives of the Seasons, and possibly in this connection acquire their triple number, if the sacred nature of the number three is not sufficient explanation of this. For these ancient peoples at first distinguished only three seasons: winter, spring, summer. Autumn was only added in late Graeco-Roman times, after which four Hours were often represented in art.

The relation to time remained attached to the Hours: later they presided over the time of day, as at first over the periods of the year: at last their name came to be merely a designation for the period of sixty minutes (hour, *heure, ora*). The Norns of German mythology are akin to the Hours and the Moerae and exhibit this time-signification in their names. The nature of these deities could not fail, however, to be apprehended more profoundly in time, so that the essential thing about them was shifted until it came to consist of the abiding law at work in the passage of time: the Hours thus became guardians of the law of Nature, and of the divine order of things whereby the constant recurrence of the same things in unalterable succession in the natural world takes place.

This knowledge of nature reacted on the conception of human life. The nature-myth changed into a myth of human life: the weather-goddesses became goddesses of destiny. But this aspect of the Hours only found expression in the Moerae, who watch over the needful ordering of human life as inexorably as do the Hours over the regular order of nature. The implacable severity of this law, the affinity of it with death and ruin, avoided in the winsome figures of the Hours, was now stamped upon the Moerae, as though mankind had only perceived the full solemnity of natural law when he had to submit his own personality to its working.

The names of the three spinners have been interpreted significantly by mythologists. Lachesis, the name of the second, seems to mean "the accidental within the decrees of destiny"[9]—we might say "that which is experienced"—

while Atropos means "the inevitable"—Death—, and then for Clotho there remains "the fateful tendencies each one of us brings into the world."

And now it is time to return to the idea contained in the choice between the three sisters, which we are endeavouring to interpret. It is with deep dissatisfaction that we find how unintelligible insertion of the new interpretation makes the situations we are considering and what contradictions of the apparent content then result. The third of the sisters should be the Goddess of Death, nay, Death itself; in the Judgement of Paris she is the Goddess of Love, in the tale of Apuleius one comparable to the goddess for her beauty, in *The Merchant of Venice* the fairest and wisest of women, in *Lear* the one faithful daughter. Can a contradiction be more complete? Yet perhaps close at hand there lies even this, improbable as it is—the acme of contradiction. It is certainly forthcoming if every time in this theme of ours there occurs a free choice between the women, and if the choice is thereupon to fall on death— that which no man chooses, to which by destiny alone man falls a victim.

However, contradictions of a certain kind, replacements by the exact opposite, offer no serious difficulty to analytic interpretation. We shall not this time take our stand on the fact that contraries are constantly represented by one and the same element in the modes of expression used by the unconscious, such as dreams. But we shall remember that there are forces in mental life tending to bring about replacement by the opposite, such as the so-called reaction-formation, and it is just in the discovery of such hidden forces that we look for the reward of our labours. The Moerae were created as a result of a recognition which warns man that he too is a part of nature and therefore subject to the immutable law of death. Against this subjection something in man was bound to struggle, for it is only with extreme unwillingness that he gives up his claim to an exceptional position. We know that man makes use of his imaginative faculty (phantasy) to satisfy those wishes that reality does not satisfy. So his imagination rebelled against the recognition of the truth embodied in the myth of the Moerae, and constructed instead the myth derived from it, in which the Goddess of Death was replaced by the Goddess of Love and by that which most resembles her in human shape. The third of the sisters is no longer Death, she is the fairest, best, most desirable and the most lovable among women. Nor was this substitution in any way difficult: it was prepared for by an ancient ambivalence, it fulfilled itself along the lines of an ancient context which could at that time not long have been forgotten. The Goddess of Love herself, who now took the place of the Goddess of Death, had once been identical with her. Even the Greek Aphrodite had not wholly relinquished her connection with the underworld, although she had long surrendered her rôle of goddess of that region to other divine shapes, to Persephone, or to the tri-form Artemis-Hecate. The great Mother-goddesses of the oriental peoples, however, all seem to have been both founts of being and destroyers; goddesses of life and of fertility, and death-goddesses. Thus the replacement by the wish-opposite of which we have spoken in our theme is built upon an ancient identity.

The same consideration answers the question how the episode of a choice

came into the myth of the three sisters. A wished-for reversal is again found
here. Choice stands in the place of necessity, of destiny. Thus man overcomes
death, which in thought he has acknowledged. No greater triumph of
wish-fulfilment is conceivable. Just where in reality he obeys compulsion, he
exercises choice; and that which he chooses is not a thing of horror, but the
fairest and most desirable thing in life.

On a closer inspection we observe, to be sure, that the original myth is not
so much disguised that traces of it do not show through and betray its
presence. The free choice between the three sisters is, properly speaking, no
free choice, for it must necessarily fall on the third if every kind of evil is not
to come about, as in *Lear*. The fairest and the best, she who has stepped into
the place of the Death-goddess, has kept certain characteristics that border on
the uncanny, so that from them we might guess at what lay beneath.[10]

So far we have followed out the myth and its transformation, and trust that
we have rightly indicated the hidden causes of this transformation. Now we
may well be interested in the way in which the poet has made use of the idea.
We gain the impression that in his mind a reduction to the original idea of the
myth is going on, so that we once more perceive the original meaning
containing all the power to move us that had been weakened by the distortion
of the myth. It is by means of this undoing of the distortion and partial return
to the original that the poet achieves his profound effect upon us.

To avoid misunderstandings, I wish to say that I have no intention of
denying that the drama of *King Lear* inculcates the two prudent maxims: that
one should not forgo one's possessions and privileges in one's lifetime and that
one must guard against accepting flattery as genuine. These and similar
warnings do undoubtedly arise from the play; but it seems to me quite
impossible to explain the overpowering effect of *Lear* from the impression that
such a train of thought would produce, or to assume that the poet's own
creative instincts would not carry him further than the impulse to illustrate
these maxims. Moreover, even though we are told that the poet's intention was
to present the tragedy of ingratitude, the sting of which he probably felt in his
own heart, and that the effect of the play depends on the purely formal
element, its artistic trappings, it seems to me that this information cannot
compete with the comprehension that dawns upon us after our study of the
theme of a choice between the three sisters.

Lear is an old man. We said before that this is why the three sisters appear
as his daughters. The paternal relationship, out of which so much fruitful
dramatic situations might arise, is not turned to further account in the drama.
But Lear is not only an old man; he is a dying man. The extraordinary project
of dividing the inheritance thus loses its strangeness. The doomed man is
nevertheless not willing to renounce the love of women; he insists on hearing
how much he is loved. Let us now recall that most moving last scene, one of
the culminating points reached in modern tragic drama: "Enter Lear with
Cordelia dead in his arms." Cordelia is Death. Reverse the situation and it
becomes intelligible and familiar to us—the Death-goddess bearing away the
dead hero from the place of battle, like the Valkyr in German mythology.

Eternal wisdom, in the garb of the primitive myth, bids the old man renounce love, choose death and make friends with the necessity of dying.

The poet brings us very near to the ancient idea by making the man who accomplishes the choice between the three sisters aged and dying. The regressive treatment he has thus undertaken with the myth, which was disguised by the reversal of the wish, allows its original meaning so far to appear that perhaps a superficial allegorical interpretation of the three female figures in the theme becomes possible as well. One might say that the three inevitable relations man has with woman are here represented: that with the mother who bears him, with the companion of his bed and board, and with the destroyer. Or it is the three forms taken on by the figure of the mother as life proceeds: the mother herself, the beloved who is chosen after her pattern, and finally the Mother Earth who receives him again. But it is in vain that the old man yearns after the love of woman as once he had it from his mother; the third of the Fates alone, the silent goddess of Death, will take him into her arms.

NOTES

1. G. Brandes, *William Shakespeare*, 1896.

2. *Astralmythen*, p. 655.

3. O. Rank, *Der Mythus von der Geburt des Helden* (Vienne, 1909), p. 8 *et seq.*

4. I have to thank Dr. Otto Rank for calling my attention to these similarities.

5. In Schlegel's translation this allusion is quite lost; indeed, changed into the opposite meaning: *Dein schlichtes Wesen spricht beredt mich an.* (Thy plainness speaks to me with eloquence.)

6. In Stekel's *Sprache des Traumes* (1911), dumbness is also mentioned among the "death" symbols (p. 351).

7. Stekel, *loc. cit.*

8. What follows is taken from Roscher's *Lexikon der griechischen und römanischen Mythologie,* under the relevant headings.

9. Roscher, after Preller-Robert's *Griechische Mythologie.*

10. The Psyche of Apuleius' story has kept many traits that remind us of her kinship with death. Her wedding is celebrated like a funeral, she has to descend into the underworld, and afterwards sinks into a death-like sleep (Otto Rank).

On the significance of Psyche as goddess of the spring and as "Bride of Death," cf. A. Zinzow, *Psyche und Eros.*

In another of Grimm's Tales ("The Goose-girl at the Fountain") there is, as in "Cinderella," an alternation between the ugly and the beautiful aspect of the third sister, in which may be seen an indication of her double nature—before and after the substitution. This third one is repudiated by her father, after a test which nearly corresponds with that in *King Lear.* Like the other sisters, she has to say how dear she holds their father, and finds no expression for her love except the comparison of it with salt. (Kindly communicated by Dr. Hanns Sachs.)

HUMOUR

In my work on *Wit and Its Relation to the Unconscious* I considered humour really from the economic point of view alone. My object was to discover the source of the pleasure derived from humour, and I think I was able to show that that pleasure proceeds from a saving in expenditure of affect.

There are two ways in which the process at work in humour may take place. Either one person may himself adopt a humorous attitude, while a second person acts as spectator, and derives enjoyment from the attitude of the first; or there may be two people concerned, one of whom does not himself take any active share in producing the humorous effect, but is regarded by the other in a humorous light. To take a very crude example: when a criminal who is being led to the gallows on a Monday observes, "Well, this is a good beginning to the week," he himself is creating the humour; the process works itself out in relation to himself and evidently it affords him a certain satisfaction. I am merely a listener who has not assisted in this functioning of his sense of humour, but I feel its effect, as it were from a distance. I detect in myself a certain humorous satisfaction, possibly much as he does.

We have an instance of the second type of humour when a writer or a narrator depicts the behaviour of real or imaginary people in a humorous fashion. There is no need for the people described to display any humour; the humorous attitude only concerns the person who makes them the object of it, and the reader or hearer shares his enjoyment of the humour, as in the former instance. To sum up, then, we may say that the humorous attitude—in whatever it consists—may have reference to the subject's self or to other people; further, we may assume that it is a source of enjoyment to the person who adopts it, and, finally, a similar pleasure is experienced by observers who take no actual part in it.

We shall best understand the origin of the pleasure derived from humour if we consider the process which takes place in the mind of anyone listening to another man's jest. He sees this other person in a situation which leads him to anticipate that the victim will show signs of some affect; he will get angry, complain, manifest pain, fear, horror, possibly even despair. The person who is watching or listening is prepared to follow his lead, and to call up the same emotions. But his anticipations are deceived; the other man does not display any affect—he makes a joke. It is from the saving of expenditure in feeling that the hearer derives the humorous satisfaction.

It is easy to get so far, but we soon say to ourselves that it is the process in the other man, the "humorist," which calls for the greater attention. There is no doubt that the essence of humour is that one spares oneself the affects to which the situation would naturally give rise and overrides with a jest the possibility of such an emotional display. Thus far, the process must be the same in the humorist and his hearer. Or, to put it more accurately, the hearer must have copied the process in the mind of the humorist. But how does the latter arrive at that mental attitude, which makes the discharge of affect superfluous? What is the dynamic process underlying the "humorous attitude"? Clearly, the solution of this problem is to be found in the humorist himself; in the listener we may suppose there is only an echo, a copy of this unknown process.

It is now time to acquaint ourselves with some of the characteristics of humour. Like wit and the comic, humour has in it a *liberating* element. But it has also something fine and elevating, which is lacking in the other two ways of deriving pleasure from intellectual activity. Obviously, what is fine about it is the triumph of narcissism, the ego's victorious assertion of its own invulnerability. It refuses to be hurt by the arrows of reality or to be compelled to suffer. It insists that it is impervious to wounds dealt by the outside world, in fact, that these are merely occasions for affording it pleasure. This last trait is a fundamental characteristic of humour. Suppose the criminal being led to execution on a Monday had said: "It doesn't worry me. What does it matter, after all, if a fellow like me is hanged? The world won't come to an end." We should have to admit that this speech of his displays the same magnificent rising superior to the real situation; what he says is wise and true, but it does not betray a trace of humour. Indeed, it is based on an appraisal of reality which runs directly counter to that of humour. Humour is not resigned; it is rebellious. It signifies the triumph not only of the ego, but also of the pleasure principle, which is strong enough to assert itself here in the face of the adverse real circumstances.

These last two characteristics, the denial of the claim of reality and the triumph of the pleasure principle, cause humour to approximate to the regressive or reactionary processes which engage our attention so largely in psychopathology. By its repudiation of the possibility of suffering, it takes its place in the great series of methods devised by the mind of man for evading the compulsion to suffer—a series which begins with neurosis and culminates in delusions, and includes intoxication, self-induced states of abstraction and ecstasy. Owing to this connection, humour possesses a dignity which is wholly lacking, for instance, in wit, for the aim of wit is either simply to afford gratification, or, in so doing, to provide an outlet for aggressive tendencies. Now in what does this humorous attitude consist, by means of which one refuses to undergo suffering, asseverates the invincibility of one's ego against the real world and victoriously upholds the pleasure principle, yet all without quitting the ground of mental sanity, as happens when other means to the same end are adopted? Surely it seems impossible to reconcile the two achievements.

If we turn to consider the situation in which one person adopts a humorous attitude towards others, one view which I have already tentatively suggested in my book on wit will seem very evident. It is this: that the one is adopting towards the other the attitude of an adult towards a child, recognizing and smiling at the triviality of the interests and sufferings which seem to the child so big. Thus the humorist acquires his superiority by assuming the role of the grown-up, identifying himself to some extent with the father, while he reduces the other people to the position of children. This supposition is probably true to fact, but it does not seem to take us very far. We ask ourselves what makes the humorist arrogate to himself this role?

Here we must recall the other, perhaps the original and more important, situation in humour, in which a man adopts a humorous attitude towards himself in order to ward off possible suffering. Is there any sense in saying that someone is treating himself like a child and is at the same time playing the part of the superior adult in relation to this child?

This idea does not seem very plausible, but I think that if we consider what we have learnt from pathological observations of the structure of our ego, we shall find a strong confirmation of it. This ego is not a simple entity; it harbours within it, as its innermost core, a special agency: the super-ego. Sometimes it is amalgamated with this, so that we cannot distinguish the one from the other, while in other circumstances the two can be sharply differentiated. Genetically the super-ego inherits the parental function; it often holds the ego in strict subordination, and still actually treats it as the parents (or the father) treated the child in his early years. We obtain a dynamic explanation of the humorous attitude, therefore, if we conclude that it consists in the subject's removing the accent from his own ego and transferring it on to his super-ego. To the super-ego, thus inflated, the ego can appear tiny and all its interests trivial, and with this fresh distribution of energy it may be an easy matter for it to suppress the potential reactions of the ego.

To preserve our customary phraseology, let us not speak of transferring the accent, but rather of displacing large quantities of cathexis. We shall then ask whether we are justified in imagining such extensive displacements from one agency in the mental apparatus to another. It looks like a new hypothesis, conceived *ad hoc;* yet we may recollect that repeatedly, even if not often enough, we have taken such a factor into account when endeavouring to form some metapsychological conception of the mental processes. For instance, we assumed that the difference between ordinary erotic object-cathexis and the state of being in love was that in the latter case incomparably more cathexis passes over to the object, the ego as it were emptying itself into the object. The study of some cases of paranoia proved to me that ideas of persecution are formed early, and exist for a long time without any perceptible effect, until as the result of some definite occasion they receive a sufficient amount of cathexis to cause them to become dominant. The cure of paranoiac attacks of this sort, too, would lie not so much in resolving and correcting the delusional ideas as in withdrawing from them the cathexis they have attracted. The alternation between melancholia and mania, between a cruel suppressing of the ego by the super-ego and the liberation of the ego after this oppression, suggests some such shifting of cathexis; and this conception would, moreover, explain a number of phenomena in normal mental life. If, hitherto, we have but seldom had recourse to this explanation, it has been on account of our customary caution, which is surely rather praiseworthy than otherwise. The ground on which we feel ourselves secure is that of mental pathology; it is here that we make our observations and win our convictions. For the present we commit ourselves to an opinion concerning the normal only in so far as we detect it amongst the isolated and distorted features of the morbid. When once this hesitation is overcome, we shall recognize how greatly the static conditions as well as the dynamic alteration in the quantity of the energic cathexis contribute to our understanding of mental processes.

I think, therefore, that the possibility I have suggested, namely, that in a given situation the subject suddenly effects a hyper-cathexis of the super-ego, which in its turn alters the reactions of the ego, is one which deserves to be retained. Moreover, we find a striking analogy to this hypothesis of mine about humour in the kindred field of wit. I was led to assume that wit originates in the momentary abandoning of a conscious thought to unconscious elaboration, wit being therefore the contribution of the unconscious to the comic. In just the same way humour would be a contribution to the comic made through the agency of the super-ego.

In other respects we know that the super-ego is a stern master. It may be said that it accords ill with its character that it should wink at affording the ego a little gratification. It is true that the pleasure derived from humour is never so intense as that produced by the comic or by wit and never finds a vent in hearty laughter. It is also true that, in bringing about the humorous attitude, the super-ego is in fact repudiating reality and serving an illusion. But (without quite knowing why) we attribute to this less intensive pleasure a high value: we feel it to have a peculiarly liberating and elevating effect. Besides, the jest made in humour is not the essential; it has only the value of a demonstration. The principal thing is the intention which humour fulfils, whether it concerns the subject's self or other people. Its meaning is: "Look here! This is all that this seemingly dangerous world amounts to. Child's play—the very thing to jest about!"

If it is really the super-ego which, in humour, speaks such kindly words of comfort to the intimidated ego, this teaches us that we have still very much to learn about the nature of that energy. Further we note that it is not everyone who is capable of the humorous attitude: it is a rare and precious gift, and there are many people who have not even the capacity for deriving pleasure from humour when it is presented to them by others. Finally, if the super-ego does try to comfort the ego by humour and to protect it from suffering, this does not conflict with its derivation from the parental function.

DOSTOEVSKY AND PARRICIDE

Four facets may be distinguished in the rich personality of Dostoevsky: the creative artist, the neurotic, the moralist and the sinner. How is one to find one's way in this bewildering complexity?

The creative artist is the least doubtful: Dostoevsky's place is not far behind Shakespeare. *The Brothers Karamazov* is the most magnificent novel ever written; the episode of the Grand Inquisitor, one of the peaks in the literature of the world, can hardly be valued too highly. Before the problem of the creative artist analysis must, alas, lay down its arms.

The moralist in Dostoevsky is the most readily assailable. If we seek to rank him high as a moralist on the plea that only a man who has gone through the depths of sin can reach the highest summit of morality, we are neglecting a doubt that arises. A moral man is one who reacts to temptation as soon as he feels it in his heart, without yielding to it. A man who alternately sins and then in his remorse erects high moral standards lays himself open to the reproach that he has made things too easy for himself. He has not achieved the essence of morality, renunciation, for the moral conduct of life is a practical human interest. He reminds one of the barbarians of the great migrations, who murdered and did penance for it, till penance became an actual technique for enabling murder to be done. Ivan the Terrible behaved in exactly this way; indeed, this compromise with morality is a characteristic Russian trait. Nor was the final outcome of Dostoevsky's moral strivings anything very glorious. After the most violent struggles to reconcile the instinctual demands of the individual with the claims of the community, he landed in the retrograde position of submission both to temporal and spiritual authority, of veneration both for the Tsar and for the God of the Christians, and of a narrow Russian nationalism—a position which lesser minds have reached with smaller effort. This is the weak point in that great personality. Dostoevsky threw away the chance of becoming a teacher and liberator of humanity and made himself one with their gaolers. The future of human civilization will have little to thank him for. It seems probable that he was condemned to this failure by his neurosis. The greatness of his intelligence and the strength of his love for humanity might have opened to him another, an apostolic, way of life.

To consider Dostoevsky as a sinner or a criminal rouses violent opposition, which need not be based upon a philistine assessment of crime. The real motive for this opposition soon becomes apparent. Two traits are essential in a criminal: boundless egoism and a strong destructive impulse. Common to both of these, and a necessary condition for their expression, is absence of love, lack of an emotional appreciation of (human) objects. One at once recalls the contrast to this presented by Dostoevsky—his great need of love and his enormous capacity for love, which is to be seen in manifestations of exaggerated kindness and caused him to love and to help where he had a right to

56

hatred and revenge, as, for example, in his relations with his first wife and her lover. That being so, it must be asked why there is any temptation to reckon Dostoevsky among the criminals. The answer is that it comes from his choice of material, which singles out from all others violent, murderous and egoistic characters, thus pointing to the existence of similar tendencies in his own soul, and also from certain facts in his life, like his passion for gambling and his possible admission of a sexual assault upon a young girl.[1] The contradiction is resolved by the realization that Dostoevsky's very strong destructive instinct, which might easily have made him a criminal, was in his actual life directed mainly against his own person (inward instead of outward) and thus found expression as masochism and a sense of guilt. Nevertheless, his personality retained sadistic traits in plenty, which show themselves in his irritability, his love of tormenting and his intolerance even towards people he loved, and which appear also in the way in which, as an author, he treats his readers. Thus in little things he was a sadist towards others, and in bigger things a sadist towards himself, in fact a masochist, that is to say the mildest, kindliest, most helpful person possible.

We have selected three factors from Dostoevsky's complex personality, one quantitative and two qualitative: the extraordinary intensity of his emotional life, his perverse instinctual predisposition, which inevitably marked him out to be a sadomasochist or a criminal, and his unanalysable artistic endowment. This combination might very well exist without neurosis; there are people who are complete masochists without being neurotic. Nevertheless, the balance of forces between his instinctual demands and the inhibitions opposing them (plus the available methods of sublimation) would even so make it necessary to classify Dostoevsky as what is known as an "instinctual character." But the position is obscured by the simultaneous presence of neurosis, which, as we have said, was not in the circumstances inevitable, but which comes into being the more readily, the richer the complication which has to be mastered by the ego. For neurosis is after all only a sign that the ego has not succeeded in making a synthesis, that in attempting to do so it has forfeited its unity.

How then, strictly speaking, does his neurosis show itself? Dostoevsky called himself an epileptic, and was regarded as such by other people, on account of his severe seizures, which were accompanied by loss of consciousness, muscular convulsions and subsequent depression. Now it is highly probable that this so-called epilepsy was only a symptom of his neurosis and must accordingly be classified as hystero-epilepsy, that is, as severe hysteria. We cannot be completely certain on this point for two reasons, first, because the anamnestic data on Dostoevsky's alleged epilepsy are defective and untrustworthy, and secondly, because our understanding of pathological states combined with epileptiform seizures is imperfect.

To take the second point first. It is unnecessary here to reproduce the whole pathology of epilepsy, for it would throw no decisive light on the problem. But this may be said. The old *morbus sacer* is still in evidence as an ostensible clinical entity, the uncanny disease with its incalculable, apparently

unprovoked convulsive seizures, its changing of the character into irritability
and aggressiveness, and its progressive lowering of all the mental faculties.
But the outlines of this picture are quite lacking in precision. The seizures, so
savage in their onset, accompanied by biting of the tongue and incontinence of
urine and working up to the dangerous *status epilepticus* with its risk of severe
self-injuries, may, nevertheless, be reduced to brief periods of absence, or
rapidly passing attacks of vertigo or may be replaced by short spaces of time
during which the patient does something out of character, as though he were
under the control of his unconscious. These seizures, though as a rule
determined, in a way we do not understand, by purely physical causes, may
nevertheless owe their first appearance to some purely mental cause (a fright,
for instance) or may react in other respects to mental excitations. However
characteristic intellectual impairment may be in the overwhelming majority of
cases, at least *one* case is known to us (that of Helmholtz) in which the
affliction did not interfere with the highest intellectual achievement. (Other
cases of which the same assertion has been made are either disputable or open
to the same doubts as the case of Dostoevsky himself.) People who are victims
of epilepsy may give an impression of dullness and arrested development, just
as the disease often accompanies the most palpable idiocy and the grossest
cerebral defects, even though not as a necessary component of the clinical
picture. But these seizures, with all their variations, also occur in other people
who display complete mental development and, if anything, an excessive and
as a rule insufficiently controlled emotional life. It is no wonder in these
circumstances that it has been found impossible to maintain that "epilepsy" is
a single clinical entity. The similarity that we find in the manifest symptoms
seems to call for the functional view of them. It is as though a mechanism for
abnormal instinctual discharge had been laid down originally, which could be
made use of in quite different circumstances—both in the case of disturbances
of cerebral activity due to severe histolytic or toxic affections, and also in the
case of inadequate control over the mental economy and at times when the
activity of the energy operating in the mind reaches crisis-pitch. Behind this
dichotomy we have a glimpse of the identity of the underlying mechanism of
instinctual discharge. Nor can that mechanism stand remote from the sexual
processes, which are fundamentally of toxic origin: the earliest physicians
described copulation as a minor epilepsy, and thus recognized in the sexual act
a mitigation and adaptation of the epileptic method of discharging stimuli.

The "epileptic reaction," as this common element may be called, is also
undoubtedly at the disposal of the neurosis whose essence it is to get rid by
somatic means of quantities of excitation which it cannot deal with psychi-
cally. Thus the epileptic seizure becomes a symptom of hysteria and is adapted
and modified by it just as it is by the normal sexual process of discharge. It is
therefore quite right to distinguish between an organic and an "affective"
epilepsy. The practical significance of this is that a person who suffers from the
first kind has a disease of the brain, while a person who suffers from the second
kind is a neurotic. In the first case his mental life is subjected to an alien

disturbance from without, in the second case the disturbance is an expression of his mental life itself.

It is extremely probable that Dostoevsky's epilepsy was of the second kind. This cannot, strictly speaking, be proved. To do so we should have to be in a position to insert the first appearance of the seizures and their subsequent fluctuations into the thread of his mental life; and for that we know too little. The descriptions of the seizures themselves teach us nothing and our information about the relations between the seizures and Dostoevsky's experiences is defective and often contradictory. The most probable assumption is that the seizures went back far into his childhood, that their place was taken to begin with by milder symptoms and that they did not assume an epileptic form until after the shocking experience of his eighteenth year—the murder of his father.[2] It would be very much to the point if it could be established that they ceased completely during his exile in Siberia, but other accounts contradict this.[3]

The unmistakable connection between the murder of the father in *The Brothers Karamazov* and the fate of Dostoevsky's own father has struck more than one of his biographers, and has led them to refer to "a certain modern school of psychology." From the standpoint of psychoanalysis (for that is what is meant), we are tempted to see in that event the severest trauma and to regard Dostoevsky's reaction to it as the turning-point of his neurosis. But if I undertake to substantiate this view psychoanalytically, I am bound to risk the danger of being unintelligible to all those readers who are unfamiliar with the language and theories of psychoanalysis.

We have one certain starting-point. We know the meaning of the first attacks from which Dostoevsky suffered in his early years, long before the incidence of the "epilepsy." These attacks had the significance of death: they were heralded by a fear of death and consisted of lethargic, somnolent states. The illness first came over him, while he was still a boy, in the form of a sudden, groundless melancholy, a feeling, as he later told his friend Soloviev, as though he were going to die on the spot. And there in fact followed a state exactly similar to real death. His brother Andrei tells us that even when he was quite young Feodor used to leave little notes about before he went to sleep, saying that he was afraid he might fall into this death-like sleep during the night and therefore begged that his burial should be postponed for five days. (Fülöp-Miller and Eckstein, 1925, lx.)

We know the meaning and intention of such death-like seizures. They signify an identification with a dead person, either with someone who is really dead or with someone who is still alive and whom the subject wishes dead. The latter case is the more significant. The attack then has the value of a punishment. One has wished another person dead, and now one *is* this other person and is dead oneself. At this point psychoanalytical theory brings in the assertion that for a boy this other person is usually his father and that the attack (which is termed hysterical) is thus a self-punishment for a death-wish against a hated father.

Parricide, according to a well-known view, is the principal and primal crime of humanity as well as of the individual. (See my essays on *Totem und Tabu*, 1912–13.) It is in any case the main source of the sense of guilt, though we do not know if it is the only one: researches have not yet been able to establish with certainty the mental origin of guilt and the need for expiation. But it is not necessary for it to be the only one. The psychological situation is complicated and requires elucidation. The relation of a boy to his father is, as we say, an "ambivalent" one. In addition to the hate which seeks to get rid of the father as a rival, a measure of tenderness for him is also habitually present. The two attitudes of mind combine to produce identification with the father; the boy wants to be in his father's place because he admires him and wants to be like him, and also because he wants to put him out of the way. This whole development now comes up against a powerful obstacle. At a certain moment the child comes to understand that an attempt to remove his father as a rival would be punished by him with castration. So from fear of castration, that is, in the interests of preserving his masculinity, he gives up his wish to possess his mother and get rid of his father. In so far as this wish remains in the unconscious it forms the basis of the sense of guilt. We believe that what we have here been describing are the normal processes, the normal fate of the so-called "Oedipus complex"; nevertheless it requires an important amplification.

A further complication arises when the constitutional factor we call bisexuality is comparatively strongly developed in the child. For then, under the threat to the boy's masculinity by castration, his inclination becomes strengthened to deflect in the direction of femininity, to put himself instead in his mother's place and take over her role as object of his father's love. But the fear of castration makes *this* solution impossible as well. The boy understands that he must also submit to castration if he wants to be loved by his father as a woman. Thus both impulses, hatred of the father and being in love with the father, undergo repression. There is a certain psychological distinction in the fact that the hatred of the father is given up on account of fear of an *external* danger (castration), while the being in love with the father is treated as an *internal* instinctual danger, though fundamentally it goes back to the same external danger.

What makes hatred of the father unacceptable is *fear* of the father; castration is terrible, whether as a punishment or as the price of love. Of the two factors which repress hatred of the father, the first, the direct fear of punishment and castration, may be called the normal one; its pathogenic intensification seems to come only with the addition of the second factor, the fear of the feminine attitude. Thus a strong bisexual predisposition becomes one of the pre-conditions or reinforcements of neurosis. Such a predisposition must certainly be assumed in Dostoevsky, and it shows itself in a viable form (as latent homosexuality) in the important part played by male friendships in his life, in his strangely tender attitude towards rivals in love and in his remarkable understanding of situations which are explicable only by repressed homosexuality, as many examples from his novels show.

I am sorry, though I cannot alter the facts, if this exposition of the attitudes of hatred and love towards the father and their transformations under the influence of the threat of castration seems to readers unfamiliar with psychoanalysis unsavoury and incredible. I should myself expect that it is precisely the castration complex that would be bound to arouse the most universal repugnance. But I can only insist that psychoanalytic experience has put these relations in particular beyond the reach of doubt and has taught us to recognize in them the key to every neurosis. This key, then, we must apply to our author's so-called epilepsy. So alien to our consciousness are the things by which our unconscious mental life is governed!

But what has been said so far does not exhaust the consequences of the repression of the hatred of the father in the Oedipus complex. There is something fresh to be added: namely that in spite of everything the identification with the father finally makes a permanent place for itself in the ego. It is received into the ego, but establishes itself there as a separate agency in contrast to the rest of the content of the ego. We then give it the name of super-ego and ascribe to it, the inheritor of the parental influence, the most important functions. If the father was hard, violent and cruel, the super-ego takes over those attributes from him and, in the relations between the ego and it, the passivity which was supposed to have been repressed is re-established. The super-ego has become sadistic, and the ego becomes masochistic, that is to say, at bottom passive in a feminine way. A great need for punishment develops in the ego, which in part offers itself as a victim to fate, and in part finds satisfaction in ill-treatment by the super-ego (that is, in the sense of guilt). For every punishment is ultimately castration and, as such, a fulfilment of the old passive attitude towards the father. Even fate is, in the last resort, only a later father-projection.

The normal processes in the formation of conscience must be similar to the abnormal ones described here. We have not yet succeeded in fixing the boundary line between them. It will be observed that here the largest share in the event is ascribed to the passive component of repressed femininity. Moreover, it must be of importance as an accidental factor whether the father, who is feared in any case, is also especially violent in reality. This was true in Dostoevsky's case, and we can trace back the fact of his extraordinary sense of guilt and of his masochistic conduct of life to a specially strong feminine component. Thus the formula for Dostoevsky is as follows: a person of specially strong bisexual predisposition, who can defend himself with special intensity against dependence on a specially severe father. This characteristic of bisexuality comes as an addition to the components of his nature that we have already recognized. His early symptom of death-like seizures can thus be understood as a father-identification on the part of his ego, permitted by his super-ego as a punishment. "You wanted to kill your father in order to be your father yourself. Now you *are* your father, but a dead father"—the regular mechanism of hysterical symptoms. And further: "Now your father is killing *you*." For the ego the death symptom is a satisfaction in phantasy of the masculine wish and at the same time a masochistic satisfaction; for the super-ego it is a punishment satisfaction, that is, a sadistic satisfaction. Both of them, the ego and the super-ego, carry on the role of father.

To sum up, the relation between the subject and his father-object, while retaining its content, has been transformed into a relation between the ego and the super-ego—a new setting on a fresh stage. Infantile reactions from the Oedipus complex such as these may disappear if reality gives them no further nourishment. But the characteristics of the father remain the same, or rather, they deteriorate with the years, and so too Dostoevsky's hatred for his father and his death-wish against that wicked father were maintained. Now it is a dangerous thing if reality fulfils such repressed wishes. The phantasy has become reality and all defensive measures are thereupon reinforced. Dostoevsky's attacks now assumed an epileptic character; they still undoubtedly signified an identification with his father as a punishment, but they had become terrible, like his father's frightful death itself. What further content they had absorbed, particularly what sexual content, escapes conjecture.

One thing is remarkable: in the aura of the epileptic attack, one moment of supreme bliss is experienced. This may very well be a record of the triumph and sense of liberation felt on hearing the news of the death, to be followed immediately by an all the more cruel punishment. We have divined just such a sequence of triumph and mourning, of festive joy and mourning, in the brothers of the primal horde who murdered their father, and we find it repeated in the ceremony of the totem meal. If it proved to be the case that Dostoevsky was free from his seizures in Siberia, that would merely substantiate the view that his seizures were his punishment. He did not need them any longer when he was being punished in another way. But that cannot be proved. Rather does this necessity for punishment on the part of Dostoevsky's mental economy explain the fact that he passed unbroken through these years of misery and humiliation. Dostoevsky's condemnation as a political prisoner was unjust and he must have known it, but he accepted the undeserved punishment at the hands of the Little Father, the Tsar, as a substitute for the punishment he deserved for his sin against his real father. Instead of punishing himself, he got himself punished by his father's deputy. Here we have a glimpse of the psychological justification of the punishments inflicted by society. It is a fact that large groups of criminals long for punishment. Their super-ego demands it and so saves itself the necessity for inflicting the punishment itself.

Everyone who is familiar with the complicated transformation of meaning undergone by hysterical symptoms will understand that no attempt can be made here to follow out the meaning of Dostoevsky's attacks beyond this beginning.[4] It is enough that we may assume that their original meaning remained unchanged behind all later accretions. We can safely say that Dostoevsky never got free from the feelings of guilt arising from his intention of murdering his father. They also determined his attitude in the two other spheres in which the father-relation is the decisive factor, his attitude towards the authority of the State and towards belief in God. In the first of these he ended up with complete submission to his Little Father, the Tsar, who had once performed with him in *reality* the comedy of killing which his seizures had so often represented in *play*. Here penitence gained the upper hand. In the religious sphere he retained more freedom: according to apparently trustworthy reports he wavered, up to the last moment of his life, between faith and atheism. His great intellect made it possible for him to overlook any of the intellectual difficulties to which faith leads. By an individual recapitulation of a development in world-history he hoped to find a way out and a liberation from guilt in the Christ ideal, and even to make use of his sufferings as a claim to be playing a Christ-like role. If on the whole he did not achieve freedom and became a reactionary, that was because the filial guilt, which is present in human beings generally and on which religious feeling is built, had in him attained a super-individual intensity and remained insurmountable even to his great intelligence. In writing this we are laying ourselves open to the charge of having abandoned the impartiality of analysis and of subjecting Dostoevsky to judgements that can only be justified from the partisan standpoint of a particular philosophy of life. A conservative would take the side of the Grand Inquisitor and would judge Dostoevsky differently. The objection is just; and one can only say in extenuation that Dostoevsky's decision has every appearance of having been determined by an intellectual inhibition due to his neurosis.

It can scarcely be owing to chance that three of the masterpieces of the literature of all time—the *Oedipus Rex* of Sophocles, Shakespeare's *Hamlet* and Dostoevsky's *The Brothers Karamazov*—should all deal with the same subject, parricide. In all three, moreover, the motive for the deed, sexual rivalry for a woman, is laid bare.

The most straightforward is certainly the representation in the drama derived from the Greek legend. In this it is still the hero himself who commits the crime. But poetic treatment is impossible without softening and disguise. The naked admission of an intention to commit parricide, as we arrive at it in analysis, seems intolerable without analytical preparation. The Greek drama, while retaining the crime, introduces the indispensable toning-down in a masterly fashion by projecting the hero's unconscious motive into reality in the form of a compulsion by a destiny which is alien to him. The hero commits the deed unintentionally and apparently uninfluenced by the woman; this latter element is however taken into account in the circumstance that the hero can only obtain possession of the queen mother after he has repeated his deed upon the monster who symbolizes the father. After his guilt has been revealed and made conscious, the hero makes no attempt to exculpate himself by appealing to the artificial expedient of the compulsion of destiny. His crime is acknowledged and punished as though it were fully conscious—which is bound to appear unjust to our reason, but which psychologically is perfectly correct.

In the English play the presentation is more indirect; the hero does not commit the crime himself; it is carried out by someone else, for whom it is not parricide. The forbidden motive of sexual rivalry for the woman does not need, therefore, to be disguised. Moreover, we see the hero's Oedipus complex, as it were, in a reflected light, by learning the effect upon him of the other's crime. He ought to avenge the crime, but finds himself, strangely enough, incapable of doing so. We know that it is his sense of guilt that is paralysing him; but, in a manner entirely in keeping with neurotic processes, the sense of guilt is displaced on to the perception of his inadequacy for fulfilling his task. There are signs that the hero feels this guilt as a super-individual one. He despises others no less than himself: "Use every man after his desert, and who should 'scape whipping?"

The Russian novel goes a step further in the same direction. There also the murder is committed by someone else. This other person, however, stands to the murdered man in the same filial relation as the hero, Dmitri; in this other person's case the motive of sexual rivalry is openly admitted; he is a brother of the hero's, and it is a remarkable fact that Dostoevsky has attributed to him his own illness, the alleged epilepsy, as though he were seeking to confess that the epileptic, the neurotic, in himself was a parricide. Then, again, in the speech for the defence at the trial, there is the famous joke at the expense of psychology—it is a "knife that cuts both ways": a splendid piece of disguise, for we have only to reverse it in order to discover the deepest meaning of Dostoevsky's view of things. It is not psychology that deserves to be laughed at, but the procedure of judicial enquiry. It is a matter of indifference who actually committed the crime; psychology is only concerned to know who desired it emotionally and who welcomed it when it was done. And for that reason all of the brothers, except the contrasted figure of Alyosha, are equally guilty, the impulsive sensualist, the sceptical cynic and the epileptic criminal. In *The Brothers Karamazov* there is one particularly revealing scene. In the course of his talk with Dmitri, Father Zossima recognizes that Dmitri is prepared to commit parricide, and he bows down at his feet. It is impossible that this can be meant as an expression of admiration; it must mean that the holy man is rejecting the temptation to despise or detest the murderer and for that reason humbles himself before him. Dostoevsky's sympathy for the criminal is, in fact, boundless; it goes far beyond the pity which the unhappy wretch might claim, and reminds us of the "holy awe" with which epileptics and lunatics were regarded in the past. A criminal is to him almost a Redeemer, who has taken on himself the guilt which must else have been borne by others. There is no longer any need for one to murder, since *he* has already murdered; and one must be grateful to him, for, except for him, one would have been obliged oneself to murder. That is not just kindly pity, it is identification on the basis of a similar murderous impulse—in fact, a slightly displaced narcissism. (In saying this, we are not disputing the ethical value of this kindliness.) This may perhaps be quite generally the mechanism of kindly sympathy with other people, a mechanism which one can discern with especial ease in the extreme case of the guilt-ridden novelist. There is no doubt that this sympathy by identification was a decisive factor in determining Dostoevsky's choice of material. He dealt first with the common criminal (whose motives are egotistical) and the political and religious criminal; and not until the end of his life did he come back to the primal criminal, the parricide, and use him, in a work of art, for making his confession.

The publication of Dostoevsky's posthumous papers and of his wife's diaries has thrown a glaring light on one episode in his life, namely the period in Germany when he was obsessed with a mania for gambling (cf. Fülöp-Miller and Eckstein, 1925), which no one could regard as anything but an unmistakable fit of pathological passion. There was no lack of rationalizations for this remarkable and unworthy behaviour. As often happens with neurotics, Dostoevsky's burden of guilt had taken a tangible shape as a burden of debt, and he was able to take refuge behind the pretext that he was trying by his winnings at the tables to make it possible for him to return to Russia without being arrested by his creditors. But this was no more than a pretext; and Dostoevsky was acute enough to recognize the fact and honest enough to admit it. He knew that the chief thing was gambling for its own sake—*le jeu pour le jeu*.[5] All the details of his impulsively irrational conduct show this and something more besides. He never rested until he had lost everything. For him gambling was another method of self-punishment. Time after time he gave his young wife his promise or his word of honour not to play any more or not to play any more on that particular day; and, as she says, he almost always broke it. When his losses had reduced himself and her to the direst need, he derived a second pathological satisfaction from that. He could then scold and humiliate himself before her, invite her to despise him and to feel sorry that she had married such an old sinner; and when he had thus unburdened his conscience, the whole business would begin again next day. His young wife accustomed herself to this cycle, for she had noticed that the one thing which offered any real hope of salvation—his literary production—never went better than when they had lost everything and pawned their last possessions. Naturally she did not understand the connection. When his sense of guilt was satisfied by the punishments he had inflicted on himself, the inhibitions upon his work became less severe and he allowed himself to take a few steps along the way to success.[6]

What part of a gambler's long-buried childhood is it that forces its way to repetition in his obsession for play? The answer may be divined without difficulty from a story by one of our younger writers. Stefan Zweig, who has incidentally devoted a study to Dostoevsky himself (1920), has included in his collection of three stories *Die Verwirrung der Gefühle* (1927) one which he calls "Vierundzwanzig Stunden aus dem Leben einer Frau" ["Four-and-Twenty Hours in a Woman's Life"]. This little masterpiece ostensibly sets out only to show what an irresponsible creature woman is, and to what excesses, surprising even to herself, an unexpected experience may drive her. But the story tells far more than this. If it is subjected to an analytical interpretation, it will be found to represent (without any apologetic intent) something quite different, something universally human, or rather something masculine. And such an interpretation is so extremely obvious that it cannot be resisted. It is characteristic of the nature of artistic creation that the author, who is a personal friend of mine, was able to assure me, when I asked him, that the interpretation which I put to him had been completely strange to his knowledge and intention, although some of the details woven into the narrative seemed expressly designed to give a clue to the hidden secret.

In this story, an elderly lady of distinction tells the author of an experience she has had more than twenty years earlier. She has been left a widow when still young and is the mother of two sons, who no longer need her. In her forty-second year, expecting nothing further of life, she happens, on one of her aimless journeyings, to visit the Rooms at Monte Carlo. There, among all the remarkable impressions which the place produces, she is soon fascinated by the sight of a pair of hands which seem to betray all the feelings of the unlucky gambler with terrifying sincerity and intensity. These hands "belong to a handsome young man—the author, as though unintentionally, makes him of the same age as the narrator's elder son—who, after losing everything, leaves the Rooms in the depths of despair, with the evident intention of ending his hopeless life in the Casino gardens. An inexplicable feeling of sympathy compels her to follow him and make every effort to save him. He takes her for one of the importunate women so common there and tries to shake her off; but she stays with him and finds herself obliged, in the most natural way possible, to join him in his apartment at the hotel, and finally to share his bed. After this improvised night of love, she exacts a most solemn vow from the young man, who has now apparently calmed down, that he will never play again, provides him with money for his journey home and promises to meet him at the station before the departure of his train. Now, however, she begins to feel a great tenderness for him, is ready to sacrifice all she has in order to keep him and makes up her mind to go with him instead of saying goodbye. Various mischances delay her, so that she misses the train. In her longing for the lost one she returns once more to the Rooms and there, to her horror, sees once more the hands which had first excited her sympathy: the faithless youth had gone back to his play. She reminds him of his promise, but, obsessed by his passion, he calls her a spoil-sport, tells her to go and flings back the money with which she has tried to rescue him. She hurries away in deep mortification and learns later that she has not succeeded in saving him from suicide.

The brilliantly told, faultlessly motivated story is of course complete in itself and is certain to make a deep effect upon the reader. But analysis shows us that its invention is based fundamentally upon a wishful phantasy belonging to the period of puberty, which a number of people actually remember consciously. The phantasy embodies a boy's wish that his mother should herself initiate him into sexual life in order to save him from the dreaded injuries caused by masturbation. (The numerous creative works that deal with the theme of redemption have the same origin.) The "vice" of masturbation is replaced by the mania for gambling; and the emphasis laid upon the passionate activity of the hands betrays this derivation. The passion for play is an equivalent of the old compulsion to masturbate; "playing" is the actual word used in the nursery to describe the activity of the hands upon the genitals. The irresistible nature of the temptation, the solemn resolutions, which are nevertheless invariably broken, never to do it again, the numbing pleasure and the bad conscience which tells the subject that he is ruining himself (committing suicide)—all these elements remain unaltered in the process of substitution. It is true that Zweig's story is told by the mother, not by the son. It must flatter the son to think: "if my mother only knew what dangers masturbation involves me in, she would certainly save me from them by allowing me to lavish all my tenderness on her own body." The equation of the mother with a prostitute, which is made by the young man in the story, is linked up with the same phantasy. It brings the unattainable within easy reach. The bad conscience which accompanies the phantasy brings about the unhappy ending of the story. It is also interesting to notice how the *façade* given to the story by its author seeks to disguise its analytic meaning. For it is extremely questionable whether the erotic life of women is dominated by sudden and mysterious impulses. On the contrary, analysis reveals an adequate motivation for the surprising behaviour of this woman who had hitherto turned away from love. Faithful to the memory of her dead husband, she had armed herself against all similar attractions; but—and here the son's phantasy is right—she did not, as a mother, escape her quite unconscious transference of love on to her son, and fate was able to catch her at this undefended spot.

If the mania for gambling, with the unsuccessful struggles to break the habit and the opportunities it affords for self-punishment, is a repetition of the compulsion to masturbate, we shall not be surprised to find that it occupied such a large space in Dostoevsky's life. After all, we find no cases of severe neuroses in which the autoerotic satisfaction of early childhood and of puberty has not played a part; and the relation between efforts to suppress it and fear of the father are too well known to need more than a mention.[7]

NOTES

1. See the discussion on this point in Fülöp-Miller and Eckstein (1926). Stefan Zweig (1920) writes: "He was not halted by the barriers of bourgeois morality; and no one can say exactly how far he transgressed the bounds of law in his own life or how much of the criminal instincts of his heroes was realized in himself." For the intimate connection between Dostoevsky's characters and his own experiences, see René Fülöp-Miller's remarks in the introduction section of Fülöp-Miller and Eckstein (1925), which are based upon Nikolai Strakhov.

2. See René Fülöp-Miller (1924). Of especial interest is the information that in the novelist's childhood "something terrible, unforgettable and agonizing" happened, to which the first signs of his illness were to be traced (from an article by Suvorin in the newspaper *Novoe Vremya*, 1881, quoted in the introduction to Fülöp-Miller and Eckstein, 1925, xlv). See also Orest Miller (1882), 140: "There is, however, another special piece of evidence about Feodor Mikhailovich's illness, which relates to his earliest youth and brings the illness into connection with a tragic event in the family life of his parents. But, although this piece of evidence was given to me orally by one who was a close friend of Feodor Mikhailovich, I cannot bring myself to reproduce it fully and precisely since I have had no confirmation of this rumour from any other quarter." Biographers and scientific research workers cannot feel grateful for this discretion.

3. Most of the accounts, including Dostoevsky's own, assert on the contrary that

the illness only assumed its final, epileptic character during the Siberian exile. Unfortunately there is reason to distrust the autobiographical statements of neurotics. Experience shows that their memories introduce falsifications, which are designed to interrupt disagreeable causal connections. Nevertheless, it appears certain that Dostoevsky's detention in the Siberian prison markedly altered his pathological condition. Cf. Fülöp-Miller (1924, 1186).

4. See *Totem und Tabu* (1912–13). The best account of the meaning and content of his seizures was given by Dostoevsky himself, when he told his friend Strakhov that his irritability and depression after an epileptic attack were due to the fact that he seemed to himself a criminal and could not get rid of the feeling that he had a burden of unknown guilt upon him, that he had committed some great misdeed, which oppressed him. (Fülöp-Miller, 1924, 1188.) In self-accusations like these psycho-analysis sees signs of a recognition of "psychical reality," and it endeavours to make the unknown guilt known to consciousness.

5. "The main thing is the play itself," he writes in one of his letters. "I swear that greed for money has nothing to do with it, although Heaven knows I am sorely in need of money."

6. "He always remained at the gaming tables till he had lost everything and was totally ruined. It was only when the damage was quite complete that the demon at last retired from his soul and made way for the creative genius." (Fülöp-Miller and Eckstein, 1925, lxxxvi.)

7. Most of the views which are here expressed are also contained in an excellent book by Jolan Neufeld (1923).

W. B. Yeats

1865–1939

William Butler Yeats, poet, dramatist, and critic, was born at Sandymount, a suburb of Dublin, on June 13, 1865. He was the eldest son of John Butler Yeats and brother of Jack Yeats, both celebrated painters, and was educated at the Godolphin School, London, and the Erasmus High School, Dublin. Between 1883 and 1886 he studied painting at the Metropolitan School of Art, Dublin, where with his fellow student George William Russell (A.E.) he became interested in mysticism and the occult. In 1887, after deciding to abandon art in favor of literature, he returned with his family to London, where he joined the Blavatsky Lodge of the Theosophical Society and had his first poems published in English magazines. In the following year he made the acquaintance of William Morris, G. B. Shaw, W. E. Henley, and Oscar Wilde, and published his compilation *Fairy and Folk Tales of the Irish Peasantry* (1888). His first collection of verse, *The Wanderings of Oisin and Other Poems*, was published to good reviews in 1889, and attracted the friendship of the revolutionary Maud Gonne, to whom Yeats several times unsuccessfully proposed; she was to be a primary source of inspiration for the rest of Yeats' poetic career.

In 1890 Yeats joined the Hermetic Order of the Golden Dawn, a group of theosophists involved in cabalistic magic, and in the following two years he was a founding member of the Rhymers' Club, the Irish Literary Society, London (1891), and the Irish Literary Society, Dublin (1892). Yeats' autobiographical novel *John Sherman and Dhoya* (1891) was followed by his first play, *The Countess Cathleen* (1892); two collections of Irish folklore, *The Celtic Twilight* (1893) and *The Secret Rose* (1897); a book of poems, *The Wind among the Reeds* (1899); and his edition of the *Poems of William Blake* (1893).

One of Yeats' ambitions was to create an Irish national theatre, and this was eventually achieved, with the help of Lady Gregory and others, by the foundation of first the Irish Literary Theatre (1899), and then of the Irish National Theatre Company (1902), which acquired the Abbey Theatre in Dublin and opened it to the public in 1904. Among Yeats' plays that became part of the Abbey Theatre's repertoire are *The Land of Heart's Desire* (1894), *Cathleen ni Houlihan* (1902), *The King's Threshhold* (1903), *On Baile's Strand* (1904), and *Deirdre* (1906). Yeats' later dramatic style bears the mark of his exposure to the Japanese Noh theatre through his friendship with Ezra Pound; his plays became simplified and stylized, as well as highly symbolic, and in such works as *Four Plays for Dancers* (1921), *Calvary* (1930), and *The Resurrection* (1931) he made use of music, masks, and dancers. Other important plays include *At the Hawk's Well* (1916), *The Only Jealousy of Emer* (1918), Yeats' translation of *Oedipus Rex* (1928), and *Purgatory* (1938).

With the turn of the century Yeats' poetic style also began to change; with each successive collection of verse he moved further away from the Pre-Raphaelite style of the 1890s and gradually discarded certain Celtic and esoteric influences. *In the Seven Woods* (1903) was followed by *The Green Helmet and Other Poems* (1910), *Poems Written in Discouragement* (1913), *Responsibilities: Poems and a Play* (1914), and *The Wild Swans at Coole* (1917). The nationalistic element of Yeats' poetry was given added stimulus by the Easter Rising of 1916, which he mythologized and associated with the legend of Cuchulain, although he treated it with increasing ambivalence as time went on. His marriage in 1917 to George Hyde-Lees also had an important effect on his poetry, since her practice of automatic writing eventually provided Yeats with the symbolic system described in *A Vision* (1925). This system is the basis for many of the poems in *Michael Robartes and the Dancer* (1920), *The Tower* (1928), *The Winding Stair* (1933), *Wheels and Butterflies* (1934), *A Full Moon in March* (1935), *New Poems* (1938), *Last Poems and Two Plays* (1939), and many others.

In 1922 Yeats was elected a senator of the Irish Free State; later, however, he became increasingly disillusioned with the Irish political scene. He was awarded the Nobel Prize for Literature in 1923. Yeats died on January 28, 1939, in the south of France; nine years later his remains were returned to Ireland. In addition to the works mentioned above, Yeats published several collections of essays, the most important of which are *Ideas of Good and Evil* (1903), *Discoveries* (1907), *Per Amica Silentia Lunae* (1918), *The Cutting of an Agate* (1919), and *On the Boiler* (1939). He also edited *The Oxford Book of Modern Verse* (1936). A projected twelve-volume edition of his *Collected Letters* is being published by Oxford University Press.

THE PHILOSOPHY OF
SHELLEY'S POETRY

His Ruling Ideas

When I was a boy in Dublin I was one of a group who rented a room in a mean street to discuss philosophy. My fellow-students got more and more interested in certain modern schools of mystical belief, and I never found anybody to share my one unshakable belief. I thought that whatever of philosophy has been made poetry is alone permanent, and that one should begin to arrange it in some regular order, rejecting nothing as the make-believe of the poets. I thought, so far as I can recollect my thoughts after so many years, that if a powerful and benevolent spirit has shaped the destiny of this world, we can better discover that destiny from the words that have gathered up the heart's desire of the world, than from historical records, or from speculation, wherein the heart withers. Since then I have observed dreams and visions very carefully, and am now certain that the imagination has some way of lighting on the truth that the reason has not, and that its commandments, delivered when the body is still and the reason silent, are the most binding we can ever know. I have reread *Prometheus Unbound,* which I had hoped my fellow-students would have studied as a sacred book, and it seems to me to have an even more certain place than I had thought, among the sacred books of the world. I remember going to a learned scholar to ask about its deep meanings, which I felt more than understood, and his telling me that it was Godwin's *Political Justice* put into rhyme, and that Shelley was a crude revolutionist, and believed that the overturning of kings and priests would regenerate mankind. I quoted the lines which tell how the halcyons ceased to prey on fish, and how poisonous leaves became good for food, to show that he foresaw more than any political regeneration, but was too timid to push the argument. I still believe that one cannot help believing him, as this scholar I know believes him, a vague thinker, who mixed occasional great poetry with a phantastic rhetoric, unless one compares such passages, and above all such passages as describe the liberty he praised, till one has discovered the system of belief that lay behind them. It should seem natural to find his thought full of subtlety, for Mrs. Shelley has told how he hesitated whether he should be a metaphysician or a poet, and has spoken of his 'huntings after the obscure' with regret, and said of that *Prometheus Unbound,* which so many for three generations have thought *Political Justice* put into rhyme, 'It requires a mind as subtle and penetrating as his own to understand the mystic meanings scattered throughout the poem. They elude the ordinary reader by their abstraction and delicacy of distinction, but they are far from vague. It was his design to write prose metaphysical essays on the Nature of Man, which would have served to explain much of what is obscure in his poetry; a few scattered fragments of observation and remarks alone remain. He considered these philosophical views of mind and nature to be instinct with the intensest spirit of poetry.' From these scattered fragments and observations, and from many passages read in their light, one soon comes to understand that his liberty was so much more than the liberty of *Political Justice* that it was one with Intellectual Beauty, and that the regeneration he foresaw was so much more than the regeneration many political dreamers have foreseen, that it could not come in its perfection till the hours bore 'Time to his grave in eternity.' In *A Defence of Poetry,* he will have it that the poet and the lawgiver hold their station by the right of the same faculty, the one uttering in words and the other in the forms of society, his vision of the divine order, the Intellectual Beauty. 'Poets, according to the circumstances of the age and nation in which they appeared, were called in the earliest epoch of the world legislators or prophets, and a poet essentially comprises and unites both these characters. For he not only beholds intensely the present as it is, and discovers those laws according to which present things are to be ordained, but he beholds the future in the present, and his thoughts are the germs of the flowers and the fruit of latest time.' 'Language, colour, form, and religious and civil habits of action are all the instruments and materials of poetry.' Poetry is 'the creation of actions according to the unchangeable process of human nature as existing in the mind of the creator, which is itself the image of all other minds.' 'Poets have been challenged to resign the civic crown to reasoners and merchants. . . . It is admitted that the exercise of the imagination is the most delightful, but it is alleged that that of reason is the most useful. . . . Whilst the mechanist abridges and the political economist combines labour, let them be sure that their speculations, for want of correspondence with those first principles which belong to the imagination, do not tend, as they have in modern England, to exasperate at once the extremes of luxury and want. . . . The rich have become richer, the poor have become poorer, . . . such are the effects which must ever flow from an unmitigated exercise of the calculating faculty.' The speaker of these things might almost be Blake, who held that the Reason not only created Ugliness, but all other evils. The books of all wisdom are hidden in the cave of the Witch of Atlas, who is one of his personifications of beauty, and when she moves over the enchanted river that is an image of all life, the priests cast aside their deceits, and the king crowns an ape to mock his own sovereignty, and the soldiers gather about the anvils to beat their swords to ploughshares, and lovers cast away their timidity, and friends are united; while the power, which in 'Laon and Cythna,' awakens the mind of the reformer to contend, and itself contends, against the tyrannies of the world, is first seen, as the star of love or beauty. And at the end of the 'Ode to Naples,' he cries out to 'the spirit of beauty' to overturn the tyrannies of the world, or to fill them with its 'harmonising ardours.' He calls the spirit of beauty liberty, because despotism, and perhaps, as 'the man of virtuous soul commands not nor obeys,' all authority, pluck virtue from her path towards beauty, and because it leads us by that love whose service is perfect freedom. It leads all things by love, for he cries again and again that love is the perception of beauty in thought and things, and it orders all things by love, for it is love that impels the soul to its expressions in thought and in action, by making us 'seek to awaken in all things that are, a community with what we experience within ourselves.' 'We are born into the world, and there is something within us which, from the instant that we live, more and more thirsts after its likeness.' We have 'a soul within our soul that describes a circle around its proper paradise which pain and sorrow and evil dare not overleap,' and we labour to see this soul in many mirrors, that we may possess it the more abundantly. He would hardly seek the progress of the world by any less gentle labour, and would hardly have us resist evil itself. He bids the reformers in *The Philosophical Review of Reform* receive 'the onset of the cavalry,' if it be sent to disperse their meetings, 'with folded arms,' and 'not because active resistance is not justifiable, but because temperance and courage would produce greater advantages than the most decisive victory'; and he gives them like advice in *The Masque of Anarchy,* for liberty, the poem cries, 'is love,' and can make the rich man kiss its feet, and, like those who followed Christ, give away his goods and follow it throughout the world.

He does not believe that the reformation of society can bring this beauty, this divine order, among men without the regeneration of the hearts of men. Even in *Queen Mab,* which was written before he had found his deepest thought, or rather perhaps before he had found words to utter it, for I do not think men change much in their deepest thought, he is less anxious to challenge men's beliefs, as I think, than to cry out against that serpent more subtle than any beast of the field, 'the cause and the effect of tyranny.' He affirms again and again that the virtuous, those who have 'pure desire and universal love,' are happy in the midst of tyranny, and he foresees a day when 'the spirit of nature,' the spirit of beauty of his later poems, who has her 'throne of power unappealable in every human heart,' shall have made men so virtuous that 'kingly glare will lose its power to dazzle and silently pass by,' and as it seems commerce, 'the venal interchange of all that human art or nature yields, which wealth should purchase not,' come as silently to an end.

He was always, indeed in chief, a witness for that 'power unappealable.' Maddalo, in *Julian and Maddalo,* says that the soul is powerless, and can only, like a 'dreary bell hung in a heaven-illumined tower, toll our thoughts and our desires to meet round the rent heart and pray'; but Julian, who is Shelley himself, replies, as the makers of all religions have replied—

> Where is the love, beauty and truth we seek
> But in our mind? And if we were not weak,
> Should we be less in deed than in desire?

while 'Mont Blanc' is an intricate analogy to affirm that the soul has its sources in 'the secret strength of things,' 'which governs thought and to the infinite heavens is a law.' He even thought that men might be immortal were they sinless, and his Cythna bids the sailors be without remorse, for all that live are stained as they are. It is thus, she says, that time marks men and their thoughts for the tomb. And the 'Red Comet,' the image of evil in 'Laon and Cythna,' when it began its war with the star of beauty, brought not only 'Fear, Hatred, Fraud and Tyranny,' but 'Death, Decay, Earthquake, and Blight and Madness pale.'

When the Red Comet is conquered, when Jupiter is overthrown by Demogorgon, when the prophecy of Queen Mab is fulfilled, visible nature will put on perfection again. He declares in one of the notes to *Queen Mab*, that 'there is no great extravagance in presuming . . . that there should be a perfect identity between the moral and physical improvement of the human species,' and thinks it 'certain that wisdom is not compatible with disease, and that, in the present state of the climates of the earth, health in the true and comprehensive sense of the word is out of the reach of civilised man.' In *Prometheus Unbound* he sees, as in the ecstasy of a saint, the ships moving among the seas of the world without fear of danger

>   by the light
> Of wave-reflected flowers, and floating odours,
> And music soft,

and poison dying out of the green things, and cruelty out of all living things, and even the toads and efts becoming beautiful, and at last Time being borne 'to his tomb in eternity.'

This beauty, this divine order, whereof all things shall become a part in a kind of resurrection of the body, is already visible to the dead and to souls in ecstasy, for ecstasy is a kind of death. The dying Lionel hears the song of the nightingale, and cries—

> Heardst thou not sweet words among
> That heaven-resounding minstrelsy?
> Heardst thou not that those who die
> Awake in a world of ecstasy?
> That love, when limbs are interwoven,
> And sleep, when the night of life is cloven,
> And thought, to the world's dim boundaries clinging,
> And music when one beloved is singing,
> Is death? Let us drain right joyously
> The cup which the sweet bird fills for me.

And in the most famous passage in all his poetry he sings of Death as of a mistress. 'Life, like a dome of many-coloured glass, stains the white radiance of eternity.' 'Die, if thou wouldst be with that which thou wouldst seek'; and he sees his own soon-coming death in a rapture of prophecy, for 'the fire for which all thirst' beams upon him, 'consuming the last clouds of cold mortality.' When he is dead he will still influence the living, for though Adonais has fled 'to the burning fountains whence he came,' and 'is a portion of the eternal which must glow through time and change unquenchably the same,' and has 'awaked from the dream of life,' he has not gone from 'the young dawn,' or the 'caverns in the forests,' or 'the faint flowers and the fountains.' He has been 'made one with nature,' and his voice is 'heard in all her music,' and his presence is felt wherever 'that power may move which has withdrawn his being to its own,' and he bears 'his part' when it is compelling mortal things to their appointed forms, and he overshadows men's minds at their supreme moments, for

> when lofty thought
> Lifts a young heart above its mortal lair,
> And love and life contend in it for what
> Shall be its earthly doom, the dead live there,
> And move like winds of light on dark and stormy air.

'Of his speculations as to what will befall this inestimable spirit when we appear to die,' Mrs. Shelley has written, 'a mystic ideality tinged these speculations in Shelley's mind; certain stanzas in the poem of 'The Sensitive Plant' express, in some degree, the almost inexpressible idea, not that we die into another state, when this state is no longer, from some reason, unapparent as well as apparent, accordant with our being—but that those who rise above the ordinary nature of man, fade from before our imperfect organs; they remain in their "love, beauty, and delight," in a world congenial to them, and we, clogged by "error, ignorance, and strife," see them not till we are fitted by purification and improvement to their higher state.' Not merely happy souls, but all beautiful places and movements and gestures and events, when we think they have ceased to be, have become portions of the eternal.

> In this life
> Of error, ignorance, and strife,
> Where nothing is, but all things seem,
> And we the shadow of the dream,
>
> It is a modest creed, and yet
> Pleasant, if one considers it,
> To own that death itself must be,
> Like all the rest, a mockery.
>
> That garden sweet, that lady fair,
> And all sweet shapes and odours there,
> In truth have never passed away;
> 'Tis we, 'tis ours are changed, not they.
>
> For love and beauty and delight
> There is no death, nor change; their might
> Exceeds our organs, which endure
> No light, being themselves obscure.

He seems in his speculations to have lit on that memory of nature the visionaries claim for the foundation of their knowledge; but I do not know whether he thought, as they do, that all things good and evil remain for ever, 'thinking the thought and doing the deed,' though not, it may be, self-conscious; or only thought that 'love and beauty and delight' remain forever. The passage where Queen Mab awakes 'all knowledge of the past,' and the good and evil 'events of old and wondrous times,' was no more doubtless than a part of the machinery of the poem, but all the machineries of poetry are parts of the convictions of antiquity, and readily become again convictions in minds that brood over them with visionary intensity.

Intellectual Beauty has not only the happy dead to do her will, but ministering spirits who correspond to the Devas of the East, and the Elemental Spirits of mediæval Europe, and the Sidhe of ancient Ireland, and whose too constant presence, and perhaps Shelley's ignorance of their more traditional forms, give some of his poetry an air of rootless phantasy. They change continually in his poetry, as they do in the visions of the mystics everywhere and of the common people in Ireland, and the forms of these changes display, in an especial sense, the flowing forms of his mind when freed from all impulse not out of itself or out of super-sensual power. These are 'gleams of a remoter world which visit us in sleep,' spiritual essences whose shadows are the delights of all the senses, sounds 'folded in cells of crystal silence,' 'visions swift and sweet and quaint,' which lie waiting their moment 'each in his thin sheath like a chrysalis,' 'odours' among 'ever-blooming eden trees,' 'liquors' that can give 'happy sleep,' or can make tears 'all wonder and delight'; 'the golden genii who spoke to the poets of Greece in dreams'; 'the phantoms' which become the forms of the arts when 'the mind, arising bright from the embrace of beauty,' 'casts on them the gathered rays which are reality'; 'the guardians' who move in 'the atmosphere of human thought,' as 'the birds within the wind, or the fish within the wave,' or man's thought itself through all things; and who join the throng of the happy hours when Time is passing away—

> As the flying fish leap
> From the Indian deep,
> And mix with the seabirds half asleep.

It is these powers which lead Asia and Panthea, as they would lead all the affections of humanity, by words written upon leaves, by faint songs, by eddies of echoes that draw 'all spirits on that secret way,' by the 'dying odours' of flowers and by 'the sunlight of the sphered dew,' beyond the gates of birth and death to awake Demogorgon, eternity, that 'the painted veil called life' may be 'torn aside.'

There are also ministers of ugliness and all evil, like those that came to Prometheus—

> As from the rose which the pale priestess kneels
> To gather for her festal crown of flowers,
> The aerial crimson falls, flushing her cheek,
> So from our victim's destined agony
> The shade which is our form invests us round;
> Else we are shapeless as our mother Night.

Or like those whose shapes the poet sees in *The Triumph of Life,* coming from the procession that follows the car of life, as 'hope' changes to 'desire,' shadows 'numerous as the dead leaves blown in autumn evening from a poplar tree'; and resembling those they come from, until, if I understand an obscure phrase aright, they are 'wrapt' round 'all the busy phantoms that live there as the sun shapes the clouds.' Some to sit 'chattering like apes,' and some like 'old anatomies' 'hatching their bare broods under the shade of dæmons' wings,' laughing 'to reassume the delegated powers' they had given to the tyrants of the earth, and some 'like small gnats and flies' to throng 'about the brow of lawyers, statesmen, priest and theorist,' and some 'like discoloured shapes of snow' to fall 'on fairest bosoms and the sunniest hair,' to be 'melted by the youthful glow which they extinguish,' and many to 'fling shadows of shadows yet unlike themselves,' shadows that are shaped into new forms by that 'creative ray' in which all move like motes.

These ministers of beauty and ugliness were certainly more than metaphors or picturesque phrases to one who believed the 'thoughts which are called real or external objects' differed but in regularity of recurrence from 'hallucinations, dreams, and the ideas of madness,' and lessened this difference by telling how he had dreamed 'three several times, between intervals of two or more years, the same precise dream,' and who had seen images with the mind's eye that left his nerves shaken for days together. Shadows that were as when there

> hovers
> A flock of vampire bats before the glare
> Of the tropic sun, bringing, ere evening,
> Strange night upon some Indian isle,

could not but have had more than a metaphorical and picturesque being to one who had spoken in terror with an image of himself, and who had fainted at the apparition of a woman with eyes in her breasts, and who had tried to burn down a wood, if we can trust Mrs. Williams' account, because he believed a devil, who had first tried to kill him, had sought refuge there.

It seems to me, indeed, that Shelley had reawakened in himself the age of faith, though there were times when he would doubt, as even the saints have doubted, and that he was a revolutionist, because he had heard the commandment, 'If ye know these things, happy are ye if ye do them.' I have re-read his *Prometheus Unbound* for the first time for many years, in the woods of Drim-da-rod, among the Echte hills, and sometimes I have looked towards Slieve-nan-Orr, where the country people say the last battle of the world shall be fought till the third day, when a priest shall lift a chalice, and the thousand years of peace begin. And I think this mysterious song utters a faith as simple and as ancient as the faith of those country people, in a form suited to a new age, that will understand with Blake that the Holy Spirit is 'an intellectual fountain,' and that the kinds and degrees of beauty are the images of its authority.

His Ruling Symbols

At a comparatively early time Shelley made his imprisoned Cythna become wise in all human wisdom through the contemplation of her own mind, and write out this wisdom upon the sands in 'signs' that were 'clear elemental shapes whose smallest change' made 'a subtler language within language,' and were 'the key of truths, which once were dimly taught in old Crotona.' His early romances and much throughout his poetry show how strong a fascination the traditions of magic and of the magical philosophy had cast over his mind, and one can hardly suppose that he had not brooded over their doctrine of symbols or signatures, though I do not find anything to show that he gave it any deep study. One finds in his poetry, besides innumerable images that have not the definiteness of symbols, many images that are certainly symbols, and as the years went by he began to use these with a more and more deliberately symbolic purpose. I imagine that, when he wrote his earlier poems he allowed the subconscious life to lay its hands so firmly upon the rudder of his imagination, that he was little conscious of the abstract meaning of the images that rose in what seemed the idleness of his mind. Any one who has any experience of any mystical state of the soul knows how there float up in the mind profound symbols,[1] whose meaning, if indeed they do not delude one into the dream that they are meaningless, one does not perhaps understand for years. Nor I think has any one, who has known that experience with any constancy, failed to find some day in some old book or on some old monument, a strange or intricate image, that had floated up before him, and to grow perhaps dizzy with the sudden conviction that our little memories are but a part of some great memory that renews the world and men's thoughts age after age, and that our thoughts are not, as we suppose, the deep but a little foam upon the deep. Shelley understood this as is proved by what he says of the eternity of beautiful things and of the influence of the dead, but whether he understood that the great memory is also a dwelling-house of symbols, of images that are living souls, I cannot tell. He had certainly experience of all but the most profound of the mystical states, and known that union with created things which assuredly must precede the soul's union with the uncreated spirit. He says, in his fragment of an essay 'On Life,' mistaking a unique experience for the common experience of all: 'Let us recollect our sensations as children . . . we less habitually distinguish all that we saw and felt from ourselves. They seemed as it were to constitute one mass. There are some persons who in this respect are always children. Those who are subject to the state called reverie, feel as if their nature were resolved into the surrounding universe or as if the surrounding universe were resolved into their being,' and he must have expected to receive thoughts and images from beyond his own mind, just in so far as that mind transcended its preoccupation with particular time and place, for he believed inspiration a kind of death; and he could hardly have helped perceiving that an image that has transcended particular time and place becomes a symbol, passes beyond death, as it were, and becomes a living soul.

When Shelley went to the Continent with Godwin's daughter in 1814 they sailed down certain great rivers in an open boat, and when he summed up in his preface to 'Laon and Cythna' the things that helped to make him a poet, he spoke of these voyages: 'I have sailed down mighty rivers and seen the sun rise and set and the stars come forth whilst I sailed night and day down a rapid stream among mountains.'

He may have seen some cave that was the bed of a rivulet by some river side, or have followed some mountain stream to its source in a cave, for from his return to England rivers and streams and wells, flowing through caves or rising in them, came into every poem of his that was of any length, and always with the precision of symbols. Alastor passed in his boat along a river in a cave; and when for the last time he felt the presence of the spirit he loved and followed, it was when he watched his image in a silent well; and when he died it was where a river fell into 'an abysmal chasm'; and the Witch of Atlas in her gladness, as he in his sadness, passed in her boat along a river in a cave, and it was where it bubbled out of a cave that she was born; and when Rousseau, the typical poet of *The Triumph of Life,* awoke to the vision that was life, it was where a rivulet bubbled out of a cave; and the poet of *Epipsychidion* met the evil beauty 'by a well under blue nightshade bowers'; and Cythna bore her child imprisoned in a great cave beside 'a fountain round and vast, in which the wave imprisoned leaped and boiled perpetually'; and her lover Laon was brought to his prison in a high column through a cave where there was 'a putrid pool,' and when he went to see the conquered city he dismounted beside a polluted fountain in the marketplace, foreshadowing thereby that spirit who at the end of *Prometheus Unbound* gazes at a regenerated city from 'within a fountain in the public square'; and when Laon and Cythna are dead they awake beside a fountain and drift into Paradise along a river; and at the end of things Prometheus and Asia are to live amid a happy world in a cave where a fountain 'leaps with an awakening sound'; and it was by a fountain, the meeting-place of certain unhappy lovers, that Rosalind and Helen told their unhappiness to one another; and it was under a willow by a fountain that the enchantress and her lover began their unhappy love; while his lesser poems and his prose fragments use caves and rivers and wells and fountains continually as metaphors. It may be that his subconscious life seized upon some passing scene, and moulded it into an ancient symbol without help from anything but that great memory; but so good a Platonist as Shelley could hardly have thought of any cave as a symbol, without thinking of Plato's cave that was the world; and so good a scholar may well have had Porphyry on 'the Cave of the Nymphs' in his mind. When I compare Porphyry's description of the cave where the Phæacian boat left Odysseus, with Shelley's description of the cave of the Witch of Atlas, to name but one of many, I find it hard to think otherwise. I quote Taylor's translation, only putting Mr. Lang's prose for Taylor's bad verse. 'What does Homer obscurely signify by the cave in Ithaca which he describes in the following verses? "Now at the harbour's head is a long-leaved olive tree, and hard by is a pleasant cave and shadowy, sacred to the nymphs, that are called Naiads. And therein are mixing bowls and jars of stone, and there moreover do bees hive. And there are great looms of stone, whereon the nymphs weave raiment of purple stain, a marvel to behold; and there are waters welling evermore. Two gates there are to the cave, the one set towards the North wind, whereby men may go down, but the portals towards the South pertain rather to the gods, whereby men may not enter: it is the way of the immortals."' He goes on to argue that the cave was a temple before Homer wrote, and that 'the ancients did not establish temples without fabulous symbols,' and then begins to interpret Homer's description in all its detail. The ancients, he says, 'consecrated a cave to the world' and held 'the flowing waters' and the 'obscurity of the cavern' 'apt symbols of what the world contains,' and he calls to witness Zoroaster's cave with fountains; and often caves are, he says, symbols of 'all invisible power; because as caves are obscure and dark, so the essence of all these powers is occult,' and quotes a lost hymn to Apollo to prove that nymphs living in caves fed men 'from intellectual fountains'; and he contends that fountains and rivers symbolise generation, and that the word nymph 'is commonly applied to all souls descending into generation,' and that the two gates of Homer's cave are the gate of generation and the gate of ascent through death to the gods, the gate of cold and moisture, and the gate of heat and fire. Cold, he says, causes life in the world, and heat causes life among the gods, and the constellation of the Cup is set in the heavens near the sign Cancer, because it is there that the souls descending from the Milky Way receive their draught of the intoxicating cold drink of generation. 'The mixing bowls and jars of stone' are consecrated to the Naiads, and are also, as it seems, symbolical of Bacchus, and are of stone because of the rocky beds of the rivers. And 'the looms of stone' are the symbols of the 'souls that descend into generation.' 'For the formation of the flesh is on or about the bones, which in the bodies of animals resemble stones,' and also because 'the body is a garment' not only about the soul, but about all essences that become visible, for 'the heavens are called by the ancients a veil, in consequence of being as it were the vestments of the celestial gods.' The bees hive in the mixing bowls and jars of stone, for so Porphyry understands the passage, because honey was the symbol adopted by the ancients for 'pleasure arising from generation.' The ancients, he says, called souls not only Naiads but bees, 'as the efficient cause of sweetness'; but not all souls 'proceeding into generation' are called bees, 'but those who will live in it justly and who after having performed such things as are acceptable to the gods will again return (to their kindred stars). For this insect loves to return to the place from whence it came and is eminently just and sober.' I find all these details in the cave of the Witch of Atlas, the most elaborately described of Shelley's caves, except the two gates, and these have a far-off echo in her summer journeys on her cavern river and in her winter sleep in 'an inextinguishable well of crimson fire.' We have for the mixing bowls, and jars of stone full of honey, those delights of the senses, 'sounds of air' 'folded in cells of crystal silences,' 'liquors clear and sweet' 'in crystal vials,' and for the bees, visions 'each in his thin sheath like a chrysalis,' and for 'the looms of stone' and 'raiment of purple stain' the Witch's spinning and embroidering; and the Witch herself is a Naiad, and was born from one of the Atlantides, who lay in 'a chamber of grey rock' until she was changed by the sun's embrace into a cloud.

When one turns to Shelley for an explanation of the cave and fountain one finds how close his thought was to Porphyry's. He looked upon thought as a condition of life in generation and believed that the reality beyond was something other than thought. He wrote in his fragment 'On Life,' 'That the basis of all things cannot be, as the popular philosophy alleges, mind is sufficiently evident. Mind, as far as we have any experience of its properties, and beyond that experience how vain is argument, cannot create, it can only perceive'; and in another passage he defines mind as existence. Water is his great symbol of existence, and he continually meditates over its mysterious source. In his prose he tells how 'thought can with difficulty visit the intricate and winding chambers which it inhabits. It is like a river, whose rapid and perpetual stream flows outward. . . . The caverns of the mind are obscure and shadowy; or pervaded with a lustre, beautiful and bright indeed, but shining not beyond their portals.' When the Witch has passed in her boat from the caverned river, that is doubtless her own destiny, she passes along the Nile 'by Moeris and the Mareotid lakes,' and sees all human life shadowed upon its waters in shadows that 'never are erased but tremble ever'; and in many a dark and subterranean street under the Nile—new caverns—and along the bank of the Nile; and as she bends over the unhappy, she compares unhappiness to the strife that 'stirs the liquid surface of man's life'; and because she can see the reality of things she is described as journeying 'in the calm depths' of 'the wide lake' we journey over unpiloted. Alastor calls the river that he follows an image of his mind, and thinks that it will be as hard to say where his thought will be when he is dead as where its waters will be in ocean or cloud in a little while. In 'Mont Blanc,' a poem so overladen with descriptions in parentheses that one loses sight of its logic, Shelley compares the flowing through our mind of 'the universe of things,' which are, he has explained elsewhere, but thoughts, to the flowing of the Arve through the ravine, and compares the unknown sources of our thoughts in some 'remoter world' whose 'gleams' 'visit the soul in sleep,' to Arve's sources among the glaciers on the mountain heights. Cythna in the passage where she speaks of making signs 'a subtle language within language' on the sand by the 'fountain' of sea water in the cave where she is imprisoned, speaks of the 'cave' of her mind which gave its secrets to her, and of 'one mind the type of all' which is a 'moveless wave' reflecting 'all moveless things that are'; and then passing more completely under the power of the symbol, she speaks of growing wise through contemplation of the images that rise out of the fountain at the call of her will. Again and again one finds some passing allusion to the cave of man's mind, or to the caves of his youth, or to the cave of mysteries we enter at death, for to Shelley as to Porphyry it is more than an image of life in the world. It may mean any enclosed life, as when it is the dwelling-place of Asia and Prometheus, or when it is 'the still cave of poetry,' and it may have all meanings at once, or it may have as little meaning as some ancient religious symbol enwoven from the habit of centuries with the patterns of a carpet or a tapestry.

As Shelley sailed along those great rivers and saw or imagined the cave that associated itself with rivers in his mind, he saw half-ruined towers upon the hilltops, and once at any rate a tower is used to symbolise a meaning that is the contrary to the meaning symbolised by caves. Cythna's lover is brought through the cave where there is a polluted fountain to a high tower, for being man's far-seeing mind, when the world has cast him out he must to the 'towers of thought's crowned powers'; nor is it possible for Shelley to have forgotten this first imprisonment when he made men imprison Lionel in a tower for a like offence; and because I know how hard it is to forget a symbolical meaning, once one has found it, I believe Shelley had more than a romantic scene in his mind when he made Prince Athanase follow his mysterious studies in a lighted tower above the sea, and when he made the old hermit watch over Laon in his sickness in a half-ruined tower, wherein the sea, here doubtless as to Cythna, 'the one mind,' threw 'spangled sands' and 'rarest sea shells.' The tower, important in Maeterlinck, as in Shelley, is, like the sea, and rivers, and caves with fountains, a very ancient symbol, and would perhaps, as years went by, have grown more important in his poetry. The contrast between it and the cave in 'Laon and Cythna' suggests a contrast between the mind looking outward upon men and things and the mind looking inward upon itself, which may or may not have been in Shelley's mind, but certainly helps, with one knows not how many other dim meanings, to give the poem mystery and shadow. It is only by ancient symbols, by symbols that have numberless meanings beside the one or two the writer lays an emphasis upon, or the half-score he knows of, that any highly subjective art can escape from the barrenness and shallowness of a too conscious arrangement, into the abundance and depth of nature. The poet of essences and pure ideas must seek in the half-lights that glimmer from symbol to symbol as if to the ends of the earth, all that the epic and dramatic poet finds of mystery and shadow in the accidental circumstances of life.

The most important, the most precise of all Shelley's symbols, the one he uses with the fullest knowledge of its meaning, is the Morning and Evening Star. It rises and sets for ever over the towers and rivers, and is the throne of his genius. Personified as a woman it leads Rousseau, the typical poet of *The Triumph of Life,* under the power of the destroying hunger of life, under the power of the sun that we shall find presently as a symbol of life, and it is the Morning Star that wars against the principle of evil in 'Laon and Cythna,' at first as a star with a red comet, here a symbol of all evil as it is of disorder in *Epipsychidion,* and then as a serpent with an eagle—symbols in Blake too and in the Alchemists; and it is the Morning Star that appears as a winged youth to a woman, who typifies humanity amid its sorrows, in the first canto of 'Laon and Cythna'; and it is invoked by the wailing women of *Hellas,* who call it 'lamp of the free' and 'beacon of love' and would go where it hides flying from the deepening night among those 'kingless continents sinless as Eden,' and 'mountains and islands' 'prankt on the sapphire sea' that are but the opposing hemispheres to the senses but, as I think, the ideal world, the world of the dead, to the imagination; and in the 'Ode to Liberty,' Liberty is bid lead wisdom out of the inmost cave of man's mind as the Morning Star leads the sun out of the waves. We know too that had *Prince Athanase* been finished it would have described the finding of Pandemus, the stars' lower genius, and the growing weary of her, and the coming to its true genius Urania at the coming of death, as the day finds the Star at evening. There is hardly indeed a poem of any length in which one does not find it as a symbol of love, or liberty, or wisdom, or beauty, or of some other expression of that Intellectual Beauty, which was to Shelley's mind the central power of the world; and to its faint and fleeting light he offers up all desires, that are as

> The desire of the moth for the star,
>   Of the night for the morrow,
> The devotion to something afar
>   From the sphere of our sorrow.

When its genius comes to Rousseau, shedding dew with one hand, and treading out the stars with her feet, for she is also the genius of the dawn, she brings him a cup full of oblivion and love. He drinks and his mind becomes like sand 'on desert Labrador' marked by the feet of deer and a wolf. And then the new vision, life, the cold light of day moves before him, and the first vision becomes an invisible presence. The same image was in his mind too when he wrote

> Hesperus flies from awakening night
> And pants in its beauty and speed with light,
> Fast fleeting, soft and bright.

Though I do not think that Shelley needed to go to Porphyry's account of the cold intoxicating cup, given to the souls in the constellation of the Cup near the constellation Cancer, for so obvious a symbol as the cup, or that he could not have found the wolf and the deer and the continual flight of his Star in his own mind, his poetry becomes the richer, the more emotional, and loses something of its appearance of idle phantasy when I remember that these are ancient symbols, and still come to visionaries in their dreams. Because the wolf is but a more violent symbol of longing and desire than the hound, his wolf and deer remind me of the hound and deer that Usheen saw in the Gaelic poem chasing one another on the water before he saw the young man following the woman with the golden apple; and of a Galway tale that tells how Niam, whose name means brightness or beauty, came to Usheen as a deer; and of a vision that a friend of mine saw when gazing at a dark-blue curtain. I was with a number of Hermetists, and one of them said to another, 'Do you see something in the curtain?' The other gazed at the curtain for a while and saw presently a man led through a wood by a black hound, and then the hound lay dead at a place the seer knew was called, without knowing why, 'the Meeting of the Suns,' and the man followed a red hound, and then the red hound was pierced by a spear. A white fawn watched the man out of the wood, but he did not look at it, for a white hound came and he followed it trembling, but the seer knew that he would follow the fawn at last, and that it would lead him among the gods. The most learned of the Hermetists said, 'I cannot tell the meaning of the hounds or where the Meeting of the Suns is, but I think the fawn is the Morning and Evening Star.' I have little doubt that when the man saw the white fawn he was coming out of the darkness and passion of the world into some day of partial regeneration, and that it was the Morning Star and would be the Evening Star at its second coming. I have little doubt that it was but the story of Prince Athanase and what may have been the story of Rousseau in *The Triumph of Life,* thrown outward once again from that great memory, which is still the mother of the Muses, though men no longer believe in it.

It may have been this memory, or it may have been some impulse of his nature too subtle for his mind to follow, that made Keats, with his love of embodied things, of precision of form and colouring, of emotions made sleepy by the flesh, see Intellectual Beauty in the Moon; and Blake, who lived in that energy he called eternal delight, see it in the Sun, where his personification of poetic genius labours at a furnace. I think there was certainly some reason why these men took so deep a pleasure in lights that Shelley thought of with weariness and trouble. The Moon is the most changeable of symbols, and not merely because it is the symbol of change. As mistress of the waters she governs the life of instinct and the generation of things, for, as Porphyry says, even 'the apparition of images' in the 'imagination' is through 'an excess of moisture'; and, as a cold and changeable fire set in the bare heavens, she governs alike chastity and the joyless idle drifting hither and thither of generated things. She may give God a body and have Gabriel to bear her messages, or she may come to men in their happy moments as she came to Endymion, or she may deny life and shoot her arrows; but because she only becomes beautiful in giving herself, and is no flying ideal, she is not loved by the children of desire.

Shelley could not help but see her with unfriendly eyes. He is believed to have described Mary Shelley at a time when she had come to seem cold in his eyes, in that passage of *Epipsychidion* which tells how a woman like the Moon led him to her cave and made 'frost' creep over the sea of his mind, and so bewitched Life and Death with 'her silver voice' that they ran from him crying, 'Away, he is not of our crew.' When he describes the Moon as part of some beautiful scene he can call her beautiful, but when he personifies, when his words come under the influence of that great memory or of some mysterious tide in the depth of our being, he grows unfriendly or not truly friendly or at the most pitiful. The Moon's lips 'are pale and waning,' it is 'the cold Moon,' or 'the frozen and inconstant Moon,' or it is 'forgotten' and 'waning,' or it 'wanders' and is 'weary,' or it is 'pale and grey,' or it is 'pale for weariness,' and 'wandering companionless' and 'ever changing,' and finding 'no object worth' its 'constancy,' or it is like a 'dying lady' who 'totters' 'out of her chamber led by the insane and feeble wanderings of her fading brain,' and even when it is no more than a star, it casts an evil influence that makes the lips of lovers 'lurid' or pale. It only becomes a thing of delight when Time is being borne to his tomb in eternity, for then the spirit of the Earth, man's procreant mind, fills it with his own joyousness. He describes the spirit of the Earth and of the Moon, moving above the rivulet of their lives in a passage which reads like a half-understood vision. Man has become 'one harmonious soul of many a soul' and 'all things flow to all' and 'familiar acts are beautiful through love,' and an 'animation of delight' at this change flows from spirit to spirit till the snow 'is loosened from the Moon's lifeless mountains.'

Some old magical writer, I forget who, says if you wish to be melancholy hold in your left hand an image of the Moon made out of silver, and if you wish to be happy hold in your right hand an image of the Sun made out of gold.[2] The Sun is the symbol of sensitive life, and of belief and joy and pride and energy, of indeed the whole life of the will, and of that beauty which neither lures from far off, nor becomes beautiful in giving itself, but makes all glad because it is beauty. Taylor quotes Proclus as calling it 'the Demiurgos of everything sensible.' It was therefore natural that Blake, who was always praising energy, and all exalted overflowing of oneself, and who thought art an impassioned labour to keep men from doubt and despondency, and woman's love an evil, when it would trammel man's will, should see the poetic genius not in a woman star but in the Sun, and should rejoice throughout his poetry in 'the Sun in his strength.' Shelley, however, except when he uses it to describe the peculiar beauty of Emilia Viviani, who was 'like an incarnation of the Sun when light is changed to love,' saw it with less friendly eyes. He seems to have seen it with perfect happiness only when veiled in mist, or glimmering upon water, or when faint enough to do no more than veil the brightness of his own Star; and in *The Triumph of Life,* the one poem in which it is part of the avowed symbolism, its power is the being and the source of all tyrannies. When the woman personifying the Morning Star has faded from before his eyes, Rousseau sees a 'new vision' in 'a cold bright car' with a rainbow hovering over her, and as she comes the shadow passes from 'leaf to stone' and the souls she has enslaved seem in 'that light like atomies to dance within a sunbeam,' or they dance among the flowers that grow up newly 'in the grassy verdure of the desert,' unmindful of the misery that is to come upon them. 'These are the great, the unforgotten,' all who have worn 'mitres and helms and crowns or wreaths of light,' and yet have not known themselves. Even 'great Plato' is there because he knew joy and sorrow, because life that could not subdue him by gold or pain, by 'age or sloth or slavery,' subdued him by love. All who have ever lived are there except Christ and Socrates and the 'sacred few' who put away all life could give, being doubtless followers throughout their lives of the forms borne by the flying ideal, or who, 'as soon as they had touched the world with living flame, flew back like eagles to their native noon.'

In ancient times, it seems to me that Blake, who for all his protest was glad to be alive, and ever spoke of his gladness, would have worshipped in some chapel of the Sun, but that Shelley, who hated life because he sought 'more in life than any understood,' would have wandered, lost in a ceaseless reverie, in some chapel of the Star of infinite desire.

I think too that as he knelt before an altar, where a thin flame burnt in a lamp made of green agate, a single vision would have come to him again and again, a vision of a boat drifting down a broad river between high hills where there were caves and towers, and following the light of one Star; and that voices would have told him how there is for every man some one scene, some one adventure, some one picture that is the image of his secret life, for wisdom first speaks in images, and that this one image, if he would but brood over it his life long, would lead his soul, disentangled from unmeaning circumstance and the ebb and flow of the world, into that far household, where the undying gods await all whose souls have become simple as flame, whose bodies have become quiet as an agate lamp.

But he was born in a day when the old wisdom had vanished and was content merely to write verses, and often with little thought of more than verses.

NOTES

1. 'Marianne's Dream' was certainly copied from a real dream of somebody's, but like images come to the mystic in his waking state.

2. Wilde told me that he had read this somewhere. He had suggested it to Burne-Jones as a subject for a picture. 1924.

THE SYMBOLISM OF POETRY

I

'Symbolism, as seen in the writers of our day, would have no value if it were not seen also, under one disguise or another, in every great imaginative writer,' writes Mr. Arthur Symons in *The Symbolist Movement in Literature,* a subtle book which I cannot praise as I would, because it has been dedicated to me; and he goes on to show how many profound writers have in the last few years sought for a philosophy of poetry in the doctrine of symbolism, and how even in countries where it is almost scandalous to seek for any philosophy of poetry, new writers are following them in their search. We do not know what the writers of ancient times talked of among themselves, and one bull is all that remains of Shakespeare's talk, who was on the edge of modern times; and the journalist is convinced, it seems, that they talked of wine and women and politics, but never about their art, or never quite seriously about their art. He is certain that no one, who had a philosophy of his art or a theory of how he should write, has ever made a work of art, that people have no imagination who do not write without forethought and afterthought as he writes his own articles. He says this with enthusiasm, because he has heard it at so many comfortable dinner-tables, where some one had mentioned through careless-ness, or foolish zeal, a book whose difficulty had offended indolence, or a man who had not forgotten that beauty is an accusation. Those formulas and generalisations, in which a hidden sergeant has drilled the ideas of journalists and through them the ideas of all but all the modern world, have created in their turn a forgetfulness like that of soldiers in battle, so that journalists and their readers have forgotten, among many like events, that Wagner spent seven years arranging and explaining his ideas before he began his most characteristic music; that opera, and with it modern music, arose from certain talks at the house of one Giovanni Bardi of Florence; and that the Pleiade laid the foundations of modern French literature with a pamphlet. Goethe has said, 'a poet needs all philosophy, but he must keep it out of his work,' though that is not always necessary; and almost certainly no great art, outside England, where journalists are more powerful and ideas less plentiful than elsewhere, has arisen without a great criticism, for its herald or its interpreter and protector, and it may be for this reason that great art, now that vulgarity has armed itself and multiplied itself, is perhaps dead in England.

All writers, all artists of any kind, in so far as they have had any philosophical or critical power, perhaps just in so far as they have been deliberate artists at all, have had some philosophy, some criticism of their art; and it has often been this philosophy, or this criticism, that has evoked their most startling inspiration, calling into outer life some portion of the divine life, or of the buried reality, which could alone extinguish in the emotions what their philosophy or their criticism would extinguish in the intellect. They have sought for no new thing, it may be, but only to understand and to copy the pure inspiration of early times, but because the divine life wars upon our outer life, and must needs change its weapons and its movements as we change ours, inspiration has come to them in beautiful startling shapes. The scientific movement brought with it a literature, which was always tending to lose itself in externalities of all kinds, in opinion, in declamation, in picturesque writing, in word-painting, or in what Mr. Symons has called an attempt 'to build in brick and mortar inside the covers of a book'; and now writers have begun to dwell upon the element of evocation, of suggestion, upon what we call the symbolism in great writers.

II

In 'Symbolism in Painting,' I tried to describe the element of symbolism that is in pictures and sculpture, and described a little the symbolism in poetry, but did not describe at all the continuous indefinable symbolism which is the substance of all style.

There are no lines with more melancholy beauty than these by Burns—

> The white moon is setting behind the white wave,
> And Time is setting with me, O!

and these lines are perfectly symbolical. Take from them the whiteness of the moon and of the wave, whose relation to the setting of Time is too subtle for the intellect, and you take from them their beauty. But, when all are together, moon and wave and whiteness and setting Time and the last melancholy cry, they evoke an emotion which cannot be evoked by any other arrangement of colours and sounds and forms. We may call this metaphorical writing, but it is better to call it symbolical writing, because metaphors are not profound enough to be moving, when they are not symbols, and when they are symbols they are the most perfect of all, because the most subtle, outside of pure sound, and through them one can the best find out what symbols are. If one begins the reverie with any beautiful lines that one can remember, one finds they are like those by Burns. Begin with this line by Blake—

> The gay fishes on the wave when the moon sucks up the dew;

or these lines by Nash—

> Queens have died young and fair,
> Brightness falls from the air,
> Dust hath closed Helen's eye;

or these lines by Shakespeare—

> Timon hath made his everlasting mansion
> Upon the beached verge of the salt flood;

> Who once a day with his embossed froth
> The turbulent surge shall cover;

or take some line that is quite simple, that gets its beauty from its place in a
story, and see how it flickers with the light of the many symbols that have
given the story its beauty, as a sword-blade may flicker with the light of
burning towers.

All sounds, all colours, all forms, either because of their pre-ordained
energies or because of long association, evoke indefinable and yet precise
emotions, or, as I prefer to think, call down among us certain disembodied
powers, whose footsteps over our hearts we call emotions; and when sound,
and colour, and form are in a musical relation, a beautiful relation to one
another, they become as it were one sound, one colour, one form, and evoke an
emotion that is made out of their distinct evocations and yet is one emotion.
The same relation exists between all portions of every work of art, whether it
be an epic or a song, and the more perfect it is, and the more various and
numerous the elements that have flowed into its perfection, the more powerful
will be the emotion, the power, the god it calls among us. Because an emotion
does not exist, or does not become perceptible and active among us, till it has
found its expression, in colour or in sound or in form, or in all of these, and
because no two modulations or arrangements of these evoke the same
emotion, poets and painters and musicians, and in a less degree because their
effects are momentary, day and night and cloud and shadow, are continually
making and un-making mankind. It is indeed only those things which seem
useless or very feeble that have any power, and all those things that seem
useful or strong, armies, moving wheels, modes of architecture, modes of
government, speculations of the reason, would have been a little different if
some mind long ago had not given itself to some emotion, as a woman gives
herself to her lover, and shaped sounds or colours or forms, or all of these, into
a musical relation, that their emotion might live in other minds. A little lyric
evokes an emotion, and this emotion gathers others about it and melts into
their being in the making of some great epic; and at last, needing an always
less delicate body, or symbol, as it grows more powerful, it flows out, with all
it has gathered, among the blind instincts of daily life, where it moves a power
within powers, as one sees ring within ring in the stem of an old tree. This is
maybe what Arthur O'Shaughnessy meant when he made his poets say they
had built Nineveh with their sighing; and I am certainly never certain, when
I hear of some war, or of some religious excitement or of some new
manufacture, or of anything else that fills the ear of the world, that it has not
all happened because of something that a boy piped in Thessaly. I remember
once telling a seer to ask one among the gods who, as she believed, were
standing about her in their symbolic bodies, what would come of a charming
but seeming trivial labour of a friend, and the form answering, 'the devastation
of peoples and the overwhelming of cities.' I doubt indeed if the crude
circumstance of the world, which seems to create all our emotions, does more
than reflect, as in multiplying mirrors, the emotions that have come to solitary

men in moments of poetical contemplation; or that love itself would be more than an animal hunger but for the poet and his shadow the priest, for unless we believe that outer things are the reality, we must believe that the gross is the shadow of the subtle, that things are wise before they become foolish, and secret before they cry out in the market-place. Solitary men in moments of contemplation receive, as I think, the creative impulse from the lowest of the Nine Hierarchies, and so make and unmake mankind, and even the world itself, for does not 'the eye altering alter all'?

> Our towns are copied fragments from our breast;
> And all man's Babylons strive but to impart
> The grandeurs of his Babylonian heart.

III

The purpose of rhythm, it has always seemed to me, is to prolong the moment of contemplation, the moment when we are both asleep and awake, which is the one moment of creation, by hushing us with an alluring monotony, while it holds us waking by variety, to keep us in that state of perhaps real trance, in which the mind liberated from the pressure of the will is unfolded in symbols. If certain sensitive persons listen persistently to the ticking of a watch, or gaze persistently on the monotonous flashing of a light, they fall into the hypnotic trance; and rhythm is but the ticking of a watch made softer, that one must needs listen, and various, that one may not be swept beyond memory or grow weary of listening; while the patterns of the artist are but the monotonous flash woven to take the eyes in a subtler enchantment. I have heard in meditation voices that were forgotten the moment they had spoken; and I have been swept, when in more profound meditation, beyond all memory but of those things that came from beyond the threshold of waking life. I was writing once at a very symbolical and abstract poem, when my pen fell on the ground; and as I stooped to pick it up, I remembered some phantastic adventure that yet did not seem phantastic, and then another like adventure, and when I asked myself when these things had happened, I found that I was remembering my dreams for many nights. I tried to remember what I had done the day before, and then what I had done that morning; but all my waking life had perished from me, and it was only after a struggle that I came to remember it again, and as I did so that more powerful and startling life perished in its turn. Had my pen not fallen on the ground and so made me turn from the images that I was weaving into verse, I would never have known that meditation had become trance, for I would have been like one who does not know that he is passing through a wood because his eyes are on the pathway. So I think that in the making and in the understanding of a work of art, and the more easily if it is full of patterns and symbols and music, we are lured to the threshold of sleep, and it may be far beyond it, without knowing that we have ever set our feet upon the steps of horn or of ivory.

IV

Besides emotional symbols, symbols that evoke emotions alone,—and in this sense all alluring or hateful things are symbols, although their relations with one another are too subtle to delight us fully, away from rhythm and pattern,—there are intellectual symbols, symbols that evoke ideas alone, or ideas mingled with emotions; and outside the very definite traditions of mysticism and the less definite criticism of certain modern poets, these alone are called symbols. Most things belong to one or another kind, according to the way we speak of them and the companions we give them, for symbols, associated with ideas that are more than fragments of the shadows thrown upon the intellect by the emotions they evoke, are the playthings of the allegorist or the pedant, and soon pass away. If I say 'white' or 'purple' in an ordinary line of poetry, they evoke emotions so exclusively that I cannot say why they move me; but if I bring them into the same sentence with such obvious intellectual symbols as a cross or a crown of thorns, I think of purity and sovereignty. Furthermore, innumerable meanings, which are held to 'white' or to 'purple' by bonds of subtle suggestion, and alike in the emotions and in the intellect, move visibly through my mind, and move invisibly beyond the threshold of sleep, casting lights and shadows of an indefinable wisdom on what had seemed before, it may be, but sterility and noisy violence. It is the intellect that decides where the reader shall ponder over the procession of the symbols, and if the symbols are merely emotional, he gazes from amid the accidents and destinies of the world; but if the symbols are intellectual too, he becomes himself a part of pure intellect, and he is himself mingled with the procession. If I watch a rushy pool in the moonlight, my emotion at its beauty is mixed with memories of the man that I have seen ploughing by its margin, or of the lovers I saw there a night ago; but if I look at the moon herself and remember any of her ancient names and meanings, I move among divine people, and things that have shaken off our mortality, the tower of ivory, the queen of waters, the shining stag among enchanted woods, the white hare sitting upon the hilltop, the fool of faery with his shining cup full of dreams, and it may be 'make a friend of one of these images of wonder,' and 'meet the Lord in the air.' So, too, if one is moved by Shakespeare, who is content with emotional symbols that he may come the nearer to our sympathy, one is mixed with the whole spectacle of the world; while if one is moved by Dante, or by the myth of Demeter, one is mixed into the shadow of God or of a goddess. So too one is furthest from symbols when one is busy doing this or that, but the soul moves among symbols and unfolds in symbols when trance, or madness, or deep meditation has withdrawn it from every impulse but its own. 'I then saw,' wrote Gérard de Nerval of his madness, 'vaguely drifting into form, plastic images of antiquity, which outlined themselves, became definite, and seemed to represent symbols of which I only seized the idea with difficulty.' In an earlier time he would have been of that multitude, whose souls austerity withdrew, even more perfectly than madness could withdraw his soul, from hope and memory, from desire and regret, that they might reveal those processions of symbols that men bow to before altars, and woo with incense and offerings. But being of our time, he has been like Maeterlinck, like Villiers de l'Isle Adam in *Axël*, like all who are preoccupied with intellectual symbols in our time, a foreshadower of the new sacred book, of which all the arts, as somebody has said, are begging to dream. How can the arts overcome the slow dying of men's hearts that we call the progress of the world, and lay their hands upon men's heart-strings again, without becoming the garment of religion as in old times?

V

If people were to accept the theory that poetry moves us because of its symbolism, what change should one look for in the manner of our poetry? A return to the way of our fathers, a casting out of descriptions of nature for the sake of nature, of the moral law for the sake of the moral law, a casting out of all anecdotes and of that brooding over scientific opinion that so often extinguished the central flame in Tennyson, and of that vehemence that would make us do or not do certain things; or, in other words, we should come to understand that the beryl stone was enchanted by our fathers that it might unfold the pictures in its heart, and not to mirror our own excited faces, or the boughs waving outside the window. With this change of substance, this return to imagination, this understanding that the laws of art, which are the hidden laws of the world, can alone bind the imagination, would come a change of style, and we would cast out of serious poetry those energetic rhythms, as of a man running, which are the invention of the will with its eyes always on something to be done or undone; and we would seek out those wavering, meditative, organic rhythms, which are the embodiment of the imagination, that neither desires nor hates, because it has done with time, and only wishes to gaze upon some reality, some beauty; nor would it be any longer possible for anybody to deny the importance of form, in all its kinds, for although you can expound an opinion, or describe a thing when your words are not quite well chosen, you cannot give a body to something that moves beyond the senses, unless your words are as subtle, as complex, as full of mysterious life, as the body of a flower or of a woman. The form of sincere poetry, unlike the form of the popular poetry, may indeed be sometimes obscure, or ungrammatical as in some of the best of the Songs of Innocence and Experience, but it must have the perfections that escape analysis, the subtleties that have a new meaning every day, and it must have all this whether it be but a little song made out of a moment of dreamy indolence, or some great epic made out of the dreams of one poet and of a hundred generations whose hands were never weary of the sword.

PER AMICA SILENTIA LUNAE

ANIMA HOMINIS

I

When I come home after meeting men who are strange to me, and sometimes even after talking to women, I go over all I have said in gloom and disappointment. Perhaps I have overstated everything from a desire to vex or startle, from hostility that is but fear; or all my natural thoughts have been drowned by an undisciplined sympathy. My fellow-diners have hardly seemed of mixed humanity, and how should I keep my head among images of good and evil, crude allegories.

But when I shut my door and light the candle, I invite a Marmorean Muse, an art, where no thought or emotion has come to mind because another man has thought or felt something different, for now there must be no reaction, action only, and the world must move my heart but to the heart's discovery of itself, and I begin to dream of eyelids that do not quiver before the bayonet: all my thoughts have ease and joy, I am all virtue and confidence. When I come to put in rhyme what I have found it will be a hard toil, but for a moment I believe I have found myself and not my anti-self. It is only the shrinking from toil perhaps that convinces me that I have been no more myself than is the cat the medicinal grass it is eating in the garden.

How could I have mistaken for myself an heroic condition that from early boyhood has made me superstitious? That which comes as complete, as minutely organised, as are those elaborate, brightly lighted buildings and sceneries appearing in a moment, as I lie between sleeping and waking, must come from above me and beyond me. At times I remember that place in Dante where he sees in his chamber the 'Lord of Terrible Aspect,' and how, seeming 'to rejoice inwardly that it was a marvel to see, speaking, he said, many things among the which I could understand but few, and of these this: ego dominus tuus'; or should the conditions come, not as it were in a gesture—as the image of a man—but in some fine landscape, it is of Boehme, maybe, that I think, and of that country where we 'eternally solace ourselves in the excellent beautiful flourishing of all manner of flowers and forms, both trees and plants, and all kinds of fruit.'

II

When I consider the minds of my friends, among artists and emotional writers, I discover a like contrast. I have sometimes told one close friend that her only fault is a habit of harsh judgement with those who have not her sympathy, and she has written comedies where the wickedest people seem but bold children. She does not know why she has created that world where no one is ever judged, a high celebration of indulgence, but to me it seems that her ideal of beauty is the compensating dream of a nature wearied out by over-much judgement. I know a famous actress who in private life is like the captain of some buccaneer ship holding his crew to good behaviour at the mouth of a blunderbuss, and upon the stage she excels in the representation of women who stir to pity and to desire because they need our protection, and is most adorable as one of those young queens imagined by Maeterlinck who have so little will, so little self, that they are like shadows sighing at the edge of the world. When I last saw her in her own house she lived in a torrent of words and movements, she could not listen, and all about her upon the walls were women drawn by Burne-Jones in his latest period. She had invited me in the hope that I would defend those women, who were always listening, and are as necessary to her as a contemplative Buddha to a Japanese Samurai, against a French critic who would persuade her to take into her heart in their stead a Post-Impressionist picture of a fat, flushed woman lying naked upon a Turkey carpet.

There are indeed certain men whose art is less an opposing virtue than a compensation for some accident of health or circumstance. During the riots over the first production of the *Playboy of the Western World* Synge was confused, without clear thought, and was soon ill—indeed the strain of that week may perhaps have hastened his death—and he was, as is usual with gentle and silent men, scrupulously accurate in all his statements. In his art he made, to delight his ear and his mind's eye, voluble daredevils who 'go romancing through a romping life time . . . to the dawning of the Judgement Day.' At other moments this man, condemned to the life of a monk by bad health, takes an amused pleasure in 'great queens . . . making themselves matches from the start to the end.' Indeed, in all his imagination he delights in fine physical life, in life when the moon pulls up the tide. The last act of *Deirdre of the Sorrows,* where his art is at its noblest, was written upon his death-bed. He was not sure of any world to come, he was leaving his betrothed and his unwritten play—'Oh, what a waste of time,' he said to me; he hated to die, and in the last speeches of Deirdre and in the middle act he accepted death and dismissed life with a gracious gesture. He gave to Deirdre the emotion that seemed to him most desirable, most difficult, most fitting, and maybe saw in those delighted seven years, now dwindling from her, the fulfilment of his own life.

III

When I think of any great poetical writer of the past (a realist is an historian and obscures the cleavage by the record of his eyes) I comprehend, if I know the lineaments of his life, that the work is the man's flight from his entire horoscope, his blind struggle in the network of the stars. William Morris, a happy, busy, most irascible man, described dim colour and pensive emotion, following, beyond any man of his time, an indolent muse; while Savage Landor topped us all in calm nobility when the pen was in his hand, as in the daily violence of his passion when he had laid it down. He had in his *Imaginary Conversations* reminded us, as it were, that the Venus de Milo is a stone, and yet he wrote when the copies did not come from the printer as soon as he expected: 'I have . . . had the resolution to tear in pieces all my sketches and projects and to forswear all future undertakings. I have tried to sleep away my time and pass two-thirds of the twenty-four hours in bed. I may speak of myself as a dead man.' I imagine Keats to have been born with that thirst for luxury common to many at the outsetting of the Romantic Movement, and not able, like wealthy Beckford, to slake it with beautiful and strange objects. It drove him to imaginary delights; ignorant, poor, and in poor health, and not perfectly well-bred, he knew himself driven from tangible luxury; meeting Shelley, he was resentful and suspicious because he, as Leigh Hunt recalls, 'being a little too sensitive on the score of his origin, felt inclined to see in every man of birth his natural enemy.'

IV

Some thirty years ago I read a prose allegory by Simeon Solomon, long out of print and unprocurable, and remember or seem to remember a sentence, 'a hollow image of fulfilled desire.' All happy art seems to me that hollow image, but when its lineaments express also the poverty or the exasperation that set its maker to the work, we call it tragic art. Keats but gave us his dream of luxury; but while reading Dante we never long escape the conflict, partly because the verses are at moments a mirror of his history, and yet more because that history is so clear and simple that it has the quality of art. I am no Dante scholar, and I but read him in Shadwell or in Dante Rossetti, but I am always persuaded that he celebrated the most pure lady poet ever sung and the Divine Justice, not merely because death took that lady and Florence banished her singer, but because he had to struggle in his own heart with his unjust anger and his lust; while unlike those of the great poets, who are at peace with the world and at war with themselves, he fought a double war. 'Always,' says Boccaccio, 'both in youth and maturity he found room among his virtues for lechery'; or as Matthew Arnold preferred to change the phrase, 'his conduct was exceeding irregular.' Guido Cavalcanti, as Rossetti translates him, finds 'too much baseness' in his friend:

> And still thy speech of me, heartfelt and kind,
> Hath made me treasure up thy poetry;
> But now I dare not, for thy abject life,
> Make manifest that I approve thy rhymes.

And when Dante meets Beatrice in Eden, does she not reproach him because, when she had taken her presence away, he followed in spite of warning dreams, false images, and now, to save him in his own despite, she has 'visited . . . the Portals of the Dead,' and chosen Virgil for his courier? While Gino da Pistoia complains that in his *Commedia* his 'lovely heresies . . . beat the right down and let the wrong go free':

Therefore his vain decrees, wherein he lied,
Must be like empty nutshells flung aside;
Yet through the rash false witness set to grow,
French and Italian vengeance on such pride
May fall like Anthony on Cicero.

Dante himself sings to Giovanni Guirino 'at the approach of death':

The King, by whose rich grave his servants be
With plenty beyond measure set to dwell,
Ordains that I my bitter wrath dispel,
And lift mine eyes to the great Consistory.

V

We make out of the quarrel with others, rhetoric, but of the quarrel with ourselves, poetry. Unlike the rhetoricians, who get a confident voice from remembering the crowd they have won or may win, we sing amid our uncertainty; and, smitten even in the presence of the most high beauty by the knowledge of our solitude, our rhythm shudders. I think, too, that no fine poet, no matter how disordered his life, has ever, even in his mere life, had pleasure for his end. Johnson and Dowson, friends of my youth, were dissipated men, the one a drunkard, the other a drunkard and mad about women, and yet they had the gravity of men who had found life out and were awakening from the dream; and both, one in life and art and one in art and less in life, had a continual preoccupation with religion. Nor has any poet I have read of or heard of or met with been a sentimentalist. The other self, the anti-self or the antithetical self, as one may choose to name it, comes but to those who are no longer deceived, whose passion is reality. The sentimentalists are practical men who believe in money, in position, in a marriage bell, and whose understanding of happiness is to be so busy whether at work or at play, that all is forgotten but the momentary aim. They find their pleasure in a cup that is filled from Lethe's wharf, and for the awakening, for the vision, for the revelation of reality, tradition offers us a different word—ecstasy. An old artist wrote to me of his wanderings by the quays of New York, and how he found there a woman nursing a sick child, and drew her story from her. She spoke, too, of other children who had died: a long tragic story. 'I wanted to paint her,' he wrote, 'if I denied myself any of the pain I could not believe in my own ecstasy.' We must not make a false faith by hiding from our thoughts the causes of doubt, for faith is the highest achievement of the human intellect, the only gift man can make to God, and therefore it must be offered in sincerity. Neither must we create, by hiding ugliness, a false beauty as our offering to the world. He only can create the greatest imaginable beauty who has endured all imaginable pangs, for only when we have seen and foreseen what we dread shall we be rewarded by that dazzling unforeseen wing-footed wanderer. We could not find him if he were not in some sense of our being and yet of our being but as water with fire, a noise with silence. He is of all things not impossible the most difficult, for that only which comes easily can never be a portion of our being, 'Soon got, soon gone,' as the proverb says. I shall find the dark grow luminous, the void fruitful when I understand I have nothing, that the ringers in the tower have appointed for the hymen of the soul a passing bell.

The last knowledge has often come most quickly to turbulent men, and for a season brought new turbulence. When life puts away her conjuring tricks one by one, those that deceive us longest may well be the wine-cup and the sensual kiss, for our Chambers of Commerce and of Commons have not the divine architecture of the body, nor has their frenzy been ripened by the sun. The poet, because he may not stand within the sacred house but lives amid the whirlwinds that beset its threshold, may find his pardon.

VI

I think the Christian saint and hero, instead of being merely dissatisfied, make deliberate sacrifice. I remember reading once an autobiography of a man who had made a daring journey in disguise to Russian exiles in Siberia, and his telling how, very timid as a child, he schooled himself by wandering at night through dangerous streets. Saint and hero cannot be content to pass at moments to that hollow image and after become their heterogeneous selves, but would always, if they could, resemble the antithetical self. There is a shadow of type on type, for in all great poetical styles there is saint or hero, but when it is all over Dante can return to his chambering and Shakespeare to his 'pottle pot.' They sought no impossible perfection but when they handled paper or parchment. So too will saint or hero, because he works in his own flesh and blood and not in paper or parchment, have more deliberate understanding of that other flesh and blood.

Some years ago I began to believe that our culture, with its doctrine of sincerity and self-realisation, made us gentle and passive, and that the Middle Ages and the Renaissance were right to found theirs upon the imitation of Christ or of some classic hero. St. Francis and Cæsar Borgia made themselves over-mastering, creative persons by turning from the mirror to meditation upon a mask. When I had this thought I could see nothing else in life. I could not write the play I had planned, for all became allegorical, and though I tore up hundreds of pages in my endeavour to escape from allegory, my imagination became sterile for nearly five years and I only escaped at last when I had mocked in a comedy my own thought. I was always thinking of the element of imitation in style and in life, and of the life beyond heroic imitation. I find in an old diary: 'I think all happiness depends on the energy to assume the mask of some other life, on a re-birth as something not one's self, something created in a moment and perpetually renewed; in playing a game like that of a child where one loses the infinite pain of self-realisation, in a grotesque or solemn painted face put on that one may hide from the terror of judgement. . . . Perhaps all the sins and energies of the world are but the world's flight from an infinite blinding beam'; and again at an earlier date: 'If we cannot imagine ourselves as different from what we are, and try to assume that second self, we cannot impose a discipline upon ourselves though we may accept one from others. Active virtue, as distinguished from the passive acceptance of a code, is therefore theatrical, consciously dramatic, the wearing of a mask. . . . Wordsworth, great poet though he be, is so often flat and heavy partly because his moral sense, being a discipline he had not created, a mere obedience, has no theatrical element. This increases his popularity with the better kind of journalists and politicians who have written books.'

VII

I thought the hero found hanging upon some oak of Dodona an ancient mask, where perhaps there lingered something of Egypt, and that he changed it to his fancy, touching it a little here and there, gilding the eyebrows or putting a gilt line where the cheekbone comes; that when at last he looked out of its eyes he knew another's breath came and went within his breath upon the carven lips, and that his eyes were upon the instant fixed upon a visionary world: how else could the god have come to us in the forest? The good, unlearned books say that He who keeps the distant stars within His fold comes without intermediary, but Plutarch's precepts and the experience of old women in Soho, ministering their witchcraft to servant girls at a shilling a piece, will have it that a strange living man may win for Daemon[1] an illustrious dead man; but now I add another thought: the Daemon comes not as like to like but seeking its own opposite, for man and Daemon feed the hunger in one another's hearts. Because the ghost is simple, the man heterogeneous and confused, they are but knit together when the man has found a mask whose lineaments permit the expression of all the man most lacks, and it may be dreads, and of that only.

The more insatiable in all desire, the more resolute to refuse deception or an easy victory, the more close will be the bond, the more violent and definite the antipathy.

VIII

I think that all religious men have believed that there is a hand not ours in the events of life, and that, as somebody says in *Wilhelm Meister,* accident is destiny; and I think it was Heraclitus who said: the Daemon is our destiny. When I think of life as a struggle with the Daemon who would ever set us to the hardest work among those not impossible, I understand why there is a deep enmity between a man and his destiny, and why a man loves nothing but his destiny. In an Anglo-Saxon poem a certain man is called, as though to call him something that summed up all heroism, 'Doom eager.' I am persuaded that the Daemon delivers and deceives us, and that he wove that netting from the stars and threw the net from his shoulder. Then my imagination runs from Daemon to sweetheart, and I divine an analogy that evades the intellect. I remember that Greek antiquity has bid us look for the principal stars, that govern enemy and sweetheart alike, among those that are about to set, in the Seventh House as the astrologers say; and that it may be 'sexual love,' which is 'founded upon spiritual hate,' is an image of the warfare of man and Daemon; and I even wonder if there may not be some secret communion, some whispering in the dark between Daemon and sweetheart. I remember how often women when in love, grow superstitious, and believe that they can bring their lovers good luck; and I remember an old Irish story of three young men who went seeking for help in battle into the house of the gods at Slieve-na-mon. 'You must first be married,' some god told them, 'because a man's good or evil luck comes to him through a woman.'

I sometimes fence for half an hour at the day's end, and when I close my eyes upon the pillow I see a foil playing before me the button to my face. We meet always in the deep of the mind, whatever our work, wherever our reverie carries us, that other Will.

IX

The poet finds and makes his mask in disappointment, the hero in defeat. The desire that is satisfied is not a great desire, nor has the shoulder used all its might that an unbreakable gate has never strained. The saint alone is not deceived, neither thrusting with his shoulder nor holding out unsatisfied hands. He would climb without wandering to the antithetical self of the world, the Indian narrowing his thought in meditation or driving it away in contemplation, the Christian copying Christ, the antithetical self of the classic world. For a hero loves the world till it breaks him, and the poet till it has broken faith; but while the world was yet debonair, the saint has turned away, and because he renounced Experience itself, he will wear his mask as he finds it. The poet or the hero, no matter upon what bark they found their mask, so teeming their fancy, somewhat change its lineaments, but the saint, whose life is but a round of customary duty, needs nothing the whole world does not need, and day by day he scourges in his body the Roman and Christian conquerors; Alexander and Caesar are famished in his cell. His nativity is neither in disappointment nor in defeat, but in a temptation like that of Christ in the Wilderness, a contemplation in a single instant perpetually renewed of the Kingdoms of the World; all—because all renounced—continually present showing their empty thrones. Edwin Ellis, remembering that Christ also measured the sacrifice, imagined himself in a fine poem as meeting at Golgotha the phantom of 'Christ the Less,' the Christ who might have lived a prosperous life without the knowledge of sin, and who now wanders 'companionless a weary spectre day and night.'

> I saw him go and cried to him
> 'Eli, thou hast forsaken me.'
> The nails were burning through each limb,
> He fled to find felicity.

And yet is the saint spared—despite his martyr's crown and his vigil of desire—defeat, disappointed love, and the sorrow of parting.

O Night, that did'st lead thus,
O Night, more lovely than the dawn of light,
O Night, that broughtest us
Lover to lover's sight,
Lover with loved in marriage of delight!"

Upon my flowery breast,
Wholly for him, and save himself for none,
There did I give sweet rest
To my beloved one;
The fanning of the cedars breathed thereon.

When the first morning air
Blew from the tower, and waved his locks aside,
His hand, with gentle care,
Did wound me in the side,
And in my body all my senses died.

All things I then forgot,
My cheek on him who for my coming came;
All ceased and I was not,
Leaving my cares and shame
Among the lilies, and forgetting them.[2]

X

It is not permitted to a man, who takes up pen or chisel, to seek originality, for passion is his only business, and he cannot but mould or sing after a new fashion because no disaster is like another. He is like those phantom lovers in the Japanese play who, compelled to wander side by side and never mingle, cry: 'We neither wake nor sleep and passing our nights in a sorrow which is in the end a vision, what are these scenes of spring to us?' If when we have found a mask we fancy that it will not match our mood till we have touched with gold the cheek, we do it furtively, and only where the oaks of Dodona cast their deepest shadow, for could he see our handiwork the Daemon would fling himself out, being our enemy.

XI

Many years ago I saw, between sleeping and waking, a woman of incredible beauty shooting an arrow into the sky, and from the moment when I made my first guess at her meaning I have thought much of the difference between the winding movement of nature and the straight line, which is called in Balzac's *Seraphita* the 'Mark of Man,' but is better described as the mark of saint or sage. I think that we who are poets and artists, not being permitted to shoot beyond the tangible, must go from desire to weariness and so to desire again, and live but for the moment when vision comes to our weariness like terrible lightning, in the humility of the brutes. I do not doubt those heaving circles, those winding arcs, whether in one man's life or in that of an age, are mathematical, and that some in the world, or beyond the world, have foreknown the event and pricked upon the calendar the life-span of a Christ, a Buddha, a Napoleon: that every movement, in feeling or in thought, prepares in the dark by its own increasing clarity and confidence its own executioner. We seek reality with the slow toil of our weakness and are smitten from the boundless and the unforeseen. Only when we are saint or sage, and renounce Experience itself, can we, in imagery of the Christian Caballa, leave the sudden lightning and the path of the serpent and become the bowman who aims his arrow at the centre of the sun.

XII

The doctors of medicine have discovered that certain dreams of the night, for I do not grant them all, are the day's unfulfilled desire, and that our terror of desires condemned by the conscience has distorted and disturbed our dreams. They have only studied the breaking into dream of elements that have remained unsatisfied without purifying discouragement. We can satisfy in life a few of our passions and each passion but a little, and our characters indeed but differ because no two men bargain alike. The bargain, the compromise, is always threatened, and when it is broken we become mad or hysterical or are in some way deluded; and so when a starved or banished passion shows in a dream we, before awaking, break the logic that had given it the capacity of action and throw it into chaos again. But the passions, when we know that they cannot find fulfilment, become vision; and a vision, whether we wake or sleep, prolongs its power by rhythm and pattern, the wheel where the world is butterfly. We need no protection but it does, for if we become interested in ourselves, in our own lives, we pass out of the vision. Whether it is we or the vision that create the pattern, who set the wheel turning, it is hard to say, but certainly we have a hundred ways of keeping it near us: we select our images from past times, we turn from our own age and try to feel Chaucer nearer than the daily paper. It compels us to cover all it cannot incorporate, and would carry us when it comes in sleep to that moment when even sleep closes her eyes and dreams begin to dream; and we are taken up into a clear light and are forgetful even of our own names and actions and yet in perfect possession of ourselves murmur like Faust, 'Stay, moment,' and murmur in vain.

XIII

A poet, when he is growing old, will ask himself if he cannot keep his mask and his vision without new bitterness, new disappointment. Could he if he would, knowing how frail his vigour from youth up, copy Landor who lived loving and hating, ridiculous and unconquered, into extreme old age, all lost but the favour of his muses?

> The mother of the muses we are taught
> Is memory; she has left me; they remain
> And shake my shoulder urging me to sing.

Surely, he may think, now that I have found vision and mask I need not suffer any longer. He will buy perhaps some small old house where like Ariosto he can dig his garden, and think that in the return of birds and leaves, or moon and sun, and in the evening flight of the rooks he may discover rhythm and pattern like those in sleep and so never awake out of vision. Then he will remember Wordsworth withering into eighty years, honoured and empty-witted, and climb to some waste room and find, forgotten there by youth, some bitter crust.

NOTES

1. I could not distinguish at the time between the permanent Daemon and the impermanent, who may be 'an illustrious dead man,' though I knew the distinction was there. I shall deal with the matter in *A Vision*. (February 1924.)

2. Translated by Arthur Symons from *San Juan de la Cruz*.

Benedetto Croce

1866–1952

Benedetto Croce was born in Pescasseroli, Italy, on February 25, 1866. He devoted his formative years to an eclectic range of studies, including Neapolitan history (he lived in Naples from 1886 on), literary criticism, and Marx; he was for some years the editor of the writings of his former teacher Antonio Labriola, with whom he was friendly, as also with Georges Sorel. Around 1900, the year of the murder of King Umberto, Croce put aside his studies of economics to turn to the study of literary theory; his *Aesthetic* was published in 1902. Here Croce attempted to take up the thought of his fellow Neapolitan, the philosopher Giambattista Vico. In 1903 Croce founded his own journal, *La Critica,* at the same time as several younger men—Corradini, Papini and Prezzolini, Borghese—set up similar journals, all of an anti-academic, anti-democratic, and anti-positivist bent. Croce's scholarly moderation, and that of his chief collaborator Giovanni Gentile, contrasted sharply with the tendentiousness of the younger men. The *Logic* of 1905, with its continued anti-positivism, was applauded by Croce's younger admirers. *The Philosophy of the Practical* (1909), with its closing note of austerity and moral restraint, was not so well received; and by the time of the Italian colonial war of 1911–12 (the first triumph of Italian nationalism), the break between Croce and his younger collaborators, who now termed him "outmoded," was complete.

During World War I Croce turned back to poetry and spent much time studying the greatest poet of the opposing nation, Goethe. Curiously enough (since Goethe was nothing if not a free spirit), this brought him to a revision of his earlier ideas about artistic freedom: he began to see in art a moral function of quasi-religious validity. He also continued his historical studies, publishing his *History: Its Theory and Practice* (1917) and a study of Italian historiography in 1918. After the war it seemed at first that Croce would be at the center of a new regrouping of the Italian left; but Croce went along with nationalism, contributing to the nationalist journal *Politica* and then voting for Mussolini in the Senate. While he was minister of education in 1920, his old co-worker Gentile influenced him to introduce Catholic instruction into the state elementary schools. Croce's and Gentile's educational "reforms" met with harsh opposition from the left. Mussolini's speech of January 3, 1925, abruptly dispelled any illusions Croce might have had about the regime. The publication of Gentile's "Manifesto degli intellectuali fascisti" in April of that year prompted Croce to write a response that made him overnight the leader of the anti-fascist resistance.

With the outbreak of World War II Croce became displaced by the vogue for existentialism and phenomenology. By a strange twist of fate Croce chose to spend his last years in opposition to communism; this new bias led him to excise all traces of that Marxian-Hegelian dialectic which had once been so marked a feature of his thought. Croce died in Naples on November 20, 1952.

In many respects Croce never entered the century in which most of his life was spent: his preference for literary and historical studies closed him off from the new areas being opened up by phenomenology, psychology, linguistics, or even anthropology, not to mention the exact sciences. Like his great predecessor, the historian Jakob Burckhardt, he was an atheist but persisted in his adherence to the moral culture born of Christianity; but with Croce this agnostic moralism, cut off from all concrete practice (for him politics and ethics occupied two distinct spheres), was also accompanied by a vague belief in Providence, in the impenetrable "mystery" of life which could never be systematized, which must always remain bound to empirical, particular existences, facts, and situations. Croce documented the limits of his own time rather than seeing beyond them, and like them he has had little influence beyond his own lifetime. His philosophical "system" was too idiosyncratic and eclectic to have much lasting resonance. Where he will continue to inspire respect is among historians: as Arnaldo Momigliano has written, "Croce the scholar will be indispensable for a long time to come even to those who care little for Croce the philosopher."

TASTE AND THE
REPRODUCTION OF ART

When the entire æsthetic and externalizing process has been completed, when a beautiful expression has been produced and it has been fixed in a definite physical material, what is meant by *judging it*? *To reproduce it in oneself,* answer the critics of art, almost with one voice. Very good. Let us try thoroughly to understand this fact, and with that object in view, let us represent it schematically.

The individual A is seeking the expression of an impression which he feels or anticipates, but has not yet expressed. See him trying various words and phrases which may give the sought-for expression, that expression which must exist, but which he does not possess. He tries the combination *m,* but rejects it as unsuitable, inexpressive, incomplete, ugly: he tries the combination *n,* with a like result. *He does not see at all, or does not see clearly.* The expression still eludes him. After other vain attempts, during which he sometimes approaches, sometimes retreats from the mark at which he aims, all of a sudden (almost as though formed spontaneously of itself) he forms the sought-for expression, and *lux facta est.* He enjoys for an instant æsthetic pleasure or the pleasure of the beautiful. The ugly, with its correlative displeasure, was the æsthetic activity which had not succeeded in conquering the obstacle; the beautiful is the expressive activity which now displays itself triumphant.

We have taken this example from the domain of speech, as being nearer and more accessible, and because we all talk, though we do not all draw or paint. Now if another individual, whom we shall call B, is to judge that expression and decide whether it be beautiful or ugly, he *must of necessity place himself at A's point of view,* and go through the whole process again, with the help of the physical sign supplied to him by A. If A has seen clearly, then B (who has placed himself at A's point of view) will also see clearly and will see this expression as beautiful. If A has not seen clearly, then B also will not see clearly, and will find the expression more or less ugly, *just as A did.*

It may be observed that we have not taken into consideration two other cases: that of A having a clear and B an obscure vision; and that of A having an obscure and B a clear vision. Strictly speaking, these two cases are *impossible.*

Expressive activity, just because it is activity, is not caprice, but spiritual necessity; it cannot solve a definite æsthetic problem save in one way, which is the right way. It will be objected to this plain statement that works which seem beautiful to the artists are afterwards found to be ugly by the critics; while other works with which the artists were discontented and held to be imperfect or failures are, on the contrary, held to be beautiful and perfect by the critics. But in this case, one of the two is wrong: either the critics or the artists, sometimes the artists, at other times the critics. Indeed, the producer of an expression does not always fully realize what is happening in his soul. Haste, vanity, want of reflexion, theoretic prejudices, make people say, and others sometimes almost believe, that works of ours are beautiful, which, if we really looked into ourselves, we should see to be ugly, as they are in reality. Thus poor Don Quixote, when he had reattached to his helmet as well as he could the vizor of cardboard—the vizor that had showed itself to possess but the feeblest force of resistance at the first encounter,—took good care not to test it again with a well-delivered sword-thrust, but simply declared and maintained it to be (says the author) *por celada finisima de encaxe*. And in other cases, the same reasons, or opposite but analogous ones, trouble the consciousness of the artist, and cause him to value badly what he has successfully produced, or to strive to undo and do again for the worse what he has done well in artistic spontaneity. An instance of this is Tasso and his passage from the *Gerusalemme liberata* to the *Gerusalemme conquistata*. In the same way, haste, laziness, want of reflexion, theoretic prejudices, personal sympathies or animosities, and other motives of a similar sort, sometimes cause the critics to proclaim ugly what is beautiful, and beautiful what is ugly. Were they to eliminate such disturbing elements, they would feel the work of art as it really is, and would not leave it to posterity, that more diligent and more dispassionate judge, to award the palm, or to do that justice which they have refused.

It is clear from the preceding theorem that the activity of judgement which criticizes and recognizes the beautiful is identical with what produces it. The only difference lies in the diversity of circumstances, since in the one case it is a question of æsthetic production, in the other of reproduction. The activity which judges is called *taste;* the productive activity is called *genius:* genius and taste are therefore substantially *identical.*

The common remark that the critic should possess something of the genius of the artist and that the artist should possess taste, gives a glimpse of this identity; or the remark that there exists an active (productive) and a passive (reproductive) taste. But it is also negated in other equally common remarks, as when people speak of taste without genius, or of genius without taste. These last observations are meaningless, unless they allude to quantitative or psychological differences, those being called geniuses without taste who produce works of art, inspired in their chief parts and neglected or defective in their secondary parts, and men of taste without genius, those who, while they succeed in obtaining certain isolated or secondary merits, do not possess sufficient power for a great artistic synthesis. Analogous explanations can easily be given of other similar expressions. But to posit a substantial difference between genius and taste, between artistic production and reproduction, would render both communication and judgement alike inconceivable. How could we judge what remained external to us? How could that which is produced by a given activity be judged by a *different* activity? The critic may be a small genius, the artist a great one; the former may have the strength of ten, the latter of a hundred; the former, in order to reach a certain height, will have need of the assistance of the other; but the nature of both must remain the same. To judge Dante, we must raise ourselves to his level: let it be well understood that empirically we are not Dante, nor Dante we; but in that moment of contemplation and judgement, our spirit is one with that of the poet, and in that moment we and he are one thing. In this identity alone resides the possibility that our little souls can echo great souls, and grow great with them in the universality of the spirit.

Let us remark in passing that what has been said of the æsthetic judgement holds good equally for every other activity and for every other judgement; and that scientific, economic, and ethical criticism is effected in a like manner. To limit ourselves to this last, only if we place ourselves ideally in the same conditions in which he found himself who took a given resolution, can we form a judgement as to whether his decision were moral or immoral. An action would otherwise remain incomprehensible and therefore impossible to judge. A homicide may be a rascal or a hero: if this be, within limits, indifferent as regards the defence of society, which condemns both to the same punishment, it is not indifferent to one who wishes to distinguish and judge from the moral point of view, and we therefore cannot dispense with reconstructing the individual psychology of the homicide, in order to determine the true nature of his deed, not merely in its legal, but also in its moral aspect. In Ethics, a moral taste or tact is sometimes mentioned, answering to what is generally called the moral consciousness, that is to say, to the activity of the good will itself.

The explanation above given of æsthetic judgement or reproduction both agrees with and condemns the absolutists and relativists, those who affirm and those who deny the absoluteness of taste.

In affirming that the beautiful can be judged, the absolutists are right; but the theory on which they found their affirmation is not tenable, because they conceive of the beautiful, that is, æsthetic value, as something placed outside the æsthetic activity, as a concept or a model which an artist realizes in his work, and of which the critic avails himself afterwards in judging the work itself. These concepts and models have no existence in art, for when proclaiming that every art can be judged only in itself and that it has its model in itself, they implicitly denied the existence of objective models of beauty, whether these are intellectual concepts, or ideas suspended in a metaphysical heaven.

In proclaiming this, their adversaries, the relativists, are perfectly right, and effect an advance upon them. However, the initial rationality of their thesis in its turn becomes converted into a false theory. Repeating the ancient adage that there is no accounting for tastes, they believe that æsthetic expression is of the same nature as the pleasant and the unpleasant, which every one feels in his own way, and about which there is no dispute. But we know that the pleasant and the unpleasant are utilitarian, practical facts. Thus the relativists deny the specific character of the æsthetic fact, and again confound expression with impression, the theoretic with the practical.

The true solution lies in rejecting alike relativism or psychologism and false absolutism; and in recognizing that the criterion of taste is absolute, but absolute in a different way from that of the intellect, which expresses itself in ratiocination. The criterion of taste is absolute, with the intuitive absoluteness of the imagination. Thus any act of expressive activity, which is so really, is to be recognized as beautiful, and any fact as ugly in which expressive activity and passivity are found engaged with one another in an unfinished struggle.

Between absolutists and relativists is a third class, which may be called that of the relative relativists. These affirm the existence of absolute values in other fields, such as Logic and Ethic, but deny it in the field of Æsthetic. To dispute about science or morals seems to them to be rational and justifiable, because science depends upon the universal, common to all men, and morality upon duty, which is also a law of human nature; but how dispute about art, which depends upon imagination? Not only, however, is the imaginative activity universal and no less inherent in human nature than the logical concept and practical duty; but there is a preliminary objection to the thesis in question. If the absoluteness of the imagination be denied, we must also deny intellectual or conceptual truth and implicitly morality. Does not morality presuppose logical distinctions? How could these be known, otherwise than in expressions and words, that is to say, in imaginative form? If the absoluteness of the imagination were removed, the life of the spirit would tremble to its foundations. One individual would no longer understand another, nor indeed his own self of a moment before, which is already another individual considered a moment after.

Nevertheless, variety of judgements is an indubitable fact. Men disagree as to logical, ethical, and economical valuations; and they disagree equally or even more as to the æsthetic. If certain reasons recorded by us above, such as haste, prejudices, passions, etc., may lessen the importance of this disagreement, they do not on that account annul it. When speaking of the stimuli of reproduction we have added a caution, for we said that reproduction takes place, *if all the other conditions remain equal.* Do they remain equal? Does the hypothesis correspond to reality?

It would appear not. In order to reproduce an impression several times by means of a suitable physical stimulus it is necessary that this stimulus be not changed, and that the organism remain in the same psychical conditions as those in which was experienced the impression that it is desired to reproduce. Now it is a fact that the physical stimulus is continually changing, and in like manner the psychological conditions.

Oil-paintings grow dark, frescoes fade, statues lose noses, hands and legs, architecture becomes totally or partially a ruin, the tradition of the execution of a piece of music is lost, the text of a poem is corrupted by bad copyists or bad printing. These are obvious instances of the changes which daily occur in objects or physical stimuli. As regards psychological conditions, we will not dwell upon the cases of deafness or blindness, that is to say, upon the loss of entire orders of psychical impressions; these cases are secondary and of less importance compared with the fundamental, daily, inevitable and perpetual changes of the society around us and of the internal conditions of our individual life. The phonetic manifestations or words and verses of Dante's *Commedia* must produce a very different impression on an Italian citizen engaged in the politics of the third Rome, from that experienced by a well-informed and intimate contemporary of the poet. The Madonna of Cimabue is still in the Church of Santa Maria Novella; but does she speak to the visitor of to-day as to the Florentines of the thirteenth century? Even though she were not also darkened by time, must we not suppose that the impression which she now produces is altogether different from that of former times? And even in the case of the same individual poet, will a poem composed by him in youth make the same impression upon him when he re-reads it in his old age, with psychic conditions altogether changed?

It is true that certain æstheticians have attempted a distinction between stimuli and stimuli, between *natural* and *conventional* signs. The former are held to have a constant effect upon all; the latter only upon a limited circle. In their belief, signs employed in painting are natural, those used in poetry conventional. But the difference between them is at the most only one of degree. It has often been said that painting is a language understood by all, while with poetry it is otherwise. Here, for example, Leonardo found one of the prerogatives of his art, "which hath not need of interpreters of different tongues as have letters," and it pleases man and beast. He relates the anecdote of that portrait of the father of a family "which the little grandchildren were wont to caress while they were still in swaddling-clothes, and the dogs and cats of the house in like manner." But other anecdotes, such as those of the savages who took the portrait of a soldier for a boat, or considered the portrait of a man on horseback to be furnished with only one leg, are apt to shake one's faith in the understanding of painting by sucklings, dogs and cats. Fortunately, no arduous researches are necessary to convince oneself that pictures, poetry and all works of art only produce effects upon souls prepared to receive them. Natural signs do not exist; because all are equally conventional, or, to speak with greater exactness, *historically conditioned.*

Granting this, how are we to succeed in causing the expression to be reproduced by means of the physical object? How obtain the same effect, when the conditions are no longer the same? Would it not, rather, seem necessary to conclude that expressions cannot be reproduced, despite the physical instruments made for the purpose, and that what is called reproduction consists in ever new expressions? Such would indeed be the conclusion if the varieties of physical and psychical conditions were intrinsically insurmountable. But since the insuperability has none of the characteristics of necessity we must on the contrary conclude that reproduction always occurs when we can replace ourselves in the conditions in which the stimulus (physical beauty) was produced.

Not only can we replace ourselves in these conditions as an abstract possibility, but as a matter of fact we do so continually. Individual life, which is communion with ourselves (with our past), and social life, which is communion with our like, would not otherwise be possible.

As regards the physical object, palæographers and philologists, who *restore* to texts their original physiognomy, *restorers* of pictures and of statues and other industrious toilers strive precisely to preserve or to restore to the physical object all its primitive energy. These efforts are certainly not always successful, or are not completely successful, for it is never or hardly ever possible to obtain a restoration complete in its smallest details. But the insurmountable is here only present accidentally and must not lead us to overlook the successes which actually are achieved.

Historical interpretation labours for its part to reintegrate in us the psychological conditions which have changed in the course of history. It revives the dead, completes the fragmentary, and enables us to see a work of art (a physical object) as its author saw it in the moment of production.

A condition of this historical labour is tradition, with the help of which it is possible to collect the scattered rays and concentrate them in one focus. With the help of memory we surround the physical stimulus with all the facts among which it arose; and thus we enable it to act upon us as it acted upon him who produced it.

Where the tradition is broken, interpretation is arrested; in this case, the products of the past remain silent for us. Thus the expressions contained in the Etruscan or Mexican inscriptions are unattainable; thus we still hear discussions among ethnographers as to whether certain products of the art of savages are pictures or writings; thus archæologists and prehistorians are not always able to establish with certainty whether the figures found on the pottery of a certain region, and on other instruments employed, are of a religious or profane nature. But the arrest of interpretation, as that of restoration, is never a definitely insurmountable barrier; and the daily discoveries of new historical sources and of new methods of better exploiting the old, which we may hope to see ever improving, link up again broken traditions.

We do not wish to deny that erroneous historical interpretation sometimes produces what may be called *palimpsests*, new expressions imposed upon the ancient, artistic fancies instead of historical reproductions. The so-called "fascination of the past" depends in part upon these expressions of ours, which we weave upon the historical. Thus has been discovered in Greek plastic art the calm and serene intuition of life of those peoples, who nevertheless felt the universal sorrow so poignantly; thus "the terror of the year 1000" has recently been discerned on the faces of the Byzantine saints, a terror which is a misunderstanding, or an artificial legend invented later by men of learning. But *historical criticism* tends precisely to circumscribe fancies and to establish exactly the point of view from which we must look.

By means of the above process we live in communication with other men of the present and of the past; and we must not conclude because we sometimes, and indeed often, meet with an unknown or an ill-known, that therefore, when we believe we are engaged in a dialogue, we are always speaking a monologue; or that we are unable even to repeat the monologue which we formerly held with ourselves.

FOLK POETRY AND POETS' POETRY

In the abundant literature dealing with popular or folk poetry admissions abound that while "folk poetry" is easily talked of, and it is not hard to agree on what works the description covers, yet it is very difficult to "define" it. Is it not better, it is then suggested,[1] to go ahead without seeking a definition, thus sparing much headscratching?

For all that, the attempt is not abandoned to define folk poetry at the very least by contrasting it with the poetry of poets, the poetry of literary artists. Folk poetry, it is said, by contrast with poets' poetry, is anonymous, improvised, springs from the people, that is from the humble ranks of peasants and shepherds, originates and spreads itself collectively, is passed on by word of mouth, is always undergoing change, and so on and so on.[2] But such descriptions lack any method or consistency. Folk poetry is not always anonymous, nor has the other always an author's name attached to it. Improvisation, or rapidity of composition, is not the mark of one or of the other, nor yet is a slow deliberate rate of composition. It is not only the humbler ranks who compose folk poetry, nor the higher ranks alone who produce cultured and sophisticated poems. No poem can have a collective origin: a personal poet's work is indispensable at the birth of a poem. Poetry of every sort can or does spread through the society of its place of origin, and more or less far afield. Transmission by word of mouth was the rule for complex literary poems in times when writing was little practised. It serves even today for the circulation of epigrams and satirical sayings of anything but popular origin and character, which it is preferred not to commit to writing. As to the "fluidity" supposedly characterizing folk poetry, what is meant is simply the incessant imitation, adaptation, modification which happens equally to literary poetry at the hands of authors, copyists, publishers, interpreters, and other conveyers.[3] Even if all or some of all those descriptions of folk poetry were to the point, they would in any case cover only external characters and would thus be useless for the definition of a quality of poetry. For such a definition could not be (like the descriptions already mentioned) drawn from external circumstances, but would have to penetrate to the interior. It would have to be not, so to speak, philological, but psychological.

There are, in fact, other definitions attempted on more psychological lines. It is said that folk poetry is impersonal or general, indifferent to or lacking in technique, unhistorical (that is, not assignable to any historical phase), asynthetic, expressed in propositions not built into sentence form, or in verses not composed in a chain of stanzas, or composed in imperfect stanzas, or in episodes through which there runs no connecting story, or in successions of scenes lacking the link of drama, and so on.[4] Some of these latter descriptions do indeed point to genuine and characteristic features in the thing described, yet they do not bring this into a clear light, and when formulated in this manner are easily confuted. For one might retort that all poetry is both personal and impersonal, personal in that its content is the passion of a human heart, but impersonal in that this passion, becoming poetry, must have surpassed and overcome itself in the universally human. Accordingly poetry can never reside in the abstraction or type, yet any poetry may become typical for whoever generalizes its content. On the other hand, no poetry is ever void of technique, even in the sense in which the word is here used to indicate formal precedent, discipline, school. Nay, it might even be said that folk poetry, disposing of a small number of patterns, and repeating these, is outstandingly technical. And then, there is no poetry outside of history, and as to the supposed asynthetic character of folk poetry, if synthesis were lacking all would be lacking, for there is no act of the human spirit that is not synthetic. If the syntheses of folk poetry are genuine syntheses, yet different from the syntheses of literary poetry, the right proceeding is to investigate and locate the quality of this differentiation in folk poetry, not to deny that the synthesis is there.

Naturally, the difference whose quality is sought out cannot be absolute or pertain to the essence, because there are no categories in poetry, that which is poetry being purely and simply poetry. Here too then the temptation of violating unity must be resisted. Let it be remarked that the contrast between *Volkslied* and *Kunstlied* was primarily proclaimed by that same people which invented the contrasting pairs "classical and romantic", "Latin and Germanic", and others of the same order, a conceptual corruption of the pure aesthetic judgement.[5] It is not to be denied that there is beautiful folk poetry and unbeautiful (non-poetic) folk poetry, just as poets' poetry can be beautiful or unbeautiful; and folk poetry can be as ugly, awkward, facetious, mechanical as the other, and includes also no less abundance and variety of gnomic, admonitory, anecdotic, playful verse which is not and does not pretend to be poetry properly so called.[6] Nor, when folk poetry is poetry, is it distinguishable from literary poetry: its modes are enthralling and delightful.[7] The difference to be investigated and the resultant definition will have to be, then, as already said, merely psychological, a difference not of essence but of tendency or stress. Within this limit, it may be useful to the ends of criticism.

By way of introduction we may consider the analogy with other spheres of spiritual life in which a cognate psychological difference is found. We will at once recall, in the intellectual sphere, how "common sense"[8] is distinguished from critical and systematic thought, without any intention of asserting that there could be a common sense wholly uncritical and unsystematic, or a critical and systematic thought wanting in common sense. Nevertheless it is clear that common sense is that attitude of the intellect which effortlessly asserts obvious truths, whereas critical and systematic thought takes up matters of doubt, struggles and wrestles with them, overcomes them, and, with often painful effort and unravelling of complications, proclaims its truths. Which truths often seem the very same as those proclaimed by common sense, yet they are not the same, for they carry a weight which is absent from the pronouncement of common sense, in that they sum up a great number of judgements which common sense never bothered itself to formulate, carry in themselves the results of a long process, and are forearmed against the emergence or re-emergence of doubts against which common sense was unprepared (and common sense may never have experienced them, but could not prevent them from raising their head, nor find any means of safety except to take flight, that is, to shut itself in itself). The linguistic monument of common sense is to be found in popular literature, and is built up of proverbs, and of what is called the wisdom of the ages, the wisdom of the world, so often praised for its utterly solid soundness, but no one, even when quoting such proverbial wisdom with approval, will ever mistake its maxims for the works of criticism, learning, philosophy, with their series of enquiries, discussions, treatises, systems.[9] Many philosophical discussions may be aptly concluded with the quotation of some old and familiar saying or proverb, but this, precisely because it is placed at the conclusion of the discussion, no longer bears merely its old and familiar sense.

In the practical sphere, a difference is recognized between the natural insight of the child or the peasant, and the insight of the trained man. In morals, we distinguish between sheer innocence, which scarcely lights upon evil, hardly knows of its existence, does good naturally as though knowing of no other course, and is itself a bright and happy goodness; and, on the other hand, a forearmed and forewarned goodness, aware of the passions and their perils, having measured these, struggled against them, mustered strength to subdue them. Such goodness is ever watchful and is austere rather than happy. But the distinction here, once again, is not absolute. There is really no natural goodness that has never experienced or been stung by evil, nor is there any goodness so austere and effortfully acquired as to have wholly lost the element of innocent, natural goodness. All the same the two attitudes are differentiated, and all can see which of them prevails or dominates in any given character. *Beati sunt possidentes:* true enough, but we give our admiration to those who work and achieve, fight and win.

Now popular or folk poetry is the analogue in the aesthetic sphere of common sense in the intellectual and wide-eyed innocence in the moral. It expresses emotions which have no immediate background and precedent of arduous thought and passion, but simple feelings which receive a correspondingly simple form. The poetry of great poets excites and stirs in us vast stores of memories, experiences, thoughts, multiple feelings, and ever finer shades of feeling. Folk poetry makes no such ample circling and wheeling flight towards the goal, but speeds straight for it. The words and rhythms in which folk poetry takes its shape are fully adequate for its aims, just as the words and rhythms proper to high poetry, charged with suggestions peculiar to it alone, are adequate for its own aims. For an example, take the celebrated popular stanza on the turtle-dove that has lost its mate, and compare this with the words expressive of almost the same image, which Tommaseo puts in the heart of Matilda of Canossa, bereft of her mate, pining for love. It will be seen that there is here no contrast between a greater and a lesser artistic perfection. The contrast is, that behind the popular verse lies the simple experience of the desolate restlessness of widowhood, but behind the other the whole agitation of the senses and mysticism of the Dalmatian poet.

The popular octave thus describes the misery of the dove that has lost its mate and now drinks alone in the stream, abandons the choirs of birds on the flowery branch, beats its wings, lamenting, on its breast:

> La tortora, che ha perso la compagna,
> fa una vita molto dolorosa:
> va in un fiumicello e vi si bagna,
> e beve di quell'acqua torbidosa;
> cogli altri uccelli non ci s'accompagna,
> sugli alberi fioriti non si posa;
> si batte con le ali sopra il cuore:
> —Povera me, c'ho perso lo mio amore!

Tommaseo's Matilda found no relief in sighs, but like a forlorn bird lamented to God, the pain unsilenced in her heart:

> Né mai dal chiuso petto si partìo
> il sospiro dell'anima solinga;
> e per la notte lamentava a Dio,
> quale su' tetti passera raminga . . .
> . . . Ancóra, o padre, ancóra
> l'acuto grido del mio cor non tace! . . .

The tone of feeling, rhythm, word-stuff of these last verses mark a depth by the side of which the popular verse seems to be but on the surface of things. But the popular verse is no more superficial than the other: in it, too, there is a vibration of feeling, and it is deeply human.

Such is the character of all the folk poetry that comes easily to mind. In the Tuscan *stornello*

> Fior d'erbe amare!
> Se il capezzale lo potesse dire,
> oh quanti pianti potrebbe contare!

what else is there but desolate weeping by night, the face pressed down on the pillow, for a sorrow which is just any sorrow, sorrow viewed simply as sorrow.—There is another folk song which echoes the answer which so pleased Alceste in the *vieille chanson* of *ma mie, le roi Henri, Paris sa grande ville;* the singer would keep his love though the Pope should offer him all Rome in its stead:

> Se il papa mi donasse tutta Roma,
> e mi dicesse:—Lascia andar chi t'ama—
> io gli direi di no, Sacra Corona.

There is nothing here save the eternal "no" with which man rejects the proposal that he should give up what stands highest in his heart, what he has come to live and breathe for, and has no equivalent in anything else, and is thus priceless.—Again, a lover has quarrelled with his mistress and thinks he has broken with her, but in a little while the name returns to his mind with all its old charm, and he dreams of and hastens on the reconciliation and the renewal of his love:

> Nel passar per la vetta di quel monte,
> al tuo bel nome mi venne pensato;
> mi messi in ginocchioni a mani gionte
>
> e di lasciarti mi parve peccato;
> mi messi in ginocchioni in sulla via:
> ritorni il nostro amor com'era pria!

Goethe took pleasure in bright imaginations of girls with their longings, their ruses and caprices, their anxieties, their throbbing hearts: he served up these miniature portraits and scenes with a smile of indulgent irony. But in the folksong the image emerges unassisted, yet radiating the grace of such girlish desire and expectation (the girl too young for a lover tells what kind of song she would sing were she not so small, and had she but, like the elders, a lover for herself):

> Son piccinina, e volete che canti?
> Queste più grandi l'averan per male.
> Tutte quest'altre ci hanno i loro amanti;
> sotto di me non ci vorranno stare.
>   Ma, se lo avessi lo mio amante anch'io,
> vorrei cantare e dire il fatto mio!
>   Se ce lo avessi lo mio amante ancora,
> vorrei cantare e dir la mia canzona!

Greuze painted his famous La cruche cassée, now at the Louvre, with a mixture of the innocent and the vicious, the moralistic and the sensual, typical of all his painting and in general of his age. But the same transparent symbol, untainted by corrupt and overrefined eroticism, expressive simply of the fear and bewilderment brought on by the event, together with a tragicomic apprehension of the impending wrath of Mamma, is given us in an Italian lay of the sixteenth century.

> Meschina me, che ho rotta la langella,
> alla fontana la me s'è spezzata:
> trista la sfortunata sorte mia!
> Mo saccio, mo saccio, mo saccio,
> mo saccio che m'occide mamma mia!

A poor woman of Naples sings a lullaby for her child, invoking the Saint who gives sleep, Saint Nicholas of Bari whose church is near the Dogana:

> *Santo Nicola mio della Dogana,*
> *con l'acqua tua li malati sani;*
> *e sani li malati poverelli,*
> *e sonno porti sotto lo mantello . . .*

And she seems to see the good Saint, answering her prayer: he leaves heaven and draws near to the child and makes ready to immerse him in sleep by knocking on his forehead one of his balls of gold. The mother who has invoked this magic yet watches in vigilant anxiety for the result:

> *Vieni, palluccia d'oro, e dàgli in fronte,*
> *dagliela in fronte, e non me gli far male . . .*

We are still within the range of the simplest feelings, but these are caught on the wing and poetically expressed. There is much beauty in that fear of the Saint himself, that raising of the voice and stretching of the hand to protect the child even against him.—And here is the woman whose anxiety for her lover gone to the wars is also a motherly sentiment:—

> *Giovanottini che andate alla guerra,*
> *tenete conto del mio innamorato.*
> *Badate che non pòsi l'arme in terra,*
> *perché alla guerra non c'è mai più stato.*
> *Non me lo fate dormire al sereno:*
> *è tanto gentilin che verrà meno.*
> *Non me lo fate dormire alla luna:*
> *è tanto gentilin, me lo consuma.*

This is war seen through the eyes of a woman, taking its significance from the thought that now there will be nobody to take care of her young man in all the little ways in which she used to do so.

Here is a song of quite different feeling, celebrating the most elementary vitality; an old song, for I have found it in collections of the late seventeenth century, of the impetuous expansion of physical energies in their prime:

> *Tanta ho una fame che mi mangerei*
> *Napoli attorniata di panelle;*
> *tanta ho una sete che mi beverei*
> *Castellamare con le fontanelle;*
> *tanto è il mio passo che camminerei*
> *Carotto, Pozzopiano e Tresaelle;*
> *tanto è il mio sonno che mi dormirei*
> *cinquecent'anni con nennella bella!*

To appreciate also in the case of this song (in which the singer would like to eat all Naples, drink the fountains, sleep five hundred years) what differentiates it from literary poetry, it would suffice to recall similar expressions of gaily exuberant energy in the works of refined poets, where we should always find the sense close at hand of something higher, holding the gaiety within bounds, tempering it with humour, or opening up a vista of wicked and perilous inebriation; or some such complications.

I will close this little collection of examples, drawn, as I said, from my own memory rather than from laborious research, by citing three lines of a veritably grim and balefully mocking character, lines from a ballad sung in a village of the Basilicata in 1799 on the occasion of a semi-political and semi-brigandish encounter in which a man of the other side was caught and killed in spite of all the precautions that he had taken. It is the dead man who is made to speak and to relate the vanity of all the precautions taken ("mother made me breeches of cloth") when he came up against so astute and victoriously powerful an enemy ("when the blow fell, I went all cold"):

> *Mamma mi fece le calze di tela,*
> *ed io me le imbottii di canavaccio,*
> *eppure freddo, allo colpo, mi feci!*[10]

Here there is no doubt a great efficacy in the images expressing the mockery and the tragedy, sprung from an elemental human delight in savagery.

We shall now no longer, after thus defining it, be led to confound folk poetry with other types of poetry with which it has sometimes been identified or confounded. It is not "primitive" poetry in the usual meaning of a poetry poor in intellectuality but rich in sensibility and fancy; nor yet the poetry of a "puerile" or "childlike" art corresponding to the disposition and mentality of the child (as contrasted with the disposition and mentality of the simple, the elemental). It is not vernacular poetry, though the expressions of dialect often well fit it: for dialect may be and sometimes is the vehicle for the ways of thought of the educated, and for literary poetry. But our definition enables us to see why folk poetry has been variously felt to be impersonal, typical, generic, non-technical, non-historical, all of these being indistinct approximations to the character which we have assigned to it, and by the light of which the approximations should be interpreted so as to reveal the sense in which they are true. Thus "impersonal" must signify not that the expressions of folk poetry are not personal, but that they are not so strongly diversified as in the poetry of the poets, where the personality of these is illustrated in prolonged compositions. It is for the same reason that folk poems are felt to be "typical" or "generic" and not individual. In the same way it is not true that they lack technique, that is, are not linked to a certain artistic tradition, but only that the tradition to which the poets' poems are linked is by comparison much more substantial. Folk poems are certainly not outside of history: those of the Christian peoples have different accents from those of Greek or Roman antiquity. Yet history means culture, and a cultural specification and diversification is lacking in folk poetry, hence its preference for dialect rather than for the strongly historicized ways of speech of the courtly and cultivated world. Folk poems are, in their way, synthetic, but not with that synthesis of multiple feelings and great contrasts which is found in the poems and dramas, and even the short lyrics, of the poets.[11] The almost constant combination of folk poems, but not of literary poems, with the singing voice and with instrumental music is explained by the consideration of the elementarity of folk poetry.[12]

Our psychological definition which sees the essential mark of folk poetry in a disposition of mind or a "tone" of feeling and expression, forbids us to identify folk poetry with the poetry of the so-called people, or of other such extrinsically and materially delimited milieux. There is plenty of folk poetry to be found under the guise and in the purlieus of literary poetry, and in the so-called sphere of popular or semi-popular art there is to be found not merely literary art, but artifice. The true distinction can be established only on the ideal plane, and by intrinsic standards. It may be very true that folk poetry usually flourishes in the popular class, yet not only in that, for its tone may be discerned wherever there are minds so disposed, which is far from being only in popular circles or on the part of men of the people. Anyway it is well known that much folk poetry is the work of educated or semi-educated men and very little is the product of ignorant working people (as to which ignorance much might be said and many distinctions drawn). Now for the "tone" in question to make itself heard, it is but necessary that certain men, however well educated, should have remained in a state of simple and naive feeling about life or some aspects of life, or should from time to time fall back into that state. In the same way there are men of high critical intelligence who in some ways remain simple-minded, trusting to common sense, and there are men of great practical experience who are in some ways childishly innocent. What is impossible is that having lost our innocence and won in its place another resource, we should behave innocently for example, after exercising ourselves in criticism and philosophy, take our ways of thought from proverbs; or having wholly replaced the tone of folk poetry by that of literary poetry, turn back and resume the folk tone.[13] Therefore it is that the poets, when they have applied themselves to folk poetry or something approaching it, can, if one looks closely at such work (always provided that the result has been something beautiful and vital, and not, as so often, cold and tedious), be seen to have taken up certain elements, motives, forms of folk poetry, but either deepening them in the process or letting some sort of irony play upon them, with the consequence that this apparent folk poetry turns out to be highly refined poetry. Critics have said that "all folk poetry tends to become work of the poetic art".[14] It is not, however, folk poetry that exhibits this tendency. As poetry, it is self-satisfied and independent. It is the Spirit which needs must pass from the one tone to the other, and sometimes back again to the former. It is a mere scholarly illusion to think to find summed up in the great works of poetic art the small and scattered creations of the popular Muse, which in truth only exist as small and scattered, having their own "tone" and not a different tone which has got the better of theirs, and which, even when it seems to offer them a welcome and a permanence, has in fact extinguished them, in the very act of animating their appearances, which it resuscitates, with a new soul.[15]

NOTES

Translator's Note:—It was impossible, by reason of other connotations of the words in English, to translate the title of this essay literally as "Popular Poetry and Art Poetry". Of the two sorts of poetry discussed in the essay, it has been found necessary to render *Poesia popolare* generally as folk poetry, but sometimes also as popular poetry, and *Poesia d'arte* variously as poets' poetry, literary poetry, or works of the poetic art.

1. For example, A. D'Ancona, *La poesia popolare italiana* (2nd edn., Leghorn, 1906), p. 363: "'*Poesia popolare*' is an easy enough phrase, but the genre which it denotes is hard to define." But Goethe wrote as early as 1822 concerning the *Spanische Romanzen:* "Man spricht so oft den Namen *Volkslieder* aus und weiss nicht immer ganz deutlich, was man sich dabei denken soll" (*Werke*, Stuttgart, 1840, xxxiii, 342).

2. It is unnecessary to supply quotations to illustrate the use of these descriptions which are to be found, separately or together, in all treatises about folk poetry. Suffice it to mention in connexion with the last of the list, that Steinthal gave special prominence to it in his essay on *Epos* (in *Zeitschrift für Völkerpsychologie und Sprachwissenschaft*, Vol. v, 1868, pp. 1–57). Folk poetry, he said, is a *nomen actionis*, there being in reality no such thing as a *Volksgedicht* but only a *Volksdichten*, no *Volksepos* but only a *Volksepik*. Comparetti, in an essay on *Poesia popolare* (*Rassegna settimanale*, 1878, ii, 45–47), assigns to folk poetry "certain forms which, created and kept alive by the people, are always, essentially, and in all circumstances popular", such being the *stornello, strambotto, canzone:* to wit, certain literary or even metrical genres.

3. Menéndez Pidal, in *El Romancero, Teorias y investigaciones* (Madrid, undated, but 1928), p. 38 etc., draws a distinction between 'strictly popular, poetry' (which he defines as 'that which becomes popular'), and traditional poetry which the people accepts, reproduces with emotion and imagination, and more or less reforms and refashions, as happens not only to oral but also to written traditional poetry, witness the case of the French epic and of the *Chanson de Roland* itself, and their elaboration through the series of codices in which they have been transmitted. This amounts to eliminating all substantial differentiation between so-called "popular" and "individual" poetry, though Menéndez Pidal feels that there must be a difference underlying the ill-formulated distinction drawn and upheld by several generations of scholars.

4. Once again I refrain from piling up quotations, but see Hegel, *Vorlesungen über die Aesthetik*, Hotho's edn. (Berlin 1838), pp. 435–40, concerning folk poetry; also the comments of Vischer, *Aesthethik oder Wissenschaft des schönen* (Reutlingen and Leipzig, 1946, etc.), specially iii, 90, 990, 1147, 1194, 1356–8; and Carrière, *Aesthetik* (3rd edn., Leipzig, 1885), ii, 535–9.

5. In this connexion Goethe wrote as follows on the unity of all poetry, in an essay of 1825 (*Dainos*): "Es kommt mir bei stiller Betrachtung sehr oft wundersam vor, dass man die Volkslieder so sehr anstaunt und sie so hoch erhebt. Es giebt nur *eine* Poesie, die echte, wahre; alles andere ist nur Annäherung und Schein. Das poetische Talent ist dem Bauer so gut gegeben, als dem Ritter. Es kommt mir darauf an, ob Jeder seinen Zustand ergreift und ihn nach Würden behandelt, und da haben denn die einfachsten Verhältnisse die grössten Vortheile; daher denn auch die höhern, gebildeten Stände meistens wieder, insofern sie zur Dichtung wenden, die Natur in ihrer Einfalt aufsuchen" (*Werke,* ed. cit., xxxiii, 341).

6. There are even series of words and songs having an almost exclusively physiological purpose, e.g. to regulate work, wherein lies the partial truth of the investigation of Bücher, *Arbeit und Rhythmus* (4th edn., Leipzig-Berlin, 1909).

7. I analysed some exquisite Italian folksongs in *Critica* ix (1911), now printed in

Conversazioni critiche, 3rd edn., Bari, 1942, II, 245–50. I called then for a selection to be made, on aesthetic lines, from the vast mass of Italian folksongs collected by the folklorists. My hope has not been wholly disappointed. See the anthology of religious folk poetry by Toschi, and my review of it in *Critica*, XXI (1923), 102–4, reprinted in *Conversazioni critiche*, Bari, 1932, III, 266–9.

8. Descartes, *Discours de la méthode*, I, 1: "La puissance de bien juger et distinguer le vrai d'avec le faux, qui est proprement ce qu'on nomme le bon sens ou la raison, est naturellement égale en tous les hommes."

9. A persistently returning illusion is illustrated in these well-known words of Tommaseo: "If we could collect and group under certain headings all the proverbs of Italy, of all peoples, of all ages, with all the variants in language, images, concepts, the result would be, after the Bible, the weightiest of all books of Thought."

10. To assist easy understanding, I have given here an Italian shape to the dialect poems.

11. The theory of folk poetry and literary poetry given by Hegel in the already cited work, points broadly, on the basis of a distinction between people (or nation), and individual, towards the truth of the matter: "Obschon sich im Volksliede die koncentrirteste Innigkeit des Gemüths aussprechen kann, so ist es dennoch nicht ein einzelnes Individuum, welches sich darin auch mit seiner subjektiven Eigen- thümlichkeit künstlerischer Darstellung kenntlich macht; sondern nur eine Volksempfindung, die das Individuum ganz und voll in sich trägt, insofern es für sich selbst noch kein von der Nation und deren Daseyn und Interessen abgelöstes, inneres Vorstellen und Empfinden hat. Als Voraussetzung für solche ungetrennte Einheit ist ein Zustand nothwendig, in welchem die selbstständige Reflexion und Bildung noch nicht erwacht ist, so dass nun also der Dichter ein als Subjekt zurücktretendes blosses Organ wird, vermittelst dessen sich das nationale Leben in seiner lyrischen Empfindung und Anschauungsweise äussert. Diese unmittelbare Ursprünglichkeit giebt dem Volksliede allerdings eine reflexionslose Frische kerniger Gedrungenheit und schlagender Wahrheit, die oft von der grössten Wirkung ist, aber es erhält dadurch zugleich auch leicht etwas Fragmentarisches, Abgerissenes, und einen Mangel an Explikation, der bis zur Unklarheit fortgehen kann. Die Empfindung versteckt sich tief, und kann und will nicht zum vollständigen Aussprechen kommen. Ausserdem fehlt dem ganzen Standpunkte gemäss, obschon die Form im allgemeinen vollständig lyrischer d. h. subjektiver Art ist, dennoch, wie gesagt, das Subjekt, das diese Form und deren Inhalt als Eigenthum gerade seines Herzens und Geistes, und als Produkt seiner Kunstbildung ausspricht." "Das Volkslied singt sich gleichsam unmittelbar wie ein Naturlaut aus dem Herzen heraus; die freie Kunst aber ist sich ihrer selbst bewusst, sie verlangt ein Wissen und Wollen dessen, was sie producirt, und bedarf einer Bildung zu diesem Wissen, so wie einer zur Vollendung durchgeübten Virtuosität des Her- vorbringens." "In diesem Extreme aber darf jener Satz nicht aufgefasst werden, sondern er ist nur in dem Sinne richtig, dass die subjektive Phantasie und Kunst eben um der selbstständigen Subjektivität willen, die ihr Princip ausmacht, für ihre wahre Vollendung auch das freie ausgebildete Selbstbewusstsein des Vorstellens wie der künstlerischen Thätigkeit zur Voraussetzung und Grundlage haben müsse."

12. This last, just observation I owe to V. Santoli, *Nuove questioni di poesia popolare* (Turin, 1930; *Pallante*, f. 5), pp. 38–39.

13. This is the reason for the distaste aroused by that pseudo-folk poetry which was cultivated, principally in Germany (but by reflection in Italy and also elsewhere). One may recall Heine's satire upon it in the first book of the *Romantische Schule*, culminating in the comparison with the woman in the tale, who, to regain youth, drank

a great draught of magic *elixir*, of which the proper dose was a single drop and found herself turning to a tiny babe! Heine had his doubts even about the best or skilfullest products of this sort of art: "So schön auch die Tieck'sche *Genofeva* ist, so habe ich doch weit lieber da alte, zu Koln am Rhein sehr schlecht gedruckte Volksbuch mit seinen schlechten Holzschnitten, worauf aber gar rührend zu schauen ist, wie die arme nackte Pfalzgräfin nur ihre langen Haare zur keuschen Bedeckung hat und ihren kleinen Schmerzenreich an den Zitzen einer mitleidigen Hirschkuh saugen lässt" (op. cit., book II).

14. "The popular lyric is always striving to become art-poetry." Thus I find summed up in the manual of Gayley-Kurtz, *Methods and Materials of Literary Criticism* (Boston, 1920), p. 135, the conclusions of an essay of L. Jacobowski (1896) which I have not seen.

15. Not to complicate the exposition, I have spoken here only of "poetry"; but it is clear that the psychological distinction of the two tones is to be found in all the other forms of art, and the same criterion is valid for popular painting, popular music, and so on. If I myself do not, later, extend the argument so as to embrace these other cases, I hope that someone else will.

Paul Valéry

1871–1945

Ambroise Paul Toussaint Valéry was born on October 30, 1871, in the French Mediterranean town of Sète; his parents were of Corsican and Italian descent. In 1884 the family moved to Montpellier, where Valéry finished his degree. Unable to pursue a naval career because of his weakness in mathematics, he took up, with little enthusiasm, the study of law. In 1890, between periods of unwanted military service, he met Pierre Loüys and read J. K. Huysmans' *À Rebours,* which introduced him not only to the poetry of Verlaine and Mallarmé but also to a certain notion of rarefied aesthetic existence. Loüys helped Valéry publish one of his first poems in that year, and further introduced him to the young André Gide and to Mallarmé himself, then established as the master of the most intellectually severe and formally complex poetic styles of his day. Mallarmé quickly recognized the younger man's gifts, and the two corresponded frequently over the next few years, Mallarmé often giving encouragement to the self-doubting Valéry. The influence of Mallarmé went beyond youthful enthusiasm, and helped form Valéry's ideal of a "pure" poetry (secret, arcane, "Gnostic"), so that some critics have seen Valéry as Mallarmé's successor. Valéry perceived Mallarmé's art, at this time, as inimitable; out of his despair of his own technical facility and the impossibility of equaling his master he affected scorn for the inadequacies of language and the vulgarity of mere literary fame, adopting in 1892 a resolution to give up the writing of poetry.

From 1897 to 1900 Valéry worked as a civil servant in the War Office in Paris and spent the next twenty years engaged largely in the pursuit of "pure" speculative thought, reading such physicists as James Clerk Maxwell and William Thomson Kelvin. He had little interest in established philosophy as such, which he felt was too abstract; his researches became increasing empirical and Cartesian, concerned with the structure of immediate sense impressions and thought processes. Much of his work is contained within the *Cahiers (Notebooks),* not published until after the author's death. The first finished product of these years was the *Introduction to the Method of Leonardo da Vinci* (1894), a kind of manifesto of Valéry's own "method of thought"; more important was *The Evening with Monsieur Teste* (1896), the portrait of a fictive character who represents all of Valéry's longings for a pure and omnipotent disembodied intellectualism.

By 1913 Valéry had given up his attempts at becoming a "universal mind"; when Gide asked him for permission to reprint his early poetry, he agreed after some hesitation, on condition that he be allowed to make revisions and add, as a conclusion, a short "farewell to poetry." That "pendant" grew to more than 500 lines of *La Jeune Parque;* in it Valéry attempts to unite the technical precocity of his early work with the knowledge gained in his self-imposed withdrawal of twenty years. The poem is an "epic" of the intelligence of the "young Fate" (Valéry himself), her internal doubts and debates, her alterations in consciousness; but it is also, in somewhat Mallarméan fashion, a poem about the writing of poetry. *La Jeune Parque* was an unexpected sensation when it appeared in 1917, and Valéry became a literary celebrity; the "exercise" of the poem had, moreover, opened his poetic vein again, and many other poems were written shortly thereafter, including "Le Cimetière marin" (1920), along with the publication of a collection of his early work. Two years later came *Charmes,* his last important collection; little poetry followed.

From 1900 to 1922 Valéry was employed as private secretary to Edouard Lebey, director of the Havas New Agency; Lebey's death in 1922 left Valéry without means of support and he was forced to publish a great number of prose essays, later collected in the volumes *Tel Quel* (2 vols., 1941–43) and *Variété* (5 vols., 1924–44), and to give lectures both in France and abroad. In 1925 he became a member of the Académie Française. His last works were a series of brief plays (envisioned as ritual or cultic spectacles, like the Mass), including his allegorical reworking of Goethe, *Mon Faust,* begun in 1940 and unfinished at his death; it was published in 1946. Valéry lived to see the liberation of France and died on July 20, 1945.

POETRY AND ABSTRACT THOUGHT

The idea of Poetry is often contrasted with that of Thought, and particularly "Abstract Thought." People say "Poetry and Abstract Thought" as they say Good and Evil, Vice and Virtue, Hot and Cold. Most people, without thinking any further, believe that the analytical work of the intellect, the efforts of will and precision in which it implicates the mind, are incompatible with that freshness of inspiration, that flow of expression, that grace and fancy which are the signs of poetry and which reveal it at its very first words. If a poet's work is judged profound, its profundity seems to be of a quite different order from that of a philosopher or a scientist. Some people go so far as to think that even meditation on his art, the kind of exact reasoning applied to the cultivation of roses, can only harm a poet, since the principal and most charming object of his desire must be to communicate the impression of a newly and happily born state of creative emotion which, through surprise and pleasure, has the power to remove the poem once and for all from any further criticism.

This opinion may possibly contain a grain of truth, though its simplicity makes me suspect it to be of scholarly origin. I feel we have learned and adopted this antithesis without reflection, and that we now find it firmly fixed in our mind, as a verbal contrast, as though it represented a clear and real relationship between two well-defined notions. It must be admitted that that character always in a hurry to have done, whom we call *our mind*, has a weakness for this kind of simplification, which freely enables him to form all kinds of combinations and judgments, to display his logic, and to develop his rhetorical resources—in short, to carry out as brilliantly as possible his business of being a mind.

At all events, this classic contrast, crystallized, as it were, by language, has always seemed to me too abrupt, and at the same time too facile, not to provoke me to examine the things themselves more closely.

Poetry, Abstract Thought. That is soon said, and we immediately assume that we have said something sufficiently clear and sufficiently precise for us to proceed, without having to go back over our experiences; and to build a theory or begin a discussion using this contrast (so attractive in its simplicity) as pretext, argument, and substance. One could even fashion a whole metaphysics—or at the least a "psychology"—on this basis, and evolve for oneself a system of mental life, of knowledge, and of the invention and production of works of the mind, whose consequence would inevitably be the same terminological dissonance that had served as its starting point. . . .

For my part I have the strange and dangerous habit, in every subject, of wanting to begin at the beginning (that is, at my *own* beginning), which entails beginning again, going back over the whole road, just as though many others had not already mapped and traveled it. . . .

This is the road offered to us, or imposed on us, by *language*.

With every question, before making any deep examination of the content, I take a look at the language; I generally proceed like a surgeon who sterilizes his hands and prepares the area to be operated on. This is what I call *cleaning up the verbal situation*. You must excuse this expression equating the words and forms of speech with the hands and instruments of a surgeon.

I maintain that we must be careful of a problem's first contact with our minds. We should be careful of the first words a question utters in our mind. A new question arising in us is in a state of infancy; it stammers; it finds only strange terms, loaded with adventitious values and associations; it is forced to borrow these. But it thereby insensibly deflects our true need. Without realizing it we desert our original problem, and in the end we shall come to believe that we have chosen an opinion wholly our own, forgetting that our choice was exercised only on a mass of opinions that are the more or less blind work of other men and of chance. This is what happens with the programs of political parties, no one of which is (or can be) the one that would exactly match our temperament and our interests. If we choose one among them, we gradually become the man suited to that party and to that program.

Philosophical and aesthetic questions are so richly obscured by the quantity, diversity, and antiquity of researches, arguments, and solutions, all produced within the orbit of a very restricted vocabulary, of which each author uses the words according to his own inclinations, that taken as a whole such works give me the impression of a district in the classical Underworld especially reserved for deep thinkers. Here, are the Danaïdes, Ixions, and Sisyphuses, eternally laboring to fill bottomless casks and to push back the falling rock, that is, to redefine the same dozen words whose combinations form the treasure of Speculative Knowledge.

Allow me to add to these preliminary considerations one last remark and one illustration. Here is the remark: you have surely noticed the curious fact that a certain *word,* which is perfectly clear when you hear or use it in *everyday* speech, and which presents no difficulty when caught up in the rapidity of an ordinary sentence, becomes mysteriously cumbersome, offers a strange resistance, defeats all efforts at definition, the moment you withdraw it from circulation for separate study and try to find its meaning after taking away its temporary function. It is almost comic to inquire the exact meaning of a term that one uses constantly with complete satisfaction. For example: I stop the word *Time* in its flight. This word was utterly limpid, precise, honest, and faithful in its service as long as it was part of a remark and was uttered by someone who wished to say something. But here it is, isolated, caught on the wing. It takes its revenge. It makes us believe that it has more meanings than uses. It was only a *means*, and it has become an *end*, the object of a terrible philosophical desire. It turns into an enigma, an abyss, a torment of thought. . . .

It is the same with the word *Life* and all the rest.

This readily observed phenomenon has taken on great critical value for me. Moreover, I have drawn from it an illustration that, for me, nicely conveys this strange property of our verbal material.

Each and every word that enables us to leap so rapidly across the chasm of thought, and to follow the prompting of an idea that constructs its own expression, appears to me like one of those light planks which one throws across a ditch or a mountain crevasse and which will bear a man crossing it rapidly. But he must pass without weighing on it, without stopping—above all, he must not take it into his head to dance on the slender plank to test its resistance! . . . Otherwise the fragile bridge tips or breaks immediately, and all is hurled into the depths. Consult your own experience; and you will find that we understand each other, and ourselves, only thanks to our *rapid passage over words*. We must not lay stress upon them, or we shall see the clearest discourse dissolve into enigmas and more or less learned illusions.

But how are we to think—I should say *rethink,* study deeply whatever seems to merit deep study—if we hold language to be something essentially provisional, as a banknote or a check is provisional, what we call its "value" requiring us to forget its true nature, which is that of a piece of paper, generally dirty? The paper has passed through so many hands. . . . But words have passed through so many mouths, so many phrases, so many uses and abuses, that the most delicate precautions must be taken to avoid too much confusion in our minds between what we think and are trying to think, and what dictionaries, authors, and, for that matter, the whole human race since the beginning of language, want us to think. . . .

I shall therefore take care not to accept what the words *Poetry* and *Abstract Thought* suggest to me the moment they are pronounced. But I shall look into myself. There I shall seek my real difficulties and my actual observations of my real states; there I shall find my own sense of the rational and the irrational; I shall see whether the alleged antithesis exists and how it exists in a living condition. I confess that it is my habit, when dealing with problems of the mind, to distinguish between those which I might have invented and which represent a need truly felt by my mind, and the rest, which are other people's problems. Of the latter, more than one (say forty per cent) seem to me to be nonexistent, to be no more than apparent problems: *I do not feel them.* And as for the rest, more than one seem to me to be badly stated. . . . I do not say I am right. I say that I observe what occurs within myself when I attempt to replace the verbal formulas by values and meanings that are nonverbal, that are independent of the language used. I discover naïve impulses and images, raw products of my needs and of my personal experiences. *It is my life itself that is surprised,* and my life must, if it can, provide my answers, for it is only in the reactions of our life that the full force, and as it were the necessity, of our truth can reside. The thought proceeding from that life never uses for its own account certain words which seem to it fit only for external consumption; nor certain others whose depths are obscure and which may only deceive thought as to its real strength and value.

I have, then, noticed in myself certain states which I may well call *poetic,* since some of them were finally realized in poems. They came about from no apparent cause, arising from some accident or other; they developed according to their own nature, and consequently I found myself for a time jolted out of my habitual state of mind. Then, the cycle completed, I returned to the rule of ordinary exchanges between my life and my thought. But meanwhile *a poem had been made,* and in completing itself the cycle left something behind. This closed cycle is the cycle of an act which has, as it were, aroused and given external form to a poetic power. . . .

On other occasions I have noticed that some no less insignificant incident caused—or seemed to cause—a quite different excursion, a digression of another nature and with another result. For example, a sudden concatenation of ideas, an analogy, would strike me in much the way the sound of a horn in the heart of a forest makes one prick up one's ears, and virtually directs the co-ordinated attention of all one's muscles toward some point in the distance, among the leafy depths. But this time, instead of a poem, it was an analysis of the sudden intellectual sensation that was taking hold of me. It was not verses that were being formed more or less easily during this phase, but some proposition or other that was destined to be incorporated among my habits of thought, some formula that would henceforward serve as an instrument for further researches. . . .

I apologize for thus revealing myself to you; but in my opinion it is more useful to speak of what one has experienced than to pretend to a knowledge that is entirely impersonal, an observation with no observer. In fact there is no theory that is not a fragment, carefully prepared, of some autobiography.

I do not pretend to be teaching you anything at all. I will say nothing you do not already know; but I will, perhaps, say it in a different order. You do not need to be told that a poet is not always incapable of solving a *rule of three;* or that a logician is not always incapable of seeing in words something other than concepts, categories, and mere pretexts for syllogisms.

On this point I would add this paradoxical remark: if the logician could never be other than a logician, he would not, and could not, be a logician; and if the poet were never anything but a poet, without the slightest hope of being able to reason abstractly, he would leave no poetic traces behind him. I believe in all sincerity that if each man were not able to live a number of other lives besides his own, he would not be able to live his own life.

My experience has thus shown me that the same *self* can take very different forms, can become an abstract thinker or a poet, by successive specializations, each of which is a deviation from that entirely unattached state which is superficially in accord with exterior surroundings and which is the average state of our existence, the state of undifferentiated exchanges.

Let us first see in what may consist that initial and *invariably accidental* shock which will construct the poetic instrument within us, and above all, what are its effects. The problem can be put in this way: Poetry is an art of Language; certain combinations of words can produce an emotion that others do not produce, and which we shall call *poetic.* What kind of emotion is this?

I recognize it in myself by this: that all possible objects of the ordinary world, external or internal, beings, events, feelings, and actions, while keeping their usual appearance, are suddenly placed in an indefinable but wonderfully fitting relationship with the modes of our general sensibility. That is to say that these well-known things and beings—or rather the ideas that represent them—somehow change in value. They attract one another, they are connected in ways quite different from the ordinary; they become (if you will permit the expression) *musicalized,* resonant, and, as it were, harmonically related. The poetic universe, thus defined, offers extensive analogies with what we can postulate of the dream world.

Since the word *dream* has found its way into this talk, I shall say in passing that in modern times, beginning with Romanticism, there has arisen a fairly understandable confusion between the notion of the dream and that of poetry. Neither the dream nor the daydream is necessarily poetic; it may be so: but figures formed *by chance* are only *by chance* harmonious figures.

In any case, our memories of dreams teach us, by frequent and common experience, that our consciousness can be invaded, filled, entirely absorbed by the production of an *existence* in which objects and beings seem the same as those in the waking state; but their meanings, relationships, modes of variation and of substitution are quite different and doubtless represent, like symbols or allegories, the immediate fluctuations of our *general* sensibility uncontrolled by the sensitivities of our *specialized* senses. In very much the same way the *poetic state* takes hold of us, develops, and finally disintegrates.

This is to say that the *state of poetry* is completely irregular, inconstant, involuntary, and fragile, and that we lose it, as we find it, *by accident*. But this state is not enough to make a poet, any more than it is enough to see a treasure in a dream to find it, on waking, sparkling at the foot of one's bed.

A poet's function—do not be startled by this remark—is not to experience the poetic state: that is a private affair. His function is to create it in others. The poet is recognized—or at least everyone recognizes his own poet—by the simple fact that he causes his reader to become "inspired." Positively speaking, inspiration is a graceful attribute with which the reader endows his poet: the reader sees in us the transcendent merits of virtues and graces that develop in him. He seeks and finds in us the wondrous cause of his own wonder.

But poetic feeling and the artificial synthesis of this state in some work are two quite distinct things, as different as sensation and action. A sustained action is much more complex than any spontaneous production, particularly when it has to be carried out in a sphere as conventional as that of language. Here you see emerging through my explanations the famous ABSTRACT THOUGHT which custom opposes to POETRY. We shall come back to that in a moment. Meanwhile I should like to tell you a true story, so that you may feel as I felt, and in a curiously clear way, the whole difference that exists between the poetic state or emotion, even creative and original, and the production of a work. It is a rather remarkable observation of myself that I made about a year ago.

I had left my house to relax from some tedious piece of work by walking and by a consequent change of scene. As I went along the street where I live,

I was suddenly *gripped* by a rhythm which took possession of me and soon gave me the impression of some force outside myself. It was as though someone else were making use of my *living-machine*. Then another rhythm overtook and combined with the first, and certain strange *transverse* relations were set up between these two principles (I am explaining myself as best I can). They combined the movement of my walking legs and some kind of song I was murmuring, or rather which was being murmured *through me*. This composition became more and more complicated and soon in its complexity went far beyond anything I could reasonably produce with my ordinary, usable rhythmic faculties. The sense of strangeness that I mentioned became almost painful, almost disquieting. I am no musician; I am completely ignorant of musical technique; yet here I was, prey to a development in several parts more complicated than any poet could dream. I argued that there had been an error of person, that this grace had descended on the wrong head, since I could make no use of a gift which for a musician would doubtless have assumed value, form, and duration, while these parts that mingled and separated offered me in vain a composition whose cunningly organized sequence amazed my ignorance and reduced it to despair.

After about twenty minutes the magic suddenly vanished, leaving me on the bank of the Seine, as perplexed as the duck in the fable, that saw a swan emerge from the egg she had hatched. As the swan flew away, my surprise changed to reflection. I knew that walking often induces in me a quickened flow of ideas and that there is a certain reciprocity between my pace and my thoughts—my thoughts modify my pace; my pace provokes my thoughts— which after all is remarkable enough, but is fairly understandable. Our various "reaction periods" are doubtless synchronized, and it is interesting to have to admit that a reciprocal modification is possible between a form of action which is purely muscular and a varied production of images, judgments, and reasonings.

But in the case I am speaking of, my movement in walking became in my consciousness a very subtle system of rhythms, instead of instigating those images, interior words, and potential actions which one calls *ideas*. As for ideas, they are things of a species familiar to me; they are things that I can note, provoke, and handle. . . . *But I cannot say the same of my unexpected rhythms*.

What was I to think? I supposed that mental activity while walking must correspond with a general excitement exerting itself in the region of my brain; this excitement satisfied and relieved itself as best it could, and so long as its energy was expended, it mattered little whether this was on ideas, memories, or rhythms unconsciously hummed. On that day, the energy was expended in a rhythmical intuition that developed before the awakening in my consciousness of *the person who knows that he does not know music*. I imagine it is the same as when *the person who knows he cannot fly* has not yet become active in the man who dreams he is flying.

I apologize for this long and true story—as true, that is, as a story of this kind can be. Notice that everything I have said, or tried to say, happened in relation to what we call the *External World,* what we call *Our Body,* and what we call *Our Mind,* and requires a kind of vague collaboration between these three great powers.

Why have I told you this? In order to bring out the profound difference existing between spontaneous production by the mind—or rather by our *sensibility as a whole*—and the fabrication of works. In my story, the substance of a musical composition was freely given to me, but the organization which would have seized, fixed, and reshaped it was lacking. The great painter Degas often repeated to me a very true and simple remark by Mallarmé. Degas occasionally wrote verses, and some of those he left were delightful. But he often found great difficulty in this work accessory to his painting. (He was, by the way, the kind of man who would bring all possible difficulty to any art whatever.) One day he said to Mallarmé: "Yours is a hellish craft. I can't manage to say what I want, and yet I'm full of ideas. . . ." And Mallarmé answered: "My dear Degas, one does not make poetry with ideas, but with *words.*"

Mallarmé was right. But when Degas spoke of ideas, he was, after all, thinking of inner speech or of images, which might have been expressed in *words.* But these words, these secret phrases which he called ideas, all these intentions and perceptions of the mind, do not make verses. There is something else, then, a modification, or a transformation, sudden or not, spontaneous or not, laborious or not, which must necessarily intervene between the thought that produces ideas—that activity and multiplicity of inner questions and solutions—and, on the other hand, that discourse, so different from ordinary speech, which is verse, which is so curiously ordered, which answers no need *unless it be the need it must itself create,* which never speaks but of absent things or of things profoundly and secretly felt: strange discourse, as though made by someone *other* than the speaker and addressed to someone *other* than the listener. In short, it is a *language within a language.*

Let us look into these mysteries.

Poetry is an art of language. But language is a practical creation. It may be observed that in all communication between men, certainty comes only from practical acts and from the verification which practical acts give us. *I ask you for a light. You give me a light:* you have understood me.

But in asking me for a light, you were able to speak those few unimportant words with a certain intonation, a certain tone of voice, a certain inflection, a certain languor or briskness perceptible to me. I have understood your words, since without even thinking I handed you what you asked for—a light. But the matter does not end there. The strange thing: the sound and as it were the features of your little sentence come back to me, echo within me, as though they were pleased to be there; I, too, like to hear myself repeat this little phrase, which has almost lost its meaning, which has stopped being of use, and which can yet go on living, though with quite another life. It has acquired a value; and has acquired it *at the expense of its finite significance.* It has created the need to be heard again. . . . Here we are on the very threshold of the poetic state. This tiny experience will help us to the discovery of more than one truth.

It has shown us that language can produce effects of two quite different kinds. One of them tends to bring about the complete negation of language itself. I speak to you, and if you have understood my words, those very words are abolished. If you have understood, it means that the words have vanished from your minds and are replaced by their counterpart, by images, relationships, impulses; so that you have within you the means to retransmit these ideas and images in a language that may be very different from the one you received. *Understanding* consists in the more or less rapid replacement of a system of sounds, intervals, and signs by something quite different, which is, in short, a modification or interior reorganization of the person to whom one is speaking. And here is the counterproof of this proposition: the person who does not understand *repeats* the words, or *has them repeated* to him.

Consequently, the perfection of a discourse whose sole aim is comprehension obviously consists in the ease with which the words forming it are transformed into something quite different: the *language* is transformed first into *non-language* and then, if we wish, into a form of language differing from the original form.

In other terms, in practical or abstract uses of language, the form—that is the physical, the concrete part, the very act of speech—does not last; it does not outlive understanding; it dissolves in the light; it has acted; it has done its work; it has brought about understanding; it has lived.

But on the other hand, the moment this concrete form takes on, by an effect of its own, such importance that it asserts itself and makes itself, as it were, respected; and not only remarked and respected, but desired and therefore repeated—then something new happens: we are insensibly transformed and ready to live, breathe, and think in accordance with a rule and under laws which are no longer of the practical order—that is, nothing that may occur in this state will be resolved, finished, or abolished by a specific act. We are entering the poetic universe.

Permit me to support this notion of a *poetic universe* by referring to a similar notion that, being much simpler, is easier to explain: the notion of a *musical universe*. I would ask you to make a small sacrifice: limit yourselves for a moment to your faculty of hearing. One simple sense, like that of hearing, will offer us all we need for our definition and will absolve us from entering into all the difficulties and subtleties to which the conventional structure and historical complexities of ordinary language would lead us. We live by ear in the world of noises. Taken as a whole, it is generally incoherent and irregularly supplied by all the mechanical incidents which the ear may interpret as it can. But the same ear isolates from this chaos a group of noises particularly remarkable and simple—that is, easily recognizable by our sense of hearing and furnishing it with points of reference. These elements have relations with one another which we sense as we do the elements themselves. The interval between two of these privileged noises is as clear to us as each of them. These are the *sounds,* and these units of sonority tend to form clear combinations, successive or simultaneous implications, series, and intersections which one may term *intelligible:* this is why abstract possibilities exist in music. But I must return to my subject.

I will confine myself to saying that the contrast between noise and sound is the contrast between pure and impure, order and disorder; that this differentiation between pure sensations and others has permitted the constitution of music; that it has been possible to control, unify, and codify this constitution, thanks to the intervention of physical science, which knows how to adjust measure to sensation so as to obtain the important result of teaching us to produce this sonorous sensation consistently, and in a continuous and identical fashion, by instruments that are, in reality, *measuring instruments.*

The musician is thus in possession of a perfect system of well-defined means which exactly match sensations with acts. From this it results that music has formed a domain absolutely its own. The world of the art of music, a world of sounds, is distinct from the world of noises. Whereas a *noise* merely rouses in us some isolated event—a dog, a door, a motor car—*a sound evokes, of itself, the musical universe.* If, in this hall where I am speaking to you and where you hear the noise of my voice, a tuning fork or a well-tempered instrument began to vibrate, you would at once, as soon as you were affected by this pure and exceptional noise that cannot be confused with others, have the feeling of a beginning, the beginning of a world; a quite different atmosphere would immediately be created, a new order would arise, and you yourselves would unconsciously *organize* yourselves to receive it. The musical universe, therefore, was within you, with all its associations and proportions— as in a saturated salt solution a crystalline universe awaits the molecular shock of a minute crystal in order *to declare itself.* I dare not say: the crystalline idea of such a system awaits. . . .

And here is the counterproof of our little experiment: if, in a concert hall dominated by a resounding symphony, a chair happens to fall, someone coughs, or a door shuts, we immediately have the impression of a kind of rupture. Something indefinable, something like a spell or a Venetian glass, has been broken or cracked. . . .

The poetic universe is not created so powerfully or so easily. It exists, but the poet is deprived of the immense advantages possessed by the musician. He does not have before him, ready for the uses of beauty, a body of resources expressly made for his art. He has to borrow *language*—the voice of the public, that collection of traditional and irrational terms and rules, oddly created and transformed, oddly codified, and very variedly understood and pronounced. Here there is no physicist who has determined the relations between these elements; no tuning forks, no metronomes, no inventors of scales or theoreticians of harmony. Rather, on the contrary, the phonetic and semantic fluctuations of vocabulary. Nothing pure; but a mixture of completely incoherent auditive and psychic stimuli. Each word is an instantaneous coupling of a *sound* and a *sense* that have no connection with each other. Each sentence is an act so complex that I doubt whether anyone has yet been able to provide a tolerable definition of it. As for the use of the resources of language and the

modes of this action, you know what diversity there is, and what confusion
sometimes results. A discourse can be logical, packed with sense, but devoid of
rhythm and measure. It can be pleasing to the ear, yet completely absurd or
insignificant; it can be clear, yet useless; vague, yet delightful. But to grasp its
strange multiplicity, which is no more than the multiplicity of life itself, it
suffices to name all the sciences which have been created to deal with this
diversity, each to study one of its aspects. One can analyze a text in many
different ways, for it falls successively under the jurisdiction of phonetics,
semantics, syntax, logic, rhetoric, philology, not to mention metrics, prosody,
and etymology. . . .

So the poet is at grips with this verbal matter, obliged to speculate on
sound and sense at once, and to satisfy not only harmony and musical timing
but all the various intellectual and aesthetic conditions, not to mention the
conventional rules. . . .

You can see what an effort the poet's understanding would require if he
had *consciously* to solve all these problems. . . .

It is always interesting to try to reconstruct one of our complex activities,
one of those complete actions which demand a specialization at once mental,
sensuous, and motor, supposing that in order to accomplish this act we were
obliged to understand and organize all the functions that we know play their
part in it. Even if this attempt, at once imaginative and analytical, is clumsy,
it will always teach us something. As for myself, who am, I admit, much more
attentive to the formation or fabrication of works than to the works themselves,
I have a habit, or obsession, of appreciating works only as actions. In my eyes
a poet is a man who, as a result of a certain incident, undergoes a hidden
transformation. He leaves his ordinary condition of general disposability, and I
see taking shape in him an agent, a living system for producing verses. As
among animals one suddenly sees emerging a capable hunter, a nest maker, a
bridge builder, a digger of tunnels and galleries, so in a man one sees a
composite organization declare itself, bending its functions to a specific piece
of work. Think of a very small child: the child we have all been bore many
possibilities within him. After a few months of life he has learned, at the same
or almost the same time, to speak and to walk. He has acquired two types of
action. That is to say that he now possesses two kinds of potentiality from
which the accidental circumstances of each moment will draw what they can,
in answer to his varying needs and imaginings.

Having learned to use his legs, he will discover that he can not only walk,
but run; and not only walk and run, but dance. This is a great event. He has
at that moment both invented and discovered a kind of *secondary use* for his
limbs, a generalization of his formula of movement. In fact, whereas walking
is after all a rather dull and not easily perfectible action, this new form of
action, the Dance, admits of an infinite number of creations and variations or
figures.

But will he not find an analogous development in speech? He will explore
the possibilities of his faculty of speech; he will discover that more can be done
with it than to ask for jam and deny his little sins. He will grasp the power of

reasoning; he will invent stories to amuse himself when he is alone; he will repeat to himself words that he loves for their strangeness and mystery.

So, parallel with *Walking* and *Dancing,* he will acquire and distinguish the divergent types, *Prose and Poetry.*

This parallel has long struck and attracted me; but someone saw it before I did. According to Racan, Malherbe made use of it. In my opinion it is more than a simple comparison. I see in it an analogy as substantial and pregnant as those found in physics when one observes the identity of formulas that represent the measurement of seemingly very different phenomena. Here is how our comparison develops.

Walking, like prose, has a definite aim. It is an act directed at something we wish to reach. Actual circumstances, such as the need for some object, the impulse of my desire, the state of my body, my sight, the terrain, etc., which order the manner of walking, prescribe its direction and its speed, and give it a *definite end.* All the characteristics of walking derive from these instantaneous conditions, which combine *in a novel way* each time. There are no movements in walking that are not special adaptations, but, each time, they are abolished and, as it were, absorbed by the accomplishment of the act, by the attainment of the goal.

The dance is quite another matter. It is, of course, a system of actions; but of actions whose end is in themselves. It goes nowhere. If it pursues an object, it is only an ideal object, a state, an enchantment, the phantom of a flower, an extreme of life, a smile—which forms at last on the face of the one who summoned it from empty space.

It is therefore not a question of carrying out a limited operation whose end is situated somewhere in our surroundings, but rather of creating, maintaining, and exalting a certain *state,* by a periodic movement that can be executed on the spot; a movement which is almost entirely dissociated from sight, but which is stimulated and regulated by auditive rhythms.

But please note this very simple observation, that however different the dance may be from walking and utilitarian movements, it uses the same organs, the same bones, the same muscles, only differently co-ordinated and aroused.

Here we come again to the contrast between prose and poetry. Prose and poetry use the same words, the same syntax, the same forms, and the same sounds or tones, but differently co-ordinated and differently aroused. Prose and poetry are therefore distinguished by the difference between certain links and associations which form and dissolve in our psychic and nervous organism, whereas the components of these modes of functioning are identical. This is why one should guard against reasoning about poetry as one does about prose. What is true of one very often has no meaning when it is sought in the other. But here is the great and decisive difference. When the man who is walking has reached his goal—as I said—when he has reached the place, book, fruit, the object of his desire (which desire drew him from his repose), this possession at once entirely annuls his whole act; the effect swallows up the cause, the end absorbs the means; and, whatever the act, only the result remains. It is the same with utilitarian language: the language I use to express my design, my desire, my command, my opinion; this language, when it has served its purpose, evaporates almost as it is heard. I have given it forth to perish, to be radically transformed into something else in your mind; and I shall know that I was *understood* by the remarkable fact that my speech no longer exists: it has been completely replaced by its *meaning*—that is, by images, impulses, reactions, or acts that belong to you: in short, by an interior modification in you.

As a result the perfection of this kind of language, whose sole end is to be understood, obviously consists in the ease with which it is transformed into something altogether different.

The poem, on the other hand, does not die for having lived: it is expressly designed to be born again from its ashes and to become endlessly what it has just been. Poetry can be recognized by this property, that it tends to get itself reproduced in its own form: it stimulates us to reconstruct it identically.

That is an admirable and uniquely characteristic property.

I should like to give you a simple illustration. Think of a pendulum oscillating between two symmetrical points. Suppose that one of these extremes represents *form:* the concrete characteristics of the language, sound, rhythm, accent, tone, movement—in a word, the *Voice* in action. Then associate with the other point, the acnode of the first, all significant values, images and ideas, stimuli of feeling and memory, virtual impulses and structures of understanding—in short, everything that makes the *content,* the meaning of a discourse. Now observe the effect of poetry on yourselves. You will find that at each line the meaning produced within you, far from destroying the musical form communicated to you, recalls it. The living pendulum that has swung from *sound* to *sense* swings back to its felt point of departure, as though the very sense which is present to your mind can find no other outlet or expression, no other answer, than the very music which gave it birth.

So between the form and the content, between the sound and the sense, between the poem and the state of poetry, a symmetry is revealed, an equality between importance, value, and power, which does not exist in prose; which is contrary to the law of prose—the law which ordains the inequality of the two constituents of language. The essential principle of the mechanics of poetry— that is, of the conditions for producing the poetic state by words—seems to me to be this harmonious exchange between expression and impression.

I introduce here a slight observation which I shall call "philosophical," meaning simply that we could do without it.

Our poetic pendulum travels from our sensation toward some idea or some sentiment, and returns toward some memory of the sensation and toward the potential act which could reproduce the sensation. Now, whatever is sensation is essentially *present.* There is no other definition of the present except sensation itself, which includes, perhaps, the impulse to action that would modify that sensation. On the other hand, whatever is properly thought, image, sentiment, is always, in some way, *a production of absent things.*

Memory is the substance of all thought. Anticipation and its gropings, desire, planning, the projection of our hopes, of our fears, are the main interior activity of our being.

Thought is, in short, the activity which causes what does not exist to come alive in us, lending to it, whether we will or no, our present powers, making us take the part for the whole, the image for reality, and giving us the illusion of seeing, acting, suffering, and possessing independently of our dear old body, which we leave with its cigarette in an armchair until we suddenly retrieve it when the telephone rings or, no less strangely, when our stomach demands provender. . . .

Between Voice and Thought, between Thought and Voice, between Presence and Absence, oscillates the poetic pendulum.

The result of this analysis is to show that the value of a poem resides in the indissolubility of sound and sense. Now this is a condition that seems to demand the impossible. There is no relation between the sound and the meaning of a word. The same thing is called HORSE in English, HIPPOS in Greek, EQUUS in Latin, and CHEVAL in French; but no manipulation of any of these terms will give me an idea of the animal in question; and no manipulation of the idea will yield me any of these words—otherwise, we should easily know all languages, beginning with our own.

Yet it is the poet's business to give us the feeling of an intimate union between the word and the mind.

This must be considered, strictly speaking, a marvelous result. I say *marvelous*, although it is not exceptionally rare. I use *marvelous* in the sense we give that word when we think of the miracles and prodigies of ancient magic. It must not be forgotten that for centuries poetry was used for purposes of enchantment. Those who took part in these strange operations had to believe in the power of the word, and far more in the efficacy of its sound than in its significance. Magic formulas are often without meaning; but it was never thought that their power depended on their intellectual content.

Let us listen to lines like these:

> *Mère des souvenirs, maîtresse des maîtresses . . .*

or

> *Sois sage, ô ma Douleur, et tiens-toi plus tranquille. . . .*

These words work on us (or at least on some of us) without telling us very much. They tell us, perhaps, that they have nothing to tell us; that, by the very means which usually tell us something, they are exercising a quite different function. They act on us like a chord of music. The impression produced depends largely on resonance, rhythm, and the number of syllables; but it is also the result of the simple bringing together of meanings. In the second of these lines the accord between the vague ideas of Wisdom and Grief, and the tender solemnity of the tone produce the inestimable value of a spell: the *momentary being* who made that line could not have done so had he been in a state where the form and the content occurred separately to his mind. On the contrary, he was in a special phase in the domain of his psychic existence, a phase in which the sound and the meaning of the word acquire or keep an equal importance—which is excluded from the habits of practical language, as from the needs of abstract language. The state in which the inseparability of sound and sense, in which the desire, the expectation, the possibility of their intimate and indissoluble fusion are required and sought or given, and sometimes anxiously awaited, is a comparatively rare state. It is rare, firstly because all the exigencies of life are against it; secondly because it is opposed to the crude simplifying and specializing of verbal notations.

But this state of inner modification, in which all the properties of our language are indistinctly but harmoniously summoned, is not enough to produce that complete object, that compound of beauties, that collection of happy chances for the mind which a noble poem offers us.

From this state we obtain only fragments. All the precious things that are found in the earth, gold, diamonds, uncut stones, are there scattered, strewn, grudgingly hidden in a quantity of rock or sand, where chance may sometimes uncover them. These riches would be nothing without the human labor that draws them from the massive night where they were sleeping, assembles them, alters and organizes them into ornaments. These fragments of metal embedded in formless matter, these oddly shaped crystals, must owe all their luster to intelligent labor. It is a labor of this kind that the true poet accomplishes. Faced with a beautiful poem, one can indeed feel that it is most unlikely that any man, however gifted, could have improvised without a backward glance, with no other effort than that of writing or dictating, such a simultaneous and complete system of lucky finds. Since the traces of effort, the second thoughts, the changes, the amount of time, the bad days, and the distaste have now vanished, effaced by the supreme return of a mind over its work, some people, seeing only the perfection of the result, will look on it as due to a sort of magic that they call INSPIRATION. They thus make of the poet a kind of temporary *medium*. If one were strictly to develop this doctrine of pure inspiration, one would arrive at some very strange results. For example, one would conclude that the poet, since he merely transmits what he receives, merely delivers to unknown people what he has taken from the unknown, has no need to understand what he writes, which is dictated by a mysterious voice. He could write poems in a language he did not know. . . .

In fact, the poet has indeed a kind of spiritual energy of a special nature: it is manifested in him and reveals him to himself in certain moments of infinite worth. Infinite for him. . . . I say, *infinite for him,* for, alas, experience shows us that these moments which seem to us to have a universal value are sometimes without a future, and in the end make us ponder on this maxim: *what is of value for one person only has no value.* This is the iron law of Literature.

But every true poet is necessarily a first-rate critic. If one doubts this, one can have no idea of what the work of the mind is: that struggle with the inequality of moments, with chance associations, lapses of attention, external distractions. The mind is terribly variable, deceptive and self-deceiving, fertile in insoluble problems and illusory solutions. How could a remarkable work emerge from this chaos if this chaos that contains everything did not also contain some serious chances to know oneself and to choose within oneself whatever is worth taking from each moment and using carefully?

That is not all. Every true poet is much more capable than is generally known of right reasoning and abstract thought.

But one must not look for his real philosophy in his more or less philosophical utterances. In my opinion, the most authentic philosophy lies not so much in the objects of our reflection as in the very act of thought and in its handling. Take from metaphysics all its pet or special terms, all its traditional vocabulary, and you may realize that you have not impoverished the thought. Indeed, you may perhaps have eased and freshened it, and you will have got rid of other people's problems, so as to deal only with your own difficulties, your surprises that owe nothing to anyone, and whose intellectual spur you feel actually and directly.

It has often happened, however, as literary history tells us, that poetry has been made to enunciate theses or hypotheses and that the *complete* language which is its own—the language whose *form*, that is to say the action and sensation of the *Voice*, is of the same power as the *content*, that is to say the eventual modification of a *mind*—has been used to communicate "abstract" ideas, which are on the contrary independent of their form, or so we believe. Some very great poets have occasionally attempted this. But whatever may be the talent which exerts itself in this very noble undertaking, it cannot prevent the attention given to following the ideas from competing with the attention that follows the song. The DE RERUM NATURA is here in conflict with the nature of things. The state of mind of the reader of poems is not the state of mind of the reader of pure thought. The state of mind of a man dancing is not that of a man advancing through difficult country of which he is making a topographical survey or a geological prospectus.

I have said, nevertheless, that the poet has his abstract thought and, if you like, his philosophy; and I have said that it is at work in his very activity as a poet. I said this because I have observed it, in myself and in several others. Here, as elsewhere, I have no other reference, no other claim or excuse, than recourse to my own experience or to the most common observation.

Well, every time I have worked as a poet, I have noticed that my work exacted of me not only that presence of the poetic universe I have spoken of, but many reflections, decisions, choices, and combinations, without which all possible gifts of the Muses, or of Chance, would have remained like precious materials in a workshop without an architect. Now an architect is not himself necessarily built of precious materials. In so far as he is an architect of poems, a poet is quite different from what he is as a producer of those precious elements of which all poetry should be composed, but whose composition is separate and requires an entirely different mental effort.

One day someone told me that lyricism is enthusiasm, and that the odes of the great lyricists were written at a single stroke, at the speed of the voice of delirium, and with the wind of inspiration blowing a gale. . . .

I replied that he was quite right; but that this was not a privilege of poetry alone, and that everyone knew that in building a locomotive it is indispensable for the builder to work at eighty miles an hour in order to do his job.

A poem is really a kind of machine for producing the poetic state of mind by means of words. The effect of this machine is uncertain, for nothing is certain about action on other minds. But whatever may be the result, in its uncertainty, the construction of the machine demands the solution of many problems. If the term *machine* shocks you, if my mechanical comparison seems crude, please notice that while the composition of even a very short poem may absorb years, the action of the poem on the reader will take only a few minutes. In a few minutes the reader will receive his shock from discoveries, connections, glimmers of expression that have been accumulated during months of research, waiting, patience, and impatience. He may attribute much more to inspiration than it can give. He will imagine the kind of person it would take to create, without pause, hesitation, or revision, this powerful and perfect work which transports him into a world where things and people, passions and thoughts, sonorities and meanings proceed from the same energy, are transformed one into another, and correspond according to exceptional laws of harmony, for it can only be an exceptional form of stimulus that simultaneously produces the exaltation of our sensibility, our intellect, our memory, and our powers of verbal action, so rarely granted to us in the ordinary course of life.

Perhaps I should remark here that the execution of a poetic work—if one considers it as the engineer just mentioned would consider the conception and construction of his locomotive, that is, making explicit the problems to be solved—would appear impossible. In no other art is the number of conditions and independent functions to be co-ordinated so large. I will not inflict on you a detailed demonstration of this proposition. It is enough for me to remind you of what I said regarding sound and sense, which are linked only by pure convention, but which must be made to collaborate as effectively as possible. From their double nature words often make me think of those complex quantities which geometricians take such pleasure in manipulating.

Fortunately, some strange virtue resides in certain moments in certain people's lives which simplifies things and reduces the insurmountable difficulties I spoke of to the scale of human energies.

The poet awakes within man at an unexpected event, an outward or inward incident: a tree, a face, a "subject," an emotion, a word. Sometimes it is the will to expression that starts the game, a need to translate what one feels; another time, on the contrary, it is an element of form, the outline of an expression which seeks its origin, seeks a meaning within the space of my mind. . . . Note this possible duality in ways of getting started: either something wants to express itself, or some means of expression wants to be used.

My poem "Le Cimetière marin" began in me by a rhythm, that of a French line . . . of ten syllables, divided into four and six. I had as yet no idea with which to fill out this form. Gradually a few hovering words settled in it, little by little determining the subject, and my labor (a very long labor) was before me. Another poem, "La Pythie," first appeared as an eight-syllable line whose sound came of its own accord. But this line implied a sentence, of which it was part, and this sentence, if it existed, implied many other sentences. A problem of this kind has an infinite number of solutions. But with poetry the musical and metrical conditions greatly restrict the indefiniteness. Here is what happened: my fragment acted like a living fragment, since, plunged in the (no doubt nourishing) surroundings of my desire and waiting thought, it proliferated, and engendered all that was lacking: several lines before and a great many lines after.

I apologize for having chosen my examples from my own little story: but I could hardly have taken them elsewhere.

Perhaps you think my conception of the poet and the poem rather singular. Try to imagine, however, what the least of our acts implies. Think of everything that must go on inside a man who utters the smallest intelligible sentence, and then calculate all that is needed for a poem by Keats or Baudelaire to be formed on an empty page in front of the poet.

Think, too, that of all the arts, ours is perhaps that which co-ordinates the greatest number of independent parts or factors: sound, sense, the real and the imaginary, logic, syntax, and the double invention of content and form . . . and all this by means of a medium essentially practical, perpetually changing, soiled, a maid of all work, *everyday language,* from which we must draw a pure, ideal Voice, capable of communicating without weakness, without apparent effort, without offense to the ear, and without breaking the ephemeral sphere of the poetic universe, an idea of some *self* miraculously superior to Myself.

Wallace Stevens

1879–1955

Born on October 2, 1879, in Reading, Pennsylvania, to Mary Catherine Zeller and Garrett Barckalow Stevens, a lawyer, Wallace Stevens was the second of five children. The genealogical study Stevens initiated in 1941 returned him to his mother's Dutch and German roots, Pennsylvanian locales, and domestic, familial themes that appear in such later poems as "Dutch Graves in Buck's County" and "The Bed of Old John Zeller." The Protestant family inclined toward the maternal Pennsylvania Dutch and a Puritan heritage, reflected in Stevens' later renunciation of self-indulgence, his ambiguous attitude toward pleasure and eroticism, and his ethical desire for a more solid, respectable vocation than that of poet.

Aiming for a career in journalism, Stevens entered Harvard in 1897 as a "special student" on a three-year program. Doing poorly in economics, he studied literature guided by his most influential teacher, Barrett Wendell, who began to advise him on writing. In Cambridge Stevens' friendly relationship with George Santayana included teas in the philosopher's apartment, meetings at the Laodicean Club, and an exchange of philosophic sonnets on the topic of "Cathedrals by the Sea." Stevens joined the Signet Club and became president of the *Harvard Advocate,* which published some of his Pre-Raphaelite-like sonnets under pseudonyms.

In 1900 Stevens was alone and adrift in New York City, where he worked on *The New York Herald Tribune* as a reporter, and in 1901 he entered New York University Law School. A 1903 camping trip in British Columbia, with his later fishing outings with friends in the Florida Keys, provided his rare experiences of rugged, self-sufficient, natural living. At places like the Long Key Fishing Camp, Stevens found the exotic material for poems such as "Nomad Exquisite" and "Farewell to Florida." Stevens began courting Elsie Kachel in 1904, after being admitted to the New York bar and beginning a law practice. "A Book of Verses," his first group of poems, was written for Elsie's twenty-second birthday, and they were married in 1909.

Spending evenings at the New York studio of Walter Arensberg, Stevens met Wittner Bynner, Alfred Kreymborg, and members of the literary avant-garde. After the infamous Armory Show of 1913, Stevens encountered European cubism, Dadaism, and their proponents—Marcel Duchamp, Francis Picabia, and other visual artists.

Harriet Monroe selected Stevens' group of poems, "Phases," for the November 1914 issue of *Poetry,* a special war issue that brought Stevens wide recognition. He thereafter corresponded with Monroe and gave her priority when he submitted new work for publication. His first group of published poems had appeared in *Trend;* other early forums were *Others, Broom, Contact, The Dial,* and *The New Republic.*

Firmly established as both poet and insurance attorney, in 1916 Stevens moved with Elsie to Hartford, Connecticut, to work for the Hartford Accident and Indemnity Company, where he would become vice-president. Stevens' marriage, once a source of passion and inspiration, cooled to a frozen estrangement, and the two spent much time apart.

Stevens was already forty-four when his first book of poems, *Harmonium* (1923), met a cool response. The volume includes "Sunday Morning" (which contains allusions to Elsie), "Thirteen Ways of Looking at a Blackbird," and "The Emperor of Ice-Cream." Subsequent volumes of poetry include *Ideas of Order* (1935), *The Man with the Blue Guitar* (1937), *Parts of a World* (1942), *Transport to Summer* (1947), *The Auroras of Autumn* (1950), and *Collected Poems* (1954).

Increased productivity matched a series of awards and honors. Stevens was inducted into the National Institute of Arts and Letters in 1946 and in 1949 won the Bollingen Prize for poetry. He was awarded the National Book Award for *The Auroras of Autumn* and for *Collected Poems,* which also won the 1955 Pulitzer Prize in poetry.

After being diagnosed with stomach cancer early in 1955, Stevens was hospitalized in the summer and died in Hartford on August 2, 1955. His late leaning toward religion and spirituality manifested itself in an increased quietude in the poems; Stevens was converted to Catholicism on his deathbed.

Much of Wallace Stevens' criticism is embedded in his poetry. As the preeminent twentieth-century American poet, Stevens functions as theorist—even in his overt criticism—within the context of the poems. His preoccupation with poets is indicated in the predominantly essayistic titles of poems such as "Notes toward a Supreme Fiction," "The Motive for Metaphor," "Of Modern Poetry," "Poetry Is a Destructive Force," and "The Poems of Our Climate." His critical work consists of his few reviews (on such writers as Marianne Moore and John Crowe Ransome), speeches, the seven essays (most of them originally lectures) collected in *The Necessary Angel* (1951), and notes collected in the *Opus Posthumous* (1957).

The Figure of the Youth
as Virile Poet

I

It appears that what is central to philosophy is its least valuable part. Note the three scraps that follow. First, part of a letter from Henry Bradley to Robert Bridges, as follows:

> My own attitude towards all philosophies old and new, is very sceptical. Not that I despise philosophy or philosophers; but I feel that the universe of being is too vast to be comprehended even by the greatest of the sons of Adam. We do get, I believe, glimpses of the real problems, perhaps even of the real solutions; but when we have formulated our questions, I fear we have always substituted illusory problems for the real ones.

This was in reply to a letter from Bridges, in which Bridges appears to have commented on Bergson. Then, second, it is Bergson that Paul Valéry called

> *peut-être l'un des derniers hommes qui auront exclusivement, profondément et supérieurement pensé, dans une époque du monde où le monde va pensant et méditant de moins en moins. . . . Bergson semble déjà appartenir à un âge révolu, et son nom est le dernier grand nom de l'histoire de l'intelligence européenne.*

And yet, third, it is of Bergson's *L'Evolution créatrice* that William James said in a letter to Bergson himself:

> You may be amused at the comparison, but in finishing it I found the same after-taste remaining as after finishing *Madame Bovary,* such a flavor of persistent *euphony.*

II

If these expressions speak for any considerable number of people and, therefore, if any considerable number of people feel this way about the truth and about what may be called the official view of being (since philosophic truth may be said to be the official view), we cannot expect much in respect to poetry, assuming that we define poetry as an unofficial view of being. This is a much larger definition of poetry than it is usual to make. But just as the nature of the truth changes, perhaps for no more significant reason than that philosophers live and die, so the nature of poetry changes, perhaps for no more significant reason than that poets come and go. It is so easy to say in a universe of life and death that the reason itself lives and dies and, if so, that the imagination lives and dies no less.

Once on a packet on his way to Germany Coleridge was asked to join a party of Danes and drink with them. He says:

> I went, and found some excellent wines and a dessert of grapes with a pine-apple. The Danes had christened me Doctor Teology, and dressed as I was all in black, with large shoes and black worsted stockings, I might certainly have passed very well for a Methodist missionary. However I disclaimed my title. What then may you be . . . *Un philosophe,* perhaps? It was at that time in my life in which of all possible names and characters I had the greatest disgust to that of *un philosophe. . . .* The Dane then informed me that all in the present party were Philosophers likewise. . . . We drank and talked and sung, till we talked and sung altogether; and then we rose and danced on the deck a set of dances.

As poetry goes, as the imagination goes, as the approach to truth, or, say, to being by way of the imagination goes, Coleridge is one of the great figures. Even so, just as William James found in Bergson a persistent euphony, so we find in Coleridge, dressed in black, with large shoes and black worsted stockings, dancing on the deck of a Hamburg packet, a man who may be said to have been defining poetry all his life in definitions that are valid enough but which no longer impress us primarily by their validity.

To define poetry as an unofficial view of being places it in contrast with philosophy and at the same time establishes the relationship between the two. In philosophy we attempt to approach truth through the reason. Obviously this is a statement of convenience. If we say that in poetry we attempt to approach truth through the imagination, this, too, is a statement of convenience. We must conceive of poetry as at least the equal of philosophy. If truth is the object of both and if any considerable number of people feel very sceptical of all philosophers, then, to be brief about it, a still more considerable number of people must feel very sceptical of all poets. Since we expect rational ideas to satisfy the reason and imaginative ideas to satisfy the imagination, it follows that if we are sceptical of rational ideas it is because they do not satisfy the reason and if we are sceptical of imaginative ideas it is because they do not satisfy the imagination. If a rational idea does not satisfy the imagination, it may, nevertheless, satisfy the reason. If an imaginative idea does not satisfy the reason, we regard the fact as in the nature of things. If an imaginative idea does not satisfy the imagination, our expectation of it is not fulfilled. On the other hand, and finally, if an imaginative idea satisfies the imagination, we are indifferent to the fact that it does not satisfy the reason, although we concede that it would be complete, as an idea, if, in addition to satisfying the imagination, it also satisfied the reason. From this analysis, we deduce that an idea that satisfies both the reason and the imagination, if it happened, for instance, to be an idea of God, would establish a divine beginning and end for us which, at the moment, the reason, singly, at best proposes and on which, at the moment, the imagination, singly, merely meditates. This is an illustration. It seems to be elementary, from this point of view, that the poet, in order to fulfill himself, must accomplish a poetry that satisfies both the reason and the imagination. It does not follow that in the long run the poet will find himself in the position in which the philosopher now finds himself. On the contrary, if the end of the philosopher is despair, the end of the poet is fulfillment, since the poet finds a sanction for life in poetry that satisfies the imagination. Thus, poetry, which we have been thinking of as at least the equal of philosophy, may be its superior. Yet the area of definition is almost an area of apologetics. The look of it may change a little if we consider not that the definition has not yet been found but that there is none.

III

Certainly the definition has not yet been found. You will not find it in such works as those on the art of poetry by Aristotle and Horace. In his edition of Aristotle's work Principal Fyfe says that Aristotle did not even appreciate poetry. In the time of Aristotle, there was no such word as literature in Greek. Yet today poetry is literature more often than not; for poetry partakes of what may be called the tendency to become literature. Life itself partakes of this tendency, which is a phase of the growth of sophistication. Sophistication, in turn, is a phase of the development of civilization. Aristotle understood poetry to be imitation particularly of action in drama. In Chapter 6, Aristotle states the parts of tragedy, among them thought and character, which are not to be confused. He says that character in a play is that which reveals the moral purpose of the agents, i.e., the sort of thing they seek or avoid—hence, there is no room for character in a speech on a purely indifferent subject. The annotation of the editor is this:

> A man who chooses, e.g., vengeance rather than safety reveals his character by exercise of Will. A man who at dinner chooses grouse rather than rabbit reveals nothing, because no sane man would choose otherwise.

This sort of thing has nothing to do with poetry. With our sense of the imaginative today, we are bound to consider a language that did not contain a word for literature as extraordinary even though the language was the language of Plato. With us it is not a paradox to say that poetry and literature are close together. Although there is no definition of poetry, there are impressions, approximations. Shelley gives us an approximation when he gives us a definition in what he calls "a general sense." He speaks of poetry as created by "that imperial faculty whose throne is curtained within the invisible nature of man." He says that a poem is the very image of life expressed in its eternal truth. It is "indeed something divine. It is at once the centre and circumference of knowledge . . . the record of the best and happiest moments of the happiest and best minds . . . it arrests the vanishing apparitions which haunt the interlunations of life." In spite of the absence of a definition and in spite of the impressions and approximations we are never at a loss to recognize poetry. As a consequence it is easy for us to propose a center of poetry, a *vis* or *noeud vital*, to which, in the absence of a definition, all the variations of definition are peripheral. Sometimes we think that a psychology of poetry has found its way to the center. We say that poetry is metamorphosis and we come to see in a few lines descriptive of an eye, a hand, a stick, the essence of the matter, and we see it so definitely that we say that if the philosopher comes to nothing because he fails, the poet may come to nothing because he succeeds. The philosopher fails to discover. Suppose the poet discovered and had the power thereafter at will and by intelligence to reconstruct us by his transformations. He would also have the power to destroy us. If there was, or if we believed that there was, a center, it would be absurd to fear or to avoid its discovery.

Since we have no difficulty in recognizing poetry and since, at the same time, we say that it is not an attainable acme, not some breath from an altitude, not something that awaits discovery, after which it will not be subject to chance, we may be accounting for it if we say that it is a process of the personality of the poet. One does not have to be a cardinal to make the point. To say that it is a process of the personality of the poet does not mean that it involves the poet as subject. Aristotle said: "The poet should say very little *in propria persona*." Without stopping to discuss what might be discussed for so long, note that the principle so stated by Aristotle is cited in relation to the point that poetry is a process of the personality of the poet. This is the element, the force, that keeps poetry a living thing, the modernizing and ever-modern influence. The statement that the process does not involve the poet as subject, to the extent to which that is true, precludes direct egotism. On the other hand, without indirect egotism there can be no poetry. There can be no poetry without the personality of the poet, and that, quite simply, is why the definition of poetry has not been found and why, in short, there is none. In one of the really remarkable books of the day, *The Life of Forms in Art*, Henri Focillon says:

> Human consciousness is in perpetual pursuit of a language and a style. To assume consciousness is at once to assume form. Even at levels far below the zone of definition and clarity, forms, measures and relationships exist. The chief characteristic of the mind is to be constantly describing *itself*.

This activity is indirect egotism. The mind of the poet describes itself as constantly in his poems as the mind of the sculptor describes itself in his forms, or as the mind of Cézanne described itself in his "psychological landscapes." We are talking about something a good deal more comprehensive than the temperament of the artist as that is usually spoken of. We are concerned with the whole personality and, in effect, we are saying that the poet who writes the heroic poem that will satisfy all there is of us and all of us in time to come, will accomplish it by the power of his reason, the force of his imagination and, in addition, the effortless and inescapable process of his own individuality.

It was of the temperament of the artist that Cézanne spoke so frequently in his letters, and while we mean something more, so, it seems, did Cézanne. He said:

> Primary force alone, *id est* temperament, can bring a person to the end he must attain.

Again:

> With a small temperament one can be very much of a painter. It is sufficient to have a sense of art. . . . Therefore institutions, pensions, honours can only be made for cretins, rogues and rascals.

And again, this time to Emile Bernard:

> Your letters are precious to me . . . because their arrival lifts me out of the monotony which is caused by the incessant . . . search for the sole and unique aim. . . . I am able to describe to you again . . . the realization of that part of nature which, coming into our line of vision, gives the picture. Now the theme to develop is that—whatever our temperament or power in the presence of nature may be—we must render the image of what we see.

And, finally, to his son:

> Obviously one must succeed in feeling for oneself and in expressing oneself sufficiently.

IV

An attempt has been made to equate poetry with philosophy, and to do this with an indication of the possibility that an advantage, in the long run, may lie with poetry; and yet it has been said that poetry is personal. If it is personal in a pejorative sense its value is slight and it is not the equal of philosophy. What we have under observation, however, is the creative process, the personality of the poet, his individuality, as an element in the creative process; and by process of the personality of the poet we mean, to select what may seem to be a curious particular, the incidence of the nervous sensitiveness of the poet in the act of creating the poem and, generally speaking, the physical and mental factors that condition him as an individual. If a man's nerves shrink from loud sounds, they are quite likely to shrink from strong colors and he will be found preferring a drizzle in Venice to a hard rain in Hartford. Everything is of a piece. If he composes music it will be music agreeable to his own nerves. Yet it is commonly thought that the artist is independent of his work. In his chapter on "Forms in the Realm of the Mind," M. Focillon speaks of a vocation of substances, or technical destiny, to which there is a corresponding vocation of minds; that is to say, a certain order of forms corresponds to a certain order of minds. These things imply an element of change. Thus a vocation recognizes its material by foresight, before experience. As an example of this, he refers to the first state of the *Prisons* of Piranesi as skeletal. But "twenty years later, Piranesi returned to these etchings, and on taking them up again, he poured into them shadow after shadow, until one might say that he excavated this astonishing darkness not from the brazen plates, but from the living rock of some subterranean world." The way a poet feels when he is writing, or after he has written, a poem that completely accomplishes his purpose is evidence of the personal nature of his activity. To describe it by exaggerating it, he shares the transformation, not to say apotheosis, accomplished by the poem. It must be this experience that makes him think of poetry as possibly a phase of metaphysics; and it must be this experience that teases him with that sense of the possibility of a remote, a mystical *vis* or *noeud vital* to which reference has already been made. In *The Two Sources of Morality and Religion*, Bergson speaks of the morality of aspiration. It implicitly contains, he says,

> the feeling of progress. The emotion . . . is the enthusiasm of a forward movement. . . . But antecedent to this metaphysical theory . . . are the simpler representations . . . of the founders of religion, the mystics and the saints. . . . They begin by saying that what they experience is a feeling of liberation. . . .

The feeling is not a feeling peculiar to exquisite or (perhaps, as better) precise realization, and hence confined to poets who exceed us in nature as they do in speech. There is nothing rare about it although it may extend to degrees of rarity. On the contrary, just as Bergson refers to the simpler representations of aspiration occurring in the lives of the saints, so we may refer to the simpler representations of an aspiration (not the same, yet not wholly unlike) occurring in the lives of those who have just written their first essential poems. After all, the young man or young woman who has written a few poems and who wants to read them is merely the voluble convert or the person looking in a mirror who sees suddenly the traces of an unexpected genealogy. We are interested in this transformation primarily on the part of the poet. Yet it is a thing that communicates itself to the reader. Anyone who has read a long poem day after day as, for example, *The Faerie Queene*, knows how the poem comes to possess the reader and how it naturalizes him in its own imagination and liberates him there.

This sense of liberation may be examined specifically in relation to the experience of writing a poem that completely accomplishes the purpose of the poet. Bergson had in mind religious aspiration. The poet who experiences what was once called inspiration experiences both aspiration and inspiration. But that is not a difference, for it is clear that Bergson intended to include in aspiration not only desire but the fulfillment of desire, not only the petition but the harmonious decree. What is true of the experience of the poet is no doubt true of the experience of the painter, of the musician and of any artist. If, then, when we speak of liberation, we mean an exodus; if when we speak of justification, we mean a kind of justice of which we had not known and on which we had not counted; if when we experience a sense of purification, we can think of the establishing of a self, it is certain that the experience of the poet is of no less a degree than the experience of the mystic and we may be certain that in the case of poets, the peers of saints, those experiences are of no less a degree than the experiences of the saints themselves. It is a question of the nature of the experience. It is not a question of identifying or relating dissimilar figures; that is to say, it is not a question of making saints out of poets or poets out of saints.

In this state of elevation we feel perfectly adapted to the idea that moves and *l'oiseau qui chante*. The identity of the feeling is subject to discussion and, from this, it follows that its value is debatable. It may be dismissed, on the one hand, as a commonplace aesthetic satisfaction; and, on the other hand, if we say that the idea of God is merely a poetic idea, even if the supreme poetic idea, and that our notions of heaven and hell are merely poetry not so called, even if poetry that involves us vitally, the feeling of deliverance, of a release, of a perfection touched, of a vocation so that all men may know the truth and that the truth may set them free—if we say these things and if we are able to see the poet who achieved God and placed Him in His seat in heaven in all His glory, the poet himself, still in the ecstasy of the poem that completely accomplished his purpose, would have seemed, whether young or old, whether in rags or ceremonial robe, a man who needed what he had created, uttering the hymns of joy that followed his creation. This may be a gross exaggeration of a very simple matter. But perhaps that remark is true of many of the more prodigious things of life and death.

V

The centuries have a way of being male. Without pretending to say whether they get this character from their good heroes or their bad ones, it is certain that they get it, in part, from their philosophers and poets. It is curious, looking back at them, to see how much of the impression that they leave has been derived from the progress of thought in their time and from the abundance of the arts, including poetry, left behind and how little of it comes from prouder and much noisier things. Thus, when we think of the seventeenth century, it is to be remarked how much of the strength of its appearance is associated with the idea that this was a time when the incredible suffered most at the hands of the credible. We think of it as a period of hard thinking. We have only their records and memories by which to recall such eras, not the sight and sound of those that lived in them preserved in an eternity of dust and dirt. When we look back at the face of the seventeenth century, it is at the rigorous face of the rigorous thinker and, say, the Miltonic image of a poet, severe and determined. In effect, what we are remembering is the rather haggard background of the incredible, the imagination without intelligence, from which a younger figure is emerging, stepping forward in the company of a muse of its own, still half-beast and somehow more than human, a kind of sister of the Minotaur. This younger figure is the intelligence that endures. It is the imagination of the son still bearing the antique imagination of the father. It is the clear intelligence of the young man still bearing the burden of the obscurities of the intelligence of the old. It is the spirit out of its own self, not out of some surrounding myth, delineating with accurate speech the complications of which it is composed. For this Aeneas, it is the past that is Anchises.

The incredible is not a part of poetic truth. On the contrary, what concerns us in poetry, as in everything else, is the belief of credible people in credible things. It follows that poetic truth is the truth of credible things, not so much that it is actually so, as that it must be so. It is toward that alone that it is possible for the intelligence to move. In one of his letters, Xavier Doudan says: "*Il y a longtemps que je pense que celui qui n'aurait que des idées claires serait assurément un sot.*" The reply to this is that it is impossible to conceive of a man who has nothing but clear ideas; for our nature is an illimitable space through which the intelligence moves without coming to an end. The incredible is inexhaustible but, fortunately, it is not always the same. We come, in this way, to understand that the moment of exaltation that the poet experiences when he writes a poem that completely accomplishes his purpose, is a moment of victory over the incredible, a moment of purity that does not become any the less pure because, as what was incredible is eliminated, something newly credible takes its place. As we come to the point at which it is necessary to be explicit in respect to poetic truth, note that, if we say that the philosopher pursues the truth in one way and the poet in another, it is implied that both are pursuing the same thing, and we overlook the fact that they are pursuing two different parts of a whole. It is as if we said that the end of logic, mathematics, physics, reason and imagination is all one. In short, it is as if we said that there is no difference between philosophic truth and poetic truth. There is a difference between them and it is the difference between logical and empirical knowledge. Since philosophers do not agree in respect to what constitutes philosophic truth, as Bertrand Russell (if any illustration whatever is necessary) demonstrates in his *Inquiry into Meaning and Truth*, even in the casual comment that truth as a static concept is to be discarded, it may not be of much use to improvise a definition of poetic truth. Nevertheless, it may be said that poetic truth is an agreement with reality, brought about by the imagination of a man disposed to be strongly influenced by his imagination, which he believes, for a time, to be true, expressed in terms of his emotions or, since it is less of a restriction to say so, in terms of his own personality. And so stated, the difference between philosophic truth and poetic truth appears to become final. As to the definition itself, it is an expedient for getting on. We shall come back to the nature of poetic truth very shortly.

In the most propitious climate and in the midst of life's virtues, the simple figure of the youth as virile poet is always surrounded by a cloud of double characters, against whose thought and speech it is imperative that he should remain on constant guard. These are the poetic philosophers and the philosophical poets. Mme. de Staël said: "*Nos meilleurs poètes lyriques, en France, ce sont peut-être nos grands prosateurs, Bossuet, Pascal, Fénelon, Buffon, Jean-Jacques. . . ."* M. Claudel added Rabelais, Chateaubriand, even Balzac, and when he did so, M. René Fernandat said: *"On remarquera que M. Claudel a supprimé les 'peut-être' de Mme. de Staël."* In English the poetic aspect of Bunyan is quite commonly recognized. This is an occasion to call attention to William Penn as an English poet, although he may never have written a line of verse. But the illustration of Descartes is irresistible. To speak of figures like Descartes as double characters is an inconceivable difficulty. In his exegesis of *The Discourse on Method,* Leon Roth says:

> His vision showed him first the "dictionary," then the "poets," and only afterwards the *est et non;* and his "rationalism," like the "anti-rationalism" of Pascal, was the product of a struggle not always completely successful. What less "rationalistic" could there be than the early thought preserved by Baillet from the *Olympica* (one may note in passing the poetical names of all these early works): "There are sentences in the writings of the poets more serious than in those of the philosophers. . . . There are in us, as in a flint, seeds of knowledge. Philosophers adduce them through the reason; poets strike them out from the imagination, and these are the brighter." It was the "rationalist" Voltaire who first called attention to the "poetic" in Descartes. . . . To the casual reader there is nothing more remarkable than the careless richness of his style. It is full of similes drawn not only from the arts, like architecture, painting and the stage, but also from the familiar scenes of ordinary and country life. . . . And this not only in his early writing. It is apparent even in his latest published work, the scientific analysis of the "passions of the soul," and it was Voltaire again who commented first on the fact that the last thing from his pen was a ballet written for the Queen of Sweden.

The philosopher proves that the philosopher exists. The poet merely enjoys existence. The philosopher thinks of the world as an enormous pastiche or, as he puts it, the world is as the percipient. Thus Kant says that the objects of perception are conditioned by the nature of the mind as to their form. But the poet says that, whatever it may be, *la vie est plus belle que les idées.* One needs hardly to be told that men more or less irrational are only more or less rational; so that it was not surprising to find Raymond Mortimer saying in the *New Statesman* that the "thoughts" of Shakespeare or Raleigh or Spenser were in fact only contemporary commonplaces and that it was a Victorian habit to praise poets as thinkers, since their "thoughts are usually borrowed or confused." But do we come away from Shakespeare with the sense that we have been reading contemporary commonplaces? Long ago, Sarah Bernhardt was playing Hamlet. When she came to the soliloquy "To be or not to be," she half turned her back on the audience and slowly weaving one hand in a small circle above her head and regarding it, she said, with deliberation and as from the depths of a hallucination:

D'être ou ne pas d'être, c'est là la question . . .

and one followed her, lost in the intricate metamorphosis of thoughts that passed through the mind with a gallantry, an accuracy of abundance, a crowding and pressing of direction, which, for thoughts that were both borrowed and confused, cancelled the borrowing and obliterated the confusion.

There is a life apart from politics. It is this life that the youth as virile poet lives, in a kind of radiant and productive atmosphere. It is the life of that atmosphere. There the philosopher is an alien. The pleasure that the poet has there is a pleasure of agreement with the radiant and productive world in which he lives. It is an agreement that Mallarmé found in the sound of

Le vierge, le vivace et le bel aujourd'hui

and that Hopkins found in the color of

The thunder-purple seabeach plumèd purple-of-thunder.

The indirect purpose or, perhaps, it would be better to say, inverted effect of soliloquies in hell and of most celestial poems and, in a general sense, of all music played on the terraces of the audiences of the moon, seems to be to produce an agreement with reality. It is the *mundo* of the imagination in which the imaginative man delights and not the gaunt world of the reason. The pleasure is the pleasure of powers that create a truth that cannot be arrived at by the reason alone, a truth that the poet recognizes by sensation. The morality of the poet's radiant and productive atmosphere is the morality of the right sensation.

VI

I have compared poetry and philosophy; I have made a point of the degree to which poetry is personal, both in its origin and in its end, and have spoken of the typical exhilaration that appears to be inseparable from genuine poetic activity; I have said that the general progress from the incredible to the credible was a progress in which poetry has participated; I have improvised a definition of poetic truth and have spoken of the integrity and peculiarity of the poetic character. Summed up, our position at the moment is that the poet must get rid of the hieratic in everything that concerns him and must move constantly in the direction of the credible. He must create his unreal out of what is real.

If we consider the nature of our experience when we are in agreement with reality, we find, for one thing, that we cease to be metaphysicians. William James said:

Most of them [i.e., metaphysicians] have been invalids. I am one, can't sleep, can't make a decision, can't buy a horse, can't do anything that befits a man; and yet you say from my photograph that I must be a second General Sherman, only greater and better! All right! I love you for the fond delusion.

For all the reasons stated by William James, and for many more, and in spite of M. Jacques Maritain, we do not want to be metaphysicians. In the crowd around the simple figure of the youth as virile poet, there are metaphysicians, among the others. And having ceased to be metaphysicians, even though we have acquired something from them as from all men, and standing in the radiant and productive atmosphere, and examining first one detail of that world, one particular, and then another, as we find them by chance, and observing many things that seem to be poetry without any intervention on our part, as, for example, the blue sky, and noting, in any case, that the imagination never brings anything into the world but that, on the contrary, like the personality of the poet in the act of creating, it is no more than a process, and desiring with all the power of our desire not to write falsely, do we not begin to think of the possibility that poetry is only reality, after all, and that poetic truth is a factual truth, seen, it may be, by those whose range in the perception of fact—that is, whose sensibility—is greater than our own? From that point of view, the truth that we experience when we are in agreement with reality is the truth of fact. In consequence, when men, baffled by philosophic truth, turn to poetic truth, they return to their starting-point, they return to fact, not, it ought to be clear, to bare fact (or call it absolute fact), but to fact possibly beyond their perception in the first instance and outside the normal range of their sensibility. What we have called elevation and elation on the part of the poet, which he communicates to the reader, may be not so much elevation as an incandescence of the intelligence and so more than ever a triumph over the incredible. Here as part of the purification that all of us undergo as we approach any central purity, and that we feel in its presence, we can say:

> No longer do I believe that there is a mystic muse, sister of the Minotaur. This is another of the monsters I had for nurse, whom I have wasted. I am myself a part of what is real, and it is my own speech and the strength of it, this only, that I hear or ever shall.

These words may very well be an inscription above the portal to what lies ahead. But if poetic truth means fact and if fact includes the whole of it as it is between the extreme poles of sensibility, we are talking about a thing as extensible as it is ambiguous. We have excluded absolute fact as an element of poetic truth. But this has been done arbitrarily and with a sense of absolute fact as fact destitute of any imaginative aspect whatever. Unhappily the more destitute it becomes the more it begins to be precious. We must limit ourselves to saying that there are so many things which, as they are, and without any intervention of the imagination, seem to be imaginative objects that it is no doubt true that absolute fact includes everything that the imagination includes. This is our intimidating thesis.

One sees demonstrations of this everywhere. For example, if we close our eyes and think of a place where it would be pleasant to spend a holiday, and if there slide across the black eyes, like a setting on a stage, a rock that sparkles, a blue sea that lashes, and hemlocks in which the sun can merely fumble, this inevitably demonstrates, since the rock and sea, the wood and sun are those that have been familiar to us in Maine, that much of the world of fact is the equivalent of the world of the imagination, because it looks like it. Here we are on the border of the question of the relationship of the imagination and memory, which we avoid. It is important to believe that the visible is the equivalent of the invisible; and once we believe it, we have destroyed the imagination; that is to say, we have destroyed the false imagination, the false conception of the imagination as some incalculable *vates* within us, unhappy Rodomontade. One is often tempted to say that the best definition of poetry is that poetry is the sum of its attributes. So, here, we may say that the best definition of true imagination is that it is the sum of our faculties. Poetry is the scholar's art. The acute intelligence of the imagination, the illimitable resources of its memory, its power to possess the moment it perceives—if we were speaking of light itself, and thinking of the relationship between objects and light, no further demonstration would be necessary. Like light, it adds nothing, except itself. What light requires a day to do, and by day I mean a kind of Biblical revolution of time, the imagination does in the twinkling of an eye. It colors, increases, brings to a beginning and end, invents languages, crushes men and, for that matter, gods in its hands, it says to women more than it is possible to say, it rescues all of us from what we have called absolute fact and while it does these things, and more, it makes sure that

> . . . *la mandoline jase,*
> *Parmi les frissons de brise.*

Having identified poetic truth as the truth of fact, since fact includes poetic fact, that is to say: the indefinite number of actual things that are indistinguishable from objects of the imagination; and having, as we hope, washed the imagination clean, we may now return, once again, to the figure of the youth as virile poet and join him, or try to do so, in coming to the decision, on which, for him and for us, too, so much depends. At what level of the truth shall he compose his poems? That is the question on which he is reflecting, as he sits in the radiant and productive atmosphere, which is his life, surrounded not only by double characters and metaphysicians, but by many men and many kinds of men, by many women and many children and many kinds of women and of children. The question concerns the function of the poet today and tomorrow, but makes no pretence beyond. He is able to read the inscription on the portal and he repeats:

> I am myself a part of what is real and it is my own speech and the strength of it, this only, that I hear or ever shall.

He says, so that we can all hear him:

> I am the truth, since I am part of what is real, but neither more nor less than those around me. And I am imagination, in a leaden time and in a world that does not move for the weight of its own heaviness.

Can there be the slightest doubt what the decision will be? Can we suppose for a moment that he will be content merely to make notes, merely to copy Katahdin, when, with his sense of the heaviness of the world, he feels his own power to lift, or help to lift, that heaviness away? Can we think that he will elect anything except to exercise his power to the full and at its height, meaning by this as part of what is real, to rely on his imagination, to make his own imagination that of those who have none, or little?

And how will he do this? It is not possible to say how an imaginative person will do a thing. Having made an election, he will be faithful to the election that he has made. Having elected to exercise his power to the full and at its height, and having identified his power as the power of the imagination, he may begin its exercise by studying it in exercise and proceed little by little, as he becomes his own master, to those violences which are the maturity of his desires. The character of the crisis through which we are passing today, the reason why we live in a leaden time, was summed up in a note on Klaus Mann's recent book on Gide, as follows:

> The main problem which Gide tries to solve—the crisis of our time— is the reconciliation of the inalienable rights of the individual to personal development and the necessity for the diminution of the misery of the masses.

When the poet has converted this into his own terms: the figure of the youth as virile poet and the community growing day by day more and more colossal, the consciousness of his function, if he is a serious artist, is a measure of his obligation. And so is the consciousness of his history. In the *Reflections on History* of Jakob Burckhardt, there are some pages of notes on the historical consideration of poetry. Burckhardt thought (citing Schopenhauer and Aristotle) that poetry achieves more for the knowledge of human nature than history. Burckhardt considers the status of poetry at various epochs, among various peoples and classes, asking each time *who* is singing or writing, and for *whom*. Poetry is the voice of religion, prophecy, mythology, history, national life and inexplicably, for him, of literature. He says:

> It is a matter for great surprise that Virgil, in those circumstances, could occupy his high rank, could dominate all the age which followed and become a mythical figure. How infinitely great are the gradations of existence from the epic rhapsodist to the novelist of today!

This was written seventy-five years ago. The present generation of poets is not accustomed to measure itself by obligations of such weight nor to think of itself as Burckhardt seems to have thought of epic bards or, to choose another example at random, of the writers of hymns, for he speaks of "the Protestant hymn as the supreme religious expression, especially of the seventeenth century."

The poet reflecting on his course, which is the same thing as a reflection by him and by us, on the course of poetry, will decide to do as the imagination bids, because he has no choice, if he is to remain a poet. Poetry is the imagination of life. A poem is a particular of life thought of for so long that one's thought has become an inseparable part of it or a particular of life so intensely felt that the feeling has entered into it. When, therefore, we say that the world is a compact of real things so like the unreal things of the imagination that they are indistinguishable from one another and when, by way of illustration, we cite, say, the blue sky, we can be sure that the thing cited is always something that, whether by thinking or feeling, has become a part of our vital experience of life, even though we are not aware of it. It is easy to suppose that few people realize on that occasion, which comes to all of us, when we look at the blue sky for the first time, that is to say: not merely see it, but look at it and experience it and for the first time have a sense that we live in the center of a physical poetry, a geography that would be intolerable except for the non-geography that exists there—few people realize that they are looking at the world of their own thoughts and the world of their own feelings. On that occasion, the blue sky is a particular of life that we have thought of often, even though unconsciously, and that we have felt intensely in those crystallizations of freshness that we no more remember than we remember this or that gust of wind in spring or autumn. The experiences of thinking and feeling accumulate particularly in the abnormal ranges of sensibility; so that, to use a bit of M. Focillon's personal language, while the "normative type" of poet is likely to be concerned with pretty much the same facts as those with which the genius, or, rather, the youth as virile poet, is concerned, the genius, because of the abnormal ranges of his sensibility, not only accumulates experiences with greater rapidity, but accumulates experiences and qualities of experience accessible only in the extreme ranges of sensibility.

But genius is not our concern. We are trying to define what we mean by the imagination of life, and, in addition, by that special illumination, special abundance and severity of abundance, virtue in the midst of indulgence and order in disorder that is involved in the idea of virility. We have been referring constantly to the simple figure of the youth, in his character of poet, as virile poet. The reason for this is that if, for the poet, the imagination is paramount, and if he dwells apart in his imagination, as the philosopher dwells in his reason, and as the priest dwells in his belief, the masculine nature that we propose for one that must be the master of our lives will be lost as, for example, in the folds of the garments of the ghost or ghosts of Aristotle. As we say these things, there begins to develop, in addition to the figure that has been seated in our midst, composed, in the radiant and productive atmosphere with which we have surrounded him, an intimation of what he is thinking as he reflects on the imagination of life, determined to be its master and ours. He is thinking of those facts of experience of which all of us have thought and which all of us have felt with such intensity, and he says:

Inexplicable sister of the Minotaur, enigma and mask, although I am part of what is real, hear me and recognize me as part of the unreal. I am the truth but the truth of that imagination of life in which with unfamiliar motion and manner you guide me in those exchanges of speech in which your words are mine, mine yours.

Two or Three Ideas

My first proposition is that the style of a poem and the poem itself are one. One of the better known poems in *Fleurs du mal* is the one (XII) entitled "La Vie antérieure" or "Former Life." It begins with the line

> *J'ai longtemps habité sous de vastes portiques*

or

> A long time I lived beneath tremendous porches.

It continues:

> Which the salt-sea suns tinged with a thousand fires
> And which great columns, upright and majestic,
> At evening, made resemble basalt grottoes.

The poem concerns the life among the images, sounds and colors of those calm, sensual presences.

> At the center of azure, of waves, of brilliances,

and so on. I have chosen this poem to illustrate my first proposition, because it happens to be a poem in which the poem itself is immediately recognizable without reference to the manner in which it is rendered. If the style and the poem are one, one ought to choose, for the purpose of illustration, a poem that illustrates this as, for example, Yeats' "Lake-Isle of Innisfree." To choose a French poem which has to be translated is to choose an example in which the style is lost in the paraphrase of translation. On the other hand, Baudelaire's poem is useful because it identifies what is meant by the poem itself. The idea of an earlier life is like the idea of a later life, or like the idea of a different life, part of the classic repertory of poetic ideas. It is part of one's inherited store of poetic subjects. Precisely, then, because it is traditional and because we understand its romantic nature and know what to expect from it, we are suddenly and profoundly touched when we hear it declaimed by a voice that says:

> I lived, for long, under huge porticoes.

It is as if we had stepped into a ruin and were startled by a flight of birds that rose as we entered. The familiar experience is made unfamiliar and from that time on, whenever we think of that particular scene, we remember how we held our breath and how the hungry doves of another world rose out of nothingness and whistled away. We stand looking at a remembered habitation. All old dwelling-places are subject to these transmogrifications and the experience of all of us includes a succession of old dwelling-places: abodes of

160

the imagination, ancestral or memories of places that never existed. It is plain that when, in this world of weak feeling and blank thinking, in which we are face to face with the poem every moment of time, we encounter some integration of the poem that pierces and dazzles us, the effect is an effect of style and not of the poem itself or at least not of the poem alone. The effective integration is not a disengaging of the subject. It is a question of the style in which the subject is presented.

Although I have limited myself to an instance of the relation between style and the familiar, one gets the same result in considering the relation between style and its own creations, that is between style and the unfamiliar. What we are really considering here are the creations of modern art and modern literature. If one keeps in mind the fact that most poets who have something to say are content with what they say and that most poets who have little or nothing to say are concerned primarily with the way in which they say it, the importance of this discussion becomes clear. I do not mean to imply that the poets who have something to say are the poets that matter; for obviously if it is true that the style of a poem and the poem itself are one, it follows that, in considering style and its own creations, that is to say, the relation between style and the unfamiliar, it may be, or become, that the poets who have little or nothing to say are, or will be, the poets that matter. Today, painters who have something to say are less admired than painters who seem to have little or nothing to say but who do at least believe that style and the painting are one. The inclination toward arbitrary or schematic constructions in poetry is, from the point of view of style, very strong; and certainly if these constructions were effective it would be true that the style and the poem were one.

In the light of this first idea the prejudice in favor of plain English, for instance, comes to nothing. I have never been able to see why what is called Anglo-Saxon should have the right to higgle and haggle all over the page, contesting the right of other words. If a poem seems to require a hierophantic phrase, the phrase should pass. This is a way of saying that one of the consequences of the ordination of style is not to limit it, but to enlarge it, not to impoverish it, but to enrich and liberate it.

The second idea relates to poetry and the gods, both ancient and modern, both foreign and domestic. To simplify, I shall speak only of the ancient and the foreign gods. I do not mean to refer to them in their religious aspects but as creations of the imagination; and I suppose that as with all creations of the imagination I have been thinking of them from the point of view of style, that is to say of their style. When we think of Jove, while we take him for granted as the symbol of omnipotence, the ruler of mankind, we do not fear him. He does have a superhuman size, but at least not so superhuman as to amaze and intimidate us. He has a large head and a beard and is a relic, a relic that makes a kindly impression on us and reminds us of stories that we have heard about him. All of the noble images of all of the gods have been profound and most of them have been forgotten. To speak of the origin and end of gods is not a light matter. It is to speak of the origin and end of eras of human belief. And while it is easy to look back on those that have disappeared as if they were the playthings of cosmic make-believe, and on those that made petitions to them and honored them and received their benefits as legendary innocents, we are bound, nevertheless, to concede that the gods were personae of a peremptory elevation and glory. It would be wrong to look back to them as if they had existed in some indigence of the spirit. They were in fact, as we see them now, the clear giants of a vivid time, who in the style of their beings made the style of the gods and the gods themselves one.

This brings me to the third idea, which is this: In an age of disbelief, or, what is the same thing, in a time that is largely humanistic, in one sense or another, it is for the poet to supply the satisfactions of belief, in his measure and in his style. I say in his measure to indicate that the figures of the philosopher, the artist, the teacher, the moralist and other figures, including the poet, find themselves, in such a time, to be figures of an importance greatly enhanced by the requirements both of the individual and of society; and I say in his style by way of confining the poet to his role and thereby of intensifying that role. It is this that I want to talk about today. I want to try to formulate a conception of perfection in poetry with reference to the present time and the near future and to speculate on the activities possible to it as it deploys itself throughout the lives of men and women. I think of it as a role of the utmost seriousness. It is, for one thing, a spiritual role. One might stop to draw an ideal portrait of the poet. But that would be parenthetical. In any case, we do not say that the philosopher, the artist or the teacher is to take the place of the gods. Just so, we do not say that the poet is to take the place of the gods.

To see the gods dispelled in mid-air and dissolve like clouds is one of the great human experiences. It is not as if they had gone over the horizon to disappear for a time; nor as if they had been overcome by other gods of greater power and profounder knowledge. It is simply that they came to nothing. Since we have always shared all things with them and have always had a part of their strength and, certainly, all of their knowledge, we shared likewise this experience of annihilation. It was their annihilation, not ours, and yet it left us feeling that in a measure, we, too, had been annihilated. It left us feeling dispossessed and alone in a solitude, like children without parents, in a home that seemed deserted, in which the amical rooms and halls had taken on a look of hardness and emptiness. What was most extraordinary is that they left no momentoes behind, no thrones, no mystic rings, no texts either of the soil or of the soul. It was as if they had never inhabited the earth. There was no crying out for their return. They were not forgotten because they had been a part of the glory of the earth. At the same time, no man ever muttered a petition in his heart for the restoration of those unreal shapes. There was always in every man the increasingly human self, which instead of remaining the observer, the non-participant, the delinquent, became constantly more and more all there was or so it seemed; and whether it was so or merely seemed so still left it for him to resolve life and the world in his own terms.

Thinking about the end of the gods creates singular attitudes in the mind of the thinker. One attitude is that the gods of classical mythology were merely aesthetic projections. They were not the objects of belief. They were expressions of delight. Perhaps delight is too active a word. It is true that they were engaged with the future world and the immortality of the soul. It is true, also, that they were the objects of veneration and therefore of religious dignity and sanctity. But in the blue air of the Mediterranean these white and a little colossal figures had a special propriety, a special felicity. Could they have been created for that propriety, that felicity? Notwithstanding their divinity, they were close to the people among whom they moved. Is it one of the normal activities of humanity, in the solitude of reality and in the unworthy treatment of solitude, to create companions, a little colossal as I have said, who, if not superficially explicative, are, at least, assumed to be full of the secret of things and who in any event bear in themselves even, if they do not always wear it, the peculiar majesty of mankind's sense of worth, neither too much nor too little? To a people of high intelligence, whose gods have benefited by having been accepted and addressed by the superior minds of a superior world, the symbolic paraphernalia of the very great becomes unnecessary and the very great become the very natural. However all that may be, the celestial atmosphere of these deities, their ultimate remote celestial residences are not matters of chance. Their fundamental glory is the fundamental glory of men and women, who being in need of it create it, elevate it, without too much searching of its identity.

The people, not the priests, made the gods. The personages of immortality were something more than the conceptions of priests, although they may have picked up many of the conceits of priests. Who were the priests? Who have always been the high priests of any of the gods? Certainly not those officials or generations of officials who administered rites and observed rituals. The great and true priest of Apollo was he that composed the most moving of Apollo's hymns. The really illustrious archimandrite of Zeus was the one that made the being of Zeus people the whole of Olympus and the Olympian land, just as the only marvelous bishops of heaven have always been those that made it seem like heaven. I said a moment ago that we had not forgotten the gods. What is it that we remember of them? In the case of those masculine do we remember their ethics or is it their port and mien, their size, their color, not to speak of their adventures, that we remember? In the case of those feminine do we remember, as in the case of Diana, their fabulous chastity or their beauty? Do we remember those masculine in any way differently from the way in which we remember Ulysses and other men of supreme interest and excellence? In the case of those feminine do we remember Venus in any way differently from the way in which we remember Penelope and other women of much mark and feeling? In short, while the priests helped to realize the gods, it was the people that spoke of them and to them and heard their replies.

Let us stop now and restate the ideas which we are considering in relation to one another. The first is that the style of a poem and the poem itself are one; the second is that the style of the gods and the gods themselves are one; the third is that in an age of disbelief, when the gods have come to an end, when we think of them as the aesthetic projections of a time that has passed, men turn to a fundamental glory of their own and from that create a style of bearing themselves in reality. They create a new style of a new bearing in a new reality. This third idea, then, may be made to conform to the way in which the other two have been expressed by saying that the style of men and men themselves are one. Now, if the style of a poem and poem itself are one; if the style of the gods and the gods themselves are one; and if the style of men and men themselves are one; and if there is any true relation between these propositions, it might well be the case that the parts of these propositions are interchangeable. Thus, it might be true that the style of a poem and the gods themselves are one; or that the style of the gods and the style of men are one; or that the style of a poem and the style of men are one. As we hear these things said, without having time to think about them, it sounds as if they might be true, at least as if there might be something to them. Most of us are prepared to listen patiently to talk of the identity of the gods and men. But where does the poem come in? And if my answer to that is that I am concerned primarily with the poem and that my purpose this morning is to elevate the poem to the level of one of the major significances of life and to equate it, for the purpose of discussion, with gods and men, I hope it will be clear that it comes in as the central interest, the fresh and foremost object.

If in the minds of men creativeness was the same thing as creation in the natural world, if a spiritual planet matched the sun, or if without any question of a spiritual planet, the light and warmth of spring revitalized all our faculties, as in a measure they do, all the bearings one takes, all the propositions one formulates would be within the scope of that particular domination. The trouble is, however, that men in general do not create in light and warmth alone. They create in darkness and coldness. They create when they are hopeless, in the midst of antagonisms, when they are wrong, when their powers are no longer subject to their control. They create as the ministers of evil. Here in New England at this very moment nothing but good seems to be returning; and in that good, particularly if we ignore the difference between men and the natural world, how easy it is suddenly to believe in the poem as one has never believed in it before, suddenly to require of it a meaning beyond what its words can possibly say, a sound beyond any giving of the ear, a motion beyond our previous knowledge of feeling. And, of course, our three ideas have not only to be thought of as deriving what they have in common from the intricacies of human nature as distinguished from what the things of the natural world have in common, derived from strengths like light and warmth. They have to be thought of with reference to the meaning of style. Style is not something applied. It is something inherent, something that permeates. It is of the nature of that in which it is found, whether the poem, the manner of a god, the bearing of a man. It is not a dress. It may be said to be a voice that is inevitable. A man has no choice about his style. When he says I am my style the truth reminds him that it is his style that is himself. If he says, as my poem is, so are my gods and so am I, the truth remains quiet and broods on what he has said. He knows that the gods of China are always Chinese; that the gods of Greece are always Greeks and that all gods are created in the images of their creators; and he sees in these circumstances the operation of a style, a basic law. He observes the uniform enhancement of all things within the category of the imagination. He sees, in the struggle between the perfectible and the imperfectible, how the perfectible prevails, even though it falls short of perfection.

It is no doubt true that the creative faculties operate alike on poems, gods and men up to a point. They are always the same faculties. One might even say that the things created are always the same things. In case of a universal artist, all of his productions are his peculiar own. When we are dealing with racial units of the creative faculties all of the productions of one unit resemble one another. We say of a painting that it is Florentine. But we say the same thing and with equal certainty of a piece of sculpture. There is no difficulty in arguing about the poems, gods and men of Egypt or India that they look alike. But if the gods of India disappeared would not the poems of India and the men of India still remain alike. And if there were no poems, a new race of poets would produce poems that would take the place of the gods that had disappeared. What, then, is the nature of poetry in a time of disbelief? The truistic nature of some of the things that I have said shows how the free-will of the poet is limited. They demonstrate that the poetry of the future can never be anything purely eccentric and dissociated. The poetry of the present cannot be purely eccentric and dissociated. Eccentric and dissociated poetry is poetry that tries to exist or is intended to exist separately from the poem, that is to say in a style that is not identical with the poem. It never achieves anything more than a shallow mannerism, like something seen in a glass. Now, a time of disbelief is precisely a time in which the frequency of detached styles is greatest. I am not quite happy about the word detached. By detached, I mean the unsuccessful, the ineffective, the arbitrary, the literary, the non-umbilical, that which in its highest degree would still be words. For the style of the poem and the poem itself to be one there must be a mating and a marriage, not an arid love-song.

Yes: but the gods—now they come into it and make it a delicious subject, as if we were here together wasting our time on something that appears to be whimsical but turns out to be essential. They give to the subject just that degree of effulgence and excess, no more, no less, that the subject requires. Our first proposition, that the style of a poem and the poem itself are one was a definition of perfection in poetry. In the presence of the gods, or of their images, we are in the presence of perfection in created beings. The gods are a definition of perfection in ideal creatures. These remarks expound the second proposition that the style of the gods and the gods themselves are one. The exhilaration of their existence, their freedom from fate, their access to station, their liberty to command fix them in an atmosphere which thrills us as we share it with them. But these are merely attributes. What matters is their manner, their style, which tells us at once that they are as we wished them to be, that they have fulfilled us, that they are us but purified, magnified, in an expansion. It is their style that makes them gods, not merely privileged beings. It is their style most of all that fulfills themselves. If they lost all their privileges, their freedom from fate, their liberty to command, and yet still retained their style, they would still be gods, however destitute. That alone would destroy them, which deprived them of their style. When the time came for them to go, it was a time when their aesthetic had become invalid in the presence not of a greater aesthetic of the same kind, but of a different aesthetic, of which from the point of view of greatness, the difference was that of an intenser humanity. The style of the gods is derived from men. The style of the gods is derived from the style of men.

One has to pierce through the dithyrambic impressions that talk of the gods makes to the reality of what is being said. What is being said must be true and the truth of it must be seen. But the truth about the poet in a time of disbelief is not that he must turn evangelist. After all, he shares the disbelief of his time. He does not turn to Paris or Rome for relief from the monotony of reality. He turns to himself and he denies that reality was ever monotonous except in comparison. He asserts that the source of comparison having been eliminated, reality is returned, as if a shadow had passed and drawn after it and taken away whatever coating had concealed what lay beneath it. Yet the revelation of reality is not a part peculiar to a time of disbelief or, if it is, it is so in a sense singular to that time. Perhaps, the revelation of reality takes on a special meaning, without effort or consciousness on the part of the poet, at such a time. Why should a poem not change in sense when there is a fluctuation of the whole of appearance? Or why should it not change when we realize that the indifferent experience of life is the unique experience, the item of ecstasy which we have been isolating and reserving for another time and place, loftier and more secluded. There is inherent in the words *the revelation of reality* a suggestion that there is a reality of or within or beneath the surface of reality. There are many such realities through which poets constantly pass to and fro, without noticing the imaginary lines that divide one from the other. We were face to face with such a transition at the outset, for Baudelaire's line

A long time I passed beneath an entrance roof

opens like a voice heard in a theatre and a theatre is a reality within a reality. The most provocative of all realities is that reality of which we never lose sight but never see solely as it is. The revelation of that particular reality or of that particular category of realities is like a series of paintings of some natural object affected, as the appearance of any natural object is affected, by the passage of time, and the changes that ensue, not least in the painter. That the revelation of reality has a character or quality peculiar to this time or that or, what is intended to be the same thing, that it is affected by states of mind, is elementary. The line from Baudelaire will not have the same effect on everyone at all times, any more than it will continue to have the same effect on the same person constantly. I remember that when a friend of mine in Ireland quoted the line, a few years ago, in a letter, my feeling about it was that it was a good instance of the value of knowing people of different educations. The chances are that my friend in Dublin and I have done much the same reading. The chances are, also, that we have retained many different things. For instance, this man had chosen Giorgione as the painter that meant most to him. For my own part, Giorgione would not have occurred to me. I should like you to be sure that in speaking of the revelation of reality I am not attempting to forecast the poetry of the future. It would be logical to conclude that, since a time of disbelief is also a time of truth-loving and since I have emphasized that I recognize that what I am trying to say is nothing unless it is true and that the truth of it must be seen, I think that the main characteristic of the poetry of the future or the near future will be an absence of the poetic. I do not think that. I cannot see what value it would have if I did, except as a value to me personally. If there is a logic that controls poetry, which everything that I have been saying may illustrate, it is not the narrow logic that exists on the level of prophecy. That there is a larger logic I have no doubt. But certainly it has to be large enough to allow for a good many irrelevancies.

One of the irrelevancies is the romantic. It looks like something completely contemptible in the light of literary intellectualism and cynicism. The romantic, however, has a way of renewing itself. It can be said of the romantic, just as it can be said of the imagination, that it can never effectively touch the same thing twice in the same way. It is partly because the romantic will not be what has been romantic in the past that it is preposterous to think of confining poetry hereafter to the revelation of reality. The whole effort of the imagination is toward the production of the romantic. When, therefore, the romantic is in abeyance, when it is discredited, it remains true that there is always an unknown romantic and that the imagination will not be forever denied. There is something a little romantic about the idea that the style of a poem and the poem itself are one. It seems to be a much more broadly romantic thing to say that the style of the gods and the gods themselves are one. It is completely romantic to say that the style of men and men themselves are one. To collect and collate these ideas of disparate things may seem to pass beyond the romantic to the fantastic. I hope, however, that you will agree that if each one of these ideas is valid separately, or more or less valid, it is permissible to have brought them together as a collective source of suppositions. What is romantic in all of them is the idea of style which I have not defined in any sense uniformly common to all three. A poem is a restricted creation of the imagination. The gods are the creation of the imagination at its utmost. Men are part of reality. The gradations of romance noticeable as the sense of style is used with reference to these three, one by one, are relevant to the difficulties of the imagination in a truth-loving time. These difficulties exist only as one foresees them. They may never exist at all. An age in which the imagination might be expected to become part of time's *rejectamenta* may behold it established and protected and enthroned on one of the few ever-surviving thrones; and, to our surprise, we may find posted in the portico of its eternal dwelling, on the chief portal, among the morning's ordinances, three regulations which if they were once rules of art will then have become rules of conduct. By that time the one that will matter most is likely to be the last, that the style of man is man himself, which is about what we have been saying.

It comes to this that we use the same faculties when we write poetry that we use when we create gods or when we fix the bearing of men in reality. That this is obvious does not make the statement less. On the contrary, it makes the statement more, because its obviousness is that of the truth. The three ideas are sources of perfection. They are of such a nature that they are instances of aesthetic ideas tantamount to moral ideas, a subject precious in itself but beyond our scope today. For today, they mean that however one time may differ from another, there are always available to us the faculties of the past, but always vitally new and strong, as the sources of perfection today and tomorrow. The unity of style and the poem itself is a unity of language and life that exposes both in a supreme sense. Its collation with the unity of style and the gods and the unity of style and men is intended to demonstrate this.

Virginia Woolf

1882–1941

Adeline Virginia Woolf (née Stephen) was born on January 25, 1882, at Hyde Park Gate, London, the daughter of Sir Leslie Stephen—a leading editor, critic, philosopher, agnostic, and dominating patriarch—whose first wife, Thackeray's daughter, was followed by Julia Duckworth, the mother of the four Stephen children who formed the nucleus of the Bloomsbury Group. Models for the fictional Mr. and Mrs. Ramsay, her parents and the childhood vacations in Cornwall are described in Woolf's novel, *To the Lighthouse* (1927). The death of Julia rendered Sir Leslie chronically gloomy, prone to violence and self-pity; the high-strung adolescent Virginia suffered a trauma and suicide attempt that foreshadowed her later recurrent breakdowns.

With the death of Sir Leslie, the four Stephen children moved from the old Kensington house to Bloomsbury, the scene of regular Thursday evening meetings with a growing circle of intellectuals and artists; Virginia and her sister, Vanessa, a painter, were hostesses. The early members, all friends and disciples of the philosopher G. E. Moore, included Lytton Strachey, Desmond MacCarthy, Saxon Sydney-Turner, and Clive Bell, who would later become Vanessa's husband. Virginia began to participate more actively, and the group became a fashionable salon, including such figures as Henry Lamb, Charles Tennyson, Augustus John, E. M. Forster, Bertrand Russell, and Roger Fry.

In 1911 Virginia and her brother Adrian shared a house with John Maynard Keynes, Duncan Grant, and Leonard Woolf. Already working on her first novel, *The Voyage Out* (1915), still realistic in style and form, Virginia in 1912 married Leonard Woolf, who had returned from colonial service in Ceylon and was to become an author, editor, social reformer, Fabian socialist, and devoted husband to Virginia.

Virginia Woolf had begun writing reviews for *The Times Literary Supplement* and *The Guardian;* these essays began her career of distinctive, witty, and impressionistic criticism, later collected as *The Common Reader* (first series, 1925; second series, 1932), *The Death of the Moth* (1942), *The Captain's Death Bed* (1950), and *Granite and Rainbow* (1958). Her breakdown on completing *The Voyage Out* in 1915 was typical of her creative cycle, where depression would ensue near the end of a serious work. That year the Woolfs moved to Hogarth House, Richmond, where they began a printing press, partially as therapy for Virginia. The

Hogarth Press published many of Virginia Woolf's novels, as well as those of such new authors as T. S. Eliot, Katherine Mansfield, and Maxim Gorky.

Woolf's early novels, *Night and Day* (1919), concerning woman suffrage, and *Jacob's Room* (1922), depicting the short life of a young man similar to her brother Thoby who died in 1906, were followed by increasingly unrealistic, stream-of-consciousness novels: *Mrs. Dalloway* (1925), *To the Lighthouse* (1927), and *The Waves* (1931). These established her reputation as a Modernist. Like the later novels, psychological studies in an impressionistic manner, Woolf's important treatise on modern fiction, "Mr. Bennett and Mrs. Brown" (1923), addresses characterization and human relations, arguing against realism. "Modern Fiction" (1919) also proposes an agenda for the new novelists and an end to materialism.

Intermittently, Woolf produced playful and fantastic works. The whimsical biography of Elizabeth Barrett Browning's spaniel, *Flush* (1933), and the biography of an androgynous, magical, historical figure, *Orlando* (1928), were practical jokes that proved therapeutic and widely popular. Orlando, a figure modeled after the outrageous Vita Sackville-West, with whom Woolf had an intimate relationship in the 1920s, represents Woolf's growing concern with women's issues. The love affair with Vita and Woolf's ambivalence toward sex in general led her toward a theory of women and literature that depended on androgyny.

Woolf began lecturing to workers' collectives and literary societies, informal groups and universities; the product of lectures at Cambridge was *A Room of One's Own* (1929), a polemic on the condition of women in society. Speculations about women in history, the economic structure of art production, Elizabethan and Restoration women writers, and patriarchy in general are given an impressionistic treatment, scattered throughout with creative anecdote and rhetoric.

Under tremendous psychological strain, Woolf completed *The Years* in 1936; it was published the next year. The Hogarth Press was wearing down, and *Three Guineas* (1938) proved a lesser version of the feminist perspective in *A Room of One's Own*. With her lecture to the Workers' Educational Association in Brighton, published as "The Leaning Tower" (1940), Woolf defined herself as a sort of socialist, undoubtedly influenced by Leonard. Her pacifism had emerged during the two wars, but her political ideas were vague.

Like her father, who had edited the first series of the *Dictionary of National Biography*, Woolf was interested in the lives of the great and obscure. Along with essays on "The Art of Biography" and "The New Biography," she wrote a book on Roger Fry, art critic and colleague of Vanessa's husband Clive Bell.

Firebombs of the war damaged the Woolfs' home and the Hogarth Press. By then, as Virginia was finishing her final novel, *Between the Acts* (1941), her health was deteriorating. Terrified, apparently, by the onset of madness and by her failing writing, she filled her clothes with stones and drowned herself in the river Ouse on March 28, 1941. Leonard Woolf edited the many posthumous volumes of essays (including the *Collected Essays* in four volumes in 1966) and *A Writer's Diary* (1953), a record begun in 1915 of her creative process.

A ROOM OF ONE'S OWN

Chapter III

It was disappointing not to have brought back in the evening some important statement, some authentic fact. Women are poorer than men because—this or that. Perhaps now it would be better to give up seeking for the truth, and receiving on one's head an avalanche of opinion hot as lava, discoloured as dish-water. It would be better to draw the curtains; to shut out distractions; to light the lamp; to narrow the enquiry and to ask the historian, who records not opinions but facts, to describe under what conditions women lived, not throughout the ages, but in England, say in the time of Elizabeth.

For it is a perennial puzzle why no woman wrote a word of that extraordinary literature when every other man, it seemed, was capable of song or sonnet. What were the conditions in which women lived, I asked myself; for fiction, imaginative work that is, is not dropped like a pebble upon the ground, as science may be; fiction is like a spider's web, attached ever so lightly perhaps, but still attached to life at all four corners. Often the attachment is scarcely perceptible. Shakespeare's plays, for instance, seem to hang there complete by themselves. But when the web is pulled askew, hooked up at the edge, torn in the middle, one remembers that these webs are not spun in mid-air by incorporeal creatures, but are the work of suffering human beings, and are attached to grossly material things, like health and money and the houses we live in.

I went, therefore, to the shelf where the histories stand and took down one of the latest, Professor Trevelyan's *History of England*. Once more I looked up Women, found "position of," and turned to the pages indicated. "Wife-beating," I read, "was a recognised right of man, and was practised without shame by high as well as low. . . . Similarly," the historian goes on, "the daughter who refused to marry the gentleman of her parents' choice was liable to be locked up, beaten and flung about the room, without any shock being inflicted on public opinion. Marriage was not an affair of personal affection, but of family avarice, particularly in the 'chivalrous' upper classes. . . . Betrothal often took place while one or both of the parties was in the cradle, and marriage when they were scarcely out of the nurses' charge." That was about 1470, soon after Chaucer's time. The next reference to the position of women is some two hundred years later, in the time of the Stuarts. "It was still the exception for women of the upper and middle class to choose their own husbands, and when the husband had been assigned, he was lord and master, so far at least as law and custom could make him. Yet even so," Professor Trevelyan concludes, "neither Shakespeare's women nor those of authentic seventeenth-century memoirs, like the Verneys and the Hutchinsons, seem wanting in personality and character." Certainly, if we consider it, Cleopatra must have had a way with her; Lady Macbeth, one would suppose, had a will of her own; Rosalind, one might conclude, was an attractive girl. Professor Trevelyan is speaking no more than the truth when he remarks that Shakespeare's women do not seem wanting in personality and character. Not being a historian, one might go even further and say that women have burnt like beacons in all the works of all the poets from the beginning of time—Clytemnestra, Antigone, Cleopatra, Lady Macbeth, Phèdre, Cressida, Rosalind, Desdemona, the Duchess of Malfi, among the dramatists; then among the prose writers: Millamant, Clarissa, Becky Sharp, Anna Karenina, Emma Bovary, Madame de Guermantes—the names flock to mind, nor do they recall women "lacking in personality and character." Indeed, if woman had no existence save in the fiction written by men, one would imagine her a person of the utmost importance; very various; heroic and mean; splendid and sordid; infinitely beautiful and hideous in the extreme; as great as a man, some think even greater.[1] But this is woman in fiction. In fact, as Professor Trevelyan points out, she was locked up, beaten and flung about the room.

A very queer, composite being thus emerges. Imaginatively she is of the highest importance; practically she is completely insignificant. She pervades poetry from cover to cover; she is all but absent from history. She dominates the lives of kings and conquerors in fiction; in fact she was the slave of any boy whose parents forced a ring upon her finger. Some of the most inspired words, some of the most profound thoughts in literature fall from her lips; in real life she could hardly read, could scarcely spell, and was the property of her husband.

It was certainly an odd monster that one made up by reading the historians first and the poets afterwards—a worm winged like an eagle; the spirit of life and beauty in a kitchen chopping up suet. But these monsters, however amusing to the imagination, have no existence in fact. What one must do to bring her to life was to think poetically and prosaically at one and the same moment, thus keeping in touch with fact—that she is Mrs. Martin, aged thirty-six, dressed in blue, wearing a black hat and brown shoes; but not losing sight of fiction either—that she is a vessel in which all sorts of spirits and forces are coursing and flashing perpetually. The moment, however, that one tries this method with the Elizabethan woman, one branch of illumination fails; one is held up by the scarcity of facts. One knows nothing detailed, nothing perfectly true and substantial about her. History scarcely mentions her. And I turned to Professor Trevelyan again to see what history meant to him. I found by looking at his chapter headings that it meant—

"The Manor Court and the Methods of Open-field Agriculture . . . The Cistercians and Sheep-farming . . . The Crusades . . . The University . . . The House of Commons . . . The Hundred Years' War . . . The Wars of the Roses . . . The Renaissance Scholars . . . The Dissolution of the Monasteries . . . Agrarian and Religious Strife . . . The Origin of English Sea-power . . . The Armada . . ." and so on. Occasionally an individual woman is mentioned, an Elizabeth, or a Mary; a queen or a great lady. But by no possible means could middle-class women with nothing but brains and character at their command have taken part in any one of the great movements which, brought together, constitute the historian's view of the past. Nor shall we find her in any collection of anecdotes. Aubrey hardly mentions her. She never writes her own life and scarcely keeps a diary; there are only a handful of her letters in existence. She left no plays or poems by which we can judge her. What one wants, I thought—and why does not some brilliant student at Newnham or Girton supply it?—is a mass of information; at what age did she marry; how many children had she as a rule; what was her house like; had she a room to herself; did she do the cooking; would she be likely to have a servant? All these facts lie somewhere, presumably, in parish registers and account books; the life of the average Elizabethan woman must be scattered about somewhere, could one collect it and make a book of it. It would be ambitious beyond my daring, I thought, looking about the shelves for books that were not there, to suggest to the students of those famous colleges that they should re-write history, though I own that it often seems a little queer as it is, unreal, lop-sided; but why should they not add a supplement to history? calling it, of course, by some inconspicuous name so that women might figure there without impropriety? For one often catches a glimpse of them in the lives of the great, whisking away into the background, concealing, I sometimes think, a wink, a laugh, perhaps a tear. And, after all, we have lives enough of Jane Austen; it scarcely seems necessary to consider again the influence of the tragedies of Joanna Baillie upon the poetry of Edgar Allan Poe; as for myself, I should not mind if the homes and haunts of Mary Russell Mitford were closed to the public for a century at least. But what I find deplorable, I continued, looking about the bookshelves again, is that nothing is known about women before the eighteenth century. I have no model in my mind to turn about this way and that. Here am I asking why women did not write poetry in the Elizabethan age, and I am not sure how they were educated; whether they were taught to write; whether they had sitting-rooms to themselves; how many women had children before they were twenty-one; what, in short, they did from eight in the morning till eight at night. They had no money evidently; according to Professor Trevelyan they were married whether they liked it or not before they were out of the nursery, at fifteen or sixteen very likely. It would have been extremely odd, even upon this showing, had one of them suddenly written the plays of Shakespeare, I concluded, and I thought of that old gentleman, who is dead now, but was a bishop, I think, who declared that it was impossible for any woman, past, present, or to come, to have the genius of Shakespeare. He wrote to the papers about it. He also told a lady who applied to him for information that cats do not as a matter of fact go to heaven, though they have, he added, souls of a sort. How much thinking those old gentlemen used to save one! How the borders of ignorance shrank back at their approach! Cats do not go to heaven. Women cannot write the plays of Shakespeare.

Be that as it may, I could not help thinking, as I looked at the words of Shakespeare on the shelf, that the bishop was right at least in this; it would have been impossible, completely and entirely, for any woman to have written the plays of Shakespeare in the age of Shakespeare. Let me imagine, since facts are so hard to come by, what would have happened had Shakespeare had a wonderfully gifted sister, called Judith, let us say. Shakespeare himself went, very probably—his mother was an heiress—to the grammar school, where he may have learnt Latin—Ovid, Virgil and Horace—and the elements of grammar and logic. He was, it is well known, a wild boy who poached rabbits, perhaps shot a deer, and had, rather sooner than he should have done, to marry a woman in the neighbourhood, who bore him a child rather quicker than was right. That escapade sent him to seek his fortune in London. He had, it seemed, a taste for the theatre; he began by holding horses at the stage door. Very soon he got work in the theatre, became a successful actor, and lived at the hub of the universe, meeting everybody, knowing everybody, practising his art on the boards, exercising his wits in the streets, and even getting access to the palace of the queen. Meanwhile his extraordinarily gifted sister, let us suppose, remained at home. She was as adventurous, as imaginative, as agog to see the world as he was. But she was not sent to school. She had no chance of learning grammar and logic, let alone of reading Horace and Virgil. She picked up a book now and then, one of her brother's perhaps, and read a few pages. But then her parents came in and told her to mend the stockings or mind the stew and not moon about with books and papers. They would have spoken sharply but kindly, for they were substantial people who knew the conditions of life for a woman and loved their daughter—indeed, more likely than not she was the apple of her father's eye. Perhaps she scribbled some pages up in an apple loft on the sly, but was careful to hide them or set fire to them. Soon, however, before she was out of her teens, she was to be betrothed to the son of a neighbouring wool-stapler. She cried out that marriage was hateful to her, and for that she was severely beaten by her father. Then he ceased to scold her. He begged her instead not to hurt him, not to shame him in this matter of her marriage. He would give her a chain of beads or a fine petticoat, he said; and there were tears in his eyes. How could she disobey him? How could she break his heart? The force of her own gift alone drove her to it. She made up a small parcel of her belongings, let herself down by a rope one summer's night and took the road to London. She was not seventeen. The birds that sang in the hedge were not more musical than she was. She had the quickest fancy, a gift like her brother's, for the tune of words. Like him, she had a taste for the theatre. She stood at the stage door; she wanted to act; she said. Men laughed in her face. The manager—a fat, loose-lipped man—guffawed. He bellowed, something about poodles dancing and women acting—no woman, he said, could possibly be an actress. He hinted—you can imagine what. She could get no training in her craft. Could she even seek her dinner in a tavern or roam the streets at midnight? Yet her genius was for fiction and lusted to feed abundantly upon the lives of men and women and the study of their ways. At last—for she was very young, oddly like Shakespeare the poet in her face, with the same grey eyes and rounded brows—at last Nick Greene the actor-manager took pity on her; she found herself with child by that gentleman and so—who shall measure the heat and violence of the poet's heart when caught and tangled in a woman's body?—killed herself one winter's night and lies buried at some cross-roads where the omnibuses now stop outside the Elephant and Castle.

That, more or less, is how the story would run, I think, if a woman in Shakespeare's day had had Shakespeare's genius. But for my part, I agree with the deceased bishop, if such he was—it is unthinkable that any woman in Shakespeare's day should have had Shakespeare's genius. For genius like Shakespeare's is not born among labouring, uneducated, servile people. It was not born in England among the Saxons and the Britons. It is not born today among the working classes. How, then, could it have been born among women whose work began, according to Professor Trevelyan, almost before they were out of the nursery, who were forced to it by their parents and held to it by all the power of law and custom? Yet genius of a sort must have existed among women as it must have existed among the working classes. Now and again an Emily Brontë or a Robert Burns blazes out and proves its presence. But certainly it never got itself on to paper. When, however, one reads of a witch being ducked, of a woman possessed by devils, of a wise woman selling herbs, or even of a very remarkable man who had a mother, then I think we are on the track of a lost novelist, a suppressed poet, of some mute and inglorious Jane Austen, some Emily Brontë who dashed her brains out on the moor or mopped and mowed about the highways crazed with the torture that her gift had put her to. Indeed, I would venture to guess that Anon, who wrote so many poems without signing them, was often a woman. It was a woman Edward FitzGerald, I think, suggested who made the ballads and the folk-songs, crooning them to her children, beguiling her spinning with them, or the length of the winter's night.

This may be true or it may be false—who can say?—but what is true in it, so it seemed to me, reviewing the story of Shakespeare's sister as I had made it, is that any woman born with a great gift in the sixteenth century would certainly have gone crazed, shot herself, or ended her days in some lonely cottage outside the village, half witch, half wizard, feared and mocked at. For it needs little skill in psychology to be sure that a highly gifted girl who had tried to use her gift for poetry would have been so thwarted and hindered by other people, so tortured and pulled asunder by her own contrary instincts, that she must have lost her health and sanity to a certainty. No girl could have walked to London and stood at a stage door and forced her way into the presence of actor-managers without doing herself a violence and suffering an anguish which may have been irrational—for chastity may be a fetish invented by certain societies for unknown reasons—but were none the less inevitable. Chastity had then, it has even now, a religious importance in a woman's life, and has so wrapped itself round with nerves and instincts that to cut it free and bring it to the light of day demands courage of the rarest. To have lived a free life in London in the sixteenth century would have meant for a woman who was poet and playwright a nervous stress and dilemma which might well have killed her. Had she survived, whatever she had written would have been twisted and deformed, issuing from a strained and morbid imagination. And undoubtedly, I thought, looking at the shelf where there are no plays by women, her work would have gone unsigned. That refuge she would have sought certainly. It was the relic of the sense of chastity that dictated anonymity to women even so late as the nineteenth century. Currer Bell, George Eliot, George Sand, all the victims of inner strife as their writings prove, sought ineffectively to veil themselves by using the name of a man. Thus they did homage to the convention, which if not implanted by the other sex was liberally encouraged by them (the chief glory of a woman is not to be talked of, said Pericles, himself a much-talked-of man), that publicity in women is detestable. Anonymity runs in their blood. The desire to be veiled still possesses them. They are not even now as concerned about the health of their fame as men are, and, speaking generally, will pass a tombstone or a signpost without feeling an irresistible desire to cut their names on it, as Alf, Bert or Chas. must do in obedience to their instinct, which murmurs if it sees a fine woman go by, or even a dog, Ce chien est à moi. And, of course, it may not be a dog, I thought, remembering Parliament Square, the Sièges Allée and other avenues; it may be a piece of land or a man with curly black hair. It is one of the great advantages of being a woman that one can pass even a very fine negress without wishing to make an Englishwoman of her.

That woman, then, who was born with a gift of poetry in the sixteenth century, was an unhappy woman, a woman at strife against herself. All the conditions of her life, all her own instincts, were hostile to the state of mind which is needed to set free whatever is in the brain. But what is the state of mind that is most propitious to the act of creation, I asked. Can one come by any notion of the state that furthers and makes possible that strange activity? Here I opened the volume containing the Tragedies of Shakespeare. What was Shakespeare's state of mind, for instance, when he wrote *Lear* and *Antony and Cleopatra*? It was certainly the state of mind most favourable to poetry that there has ever existed. But Shakespeare himself said nothing about it. We only know casually and by chance that he "never blotted a line." Nothing indeed was ever said by the artist himself about his state of mind until the eighteenth century perhaps. Rousseau perhaps began it. At any rate, by the nineteenth century self-consciousness had developed so far that it was the habit for men of letters to describe their minds in confessions and autobiographies. Their lives were also written, and their letters were printed after their deaths. Thus, though we do not know what Shakespeare went through when he wrote *Lear,* we do know what Carlyle went through when he wrote the *French Revolution;* what Flaubert went through when he wrote *Madame Bovary;* what Keats was going through when he tried to write poetry against the coming of death and the indifference of the world.

And one gathers from this enormous modern literature of confession and self-analysis that to write a work of genius is almost always a feat of prodigious difficulty. Everything is against the likelihood that it will come from the writer's mind whole and entire. Generally material circumstances are against it. Dogs will bark; people will interrupt; money must be made; health will break down. Further, accentuating all these difficulties and making them harder to bear is the world's notorious indifference. It does not ask people to write poems and novels and histories; it does not need them. It does not care whether Flaubert finds the right word or whether Carlyle scrupulously verifies this or that fact. Naturally, it will not pay for what it does not want. And so the writer, Keats, Flaubert, Carlyle, suffers, especially in the creative years of youth, every form of distraction and discouragement. A curse, a cry of agony, rises from those books of analysis and confession. "Mighty poets in their misery dead"—that is the burden of their song. If anything comes through in spite of all this, it is a miracle, and probably no book is born entire and uncrippled as it was conceived.

But for women, I thought, looking at the empty shelves, these difficulties were infinitely more formidable. In the first place, to have a room of her own, let alone a quiet room or a sound-proof room, was out of the question, unless her parents were exceptionally rich or very noble, even up to the beginning of the nineteenth century. Since her pin money, which depended on the good will of her father, was only enough to keep her clothed, she was debarred from such alleviations as came even to Keats or Tennyson or Carlyle, all poor men, from a walking tour, a little journey to France, from the separate lodging which, even if it were miserable enough, sheltered them from the claims and tyrannies of their families. Such material difficulties were formidable; but much worse were the immaterial. The indifference of the world which Keats and Flaubert and other men of genius have found so hard to bear was in her case not indifference but hostility. The world did not say to her as it said to them, Write if you choose; it makes no difference to me. The world said with a guffaw, Write? What's the good of your writing? Here the psychologists of Newnham and Girton might come to our help, I thought, looking again at the blank spaces on the shelves. For surely it is time that the effect of discouragement upon the mind of the artist should be measured, as I have seen a dairy company measure the effect of ordinary milk and Grade A milk upon the body of the rat. They set two rats in cages side by side, and of the two one was furtive, timid and small, and the other was glossy, bold and big. Now what food do we feed women artists upon? I asked, remembering, I suppose, that dinner of prunes and custard. To answer that question I had only to open the evening paper and to read that Lord Birkenhead is of opinion—but really I am not going to trouble to copy out Lord Birkenhead's opinion upon the writing of women. What Dean Inge says I will leave in peace. The Harley Street specialist may be allowed to rouse the echoes of Harley Street with his vociferations without raising a hair on my head. I will quote, however, Mr. Oscar Browning, because Mr. Oscar Browning was a great figure in Cambridge at one time, and used to examine the students at Girton and Newnham. Mr. Oscar Browning was wont to declare "that the impression left on his mind, after looking over any set of examination papers, was that, irrespective of the marks he might give, the best woman was intellectually the inferior of the worst man." After saying that Mr. Browning went back to his rooms—and it is this sequel that endears him and makes him a human figure of some bulk and majesty—he went back to his rooms and found a stable-boy lying on the sofa—"a mere skeleton, his cheeks were cavernous and sallow, his teeth were black, and he did not appear to have the full use of his limbs. . . . 'That's Arthur' [said Mr. Browning]. 'He's a dear boy really and most high-minded.'" The two pictures always seem to me to complete each other. And happily in this age of biography the two pictures often do complete each other, so that we are able to interpret the opinions of great men not only by what they say, but by what they do.

But though this is possible now, such opinions coming from the lips of important people must have been formidable enough even fifty years ago. Let us suppose that a father from the highest motives did not wish his daughter to leave home and become writer, painter or scholar. "See what Mr. Oscar Browning says," he would say; and there was not only Mr. Oscar Browning; there was the *Saturday Review;* there was Mr. Greg—the "essentials of a woman's being," said Mr. Greg emphatically, "are that *they are supported by, and they minister to, men*"—there was an enormous body of masculine opinion to the effect that nothing could be expected of women intellectually. Even if her father did not read out loud these opinions, any girl could read them for herself; and the reading, even in the nineteenth century, must have lowered her vitality, and told profoundly upon her work. There would always have been that assertion—you cannot do this, you are incapable of doing that— to protest against, to overcome. Probably for a novelist this germ is no longer of much effect; for there have been women novelists of merit. But for painters it must still have some sting in it; and for musicians, I imagine, is even now active and poisonous in the extreme. The woman composer stands where the actress stood in the time of Shakespeare. Nick Greene, I thought, remembering the story I had made about Shakespeare's sister, said that a woman acting put him in mind of a dog dancing. Johnson repeated the phrase two hundred years later of women preaching. And here, I said, opening a book about music, we have the very words used again in this year of grace, 1928, of women who try to write music. "Of Mlle. Germaine Tailleferre one can only repeat Dr. Johnson's dictum concerning a woman preacher, transposed into terms of music. 'Sir, a woman's composing is like a dog's walking on his hind legs. It is not done well, but you are surprised to find it done at all.'"[2] So accurately does history repeat itself.

Thus, I concluded, shutting Mr. Oscar Browning's life and pushing away the rest, it is fairly evident that even in the nineteenth century a woman was not encouraged to be an artist. On the contrary, she was snubbed, slapped, lectured and exhorted. Her mind must have been strained and her vitality lowered by the need of opposing this, of disproving that. For here again we come within range of that very interesting and obscure masculine complex which has had so much influence upon the woman's movement; that deep-seated desire, not so much that *she* shall be inferior as that *he* shall be superior, which plants him wherever one looks, not only in front of the arts, but barring the way to politics too, even when the risk to himself seems infinitesimal and the suppliant humble and devoted. Even Lady Bessborough, I remembered, with all her passion for politics, must humbly bow herself and write to Lord Granville Leveson-Gower: ". . . notwithstanding all my violence in politics and talking so much on that subject, I perfectly agree with you that no woman has any business to meddle with that or any other serious business, farther than giving her opinion (if she is ask'd)." And so she goes on to spend her enthusiasm where it meets with no obstacle whatsoever upon that immensely important subject, Lord Granville's maiden speech in the House of Commons. The spectacle is certainly a strange one, I thought. The history of men's opposition to women's emancipation is more interesting perhaps than the story of that emancipation itself. An amusing book might be made of it if some young student at Girton or Newnham would collect examples and deduce a theory—but she would need thick gloves on her hands, and bars to protect her of solid gold.

But what is amusing now, I recollected, shutting Lady Bessborough, had to be taken in desperate earnest once. Opinions that one now pastes in a book labelled cock-a-doodle-dum and keeps for reading to select audiences on summer nights once drew tears, I can assure you. Among your grandmothers and great-grandmothers there were many that wept their eyes out. Florence Nightingale shrieked aloud in her agony.[3] Moreover, it is all very well for you, who have got yourselves to college and enjoy sitting-rooms—or is it only bed-sitting-rooms?—of your own to say that genius should disregard such opinions; that genius should be above caring what is said of it. Unfortunately, it is precisely the men or women of genius who mind most what is said of them. Remember Keats. Remember the words he had cut on his tombstone. Think of Tennyson; think—but I need hardly multiply instances of the undeniable, if very unfortunate, fact that it is the nature of the artist to mind excessively what is said about him. Literature is strewn with the wreckage of men who have minded beyond reason the opinions of others.

And this susceptibility of theirs is doubly unfortunate, I thought, returning again to my original enquiry into what state of mind is most propitious for creative work, because the mind of an artist, in order to achieve the prodigious effort of freeing whole and entire the work that is in him, must be incandescent, like Shakespeare's mind, I conjectured, looking at the book which lay open at *Antony and Cleopatra*. There must be no obstacle in it, no foreign matter unconsumed.

For though we say that we know nothing about Shakespeare's state of mind, even as we say that, we are saying something about Shakespeare's state of mind. The reason perhaps why we know so little of Shakespeare—compared with Donne or Ben Jonson or Milton—is that his grudges and spites and antipathies are hidden from us. We are not held up by some "revelation" which reminds us of the writer. All desire to protest, to preach, to proclaim an injury, to pay off a score, to make the world the witness of some hardship or grievance was fired out of him and consumed. Therefore his poetry flows from him free and unimpeded. If ever a human being got his work expressed completely, it was Shakespeare. If ever a mind was incandescent, unimpeded, I thought, turning again to the bookcase, it was Shakespeare's mind.

Chapter V

I had come at last, in the course of this rambling, to the shelves which hold books by the living; by women and by men; for there are almost as many books written by women now as by men. Or if that is not yet quite true, if the male is still the voluble sex, it is certainly true that women no longer write novels solely. There are Jane Harrison's books on Greek archaeology; Vernon Lee's books on aesthetics; Gertrude Bell's books on Persia. There are books on all sorts of subjects which a generation ago no woman could have touched. There are poems and plays and criticism; there are histories and biographies, books of travel and books of scholarship and research; there are even a few philosophies and books about science and economics. And though novels predominate, novels themselves may very well have changed from association with books of a different feather. The natural simplicity, the epic age of women's writing, may have gone. Reading and criticism may have given her a wider range, a greater subtlety. The impulse towards autobiography may be spent. She may be beginning to use writing as an art, not as a method of self-expression. Among these new novels one might find an answer to several such questions.

I took down one of them at random. It stood at the very end of the shelf, was called *Life's Adventure,* or some such title, by Mary Carmichael, and was published in this very month of October. It seems to be her first book, I said to myself, but one must read it as if it were the last volume in a fairly long series, continuing all those other books that I have been glancing at—Lady Winchilsea's poems and Aphra Behn's plays and the novels of the four great novelists. For books continue each other, in spite of our habit of judging them separately. And I must also consider her—this unknown woman—as the descendant of all those other women whose circumstances I have been glancing at and see what she inherits of their characteristics and restrictions. So, with a sigh, because novels so often provide an anodyne and not an antidote, glide one into torpid slumbers instead of rousing one with a burning brand, I settled down with a notebook and a pencil to make what I could of Mary Carmichael's first novel, *Life's Adventure.*

To begin with, I ran my eye up and down the page. I am going to get the hang of her sentences first, I said, before I load my memory with blue eyes and brown and the relationship that there may be between Chloe and Roger. There will be time for that when I have decided whether she has a pen in her hand or a pickaxe. So I tried a sentence or two on my tongue. Soon it was obvious that something was not quite in order. The smooth gliding of sentence after sentence was interrupted. Something tore, something scratched; a single word here and there flashed its torch in my eyes. She was "unhanding" herself as they say in the old plays. She is like a person striking a match that will not light, I thought. But why, I asked her as if she were present, are Jane Austen's sentences not of the right shape for you? Must they all be scrapped because Emma and Mr. Woodhouse are dead? Alas, I sighed, that it should be so. For while Jane Austen breaks from melody to melody as Mozart from song to song, to read this writing was like being out at sea in an open boat. Up one went, down one sank. This terseness, this short-windedness, might mean that she was afraid of something; afraid of being called "sentimental" perhaps; or she remembers that women's writing has been called flowery and so provides a superfluity of thorns; but until I have read a scene with some care, I cannot be sure whether she is being herself or some one else. At any rate, she does not lower one's vitality, I thought, reading more carefully. But she is heaping up too many facts. She will not be able to use half of them in a book of this size. (It was about half the length of *Jane Eyre*.) However, by some means or other she succeeded in getting us all—Roger, Chloe, Olivia, Tony and Mr. Bigham—in a canoe up the river. Wait a moment, I said, leaning back in my chair, I must consider the whole thing more carefully before I go any further.

I am almost sure, I said to myself, that Mary Carmichael is playing a trick on us. For I feel as one feels on a switchback railway when the car, instead of sinking, as one has been led to expect, swerves up again. Mary is tampering with the expected sequence. First she broke the sentence; now she has broken the sequence. Very well, she has every right to do both these things if she does them not for the sake of breaking, but for the sake of creating. Which of the two it is I cannot be sure until she has faced herself with a situation. I will give her every liberty, I said, to choose what that situation shall be; she shall make it of tin cans and old kettles if she likes; but she must convince me that she believes it to be a situation; and then when she has made it she must face it. She must jump. And, determined to do my duty by her as reader if she would do her duty by me as writer, I turned the page and read . . . I am sorry to break off so abruptly. Are there no men present? Do you promise me that behind that red curtain over there the figure of Sir Chartres Biron is not concealed? We are all women, you assure me? Then I may tell you that the very next words I read were these—"Chloe liked Olivia . . ." Do not start. Do not blush. Let us admit in the privacy of our own society that these things sometimes happen. Sometimes women do like women.

"Chloe liked Olivia," I read. And then it struck me how immense a change was there. Chloe liked Olivia perhaps for the first time in literature. Cleopatra did not like Octavia. And how completely *Antony and Cleopatra* would have been altered had she done so! As it is, I thought, letting my mind, I am afraid, wander a little from *Life's Adventure,* the whole thing is simplified, conventionalised, if one dared say it, absurdly. Cleopatra's only feeling about Octavia is one of jealousy. Is she taller than I am? How does she do her hair? The play, perhaps, required no more. But how interesting it would have been if the relationship between the two women had been more complicated. All these relationships between women, I thought, rapidly recalling the splendid gallery of fictitious women, are too simple. So much has been left out, unattempted. And I tried to remember any case in the course of my reading where two women are represented as friends. There is an attempt at it in *Diana of the Crossways.* They are confidantes, of course, in Racine and the Greek tragedies. They are now and then mothers and daughters. But almost without exception they are shown in their relation to men. It was strange to think that all the great women of fiction were, until Jane Austen's day, not only seen by the other sex, but seen only in relation to the other sex. And how small a part of a woman's life is that; and how little can a man know even of that when he observes it through the black or rosy spectacles which sex puts upon his nose. Hence, perhaps, the peculiar nature of woman in fiction; the astonishing extremes of her beauty and horror; her alternations between heavenly goodness and hellish depravity—for so a lover would see her as his love rose or sank, was prosperous or unhappy. This is not so true of the nineteenth-century novelists, of course. Woman becomes much more various and complicated there. Indeed it was the desire to write about women perhaps that led men by degrees to abandon the poetic drama which, with its violence, could make so little use of them, and to devise the novel as a more fitting receptacle. Even so it remains obvious, even in the writing of Proust, that a man is terribly hampered and partial in his knowledge of women, as a woman in her knowledge of men.

Also, I continued, looking down at the page again, it is becoming evident that women, like men, have other interests besides the perennial interests of domesticity. "Chloe liked Olivia. They shared a laboratory together. . . ." I read on and discovered that these two young women were engaged in mincing liver, which is, it seems, a cure for pernicious anaemia: although one of them was married and had—I think I am right in stating—two small children. Now all that, of course, has had to be left out, and thus the splendid portrait of the fictitious woman is much too simple and much too monotonous. Suppose, for instance, that men were only represented in literature as the lovers of women, and were never the friends of men, soldiers, thinkers, dreamers; how few parts in the plays of Shakespeare could be allotted to them; how literature would suffer! We might perhaps have most of Othello; and a good deal of Antony; but no Caesar, no Brutus, no Hamlet, no Lear, no Jaques—literature would be incredibly impoverished, as indeed literature is impoverished beyond our counting by the doors that have been shut upon women. Married against their will, kept in one room, and to one occupation, how could a dramatist give a full or interesting or truthful account of them? Love was the only possible interpreter. The poet was forced to be passionate or bitter, unless indeed he chose to "hate women," which meant more often than not that he was unattractive to them.

Now if Chloe likes Olivia and they share a laboratory, which of itself will make their friendship more varied and lasting because it will be less personal; if Mary Carmichael knows how to write, and I was beginning to enjoy some quality in her style; if she has a room to herself, of which I am not quite sure; if she has five hundred a year of her own—but that remains to be proved—then I think that something of great importance has happened.

For if Chloe likes Olivia and Mary Carmichael knows how to express it she will light a torch in that vast chamber where nobody has yet been. It is all half lights and profound shadows like those serpentine caves where one goes with a candle peering up and down, not knowing where one is stepping. And I began to read the book again, and read how Chloe watched Olivia put a jar on a shelf and say how it was time to go home to her children. That is a sight that has never been since the world began, I exclaimed. And I watched too, very curiously. For I wanted to see how Mary Carmichael set to work to catch those unrecorded gestures, those unsaid or half-said words, which form themselves, no more palpably than the shadows of moths on the ceiling, when women are alone, unlit by the capricious and coloured light of the other sex. She will need to hold her breath, I said, reading on, if she is to do it; for women are so suspicious of any interest that has not some obvious motive behind it, so terribly accustomed to concealment and suppression, that they are off at the flicker of an eye turned observingly in their direction. The only way for you to do it, I thought, addressing Mary Carmichael as if she were there, would be to talk of something else, looking steadily out of the window, and thus note, not with a pencil in a notebook, but in the shortest of shorthand, in words that are hardly syllabled yet, what happens when Olivia—this organism that has been under the shadow of the rock these million years—feels the light fall on it, and sees coming her way a piece of strange food—knowledge, adventure, art. And she reaches out for it, I thought, again raising my eyes from the page, and has to devise some entirely new combination of her resources, so highly developed for other purposes, so as to absorb the new into the old without disturbing the infinitely intricate and elaborate balance of the whole.

But, alas, I had done what I had determined not to do; I had slipped unthinkingly into praise of my own sex. "Highly developed"—"infinitely intricate"—such are undeniably terms of praise, and to praise one's own sex is always suspect, often silly; moreover, in this case, how could one justify it? One could not go to the map and say Columbus discovered America and Columbus was a woman; or take an apple and remark, Newton discovered the laws of gravitation and Newton was a woman; or look into the sky and say aeroplanes are flying overhead and aeroplanes were invented by women. There is no mark on the wall to measure the precise height of women. There are no yard measures, neatly divided into the fractions of an inch, that one can lay against the qualities of a good mother or the devotion of a daughter, or the fidelity of a sister, or the capacity of a housekeeper. Few women even now have been graded at the universities; the great trials of the professions, army and navy, trade, politics, and diplomacy have hardly tested them. They remain even at this moment almost unclassified. But if I want to know all that a human being can tell me about Sir Hawley Butts, for instance, I have only to open Burke or Debrett and I shall find that he took such and such a degree; owns a hall; has an heir; was Secretary to a Board; represented Great Britain in Canada; and has received a certain number of degrees, offices, medals and other distinctions by which his merits are stamped upon him indelibly. Only Providence can know more about Sir Hawley Butts than that.

When, therefore, I say "highly developed," "infinitely intricate," of women, I am unable to verify my words either in Whitaker, Debrett or the University Calendar. In this predicament what can I do? And I looked at the bookcase again. There were the biographies: Johnson and Goethe and Carlyle and Sterne and Cowper and Shelley and Voltaire and Browning and many others. And I began thinking of all those great men who have for one reason or another admired, sought out, lived with, confided in, made love to, written of, trusted in, and shown what can only be described as some need of and dependence upon certain persons of the opposite sex. That all these relationships were absolutely Platonic I would not affirm, and Sir William Joynson Hicks would probably deny. But we should wrong these illustrious men very greatly if we insisted that they got nothing from these alliances but comfort, flattery and the pleasures of the body. What they got, it is obvious, was something that their own sex was unable to supply; and it would not be rash, perhaps, to define it further, without quoting the doubtless rhapsodical words of the poets, as some stimulus, some renewal of creative power which is in the gift only of the opposite sex to bestow. He would open the door of drawing-room or nursery, I thought, and find her among her children perhaps, or with a piece of embroidery on her knee—at any rate, the centre of some different order and system of life, and the contrast between this world and his own, which might be the law courts or the House of Commons, would at once refresh and invigorate; and there would follow, even in the simplest talk, such a natural difference of opinion that the dried ideas in him would be fertilised anew; and the sight of her creating in a different medium from his own would so quicken his creative power that insensibly his sterile mind would begin to plot again, and he would find the phrase or the scene which was lacking when he put on his hat to visit her. Every Johnson has his Thrale, and holds fast to her for some such reasons as these, and when the Thrale marries her Italian music master Johnson goes half mad with rage and disgust, not merely that he will miss his pleasant evenings at Streatham, but that the light of his life will be "as if gone out."

And without being Dr. Johnson or Goethe or Carlyle or Voltaire, one may feel, though very differently from these great men, the nature of this intricacy and the power of this highly developed creative faculty among women. One goes into the room—but the resources of the English language would be much put to the stretch, and whole flights of words would need to wing their way illegitimately into existence before a woman could say what happens when she goes into a room. The rooms differ so completely; they are calm or thunderous; open on to the sea, or, on the contrary, give on to a prison yard; are hung with washing; or alive with opals and silks; are hard as horsehair or soft as feathers—one has only to go into any room in any street for the whole of that extremely complex force of femininity to fly in one's face. How should it be otherwise? For women have sat indoors all these millions of years, so that by this time the very walls are permeated by their creative force, which has, indeed, so overcharged the capacity of bricks and mortar that it must needs harness itself to pens and brushes and business and politics. But this creative power differs greatly from the creative power of men. And one must conclude that it would be a thousand pities if it were hindered or wasted, for it was won by centuries of the most drastic discipline, and there is nothing to take its place. It would be a thousand pities if women wrote like men, or lived like men, or looked like men, for if two sexes are quite inadequate, considering the vastness and variety of the world, how should we manage with one only? Ought not education to bring out and fortify the differences rather than the similarities? For we have too much likeness as it is, and if an explorer should come back and bring word of other sexes looking through the branches of other trees at other skies, nothing would be of greater service to humanity; and we should have the immense pleasure into the bargain of watching Professor X rush for his measuring-rods to prove himself "superior."

Mary Carmichael, I thought, still hovering at a little distance above the page, will have her work cut out for her merely as an observer. I am afraid indeed that she will be tempted to become, what I think the less interesting branch of the species—the naturalist-novelist, and not the contemplative. There are so many new facts for her to observe. She will not need to limit herself any longer to the respectable houses of the upper middle classes. She will go without kindness or condescension, but in the spirit of fellowship into those small, scented rooms where sit the courtesan, the harlot and the lady with the pug dog. There they still sit in the rough and ready-made clothes that the male writer has had perforce to clap upon their shoulders. But Mary Carmichael will have out her scissors and fit them close to every hollow and angle. It will be a curious sight, when it comes, to see these women as they are, but we must wait a little, for Mary Carmichael will still be encumbered with that self-consciousness in the presence of "sin" which is the legacy of our sexual barbarity. She will still wear the shoddy old fetters of class on her feet.

However, the majority of women are neither harlots nor courtesans; nor do they sit clasping pug dogs to dusty velvet all through the summer afternoon. But what do they do then? and there came to my mind's eye one of those long streets somewhere south of the river whose infinite rows are innumerably populated. With the eye of the imagination I saw a very ancient lady crossing the street on the arm of a middle-aged woman, her daughter, perhaps, both so respectably booted and furred that their dressing in the afternoon must be a ritual, and the clothes themselves put away in cupboards with camphor, year after year, throughout the summer months. They cross the road when the lamps are being lit (for the dusk is their favourite hour), as they must have done year after year. The elder is close on eighty; but if one asked her what her life has meant to her, she would say that she remembered the streets lit for the battle of Balaclava, or had heard the guns fire in Hyde Park for the birth of King Edward the Seventh. And if one asked her, longing to pin down the moment with date and season, but what were you doing on the fifth of April 1868, or the second of November 1875, she would look vague and say that she could remember nothing. For all the dinners are cooked; the plates and cups washed; the children set to school and gone out into the world. Nothing remains of it all. All has vanished. No biography or history has a word to say about it. And the novels, without meaning to, inevitably lie.

All these infinitely obscure lives remain to be recorded, I said, addressing Mary Carmichael as if she were present; and went on in thought through the streets of London feeling in imagination the pressure of dumbness, the accumulation of unrecorded life, whether from the women at the street corners with their arms akimbo, and the rings embedded in their fat swollen fingers, talking with a gesticulation like the swing of Shakespeare's words; or from the violet-sellers and match-sellers and old crones stationed under doorways; or from drifting girls whose faces, like waves in sun and cloud, signal the coming of men and women and the flickering lights of shop windows. All that you will have to explore, I said to Mary Carmichael, holding your torch firm in your hand. Above all, you must illumine your own soul with its profundities and its shallows, and its vanities and its generosities, and say what your beauty means to you or your plainness, and what is your relation to the everchanging and turning world of gloves and shoes and stuffs swaying up and down among the faint scents that come through chemists' bottles down arcades of dress material over a floor of pseudo-marble. For in imagination I had gone into a shop; it was laid with black and white paving; it was hung, astonishingly beautifully, with coloured ribbons. Mary Carmichael might well have a look at that in passing, I thought, for it is a sight that would lend itself to the pen as fittingly as any snowy peak or rocky gorge in the Andes. And there is the girl behind the counter too—I would as soon have her true history as the hundred and fiftieth life of Napoleon or seventieth study of Keats and his use of Miltonic inversion which old Professor Z and his like are now inditing. And then I went on very warily, on the very tips of my toes (so cowardly am I, so afraid of the lash that was once almost laid on my own shoulders), to murmur that she should also learn to laugh, without bitterness, at the vanities—say rather at the peculiarities, for it is a less offensive word—of the other sex. For there is a spot the size of a shilling at the back of the head which one can never see for oneself. It is one of the good offices that sex can discharge for sex—to describe that spot the size of a shilling at the back of the head. Think how much women have profited by the comments of Juvenal; by the criticism of Strindberg. Think with what humanity and brilliancy men, from the earliest ages, have pointed out to women that dark place at the back of the head! And if Mary were very brave and very honest, she would go behind the other sex and tell us what she found there. A true picture of man as a whole can never be painted until a woman has described that spot the size of a shilling. Mr. Woodhouse and Mr. Casaubon are spots of that size and nature. Not of course that any one in their senses would counsel her to hold up to scorn and ridicule of set purpose—literature shows the futility of what is written in that spirit. Be truthful, one would say, and the result is bound to be amazingly interesting. Comedy is bound to be enriched. New facts are bound to be discovered.

However, it was high time to lower my eyes to the page again. It would be better, instead of speculating what Mary Carmichael might write and should write, to see what in fact Mary Carmichael did write. So I began to read again. I remembered that I had certain grievances against her. She had broken up Jane Austen's sentence, and thus given me no chance of pluming myself upon my impeccable taste, my fastidious ear. For it was useless to say, "Yes, yes, this is very nice; but Jane Austen wrote much better than you do," when I had to admit that there was no point of likeness between them. Then she had gone further and broken the sequence—the expected order. Perhaps she had done this unconsciously, merely giving things their natural order, as a woman would, if she wrote like a woman. But the effect was somehow baffling; one could not see a wave heaping itself, a crisis coming round the next corner. Therefore I could not plume myself either upon the depths of my feelings and my profound knowledge of the human heart. For whenever I was about to feel the usual things in the usual places, about love, about death, the annoying creature twitched me away, as if the important point were just a little further on. And thus she made it impossible for me to roll out my sonorous phrases about "elemental feelings," the "common stuff of humanity," "depths of the human heart," and all those other phrases which support us in our belief that, however clever we may be on top, we are very serious, very profound and humane underneath. She made me feel, on the contrary, that instead of being serious and profound and humane, one might be—and the thought was far less seductive—merely lazy minded and conventional into the bargain.

But I read on, and noted certain other facts. She was no "genius"—that was evident. She had nothing like the love of Nature, the fiery imagination, the wild poetry, the brilliant wit, the brooding wisdom of her great predecessors, Lady Winchilsea, Charlotte Brontë, Emily Brontë, Jane Austen and George Eliot; she could not write with the melody and the dignity of Dorothy Osborne—indeed she was no more than a clever girl whose books will no doubt be pulped by the publishers in ten years' time. But, nevertheless, she had certain advantages which women of far greater gift lacked even half a century ago. Men were no longer to her "the opposing faction"; she need not waste her time railing against them; she need not climb on the roof and ruin her peace of mind longing for travel, experience and a knowledge of the world and character that were denied her. Fear and hatred were almost gone, or traces of them showed only in a slight exaggeration of the joy of freedom, a tendency to the caustic and satirical, rather than to the romantic, in her treatment of the other sex. Then there could be no doubt that as a novelist she enjoyed some natural advantages of a high order. She had a sensibility that was very wide, eager and free. It responded to an almost imperceptible touch on it. It feasted like a plant newly stood in the air on every sight and sound that came its way. It ranged, too, very subtly and curiously, among almost unknown or unrecorded things; it lighted on small things and showed that perhaps they were not small after all. It brought buried things to light and made one wonder what need there had been to bury them. Awkward though she was and without the unconscious bearing of long descent which makes the least turn of the pen of a Thackeray or a Lamb delightful to the ear, she had—I began to think— mastered the first great lesson; she wrote as a woman, but as a woman who has forgotten that she is a woman, so that her pages were full of that curious sexual quality which comes only when sex is unconscious of itself.

All this was to the good. But no abundance of sensation or fineness of perception would avail unless she could build up out of the fleeting and the personal the lasting edifice which remains unthrown. I had said that I would wait until she faced herself with "a situation." And I meant by that until she proved by summoning, beckoning and getting together that she was not a skimmer of surfaces merely, but had looked beneath into the depths. Now is the time, she would say to herself at a certain moment, when without doing anything violent I can show the meaning of all this. And she would begin— how mistakable that quickening is!—beckoning and summoning, and there would rise up in memory, half forgotten, perhaps quite trivial things in other chapters dropped by the way. And she would make their presence felt while some one sewed or smoked a pipe as naturally as possible, and one would feel, as she went on writing, as if one had gone to the top of the world and seen it laid out, very majestically, beneath.

At any rate, she was making the attempt. And as I watched her lengthening out for the test, I saw, but hoped that she did not see, the bishops and the deans, the doctors and the professors, the patriarchs and the pedagogues all at her shouting warning and advice. You can't do this and you shan't do that! Fellows and scholars only allowed on the grass! Ladies not admitted without a letter of introduction! Aspiring and graceful female novelists this way! So they kept at her like the crowd at a fence on the race-course, and it was her trial to take her fence without looking to right or left. If you stop to curse you are lost, I said to her; equally, if you stop to laugh. Hesitate or fumble and you are done for. Think only of the jump, I implored her, as if I had put the whole of my money on her back; and she went over it like a bird. But there was a fence beyond that and a fence beyond that. Whether she had the staying power I was doubtful, for the clapping and the crying were fraying to the nerves. But she did her best. Considering that Mary Carmichael was no genius, but an unknown girl writing her first novel in a bed-sitting-room, without enough of those desirable things, time, money and idleness, she did not do so badly, I thought.

Give her another hundred years, I concluded, reading the last chapter— people's noses and bare shoulders showed naked against a starry sky, for some one had twitched the curtain in the drawing-room—give her a room of her own and five hundred a year, let her speak her mind and leave out half that she now puts in, and she will write a better book one of these days. She will be a poet, I said, putting *Life's Adventure,* by Mary Carmichael, at the end of the shelf, in another hundred years' time.

NOTES

1. "It remains a strange and almost inexplicable fact that in Athena's city, where women were kept in almost Oriental suppression as odalisques or drudges, the stage should yet have produced figures like Clytemnestra and Cassandra, Atossa and Antigone, Phèdre and Medea, and all the other heroines who dominate play after play of the 'misogynist' Euripides. But the paradox of this world where in real life a respectable woman could hardly show her face alone in the street, and yet on the stage woman equals or surpasses man, has never been satisfactorily explained. In modern

tragedy the same predominance exists. At all events, a very cursory survey of Shakespeare's work (similarly with Webster, though not with Marlowe or Jonson) suffices to reveal how this dominance, this initiative of women, persists from Rosalind to Lady Macbeth. So too in Racine; six of his tragedies bear their heroines' names; and what male characters of his shall we set against Hermione and Andromaque, Bérénice and Roxane, Phèdre and Athalie? So again with Ibsen; what men shall we match with Solveig and Nora, Hedda and Hilda Wangel and Rebecca West?"—F. L. Lucas, *Tragedy*, pp. 114–15.

    2. *A Survey of Contemporary Music*, Cecil Gray, p. 246.

    3. See *Cassandra*, by Florence Nightingale, printed in *The Cause*, by R. Strachey.

MODERN FICTION

In making any survey, even the freest and loosest, of modern fiction it is difficult not to take it for granted that the modern practice of the art is somehow an improvement upon the old. With their simple tools and primitive materials, it might be said, Fielding did well and Jane Austen even better, but compare their opportunities with ours! Their masterpieces certainly have a strange air of simplicity. And yet the analogy between literature and the process, to choose an example, of making motor cars scarcely holds good beyond the first glance. It is doubtful whether in the course of the centuries, though we have learnt much about making machines, we have learnt anything about making literature. We do not come to write better; all that we can be said to do is to keep moving, now a little in this direction, now in that, but with a circular tendency should the whole course of the track be viewed from a sufficiently lofty pinnacle. It need scarcely be said that we make no claim to stand, even momentarily, upon that vantage ground. On the flat, in the crowd, half blind with dust, we look back with envy to those happier warriors, whose battle is won and whose achievements wear so serene an air of accomplishment that we can scarcely refrain from whispering that the fight was not so fierce for them as for us. It is for the historian of literature to decide; for him to say if we are now beginning or ending or standing in the middle of a great period of prose fiction, for down in the plain little is visible. We only know that certain gratitudes and hostilities inspire us; that certain paths seem to lead to fertile land, others to the dust and the desert; and of this perhaps it may be worth while to attempt some account.

Our quarrel, then, is not with the classics, and if we speak of quarrelling with Mr. Wells, Mr. Bennett, and Mr. Galsworthy it is partly that by the mere fact of their existence in the flesh their work has a living, breathing, every-day imperfection which bids us take what liberties with it we choose. But it is also true that, while we thank them for a thousand gifts, we reserve our unconditional gratitude for Mr. Hardy, for Mr. Conrad, and in a much lesser degree for the Mr. Hudson, of *The Purple Land, Green Mansions,* and *Far Away and Long Ago.* Mr. Wells, Mr. Bennett, and Mr. Galsworthy have excited so many hopes and disappointed them so persistently that our gratitude largely takes the form of thanking them for having shown us what they might have done but have not done; what we certainly could not do, but as certainly, perhaps, do not wish to do. No single phrase will sum up the charge or grievance which we have to bring against a mass of work so large in its volume and embodying so many qualities, both admirable and the reverse. If we tried to formulate our meaning in one word we should say that these three writers are materialists. It is because they are concerned not with the spirit but with the body that they have disappointed us, and left us with the feeling that the sooner English fiction turns its back upon them, as politely as may be, and marches, if only into the desert, the better for its soul. Naturally, no single word reaches the centre of three separate targets. In the case of Mr. Wells it falls notably wide of the mark. And yet even with him it indicates to our thinking the fatal alloy in his genius, the great clod of clay that has got itself mixed up with the purity of his inspiration. But Mr. Bennett is perhaps the worst culprit of the three, inasmuch as he is by far the best workman. He can make a book so well constructed and solid in its craftsmanship that it is difficult for the most exacting of critics to see through what chink or crevice decay can creep in. There is not so much as a draught between the frames of the windows, or a crack in the boards. And yet—if life should refuse to live there? That is a risk which the creator of *The Old Wives' Tale,* George Cannon, Edwin Clayhanger, and hosts of other figures, may well claim to have surmounted. His characters live abundantly, even unexpectedly, but it remains to ask how do they live, and what do they live for? More and more they seem to us, deserting even the well-built villa in the Five Towns, to spend their time in some softly padded first-class railway carriage, pressing bells and buttons innumerable; and the destiny to which they travel so luxuriously becomes more and more unquestionably an eternity of bliss spent in the very best hotel in Brighton. It can scarcely be said of Mr. Wells that he is a materialist in the sense that he takes too much delight in the solidity of his fabric. His mind is too generous in its sympathies to allow him to spend much time in making things shipshape and substantial. He is a materialist from sheer goodness of heart, taking upon his shoulders the work that ought to have been discharged by Government officials, and in the plethora of his ideas and facts scarcely having leisure to realise, or forgetting to think important, the crudity and coarseness of his human beings. Yet what more damaging criticism can there be both of his earth and of his Heaven than that they are to be inhabited here and hereafter by his Joans and his Peters? Does not the inferiority of their natures tarnish whatever institutions and ideals may be provided for them by the generosity of their creator? Nor, profoundly though we respect the integrity and humanity of Mr. Galsworthy, shall we find what we seek in his pages.

If we fasten, then, one label on all these books, on which is one word materialists, we mean by it that they write of unimportant things; that they spend immense skill and immense industry making the trivial and the transitory appear the true and the enduring.

We have to admit that we are exacting, and, further, that we find it difficult to justify our discontent by explaining what it is that we exact. We frame our question differently at different times. But it reappears most persistently as we drop the finished novel on the crest of a sigh—Is it worth while? What is the point of it all? Can it be that owing to one of those little deviations which the human spirit seems to make from time to time Mr. Bennett has come down with his magnificent apparatus for catching life just an inch or two on the wrong side? Life escapes; and perhaps without life nothing else is worth while. It is a confession of vagueness to have to make use of such a figure as this, but we scarcely better the matter by speaking, as critics are prone to do, of reality. Admitting the vagueness which afflicts all criticism of novels, let us hazard the opinion that for us at this moment the form of fiction most in vogue more often misses than secures the thing we seek. Whether we call it life or spirit, truth or reality, this, the essential thing, has moved off, or on, and refuses to be contained any longer in such ill-fitting vestments as we provide. Nevertheless, we go on perseveringly, conscientiously, constructing our two and thirty chapters after a design which more and more ceases to resemble the vision in our minds. So much of the enormous labour of proving the solidity, the likeness to life, of the story is not merely labour thrown away but labour misplaced to the extent of obscuring and blotting out the light of the conception. The writer seems constrained, not by his own free will but by some powerful and unscrupulous tyrant who has him in thrall to provide a plot, to provide comedy, tragedy, love, interest, and an air of probability embalming the whole so impeccable that if all his figures were to come to life they would find themselves dressed down to the last button of their coats in the fashion of the hour. The tyrant is obeyed; the novel is done to a turn. But sometimes, more and more often as time goes by, we suspect a momentary doubt, a spasm of rebellion, as the pages fill themselves in the customary way. Is life like this? Must novels be like this?

Look within and life, it seems, is very far from being "like this". Examine for a moment an ordinary mind on an ordinary day. The mind receives a myriad impressions—trivial, fantastic, evanescent, or engraved with the sharpness of steel. From all sides they come, an incessant shower of innumerable atoms; and as they fall, as they shape themselves into the life of Monday or Tuesday, the accent falls differently from of old; the moment of importance came not here but there; so that if a writer were a free man and not a slave, if he could write what he chose, not what he must, if he could base his work upon his own feeling and not upon convention, there would be no plot, no comedy, no tragedy, no love interest or catastrophe in the accepted style, and perhaps not a single button sewn on as the Bond Street tailors would have it. Life is not a series of gig lamps symmetrically arranged; but a luminous halo, a semi-transparent envelope surrounding us from the beginning of consciousness to the end. Is it not the task of the novelist to convey this varying, this unknown and uncircumscribed spirit, whatever aberration or complexity it may display, with as little mixture of the alien and external as possible? We are not pleading merely for courage and sincerity; we are suggesting that the proper stuff of fiction is a little other than custom would have us believe it.

It is, at any rate, in some such fashion as this that we seek to define the quality which distinguishes the work of several young writers, among whom Mr. James Joyce is the most notable, from that of their predecessors. They attempt to come closer to life, and to preserve more sincerely and exactly what interests and moves them, even if to do so they must discard most of the conventions which are commonly observed by the novelist. Let us record the atoms as they fall upon the mind in the order in which they fall, let us trace the pattern, however disconnected and incoherent in appearance, which each sight or incident scores upon the consciousness. Let us not take it for granted that life exists more fully in what is commonly thought big than in what is commonly thought small. Any one who has read *The Portrait of the Artist as a Young Man* or, what promises to be a far more interesting work, *Ulysses*, now appearing in the *Little Review*, will have hazarded some theory of this nature as to Mr. Joyce's intention. On our part, with such a fragment before us, it is hazarded rather than affirmed; but whatever the intention of the whole there can be no question but that it is of the utmost sincerity and that the result, difficult or unpleasant as we may judge it, is undeniably important. In contrast with those whom we have called materialists Mr. Joyce is spiritual; he is concerned at all costs to reveal the flickerings of that innermost flame which flashes its messages through the brain, and in order to preserve it he disregards with complete courage whatever seems to him adventitious, whether it be probability, or coherence or any other of these signposts which for generations have served to support the imagination of a reader when called upon to imagine what he can neither touch nor see. The scene in the cemetery, for instance, with its brilliancy, its sordidity, its incoherence, its sudden lightning flashes of significance, does undoubtedly come so close to the quick of the mind that, on a first reading at any rate, it is difficult not to acclaim a masterpiece. If we want life itself here, surely we have it. Indeed, we find ourselves fumbling rather awkwardly if we try to say what else we wish, and for what reason a work of such originality yet fails to compare, for we must take high examples, with *Youth* or *The Mayor of Casterbridge*. It fails because of the comparative poverty of the writer's mind, we might say simply and have done with it. But it is possible to press a little further and wonder whether we may not refer our sense of being in a bright yet narrow room, confined and shut in, rather than enlarged and set free, to some limitation imposed by the method as well as by the mind. Is it the method that inhibits the creative power? Is it due to the method that we feel neither jovial nor magnanimous, but centred in a self which, in spite of its tremor of susceptibility, never embraces or creates what is outside itself and beyond? Does the emphasis laid, perhaps didacti-cally, upon indecency, contribute to the effect of something angular and isolated? Or is it merely that in any effort of such originality it is much easier, for contemporaries especially, to feel what it lacks than to name what it gives? In any case it is a mistake to stand outside examining "methods". Any method is right, every method is right, that expresses what we wish to express, if we are writers; that brings us closer to the novelist's intention if we are readers. This method has the merit of bringing us closer to what we were prepared to call life itself; did not the reading of *Ulysses* suggest how much of life is excluded or ignored, and did it not come with a shock to open *Tristram Shandy* or even *Pendennis* and be by them convinced that there are not only other aspects of life, but more important ones into the bargain.

However this may be, the problem before the novelist at present, as we suppose it to have been in the past, is to contrive means of being free to set down what he chooses. He has to have the courage to say that what interests him is no longer "this" but "that": out of "that" alone must he construct his work. For the moderns "that", the point of interest, lies very likely in the dark places of psychology. At once, therefore, the accent falls a little differently; the emphasis is upon something hitherto ignored; at once a different outline of form becomes necessary, difficult for us to grasp, incomprehensible to our predecessors. No one but a modern, perhaps no one but a Russian, would have felt the interest of the situation which Tchekov has made into the short story which he calls "Gusev". Some Russian soldiers lie ill on board a ship which is taking them back to Russia. We are given a few scraps of their talk and some of their thoughts; then one of them dies and is carried away; the talk goes on among the others for a time, until Gusev himself dies, and looking "like a carrot or a radish" is thrown overboard. The emphasis is laid upon such unexpected places that at first it seems as if there were no emphasis at all; and then, as the eyes accustom themselves to twilight and discern the shapes of things in a room we see how complete the story is, how profound, and how truly in obedience to his vision Tchekov has chosen this, that, and the other, and placed them together to compose something new. But it is impossible to say "this is comic", or "that is tragic", nor are we certain, since short stories, we have been taught, should be brief and conclusive, whether this, which is vague and inconclusive, should be called a short story at all.

The most elementary remarks upon modern English fiction can hardly avoid some mention of the Russian influence, and if the Russians are mentioned one runs the risk of feeling that to write of any fiction save theirs is waste of time. If we want understanding of the soul and heart where else shall we find it of comparable profundity? If we are sick of our own materialism the least considerable of their novelists has by right of birth a natural reverence for the human spirit. "Learn to make yourself akin to people. . . . But let this sympathy be not with the mind—for it is easy with the mind—but with the heart, with love towards them." In every great Russian writer we seem to discern the features of a saint, if sympathy for the sufferings of others, love towards them, endeavour to reach some goal worthy of the most exacting demands of the spirit constitute saintliness. It is the saint in them which confounds us with a feeling of our own irreligious triviality, and turns so many of our famous novels to tinsel and trickery. The conclusions of the Russian mind, thus comprehensive and compassionate, are inevitably, perhaps, of the utmost sadness. More accurately indeed we might speak of the inconclusiveness of the Russian mind. It is the sense that there is no answer, that if honestly examined life presents question after question which must be left to sound on and on after the story is over in hopeless interrogation that fills us with a deep, and finally it may be with a resentful, despair. They are right perhaps; unquestionably they see further than we do and without our gross impediments of vision. But perhaps we see something that escapes them, or why should this voice of protest mix itself with our gloom? The voice of protest is the voice of another and an ancient civilisation which seems to have bred in us the instinct to enjoy and fight rather than to suffer and understand. English fiction from Sterne to Meredith bears witness to our natural delight in humour and comedy, in the beauty of earth, in the activities of the intellect, and in the splendour of the body. But any deductions that we may draw from the comparison of two fictions so immeasurably far apart are futile save indeed as they flood us with a view of the infinite possibilities of the art and remind us that there is no limit to the horizon, and that nothing—no "method", no experiment, even of the wildest—is forbidden, but only falsity and pretence. "The proper stuff of fiction" does not exist; everything is the proper stuff of fiction, every feeling, every thought; every quality of brain and spirit is drawn upon; no perception comes amiss. And if we can imagine the art of fiction come alive and standing in our midst, she would undoubtedly bid us break her and bully her, as well as honour and love her, for so her youth is renewed and her sovereignty assured.

T. E. Hulme

1883–1917

Thomas Ernest Hulme was born on September 16, 1883, at Gratton Hall in the village of Endon, Staffordshire. Hulme attended the village church school and the high school at Newcastle-under-Lyme, where his mathematical skill, early apprehension of differential calculus, and activity in the debating society redeemed his lack of interest in sports. Admitted to Cambridge on a mathematics scholarship in 1902, Hulme distinguished himself at St. John's College, but was expelled in 1904 for reasons not entirely known. At the urging of his family he entered University College, London, where he studied science, but escaped regularly to Cambridge for philosophy lectures. In 1906 he boarded a cargo boat to Montreal in order to avoid his father's plan that he join the civil service. Working as a farmhand and lumberjack in Canada, he moved about the vast country-side, stopping for church services and leaning toward Anglo-Catholicism. On returning to Europe, Hulme studied French and German briefly in Belgium, then moved back to London in 1908, where he joined the avant-garde and established himself as a leading intellectual.

Writing regularly for A. R. Orage's *The New Age,* in which he was to publish nearly all his essays, Hulme participated in the Fabian Arts Group, which had splintered from the Webbs' Fabian Movement and included George Bernard Shaw and H. G. Wells. *The New Age* rallied contributors such as Hilaire Belloc, Arnold Bennett, Havelock Ellis, G. K. Chesterton, and, later, Richard Aldington, Katherine Mansfield, and Ezra Pound. From his association with the group Hulme co-founded the Poets' Club in 1908. Here he began developing his theories of classicism versus romanticism, presented in his most famous essay, "Romanticism and Classicism." A deep dissatisfaction with English poetry, however, led Hulme to retreat from this club and form his friendship with F. S. Flint, who introduced Hulme to contemporary French poetry and the symbolist movement.

As representative of the Aristotelian Society, under the chairmanship of the philosopher G. E. Moore, Hulme in April 1911 attended the Philosophical Conference at Bologna, where he heard a paper delivered by Henri Bergson, whose irrationalism was a major influence on Hulme; he later translated Bergson's *Introduction to Metaphysics* (1912). Hulme's impressions of the Byzantine mosaics at Ravenna and the Giotto frescoes at Assisi converted him to a theory of geometric art. His aesthetic theory was formulated mainly in the 1914 *New Age* essays on "Modern Art" and "Contemporary Drawings." At the regular Friday evening salon at the home of Ethel Kibblewhite on Frith Street (attended by Ford Madox Ford, Douglas Ainslie, Wyndham Lewis, and others), Hulme met Jacob Epstein and Henri Gaudier-Brzeska, the sculptors he would champion as great geometric modernists.

Ezra Pound took up Hulme's ideas and dissatisfaction with English poetry, becoming an evangelist of Imagism. Hulme tolerated Pound's Imagism, as the two theorists shared a commitment to classical ideals, the roots of civilization, and anti-romanticism. They also shared a skepticism of democracy; Pound was drawn to Italian-style fascism, but Hulme's political tendencies were milder. However, Hulme's translations of Bergson's *Introduction to Metaphysics* and Georges Sorel's *Reflections on Violence* (1916) link him politically to Mussolini and fascism. Sorel advocates violent action in order to restructure society; similarly, Hulme believed in action for action's sake. His interest in the classical spirit with its implication of heroic ethic appears in his 1912 series of articles, "A Tory Philosophy," written under the pseudonym Thomas Gratton.

Enthusiastically enlisting in World War I, Hulme identified himself as a militarist, countering, specifically, Bertrand Russell's pacifism and arguing for war and victory over a dangerous Germany. Unlike the poet Rupert Brooke, Hulme saw war as a necessary misfortune. As "North Staffs," Hulme wrote a sequence of "War Notes" and a series of articles known as "Humanism and the Religious Attitude," in which he explains the fallacies of humanism as applied to politics by means of the doctrine of original sin. He was killed by shellfire near Niewport on September 28, 1917.

Hulme's essays were collected posthumously by Herbert Read as *Speculations* (1924) and *Notes on Language and Style* (1929). Samuel Hynes later edited his *Further Speculations* (1955). In "Romanticism and Classicism" (from *Speculations*), Hulme advocates an ideal arrived at through fancy, not imagination, and predicts a classical revival. He connects the doctrine of original sin, or man's basic limitations, with formalism and the need for discipline. In "A Lecture on Modern Poetry" (from *Further Speculations*) Hulme postulates that the anti-classical tendencies of modern poetry are a result of the radical skepticism and lack of "absolutes" typical of his generation.

Hulme's influence on Pound, Yeats, and Eliot is significant; Eliot credited this influence in *The Idea of a Christian Society* (1939). Seven of Hulme's poems were published as the appendix to Pound's *Ripostes* (1912) under the joking title, "The Complete Poetical Works of T. E. Hulme." Several others appeared posthumously.

ROMANTICISM AND CLASSICISM

I want to maintain that after a hundred years of romanticism, we are in for a classical revival, and that the particular weapon of this new classical spirit, when it works in verse, will be fancy. And in this I imply the superiority of fancy—not superior generally or absolutely, for that would be obvious nonsense, but superior in the sense that we use the word good in empirical ethics—good for something, superior for something. I shall have to prove then two things, first that a classical revival is coming, and, secondly, for its particular purposes, fancy will be superior to imagination.

So banal have the terms Imagination and Fancy become that we imagine they must have always been in the language. Their history as two differing terms in the vocabulary of criticism is comparatively short. Originally, of course, they both mean the same thing; they first began to be differentiated by the German writers on æsthetics in the eighteenth century.

I know that in using the words "classic" and "romantic" I am doing a dangerous thing. They represent five or six different kinds of antitheses, and while I may be using them in one sense you may be interpreting them in another. In this present connection I am using them in a perfectly precise and limited sense. I ought really to have coined a couple of new words, but I prefer to use the ones I have used, as I then conform to the practice of the group of polemical writers who make most use of them at the present day, and have almost succeeded in making them political catchwords. I mean Maurras, Lasserre and all the group connected with *L'Action Française*.

At the present time this is the particular group with which the distinction is most vital. Because it has become a party symbol. If you asked a man of a certain set whether he preferred the classics or the romantics, you could deduce from that what his politics were.

The best way of gliding into a proper definition of my terms would be to start with a set of people who are prepared to fight about it—for in them you will have no vagueness. (Other people take the infamous attitude of the person with catholic tastes who says he likes both.)

About a year ago, a man whose name I think was Fauchois gave a lecture at the Odéon on Racine, in the course of which he made some disparaging remarks about his dullness, lack of invention and the rest of it. This caused an immediate riot: fights took place all over the house; several people were arrested and imprisoned, and the rest of the series of lectures took place with hundreds of gendarmes and detectives scattered all over the place. These people interrupted because the classical ideal is a living thing to them and Racine is the great classic. That is what I call a real vital interest in literature. They regard romanticism as an awful disease from which France had just recovered.

The thing is complicated in their case by the fact that it was romanticism that made the revolution. They hate the revolution, so they hate romanticism.

I make no apology for dragging in politics here; romanticism both in England and France is associated with certain political views, and it is in taking a concrete example of the working out of a principle in action that you can get its best definition.

What was the positive principle behind all the other principles of '89? I am talking here of the revolution in as far as it was an idea; I leave out material causes—they only produce the forces. The barriers which could easily have resisted or guided these forces have been previously rotted away by ideas. This always seems to be the case in successful changes; the privileged class is beaten only when it has lost faith in itself, when it has itself been penetrated with the ideas which are working against it.

It was not the rights of man—that was a good solid practical war-cry. The thing which created enthusiasm, which made the revolution practically a new religion, was something more positive than that. People of all classes, people who stood to lose by it, were in a positive ferment about the idea of liberty. There must have been some idea which enabled them to think that something positive could come out of so essentially negative a thing. There was, and here I get my definition of romanticism. They had been taught by Rousseau that man was by nature good, that it was only bad laws and customs that had suppressed him. Remove all these and the infinite possibilities of man would have a chance. This is what made them think that something positive could come out of disorder, this is what created the religious enthusiasm. Here is the root of all romanticism: that man, the individual, is an infinite reservoir of possibilities; and if you can rearrange society by the destruction of oppressive order then these possibilities will have a chance and you will get Progress.

One can define the classical quite clearly as the exact opposite to this. Man is an extraordinarily fixed and limited animal whose nature is absolutely constant. It is only by tradition and organisation that anything decent can be got out of him.

This view was a little shaken at the time of Darwin. You remember his particular hypothesis, that new species came into existence by the cumulative effect of small variations—this seems to admit the possibility of future progress. But at the present day the contrary hypothesis makes headway in the shape of De Vries's mutation theory, that each new species comes into existence, not gradually by the accumulation of small steps, but suddenly in a jump, a kind of spurt, and that once in existence, it remains absolutely fixed. This enables me to keep the classical view with an appearance of scientific backing.

Put shortly, these are the two views, then. One, that man is intrinsically good, spoilt by circumstance; and the other that he is intrinsically limited, but disciplined by order and tradition to something fairly decent. To the one party man's nature is like a well, to the other like a bucket. The view which regards man as a well, a reservoir full of possibilities, I call the romantic; the one which regards him as a very finite and fixed creature, I call the classical.

One may note here that the Church has always taken the classical view since the defeat of the Pelagian heresy and the adoption of the sane classical dogma of original sin.

It would be a mistake to identify the classical view with that of materialism. On the contrary it is absolutely identical with the normal religious attitude. I should put it in this way: That part of the fixed nature of man is the belief in the Deity. This should be as fixed and true for every man as belief in the existence of matter and in the objective world. It is parallel to appetite, the instinct of sex, and all the other fixed qualities. Now at certain times, by the use of either force or rhetoric, these instincts have been suppressed—in Florence under Savonarola, in Geneva under Calvin, and here under the Roundheads. The inevitable result of such a process is that the repressed instinct bursts out in some abnormal direction. So with religion. By the perverted rhetoric of Rationalism, your natural instincts are suppressed and you are converted into an agnostic. Just as in the case of the other instincts, Nature has her revenge. The instincts that find their right and proper outlet in religion must come out in some other way. You don't believe in a God, so you begin to believe that man is a god. You don't believe in Heaven, so you begin to believe in a heaven on earth. In other words, you get romanticism. The concepts that are right and proper in their own sphere are spread over, and so mess up, falsify and blur the clear outlines of human experience. It is like pouring a pot of treacle over the dinner table. Romanticism then, and this is the best definition I can give of it, is spilt religion.

I must now shirk the difficulty of saying exactly what I mean by romantic and classical in verse. I can only say that it means the result of these two attitudes towards the cosmos, towards man, in so far as it gets reflected in verse. The romantic, because he thinks man infinite, must always be talking about the infinite; and as there is always the bitter contrast between what you think you ought to be able to do and what man actually can, it always tends, in its later stages at any rate, to be gloomy. I really can't go any further than to say it is the reflection of these two temperaments, and point out examples of the different spirits. On the one hand I would take such diverse people as Horace, most of the Elizabethans and the writers of the Augustan age, and on the other side Lamartine, Hugo, parts of Keats, Coleridge, Byron, Shelley and Swinburne.

I know quite well that when people think of classical and romantic in verse, the contrast at once comes into their mind between, say, Racine and Shakespeare. I don't mean this; the dividing line that I intend is here misplaced a little from the true middle. That Racine is on the extreme classical side I agree, but if you call Shakespeare romantic, you are using a different definition to the one I give. You are thinking of the difference between classic and romantic as being merely one between restraint and exuberance. I should say with Nietzsche that there are two kinds of classicism, the static and the dynamic. Shakespeare is the classic of motion.

What I mean by classical in verse, then, is this. That even in the most imaginative flights there is always a holding back, a reservation. The classical poet never forgets this finiteness, this limit of man. He remembers always that he is mixed up with earth. He may jump, but he always returns back; he never flies away into the circumambient gas.

You might say if you wished that the whole of the romantic attitude seems to crystallise in verse round metaphors of flight. Hugo is always flying, flying over abysses, flying up into the eternal gases. The word infinite in every other line.

In the classical attitude you never seem to swing right along to the infinite nothing. If you say an extravagant thing which does exceed the limits inside which you know man to be fastened, yet there is always conveyed in some way at the end an impression of yourself standing outside it, and not quite believing it, or consciously putting it forward as a flourish. You never go blindly into an atmosphere more than the truth, an atmosphere too rarefied for man to breathe for long. You are always faithful to the conception of a limit. It is a question of pitch; in romantic verse you move at a certain pitch of rhetoric which you know, man being what he is, to be a little high-falutin. The kind of thing you get in Hugo or Swinburne. In the coming classical reaction that will feel just wrong. For an example of the opposite thing, a verse written in the proper classical spirit, I can take the song from *Cymbeline* beginning with "Fear no more the heat of the sun." I am just using this as a parable. I don't quite mean what I say here. Take the last two lines:

> Golden lads and girls all must,
> Like chimney sweepers come to dust.

Now, no romantic would have ever written that. Indeed, so ingrained is romanticism, so objectionable is this to it, that people have asserted that these were not part of the original song.

Apart from the pun, the thing that I think quite classical is the word lad. Your modern romantic could never write that. He would have to write golden youth, and take up the thing at least a couple of notes in pitch.

I want now to give the reasons which make me think that we are nearing the end of the romantic movement.

The first lies in the nature of any convention or tradition in art. A particular convention or attitude in art has a strict analogy to the phenomena of organic life. It grows old and decays. It has a definite period of life and must die. All the possible tunes get played on it and then it is exhausted; moreover its best period is its youngest. Take the case of the extraordinary efflorescence of verse in the Elizabethan period. All kinds of reasons have been given for this—the discovery of the new world and all the rest of it. There is a much simpler one. A new medium had been given them to play with—namely, blank verse. It was new and so it was easy to play new tunes on it.

The same law holds in other arts. All the masters of painting are born into the world at a time when the particular tradition from which they start is imperfect. The Florentine tradition was just short of full ripeness when Raphael came to Florence, the Bellinesque was still young when Titian was born in Venice. Landscape was still a toy or an appanage of figure-painting when Turner and Constable arose to reveal its independent power. When Turner and Constable had done with landscape they left little or nothing for their successors to do on the same lines. Each field of artistic activity is exhausted by the first great artist who gathers a full harvest from it.

This period of exhaustion seems to me to have been reached in romanticism. We shall not get any new efflorescence of verse until we get a new technique, a new convention, to turn ourselves loose in.

Objection might be taken to this. It might be said that a century as an organic unity doesn't exist, that I am being deluded by a wrong metaphor, that I am treating a collection of literary people as if they were an organism or state department. Whatever we may be in other things, an objector might urge, in literature in as far as we are anything at all—in as far as we are worth considering—we are individuals, we are persons, and as distinct persons we cannot be subordinated to any general treatment. At any period at any time, an individual poet may be a classic or a romantic just as he feels like it. You at any particular moment may think that you can stand outside a movement. You may think that as an individual you observe both the classic and the romantic spirit and decide from a purely detached point of view that one is superior to the other.

The answer to this is that no one, in a matter of judgment of beauty, can take a detached standpoint in this way. Just as physically you are not born that abstract entity, man, but the child of particular parents, so you are in matters of literary judgment. Your opinion is almost entirely of the literary history that came just before you, and you are governed by that whatever you may think. Take Spinoza's example of a stone falling to the ground. If it had a conscious mind it would, he said, think it was going to the ground because it wanted to. So you with your pretended free judgment about what is and what is not beautiful. The amount of freedom in man is much exaggerated. That we are free on certain rare occasions, both my religion and the views I get from metaphysics convince me. But many acts which we habitually label free are in reality automatic. It is quite possible for a man to write a book almost automatically. I have read several such products. Some observations were recorded more than twenty years ago by Robertson on reflex speech, and he found that in certain cases of dementia, where the people were quite unconscious so far as the exercise of reasoning went, that very intelligent answers were given to a succession of questions on politics and such matters. The meaning of these questions could not possibly have been understood. Language here acted after the manner of a reflex. So that certain extremely complex mechanisms, subtle enough to imitate beauty, can work by themselves—I certainly think that this is the case with judgments about beauty.

I can put the same thing in slightly different form. Here is a question of a conflict of two attitudes, as it might be of two techniques. The critic, while he has to admit that changes from one to the other occur, persists in regarding them as mere variations to a certain fixed normal, just as a pendulum might swing. I admit the analogy of the pendulum as far as movement, but I deny the further consequence of the analogy, the existence of the point of rest, the normal point.

When I say that I dislike the romantics, I dissociate two things: the part of them in which they resemble all the great poets, and the part in which they differ and which gives them their character as romantics. It is this minor element which constitutes the particular note of a century, and which, while it excites contemporaries, annoys the next generation. It was precisely that quality in Pope which pleased his friends, which we detest. Now, anyone just before the romantics who felt that, could have predicted that a change was coming. It seems to me that we stand just in the same position now. I think that there is an increasing proportion of people who simply can't stand Swinburne.

When I say that there will be another classical revival I don't necessarily anticipate a return to Pope. I say merely that now is the time for such a revival. Given people of the necessary capacity, it may be a vital thing; without them we may get a formalism something like Pope. When it does come we may not even recognise it as classical. Although it will be classical it will be different because it has passed through a romantic period. To take a parallel example: I remember being very surprised, after seeing the Post Impressionists, to find in Maurice Denis's account of the matter that they consider themselves classical in the sense that they were trying to impose the same order on the mere flux of new material provided by the impressionist movement, that existed in the more limited materials of the painting before.

There is something now to be cleared away before I get on with my argument, which is that while romanticism is dead in reality, yet the critical attitude appropriate to it still continues to exist. To make this a little clearer: For every kind of verse, there is a corresponding receptive attitude. In a romantic period we demand from verse certain qualities. In a classical period we demand others. At the present time I should say that this receptive attitude has outlasted the thing from which it was formed. But while the romantic tradition has run dry, yet the critical attitude of mind, which demands romantic qualities from verse, still survives. So that if good classical verse were to be written to-morrow very few people would be able to stand it.

I object even to the best of the romantics. I object still more to the receptive attitude. I object to the sloppiness which doesn't consider that a poem is a poem unless it is moaning or whining about something or other. I always think in this connection of the last line of a poem of John Webster's which ends with a request I cordially endorse:

> End your moan and come away.

The thing has got so bad now that a poem which is all dry and hard, a properly classical poem, would not be considered poetry at all. How many people now can lay their hands on their hearts and say they like either Horace or Pope? They feel a kind of chill when they read them.

The dry hardness which you get in the classics is absolutely repugnant to them. Poetry that isn't damp isn't poetry at all. They cannot see that accurate description is a legitimate object of verse. Verse to them always means a bringing in of some of the emotions that are grouped round the word infinite.

The essence of poetry to most people is that it must lead them to a beyond of some kind. Verse strictly confined to the earthly and the definite (Keats is full of it) might seem to them to be excellent writing, excellent craftsmanship, but not poetry. So much has romanticism debauched us, that, without some form of vagueness, we deny the highest.

In the classic it is always the light of ordinary day, never the light that never was on land or sea. It is always perfectly human and never exaggerated: man is always man and never a god.

But the awful result of romanticism is that, accustomed to this strange light, you can never live without it. Its effect on you is that of a drug.

There is a general tendency to think that verse means little else than the expression of unsatisfied emotion. People say: "But how can you have verse without sentiment?" You see what it is: the prospect alarms them. A classical revival to them would mean the prospect of an arid desert and the death of poetry as they understand it, and could only come to fill the gap caused by that death. Exactly why this dry classical spirit should have a positive and legitimate necessity to express itself in poetry is utterly inconceivable to them. What this positive need is, I shall show later. It follows from the fact that there is another quality, not the emotion produced, which is at the root of excellence in verse. Before I get to this I am concerned with a negative thing, a theoretical point, a prejudice that stands in the way and is really at the bottom of this reluctance to understand classical verse.

It is an objection which ultimately I believe comes from a bad metaphysic of art. You are unable to admit the existence of beauty without the infinite being in some way or another dragged in.

I may quote for purposes of argument, as a typical example of this kind of attitude made vocal, the famous chapters in Ruskin's *Modern Painters,* Vol. II, on the imagination. I must say here, parenthetically, that I use this word without prejudice to the other discussion with which I shall end the paper. I only use the word here because it is Ruskin's word. All that I am concerned with just now is the attitude behind it, which I take to be the romantic.

> Imagination cannot but be serious; she sees too far, too darkly, too solemnly, too earnestly, ever to smile. There is something in the heart of everything, if we can reach it, that we shall not be inclined to laugh at. . . . Those who have so pierced and seen the melancholy deeps of things, are filled with intense passion and gentleness of sympathy.
>
> (Part III, Chap. III, § 9.)

> There is in every word set down by the imaginative mind an awful undercurrent of meaning, and evidence and shadow upon it of the deep places out of which it has come. It is often obscure, often half-told; for he who wrote it, in his clear seeing of the things beneath, may have been impatient of detailed interpretation; for if we choose to

dwell upon it and trace it, it will lead us always securely back to that metropolis of the soul's dominion from which we may follow out all the ways and tracks to its farthest coasts.

(Part III, Chap. III, § 5.)

Really in all these matters the act of judgment is an instinct, an absolutely unstateable thing akin to the art of the tea taster. But you must talk, and the only language you can use in this matter is that of analogy. I have no material clay to mould to the given shape; the only thing which one has for the purpose, and which acts as a substitute for it, a kind of mental clay, are certain metaphors modified into theories of æsthetic and rhetoric. A combination of these, while it cannot state the essentially unstateable intuition, can yet give you a sufficient analogy to enable you to see what it was and to recognise it on condition that you yourself have been in a similar state. Now these phrases of Ruskin's convey quite clearly to me his taste in the matter.

I see quite clearly that he thinks the best verse must be serious. That is a natural attitude for a man in the romantic period. But he is not content with saying that he prefers this kind of verse. He wants to deduce his opinion like his master, Coleridge, from some fixed principle which can be found by metaphysic.

Here is the last refuge of this romantic attitude. It proves itself to be not an attitude but a deduction from a fixed principle of the cosmos.

One of the main reasons for the existence of philosophy is not that it enables you to find truth (it can never do that) but that it does provide you a refuge for definitions. The usual idea of the thing is that it provides you with a fixed basis from which you can deduce the things you want in æsthetics. The process is the exact contrary. You start in the confusion of the fighting line, you retire from that just a little to the rear to recover, to get your weapons right. Quite plainly, without metaphor this—it provides you with an elaborate and precise language in which you really can explain definitely what you mean, but what you want to say is decided by other things. The ultimate reality is the hurly-burly, the struggle; the metaphysic is an adjunct to clear-headedness in it.

To get back to Ruskin and his objection to all that is not serious. It seems to me that involved in this is a bad metaphysical æsthetic. You have the metaphysic which is defining beauty or the nature of art always drags in the infinite. Particularly in Germany, the land where theories of æsthetics were first created, the romantic æsthetes collated all beauty to an impression of the infinite involved in the identification of our being in absolute spirit. In the least element of beauty we have a total intuition of the whole world. Every artist is a kind of pantheist.

Now it is quite obvious to anyone who holds this kind of theory that any poetry which confines itself to the finite can never be of the highest kind. It seems a contradiction in terms to them. And as in metaphysics you get the last refuge of a prejudice, so it is now necessary for me to refute this.

Here follows a tedious piece of dialectic, but it is necessary for my purpose.

I must avoid two pitfalls in discussing the idea of beauty. On the one hand there is the old classical view which is supposed to define it as lying in conformity to certain standard fixed forms; and on the other hand there is the romantic view which drags in the infinite. I have got to find a metaphysic between these two which will enable me to hold consistently that a neo-classic verse of the type I have indicated involves no contradiction in terms. It is essential to prove that beauty may be in small, dry things.

The great aim is accurate, precise and definite description. The first thing is to recognise how extraordinarily difficult this is. It is no mere matter of carefulness; you have to use language, and language is by its very nature a communal thing; that is, it expresses never the exact thing but a compromise— that which is common to you, me and everybody. But each man sees a little differently, and to get out clearly and exactly what he does see, he must have a terrific struggle with language, whether it be with words or the technique of other arts. Language has its own special nature, its own conventions and communal ideas. It is only by a concentrated effort of the mind that you can hold it fixed to your own purpose. I always think that the fundamental process at the back of all the arts might be represented by the following metaphor. You know what I call architect's curves—flat pieces of wood with all different kinds of curvature. By a suitable selection from these you can draw approximately any curve you like. The artist I take to be the man who simply can't bear the idea of that 'approximately.' He will get the exact curve of what he sees whether it be an object or an idea in the mind. I shall here have to change my metaphor a little to get the process in his mind. Suppose that instead of your curved pieces of wood you have a springy piece of steel in the same types of curvature as the wood. Now the state of tension or concentration of mind, if he is doing anything really good in this struggle against the ingrained habit of the technique, may be represented by a man employing all his fingers to bend the steel out of its own curve and into the exact curve which you want. Something different to what it would assume naturally.

There are then two things to distinguish, first the particular faculty of mind to see things as they really are, and apart from the conventional ways in which you have been trained to see them. This is itself rare enough in all consciousness. Second, the concentrated state of mind, the grip over oneself which is necessary in the actual expression of what one sees. To prevent one falling into the conventional curves of ingrained technique, to hold on through infinite detail and trouble to the exact curve you want. Wherever you get this sincerity, you get the fundamental quality of good art without dragging in infinite or serious.

I can now get at that positive fundamental quality of verse which constitutes excellence, which has nothing to do with infinity, with mystery or with emotions.

This is the point I aim at, then, in my argument. I prophesy that a period of dry, hard, classical verse is coming. I have met the preliminary objection founded on the bad romantic æsthetic that in such verse, from which the infinite is excluded, you cannot have the essence of poetry at all.

After attempting to sketch out what this positive quality is, I can get on to the end of my paper in this way: That where you get this quality exhibited in the realm of the emotions you get imagination, and that where you get this quality exhibited in the contemplation of finite things you get fancy.

In prose as in algebra concrete things are embodied in signs or counters which are moved about according to rules, without being visualised at all in the process. There are in prose certain type situations and arrangements of words, which move as automatically into certain other arrangements as do functions in algebra. One only changes the X's and the Y's back into physical things at the end of the process. Poetry, in one aspect at any rate, may be considered as an effort to avoid this characteristic of prose. It is not a counter language, but a visual concrete one. It is a compromise for a language of intuition which would hand over sensations bodily. It always endeavours to arrest you, and to make you continuously see a physical thing, to prevent you gliding through an abstract process. It chooses fresh epithets and fresh metaphors, not so much because they are new, and we are tired of the old, but because the old cease to convey a physical thing and become abstract counters. A poet says a ship 'coursed the seas' to get a physical image, instead of the counter word 'sailed.' Visual meanings can only be transferred by the new bowl of metaphor; prose is an old pot that lets them leak out. Images in verse are not mere decoration, but the very essence of an intuitive language. Verse is a pedestrian taking you over the ground, prose—a train which delivers you at a destination.

I can now get on to a discussion of two words often used in this connection, "fresh" and "unexpected." You praise a thing for being "fresh." I understand what you mean, but the word besides conveying the truth conveys a secondary something which is certainly false. When you say a poem or drawing is fresh, and so good, the impression is somehow conveyed that the essential element of goodness is freshness, that it is good because it is fresh. Now this is certainly wrong, there is nothing particularly desirable about freshness *per se*. Works of art aren't eggs. Rather the contrary. It is simply an unfortunate necessity due to the nature of language and technique that the only way the element which does constitute goodness, the only way in which its presence can be detected externally, is by freshness. Freshness convinces you, you feel at once that the artist was in an actual physical state. You feel that for a minute. Real communication is so very rare, for plain speech is unconvincing. It is in this rare fact of communication that you get the root of æsthetic pleasure.

I shall maintain that wherever you get an extraordinary interest in a thing, a great zest in its contemplation which carries on the contemplator to accurate description in the sense of the word accurate I have just analysed, there you have sufficient justification for poetry. It must be an intense zest which heightens a thing out of the level of prose. I am using contemplation here just in the same way that Plato used it, only applied to a different subject; it is a detached interest. "The object of æsthetic contemplation is something framed apart by itself and regarded without memory or expectation, simply as being itself, as end not means, as individual not universal."

To take a concrete example. I am taking an extreme case. If you are walking behind a woman in the street, you notice the curious way in which the skirt rebounds from her heels. If that peculiar kind of motion becomes of such interest to you that you will search about until you can get the exact epithet which hits it off, there you have a properly æsthetic emotion. But it is the zest with which you look at the thing which decides you to make the effort. In this sense the feeling that was in Herrick's mind when he wrote "the tempestuous petticoat" was exactly the same as that which in bigger and vaguer matters makes the best romantic verse. It doesn't matter an atom that the emotion produced is not of dignified vagueness, but on the contrary amusing; the point is that exactly the same activity is at work as in the highest verse. That is the avoidance of conventional language in order to get the exact curve of the thing.

I have still to show that in the verse which is to come, fancy will be the necessary weapon of the classical school. The positive quality I have talked about can be manifested in ballad verse by extreme directness and simplicity, such as you get in "On Fair Kirkconnel Lea." But the particular verse we are going to get will be cheerful, dry and sophisticated, and here the necessary weapon of the positive quality must be fancy.

Subject doesn't matter; the quality in it is the same as you get in the more romantic people.

It isn't the scale or kind of emotion produced that decides, but this one fact: Is there any real zest in it? Did the poet have an actually realised visual object before him in which he delighted? It doesn't matter if it were a lady's shoe or the starry heavens.

Fancy is not mere decoration added on to plain speech. Plain speech is essentially inaccurate. It is only by new metaphors, that is, by fancy, that it can be made precise.

When the analogy has not enough connection with the thing described to be quite parallel with it, where it overlays the thing it described and there is a certain excess, there you have the play of fancy—that I grant is inferior to imagination.

But where the analogy is every bit of it necessary for accurate description in the sense of the word accurate I have previously described, and your only objection to this kind of fancy is that it is not serious in the effect it produces, then I think the objection to be entirely invalid. If it is sincere in the accurate sense, when the whole of the analogy is necessary to get out the exact curve of the feeling or thing you want to express—there you seem to me to have the highest verse, even though the subject be trivial and the emotions of the infinite far away.

It is very difficult to use any terminology at all for this kind of thing. For whatever word you use is at once sentimentalised. Take Coleridge's word "vital." It is used loosely by all kinds of people who talk about art, to mean something vaguely and mysteriously significant. In fact, vital and mechanical is to them exactly the same antithesis as between good and bad.

Nothing of the kind; Coleridge uses it in a perfectly definite and what I call dry sense. It is just this: A mechanical complexity is the sum of its parts. Put them side by side and you get the whole. Now vital or organic is merely a convenient metaphor for a complexity of a different kind, that in which the parts cannot be said to be elements as each one is modified by the other's presence, and each one to a certain extent is the whole. The leg of a chair by itself is still a leg. My leg by itself wouldn't be.

Now the characteristic of the intellect is that it can only represent complexities of the mechanical kind. It can only make diagrams, and diagrams are essentially things whose parts are separate one from another. The intellect always analyses—when there is a synthesis it is baffled. That is why the artist's work seems mysterious. The intellect can't represent it. This is a necessary consequence of the particular nature of the intellect and the purposes for which it is formed. It doesn't mean that your synthesis is ineffable, simply that it can't be definitely stated.

Now this is all worked out in Bergson, the central feature of his whole philosophy. It is all based on the clear conception of these vital complexities which he calls "intensive" as opposed to the other kind which he calls "extensive," and the recognition of the fact that the intellect can only deal with the extensive multiplicity. To deal with the intensive you must use intuition.

Now, as I said before, Ruskin was perfectly aware of all this, but he had no such metaphysical background which would enable him to state definitely what he meant. The result is that he has to flounder about in a series of metaphors. A powerfully imaginative mind seizes and combines at the same instant all the important ideas of its poem or picture, and while it works with one of them, it is at the same instant working with and modifying all in their relation to it and never losing sight of their bearings on each other—as the motion of a snake's body goes through all parts at once and its volition acts at the same instant in coils which go contrary ways.

A romantic movement must have an end of the very nature of the thing. It may be deplored, but it can't be helped—wonder must cease to be wonder.

I guard myself here from all the consequences of the analogy, but it expresses at any rate the inevitableness of the process. A literature of wonder must have an end as inevitably as a strange land loses its strangeness when one lives in it. Think of the lost ecstasy of the Elizabethans. "Oh my America, my new found land," think of what it meant to them and of what it means to us. Wonder can only be the attitude of a man passing from one stage to another, it can never be a permanently fixed thing.

A LECTURE ON MODERN POETRY

I want to begin by a statement of the attitude I take towards verse. I do that in order to anticipate criticism. I shall speak of verse from a certain rather low but quite definite level, and I think that criticism ought to be confined to that level. The point of view is that verse is simply and solely the means of expression. I will give you an example of the position exactly opposite to the one I take up. A reviewer writing in *The Saturday Review* last week spoke of poetry as the means by which the soul soared into higher regions, and as a means of expression by which it became merged into a higher kind of reality. Well, that is the kind of statement that I utterly detest. I want to speak of verse in a plain way as I would of pigs: that is the only honest way. The President told us last week that poetry was akin to religion. It is nothing of the sort. It is a means of expression just as prose is, and if you can't justify it from that point of view it's not worth preserving.

I always suspect the word soul when it is brought into discussion. It reminds me of the way that the medieval scientists spoke of God. When entirely ignorant of the cause of anything, they said God did it. If I use the word soul, or speak of higher realities, in the course of my speech, you will know that at that precise point I didn't know of any real reason and was trying to bluff you. There is a tremendous amount of hocus-pocus about most discussions of poetry. Critics attempting to explain technique make mysterious passes and mumble of the infinite and the human heart, for all the world as though they were selling a patent medicine in the market-place.

There are two ways in which one can consider this. The first as a difficulty to be conquered, the second as a tool for use. In the first case, we look upon poets as we look upon pianists, and speak of them as masters of verse. The other way is to consider it merely as a tool which we want to use ourselves for definite purposes. One daily paper compared us to the Mermaid Club, but we are not. We are a number of modern people, and verse must be justified as a means of expression for us. I have not a catholic taste but a violently personal and prejudiced one. I have no reverence for tradition. I came to the subject of verse from the inside rather than from the outside. There were certain impressions which I wanted to fix. I read verse to find models, but I could not find any that seemed exactly suitable to express that kind of impression, except perhaps a few jerky rhythms of Henley, until I came to read the French *vers-libre* which seemed to exactly fit the case.

So that I don't want any literary criticism, that would be talking on another level. I don't want to be killed with a bludgeon, and references to Dante, Milton and the rest of them.

The principle on which I rely in this paper is that there is an intimate connection between the verse form and the state of poetry at any period. All kinds of reasons are given by the academic critics for the efflorescence of verse at any period. But the true one is very seldom given. It is the invention or introduction of a new verse form. To the artist the introduction of a new art form is, as Moore says, like a new dress to a girl; he wants to see himself in it. It is a new toy. You will find the burst of poetic activity at the time of Elizabeth put down to the discovery of America. The discovery of America had about as much effect on the Courtier poets at that time as the discovery of a new asteroid would have had on the poetic activity of Swinburne. The real reason was, I take it, that the first opportunity was given for the exercise of verse composition by the introduction of all kinds of new matter and new forms from Italy and France.

It must be admitted that verse forms, like manners, and like individuals, develop and die. They evolve from their initial freedom to decay and finally to virtuosity. They disappear before the new man, burdened with the thought more complex and more difficult to express by the old name. After being too much used, their primitive effect is lost. All possible tunes have been played on the instrument. What possibility is there in that for the new men, or what attraction? It would be different if poetry, like acting and dancing, were one of the arts of which no record can be kept, and which must be repeated for each generation. The actor has not to feel the competition of the dead as the poet has. Personally I am of course in favour of the complete destruction of all verse more than twenty years old. But that happy event will not, I am afraid, take place until Plato's desire has been realized and a minor poet has become dictator. Meanwhile it is necessary to realize that as poetry is immortal, it is differentiated from those arts which must be repeated. I want to call attention to this point—it is only those arts whose expression is repeated every generation that have an immutable technique. Those arts like poetry, whose matter is immortal, must find a new technique each generation. Each age must have its own special form of expression, and any period that deliberately goes out of it is an age of insincerity.

The latter stages in the decay of an art form are very interesting and worth study because they are peculiarly applicable to the state of poetry at the present day. They resemble the latter stages in the decay of religion when the spirit has gone and there is a meaningless reverence for formalities and ritual. The carcass is dead, and all the flies are upon it. Imitative poetry springs up like weeds, and women whimper and whine of you and I alas, and roses, roses all the way. It becomes the expression of sentimentality rather than of virile thought.

The writers who would be able to use the old instrument with the old masters refuse to do so, for they find it inadequate. They know the entirely empirical nature of the old rules and refuse to be cramped by them.

It is at these periods that a new art form is created; after the decay of Elizabethan poetic drama came the heroic couplet, after the decay of the couplet came the new lyrical poetry that has lasted till now. It is interesting to notice that these changes do not come by a kind of natural progress of which the artist himself is unconscious. The new forms are deliberately introduced by people who detest the old ones. Modern lyrical verse was introduced by Wordsworth with no pretence of it being a natural progress; he announced it in good set terms as a new method.

The particular example which has most connection with what I have to say is that of the Parnassian school about 1885: itself beginning as a reaction from romanticism, it has come rapidly to decay; its main principle of an absolute perfection of rhyme and form was in harmony with the natural school of the time. It was a logical form of verse, as distinct from a symbolical one. There were prominent names in it, Monde, Prudhomme, etc., but they were not very fertile; they did not produce anything of great importance; they confined themselves to repeating the same sonnet time after time, their pupils were lost in a state of sterile feebleness.

I wish you to notice that this was not the kind of unfortunate accident which has happened by chance to a number of poets. This check to the Parnassian school marked the death of a particular form of French poetry which coincided with the birth and marvellous fertility of a new form. With the definite arrival of this new form of verse in 1880 came the appearance of a band of poets perhaps unequalled at any one time in the history of French poetry.

The new technique was first definitely stated by Kahn. It consisted in a denial of a regular number of syllables as the basis of versification. The length of the line is long and short, oscillating with the images used by the poet; it follows the contours of his thoughts and is free rather than regular; to use a rough analogy, it is clothes made to order, rather than ready-made clothes. This is a very bald statement of it, and I am not concerned here so much with French poetry as with English. The kind of verse I advocate is not the same as *vers-libre,* I merely use the French as an example of the extraordinary effect that an emancipation of verse can have on poetic activity.

The ancients were perfectly aware of the fluidity of the world and of its impermanence; there was the Greek theory that the whole world was a flux. But while they recognized it, they feared it and endeavoured to evade it, to construct things of permanence which would stand fast in this universal flux which frightened them. They had the disease, the passion, for immortality. They wished to construct things which should be proud boasts that they, men, were immortal. We see it in a thousand different forms. Materially in the pyramids, spiritually in the dogmas of religion and in the hypostatized ideas of Plato. Living in a dynamic world they wished to create a static fixity where their souls might rest.

This I conceive to be the explanation of many of the old ideas on poetry. They wish to embody in a few lines a perfection of thought. Of the thousand and one ways in which a thought might roughly be conveyed to a hearer there was one way which was the perfect way, which was destined to embody that thought to all eternity, hence the fixity of the form of poem and the elaborate rules of regular metre. It was to be an immortal thing and the infinite pains taken to fit a thought into a fixed and artificial form are necessary and understandable. Even the Greek name ποίημα seems to indicate the thing created once and for all, they believed in absolute duty as they believed in absolute truth. Hence they put many things into verse which we now do not desire to, such as history and philosophy. As the French philosopher Guyau put it, the great poems of ancient times resembled pyramids built for eternity where people loved to inscribe their history in symbolic characters. They believed they could realize an adjustment of idea and words that nothing could destroy.

Now the whole trend of the modern spirit is away from that; philosophers no longer believe in absolute truth. We no longer believe in perfection, either in verse or in thought, we frankly acknowledge the relative. We shall no longer strive to attain the absolutely perfect form in poetry. Instead of these minute perfections of phrase and words, the tendency will be rather towards the production of a general effect; this of course takes away the predominance of metre and a regular number of syllables as the element of perfection in words. We are no longer concerned that stanzas shall be shaped and polished like gems, but rather that some vague mood shall be communicated. In all the arts, we seek for the maximum of individual and personal expression, rather than for the attainment of any absolute beauty.

The criticism is sure to be made, what is this new spirit, which finds itself unable to express itself in the old metre? Are the things that a poet wishes to say now in any way different to the things that former poets say? I believe that they are. The old poetry dealt essentially with big things, the expression of epic subjects leads naturally to the anatomical matter and regular verse. Action can best be expressed in regular verse, e.g., the Ballad.

But the modern is the exact opposite of this, it no longer deals with heroic action, it has become definitely and finally introspective and deals with expression and communication of momentary phases in the poet's mind. It was well put by Mr. G. K. Chesterton in this way—that where the old dealt with the Siege of Troy, the new attempts to express the emotions of a boy fishing. The opinion you often hear expressed, that perhaps a new poet will arrive who will synthesize the whole modern movement into a great epic, shows an entire misconception of the tendency of modern verse. There is an analogous change in painting, where the old endeavoured to tell a story, the modern attempts to fix an impression. We still perceive the mystery of things, but we perceive it in entirely a different way—no longer directly in the form of action, but as an impression, for example Whistler's pictures. We can't escape from the spirit of our times. What has found expression in painting as Impressionism will soon find expression in poetry as free verse. The vision of a London street at midnight, with its long rows of light, has produced several attempts at reproduction in verse, and yet the war produced nothing worth mentioning, for Mr. Watson is a political orator rather than a poet. Speaking of personal matters, the first time I ever felt the necessity or inevitableness of verse, was in the desire to reproduce the peculiar quality of feeling which is induced by the flat spaces and wide horizons of the virgin prairie of western Canada.

You see that this is essentially different to the lyrical impulse which has attained completion, and I think once and forever, in Tennyson, Shelley and

Keats. To put this modern conception of the poetic spirit, this tentative and half-shy manner of looking at things, into regular metre is like putting a child into armour.

Say the poet is moved by a certain landscape, he selects from that certain images which, put into juxtaposition in separate lines, serve to suggest and to evoke the state he feels. To this piling-up and juxtaposition of distinct images in different lines, one can find a fanciful analogy in music. A great revolution in music when, for the melody that is one-dimensional music, was substituted harmony which moves in two. Two visual images form what one may call a visual chord. They unite to suggest an image which is different to both.

Starting then from this standpoint of extreme modernism, what are the principal features of verse at the present time? It is this: that it is read and not chanted. We may set aside all theories that we read verse internally as mere verbal quibbles. We have thus two distinct arts. The one intended to be chanted, and the other intended to be read in the study. I wish this to be remembered in the criticisms that are made on me. I am not speaking of the whole of poetry, but of this distinct new art which is gradually separating itself from the older one and becoming independent.

I quite admit that poetry intended to be recited must be written in regular metre, but I contend that this method of recording impressions by visual images in distinct lines does not require the old metric system.

The older art was originally a religious incantation: it was made to express oracles and maxims in an impressive manner, and rhyme and metre were used as aids to the memory. But why, for this new poetry, should we keep a mechanism which is only suited to the old?

The effect of rhythm, like that of music, is to produce a kind of hypnotic state, during which suggestions of grief or ecstasy are easily and powerfully effective, just as when we are drunk all jokes seem funny. This is for the art of chanting, but the procedure of the new visual art is just the contrary. It depends for its effect not on a kind of half sleep produced, but on arresting the attention, so much so that the succession of visual images should exhaust one.

Regular metre to this impressionist poetry is cramping, jangling, meaningless, and out of place. Into the delicate pattern of images and colour it introduces the heavy, crude pattern of rhetorical verse. It destroys the effect just as a barrel organ does, when it intrudes into the subtle interwoven harmonies of the modern symphony. It is a delicate and difficult art, that of evoking an image, of fitting the rhythm to the idea, and one is tempted to fall back to the comforting and easy arms of the old, regular metre, which takes away all the trouble for us.

The criticism is sure to be made that when you have abolished the regular syllabled line as the unit of poetry, you have turned it into prose. Of course this is perfectly true of a great quantity of modern verse. In fact, one of the great blessings of the abolition of regular metre would be that it would at once expose all this sham poetry.

Poetry as an abstract thing is a very different matter, and has its own life, quite apart from metre as a convention.

To test the question of whether it is possible to have poetry written without a regular metre, I propose to pick out one great difference between the two. I don't profess to give an infallible test that would enable anyone to at once say: "this is, or is not, true poetry," but it will be sufficient for the purposes of this paper. It is this: that there are, roughly speaking, two methods of communication, a direct, and a conventional language. The direct language is poetry, it is direct because it deals in images. The indirect language is prose, because it uses images that have died and become figures of speech.

The difference between the two is, roughly, this: that while one arrests your mind all the time with a picture, the other allows the mind to run along with the least possible effort to a conclusion.

Prose is due to a faculty of the mind something resembling reflex action in the body. If I had to go through a complicated mental process each time I laced my boots, it would waste mental energy; instead of that, the mechanism of the body is so arranged that one can do it almost without thinking. It is an economy of effort. The same process takes place with the images used in prose. For example, when I say that the hill was clad with trees, it merely conveys the fact to me that it was covered. But the first time that expression was used by a poet, and to him it was an image recalling to him the distinct visual analogy of a man clad in clothes; but the image has died. One might say that images are born in poetry. They are used in prose, and finally die a long, lingering death in journalists' English. Now this process is very rapid, so that the poet must continually be creating new images, and his sincerity may be measured by the number of his images.

Sometimes in reading a poem, one is conscious of gaps where the inspiration failed him, and he only used metre of rhetoric. What happened was this: the image failed him, and he fell back on a dead image, that is prose, but kept an effect by using metre. That is my objection to metre, that it enables people to write verse with no poetic inspiration, and whose mind is not stored with new images.

As an example of this, I will take the poem which now has the largest circulation. Though consisting of only four verses it is six feet long. It is posted outside the Pavilion Music-hall. We instinctively shudder at these clichés or tags of speech. The inner explanation is this: it is not that they are old, but that being old they have become dead, and so evoked no image. The man who wrote them not being a poet, did not see anything definitely himself, but imitated other poets' images.

This new verse resembles sculpture rather than music; it appeals to the eye rather than to the ear. It has to mould images, a kind of spiritual clay, into definite shapes. This material, the ὕλη of Aristotle, is image and not sound. It builds up a plastic image which it hands over to the reader, whereas the old art endeavoured to influence him physically by the hypnotic effect of rhythm.

One might sum it all up in this way: a shell is a very suitable covering for the egg at a certain period of its career, but very unsuitable at a later stage. This seems to me to represent fairly well the state of verse at the present time. While the shell remains the same, the inside character is entirely changed. It is not addled, as a pessimist might say, but has become alive, it has changed from the ancient art of chanting to the modern impressionist, but the mechanism of verse has remained the same. It can't go on doing so. I will conclude, ladies and gentlemen, by saying, the shell must be broken.

José Ortega y Gasset
1883–1955

José Ortega y Gasset was born in Madrid on May 9, 1883. He entered a
Jesuit college in 1891, and graduated with honors in 1897. In May 1898
he took university examinations at Salamanca, where he first encountered
his "eternal rival" Miguel de Unamuno as a member of the examination
board. Ortega passed his examinations and went on for six years of study
at the Universidad Central in Madrid. After a winter in Leipzig, another
year in Madrid, and three more years of philosophical study in Germany
under the influence of liberal neo-Kantians, Ortega returned to Spain
steeped in the tradition of German critical reason. In 1910 he married Rosa
Spottorno y Topete, and received an appointment to the Chair of Metaphysics of the Faculty of Philosophy and Letters of the Universidad
Central. He occupied this chair and a central position in Spanish intellectual life for twenty-five years, until 1936 when the Civil War forced him
into self-imposed exile.

Ortega first gained the attention of the Spanish people with a famous
speech announcing the death of the "old politics" of the Restoration. He
attacked the Jesuits as insincere and incompetent, the traditional republicans as too dogmatic, the old liberals as dead weight, and even contemporary socialism and anarchism as ill-conceived and irresponsible. Exhorting
Spain to join the European tradition of liberal rationalism, he called for the
establishment of secular schools and a new, open-ended experiment in
"justice and democracy" led by a select minority of intellectuals and
statesmen capable of upholding high standards for themselves and their
countrymen. In 1914 he published *Meditations on Quixote,* in which he
adumbrated an existentialist philosophy and clearly broke with his Catholic
origins by asserting that God was only a philosophical dimension, one
among many possible metaphorical ways of looking at reality.

When the political ferment which he had helped to stir up came to a
crisis in 1930, Ortega again took on a position of liberal intellectual
leadership. He wrote a highly influential essay entitled "El Error Berenger"
calling for the restoration of the Constitution after a period of martial law.
When General Berenger resigned and elections were announced, Ortega
signed a manifesto calling upon all Spanish intellectuals to come together
to defend the Republic and "to propagate what seemed best for the
common welfare." The elections gave the republicans an overwhelming
majority, and Ortega was elected representative of the Province de Leon.
His group of intellectuals decided not to participate directly in political

affairs, concentrating instead on laying an intellectual foundation for a new democratic social order.

The Republic became oppressive, however, and Ortega, despairing of the politicization of his thinking, left the political arena to return to the solitude of his books. In 1936 he accepted an invitation from Johan Huizinga to lecture in the Netherlands. He returned to Spain only to leave shortly thereafter when the Civil War began in 1936. After ten years of self-imposed exile he returned to Madrid in 1945, but the Franco regime did not permit him to resume his chair. He died on October 18, 1955.

Ortega's mature thought was set forth in four works published between 1923 and his exile in 1936: *The Modern Theme* (1923), *The Revolt of the Masses* (1929–30), *Man and Crisis* (1933), and "History as a System" (1935). In *The Revolt of the Masses,* now his most widely read work, Ortega distinguishes two basic types of men—the mass man and the noble man. By far the numerical majority, the mass man is characterized by passitivity and self-satisfaction, a contentment with things as they are. The noble men, on the other hand, are men of effort—"the ones who are active and not merely reactive, for whom life is a perpetual striving, an incessant course of training." For Ortega this distinction is emphatically not a matter of class or heritage, but rather of demonstrated character. As did Nietzsche, Ortega saw the "revolt of the masses" as a profoundly threatening rise of a vast class of people with little character except for the crude force of their numbers and the mutual reinforcement of mediocrity.

In *The Dehumanization of Art* (1925) Ortega attempts to give an historical account of the evolution of modern art. The title seems to suggest a polemic against the abstraction and obscurity of modern art. On the contrary, Ortega argues that the strangeness of the work of Debussy, Cézanne, and Mallarmé is consistent with art's perpetual task of defying a previous generation's interpretation of reality. Modern art's means of liberation are extreme because the reality it contends with is extreme—the accumulated weight of a long romantic tradition as well as the leveling pressure of the old bourgeois marketplace.

THE DEHUMANIZATION OF ART

The study of art from the sociological point of view might at first seem a barren theme, rather like studying a man from his shadow. At first sight, the social effects of art are so extrinsic, so remote from aesthetic essentials, that it is not easy to see how from this viewpoint one can successfully explore the inner nature of style. But the fruitful aspects of a sociology of art were unexpectedly revealed to me when, a few years ago, I happened to be writing about the musical era which started with Debussy. My purpose was to define as clearly as possible the difference between modern and traditional music. The problem was strictly aesthetic, yet I found the shortest road towards its solution started from a simple sociological phenomenon: the unpopularity of modern music.

I should now like to consider all the arts which are still thriving in Europe: modern music, painting, poetry, and theatre. The unity that every era maintains within its different manifestations is indeed surprising and mysterious. An identical inspiration is recognizable in the most diverse arts. Without being aware of it, the young musician is attempting to realize in sound exactly the same aesthetic values as his contemporaries, the painter, the poet and the dramatist. And this identity of artistic aspiration must, necessarily, have an identical sociological effect. The unpopularity of today's music is equalled by the unpopularity of the other arts. All new art is unpopular, necessarily so, and not by chance or accident.

It will be said that every new style must go through a period of quarantine, and one may recall the conflicts that accompanied the advent of Romanticism. The unpopularity of modern art, however, is of a very distinct kind: we would do well to distinguish between what is not popular and what is unpopular. An innovatory style takes a certain time in winning popularity; it is not popular, but neither is it unpopular. The example of the public's acceptance of Romanticism was the exact opposite of that presented by modern art.

It made a very rapid conquest of the 'people', whose affection had never been deeply held by the old classical art. The enemy with which Romanticism had to contend was precisely that select minority who had remained loyal to the archaic structure of the poetic *ancien régime*. Romantic works were the first—since the invention of printing—to enjoy large editions. Above all other movements Romanticism was the most popular. The first-born of democracy, it was treated by the masses with the greatest affection.

Modern art, on the other hand, has the masses against it, and this will always be so since it is unpopular in essence; even more, it is anti-popular. Any new work whatsoever automatically produces a curious sociological effect on the public, splitting it into two parts. One, the lesser group, is formed by a small number of persons who are favorable to it; the other, the great majority, is hostile. (Let us leave aside those equivocal creatures, the snobs.) Thus the work of art acts as a social force creating two antagonistic groups, separating the masses into two different castes of men.

What is the principle that differentiates these two classes? Every work of art awakens different responses: some people like it, others do not; some like it less, others more. No principle is involved: the accident of our individual disposition will decide where we stand. But in the case of modern art the separation occurs on a deeper plane than the mere differences in individual taste. It is not a matter of the majority of the public *not liking* the new work and the minority liking it. What happens is that the majority, the mass of the people, *does not understand* it.

In my opinion, the characteristic of contemporary art 'from the sociological point of view' is that it divides the public into these two classes of men: those who understand it and those who do not. This implies that the one group possesses an organ of comprehension denied to the other; that they are two distinct varieties of the human species. Modern art, evidently, is not for everybody, as was Romantic art, but from the outset is aimed at a special, gifted minority. Hence the irritation it arouses in the majority. When someone does not like a work of art, but has understood it, he feels superior to it and has no room for irritation. But when distaste arises from the fact of its not having been understood, then the spectator feels humiliated, with an obscure awareness of his inferiority for which he must compensate by an indignant assertion of himself. Modern art, by its mere presence, obliges the good bourgeois to feel what he is: a good bourgeois, unfit for artistic sacraments, blind and deaf to all aesthetic beauty. Obviously this cannot happen with impunity after a hundred years of all-embracing flattery of the masses and the apotheosis of 'the people'. Accustomed to dominate in everything, the masses feel that their 'rights' are threatened by modern art, which is an art of privilege, of an aristocracy of instinct. Wherever the young muses make their appearance, the crowd boos.

For a century and a half 'the people' have pretended to be the whole of society. The music of Stravinsky or the drama of Pirandello obliges them to recognize themselves for what they are—one ingredient among many in the social structure, inert material of the historical process. On the other hand, modern art also helps the élite to know and recognize each other amid the greyness of the crowd, and to learn their role which consists of being the few who have to struggle against the many.

The time is approaching when society, from politics to art, will once more organize itself into two orders: that of the distinguished and that of the vulgar. The undifferentiated unity—chaotic, amorphous, without an anatomical structure or governing discipline cannot continue. Beneath all contemporary life lies a profound and disturbing misconception: the assumption that real equality exists among men. While every step we take plainly shows us the contrary.

If the new art is not intelligible to everybody, this implies that its resources are not those generically human. It is not an art for men in general, but for a very particular class of men, who may not be of more worth than the others, but who are apparently distinct.

There is one thing above all that it would be well to define. What do the majority of people call aesthetic pleasure? What goes on in their mind when a work of art 'pleases' them? There is no doubt about the answer: people like a work of art that succeeds in involving them in the human destinies it propounds. The loves, hates, griefs and joys of the characters touch their heart: they participate in them, as if they were occurring in real life. And they say a work is 'good' when it manages to produce the quantity of illusion necessary for the imaginary characters to rate as living persons. In poetry, they will look for the loves and griefs of the man behind the poet. In painting, they will be attracted only by those pictures where they find men and women who would be interesting to know. A landscape will appear 'pretty' to them when the scene represented merits a visit on account of its pleasant or emotive characteristics.

This means that for the majority of people aesthetic enjoyment is not an attitude of mind essentially different from the one they habitually adopt in other areas of life; but it is perhaps less utilitarian, more compact, and without unpleasant consequences. In essence, the object which concerns them in art, which serves as the focus of their attention and the rest of their faculties, is the same as in everyday life; human beings and their passions. And they will call art that which provides them with the means of making contact with human things. Thus they will tolerate certain forms of unreality and fantasy only to the extent that they do not interfere with their perception of human forms and situations. As soon as the purely aesthetic elements become dominant and detached from the human story, the public loses its way and does not know what to do before the stage, the book, or the picture. Understandably, people know of no other attitude when faced with such objects than that of habit, the habit of always becoming sentimentally involved. A work which does not invite this involvement leaves them without a role to play.

Now this is a point on which we must be clear. To rejoice or suffer with the human destinies which a work of art may relate or represent, is a very different thing from true artistic enjoyment. Indeed, such concern with the human element of the work is strictly incompatible with aesthetic gratification.

It is a perfectly simple matter of optics. In order to see an object we have to adjust our eyes in a certain way. If our visual accommodation is inadequate we do not see the object, or we see it imperfectly. Imagine we are looking at a garden through a window. Our eyes adjust themselves so that our glance penetrates the glass without lingering upon it, and seizes upon the flowers and foliage. As the goal of vision towards which we direct our glance is the garden, we do not see the pane of glass and our gaze passes through it. The clearer the glass, the less we see it. But later, by making an effort, we can ignore the garden, and, by retracting our focus, let it rest on the window-pane. Then the garden disappears from our eyes, and all we see of it are some confused masses of colour which seem to adhere to the glass. Thus to see the garden and to see the window-pane are two incompatible operations: the one excludes the other and they each require a different focus.

In the same manner, the person who seeks to involve himself, through a work of art, with the destinies of John and Mary or of Tristan and Isolde and

226 JOSÉ ORTEGA Y GASSET

adjusts his spiritual perception to these matters, will not see the work of art.
The misfortunes of Tristan, as such, can only move us to the extent that they
are taken for reality. But the artistic object is artistic only to the extent that it
is not real. In order to enjoy Titian's equestrian portrait of *Charles V*, it is a
necessary condition that we do not see the authentic, living Charles V but only
a portrait of him, that is, an unreal image. The man portrayed and his portrait
are two completely distinct objects: either we are interested in the one or in the
other. In the former case, we 'associate' with Charles V; in the latter, we
'contemplate' the artistic object as such.

Now the majority of people are incapable of adjusting their attention to the
window-pane which is the work of art; instead, their gaze passes through
without lingering and hastens to involve itself passionately in the human
reality to which the work alludes. If they are invited to let go this prize and
focus their attention on the actual work of art, they will say they see nothing
in it, because in fact they do not see in it human things, but only an 'artistic'
nothingness.

Artists during the nineteenth century strayed too far from artistic purity,
reducing to the minimum the strictly aesthetic elements and making their
works consist almost entirely of this fictionalized version of human reality. In
this sense it is therefore accurate to say that all the normal art of the past
century has been realistic. Beethoven and Wagner were realists; Chateaubriand, like Zola, was a realist. Romanticism and naturalism, seen from the
viewpoint of today, come closer together and reveal their common root in
realism.

Works of this nature are only partially works of art. In order to enjoy them
we do not have to have artistic sensitivity. It is enough to possess humanity
and a willingness to sympathize with our neighbour's anguish and joy. It is
therefore understandable that the art of the nineteenth century should have
been so popular, since it was appreciated by the majority in proportion to its
not being art, but an extract from life. Remember that in all ages which have
had two different types of art—one for the few and another for the many—the
latter has always been realistic. In the Middle Ages, for example, corresponding to the twofold structure of society there was both an aristocratic
art which was 'conventional' and idealistic, and a popular art which was
realistic and satirical.

We will not discuss now whether pure art is possible. Perhaps it is not, but
the reasons are somewhat tedious and in any case do not greatly affect the
matter under discussion. Although a pure art may not be possible, there is no
doubt that there is room for a movement towards it. This would lead to a
progressive elimination of the human or too human elements characteristic of
romantic and naturalistic works of art, and a point will be reached in which the
human content of the work diminishes until it can scarcely be seen. Then we
shall have an object which can be perceived only by those who possess that
peculiar gift of artistic sensitivity. It will be an art for artists and not for the
masses; it will be an art of caste, not demotic.

Here perhaps we have found the reason why the modern artist is dividing the public into two classes, those who understand and those who do not, that is artists themselves and those who are not. For modern art is an artistic art.

I am not seeking to extol this new manner of art and still less to denigrate the custom of the last century. I am limiting myself to classifying them. Modern art is a universal fact. During the last twenty years the most avant-garde of two successive generations in Paris, Berlin, London, New York, Rome, and Madrid have found themselves struck by the ineluctable fact that traditional art not only does not interest them; they actually find it repugnant. With these modern artists it is possible to do one of two things: either shoot them or make an effort to understand them. As soon as one decides in favour of the latter course one immediately notices a new conception of art germinating in their work which is quite clear, coherent and rational. Far from being a caprice, their striving is shown to embody the inevitable, and indeed fruitful outcome of all previous artistic evolution.

It is merely capricious, and thus sterile, to resist this new style and persist in immuring oneself within forms that are already archaic and hidebound. We have to accept the imperative of work which our era imposes; submissiveness to his own period offers the individual his only chance of achievement. Even so he may still attain nothing; but his failure is much more certain if he were to compose one more Wagnerian opera or yet another naturalistic novel.

In art all repetition is valueless. Each style in the history of art is able to engender a certain number of different forms within a generic type. But there comes a day when the rich mine is completely worked out. This has happened, for example, with the romantic and naturalistic novel and play. It is an ingenuous error to believe that the present-day sterility in both fields is due to lack of personal talent. What has happened is that all possible permutations have been exhausted. It is fortunate that the emergence of a new awareness capable of exploring unworked veins should coincide with this exhaustion.

Analysing the new style, one finds in it certain closely connected tendencies: it tends towards the dehumanization of art; to an avoidance of living forms; to ensuring that a work of art should be nothing but a work of art; to considering art simply as play and nothing else; to an essential irony; to an avoidance of all falsehood; and finally, towards an art which makes no spiritual or transcendental claims whatsoever.

With vertiginous speed modern art has diverged into a great variety of directions and intentions. It is easy to emphasize the differences between one work and another. But this will be valueless unless we first determine the common basis which, at times contradictorily, modern art shares. The specific differences in the arts today are of only moderate interest to me, and, apart from some exceptions, I am concerned still less with any one work. The important thing is that there is this new artistic awareness revealed not only in the artists themselves but also in some members of the public. When I said today's art exists primarily for artists, I meant not only those who produce it but also those who have a capacity for appreciating it. Now I shall outline which single characteristic of modern art seems to me to be of greatest importance: the tendency to dehumanize art.

If we compare a modern painting with one painted in, say, 1860, we can start by contrasting the objects represented in both works—perhaps a man, a house, or a mountain. We soon notice that the artist of 1860 has above all intended the objects in his picture to have the same air and aspect as when they form part of living reality. Possibly, also, the artist of 1860 may have sought other aesthetic implications, but the important thing to note is that he began by making sure of this external likeness. Man, house and mountain are immediately recognizable: they are our old friends. On the other hand, these things in the modern painting require some effort before we can recognize them. The spectator may think that this painter is incapable of achieving a likeness. But the picture of 1860, too, may be 'painted badly'—that is to say, there may be a gulf between the objects in the picture and the reality they represent. Nevertheless, that reality is the goal towards which he stumbles. In the later painting, however, everything is the opposite: it is not a case of the painter making mistakes and so failing to achieve the 'natural' resemblance (natural here equals human): his deviations follow a road leading directly away from the human object.

The painter, far from stumbling towards reality, is seen to be proceeding in the contrary direction. He has set himself resolutely to distort reality, break its human image, dehumanize it. It is possible to envisage living in the company of the things represented in a traditional picture; association with the things shown in the new picture is impossible. In ridding them of their aspect of living actuality, the painter has severed the bridge and burnt the boats which might connect us with our customary world. He leaves us imprisoned in an abstruse world and forces us to confront objects impossible to treat humanly. We not only have to approach these paintings with a completely open mind; we have to create and invent almost unimaginable characteristics which might fit those exceptional objects. This new, invented life to which no spontaneous response can be gained from previous experience, is precisely what artistic comprehension and enjoyment is about. There is no lack in it of feelings and passions, but they belong to a psychic flora quite distinct from that which covers the landscapes of our primary and human life. They arouse secondary emotions which are specifically aesthetic.

It will be said that it would be simpler to dispense altogether with those human forms—man, house, mountain—and construct utterly original figures. But this, in the first place, is impracticable. In the most abstract ornamental line a dormant recollection of certain 'natural' forms may linger tenaciously. In the second place—and this is more important—the art of which we are speaking is not only not human in that it does not comprise human things, but its active constituent is the very operation of dehumanizing. In his flight from the human, what matters to the artist is not so much reaching the undefined goal, as getting away from the human aspect which it is destroying. It is not a case of painting something totally distinct from a man or a house or a mountain, but of painting a man with the least possible resemblance to man; a house which conserves only what is strictly necessary to reveal its metamorphosis; a cone which has miraculously emerged from what was formerly a mountain. The aesthetic pleasure for today's artist emanates from this triumph over the human; therefore it is necessary to make the victory concrete and in each case display the victim that has been overcome.

It is commonly believed that to run away from reality is easy, whereas it is the most difficult thing in the world. It is easy to say or paint a thing which is unintelligible, completely lacking in meaning: it is enough to string together words without connection, or draw lines at random. But to succeed in constructing something which is not a copy of the 'natural' and yet possesses some substantive quality implies a most sublime talent.

'Reality' constantly lurks in ambush ready to impede the artist's evasion.

In works of art popular in the last century there is always a nucleus of living reality which ultimately forms the substance of the aesthetic body. It is upon this substance that art operates, embellishing that human nucleus, giving it brilliance and resonance. For the majority of people this is the most natural, indeed the only possible, structure of a work of art. Art is a reflection of life, it is nature seen through a temperament, it is the representative of the human, etc., etc. But the fact is that, with no less conviction, today's artists insist on the opposite. Why must the old always be counted right today, when tomorrow always agrees with the young against the old? Above all, it is useless to become indignant or make an outcry. Our most rooted and unquestioned convictions are those most open to suspicion. They demonstrate our limits and our confines. Life is of small account if it is not instinct with a formidable eagerness to extend its frontiers. One lives in proportion as one yearns to live more. The obstinate desire to remain within our habitual horizon points to a decadence of vital energies. The horizon is a biological line, a living organ of our being; while we enjoy plenitude the horizon stretches, expands, undulates elastically almost in time with our breathing. On the other hand, when the horizon becomes immovable it is a sign of a hardening of the arteries and the entry into old age.

It is not quite as evident as the academics assume that a work of art must necessarily contain a human nucleus for the Muses to bedeck and embellish. This would be to reduce art to mere cosmetics. I have already pointed out that the perception of living reality and the perception of artistic form are, in principle, incompatible since they require a different adjustment of our vision. An art that tries to make us see both ways at once will be a cross-eyed art. The works of the nineteenth century, far from representing a normal art, are perhaps the greatest anomaly in the history of taste. All the great periods of art have avoided making the human element the centre of gravity in the work of art. That demand for exclusive realism which governed the tastes of the past century precisely demonstrates an aberration without parallel in the evolution of aesthetics. Whence it follows that the new inspiration, so extravagant in appearance, is again treading the true road of art, the road called 'the desire for style'. Now, to stylize is to distort the real, to make un-real. Stylization implies de-humanization. And, vice versa, there is no other manner of de-humanizing than stylization. Realism, on the other hand, invites the artist to follow docilely the form of things, invites him to abandon style. A Zurbarán enthusiast says that his pictures have 'character', just as Lucas or Sorolla, Dickens or Galdós, have character and not-style. The eighteenth century, on the contrary, which has so little character, possesses style to saturation point.

Modernists have declared that the intrusion of the human in art is taboo. Now, human contents, the component elements of our daily lives possess a hierarchy of three ranks. First comes the order of persons, then that of other living creatures, and finally, that of inorganic things. Art today exercises its veto with an energy in proportion to the hierarchial altitude of the object. The personal, by being the most human of the human, is what is most shunned by the modern artist.

This can be seen very clearly in music and poetry. From Beethoven to Wagner, the theme of music was the expression of personal feelings. The lyric artist composed grand edifices of sound in order to fill them with his autobiography. Art was more or less confession. There was no other way of aesthetic enjoyment other than by contagion of feelings. Even Nietzsche said, 'In music, the passions take pleasure from themselves'. Wagner injects his adultery with La Wesendonck into *Tristan*, and leaves us with no other remedy, if we wish to enjoy his work, than to become vaguely adulterous for a couple of hours. That music fills us with compunction, and to enjoy it we have to weep, suffer anguish, or melt with love in spasmodic voluptuousness. All the music of Beethoven or Wagner is melodrama.

The modern artist would say that this is treachery; that it plays on man's noble weakness whereby he becomes infected by the pain or joy of his fellows. This contagion is not of a spiritual order, it is merely a reflex reaction, as when one's teeth are set on edge by a knife scraped on glass, an instinctive response, no more. It is no good confusing the effect of tickling with the experience of gladness. Art cannot be subject to unconscious phenomenon for it ought to be all clarity, the high noon of cerebration. Weeping and laughter are aesthetically fraudulent. The expression of beauty never goes beyond a smile, whether melancholy or delight, and is better still without either. *'Toute maîtrise jette le froid'* (Mallarmé).

I believe the judgment of the young artist is sound enough. Aesthetic pleasures may be blind or perspicacious. The joy of the drunkard is blind; like everything, it has its cause, which is alcohol, but it lacks motive. The man who wins a prize in a lottery also rejoices, but in a different manner: he rejoices because of something definite. He is glad because he sees an object in itself gladdening.

All that seeks a spiritual, not a mechanical being will have to possess this clear-sighted character, intelligently motivated. Yet the pleasure a romantic work excites has hardly any connection with its content. What has the beauty of music to do with the melting mood it may engender in me? Instead of delighting in the artist's work, we delight in our own emotions; the work has merely been the cause, the alcohol, of our pleasure. And this will always happen when art is made to represent living realities; they move us to a sentimental participation which prevents our contemplating them objectively.

Seeing is action at a distance. A projector is operating within a work of art both moving things further away and transfiguring them. On its magic screen we contemplate them banished from the earth, absolutely remote. When this de-realization is lacking it produces in us a fatal vacillation: we do not know whether we are living the things or contemplating them.

We have all felt a peculiar unease in front of wax figures. This arises from the insistent ambiguity which inhabits them and which prevents our adopting a consistent attitude towards them. Treat them as living beings and they mock us by revealing their cadaverous and waxen secrets, yet if we look on them as dolls they seem to protest. There is no way of reducing them to mere objects. Looking at them, we become uneasy with the suspicion that it is they who are looking at us. And we end up by feeling loathing towards this species of hired corpses. The wax figure is pure melodrama.

To me it seems that the new attitudes are dominated by a loathing for the human in art very similar to the way in which discriminating men have always felt towards wax figures. These macabre mockeries, on the other hand, have always roused the enthusiasm of the common people. And, in passing, let us ask a few random questions, with the intention of leaving them unanswered for the time being. What does it signify, this loathing for the human in art? Is it by any chance a loathing of the human, of reality, of life—or is it perhaps the opposite, a respect for life and a repugnance for seeing it confused with anything as inferior as art? But what is all this about art being an inferior function—divine art, the glory of civilization, the pinnacle of culture, and so forth? I have said, these are random questions not pertinent to the immediate issue.

In Wagner, melodrama reaches its highest exaltation. And as always happens, when a form attains its maximum its conversion into the opposite at once begins. Already in Wagner the human voice is ceasing to be a protagonist and is becoming submerged in the cosmic uproar of the other instruments. A conversion of a more radical kind was inevitable; it became necessary to eradicate personal sentiments from music. This was the accomplishment of Debussy. Since his day it has become possible to hear music serenely, without rapture and without tears. All the variations and developments that have occurred in the art of music in these last decades tread upon that extra-terrestrial ground brilliantly conquered by Debussy. The conversion from the subjective to the objective is of such importance that subsequent differentiations disappear before it. Debussy dehumanized music, and for that reason the era of modern music dates from him. His was the art of sound.

The same conversion took place in poetry. It was necessary to liberate poetry, which, weighed down with human material, was sinking to earth like a deflated balloon, bruising itself against the trees and rooftops. In this case it was Mallarmé who liberated poetry and gave it back its soaring power and freedom. Perhaps he himself did not quite realize his ambition, but as captain of the new space explorations he gave the decisive command: throw the ballast overboard.

Recall what used to be the theme of poetry in the romantic era. In neat verses the poet let us share his private, bourgeois emotions: his sufferings great and small, his nostalgias, his religious or political preoccupations, and, if he were English, his pipe-smoking reveries. On occasions, individual genius allowed a more subtle emanation to envelope the human nucleus of the poem—as we find in Baudelaire, for example. But this splendour was a by-product. All the poet wished was to be a human being.

When he writes, I believe today's poet simply proposes to be a poet. Presently we shall see how all modern art, coinciding in this with modern technologies, science and politics, in short with life as it is today, loathes all blurred frontiers. It is a symptom of mental elegance to insist on clear distinctons. Life is one thing, poetry another, the young writer thinks—or, at least, feels. The poet begins where the man stops. The latter has to live out his human destiny; the mission of the former is to invent what does not exist. In this way the function of poetry is justified. The poet augments the world, adding to the real, which is already there, an unreal aspect. Mallarmé was the first poet of the nineteenth century who wanted to be nothing but a poet. As he himself says, he rejected 'nature's materials' and composed little lyrical objects, distinct from human fauna and flora. This poetry does not need to be 'felt', because, as there is nothing of the human in it, there is nothing of pathos in it either. If he speaks of a woman it is 'any woman', and if the clock strikes it is 'the missing hour on the clock face'. By a process of denial, Mallarmé's verse annuls all human echoes and presents us with figures so far beyond reality that merely to contemplate them is a delight. Among such inhuman surroundings what can the man officiating as poet do? One thing only: disappear, volatilize and be converted into a pure, anonymous voice, which speaks disembodied words, the only true protagonists of the lyrical pursuit. That pure anonymous voice, mere accoustic carrier of the verse, is the voice of the poet, who has learnt how to isolate himself from the man he is.

From every direction we come to the same conclusion: escape from the human person. The processes of dehumanization are many. Perhaps today very different processes from those employed by Mallarmé dominate, and I am aware that even in his own works there still occur romantic vibrations. But just as modern music belongs to the era that starts with Debussy, all new poetry advances in the direction pointed out by Mallarmé. The link with both names seems to me essential if we wish to follow the main outline of the new style.

Today it is difficult for anyone under thirty to become interested in a book describing under the pretext of art, the behaviour of specific men and women. He relates this to sociology and psychology, and would accept it with pleasure if, not to confuse things, it were referred to as such. But art for him is something different.

Poetry today is the higher algebra of metaphors.

Metaphor is probably the most fertile of man's resources, its effectiveness verging on the miraculous. All other faculties keep us enclosed within the real, within what already is. The most we can do is add or subtract things to or from others. Only metaphor aids our escape and creates among real things imaginary reefs, islands pregnant with allusion.

It is certainly strange, the existence of this mental activity in man whereby he supplants one thing by another, not so much out of eagerness to achieve the one as from a desire to shun the other. Metaphor palms off one object in the guise of another, and it would not make sense if, beneath it, we did not see an instinct which leads towards an avoidance of reality.

A psychologist recently enquiring into the origin of metaphor discovered that one of its roots lay in the spirit of taboo. An object of ineffable importance would be designated by another name. The instrument of metaphor came later to be employed for the most diverse ends, one of them, the one that has predominated in poetry, being to ennoble the real object. Similes have been used for decorative purposes, to adorn and embroider the beloved reality. It would be interesting to find out whether, in modern art, on turning the metaphor into substance and not ornament, the image has not acquired a curiously denigrating quality, which, instead of ennobling and enhancing, diminishes and disparages poor reality. A little while ago I read a book of modern poetry where lightning was compared to a carpenter's rule and winter's leafless trees to brooms sweeping the sky. The lyrical weapon is turned against natural things and damages, even assassinates them.

But, if metaphor is the most radical instrument of dehumanization, it cannot be said to be the only one. There are countless others of varying range.

The simplest consists in a mere change of the customary perspective. From the human point of view things have an order, a determined hierarchy. Some seem very important, others less so, others totally insignificant. In order to satisfy the urge to dehumanize it is not, therefore, necessary to alter the inherent nature of things. It is enough to invert this order of importance and make an art in which, looming up monumentally in the foreground, appear the events of minimum importance in real life.

This is the latent connection uniting apparently incompatible forms of modern art: the selfsame instinct of flight from the real is satisfied both in the surrealism of metaphor and in what might be called infra-realism. Reality can be overcome, not only by soaring to the heights of poetic exaltation, but also by paying exaggerated attention to the minutest detail. The best examples of this—of attending, lens in hand, to the microscopic aspects of life—are to be found in Proust, Ramón Gómez de la Serna, and Joyce.

As I have said, the purpose of this essay is merely to describe modern art by means of some of its distinctive features. But, in its turn, this intention finds itself serving a curiosity broader than these pages could satisfy, so that the reader is left to his private meditation. I refer to the following considerations.

Elsewhere [Ortega y Gasset's *The Modern Theme*, London 1931, New York 1961] I have pointed out that art and pure science, precisely by being the freest of activities, and less dependent on social conditions, are the first fields in which any change in the collective consciousness can be seen. When man modifies his basic attitude to life he starts by manifesting this new awareness in both artistic creation and in scientific theory. The sensitivity of both areas makes them infinitely susceptible to the lightest breath of the winds of the spirit. As in a village, on opening the windows in the morning, we look at the smoke from the chimneys in order to see which way the wind is blowing so we can look at the arts and sciences of the younger generations with a similar meteorological curiosity.

But in order to do this it was essential to define the new phenomenon. Having done so, only now can we ask what new life-style modern art heralds for the future? The reply would entail investigation into the causes of this strange change of direction which art is making, and this in turn would be an enterprise too weighty to undertake here. Why this urge to dehumanize, why this loathing of living forms? Probably, like every historical phenomenon, its roots are so tangled only the subtlest detection could unravel them.

Nevertheless, one cause stands out quite clearly, although it cannot be regarded as the decisive one.

The influence of its own past on the future of art is something that cannot be over-stated. Within the artist there goes on a constant battle, or at least a violent reaction, between his own original experiences and the art already created by others. He does not find himself confronting the world on his own; artistic tradition, like some middleman, always intervenes. He may feel an affinity with the past, regarding himself as the offspring who inherits and then perfects its traditions—or, he may discover a sudden indefinable aversion to the traditional and established artists. Should he fall into the first category he will experience pleasure in settling into the conventional mould and repeating most of the sacred rituals: if in the second he will find the same intense pleasure in giving his work a character aggressively opposed to established standards.

This is apt to be forgotten when people talk of the influence of yesterday upon today. It is not difficult to recognize in the work of one period the desire to resemble that of the preceding one. On the other hand, almost everybody seems to find it difficult to see the negative influence of the past, and to note that a new style is often formed by the conscious and complicated negation of traditional modes.

And the fact is that one cannot understand the development of art, from Romanticism to the present day, unless one takes into account that negative mood of aggressive derision as an ingredient of aesthetic pleasure. Baudelaire praises the black Venus precisely because the classical one is white. From then on, successive styles have been progressively increasing the negative and blasphemous content in things that tradition once delighted in, up to the point where today the profile of modern art consists almost entirely of a total negation of the old. That this should be so is understandable. Many centuries of continuous evolution in art, unbroken by historical catastrophes or other serious interruptions, produce an ever-growing burden of tradition to weigh down inspiration. Or, to put it another way: an ever-growing volume of traditional styles intercept direct communication between the emergent artist and the world around him. One of two things may happen: either the tradition will end by overwhelming all original talent—as was the case in Egypt, Byzantium, and the East in general—or the burden of the past upon the present will be thrown off, followed by a long period in which the arts gradually break free from the traditions that were smothering it. This has been the case in Europe, where a futurist instinct is overthrowing a positively oriental reverence for the past.

A large part of what I have called 'dehumanization' and the loathing of human forms arises from this antipathy to the traditional interpretation of reality. The vigour of the attack is in indirect ratio to the distance in time: what most repels the artists of today is the predominant style of the past century, despite the fact that it contained its own measure of opposition to older styles. On the other hand, the new artist apparently feels an affinity towards art more distant in time or space—the prehistoric, the primitive and exotic. What is probably found pleasing in these primitive works is—more than the works themselves—their ingenuousness and the absence of any recognizable tradition in them.

If we now consider what attitude to life this attack on the artistic past indicates, we are confronted by a revelation of immense dramatic quality. Because, ultimately, to assault the art of the past is to turn against *art* itself; for what else in actual fact is art, but a record of all that the artist has achieved up to the present?

Is it then the case that, under the mask of love there is hidden a satiety of art, a hatred of art? How would that be possible? Hatred of art cannot arise except where there also prevails hatred of science, hatred of the state, hatred, in short, of culture as a whole. Does Western man bear an inconceivable rancour towards his own historical essence? Does he feel something akin to the *odium professionis* of the monk, who, after long years in the cloister, is seized with an aversion to the very discipline which has informed his life?

It would be interesting to analyse the psychological mechanisms by means of which the art of yesterday negatively influences the art of tomorrow. One of these—*ennui*—is clearly evident. The mere repetition of a style blunts and wearies the senses. Wölfflin has shown, in his *Fundamental Concepts in the History of Art,* the power that fatigue has had time and again in mobilizing and transforming art.

Earlier on it was said that the new style, taken in its broadest general aspect, consists in eliminating ingredients that are 'too human', and retaining only purely artistic material. This seems to imply a great enthusiasm for art. But, on contemplating this same fact from another angle, we discover in it a contradictory aspect of loathing or disdain. The contradiction is obvious, and must be stressed. Apparently, modern art is full of ambiguity—which is not really surprising, since almost all important contemporary issues have been equivocal. One has only to do a brief analysis of the recent European political developments to find in them the same intrinsic ambiguity. However, this paradoxical love and hate for the selfsame object is somewhat easier to understand if we look more closely at contemporary works of art.

The first result of art's withdrawal into itself is to rid it of all pathos. Art, with its burden of 'humanity', used to reflect the grave character of life itself. Art was a very serious matter, almost hieratic. At times it aspired to nothing less than saving the human species—as in Schopenhauer or Wagner. Anyone bearing these examples in mind cannot but find it strange that modern inspiration is always, unfailingly, comic. The comic element may be more or less refined, it may run from frank buffoonery to the subtle wink of irony, but it is never absent. It is not that the content of the work is comic—that would be to fall back into the category of the 'human' style—but that art itself makes the jest, whatever the content. As previously indicated, to look for fiction as nothing else but fiction is an intention that cannot be held except in a humorous state of mind. One goes to art precisely because one recognizes it as farce. This is what serious people, less attuned to the present, find most difficult to understand in modern art. They think that modern painting and music are pure 'farce'—in the pejorative sense of the word—and cannot admit the possibility that art's radical and benevolent function might lie in farce itself. It would be 'farce'—again in the bad sense—if the artist of today pretended to compete with the 'serious' art of the past, or if, say, a cubist painting attempted to solicit the same type of emotional, almost religious admiration as a statue of Michelangelo. But the modern artist invites us to contemplate an art that is a jest *in itself*. For from this stems the humour of this inspiration. Instead of laughing at any particular person or thing—there is no comedy without a victim—modern art ridicules art.

One need not become too alarmed at this. Art has never better demonstrated its magical gift than in this mockery of itself. Because it makes the gesture of destroying itself, it continues to be art, and, by a marvellous dialectic, its negation is its conservation and its triumph.

I very much doubt if young people today could be interested in a verse, a brushstroke or a sound which did not carry within it some ironic reflection.

After all, this is not a completely new theory. At the beginning of the nineteenth century a group of German romantics led by the Schlegels proclaimed irony as the highest aesthetic category, and for reasons which coincide with the intentions of modern art. Art is not justified if it limits itself to reproducing reality, to vain duplications. Its mission is to conjure up an unreal horizon. To achieve this we can only deny our reality and by so doing set ourselves above it. To be an artist is not to take man as seriously as we do when we are not artists.

Clearly, this quality of irony gives modern art a monotony which is highly exasperating. But, be that as it may, the contradiction between hate and love, surfeit and enthusiasm, now appears to be resolved. Hate is aroused when art is taken seriously, love, when art succeeds as farce, laughing at everything, including itself.

There is one feature of great significance which seems to symbolize all that modern art stands for—the fact that it is stripped of all spiritual content.

Having written this sentence, I am astonished to find the number of different connotations it carries. The fact is not that the artist has little interest in his work, but that it interests him precisely because it does not have grave importance, and to the extent that it lacks it. The matter will not be properly understood if it is not considered together with the state of art thirty years ago, indeed, throughout the past century. Poetry and music were then activities of immense importance: little less was expected of them than the salvation of the human species amid the ruin of religions and the inevitable relativism of science. Art was transcendent in a noble sense. It was transcendent by reason of its themes, which included the most serious problems of humanity, itself lending justification and dignity to humanity. This was to be seen in the solemn stance adopted by the great poet or musician, the posture of a prophet or the founder of a religion, the majestic attitude of a statesman responsible for the destiny of the universe.

I suspect that an artist of today would be appalled to see himself appointed to such an enormous mission and thus obliged to deal with matters of comparable magnitude in his work. He begins to experience something of artistic value precisely when he starts to notice a lightness in the air, when his composition begins to behave frivolously, freed of all formality. For him, this is the authentic sign that the Muses exist. If it is still proper to say that art saves man, it is only because it saves him from the seriousness of life and awakens in him an unexpected youthfulness. The magic flute of Pan which makes the Fauns dance at the edge of the forest is again becoming the symbol of art.

Modern art begins to be understandable, acquiring a certain element of greatness when it is interpreted as an attempt to instill youthfulness into an ancient world. Other styles insisted on being associated with dramatic social or political upheavals or with profound philosophical or religious currents. The new style, on the contrary, asks to be associated with the triumph of sports and games. It shares the same origins with them.

In the space of a few years, we have seen the tidal wave of sport all but overwhelming the pages of our newspapers that bear serious news. Articles of depth threaten to sink into the abyss their name implies, while the yachts of the regattas skim victoriously over the surface. The cult of the body eternally speaks of youthful inspiration, because it is only beautiful and agile in youth, while the cult of the mind implies an acceptance of growing old, because it only achieves full maturity when the body has begun to fail. The triumph of sport signifies the victory of the values of youth over the values of old age. The same is true of cinema, which is *par excellence* a group art.

In my generation the manners of middle-age still enjoyed great prestige. A boy longed to stop being a boy as early as possible and preferred to imitate the jaded airs of the man past his prime. Today, little boys and girls try hard to prolong their infancy, and the young strive to retain and accentuate their youthfulness.

This should cause no surprise. History moves in accord with great biological rhythms, its greatest changes originating in primary forces of a cosmic nature. It would be strange if the major and polar differences in human beings—the differences of sex and age—did not also exercise an influence upon the times themselves. And, indeed, it can be clearly seen that history swings rhythmically from one to the other pole, at certain times stressing the masculine qualities, in others the feminine, at certain times exalting the spirit of youth and at others that of maturity.

Today, the predominant aspect in all stages of European existence is one of masculinity and youth. Women and the elderly must for a period yield the government of life to the young men, and it is no wonder that the world appears to be losing formality.

All the characteristics of modern art can be summed up in these basic attitudes, which in turn are responding to art's changed position in the hierarchy of human preoccupations. I would say that art, previously situated, like science or politics, very close to the hub of enthusiasm, that chief support of our personal identity, has moved out towards the periphery. It has lost none of its exterior attributes, but has made itself secondary, less weighty, more remote.

The aspiration to pure art is not, as is often believed, an act of arrogance, but, on the contrary, of great modesty. Art, having been emptied of human pathos, remains without any other meaning whatsoever—as art alone, with no other pretension. Isis of a myriad names, the Egyptians called their goddess. All reality has a myriad aspects. Its components, its features, are innumerable. It would be a remarkable coincidence if, out of an infinity of possibilities, the ideas we have explored in this essay, should turn out to be the correct ones. The improbability increases when we are dealing with a new-born reality, one only at the beginning of its journey through space.

It is, therefore, highly probable that this description of modern art contains nothing but errors. Having concluded my attempt, I am curious and hopeful to find whether others of greater accuracy will follow it. It would only confuse the issues if I were to try to correct any errors I have made by singling out some particular feature omitted from this analysis. Artists are apt to fall into this error when they talk about their art and do not stand far enough away to take a broad view of the facts. I have been moved solely by the pleasure of trying to understand—not by anger or enthusiasm. I have endeavoured to seek the meaning of the intentions of modern art, and this obviously pre-supposes a benevolent state of mind.

It is surely not possible to approach a theme in any other manner without condemning it to sterility?

It will be said that the new art has not produced anything worthwhile up to now, and I come very close to thinking the same. From existing works I have been trying to extract an intention and I have not concerned myself with their fulfilment. Who knows what will come out of this new order! The enterprise is fabulous—it seeks to create out of nothing. I hope that later on it will be content with less and achieve more.

But, whatever its errors may be, there is in my opinion one immovable point in the new situation: the impossibility of going back. All the objections levelled at the inspiration of these artists may be correct, but they still do not contribute sufficient reason for condemning it. Something positive would have to be added: the suggestion of another road for art which would neither dehumanize nor retravel the roads already used and abused.

It is very easy to cry that art is always possible within the tradition. But this comforting phrase is useless for the artist who awaits, with brush or pen in hand, a concrete inspiration.

D. H. Lawrence

1885–1930

David Herbert Lawrence was born in Eastwood, Nottinghamshire, on September 11, 1885. Conflicts between his father, a coalminer, and his mother, a former schoolteacher, were frequent in his childhood, and his mother held a dominant influence over him for many years. Leaving school at the age of sixteen, he became a clerk, but had to give up his job after three months because of pneumonia. After a few years as a pupil-teacher at local schools, he entered University College, Nottingham, in 1906, to study for a teacher's certificate, which he gained in 1908. Moving to London, he took a teaching position in Croydon, but devoted himself increasingly to writing, in which he was encouraged by Ford Madox Ford, who published his early poems in the *English Review*. Lawrence's mother died in December 1910, a month before the publication of his first novel, *The White Peacock*.

Giving up teaching to write full-time, Lawrence published another novel, *The Trespasser,* in 1912, the year in which he eloped to the Continent with Frieda Weekley, *née* von Richthofen. The couple traveled in Germany and Italy while Lawrence completed *Sons and Lovers* (1913) and worked on short stories, published in *The Prussian Officer* (1914), and plays, including *The Widowing of Mrs. Holroyd* (1914). After returning to England in 1914, they were married.

His German wife added to the suspicion with which Lawrence, outspoken in his opposition to World War I, was regarded. *The Rainbow* was seized and condemned as obscene after its publication in 1915, and arguments with literary friends and illness made the war years still harder, though Lawrence did manage to publish several volumes of poetry, including *Look! We Have Come Through!* (1917), and work on *Women in Love* (1920). After the war Lawrence returned with Frieda to Italy, where he spent time in Sicily and Sardinia, giving rise to the travel book *Sea and Sardinia* (1921). In 1922 he completed a collection of stories, *England, My England,* before traveling to America via Ceylon and Australia, which he wrote of in the novel *Kangaroo* (1923). Settling in Taos, New Mexico, he visited Mexico, the background for *The Plumed Serpent* (1926), and various parts of the United States. Increasingly ill, Lawrence was found to have tuberculosis, and returned to spend his last restless years in Europe. His most controversial novel, *Lady Chatterley's Lover,* was privately printed in 1928, but was widely banned for over thirty years. Lawrence also worked on paintings, exhibited in London in 1929; a number of these, too, were seized by court order as obscene.

With his health deteriorating, Lawrence entered a sanatorium in Vence, in the south of France, where he died on March 2, 1930.

Lawrence's principal work as a critic is *Studies in Classic American Literature* (1923). Other critical work, including his long *Study of Thomas Hardy* (1914), can be found in two collections of posthumous papers, *Phoenix* (1936), ed. Edward D. McDonald, and *Phoenix II* (1963), eds. Warren Roberts and Harry T. Moore. Lawrence wrote much in defense of freedom of expression and against censorship, notably *Pornography and Obscenity* (1929).

STUDIES IN CLASSIC AMERICAN LITERATURE

THE SPIRIT OF PLACE

We like to think of the old fashioned American classics as children's books. Just childishness, on our part. The old American art-speech contains an alien quality, which belongs to the American continent and to nowhere else. But, of course, so long as we insist on reading the books as children's tales, we miss all that.

One wonders what the proper highbrow Romans of the third and fourth or later centuries read into the strange utterances of Lucretius or Apuleius or Tertullian, Augustine or Athanasius. The uncanny voice of Iberian Spain, the weirdness of old Carthage, the passion of Libya and North Africa; you may bet the proper old Romans never heard these at all. They read old Latin inference over the top of it, as we read old European inference over the top of Poe or Hawthorne.

It is hard to hear a new voice, as hard as it is to listen to an unknown language. We just don't listen. There is a new voice in the old American classics. The world has declined to hear it, and has babbled about children's stories.

Why?—Out of fear. The world fears a new experience more than it fears anything. Because a new experience displaces so many old experiences. And it is like trying to use muscles that have perhaps never been used, or that have been going stiff for ages. It hurts horribly.

The world doesn't fear a new idea. It can pigeon-hole any idea. But it can't pigeon-hole a real new experience. It can only dodge. The world is a great dodger, and the Americans the greatest. Because they dodge their own very selves.

There is a new feeling in the old American books, far more than there is in the modern American books, which are pretty empty of any feeling, and proud of it. There is a "different" feeling in the old American classics. It is the shifting over from the old psyche to something new, a displacement. And displacement hurts. This hurts. So we try to tie it up, like a cut finger. Put a rag around it.

It is a cut too. Cutting away the old emotions and consciousness. Don't ask what is left.

Art-speech is the only truth. An artist is usually a damned liar, but his art, if it be art, will tell you the truth of his day. And that is all that matters. Away with eternal truth. Truth lives from day to day, and the marvellous Plato of yesterday is chiefly bosh to-day.

The old American artists were hopeless liars. But they were artists, in spite of themselves. Which is more than you can say of most living practitioners.

And you can please yourself, when you read *The Scarlet Letter,* whether you accept what that sugary, blue-eyed little darling of a Hawthorne has to say for himself, false as all darlings are, or whether you read the impeccable truth of his art-speech.

The curious thing about art-speech is that it prevaricates so terribly, I mean it tells such lies. I suppose because we always all the time tell ourselves lies. And out of a pattern of lies art weaves the truth. Like Dostoievsky posing as a sort of Jesus, but most truthfully revealing himself all the while as a little horror.

Truly art is a sort of subterfuge. But thank God for it, we can see through the subterfuge if we choose. Art has two great functions. First, it provides an emotional experience. And then, if we have the courage of our own feelings, it becomes a mine of practical truth. We have had the feelings *ad nauseam.* But we've never dared dig the actual truth out of them, the truth that concerns us, whether it concerns our grandchildren or not.

The artist usually sets out—or used to—to point a moral and adorn a tale. The tale, however, points the other way, as a rule. Two blankly opposing morals, the artist's and the tale's. Never trust the artist. Trust the tale. The proper function of a critic is to save the tale from the artist who created it.

Now we know our business in these studies; saving the American tale from the American artist.

Let us look at this American artist first. How did he ever get to America, to start with? Why isn't he a European still, like his father before him?

Now listen to me, don't listen to him. He'll tell you the lie you expect. Which is partly your fault for expecting it.

He didn't come in search of freedom of worship. England had more freedom of worship in the year 1700 than America had. Won by Englishmen who wanted freedom, and so stopped at home and fought for it. And got it. Freedom of worship? Read the history of New England during the first century of its existence.

Freedom anyhow? The land of the free! This the land of the free! Why, if I say anything that displeases them, the free mob will lynch me, and that's my freedom. Free? Why I have never been in any country where the individual has such an abject fear of his fellow-countrymen. Because, as I say, they are free to lynch him the moment he shows he is not one of them.

No, no, if you're so fond of the truth about Queen Victoria, try a little about yourself.

Those Pilgrim Fathers and their successors never came here for freedom of worship. What did they set up when they got here? Freedom, would you call it?

They didn't come for freedom. Or if they did, they sadly went back on themselves.

All right then, what did they come for? For lots of reasons. Perhaps least of all in search of freedom of any sort: positive freedom, that is.

They came largely to get *away*—that most simple of motives. To get away. Away from what? In the long run, away from themselves. Away from everything. That's why most people have come to America, and still do come. To get away from everything they are and have been.

"Henceforth be masterless."

Which is all very well, but it isn't freedom. Rather the reverse. A hopeless sort of constraint. It is never freedom till you find something you really *positively want to be*. And people in America have always been shouting about the things they are *not*. Unless, of course, they are millionaires, made or in the making.

And after all there is a positive side to the movement. All that vast flood of human life that has flowed over the Atlantic in ships from Europe to America has not flowed over simply on a tide of revulsion from Europe and from the confinements of the European ways of life. This revulsion was, and still is, I believe, the prime motive in emigration. But there was some cause, even for the revulsion.

It seems as if at times man had a frenzy for getting away from any control of any sort. In Europe the old Christianity was the real master. The Church and the true aristocracy bore the responsibility for the working out of the Christian ideals: a little irregularly, maybe, but responsible nevertheless.

Mastery, kingship, fatherhood had their power destroyed at the time of the Renaissance.

And it was precisely at this moment that the great drift over the Atlantic started. What were men drifting away from? The old authority of Europe? Were they breaking the bonds of authority, and escaping to a new more absolute unrestrainedness? Maybe. But there was more to it.

Liberty is all very well, but men cannot live without masters. There is always a master. And men either live in glad obedience to the master they believe in, or they live in a frictional opposition to the master they wish to undermine. In America this frictional opposition has been the vital factor. It has given the Yankee his kick. Only the continual influx of more servile Europeans has provided America with an obedient labouring class. The true obedience never outlasting the first generation.

But there sits the old master, over in Europe. Like a parent. Somewhere deep in every American heart lies a rebellion against the old parenthood of Europe. Yet no American feels he has completely escaped its mastery. Hence the slow, smouldering patience of American opposition. The slow, smouldering, corrosive obedience to the old master Europe, the unwilling subject, the unremitting opposition.

Whatever else you are, be masterless.

> Ca Ca Caliban
> Get a new master, be a new man.

Escaped slaves, we might say, people the republics of Liberia or Haiti. Liberia enough! Are we to look at America in the same way? A vast republic of escaped slaves. When you consider the hordes from eastern Europe, you might well say it: a vast republic of escaped slaves. But one dare not say this of the

Pilgrim Fathers, and the great old body of idealist Americans, the modern Americans tortured with thought. A vast republic of escaped slaves. Look out, America! And a minority of earnest, self-tortured people.

The masterless.

> Ca Ca Caliban
> Get a new master, be a new man.

What did the Pilgrim Fathers come for, then, when they came so gruesomely over the black sea? Oh, it was in a black spirit. A black revulsion from Europe, from the old authority of Europe, from kings and bishops and popes. And more. When you look into it, more. They were black, masterful men, they wanted something else. No kings, no bishops maybe. Even no God Almighty. But also, no more of this new "humanity" which followed the Renaissance. None of this new liberty which was to be so pretty in Europe. Something grimmer, by no means free-and-easy.

America has never been easy, and is not easy to-day. Americans have always been at a certain tension. Their liberty is a thing of sheer will, sheer tension: a liberty of Thou shalt not. And it has been so from the first. The land of Thou shalt not. Only the first commandment is: Thou shalt not presume to be a Master. Hence democracy.

"We are the masterless." That is what the American Eagle shrieks. It's a Hen-Eagle.

The Spaniards refused the post-Renaissance liberty of Europe. And the Spaniards filled most of America. The Yankees, too, refused, refused the post-Renaissance humanism of Europe. First and foremost, they hated masters. But under that, they hated the flowing ease of humour in Europe. At the bottom of the American soul was always a dark suspense, at the bottom of the Spanish-American soul the same. And this dark suspense hated and hates the old European spontaneity, watches it collapse with satisfaction.

Every continent has its own great spirit of place. Every people is polarised in some particular locality, which is home, the homeland. Different places on the face of the earth have different vital effluence, different vibration, different chemical exhalation, different polarity with different stars: call it what you like. But the spirit of place is a great reality. The Nile valley produced not only the corn, but the terrific religions of Egypt. China produces the Chinese, and will go on doing so. The Chinese in San Francisco will in time cease to be Chinese, for America is a great melting-pot.

There was a tremendous polarity in Italy, in the city of Rome. And this seems to have died. For even places die. The Island of Great Britain had a wonderful terrestrial magnetism or polarity of its own, which made the British people. For the moment, this polarity seems to be breaking. Can England die? And what if England dies?

Men are less free than they imagine; ah, far less free. The freest are perhaps least free.

Men are free when they are in a living homeland, not when they are straying and breaking away. Men are free when they are obeying some deep, inward voice of religious belief. Obeying from within. Men are free when they belong to a living, organic, *believing* community, active in fulfilling some unfulfilled, perhaps some unrealised purpose. Not when they are escaping to some wild west. The most unfree souls go west, and shout of freedom. Men are freest when they are most unconscious of freedom. The shout is a rattling of chains, always was.

Men are not free when they are doing just what they like. The moment you can do just what you like, there is nothing you care about doing. Men are only free when they are doing what the deepest self likes.

And there is getting down to the deepest self! It takes some diving.

Because the deepest self is way down, and the conscious self is an obstinate monkey. But of one thing we may be sure. If one wants to be free, one has to give up the illusion of doing what one likes, and seek what IT wishes done.

But before you can do what IT likes, you must first break the spell of the old mastery, the old IT.

Perhaps at the Renaissance, when kingship and fatherhood fell, Europe drifted into a very dangerous half-truth: of liberty and equality. Perhaps the men who went to America felt this, and so repudiated the old world altogether. Went one better than Europe. Liberty in America has meant so far the breaking away from *all* dominion. The true liberty will only begin when Americans discover IT, and proceed possibly to fulfil IT. IT being the deepest *whole* self of man, the self in its wholeness, not idealistic halfness.

That's why the Pilgrim Fathers came to America, then; and that's why we come. Driven by IT. We cannot see that invisible winds carry us, as they carry swarms of locusts, that invisible magnetism brings us as it brings the migrating birds to their unforeknown goal. But it is so. We are not the marvellous choosers and deciders we think we are. IT chooses for us, and decides for us. Unless, of course, we are just escaped slaves, vulgarly cocksure of our ready-made destiny. But if we are living people, in touch with the source, IT drives us and decides us. We are free only so long as we obey. When we run counter, and think we will do as we like, we just flee around like Orestes pursued by the Eumenides.

And still, when the great day begins, when Americans have at last discovered America and their own wholeness, still there will be a vast number of escaped slaves to reckon with, those who have no cocksure, ready-made destinies.

Which will win in America, the escaped slaves, or the new whole men?

The real American day hasn't begun yet. Or at least, not yet sunrise. So far it has been the false dawn. That is, in the progressive American consciousness there has been the one dominant desire, to do away with the old thing. Do away with masters, exalt the will of the people. The will of the people being nothing but a figment, the exalting doesn't count for much. So, in the name of the will of the people, get rid of masters. When you have got rid of masters, you are left with this mere phrase of the will of the people. Then you pause and bethink yourself, and try to recover your own wholeness.

So much for the conscious American motive, and for democracy over here. Democracy in America is just the tool with which the old master of Europe, the European spirit, is undermined. Europe destroyed, potentially, American democracy will evaporate. America will begin.

American consciousness has so far been a false dawn. The negative ideal of democracy. But underneath, and contrary to this open ideal, the first hints and revelations of IT. IT, the American whole soul.

You have got to pull the democratic and idealistic clothes off American utterance, and see what you can of the dusky body of IT underneath.

"Henceforth be masterless."

Henceforth be mastered.

WHITMAN

Post-mortem effects?

But what of Walt Whitman?

The "good grey poet".

Was he a ghost, with all his physicality?

The good grey poet.

Post-mortem effects. Ghosts.

A certain ghoulish insistency. A certain horrible pottage of human parts. A certain stridency and portentousness. A luridness about his beatitudes.

DEMOCRACY! THESE STATES! EIDOLONS! LOVERS, ENDLESS LOVERS!

ONE IDENTITY!

ONE IDENTITY!

I AM HE THAT ACHES WITH AMOROUS LOVE.

Do you believe me, when I say post-mortem effects?

When the *Pequod* went down, she left many a rank and dirty steamboat still fussing in the seas. The *Pequod* sinks with all her souls, but their bodies rise again to man innumerable tramp steamers, and ocean-crossing liners. Corpses.

What we mean is that people may go on, keep on, and rush on, without souls. They have their ego and their will; that is enough to keep them going.

So that you see, the sinking of the *Pequod* was only a metaphysical tragedy after all. The world goes on just the same. The ship of the *soul* is sunk. But the machine-manipulating body works just the same: digests, chews gum, admires Botticelli and aches with amorous love.

I AM HE THAT ACHES WITH AMOROUS LOVE.

What do you make of that? I AM HE THAT ACHES. First generalisation. First uncomfortable universalisation. WITH AMOROUS LOVE. Oh, God! Better a bellyache. A bellyache is at least specific. But the ACHE OF AMOROUS LOVE!

Think of having that under your skin. All that!

I AM HE THAT ACHES WITH AMOROUS LOVE.

Walter, leave off. You are not HE. You are just a limited Walter. And your ache doesn't include all Amorous Love, by any means. If you ache you only ache with a small bit of amorous love, and there's so much more stays outside the cover of your ache, that you might be a bit milder about it.

I AM HE THAT ACHES WITH AMOROUS LOVE.

CHUFF! CHUFF! CHUFF!

CHU-CHU-CHU-CHU-CHUFF!

Reminds one of a steam-engine. A locomotive. They're the only things that seem to me to ache with amorous love. All that steam inside them. Forty million foot-pounds pressure. The ache of AMOROUS LOVE. Steam-pressure. CHUFF!

An ordinary man aches with love for Belinda, or his Native Land, or the Ocean, or the Stars, or the Oversoul: if he feels that an ache is in the fashion.

It takes a steam-engine to ache with AMOROUS LOVE. All of it.

Walt was really too superhuman. The danger of the superhuman is that he is mechanical.

They talk of his "splendid animality". Well, he'd got it on the brain, if that's the place for animality.

I am he that aches with amorous love:
Does the earth gravitate, does not all matter, aching, attract all matter?
So the body of me to all I meet or know.

What can be more mechanical? The difference between life and matter is that life, living things, living creatures, have the instinct of turning right away from *some* matter, and of blissfully ignoring the bulk of most matter, and of turning towards only some certain bits of specially selected matter. As for living creatures all helplessly hurtling together into one great snowball, why, most very living creatures spend the greater part of their time getting out of the sight, smell or sound of the rest of living creatures. Even bees only cluster on their own queen. And that is sickening enough. Fancy all white humanity clustering on one another like a lump of bees.

No, Walt, you give yourself away. Matter *does* gravitate, helplessly. But men are tricky-tricksy, and they shy all sorts of ways.

Matter gravitates because it *is* helpless and mechanical.

And if you gravitate the same, if the body of you gravitates to all you meet or know, why, something must have gone seriously wrong with you. You must have broken your mainspring.

You must have fallen also into mechanisation.

Your Moby Dick must be really dead. That lonely phallic monster of the individual you. Dead mentalised.

I only know that my body doesn't by any means gravitate to all I meet or know. I find I can shake hands with a few people. But most I wouldn't touch with a long prop.

Your mainspring is broken, Walt Whitman. The mainspring of your own individuality. And so you run down with a great whirr, merging with everything.

You have killed your isolate Moby Dick. You have mentalised your deep sensual body, and that's the death of it.

I am everything and everything is me and so we're all One in One Identity, like the Mundane Egg, which has been addled quite a while.

> Whoever you are, to endless announcements——
> And of these one and all I weave the song of myself.

Do you? Well then, it just shows you haven't *got* any self. It's a mush, not a woven thing. A hotch-potch, not a tissue. Your self.

Oh, Walter, Walter, what have you done with it? What have you done with yourself? With your own individual self? For it sounds as if it had all leaked out of you, leaked into the universe.

Post-mortem effects. The individuality had leaked out of him.

No, no, don't lay this down to poetry. These are post-mortem effects. And Walt's great poems are really huge fat tomb-plants, great rank graveyard growths.

All that false exuberance. All those lists of things boiled in one pudding-cloth! No, no!

I don't want all those things inside me, thank you.

"I reject nothing," says Walt.

If that is so, one must be a pipe open at both ends, so everything runs through.

Post-mortem effects.

"I embrace ALL," says Whitman. "I weave all things into myself."

Do you really! There can't be much left of *you* when you've done. When you've cooked the awful pudding of One Identity.

"And whoever walks a furlong without sympathy walks to his own funeral dressed in his own shroud."

Take off your hat then, my funeral procession of one is passing.

This awful Whitman. This post-mortem poet. This poet with the private soul leaking out of him all the time. All his privacy leaking out in a sort of dribble, oozing into the universe.

Walt becomes in his own person the whole world, the whole universe, the whole eternity of time, as far as his rather sketchy knowledge of history will carry him, that is. Because to *be* a thing he had to know it. In order to assume the identity of a thing he had to know that thing. He was not able to assume one identity with Charlie Chaplin, for example, because Walt didn't know Charlie. What a pity! He'd have done poems, pæans and what not, Chants, Songs of Cinematernity.

> Oh, Charlie, my Charlie, another film is done——

As soon as Walt *knew* a thing, he assumed a One Identity with it. If he knew that an Eskimo sat in a kyak, immediately there was Walt being little and yellow and greasy, sitting in a kyak.

Now will you tell me exactly what a kyak is?

Who is he that demands petty definitions? Let him behold me *sitting in a kyak*.

I behold no such thing. I behold a rather fat old man full of a rather senile, self-conscious sensuosity.

DEMOCRACY. EN MASSE. ONE IDENTITY.

The universe in short, adds up to ONE.

ONE.

I.

Which is Walt.

His poems, *Democracy, En Masse, One Identity,* they are long sums in addition and multiplication, of which the answer is invariably MYSELF.

He reaches the state of ALLNESS.

And what then? It's all empty. Just an empty Allness. An addled egg.

Walt wasn't an Eskimo. A little, yellow, sly, cunning, greasy little Eskimo. And when Walt blandly assumed Allness, including Eskimoness, unto himself, he was just sucking the wind out of a blown egg-shell, no more. Eskimos are not minor little Walts. They are something that I am not, I know that. Outside the egg of my Allness chuckles the greasy little Eskimo. Outside the egg of Whitman's Allness too.

But Walt wouldn't have it. He was everything and everything was in him. He drove an automobile with a very fierce headlight, along the track of a fixed idea, through the darkness of this world. And he saw everything that way. Just as a motorist does in the night.

I, who happen to be asleep under the bushes in the dark, hoping a snake won't crawl into my neck; I, seeing Walt go by in his great fierce poetic machine, think to myself: What a funny world that fellow sees!

ONE DIRECTION! toots Walt in the car, whizzing along it.

Whereas there are myriads of ways in the dark, not to mention trackless wildernesses, as anyone will know who cares to come off the road—even the Open Road.

ONE DIRECTION! whoops America, and sets off also in an automobile.

ALLNESS! shrieks Walt at a cross-road, going whizz over an unwary Red Indian.

ONE IDENTITY! chants democratic En Masse, pelting behind in motor-cars, oblivious of the corpses under the wheels.

God save me, I feel like creeping down a rabbit-hole, to get away from all these automobiles rushing down the ONE IDENTITY track to the goal of ALLNESS.

A woman waits for me——

He might as well have said: "The femaleness waits for my maleness." Oh, beautiful generalisation and abstraction! Oh, biological function.

"Athletic mothers of these States——" Muscles and wombs. They needn't have had faces at all.

As I see myself reflected in Nature,
As I see through a mist, One with inexpressible completeness, sanity,
    beauty,
See the bent head, and arms folded over the breast, the Female I see.

Everything was female to him: even himself. Nature just one great function.

> This is the nucleus—after the child is born of woman, man is born of
>   woman,
> This is the bath of birth, the merge of small and large, and the outlet
>   again——

"The Female I see——"
If I'd been one of his women, I'd have given him Female, with a flea in his ear.

Always wanting to merge himself into the womb of something or other.
"The Female I see——"
Anything, so long as he could merge himself.
Just a horror. A sort of white flux.
Post-mortem effects.

He found, as all men find, that you can't really merge in a woman, though you may go a long way. You can't manage the last bit. So you have to give it up, and try elsewhere if you *insist* on merging.

In *Calamus* he changes his tune. He doesn't shout and thump and exult any more. He begins to hesitate, reluctant, wistful.

The strange calamus has its pink-tinged root by the pond, and it sends up its leaves of comradeship, comrades from one root, without the intervention of woman, the female.

So he sings of the mystery of manly love, the love of comrades. Over and over he says the same thing: the new world will be built on the love of comrades, the new great dynamic of life will be manly love. Out of this manly love will come the inspiration for the future.

Will it though? Will it?

Comradeship! Comrades! This is to be the new Democracy of Comrades. This is the new cohering principle in the world: Comradeship.

Is it? Are you sure?

It is the cohering principle of true soldiery, we are told in *Drum Taps*. It is the cohering principle in the new unison for creative activity. And it is extreme and alone, touching the confines of death. Something terrible to bear, terrible to be responsible for. Even Walt Whitman felt it. The soul's last and most poignant responsibility, the responsibility of comradeship, of manly love.

> Yet you are beautiful to me, you faint-tinged roots, you make me think
>   of death.
> Death is beautiful from you (what indeed is finally beautiful except
>   death and love?)
> I think it is not for life I am chanting here my chant of lovers, I think
>   it must be for death,
> For how calm, how solemn it grows to ascend to the atmosphere of
>   lovers,
> Death or life, I am then indifferent, my soul declines to prefer,

(I am not sure but the high soul of lovers welcomes death most)
Indeed, O death, I think now these leaves mean precisely the same as
      you mean——

This is strange, from the exultant Walt.
Death!
Death is now his chant! Death!
Merging! And Death! Which is the final merge.
The great merge into the womb. Woman.
And after that, the merge of comrades: man-for-man love.
And almost immediately with this, death, the final merge of death.
There you have the progression of merging. For the great mergers,
woman at last becomes inadequate. For those who love to extremes. Woman is
inadequate for the last merging. So the next step is the merging of man-
for-man love. And this is on the brink of death. It slides over into death.
    David and Jonathan. And the death of Jonathan.
    It always slides into death.
    The love of comrades.
    Merging.
    So that if the new Democracy is to be based on the love of comrades, it will
be based on death too. It will slip so soon into death.
    The last merging. The last Democracy. The last love. The love of
comrades.
    Fatality. And fatality.
    Whitman would not have been the great poet he is if he had not taken the
last steps and looked over into death. Death, the last merging, that was the goal
of his manhood.
    To the mergers, there remains the brief love of comrades, and then Death.

Whereto answering, the sea
Delaying not, hurrying not,
Whispered me through the night, and very plainly before daybreak,
Lisp'd to me the low and delicious word death,
And again death, death, death, death.
Hissing melodious, neither like the bird nor like my arous'd child's
      heart,
But edging near as privately for me rustling at my feet,
Creeping thence steadily up to my ears and laving me softly all over,
Death, death, death, death, death——

    Whitman is a very great poet, of the end of life. A very great post-mortem
poet, of the transitions of the soul as it loses its integrity. The poet of the soul's
last shout and shriek, on the confines of death. *Après moi le déluge.*
    But we have all got to die, and disintegrate.
    We have got to die in life, too, and disintegrate while we live.
    But even then the goal is not death.
    Something else will come.

Out of the cradle endlessly rocking.

We've got to die first, anyhow. And disintegrate while we still live.

Only we know this much: Death is not the *goal*. And Love, and merging, are now only part of the death-process. Comradeship—part of the death-process. Democracy—part of the death-process. The new Democracy—the brink of death. One Identity—death itself.

We have died, and we are still disintegrating.

But IT IS FINISHED.

Consummatum est.

Whitman, the great poet, has meant so much to me. Whitman, the one man breaking a way ahead. Whitman, the one pioneer. And only Whitman. No English pioneers, no French. No European pioneer-poets. In Europe the would-be pioneers are mere innovators. The same in America. Ahead of Whitman, nothing. Ahead of all poets, pioneering into the wilderness of unopened life, Whitman. Beyond him, none. His wide, strange camp at the end of the great high-road. And lots of new little poets camping on Whitman's camping-ground now. But none going really beyond. Because Whitman's camp is at the end of the road, and on the edge of a great precipice. Over the precipice, blue distances, and the blue hollow of the future. But there is no way down. It is a dead end.

Pisgah. Pisgah sights. And Death. Whitman like a strange, modern, American Moses. Fearfully mistaken. And yet the great leader.

The essential function of art is moral. Not æsthetic, not decorative, not pastime and recreation. But moral. The essential function of art is moral.

But a passionate, implicit morality, not didactic. A morality which changes the blood, rather than the mind. Changes the blood first. The mind follows later, in the wake.

Now Whitman was a great moralist. He was a great leader. He was a great changer of the blood in the veins of men.

Surely it is especially true of American art, that it is all essentially moral. Hawthorne, Poe, Longfellow, Emerson, Melville: it is the moral issue which engages them. They all feel uneasy about the old morality. Sensuously, passionally, they all attack the old morality. But they know nothing better, mentally. Therefore they give tight mental allegiance to a morality which all their passion goes to destroy. Hence the duplicity which is the fatal flaw in them: most fatal in the most perfect American work of art, *The Scarlet Letter*. Tight mental allegiance given to a morality which the passional self repudiates.

Whitman was the first to break the mental allegiance. He was the first to smash the old moral conception that the soul of man is something "superior" and "above" the flesh. Even Emerson still maintained this tiresome "superiority" of the soul. Even Melville could not get over it. Whitman was the first heroic seer to seize the soul by the scruff of her neck and plant her down among the potsherds.

"There!" he said to the soul. "Stay there!"

Stay there. Stay in the flesh. Stay in the limbs and lips and in the belly. Stay in the breast and womb. Stay there, O Soul, where you belong.

Stay in the dark limbs of negroes. Stay in the body of the prostitute. Stay in the sick flesh of the syphilitic. Stay in the marsh where the calamus grows. Stay there, Soul, where you belong.

The Open Road. The great home of the Soul is the open road. Not heaven, not paradise. Not "above". Not even "within". The soul is neither "above" nor "within". It is a wayfarer down the open road.

Not by meditating. Not by fasting. Not by exploring heaven after heaven, inwardly, in the manner of the great mystics. Not by exaltation. Not by ecstasy. Not by any of these ways does the soul come into her own.

Only by taking the open road.

Not through charity. Not through sacrifice. Not even through love. Not through good works. Not through these does the soul accomplish herself.

Only through the journey down the open road.

The journey itself, down the open road. Exposed to full contact. On two slow feet. Meeting whatever comes down the open road. In company with those that drift in the same measure along the same way. Towards no goal. Always the open road.

Having no known direction even. Only the soul remaining true to herself in her going.

Meeting all the other wayfarers along the road. And how? How meet them, and how pass? With sympathy, says Whitman. Sympathy. He does not say love. He says sympathy. Feeling with. Feel with them as they feel with themselves. Catching the vibration of their soul and flesh as we pass.

It is a new great doctrine. A doctrine of life. A new great morality. A morality of actual living, not of salvation. Europe has never got beyond the morality of salvation. America to this day is deathly sick with saviourism. But Whitman, the greatest and the first and the only American teacher, was no Saviour. His morality was no morality of salvation. His was a morality of the soul living her life, not saving herself. Accepting the contact with other souls along the open way, as they lived their lives. Never trying to save them. As leave try to arrest them and throw them in gaol. The soul living her life along the incarnate mystery of the open road.

This was Whitman. And the true rhythm of the American continent speaking out in him. He is the first white aboriginal.

"In my Father's house are many mansions."

"No," said Whitman. "Keep out of mansions. A mansion may be heaven on earth, but you might as well be dead. Strictly avoid mansions. The soul is herself when she is going on foot down the open road."

It is the American heroic message. The soul is not to pile up defences round herself. She is not to withdraw and seek her heavens inwardly, in mystical ecstasies. She is not to cry to some God beyond, for salvation. She is to go down the open road, as the road opens, into the unknown, keeping company with those whose soul draws them near to her, accomplishing nothing save the journey, and the works incident to the journey, in the long life-travel into the unknown, the soul in her subtle sympathies accomplishing herself by the way.

This is Whitman's essential message. The heroic message of the American future. It is the inspiration of thousands of Americans to-day, the best souls of to-day, men and women. And it is a message that only in America can be fully understood, finally accepted.

Then Whitman's mistake. The mistake of his interpretation of his watchword: Sympathy. The mystery of SYMPATHY. He still confounded it with Jesus's LOVE, and with Paul's CHARITY. Whitman, like all the rest of us, was at the end of the great emotional highway of Love. And because he couldn't help himself, he carried on his Open Road as a prolongation of the emotional highway of Love, beyond Calvary. The highway of Love ends at the foot of the Cross. There is no beyond. It was a hopeless attempt to prolong the highway of Love.

He didn't follow his Sympathy. Try as he might, he kept on automatically interpreting it as Love, as Charity. Merging!

This merging, *en masse,* One Identity, Myself monomania was a carry-over from the old Love idea. It was carrying the idea of Love to its logical physical conclusion. Like Flaubert and the leper. The decree of unqualified Charity, as the soul's one means of salvation, still in force.

Now Whitman wanted his soul to save itself; *he* didn't want to save it. Therefore he did not need the great Christian receipt for saving the soul. He needed to supersede the Christian Charity, the Christian Love, within himself, in order to give his Soul her last freedom. The highroad of Love is no Open Road. It is a narrow, tight way, where the soul walks hemmed in between compulsions.

Whitman wanted to take his Soul down the open road. And he failed in so far as he failed to get out of the old rut of Salvation. He forced his Soul to the edge of a cliff, and he looked down into death. And there he camped, powerless. He had carried out his Sympathy as an extension of Love and Charity. And it had brought him almost to madness and soul-death. It gave him his forced, unhealthy, post-mortem quality.

His message was really the opposite of Henley's rant:

> I am the master of my fate,
> I am the captain of my soul.

Whitman's essential message was the Open Road. The leaving of the soul free unto herself, the leaving of his fate to her and to the loom of the open road. Which is the bravest doctrine man has ever proposed to himself.

Alas, he couldn't quite carry it out. He couldn't quite break the old maddening bond of the love-compulsion; he couldn't quite get out of the rut of the charity habit—for Love and Charity have degenerated now into habit: a bad habit.

Whitman said Sympathy. If only he had stuck to it! Because Sympathy means feeling with, not feeling for. He kept on having a passionate feeling *for* the negro slave, or the prostitute, or the syphilitic—which is merging. A sinking of Walt Whitman's soul into the souls of these others.

He wasn't keeping to his open road. He was forcing his soul down an old rut. He wasn't leaving her free. He was forcing her into other people's circumstances.

Supposing he had felt true sympathy with the negro slave? He would have felt *with* the negro slave. Sympathy—compassion—which is partaking of the passion which was in the soul of the negro slave.

What was the feeling in the negro's soul?

"Ah, I am a slave! Ah, it is bad to be a slave! I must free myself. My soul will die unless she frees herself. My soul says I must free myself."

Whitman came along, and saw the slave, and said to himself: "That negro slave is a man like myself. We share the same identity. And he is bleeding with wounds. Oh, oh, is it not myself who am also bleeding with wounds?"

This was not *sympathy*. It was merging and self-sacrifice. "Bear ye one another's burdens": "Love thy neighbour as thyself": "Whatsoever ye do unto him, ye do unto me."

If Whitman had truly *sympathised*, he would have said: "That negro slave suffers from slavery. He wants to be free himself. His soul wants to free him. He has wounds, but they are the price of freedom. The soul has a long journey from slavery to freedom. If I can help him I will: I will not take over his wounds and his slavery to myself. But I will help him fight the power that enslaves him when he wants to be free, if he wants my help, since I see in his face that he needs to be free. But even when he is free, his soul has many journeys down the open road, before it is a free soul."

And of the prostitute Whitman would have said:

"Look at that prostitute! Her nature has turned evil under her mental lust for prostitution. She has lost her soul. She knows it herself. She likes to make men lose their souls. If she tried to make me lose my soul, I would kill her. I wish she may die."

But of another prostitute he would have said:

"Look! She is fascinated by the Priapic mysteries. Look, she will soon be worn to death by the Priapic usage. It is the way of her soul. She wishes it so."

Of the syphilitic he would say:

"Look! She wants to infect all men with syphilis. We ought to kill her."

And of still another syphilitic:

"Look! She has a horror of her syphilis. If she looks my way I will help her to get cured."

This is sympathy. The soul judging for herself, and preserving her own integrity.

But when, in Flaubert, the man takes the leper to his naked body; when Bubu de Montparnasse takes the girl because he knows she's got syphilis; when Whitman embraces an evil prostitute: that is not sympathy. The evil prostitute has no desire to be embraced with love; so if you sympathise with her, you won't try to embrace her with love. The leper loathes his leprosy, so if you sympathise with him, you'll loathe it too. The evil woman who wishes to infect all men with her syphilis hates you if you haven't got syphilis. If you sympathise, you'll feel her hatred, and you'll hate too, you'll hate her. Her feeling is hate, and you'll share it. Only your soul will choose the direction of its own hatred.

The soul is a very perfect judge of her own motions, if your mind doesn't dictate to her. Because the mind says Charity! Charity! you don't have to force your soul into kissing lepers or embracing syphilitics. Your lips are the lips of your soul, your body is the body of your soul; your own single, individual soul. That is Whitman's message. And your soul hates syphilis and leprosy. Because it *is* a soul, it hates these things, which are against the soul. And therefore to force the body of your soul into contact with uncleanness is a great violation of your soul. The soul wishes to keep clean and whole. The soul's deepest will is to preserve its own integrity, against the mind and the whole mass of disintegrating forces.

Soul sympathises with soul. And that which tries to kill my soul, my soul hates. My soul and my body are one. Soul and body wish to keep clean and whole. Only the mind is capable of great perversion. Only the mind tries to drive my soul and body into uncleanness and unwholesomeness.

What my soul loves, I love.

What my soul hates, I hate.

When my soul is stirred with compassion, I am compassionate.

What my soul turns away from, I turn away from.

That is the *true* interpretation of Whitman's creed: the true revelation of his Sympathy.

And my soul takes the open road. She meets the souls that are passing, she goes along with the souls that are going her way. And for one and all, she has sympathy. The sympathy of love, the sympathy of hate, the sympathy of simple proximity; all the subtle sympathisings of the incalculable soul, from the bitterest hate to passionate love.

It is not I who guide my soul to heaven. It is I who am guided by my own soul along the open road, where all men tread. Therefore, I must accept her deep motions of love, or hate, or compassion, or dislike, or indifference. And I must go where she takes me, for my feet and my lips and my body are my soul. It is I who must submit to her.

This is Whitman's message of American democracy.

The true democracy, where soul meets soul, in the open road. Democracy. American democracy where all journey down the open road, and where a soul is known at once in its going. Not by its clothes or appearance. Whitman did away with that. Not by its family name. Not even by its reputation. Whitman and Melville both discounted that. Not by a progression of piety, or by works of Charity. Not by works at all. Not by anything, but just itself. The soul passing unenhanced, passing on foot and being no more than itself. And recognised, and passed by or greeted according to the soul's dictate. If it be a great soul, it will be worshipped in the road.

The love of man and woman: a recognition of souls, and a communion of worship. The love of comrades: a recognition of souls, and a communion of worship. Democracy: a recognition of souls, all down the open road, and a great soul seen in its greatness, as it travels on foot among the rest, down the common way of the living. A glad recognition of souls, and a gladder worship of great and greater souls, because they are the only riches.

Love, and Merging, brought Whitman to the Edge of Death! Death! Death!

But the exultance of his message still remains. Purified of MERGING, purified of MYSELF, the exultant message of American Democracy, of souls in the Open Road, full of glad recognition, full of fierce readiness, full of the joy of worship, when one soul sees a greater soul.

The only riches, the great souls.

Georg Lukács
1885–1971

Georg Lukács was born on April 13, 1885, in Budapest. His mother came from an aristocratic Viennese family; his father, a wealthy businessman, eventually became the director of a large bank in Budapest and was ennobled by the Hapsburgs; the younger Lukács would abandon the "von" before long. His early interests were as much literary as philosophical: Ibsen, Novalis, and Kierkegaard. His first book, *Soul and Form* (1911), deals more with aesthetics than politics; in it, Lukács is occupied with a quasi-Platonist opposition between mind and intelligible forms on the one hand and the "chaos" of matter on the other: he takes the side of the Romantics, notably Novalis, with his defense of an unrealizable inward Utopia, against the objectivity of Goethe's classicism, and finds an unbridgeable abyss between art and life, soul and material.

The absolute contradictions of this first work were unsatisfactory to Lukács, who spent the next several years in eclectic studies of the works of Max Weber, Georg Simmel, Wilhelm Dilthey, Emil Lask, and, although in still undigested fashion, Karl Marx. Lukács was attempting to draw at once on Weber's positivism, Marx's materialism, and the idealism of Simmel—a Sisyphean endeavor that led him to a renewed study of Hegel. In 1914–15 he wrote his most well-known work, *The Theory of the Novel* (published 1920). Lukács here attempts a sociology of genre—even an ethics of genre—and here the ethical and ideological primacy of realism that was to be central to Lukác's work is clearly in evidence. For Lukács the novel was not only a means to social criticism, but is a means to understanding the *totality* of human existence, a totality determined by the contradiction of soul and form, which the novel attempts to resolve. During World War I Lukács read Marx again while living alternately in Heidelberg and Budapest; in late 1918 he suddenly joined the Hungarian Communist Party, and was a member of Béla Kun's short-lived Communist regime in 1919. When the government fell, Lukács was arrested, but was released after intervention was made on his behalf by many writers (including Thomas Mann).

It can be argued that Lukács never overcame his earlier extreme and eclectic idealism (that of *Soul and Form*), in that he always maintained an undialectical opposition between an objective reality conceived of as a closed totality (in the manner of Hegel's idealism, which declared that "all that is real is rational") and the groundless ethical imperative of individual human will. Thus, Lukács' Marxism was determined by absolute moral imperatives as much as by economic diagnosis and revolutionary praxis. The unorthodoxy of this approach did not escape his fellow party members when *History and Class Consciousness* appeared in 1923 (to be followed by the pseudonymous *Blum-Theses* of 1928). After Lenin's death in 1924, there was a general crackdown on inner-party dissidence—i.e., on virtually all theoretical speculation as such—in favor of militant and bureaucratized "unity" under Stalin's leadership. Lukács learned the distasteful art of self-repudiation, and was to practice it coolly and eloquently over the years while never changing his true opinions.

The internal inconsistencies of Lukács' philosophy were to be matched by those of his aesthetics. During the early 1930s he was involved in a stubborn defense of nineteenth-century novelistic realism against both "socialist realism" and the techniques of literary modernism. (The one twentieth-century writer he championed—for what Lukács apparently saw as his "realism"—was Thomas Mann!) His upholding of Balzac and Tolstoy against Joyce and Proust was attacked by many colleagues on the left, including Ernst Bloch and Bertolt Brecht (who heaped scorn on Lukács' conservatism as being more "formalist" than the contemporary experiments he tried to suppress). Lukács spent the years from 1933 to 1944 in isolation in Moscow, returning to Budapest only to meet with more party criticism; his participation in the 1956 anti-Soviet uprising nearly cost him his life. He had found another enemy in Sartre, whose work he attacked often after 1945, at times in monolithic terminology reminiscent of the same Stalin whose power had so curtailed his own freedom; Sartre responded by quoting Lukács against himself, exposing contradictions in the latter's position. Lukács, apparently, never regretted the dishonesty forced upon him by dictatorship: in an interview held in 1970 he remarked that "the worst socialism is better than the best form of capitalism." He died on June 4, 1971.

SOUL AND FORM

On the Nature and Form of the Essay:
A Letter to Leo Popper

My friend,

The essays intended for inclusion in this book lie before me and I ask myself whether one is entitled to publish such works—whether such works can give rise to a new unity, a book. For the point at issue for us now is not what these essays can offer as "studies in literary history", but whether there is something in them that makes them a new literary form of its own, and whether the principle that makes them such is the same in each one. What is this unity—if unity there is? I make no attempt to formulate it because it is not I nor my book that should be the subject under discussion here. The question before us is a more important, more general one. It is the question whether such a unity is possible. To what extent have the really great writings which belong to this category been given literary form, and to what extent is this form of theirs an independent one? To what extent do the standpoint of such a work and the form given to this standpoint lift it out of the sphere of science and place it at the side of the arts, yet without blurring the frontiers of either? To what extent do they endow the work with the force necessary for a conceptual re-ordering of life, and yet distinguish it from the icy, final perfection of philosophy? That is the only profound apology to be made for such writings, as well as the only profound criticism to be addressed to them; for they are measured first and foremost by the yardstick of these questions, and the determining of such an objective will be the first step towards showing how far they fall short of attaining it.

The critique, the essay—call it provisionally what you will—as a work of art, a genre? I know you think the question tedious; you feel that all the arguments for and against have been exhausted long ago. Wilde and Kerr merely made familiar to everyone a truth that was already known to the German Romantics, a truth whose ultimate meaning the Greeks and Romans felt, quite unconsciously, to be self-evident: that criticism is an art and not a science. Yet I believe—and it is for this reason alone that I venture to importune you with these observations—that all the discussions have barely touched upon the essence of the real question: what *is* an essay? What is its intended form of expression, and what are the ways and means whereby this expression is accomplished? I believe that the aspect of "being well written" has been too one-sidedly emphasized in this context. It has been argued that the essay can be stylistically of equal value to a work of the imagination, and that, for this reason, it is unjust to speak of value differences at all. Yet what does that mean? Even if we consider criticism to be a work of art in this sense, we have not yet said anything at all about its essential nature. "Whatever is well written is a work of art." Is a well-written advertisement or news item a work of art? Here I can see what so disturbs you about such a view of criticism: it is anarchy, the denial of form in order that an intellect which believes itself to be sovereign may have free play with possibilities of every kind. But if I speak here of criticism as a form of art, I do so in the name of order (i.e. almost purely symbolically and non-essentially), and solely on the strength of my feeling that the essay has a form which separates it, with the rigour of a law, from all other art forms. I want to try and define the essay as strictly as is possible, precisely by describing it as an art form.

Let us not, therefore, speak of the essay's similarities with works of literary imagination, but of what divides it from them. Let any resemblance serve here merely as a background against which the differences stand out all the more sharply; the purpose of mentioning these resemblances at all will be to limit our attention to genuine essays, leaving aside those writings which, useful though they are, do not deserve to be described as essays because they can never give us anything more than information, facts and "relationships". Why, after all, do we read essays? Many are read as a source of instruction, but there are others whose attraction is to be found in something quite different. It is not difficult to identify these. Our view, our appreciation of classical tragedy is quite different today, is it not, from Lessing's in the *Dramaturgy;* Winckelmann's Greeks seem strange, almost incomprehensible to us, and soon we may feel the same about Burckhardt's Renaissance. And yet we read them: why? On the other hand there are critical writings which, like a hypothesis in natural science, like a design for a machine part, lose all their value at the precise moment when a new and better one becomes available. But if—as I hope and expect—someone were to write a new *Dramaturgy,* a *Dramaturgy* in favour of Corneille and against Shakespeare—how could it damage Lessing's? And what did Burckhardt and Pater, Rhode and Nietzsche do to change the effect upon us of Winckelmann's dreams of Greece?

"Of course, if criticism were a science . . ." writes Kerr. "But the imponderables are too strong. Criticism is, at the very best, an art." And if it were a science—it is not so impossible that it will become one—how would that change our problem? We are not concerned here with replacing something by something else, but with something essentially new, something that remains untouched by the complete or approximate attainment of scientific goals. Science affects us by its contents, art by its forms; science offers us facts and the relationships between facts, but art offers us souls and destinies. Here the ways part; here there is no replacement and no transition. In primitive, as yet undifferentiated epochs, science and art (and religion and ethics and politics) are integrated, they form a single whole; but as soon as science has become separate and independent, everything that has led up to it loses its value. Only when something has dissolved all its content in form, and thus become pure art, can it no longer become superfluous; but then its previous scientific nature altogether forgotten and emptied of meaning.

There is, then, a science of the arts; but there is also an entirely different kind of expression of the human temperament, which usually takes the form of writing about the arts. Usually, I say, for there are many writings which are engendered by such feelings without ever touching upon literature or art—writings in which the same life-problems are raised as in the writings which call themselves criticism, but with the difference that here the questions are addressed directly to life itself: they do not need the mediation of literature or art. And it is precisely the writings of the greatest essayists which belong to this category: Plato's *Dialogues*, the texts of the mystics, Montaigne's *Essays*, Kierkegaard's imaginary diaries and short stories.

An endless series of almost imperceptible, subtle transitions leads from here to imaginative writing. Think of the last scene in the *Heracles* of Euripides: the tragedy is already over when Theseus appears and discovers everything that has happened—Hera's terrible vengeance on Heracles. Then begins the dialogue about life between the mourning Heracles and his friend; questions akin to those of the Socratic dialogues are asked, but the questioners are stiffer and less human, and their questions more conceptual, less related to direct experience than in Plato. Think of the last act of *Michael Kramer,* of the *Confessions of a Beautiful Soul,* of Dante, of *Everyman,* of Bunyan—must I quote further examples?

Doubtless you will say that the end of *Heracles* is undramatic and Bunyan is. . . . Certainly, certainly, but why? The *Heracles* is undramatic because every dramatic style has this natural corollary, that whatever happens within human souls is projected into human actions, movements and gestures and is thus made visible and palpable to the senses. Here you see Hera's vengeance overtaking Heracles, you see Heraclcs in the blissful enjoyment of victory before vengeance is upon him, you see his frenzied gestures in the madness which Hera has dealt to him and his wild despair after the storm, when he sees what has happened to him. But of what comes after you see nothing at all. Theseus comes—and you try in vain to determine by other than conceptual means what happens next: what you see and hear is no longer a true means of expression of the real event, and that the event occurs at all is deep down a matter of indifference to you. You see no more than that Theseus and Heracles leave the stage together. Prior to that some questions are asked: what is the true nature of the gods? Which gods may we believe in, and which not? What is life and what is the best way of bearing one's sufferings manfully? The concrete experience which has led up to these questions is lost in an infinite distance. And when the answers return once more into the world of facts, they are no longer answers to questions posed by real life—questions of what these men must do or refrain from doing in this particular situation. These answers cast a stranger's eye upon all facts, for they have come from life and from the gods and know scarcely anything of Heracles' pain or of its cause in Hera's vengeance. Drama, I know, also addresses questions to life, and in drama, too, the answer comes from destiny—and in the last analysis the questions and answers, even in drama, are tied to certain definite facts. But the true dramatist (so long as he is a true poet, a genuine representative of the poetic principle) will see *a life* as being so rich and so intense that almost imperceptibly it

becomes *life*. Here, however, everything becomes undramatic because here the
other principle comes into effect: for the life that here poses the question loses
all its corporeality at the moment when the first word of the question is uttered.

There are, then, two types of reality of the soul: one is *life* and the other
living; both are equally effective, but they can never be effective at the same
time. Elements of both are contained in the lived experience of every human
being, even if in always varying degrees of intensity and depth; in memory too,
there is now one, now the other, but at any one moment we can only feel one
of these two forms. Ever since there has been life and men have sought to
understand and order life, there has been this duality in their lived experience.
But the struggle for priority and pre-eminence between the two has mostly
been fought out in philosophy, so that the battle-cries have always had a
different sound, and for this reason have gone unrecognized by most men and
have been unrecognizable to them. It would seem that the question was posed
most clearly in the Middle Ages, when thinkers divided into two camps, the
ones maintaining that the *universalia*—concepts, or Plato's Ideas if you will—
were the sole true realities, while the others acknowledged them only as words,
as names summarizing the sole true and distinct *things*.

The same duality also separates means of expression: the opposition here
is between image and "significance". One principle is an image-creating one,
the other a significance-supposing one. For one there exist only things, for the
other only the relationships between them, only concepts and values. Poetry in
itself knows of nothing beyond things; for it, every thing is serious and unique
and incomparable. That is also why poetry knows no questions: you do not
address questions to pure *things*, only to their relationships, for—as in
fairy-tales—every question here turns again into a thing resembling the one
that called it into being. The hero stands at the crossroads or in the midst of the
struggle, but the crossroads and the struggle are not destinies about which
questions may be asked and answers given; they are simply and literally
struggles and crossroads. And the hero blows his miraculous horn and the
expected miracle occurs: a thing which once more orders life. But in really
profound criticism there is no life of things, no image, only transparency, only
something that no image would be capable of expressing completely. An
"imagelessness of all images" is the aim of all mystics, and Socrates speaks
mockingly and contemptuously to Phaedrus of poets, who never have nor ever
could worthily celebrate the true life of the soul. "For the great existence which
the immortal part of the soul once lived is colourless and without form and
impalpable, and only the soul's guide, the mind, can behold it."

You may perhaps reply that my poet is an empty abstraction and so, too,
is my critic. You are right—both are abstractions, but not, perhaps, quite empty
ones. They are abstractions because even Socrates must speak in images of his
"world without form", his world on the far side of form, and even the German
mystic's "imagelessness" is a metaphor. Nor is there any poetry without some
ordering of things. Matthew Arnold once called it *criticism of life*. It represents
the ultimate relationships between man and destiny and world, and without
doubt it has its origin in those profound regions, even if, often, it is unaware of

it. If poetry often refuses all questioning, all taking up of positions, is not the denial of all questions in itself an asking of questions, and is not the conscious rejection of any position in itself a position? I shall go further: the separation of image and significance is itself an abstraction, for the significance is always wrapped in images and the reflection of a glow from beyond the image shines through every image. Every image belongs to our world and the joy of being in the world shines in its countenance; yet it also reminds us of something that was once there, at some time or another, a somewhere, its home, the only thing that, in the last analysis, has meaning and significance for the soul. Yes, in their naked purity they are merely abstractions, those two limits of human feeling, but only with the help of such abstractions can I define the two poles of possible literary expression. And the writings which most resolutely reject the image, which reach out most passionately for what lies behind the image, are the writings of the critics, the Platonists and the mystics.

But in saying this I have already explained why this kind of feeling calls for an art form of its own—why every expression of this kind of feeling must always disturb us when we find it in other forms, in poetry. It was you who once formulated the great demand which everything that has been given form must satisfy, the only absolutely universal demand, perhaps, but one that is inexorable and allows of no exception: the demand that everything in a work must be fashioned from the same material, that each of its parts must be visibly ordered from one single point. And because all writing aspires to both unity and multiplicity, this is the universal problem of style: to achieve equilibrium in a welter of disparate things, richness and articulation in a mass of uniform matter. Something that is viable in one art form is dead in another: here is practical, palpable proof of the inner divorce of forms. Do you remember how you explained to me the living quality of human figures in certain heavily stylized mural paintings? You said: these frescoes are painted between pillars, and even if the gestures of the men depicted in them are stiff like those of puppets and every facial expression is only a mask, still all this is more alive than the columns which frame the pictures and form a decorative unity with them. Only a little more alive, for the unity must be preserved; but more alive all the same, so that there may be an illusion of life. Here, however, the problem of equilibrium is posed in this way: the world and the beyond, image and transparency, idea and emanation lie in the two cups of a scale which is to remain balanced. The deeper down the question reaches—you need only compare the tragedy with the fairy-tale—the more linear the images become, the smaller the number of planes into which everything is compressed, the paler and more matt the radiance of the colours, the simpler the richness and multiplicity of the world, the more mask-like the expressions of the characters. But there are other experiences, for the expression of which even the simplest and most measured gesture would be too much—and too little; there are questions which are asked so softly that beside them the sound of the most toneless of events would be crude noise, not musical accompaniment; there are destiny-relationships which are so exclusively relationships between destinies as such that anything human would merely disturb their abstract

purity and grandeur. I am not speaking here of subtlety or depth: those are
value categories and are therefore valid only within a particular form. We are
speaking of the fundamental principles which separate forms from one
another—of the material from which the whole is constructed, of the standpoint, the world-view which gives unity to the entire work. Let me put it
briefly: were one to compare the forms of literature with sunlight refracted in
a prism, the writings of the essayists would be the ultra-violet rays.

There are experiences, then, which cannot be expressed by any gesture
and which yet long for expression. From all that has been said you will know
what experiences I mean and of what kind they are. I mean intellectuality,
conceptuality as sensed experience, as immediate reality, as spontaneous
principle of existence; the world-view in its undisguised purity as an event of
the soul, as the motive force of life. The question is posed immediately: what
is life, what is man, what is destiny? But posed as a question only: for the
answer, here, does not supply a "solution" like one of the answers of science or,
at purer heights, those of philosophy. Rather, as in poetry of every kind, it is
symbol, destiny and tragedy. When a man experiences such things, then
everything that is outward about him awaits in rigid immobility the outcome of
the struggle between invisible forces to which the senses have no access. Any
gesture with which such a man might wish to express something of his
experience would falsify that experience, unless it ironically emphasized its
own inadequacy and thus cancelled itself out. A man who experiences such
things cannot be characterized by any outward feature—how then can he be
given form in a work of literature? All writings represent the world in the
symbolic terms of a destiny-relationship; everywhere, the problem of destiny
determines the problem of form. This unity, this coexistence is so strong that
neither element ever occurs without the other; here again a separation is
possible only by way of abstraction. Therefore the separation which I am trying
to accomplish here appears, in practice, merely as a shift of emphasis: poetry
receives its profile and its form from destiny, and form in poetry appears always
only as destiny; but in the works of the essayists form *becomes* destiny, it is the
destiny-creating principle. This difference means the following: destiny lifts
things up outside the world of things, accentuating the essential ones and
eliminating the inessential; but form sets limits round a substance which
otherwise would dissolve like air in the All. In other words, destiny comes from
the same source as everything else, it is a thing among things, whereas form—
seen as something finished, i.e. seen from outside—defines the limits of the
immaterial. Because the destiny which orders things is flesh of their flesh and
blood of their blood, destiny is not to be found in the writings of the essayists.
For destiny, once stripped of its uniqueness and accidentality, is just as airy
and immaterial as all the rest of the incorporeal matter of these writings, and
is no more capable of giving them form than they themselves possess any
natural inclination or possibility of condensing themselves into form.

That is why such writings speak of forms. The critic is one who glimpses
destiny in forms: whose most profound experience is the soul-content which
forms indirectly and unconsciously conceal within themselves. Form is his

great experience, form—as immediate reality—is the image-element, the really living content of his writings. This form, which springs from a symbolic contemplation of life-symbols, acquires a life of its own through the power of that experience. It becomes a world-view, a standpoint, an attitude vis-à-vis the life from which it sprang: a possibility of reshaping it, of creating it anew. The critic's moment of destiny, therefore, is that moment at which things become forms—the moment when all feelings and experiences on the near or the far side of form receive form, are melted down and condensed into form. It is the mystical moment of union between the outer and the inner, between soul and form. It is as mystical as the moment of destiny in tragedy when the hero meets his destiny, in the short story when accident and cosmic necessity converge, in poetry when the soul and its world meet and coalesce into a new unity that can no more be divided, either in the past or in the future. Form *is* reality in the writings of critics; it is the voice with which they address their questions to life. That is the true and most profound reason why literature and art are the typical, natural subject-matter of criticism. For here the end-point of poetry can become a starting-point and a beginning; here form appears, even in its abstract conceptuality, as something surely and concretely real. But this is only the typical subject-matter of the essay, not the sole one. For the essayist needs form only as lived experience and he needs only its life, only the living soul-reality it contains. But this reality is to be found in every immediate sensual expression of life, it can be read out of and read into every such experience; life itself can be lived and given form through such a scheme of lived experience. Because literature, art and philosophy pursue forms openly and directly, whereas in life they are no more than the ideal demand of a certain kind of men and experiences, a lesser intensity of critical capacity is needed to experience something formed than to experience something lived; and that is why the reality of form-vision appears, at the first and most superficial glance, less problematic in the sphere of art than in life. But this only seems to be so at the first and most superficial glance, for the form of life is no more abstract than the form of a poem. Here as there, form becomes perceptible only through abstraction, and there as here the reality of form is no stronger than the force with which it is experienced. It would be superficial to distinguish between poems according to whether they take their subject-matter from life or elsewhere; for in any case the form-creating power of poetry breaks and scatters whatever is old, whatever has already been formed, and everything becomes unformed raw material in its hands. To draw such a distinction here seems to me just as superficial, for both ways of contemplating the world are merely standpoints taken up in relation to things, and each is applicable everywhere, although it is true that for both there exist certain things which, with a naturalness decreed by nature, submit themselves to one particular standpoint and others which can only be forced to do so by violent struggles and profound experiences.

As in every really essential relationship, natural effect and immediate usefulness coincide here: the experiences which the writings of the essayists were written to express become conscious in the minds of most people only when they look at the pictures or read the poem discussed and even then they rarely have a force that could move life itself. That is why most people have to believe that the writings of the essayists are produced only in order to explain books and pictures, to facilitate their understanding. Yet this relationship is profound and necessary, and it is precisely the indivisible and organic quality of this mixture of being-accidental and being-necessary which is at the root of that humour and that irony which we find in the writings of every truly great essayist—that peculiar humour which is so strong that to speak of it is almost indecent, for there is no use in pointing it out to someone who does not spontaneously feel it. And the irony I mean consists in the critic always speaking about the ultimate problems of life, but in a tone which implies that he is only discussing pictures and books, only the inessential and pretty ornaments of real life—and even then not their innermost substance but only their beautiful and useless surface. Thus each essay appears to be removed as far as possible from life, and the distance between them seems the greater, the more burningly and painfully we sense the actual closeness of the true essence of both. Perhaps the great Sieur de Montaigne felt something like this when he gave his writings the wonderfully elegant and apt title of "Essays". The simple modesty of this word is an arrogant courtesy. The essayist dismisses his own proud hopes which sometimes lead him to believe that he has come close to the ultimate: he has, after all, no more to offer than explanations of the poems of others, or at best of his own ideas. But he ironically adapts himself to this smallness—the eternal smallness of the most profound work of the intellect in face of life—and even emphasizes it with ironic modesty. In Plato, conceptuality is underlined by the irony of the small realities of life. Eryximachos cures Aristophanes of hiccups by making him sneeze before he can begin his deeply meaningful hymn to Eros. And Hippothales watches with anxious attention while Socrates questions his beloved Lysis—and little Lysis, with childish malice, asks Socrates to torment his friend Menexenos with questions just as he has tormented him. Rough guardians come and break up the gently scintillating dialogue, and drag the boys off home. Socrates, however, is more amused than anything else: "Socrates and the two boys wanted to be friends, yet were not even able to say what a friend really is." I see a similar irony in the vast scientific apparatus of certain modern essayists (think only of Weininger), and only a different expression of it in the discreetly reserved manner of a Dilthey. We can always find the same irony in every text by every great essayist, though admittedly always in a different form. The mystics of the Middle Ages are the only ones without inner irony—I surely need not tell you why.

We see, then, that criticism and the essay generally speak of pictures, books and ideas. What is their attitude towards the matter which is represented? People say that the critic must always speak the truth, whereas the poet is not obliged to tell the truth about his subject-matter. It is not our intention here to ask Pilate's question nor to enquire whether the poet, too, is not impelled towards an inner truthfulness and whether the truth of any criticism can be stronger or greater than this. I do not propose to ask these questions because I really do see a difference here, but once again a difference which is altogether pure, sharp and without transitions only at its abstract poles. When I wrote about Kassner I pointed out that the essay always speaks of something that has already been given form, or at least something that has already been there at some time in the past; hence it is part of the nature of the essay that it does not create new things from an empty nothingness but only orders those which were once alive. And because it orders them anew and does not form something new out of formlessness, it is bound to them and must always speak "the truth" about them, must find expression for their essential nature. Perhaps the difference can be most briefly formulated thus: poetry takes its motifs from life (and art); the essay has its models in art (and life). Perhaps this is enough to define the difference: the paradoxy of the essay is almost the same as that of the portrait. You see why, do you not? In front of a landscape we never ask ourselves whether this mountain or that river really is as it is painted there; but in front of every portrait the question of likeness always forces itself willy-nilly upon us. Give a little more thought, therefore, to this problem of likeness—this problem which, foolish and superficial as it is, drives true artists to despair. You stand in front of a Velásquez portrait and you say: "What a marvellous likeness," and you feel that you have really said something about the painting. Likeness? Of whom? Of no one, of course. You have no idea whom it represents, perhaps you can never find out; and if you could, you would care very little. Yet you feel that it is a likeness. Other portraits produce their effect only by colour and line, and so you do not have this feeling. In other words, the really significant portraits give us, besides all other artistic sensations, also this: the life of a human being who once was really alive, forcing us to feel that his life was exactly as shown by the lines and colours of the painting. Only because we see painters in front of their models fight such a hard battle for this ideal expression—because the look and the battle-cry of this battle are such that it cannot be anything else than a battle for likeness—only for this reason do we give this name to the portrait's suggestion of real life, even though there is no one in the world whom the portrait could be like. For even if we know the person represented, whose portrait we may call "like" or "unlike"—is it not an abstraction to say of an arbitrarily chosen moment or expression that *this* is that person's likeness? And even if we know thousands of such moments or expressions, what do we know of the immeasurably large part of his life when we do not see him, what do we know of the inner light which burns within this "known" person, what of the way this inner light is reflected in others? And that, you see, is more or less how I imagine the truth of the essay to be. Here too there is a struggle for truth, for the incarnation of a life which someone has seen in a man, an epoch or a form; but it depends only on the intensity of the work and its vision whether the written text conveys to us this suggestion of that particular life.

The great difference, then, is this: poetry gives us the illusion of life of the person it represents; nowhere is there a conceivable someone or something against which the created work can be measured. The hero of the essay was once alive, and so his life must be given form; but this life, too, is as much inside the work as everything is in poetry. The essay has to create from within itself all the preconditions for the effectiveness and validity of its vision. Therefore two essays can never contradict one another: each creates a different world, and even when, in order to achieve a higher universality, it goes beyond that created world, it still remains inside it by its tone, colour and accent; that is to say, it leaves that world only in the inessential sense. It is simply not true that there exists an objective, external criterion of life and truth, e.g. that the truth of Grimm's, Dilthey's or Schlegel's Goethe can be tested against the "real" Goethe. It is not true because many Goethes, different from one another and each profoundly different from *our* Goethe, may convince us of their life: and, conversely, we are disappointed if our own visions are presented by others, yet without that vital breath which would give them autonomous life. It is true that the essay strives for truth: but just as Saul went out to look for his father's she-asses and found a kingdom, so the essayist who is really capable of looking for the truth will find at the end of his road the goal he was looking for: life.

The illusion of truth! Do not forget how slowly and with how much difficulty poetry abandoned that ideal. It happened not so very long ago, and it is highly questionable whether the disappearance of the illusion was entirely advantageous. It is highly questionable whether man should want the precise thing he sets out to attain, whether he has the right to walk towards his goal along straight and simple paths. Think of the chivalresque epics of the Middle Ages, think of the Greek tragedies, think of Giotto and you will see what I am trying to say. We are not speaking here of ordinary truth, the truth of naturalism which it would be more accurate to call the triviality of everyday life, but of the truth of the myth by whose power ancient tales and legends are kept alive for thousands of years. The true poets of myths looked only for the true meaning of their themes; they neither could nor wished to check their pragmatic reality. They saw these myths as sacred, mysterious hieroglyphics which it was their mission to read. But do you not see that both worlds can have a mythology of their own? It was Friedrich Schlegel who said long ago that the national gods of the Germans were not Hermann or Wotan but science and the arts. Admittedly, that is not true of the *whole* life of Germany, but it is all the more apt as a description of *part* of the life of every nation in every epoch—that part, precisely, of which we are speaking. That life, too, has its golden ages and its lost paradises; we find in it rich lives full of strange adventures and enigmatic punishments of dark sins; heroes of the sun appear and fight out their harsh feuds with the forces of darkness; here, too, the magic words of wise magicians and the tempting songs of beautiful sirens lead weaklings into perdition; here too there is original sin and redemption. All the struggles of life are present here, but the stuff of which everything is made is different from the stuff of the "other" life.

We want poets and critics to give us life-symbols and to mould the still-living myths and legends in the form of our questions. It is a subtle and poignant irony, is it not, when a great critic dreams our longing into early Florentine paintings or Greek torsos and, in that way, gets something out of them for us that we would have sought in vain everywhere else—and then speaks of the latest achievements of scientific research, of new methods and new facts? Facts are always there and everything is always contained in facts, but every epoch needs its own Greece, its own Middle Ages and its own Renaissance. Every age creates the age it needs, and only the next generation believes that its fathers' dreams were lies which must be fought with its own new "truths". The history of the effect of poetry follows the same course, and in criticism, too, the continuing life of the grandfather's dreams—not to mention those of earlier generations—is barely touched by the dreams of men alive today. Consequently the most varied "conceptions" of the Renaissance can live peacefully side by side with one another, just as a new poet's new Phèdre, Siegfried or Tristan must always leave intact the Phèdre, Siegfried or Tristan of his predecessors.

Of course there is a science of the arts; there has to be one. The greatest essayists are precisely those who can least well do without it: what they create must be science, even when their vision of life has transcended the sphere of science. Sometimes its free flight is constrained by the unassailable facts of dry matter; sometimes it loses all scientific value because it is, after all, a vision, because it precedes facts and therefore handles them freely and arbitrarily. The essay form has not yet, today, travelled the road to independence which its sister, poetry, covered long ago—the road of development from a primitive, undifferentiated unity with science, ethics and art. Yet the beginning of that road was so tremendous that subsequent developments have rarely equalled it. I speak, of course, of Plato, the greatest essayist who ever lived or wrote, the one who wrested everything from life as it unfolded before his eyes and who therefore needed no mediating medium; the one who was able to connect his questions, the most profound questions ever asked, with life as lived. This greatest master of the form was also the happiest of all creators: man lived in his immediate proximity, man whose essence and destiny constituted the paradigmatic essence and destiny of his form. Perhaps they would have become paradigmatic in this way even if Plato's writing had consisted of the driest notations—not just because of his glorious form-giving—so strong was the concordance of life and form in this particular case. But Plato met Socrates and was able to give form to the myth of Socrates, to use Socrates' destiny as the vehicle for the questions he, Plato, wanted to address to life about destiny. The life of Socrates is the typical life for the essay form, as typical as hardly any other life is for any literary form—with the sole exception of Oedipus' life for tragedy. Socrates always lived in the ultimate questions; every other living reality was as little alive for him as his questions are alive for ordinary people. The concepts into which he poured the whole of his life were lived by him with the most direct and immediate life-energy; everything else was but a parable of that sole true reality, useful only as a means of expressing those experiences. His life rings with the sound of the deepest, the most hidden longing and is full of the most violent struggles; but that longing is—simply—longing, and the form in which it appears is the attempt to comprehend the nature of longing and to capture it in concepts, while the struggles are simply verbal battles fought solely in order to give more definite limits to a few concepts. Yet the longing fills that life completely and the struggles are always, quite literally, a matter of life and death. But despite everything the longing which seems to fill that life is not the essential thing about life, and neither Socrates' life nor his death was able to express those life-and-death struggles. If this had been possible, the death of Socrates would have been a martyrdom or a tragedy—which means that it could be represented in epic or dramatic form. But Plato knew exactly why he burned the tragedy he wrote in his youth. For a tragic life is crowned only by its end, only the end gives meaning, sense and form to the whole, and it is precisely the end which is always arbitrary and ironic here, in every dialogue and in Socrates' whole life. A question is thrown up and extended so far in depth that it becomes the question of all questions, but after that everything remains open; something comes from outside—from a reality which has no connection with the question nor with that which, as the possibility of an answer, brings forth a new question to meet it—and interrupts everything. This interruption is not an end, because it does not come from within, and yet it is the most profound ending because a conclusion from within would have been impossible. For Socrates every event was only an occasion for seeing concepts more clearly, his defence in front of the judges only a way of leading weak logicians *ad absurdum*—and his death? Death does not count here, it cannot be grasped by concepts, it interrupts the great dialogue—the only true reality—just as brutally, and merely from the outside, as those rough tutors who interrupted the conversation with Lysis. Such an interruption, however, can only be viewed humoristically, it has so little connection with that which it interrupts. But it is also a profound life-symbol—and, for that reason, still more profoundly humorous—that the essential is always interrupted by such things in such a way.

The Greeks felt each of the forms available to them as a reality, as a living thing and not as an abstraction. Alcibiades already saw clearly what Nietzsche was to emphasize centuries later—that Socrates was a new kind of man, profoundly different in his elusive essence from all other Greeks who lived before him. But Socrates, in the same dialogue, expressed the eternal ideal of men of his kind, an ideal which neither those whose way of feeling remains tied to the purely human nor those who are poets in their innermost being will ever understand: that tragedies and comedies should be written by the same man; that "tragic" and "comic" is entirely a matter of the chosen standpoint. In saying this, the critic expressed his deepest life-sense: the primacy of the standpoint, the concept, over feeling; and in saying it he formulated the profoundest anti-Greek thought.

Plato himself, as you see, was a "critic", although criticism, like everything else, was for him only an occasion, an ironic means of expressing himself. Later on, criticism became its own content; critics spoke only of poetry and art, and they never had the fortune to meet a Socrates whose life might have served them as a springboard to the ultimate. But Socrates was the first to condemn such critics. "It seems to me," he said to Protagoras, "that to make a poem the subject of a conversation is too reminiscent of those banquets which uneducated and vulgar people give in their houses. . . . Conversations like the one we are now enjoying—conversations among men such as most of us would claim to be—do not need outside voices or the presence of a poet. . . ."

Fortunately for us, the modern essay does not always have to speak of books or poets; but this freedom makes the essay even more problematic. It stands too high, it sees and connects too many things to be the simple exposition or explanation of a work; the title of every essay is preceded in invisible letters, by the words "Thoughts occasioned by. . . ." The essay has become too rich and independent for dedicated service, yet it is too intellectual and too multiform to acquire form out of its own self. Has it perhaps become even more problematic, even further removed from life-values than if it had continued to report faithfully on books?

When something has once become problematic—and the way of thinking that we speak of, and its way of expression, have not become problematic but have always been so—then salvation can only come from accentuating the problems to the maximum degree, from going radically to its root. The modern essay has lost that backdrop of life which gave Plato and the mystics their strength; nor does it any longer possess a naïve faith in the value of books and what can be said about them. The problematic of the situation has become accentuated almost to the point of demanding a certain frivolity of thought and expression, and this, for most critics, has become their life-mood. This has shown, however, that salvation is necessary and is therefore becoming possible and real. The essayist must now become conscious of his own self, must find himself and build something of his own out of himself. The essayist speaks of a picture or a book, but leaves it again at once—why? Because, I think, the idea of the picture or book has become predominant in his mind, because he has forgotten all that is concretely incidental about it, because he has used it only as a starting-point, a springboard. Poetry is older and greater—a larger, more important thing—than all the works of poetry: that was once the mood with which critics approached literature, but in our time it has had to become a conscious attitude. The critic has been sent into the world in order to bring to light this *a priori* primacy over great and small, to proclaim it, to judge every phenomenon by the scale of values glimpsed and grasped through this recognition. The idea is there before any of its expressions, it is a soul-value, a world-moving and life-forming force in itself: and that is why such criticism will always speak of life where it is most alive. The idea is the measure of everything that exists, and that is why the critic whose thinking is "occasioned by" something already created, and who reveals its idea, is the one who will write the truest and most profound criticism. Only something that is great and true can live in the proximity of the idea. When this magic word has been spoken, then everything that is brittle, small and unfinished falls apart, loses its usurped wisdom, its badly fitting essence. It does not have to be "criticism": the atmosphere of the idea is enough to judge and condemn it.

Yet it is now that the essayist's possibility of existence becomes profoundly problematic. He is delivered from the relative, the inessential, by the force of judgement of the idea he has glimpsed; but who gives him the right to judge?

It would be almost true to say that he seizes that right, that he creates his judgement-values from within himself. But nothing is separated from true judgement by a deeper abyss than its approximation, the squint-eyed category of complacent and self-satisifed knowledge. The criteria of the essayist's judgement are indeed created within him, but it is not he who awakens them to life and action: the one who whispers them into his ear is the great value-definer of aesthetics, the one who is always about to arrive, the one who is never quite yet there, the only one who has been called to judge. The essayist is a Schopenhauer who writes his *Parerga* while waiting for the arrival of his own (or another's) *The World as Will and Idea,* he is a John the Baptist who goes out to preach in the wilderness about another who is still to come, whose shoelace he is not worthy to untie. And if that other does not come—is not the essayist then without justification? And if the other does come, is he not made superfluous thereby? Has he not become entirely problematic by thus trying to justify himself? He is the pure type of the precursor, and it seems highly questionable whether, left entirely to himself—i.e., independent from the fate of that other of whom he is the herald—he could lay claim to any value or validity. To stand fast against those who deny his fulfilment within the great, redeeming system is easy enough: a true longing always triumphs over those who lack the energy to rise above the vulgar level of given facts and experiences; the existence of the longing is enough to decide the outcome. For it tears the mask off everything that is only apparently positive and immediate, reveals it as petty longing and cheap fulfilment, points to the measure and order to which even they who vainly and contemptibly deny its existence— because measure and order seem inaccessible to them—unconsciously aspire. The essay can calmly and proudly set its fragmentariness against the petty completeness of scientific exactitude or impressionistic freshness; but its purest fulfilment, its most vigorous accomplishment becomes powerless once the great aesthetic comes. Then all its creations are only an application of the measure which at last has become undeniable, it is then something merely provisional and occasional, its results can no longer be justified purely from within themselves. Here the essay seems truly and completely a mere precursor, and no independent value can be attached to it. But this longing for value and form, for measure and order and purpose, does not simply lead to an end that must be reached so that it may be cancelled out and become a presumptuous tautology. Every true end is a real end, the end of a road, and although road and end do not make a unity and do not stand side by side as equals, they nevertheless coexist: the end is unthinkable and unrealizable without the road being travelled again and again; the end is not standing still but arriving there, not resting but conquering a summit. Thus the essay seems justified as a necessary means to the ultimate end, the penultimate step in this hierarchy. This, however, is only the value of what it *does;* the fact of what it *is* has yet another, more independent value. For in the system of values yet to be found, the longing we spoke of would be satisfied and therefore abolished; but this longing is more than just something waiting for fulfilment, it is a fact of the soul with a value and existence of its own: an original and deep-rooted attitude towards the whole of life, a final, irreducible category of possibilities of experience. Therefore it needs not only to be satisfied (and thus abolished) but also to be given form which will redeem and release its most essential and now indivisible substance into eternal value. That is what the essay does. Think again of the example of the *Parerga:* whether they occurred before or after the system is not a matter simply of a time-sequence; the time-historical difference is only a symbol of the difference between their two natures. The *Parerga* written before the system create their preconditions from within themselves, create the whole world out of their longing for the system, so that—it seems— they can give an example, a hint; immanently and inexpressibly, they contain the system and its connection with lived life. Therefore they must always occur before the system; even if the system had already been created, they would not be a mere application but always a new creation, a coming-alive in real experience. This "application" creates both that which judges and that which is judged, it encompasses a whole world in order to raise to eternity, in all its uniqueness, something that was once there. The essay is a judgement, but the essential, the value-determining thing about it is not the verdict (as is the case with the system) but the process of judging.

Only now may we write down the opening words: the essay is an art form, an autonomous and integral giving-of-form to an autonomous and complete life. Only now would it not be contradictory, ambiguous and false to call it a work of art and yet insist on emphasizing the thing that differentiates it from art: it faces life with the same gesture as the work of art, but only the gesture, the sovereignty of its attitude is the same; otherwise there is no correspondence between them.

It was of this possibility of the essay that I wanted to speak to you here, of the nature and form of these "intellectual poems", as the older Schlegel called those of Hemsterhuys. This is not the place to discuss or decide whether the essayists' becoming conscious of their own nature, as they have been doing for some time past, has brought perfection or can bring it. The point at issue was only the possibility, only the question of whether the road upon which this book attempts to travel is really a road; it was not a question of who has already travelled it or how—nor, least of all, the distance this particular book has travelled along it. The critique of this book is contained, in all possible sharpness and entirety, in the very approach from which it sprang.

ART AND OBJECTIVE TRUTH

I

The Objectivity of Truth in Marxist-Leninist Epistemology

The basis for any correct cognition of reality, whether of nature or society, is the recognition of the objectivity of the external world, that is, its existence independent of human consciousness. Any apprehension of the external world is nothing more than a reflection in consciousness of the world that exists independently of consciousness. This basic fact of the relationship of consciousness to being also serves, of course, for the artistic reflection of reality.

The theory of reflection provides the common basis for *all* forms of theoretical and practical mastery of reality through consciousness. Thus it is also the basis for the theory of the artistic reflection of reality. In this discussion, we will seek to elaborate the *specific* aspects of artistic reflection within the scope of the general theory.

A valid, comprehensive theory of reflection first arose with dialectical materialism, in the works of Marx, Engels and Lenin. For the bourgeois mind a correct theory of objectivity and of the reflection in consciousness of a reality existing independent of consciousness, a materialist, dialectical theory, is an impossibility. Of course, in practice, in bourgeois science and art there are countless instances of an accurate reflection of reality, and there have even been a number of attempts at a correct theoretical posing and solution of the question. Once the question is elevated, however, into a question of epistemology, bourgeois thinkers become trapped in mechanistic materialism or sink into philosophic idealism. Lenin characterized and exposed the limitations of both directions of bourgeois thinking with unsurpassed clarity. Of mechanistic materialism he declared: "Its chief failure lies in its incapacity to apply dialectics to the theory of images, to the process and evolution of knowledge." Philosophic idealism he went on to characterize thus: "Contrarily, from the standpoint of *dialectical* materialism, philosophical idealism is a *one-sided,* exaggerated, extravagant . . . development, a pompous inflation of one aspect, of one side, of one frontier of knowledge to a sanctified absolute divorced from matter, from nature. . . . Single-dimensionality, one-sidedness, frigidity, subjectivism and subjective blindness, *voilà,* the epistemological roots of idealism."

This double-faceted inadequacy of bourgeois epistemology appears in all areas and in all problems of the reflection of reality through consciousness. In this connection we cannot investigate the entire realm of epistemology or trace the history of human knowledge. We must limit ourselves to a few important

aspects of the epistemology of Marxism-Leninism which are especially significant for the *problem of objectivity* in the *artistic reflection of reality*.

The first problem to deal with is that of the direct reflections of the
external world. All knowledge rests on them; they are the foundation, the point
of departure for all knowledge. But they are *only* the point of departure and not
all there is to the process of knowing. Marx expressed himself with unmistakable clarity on this question, declaring: "Science would be superfluous if there
were an immediate coincidence of the appearance and reality of things." And
in his study of Hegel's logic, Lenin analysed this question and arrived at this
formulation: "Truth is not to be found at the beginning but at the end, more
particularly within the process. Truth is not the *initial impression*." Following
Marx he illustrated this observation with an example from political economy:
"Value is a category which deprives goods of their materiality, but it is *truer*
than the law of supply and demand." From this introductory observation Lenin
goes on to define the function of abstract terms, concepts, laws, etc., in the
total human comprehension of reality and to define their place in the over-all
theory of reflection and of the objective knowledge of reality. "Just as the
simple incorporation of value, the single act of exchanging goods, includes in
microcosm, in embryo, *all* the principal contradictions of capitalism—so the
simplest generalization, the initial and simplest formulation of *concepts*
(judgments, conclusions) implies man's ever-expanding apprehension of the
objective macrocosm." On this basis he is able to state in summary: "The
abstractions of matter, natural *law,* value, etc., in a word, *all* scientific
(accurate, seriously considered, not irrational) abstractions reflect nature more
profoundly, more faithfully, more *completely*. From active observation to
abstract thought and from there to practical activity—such is the dialectical
path of apprehending truth and objective reality."

By analysing the place of various abstractions in epistemology, Lenin
underscores with the greatest precision the dialectical dichotomy within them.
He says: "The significance of the *universal* is contradictory: it is inert, impure,
incomplete, etc., but it is also only a *stage* in the cognition of the concrete, for
we never apprehend the concrete completely. The infinite sum of general
concepts, laws, etc., provides the concrete in its completeness." This dichotomy alone clarifies the dialectic of appearance and reality. Lenin says: "The
phenomenon is *richer* than the law." And he goes on to comment on a
definition of Hegel's: "That (the word 'passive') is an excellent materialist and
remarkably apt description. Every law deals with the passive—and that is why
a law, every law, is restricted, incomplete, approximate."

With this profound insight into the incompleteness of the intellectual
reproduction of reality, both in the direct mirroring of phenomena as well as in
concepts and laws (when they are considered one-sidedly, undialectically,
outside the infinite process of dialectical interaction), Lenin arrived at a
materialist elimination of all false formulations of bourgeois epistemology. For
every bourgeois epistemology has one-sidedly emphasized the priority of one
approach to apprehending reality, one mode in the conscious reproduction of
reality. Lenin concretely presents the dialectical interaction in the process of

cognition. "Is the perceptual image *closer* to reality than thought? Both yes and no. The perceptual image cannot entirely comprehend motion; for example, it cannot comprehend speed of three hundred thousand kilometres per second, but *thought* can and should do so. Thus thought derived from perception mirrors reality." In this way the idealistic depreciation of the "lower" faculties of cognition is overcome through dialectics. With the strict materialism of his epistemology and his unwavering insistence on the principle of objectivity, Lenin is able to grasp the correct dialectical relationship of the modes of human perception of reality in their dynamics. Regarding the role of fantasy in cognition, he says: "The approach of human reason to the individual thing, obtaining an impression (a concept) of it is no simple, direct, lifeless mirroring but a complicated, dichotomous, zigzag act which by its very nature encompasses the possibility that imagination can soar away from life. . . . For even in the simplest generalization of the most elementary universal idea (like the idea of a table) there lurks a shred of imagination (vice versa, it is foolish to deny the role of imagination in the most exact science)."

Only through dialectics is it possible to overcome the incompleteness, the rigidity and the barrenness of any one-sided conception of reality. Only through the correct and conscious application of dialectics can we overcome the incompleteness in the infinite process of cognition and bring our thinking closer to the dynamic infinity in objective reality. Lenin says: "We cannot imagine motion, we cannot express it, measure it, imitate it without interrupting its continuity, without simplifying, vulgarizing, disintegrating and stifling its dynamism. The intellectual representation of motion is always vulgarized and devitalized and not only through thoughts but through the senses as well and not only of motion, but of any concept at all. And precisely in this is the essence of dialectics. *Precisely this essence* is to be expressed through the formula: unity, identity of opposites."

The union of materialist dialectics with *practice*, its derivation from practice, its control through practice, its directive role in practice, rest on this profound conception of the dialectical nature of objective reality and of the dialectic of its reflection in consciousness. Lenin's theory of revolutionary practice rests on his recognition of the fact that reality is always richer and more varied than the best and most comprehensive theory that can be developed to apprehend it, and at the same time, however, on the consciousness that with the active application of dialectics one can learn from reality, apprehend important new factors in reality and apply them in practice. "History," Lenin said, "especially the history of revolution, was always richer in content, more complex, more dynamic, subtler than the most effective parties, the most class-conscious vanguard of the most progressive classes ever imagined." The extraordinary elasticity in Lenin's tactics, his ability to adapt himself swiftly to sudden changes in history and to derive the maximum from these changes rested on his profound grasp of objective dialectics.

This relationship between the strict objectivity in epistemology[1] and its integral relationship to practice is one of the significant aspects of the materialist dialectic of Marxism-Leninism. The objectivity of the external world is no inert, rigid objectivity fatalistically determining human activity; because of its very independence of consciousness it stands in the most intimate indissoluble interaction with practice. In his early youth Lenin had already rejected any mere fatalistic, abstract, undialectical conception of objectivity as false and conducive to apologetics. In his struggle against Michailowsky's subjectivism he also criticized Struve's blatantly apologetic "objectivism". He grasped the objectivism in dialectical materialism correctly and profoundly as an objectivism of practice, of *partisanship*. Materialism implies, Lenin said in summarizing his objections against Struve, "so to speak the element of partisanship within itself in setting itself the task of evaluating any event directly and openly from the standpoint of a particular social group".

II

The Theory of Reflection in Bourgeois Aesthetics

This contradictory basis in man's apprehension of the external world, this immanent contradiction in the structure of the reflection of the eternal world in consciousness appears in all theoretical concepts regarding the artistic reproduction of reality. When we investigate the history of aesthetics from the standpoint of Marxism-Leninism, we discover everywhere the one-sidedness of the two tendencies so profoundly analysed by Lenin: on the one hand, the incapacity of mechanical materialism "to apply dialectics to the theory of images", and on the other hand, the basic error inherent in idealism: "the universal (the concept, the idea) as a *peculiar entity in itself*." Naturally, these two tendencies rarely appear as absolutes in the history of aesthetics. Mechanical materialism, whose strength lies in its insistence upon the concept of the reflection of objective reality and in its maintenance of this view in aesthetics, is transformed into idealism as a result of its incapacity to comprehend motion, history, etc., as Engels so convincingly demonstrated. In the history of aesthetics, as in epistemology generally, objective idealists (Aristotle, Hegel) made heroic attempts at overcoming dialectically the inadequacy, one-sidedness and rigidity of idealism. But since their attempts were made on an idealistic basis, they achieved individual astute formulations regarding objectivity, but their systems as a whole fall victim to the one-sidedness of idealism.

To expose the contradictory, one-sided and inadequate approaches of mechanical materialism and idealism, we can cite in this discussion only one classical illustration of each. We refer to the works of the classics because they expressed their opinions with a straightforward, honest frankness, quite in contrast to the aestheticians of the decadence of bourgeois ideology with their eclectic and apologetic temporizing and chicanery.

In his novel *Les Bijoux indiscrets,* Diderot, a leading exponent of the mechanistic theory of the direct imitation of nature, expressed this theory in its crassest form. His heroine, the spokesman for his own points of view, offers the following critique of French classicism: "But I know that only truth pleases and moves. Besides, I know that the perfection in a play consists in such a precise imitation of an action that the audience is deceived into believing that they are present at the action." And to eliminate any doubt that he means by this deception the photographic imitation of reality, Diderot has his heroine imagine a case where a person is told the plot of a tragedy as though it were a real court intrigue; then he goes to the theatre to witness the continuation of this actual event: "I conduct him to his loge behind a grille in the theatre; from it he sees the stage, which he takes to be the palace of the Sultan. Do you believe that the man will let himself be deceived for a moment even if I put on a serious face? On the contrary." For Diderot this comment represents an annihilating aesthetic judgment on this drama. Clearly, on the basis of such a theory, which strives for the ultimate in objectivity in art, not a single real problem of specifically artistic objectivity can be resolved. (That Diderot does formulate and resolve a whole series of problems both in his theory and more especially in his creative work is beside the point, for he resolves them solely by departing from this crude theory.)

For the opposite extreme, we can examine Schiller's aesthetics. In the very interesting preface to his *Braut von Messina*, Schiller provides an impressive critique of the inadequacy of the aesthetic theory of imitation. He correctly poses the task of art—"not to be content simply with the appearances of truth," but to build its edifices "on truth itself". As a thorough idealist, however, Schiller considers truth not as a more profound and comprehensive reflection of objective reality than is given in mere appearance; instead he isolates truth from material reality and makes it an autonomous entity, contrasting it crudely and exclusively with reality. He says: "Nature itself is only an idea of the Spirit, which is never captured by the senses." That is why the product of artistic fantasy in Schiller's eyes is "truer than reality and more real than experience". This idealistic attenuation and petrification of what is normal and beyond immediate experience undermines all Schiller's correct and profound insights. Although in principle he expresses a correct insight when he says "that the artist cannot utilize a single element of reality just as he finds it", he carries this correct observation too far, considering only what is immediately at hand as real and holding truth to be a supernatural principle instead of a more incisive, comprehensive reflection of objective reality— opposing the two idealistically and absolutely. Thus from correct initial insights he arrives at false conclusions, and through the very theoretical approach by which he establishes a basis for objectivity in art more profound than that provided by mechanical materialism, he eliminates all objectivity from art.

In the contemporary evolution of aesthetics we find the same two extremes: on the one hand, the insistence on immediate reality; on the other hand, the isolation from material reality of any aspects reaching beyond immediate reality. As a result of the general turn in ideology in bourgeois decadence, however, to a hypocritical, foggy idealism, both theoretical approaches suffer considerable modification. The theory of the direct reproduction of reality more and more loses its mechanical materialist character as a theory of the reflection of the external world. Direct experience becomes even more strongly subjectivized, more firmly conceived as an independent and autonomous function of the individual (as impression, emotional response, etc., abstractly divorced from the objective reality which generates it). Naturally, in actual practice the outstanding realists even of this period continue to create on the basis of an artistic imitation of reality, no longer, however, with the subtlety and (relative) consequence of the realists of the period of bourgeois ascendency. More and more, theories become permeated with an eclectism of a false objectivism and a false subjectivism. They isolate objectivity from practice, eliminate all motion and vitality and set it in crass, fatalistic, romantic opposition to an equally isolated subjectivity. Zola's famous definition of art, "un coin de la nature vu à travers un tempérament", is a prime example of such eclecticism. A scrap of reality is to be reproduced mechanically and thus with a false objectivity, and is to become poetic by being viewed in the light of the observer's subjectivity, a subjectivity divorced from practice and from interaction with practice. The artist's subjectivity is no longer what it was for the old realists, the means for achieving the fullest possible reflection of motion of a totality, but a garnish to a mechanical reproduction of a chance scrap of experience.

The resultant subjectivizing of the direct reproduction of reality reaches its ultimate extension in naturalism and enjoys the most varied theoretical exposition. The most famous and influential of these theories is the so-called theory of "empathy". This theory denies any imitation of reality independent of consciousness. The leading modern exponent of this theory, Lipps, declares, for example: "The form of an object is always determined by me, through my inner activity." And he concludes, "Aesthetic pleasure is objectivized self-gratification." According to this view, the essence of art is the introduction of human thoughts, feelings, etc., into an external world regarded as unknowable. This theory faithfully mirrors the ever-intensifying subjectivization in artistic practice apparent in the transition from naturalism to impressionism, etc., in the growing subjectivization of subject matter and of creative method and in the increasing alienation of art from great social problems.

Thus the theory of realism of the imperialist period reveals an intensifying dissolution and disintegration of the ideological preconditions for realism. And it is clear that with the undisguised reactions against realism, idealistic subjectivism attains a theoretical extremism unknown to earlier idealism. The extreme idealistic rigidity is further intensified insofar as idealism under imperialism has become an idealism of imperialist parasitism. Whereas the great exponents of classical idealism sought an effective intellectual mastery of the great problems of their time, even if in their idealism their formulations were distorted and inverted, this new idealism is an ideology of reaction, of flight from the great issues of the era, a denial of reality by "abstracting it out of existence". The well-known, influential aesthetician Worringer, founder and theoretician of the so-called "theory of abstraction", derives the need for abstraction from man's "spiritual space-phobia" (*geistige Raumscheu*), his "overwhelming need for tranquillity" (*ungeheures Ruhebeduerfnis*). Accordingly, he rejects modern realism as too imitative, as too close to reality. He bases his theory on an "absolute will to art", by which he means "a potential inner drive completely independent of the object . . . existing for itself and acting as will to form". The faddish pretension of this theory to the highest artistic objectivity is characteristic of the theories of the imperialist period; they never come out in the open but always mask their intentions. In his characterization of the "struggle" of the Machians against idealism, Lenin exposed this manœuvre of imperialist idealism. The theory of abstraction, which subsequently provided the theoretical base for expressionism, represented a culmination of the subjectivist elimination of all content from aesthetics; it is a theory of the subjectivist petrification and decay of artistic forms in the period of capitalist degeneration.

III

The Artistic Reflection of Reality

The artistic reflection of reality rests on the same contradiction as any other reflection of reality. What is specific to it is that it pursues another resolution of these contradictions than science. We can best define the specific character of the artistic reflection of reality by examining first in the abstract the goal it sets itself, in order then to illuminate the preconditions for attaining this goal. The goal for all great art is to provide a picture of reality in which the contradiction between appearance and reality, the particular and the general, the immediate and the conceptual, etc., is so resolved that the two converge into a spontaneous integrity in the direct impression of the work of art and provide a sense of an inseparable integrity. The universal appears as a quality of the individual and the particular, reality becomes manifest and can be experienced within appearance, the general principle is exposed as the specific impelling cause for the individual case being specially depicted. Engels characterized this essential mode of artistic creation clearly in a comment about characterization in a novel: "Each is simultaneously a type and a particular individual, a 'this one' (Dieser), as old Hegel expressed it, and so it must be."

It follows then that every work of art must present a circumscribed, self-contained and complete context with its own *immediately* self-evident movement and structure. The necessity for the immediate obviousness of the special context is clearest in literature. The true, fundamental interrelationships in any novel or drama can be disclosed only at the end. Because of the very nature of their construction and effect, only the conclusion provides full clarification of the beginning. Furthermore, the composition would fail utterly and have no impact if the path to this culmination were not clearly demarcated at every stage. The motivating factors in the world depicted in a literary work of art are revealed in an artistic sequence and climaxing. But this climaxing must be accomplished within a direct unity of appearance and reality present from the very beginning; in the intensifying concretizing of both aspects, it must make their unity ever more integral and self-evident.

This self-contained immediacy in the work of art presupposes that every work of art evolve within itself all the preconditions for its characters, situations, events, etc. The unity of appearance and reality can become direct experience only if the reader experiences every important aspect of the growth or change with all their primary determining factors, if the outcome is never simply handed to him but he is conducted to the outcome and directly experiences the process leading to the outcome. The basic materialism of all great artists (no matter whether their ostensible philosophy is partly or completely idealistic) appears in their clear depiction of the pertinent preconditions and motivations out of which the consciousness of their characters arises and develops.

Thus every significant work of art creates its "own world". Characters, situations, actions, etc., in each have a unique quality unlike that in any other work of art and entirely distinct from anything in everyday reality. The greater the artist, the more intensely his creative power permeates all aspects of his work of art and the more pregnantly his fictional "world" emerges through all the details of the work. Balzac said of his *Comédie humaine:* "My work has its own geography as well as its own genealogy and its own families, its places and its objects, its people and its facts; even as it possesses its heraldry, its aristocracy and its bourgeoisie, its workmen and its peasants, its politicians and its dandies and its army—in short, its world."

Does not the establishment of such particularity in a work of art preclude the fulfilment of its function as a reflection of reality? By no means! It merely affirms the special character, the peculiar kind of reflection of reality there is in art. The apparently circumscribed world in the work of art and its apparent non-correspondence with reality are founded on this peculiar character of the artistic reflection of reality. For this non-correspondence is merely an illusion, though a necessary one, essential and intrinsic to art. The effect of art, the immersion of the receptant in the action of the work of art, his complete penetration into the special "world" of the work of art, results from the fact that the work by its very nature offers a truer, more complete, more vivid and more dynamic reflection of reality than the receptant otherwise possesses, that it conducts him on the basis of his own experiences and on the basis of the organization and generalization of his previous reproduction of reality beyond the bounds of his experiences toward a more concrete insight into reality. It is therefore only an illusion—as though the work itself were not a reflection of reality, as though the reader did not conceive of the special "world" as a reflection of reality and did not compare it with his own experiences. He acts consistently in accordance with this pretence, and the effect of the work of art ceases once the reader becomes aware of a contradiction, once he senses that the work of art is not an accurate reflection of reality. But this illusion is in any case necessary. For the reader does not consciously compare an individual experience with an isolated event of the work of art but surrenders himself to the general effect of the work of art on the basis of his own assembled general experience. And the comparison between both reflections of reality remains unconscious so long as the reader is engrossed, that is, so long as his experiences regarding reality are broadened and deepened by the fiction of the work of art. Thus Balzac is not contradicting his statement about his "own world" when he says, "To be productive one needs only to study. French society should be the historian, I only its amanuensis."

The self-containment of a work of art is therefore the reflection of the process of life in motion and in concrete dynamic context. Of course, science sets itself the same goal. It achieves dialectical concreteness by probing more profoundly into the laws of motion. Engels says: "The universal law of the transformation of form is far more concrete than any individual 'concrete' example of it." This progression in the scientific cognition of reality is endless. That is, objective reality is correctly reflected in any accurate scientific cognition; to this extent this cognition is absolute. Since, however, reality is always richer, more multifaceted than any law, it is in the nature of knowledge that knowledge must always be expanded, deepened, enriched, and that the absolute always appears as relative and as an approximation. Artistic concreteness too is a unity of the absolute and the relative, but a unity which cannot go beyond the framework of the work of art. Objective progress is the historical process and the further development of our knowledge of this process do not eliminate the artistic value, the validity and effect of great works of art which depict their times correctly and profoundly.

There is a second and more important difference between the scientific and the artistic reflections of reality in that individual scientific cognitions (laws, etc.) are not independent of each other but form an integral system. And this context becomes the more intensive the more science develops. Every work of art, however, must stand on its own. Naturally, there is development in art, and this development follows an objective pattern with laws that can be analysed. But the fact that this objective pattern in the development of art is a part of the general social development does not eliminate the fact that a work of art becomes such by possessing this self-containment, this capacity to achieve its effect on its own.

The work of art must therefore reflect correctly and in proper proportion all important factors objectively determining the area of life it represents. It must so reflect these that this area of life becomes comprehensible from within and from without, re-experiencable, that it appears as a totality of life. This does not mean that every work of art must strive to reflect the objective, extensive totality of life. On the contrary, the extensive totality of reality necessarily is beyond the possible scope of any artistic creation; the totality of reality can only be reproduced intellectually in ever-increasing approximation through the infinite process of science. The totality of the work of art is rather intensive: the circumscribed and self-contained ordering of those factors which objectively are of decisive significance for the portion of life depicted, which determine its existence and motion, its specific quality and its place in the total life process. In this sense the briefest song is as much an intensive totality as the mightiest epic. The objective character of the area of life represented determines the quantity, quality, proportion, etc., of the factors that emerge in interaction with the specific laws of the literary form appropriate for the representation of this portion of life.

The self-containment implies first of all that the goal of the work of art is depicting that subtlety, richness and inexhaustibility of life about which we have quoted Lenin, and bringing it dynamically and vividly to life. No matter whether the intention in the work of art is the depiction of the whole of society or only an artificially isolated incident, the aim will still be to depict the intensive inexhaustibility of the subject. This means that it will aim at involving creatively in its fiction all important factors which in objective reality provide the basis for a particular event or complex of events. And artistic involvement means that all these factors will appear as personal attributes of the persons in the action, as the specific qualities of the situations depicted, etc.; thus in a directly perceptible unity of the individual and the universal. Very few people are capable of such an experience of reality. They achieve knowledge of general determinants in life only through the abandonment of the immediate, only through abstraction, only through generalized comparison of experiences. (In this connection, the artist himself is no exception. His work consists rather in elevating the experiences he obtains ordinarily to artistic form, to a representation of the unity of the immediate and the universal.) In representing individual men and situations, the artist awakens the illusion of life. In depicting them as exemplary men and situations (the unity of the individual and the typical), in bringing to life the greatest possible richness of the objective conditions of life as the particular attributes of individual people and situations, he makes his "own world" emerge as the reflection of life in its total motion, as process and totality, in that it intensifies and surpasses in its totality and in its particulars the common reflection of the events of life.

This depiction of the subtlety of life, of a richness beyond ordinary experience, is only one side in the special mode of the artistic representation of reality. If a work of art depicted only the overflowing abundance of new concepts, only those aspects which provide new insights, only the subtlety beyond the common generalization about ordinary experience, then the reader would merely be confused instead of being involved, for the appearance of such aspects in life generally confuses people and leaves them at a loss. It is therefore necessary that *within* this richness and subtlety the artist introduce a new order of things which displaces or modifies the old abstractions. This is also a reflection of objective reality. For such a new order is never simply imposed on life but is derived from the new phenomena of life through reflection, comparison, etc. But in life itself it is always a question of two steps; in the first place, one is surprised by the new facts and sometimes even overwhelmed by them and then only does one need to deal with them intellectually by applying the dialectical method. In art these two steps coincide, not in the sense of a mechanical unity (for then the newness of the individual phenomena would again be annihilated) but in the sense of a process in which from the outset the order within the new phenomena manifesting the subtlety of life is sensed and emerges in the course of the artistic climaxing ever more sharply and clearly.

This representation of life, structured and ordered more richly and strictly than ordinary life experience, is in intimate relation to the active social function, the propaganda effect of the genuine work of art. Such a depiction cannot possibly exhibit the lifeless and false objectivity of an "impartial" imitation which takes no stand or provides no call to action. From Lenin, however, we know that this partisanship is not introduced into the external world arbitrarily by the individual but is a motive force inherent in reality which is made conscious through the correct dialectical reflection of reality and introduced into practice. This partisanship of objectivity must therefore be found intensified in the work of art—intensified in clarity and distinctness, for the subject matter of a work of art is consciously arranged and ordered by the artist toward this goal, in the sense of this partisanship; intensified, however, in objectivity too, for a genuine work of art is directed specifically toward depicting this partisanship as a quality in the subject matter, presenting it as a motive force inherent in it and growing organically out of it. When Engels approves of tendentiousness in literature he always means, as does Lenin after him, this "partisanship of objectivity" and emphatically rejects any subjective superimposed tendentiousness: "But I mean that the tendentiousness must spring out of the situation and action without being expressly pointed out."

All bourgeois theories treating the problem of the aesthetic illusion allude to this dialectic in the artistic reflection of reality. The paradox in the effect of a work of art is that we surrender ourselves to the work as though it presented reality to us, accept it as reality and immerse ourselves in it although we are always aware that it is not reality but simply a special form of reflecting reality. Lenin correctly observes: "Art does not demand recognition as *reality*." The illusion in art, the aesthetic illusion, depends therefore on the self-containment we have examined in the work of art and on the fact that the work of art in its totality reflects the full process of life and does not represent in its details reflections of particular phenomena of life which can be related individually to aspects of actual life on which they are modelled. Non-correspondence in this respect is the precondition of the artistic illusion, an illusion absolutely divorced from any such correspondence. On the other hand and inseparable from it is the fact that the aesthetic illusion is only possible when the work of art reflects the total objective process of life with *objective accuracy*.

This objective dialectic in the artistic reflection of reality is beyond the ken of bourgeois theory, and bourgeois theory always degenerates into subjectivism at least in specific points, if not in totality. Philosophic idealism must, as we have seen, isolate this characteristic of self-containment in a work of art and its elevation above ordinary reality, from material and objective reality; it must oppose the self-containment, the perfection of form in the work of art, to the theory of reflection. When objective idealism seeks to rescue and establish the objectivity of art abstractly, it inevitably falls into mysticism. It is by no means accidental that the Platonic theory of art as the reflection of "ideas" exerts such a powerful historical influence right up to Schelling and Schopenhauer. And when the mechanical materialists fall into idealism because of the inadequacy of their philosophic conception of social phenomena, they usually go from a mechanical photographic theory of imitation to Platonism, to a theory of the artistic imitation of "ideas". (This is especially apparent with Shaftesbury and at times evident with Diderot.) But this mystical objectivism is always and inevitably transformed into subjectivism. The more the aspects of the self-containment of a work and of the dynamic character of the artistic elaboration and reshaping of reality are opposed to the theory of reflection instead of being derived from it dialectically, the more the principle of form, beauty and artistry is divorced from life; the more it becomes an unclear, subjective and mystical principle. The Platonic "ideas" occasionally inflated and attenuated in the idealism of the period of bourgeois ascendancy, though artificially isolated from social reality, were reflections of decisive social problems and thus for all their idealistic distortion were full of content and were not without relevance; but with the decline of the class they more and more lose content. The social isolation of the personally dedicated artist in a declining society is mirrored in this mystical, subjective inflation of the principle of form divorced from any connection with life. The original despair of genuine artists over this situation passes to parasitic resignation and the self-complacency of "art for art's sake" and its theory of art. Baudelaire sings of beauty in a tone of despondent subjective mysticism: "Je trône dans l'azure comme un sphinx incompris." In the later art for art's sake of the imperialist period such subjectivism evolves into a theory of a contemptuous, parasitic divorce of art from life, into a denial of any objectivity in art, a glorification of the "sovereignty" of the creative individual and a theory of indifference to content and arbitrariness in form.

We have already seen that mechanical materialism tends toward an opposite direction. Sticking to the mechanical imitation of life as it is immediately perceived in all its superficial detail, it must deny the special character of the artistic reflection of reality or fall into idealism with all its distortions and subjectivism. The pseudo-objectivity of mechanical materialism, of the mechanical, direct imitation of the immediate world of phenomena, is thus inevitably transformed into idealistic subjectivism since it does not acknowledge the objectivity of the underlying laws and relationships that cannot immediately be perceived and since it sees in these laws and relationships no reflection of objective reality but simply technical means for superficial groupings of sense data. The weakness of the direct imitation of life in its particularity must intensify and develop further into subjective idealism without content as the general ideological development of the bourgeoisie transforms the philosophic materialist basis of this sort of artistic imitation of reality into agnostic idealism (the theory of empathy).

The objectivity of the artistic reflection of reality depends on the correct reflection of the totality. The artistic correctness of a detail thus has nothing to do with whether the detail corresponds to any similar detail in reality. The detail in a work of art is an accurate reflection of life when it is a necessary aspect of the accurate reflection of the total process of objective reality, no matter whether it was observed by the artist in life or created through imagination out of direct or indirect experience. On the other hand, the artistic truth of a detail which corresponds photographically to life is purely accidental, arbitrary and subjective. When, for example, the detail is not directly and obviously necessary to the context, then it is incidental to a work of art, its inclusion is arbitrary and subjective. It is therefore entirely possible that a collage of photographic material may provide an incorrect, subjective and arbitrary reflection of reality. For merely arranging thousands of chance details in a row never results in artistic necessity. In order to discipline accident into a proper context with artistic necessity, the necessity must be latent within the accidental and must appear as an inner motivation within the details themselves. The detail must be so selected and so depicted from the outset that its relationship with the totality may be organic and dynamic. Such selection and ordering of details depends solely on the artistic, objective reflection of reality. The isolation of details from the general context and their selection on the basis of a photographic correspondence with reality imply a rejection of the more profound problem of objective necessity, even a denial of the existence of this necessity. Artists who create thus, choose and organize material not out of the objective necessity in the subject matter but out of pure subjectivity, a fact which is manifested in the work as an objective anarchy in the selection and arrangement of their material.

Ignoring deeper objective necessity in the reflection of reality is manifested also in creative art as annihilation of objectivity. We have already seen how for Lenin and Engels partisanship in the work of art is a component of objective reality and of a correct, objective artistic reflection of life. The tendency in the work of art speaks forth from the objective context of the world depicted within the work; it is the language of the work of art transmitted through the artistic reflection of reality and therefore the speech of reality itself, not the subjective opinion of the writer exposed baldly or explicitly in a personal commentary or in a subjective, ready-made conclusion. The concept of art as *direct* propaganda, a concept particularly exemplified in recent art by Upton Sinclair, rejects the deeper, objective propaganda potential of art in the Leninist conception of partisanship and substitutes pure personal propaganda which does not grow organically out of the logic of the subject matter but remains a mere subjective expression of the author's views.

IV

The Objectivity of Artistic Form

Both the tendencies to subjectivism just analysed disrupt the dialectical unity of form and content in art. In principle it is not decisive whether the form or the content is wrenched out of the dialectical unity and inflated to an autonomy. In either case the concept of the objectivity of form is abandoned. Either means that the form becomes a "device" to be manipulated subjectively and wilfully; in either case form loses its character as a specific mode of the reflection of reality. Of similar tendencies in logic Lenin declared sharply and unequivocally: "Objectivism: the categories of thought are not tools for men but the expression of the order governing nature and men." This rigorous and profound formulation provides a natural basis for the investigation of form in art, with the emphasis, naturally, on the specific, essential characteristics of artistic reflection; always within the framework of the dialectical materialist conception of the nature of form.

The question of the objectivity of form is among the most difficult and least investigated in Marxist aesthetics. Marxist-Leninist epistemology indicates unequivocally indeed, as we have seen, the direction in which the solution of the problem is to be sought. But contemporary bourgeois concepts have so influenced our Marxist theory of literature and our literary practice as to introduce confusion and reserve in the face of a correct Marxist formulation and even a hesitation about recognizing an objective principle in artistic form. The fear that to emphasize objectivity of form in art will mean a relapse into bourgeois aestheticism has its epistemological base in the failure to recognize the dialectical unity of content and form. Hegel defines this unity thus: ". . . content is nothing but the conversion of form into content, and form is nothing but the conversion of content into form." Though this concept seems abstractly expressed, we will see as we proceed that Hegel did indeed correctly define the interrelationship of form and content.

Of course, merely in connection with their interrelationship. Hegel must be "turned upside down" materialistically in that the mirroring quality of both content and form must be established as the key to our investigation. The difficulty consists in grasping the fact that artistic form is just as much a mode of reflecting reality as the terminology of logic (as Lenin demonstrated so convincingly). Just as in the process of the reflection of reality through thought, the categories that are most general, the most abstracted from the surface of the world of phenomena, from sense data, therefore, express the most abstract laws governing nature and men; so is it with the forms of art. It is only a question of making clear what this highest level of abstraction signifies in art.

That the artistic forms carry out the process of abstraction, the process of generalization, is a fact long recognized. Aristotle contrasted poetry and history from this point of view (it should be noted by the contemporary reader that Aristotle understood by history a narrative chronicle of loosely related events in the manner of Herodotus). Aristotle says: "Historians and poets do not differ in the fact that the latter write in verse, the former in prose. . . . The difference lies rather in the fact that the one reports what actually happened, the other what could happen. Thus poetry is more philosophical than history, for poetry tends to express the universal, history the particular." Aristotle obviously meant that because poetry expresses the universal it is more philosophical than history. He meant that poetry (fiction) in its characters, situations and plots not merely imitates individual characters, situations and actions but expresses simultaneously the regular, the universal and the typical. In full agreement Engels declares the task of realism to be to create "typical characters under typical conditions". The difficulty in grasping abstractly what great art of all time has achieved in practice is twofold: in the first place, the error must be avoided of opposing the typical, the universal and the regular to the individual, of disrupting intellectually the inseparable unity of the individual and universal which determines the practice of all great poets from Homer to Gorki. In the second place, it must be understood that this unity of the particular and the universal, of the individual and the typical, is not a quality of literary content that is considered in isolation, a quality for the expression of which the artistic form is merely a "technical aid", but that it is a product of that interpenetration of form and content defined abstractly by Hegel.

The first difficulty can only be resolved from the standpoint of the Marxist conception of the concrete. We have seen that mechanical materialism as well as idealism—each in its own way, and, in the course of historical development, in different forms—bluntly oppose the direct reflection of the external world, the foundation for any understanding of reality, to the universal and the typical, etc. As a result, the typical appears as the product of a merely subjective intellectual operation, as a mere intellectual, abstract and thus ultimately purely subjective accessory to the world of immediate experience; not as a component of objective reality. From such a counterposing of opposites it is impossible to arrive at a conception of the unity of the individual and the typical in a work of art. Either a false conception of the concrete or an equally false conception of the abstract becomes the key to the aesthetic, or at most an eclectic one-or-the-other is propounded. Marx defined the concrete with extraordinary incisiveness: "The concrete is concrete because it is the synthesis of many determinants, the unity within diversity. In our thinking the concrete thus appears as the process of synthesis, as the result, not as the point of departure, although it is really the point of departure and hence also the point of departure for perception and conception." In our introductory remarks we noted how Lenin defines the dialectical approach to the intellectual reflection of the concrete in Marxist epistemology.

The task of art is the reconstitution of the concrete—in this Marxist sense—in a direct, perceptual self-evidence. To that end those factors must be discovered in the concrete and rendered perceptible whose unity makes the concrete concrete. Now in reality every phenomenon stands in a vast, infinite context with all other simultaneous and previous phenomena. A work of art, considered from the point of view of its content, provides only a greater or lesser extract of reality. Artistic form therefore has the responsibility of preventing this extract from giving the effect of an extract and thus requiring the addition of an environment of time and space; on the contrary, the extract must seem to be a self-contained whole and to require no external extension.

When the artist's intellectual disciplining of reality before he begins a work of art does not differ in principle from any other intellectual ordering of reality, the more likely the result will be a work of art.

Since the work of art has to act as a self-contained whole and since the concreteness of objective reality must be reconstituted in perceptual immediacy in the work of art, all those factors which objectively make the concrete concrete must be depicted in their interrelation and unity. In reality itself these conditions emerge quantitatively as well as qualitatively in extraordinary variety and dispersion. The concreteness of a phenomenon depends directly upon this extensive, infinite total context. In the work of art, any extract, any event, any individual or any aspect of the individual's life must represent such a context in its concreteness, thus in the unity of all its inherent important determinants. These determinants must in the first place be present from the start of the work; secondly, they must appear in their greatest purity, clarity and typicality; thirdly, the proportions in the relationships of the various determinants must reflect that objective partisanship with which the work is infused; fourthly, despite the fact that they are present in greater purity, profundity and abstraction than is found in any individual instance in actual life, these determinants may not offer any abstract contrast to the world of phenomena that is directly perceptible, but, contrarily, must appear as concrete, direct, perceptible qualities of individual men and situations. Any artistic process conforming to the intellectual reflection of reality through the aid of abstractions, etc., which seems artistically to "overload" the particular with typical aspects intensified to the utmost quantitatively and qualitatively requires a consequent artistic intensification of concreteness. No matter how paradoxical it may sound, an intensification of concreteness in comparison with life must therefore accompany the process of developing artistic form and the path to generalization.

Now when we pass to our second question, the role of form in the establishment of this concreteness, the reader will perhaps no longer consider Hegel's quotation regarding the transformation of content into form and form into content so abstract. Consider the determinants in a work of art we have so far derived exclusively from the most general conception of artistic form—the self-containment of a work of art: on the one hand, the intensive infinity, the apparent inexhaustibility of a work of art and the subtlety of the development by which it recalls life in its most intensive manifestation; on the other hand, the fact that it discloses simultaneously within this inexhaustibility and life-like subtlety the laws of life in their freshness, inexhaustibility and subtlety. All these factors seem merely to be factors of content. They are. But they are at the same time, and even primarily, factors emerging and becoming apparent through artistic form. They are the result of the transformation of content into form and result in the transformation of form into content.

Let us illustrate this very important fact of art with a few examples. Take a simple example, one might almost say a purely quantitative example. Whatever objections one might level against Gerhart Hauptmann's *Weavers* as a drama, there is no question that it succeeds in awakening an illusion that we are not involved merely with individuals but with the grey, numberless masses of Silesian weavers. The depiction of the masses as masses is the artistic achievement of this drama. When we investigate how many characters Hauptmann actually used to depict these masses, we are surprised to discover that he used scarcely ten to a dozen weavers, a number much smaller than is to be found in many other dramas which do not even begin to provide an impression of great masses of people. The effect arises from the fact that the few characters depicted are so selected and characterized and set in such situations and in such relationships that within the context and in the formal proportionality in the aesthetic illusion, we have the impression of a great mass. How little this aesthetic illusion depends on the actual number of characters is clear from the same author's drama of the peasants' revolt, *Florian Geyer*, where Hauptmann creates an incomparably greater cast of characters, some of which are even very clearly delineated as individuals; nevertheless the audience only intermittently has the sense of a real mass, for here Hauptmann did not succeed in representing a relationship of the characters to each other which would give the sense of a mass and would endow the mass with its own artistic physiognomy and its own capacity to act.

This significance of form emerges even more clearly in more complicated cases. Take the depiction of the typical in Balzac's *Père Goriot*. In this novel Balzac exposes the contradictions in bourgeois society, the inevitable inner contradictions appearing in every institution in bourgeois society, the varied forms of conscious and unconscious rebellion against the enslavement and crippling of the institutions in which men are imprisoned. Every manifestation of these contradictions in an individual or a situation is intensified to an extreme by Balzac and with merciless consequence. Among his characters he depicts men representing ultimate extremes: being lost or in revolt, thirsting for power or degenerate: Goriot and his daughters, Rastignac, Vautrin, the Viscountess de Beauséant, Maxime de Trailles. The events through which these characters expose themselves follow upon each other in an avalanche that appears incredible if the content is considered in isolation—an avalanche impelled by scarcely credible explosions. Consider what happens in the course of the action: the final tragedy of Goriot's family, the tragedy of Mme de Beauséant's love affair, the exposure of Vautrin, the tragedy arranged by Vautrin in the Taillefer house, etc. And yet, or rather precisely on account of this rush of events, the novel provides the effect of a terrifyingly accurate and typical picture of bourgeois society. The basis for its effectiveness is Balzac's accurate exposure of the typical aspects of the basic contradiction in bourgeois society—a necessary precondition to the effect but not in itself the effect. The effect itself results from the composition, from the context provided by the relationships of the extreme cases, a context in which the apparent outlandishness of the individual cases is eliminated. Extract any one of the conflicts from the general context and you discover a fantastic, melodramatic, improbable tale. But it is just because of the exaggeration in the individual events, in the characterization and even in the language within the relationships established among those extreme events through Balzac's composition that the common social background emerges. Only with such an extreme intensification of improbable events could Balzac depict how Vautrin and Goriot are similarly victims of capitalist society and rebels against its consequences, how Vautrin and Mme de Beauséant are motivated by a similar incomplete conception of society and its contradictions, how the genteel salon and the prison differ only quantitatively and incidentally and resemble each other in profound respects and how bourgeois morality and open crime shade into each other imperceptibly. And furthermore—through the piling up of extreme cases and on the basis of the accurate reflection of the social contradictions which underlie them in their extremeness, an atmosphere arises which eliminates any sense of their being extreme and improbable, an atmosphere in which the social reality of capitalist society emerges out of these instances and through them in a crassness and fullness that could not otherwise be realized.

Thus the content of the work of art must be transformed into a form through which it can achieve its full artistic effectiveness. Form is nothing but the highest abstraction, the highest mode of condensation of content, of the extreme intensification of motivations, of constituting the proper proportion among the individual motivations and the hierarchy of importance among the individual contradictions of the life mirrored in the work of art.

It is, of course, necessary to study this characteristic form in individual categories of form, not simply generally in composition, as we have done so far. We cannot investigate the particular categories since our task is more general—to define form and to investigate its objective existence. We will select only one example, plot, which has been considered central in discussions of literary form since Aristotle.

It is a formal principle of epic and drama that their construction be based on a plot. Is this *merely* a formal requirement, abstracted from content? Not at all. When we analyse this formal requirement precisely in its formal abstractness, we come to the conclusion that only through plot can the dialectic of human existence and consciousness be expressed, that only through a character's action can the contrast between what he is objectively and what he imagines himself to be, be expressed in a process that the reader can experience. Otherwise the writer would either be forced to take his characters as they take themselves to be and to present them then from their own limited subjective perspective, or he would have to merely assert the contrast between their view of themselves and the reality and would not be able to make his readers perceive and experience the contrast. The requirement for representing the artistic reflection of social reality through plot is therefore no mere invention of aestheticians; it derives from the basic materialist dialectical practice of the great poets (regardless of their frequent idealist ideologies) formulated by aesthetics and established as a formal postulate—without being recognized as the most general, abstract reflection of a fundamental fact of objective reality. It will be the task of Marxist aesthetics to reveal the quality of the formal aspects of art concretely as modes of reflecting reality. Here we can merely point to the problem, which even in regard to plot alone is far too complicated for adequate treatment in this essay. (Consider, for example, the significance of the plot as a means for depicting process.)

The dialectic of content and form, the transformation from the one into the other, can naturally be studied in all the stages of origin, development and effect of a work of art. We will merely allude to a few important aspects here. When we take the problem of subject matter, we seem at first glance to be dealing again with a problem of content. If we investigate more closely, however, we see that breadth and depth of subject matter convert into decisive problems of form. In the course of investigating the history of individual forms, one can see clearly how the introduction and mastery of new thematic material calls forth a new form with significantly new principles within the form, governing everything from composition to diction. (Consider the struggle for bourgeois drama in the eighteenth century and the birth of an entirely new type of drama with Diderot, Lessing and the young Schiller.)

When we follow this process over a long period of history, the conversion of content into form and vice versa in the effect of works of art is even more impressive. Precisely in those works in which this conversion of one into the other is most developed, does the resultant new form attain the fullest consummation and seem entirely "natural" (one thinks of Homer, Cervantes, Shakespeare, etc.). This "artlessness" in the greatest masterpieces illuminates not only the problem of the mutual conversion of content and form into each other but also the significance of this conversion: the establishment of the objectivity of the work of art itself. The more "artless" a work of art, the more it gives the effect of life and nature, the more clearly it exemplifies an actual concentrated reflection of its times and the more clearly it demonstrates that the only function of its form is the expression of this objectivity, this reflection of life in the greatest concreteness and clarity and with all its motivating contradictions. On the other hand, every form of which the reader is conscious as form, in its very independence of the content and in its incomplete conversion into content necessarily gives the effect of a subjective expression rather than a full reflection of the subject matter itself (Corneille and Racine in contrast to the Greek tragedians and Shakespeare). That content which emerges as an independent entity (like its antithesis, form as an independent entity) also has a subjective character, we have already seen.

This interrelationship of form and content did not escape the important aestheticians of earlier periods, of course. Schiller, for example, recognized one side of this dialectic and acutely formulated it, viewing the role of art as the annihilation of subject matter through form. In this statement, however, he provided an idealistic and one-sided subjectivist formulation of the problem. For the simple transfer of content into form without the dialectical counter-action necessarily leads to an artificial independence of form, to the subjectiv-izing of form, as is often the case not only in Schiller's theory but in his creative practice as well.

It would be the task of a Marxist aesthetic to demonstrate concretely how objectivity of form is an aspect of the creative process. The comments of great artists of the past provide an almost inexhaustible source for this investigation, an investigation we have hardly begun. Bourgeois aesthetics can scarcely begin any study of this material, for when it recognizes the objectivity of forms, it conceives of this objectivity only in some mystical fashion and makes of objectivity of form a sterile mystique about form. It becomes the responsibility of a Marxist aesthetic in developing the concept of form as a mode of reflection to demonstrate how this objectivity emerges in the creative process as objectivity, as truth independent of the artist's consciousness.

This objective independence from the artist's consciousness begins im-mediately with a selection of the subject matter. In all subject matter there are certain artistic possibilities. The artist, of course, is "free" to select any one of these or to use the subject matter as the springboard to a different sort of artistic expression. In the latter case a contradiction inevitably arises between the thematic content and the artistic elaboration, a contradiction which cannot be eliminated no matter how skilfully the artist may manipulate. (One recalls Maxim Gorki's striking critique of Leonid Andreyev's *Darkness*.) This objectivity reaches beyond the relationship of content, theme and artistic form.

When we obtain a Marxist theory of genres, we will then be able to see that every genre has its own specific, objective laws which no artist can ignore without peril. When Zola, for example, in his novel *The Masterpiece* adopted the basic structure of Balzac's masterly short story "The Unknown Masterpiece", extending the work to novel length, he demonstrated in his failure Balzac's profound artistic insight in selecting the short story to represent the tragedy of an artist.

With Balzac the short-story form grows out of the essential quality of the theme and subject matter. Balzac compressed into the narrowest form the tragedy of the modern artist, the tragic impossibility of creating a classical work of art with the specific means of expression of modern art—means of expression which themselves merely reflect the specific character of modern life and its ideology. He simply depicted the collapse of such an artist and contrasted him with two other important, less dedicated (therefore not tragic) artists. Thus he concentrated everything on the single, decisive problem, adequately expressed in a tight and fast-moving plot of artistic disintegration through an artist's suicide and destruction of his work. To treat this theme in a novel instead of a short story would require entirely different subject matter and an entirely different plot. In a novel the writer would have to expose and develop in breadth the entire process arising out of the social conditions of modern life and leading to these artistic problems. (Balzac had followed such an approach in analysing the relationship of literature to journalism in *Lost Illusions*.) To accomplish this task the novelist would have to go beyond the bounds of the short story with its single and restricted climax and would have to find subject matter suitable for transforming the additional breadth and diversity in motivations into a dynamic plot. Such a transformation is missing from Zola's work. He did indeed introduce a series of additional motivations in an attempt at providing novelistic breadth to the short-story material. But the new motivations (the struggle of the artist with society, the struggle between the dedicated and the opportunistic artists, etc.) do not arise out of the inner dialectic of the original short-story material but remain unrelated and superficial in the development and do not provide the broad, varied complex necessary for the construction of a novel.

Once sketched, characters and plots show the same independence of the artist's consciousness. Although originating in the writer's head, they have their own dialectic, which the writer must obey and pursue consequently if he does not want to destroy his work. Engels noted the objective independent existence of Balzac's characters and their life careers when he pointed out that the dialectics of the world depicted by Balzac led the author to conclusions in opposition to his own conscious ideology. Contrary examples are to be found in such strongly subjective writers as Schiller or Dostoyevski. In the struggle between the writer's ideology and the inner dialectic of his characters, the writer's subjectivity is often victorious with the result that he dissipates the significant material he has projected. Thus Schiller distorts the profound conflict he had planned between Elizabeth and Mary Stuart (the struggle between the Reformation and the Counter-Reformation) out of Kantian moralizing; thus Dostoyevski, as Gorki once acutely remarked, ends by slandering his own characters.

The objective dialectic of form because of its very objectivity is an *historical* dialectic. The idealistic inflation of form becomes most obvious in the transformation of forms not merely into mystical and autonomous but even "eternal" entities. Such idealistic de-historicizing of form eliminates any concreteness and all dialectic. Form becomes a fixed model, a schoolbook example, for mechanical imitation. The leading aestheticians of the classical period often advanced beyond this undialectical conception. Lessing, for example, recognized clearly the profound truths in Aristotle's Poetics as the expression of definite laws of tragedy. At the same time he saw clearly that what was important was the living essence, the ever-new, ever-modified application of these laws without mechanical subservience to them. He revealed sharply and vividly how Shakespeare, who ostensibly did not follow Aristotle and probably did not even know Aristotle, consistently fulfilled afresh Aristotle's important prescriptions, which Lessing considered the most profound laws of the drama; while the servile, dogmatic students of Aristotle's words, the French classicists, ignored the essential issues in Aristotle's vital legacy.

But a truly historical, dialectical and systematic formulation of the objectivity of form and its specific application to ever-changing historical reality only became possible with a materialist dialectic. In the fragmentary introduction to his *A Critique of Political Economy,* Marx defined precisely the two great problems in the historical dialectic of the objectivity of form in regard to the epic. He showed first that every artistic form is the outgrowth of definite social conditions and of ideological premises of a particular society and that only on these premises can subject matter and formal elements emerge which cause a particular form to flourish (mythology as the foundation of the epic). For Marx the concept of the objectivity of artistic forms here too offered the basis for the analysis of the historical and social factors in the generation of artistic forms. His emphasis on the law of uneven development, on the fact "that certain flourishing periods (of art) by no means stand in direct relation to the general social development", shows that he saw in those periods of extraordinary creative activity (the Greeks, Shakespeare) objective culminations in the development of art and that he considered artistic value as objectively recognizable and definable. Transformation of this profound dialectical theory into relativistic, vulgar sociology means the degradation of Marxism into the mire of bourgeois ideology.

The dialectical objectivity in Marx's second formulation regarding the development of art is even more striking. It is an indication of the primitive

level of Marxist aesthetics and of our lag behind the general development of
Marxist theory that this second formulation has enjoyed little currency among
Marxist aestheticians and was practically never applied concretely before the
appearance of Stalin's work on questions of linguistics. Marx said: "But the
difficulty does not lie in understanding that Greek art and epic were related to
certain forms of social development. The difficulty is that they still provide us
with aesthetic pleasure and serve in certain measure as norms and unattainable models." Here the problem of the objectivity of artistic form is posed with
great clarity. If Marx dealt in the first question with the genesis of artistic form,
form *in statu nascendi*, here he deals with the question of the objective validity
of a finished work of art, of the artistic form, and he does so in such a way that
he sets the investigation of this objectivity as the task at hand but leaves no
doubt of the objectivity itself—of course, within the framework of a concrete
historical dialectic. Marx's manuscript unfortunately breaks off in the middle
of his profound exposition. But his extant remarks show that for him Greek art
forms spring out of the specific content of Greek life and that form arises out
of social and historical content and has the function of raising this content to
the level of objectivity in artistic representation.

Marxist aesthetics must set out from this concept of the dialectical
objectivity of artistic form as seen in its historical concreteness. It must reject
any attempt at making artistic forms either sociologically relative, at transforming dialectics into sophistry or at effacing the difference between periods of
flourishing creativity and of decadence, between serious art and mere dab-
bling, to the elimination of the objectivity of artistic form. Marxist aesthetics
must decisively reject, in addition, any attempt at assigning artistic forms an
abstract formalistic pseudo-objectivity in which artistic form and distinction
among formal genres are construed abstractly as independent of the historical
process and as mere formal considerations.

This concretizing of the principle of objectivity within artistic form can be
achieved by Marxist aesthetics only in constant struggle against bourgeois
currents dominant today in aesthetics and against their influence on our
aestheticians. Simultaneous with the dialectical and critical reinvestigation of
the great heritage from the periods of history when artistic theory and practice
flourished, a relentless struggle against the subjectivization of art dominant in
contemporary bourgeois aesthetics must be waged. In the end it makes no
difference whether form is eliminated subjectively and transformed into the
mere expression of a so-called great personality (the Stefan George school),
whether it is exaggerated into a mystical objectivity and inflated to an
independent reality (neo-classicism) or denied and eliminated with mechanistic objectivity (the stream-of-consciousness theory). All these directions ultimately lead to the separation of form from content, to the blunt opposition of
one to the other and thus to the destruction of the dialectical basis for the
objectivity of form. We must recognize and expose in these tendencies the
same imperialistic parasitism which Marxist-Leninist epistemology exposed
long ago in the philosophy of the imperialist period. (In this respect the
development of a concrete Marxist aesthetic lags behind the general develop-

ment of Marxism.) Behind the collapse of artistic form in bourgeois decadence, behind the aesthetic theories glorifying the subjectivist disintegration or petrification of forms, there is to be found the same rot of bourgeois decadence as in other ideological areas. One would be distorting Marx's profound theory of the uneven development of art into a relativistic caricature if on the basis of this Marxist insight one were to mistake this collapse for the genesis of new form.

Especially significant because it is such a widely disseminated and misleading aspect of the trend to the subjectivization of art is the confusion of form with technique which is so fashionable today. Recently too a technological concept of thought has become dominant in bourgeois logic, a theory of logic as a formalist instrument. Marxist-Leninist epistemology has exposed such tendencies as idealist and agnostic. The identification of technique and form, the conception of aesthetics as mere technology of art, is on the same epistemological level as these subjectivist, agnostic ideological tendencies. That art has a technical side, that this technique must be mastered (indeed can be mastered only by true artists) has nothing to do with the question—the supposed identity of technique and form. Logical thinking requires schooling, too, and is a technique that can be learned and mastered; but that the categories of logic have merely a technical and auxiliary character is a subjective and agnostic deduction from this fact. Every artist must possess a highly developed technique by which he can represent the world that shimmers before him, with artistic conviction. Acquiring and mastering this technique are extraordinarily important tasks.

To eliminate any confusion, however, one must define the place of technique in aesthetics correctly, from a dialectical materialist point of view. In his remarks about the dialectics of intentions and subjective intentional activity Lenin gave a clear response and exposed subjectivist illusions about this relationship. He wrote: "In reality human intentions are created by an objective world and presuppose it—accept it as given, existing. But to man it *appears* that his intentions come from beyond and are independent of the world." Technician theories identifying technique with form arise exclusively out of this subjectivist illusion, which fails to see the dialectical interrelationship of reality, content, form and technique or how the quality and efficacy of technique are necessarily determined by these objective factors; or that technique is a means for expressing the reflection of objective reality through the alternating conversion of content and form; or that technique is *merely* a means to this end and can only be correctly understood in this context, in its dependence upon this context. When one defines technique thus, in its proper dependence upon the objective problem of content and form, its necessarily subjective character is seen as a necessary aspect of the dialectical general context of aesthetics.

Only when technique is rendered autonomous, when in this artificial independence it replaces objective form, does the danger arise of subjectivization of the problems of aesthetics, and in a two-fold respect: in the first place, technique considered in isolation becomes divorced from the objective problems of art and appears as an independent instrument at the service of the artist's subjectivity, an independent instrument with which one can approach any subject matter and produce any form. Rendering technique independent can easily lead to a degeneration into an ideology of subjectivist virtuosity of form, to the cult of "perfection of form" for its own sake, into aestheticism. Secondly, and closely related to this, the exaggeration of the relevance of purely technical problems in artistic representation obscures the more profound problems of artistic form that are much more difficult to comprehend. Such obscurantism in bourgeois ideology accompanies the disintegration and congelation of artistic forms and the loss of a sense for the special problems of artistic form. The great aestheticians of the past always put the decisive problem of form in the foreground and thus maintained a proper hierarchy within aesthetics. Aristotle said that the poet must demonstrate his power rather in the action than in verse. And it is very interesting to see that Marx's and Engels' aversion to the "petty clever defecations" (Engels) of contemporary virtuosos of form without content, of the banal "masters of technique" went so far that they treated the bad verse of Lassalle's *Sickingen* with indulgence because Lassalle had at least dared in this tragedy—admittedly a failure and considered so by them—to grapple with real, basic problems of dramatic content and form. The same Marx praised this attempt who in his correspondence with Heine showed that he had so steeped himself in the fundamental problems of art as well as in the details of artistic technique that he was able to offer the great poet specific technical suggestions to improve his poetry.

NOTES

1. Objectivity not in the sense of a pretension to non-partisan tolerance of all positions but in the sense of the conviction of the strict objectivity in nature and society and their laws.

Ezra Pound

1885–1972

Ezra Weston Loomis Pound was born to Quaker parents in Hailey, Idaho, on October 30, 1885. He received an education in Romance philology at the University of Pennsylvania (B.A., 1905) and at Hamilton College (M.A., 1906). He taught briefly at Wabash College, Indiana, but was fired after only four months, in January 1908. In February of that year he sailed for Europe and, while in Venice somewhat later, published his first volume of poetry, *A Lume Spento* (1908). He then moved to London, where he quickly established a literary reputation, and joined Wyndham Lewis and others in the short-lived Vorticist movement. Along with F. S. Flint, Richard Aldington, and Hilda Doolittle (H.D.), Pound also involved himself in the Imagist movement, which, inspired in part by the aesthetic theories of T. E. Hulme, produced poetry characterized by free rhythms, concreteness, and concision of language and imagery. *Des Imagistes,* an anthology of Imagist poems edited by Pound, appeared in 1914. Pound also championed the work of such Modernist writers as James Joyce and T. S. Eliot, and later edited Eliot's *Waste Land* (1922). During this period he published several volumes of his own verse, including *Personae* (1909), *Canzoni* (1911), *Ripostes* (1912), and *Lustra* (1916). In addition, Pound's wide interests led him to a series of translations which foreshadowed the pan-cultural diversity of his *Cantos;* early volumes contained translations from Provençal and archaic Italian, as well as a loose translation of the Old English poem *The Seafarer.* In 1915 he published *Cathay,* translations of Chinese poems by Li Bai (Li Po). Further volumes of original poetry appeared, including *Quia Pauper Amavi* (1919), containing *Homage to Sextus Propertius,* and *Hugh Selwyn Mauberley* (1920).

By the 1920s Pound began to move away from the principles of Imagism, which had become too restrictive for him. Pound left London for Paris in 1920 with his English wife, Dorothy Shakespear, whom he had married in 1914; in Paris he became part of a literary circle which included Gertrude Stein and Ernest Hemingway. In 1925 he settled in Rapallo, Italy, where he remained for the next twenty years; here he continued work on the *Cantos,* the first three of which had been published in 1917. These appeared intermittently over several decades until his death.

In Italy Pound's support for Mussolini's Fascism led him during the war years to give a series of talks on Italian radio; these were on a variety of subjects ranging from Confucianism to Social Credit theories to allegations of Jewish control of the American Government. In 1945 he was arrested at Genoa, and sent to a U.S. Army Disciplinary Training Center near Pisa. While in internment Pound produced *The Pisan Cantos* (1948), which was selected by the Fellows of the Library of Congress to receive the Bollingen Prize for 1948. This caused major political repercussions in the United States and led to a demand for the investigation of the Fellows themselves. In 1946 Pound was moved to Washington to stand trial for treason, but was found incompetent to do so by reason of insanity. Until 1958 he was confined in a mental institution, where he continued to write, and from which he issued various unsigned or pseudonymous articles. On his release he returned to Italy, where he continued to work on his *Cantos*. He died there on November 1, 1972.

After the early, modest *Spirit of Romance* (1910), Pound's criticism includes *Instigations* (1920); *How to Read* (1931); *ABC of Reading* (1934); *Make It New* (1934), *Polite Essays* (1937); and *Guide to Kulchur* (1938). He also has a memoir of *Gaudier-Brzeska* (1916) and the collected *Literary Essays* (1954), edited by T. S. Eliot.

Pound was a pedagogue by nature; he also wanted to perform a hieratic function in the sanctuary of literary history. In an epigraph to "The Renaissance" (1914) he says, "All criticism is an attempt to define the classic." *How to Read* might better be called *What to Read*. Interested not in theory but in hierarchy, Pound's criticism constitutes a ranking, a checklist, a sort of handbook to world literature for future writers. In *ABC* he defines the Greek verb *krino* (from which *criticism* is derived) as "*to pick out for oneself, to choose*. That's what the word means." When he chooses, he chooses Dante, Villon, and Cavalcanti, and prefers Chaucer to Shakespeare. He has no use for Elizabethan literature, the Renaissance in general, most of the Romantics, the Victorians, and especially Milton. He liked ordinary speech patterns in verse, and wanted to formulate a lingua franca where English could compete with the Romance languages. With his dogmatic opinion he changed the taste of a generation. Canon-formation and reformation was his aim.

THE SPIRIT OF ROMANCE

PRAEFATIO AD LECTOREM ELECTUM

This book is not a philological work. Only by courtesy can it be said to be a study in comparative literature.

I am interested in poetry. I have attempted to examine certain forces, elements or qualities which were potent in the mediæval litcrature of the Latin tongues, and are, I believe, still potent in our own.

The history of an art is the history of masterwork, not of failures, or mediocrity. The omniscient historian would display the masterpieces, their causes and their inter-relation. The study of literature is hero-worship. It is a refinement, or, if you will, a perversion of that primitive religion.

I have floundered somewhat ineffectually through the slough of philology, but I look forward to the time when it will be possible for the lover of poetry to study poetry—even the poetry of recondite times and places—without burdening himself with the rags of morphology, epigraphy, *privatleben* and the kindred delights of the archaeological or "scholarly" mind. I consider it quite as justifiable that a man should wish to study the poetry and nothing but the poetry of a certain period, as that he should study its antiquities, phonetics or paleography and be, at the end of his labours, incapable of discerning a refinement of style or a banality of diction.

There are a number of sciences connected with the study of literature. There is in literature itself the Art, which is not, and never will be, a science.

Art is a fluid moving above or over the minds of men.

Having violated one canon of modern prose by this metaphysical generality, I shall violate another. I shall make a florid and metaphorical comparison.

Art or an art is not unlike a river, in that it is perturbed at times by the quality of the river bed, but is in a way independent of that bed. The color of the water depends upon the substance of the bed and banks immediate and preceding. Stationary objects are reflected, but the quality of motion is of the river. The scientist is concerned with all of these things, the artist with that which flows.

It is dawn at Jerusalem while midnight hovers above the Pillars of Hercules. All ages are contemporaneous. It is B.C., let us say, in Morocco. The Middle Ages are in Russia.[1] The future stirs already in the minds of the few. This is especially true of literature, where the real time is independent of the apparent, and where many dead men are our grandchildren's contemporaries, while many of our contemporaries have been already gathered into Abraham's bosom, or some more fitting receptacle.

What we need is a literary scholarship, which will weigh Theocritus and Yeats with one balance, and which will judge dull dead men as inexorably as dull writers of today, and will, with equity, give praise to beauty before referring to an almanack.

Art is a joyous thing. Its happiness antedates even Whistler; apropos of which I would in all seriousness plead for a greater levity, a more befitting levity, in our study of the arts.

Good art never bores one. By that I mean that it is the business of the artist to prevent ennui; in the literary art, to relieve, refresh, revive the mind of the reader—at reasonable intervals—with some form of ecstasy, by some splendor of thought, some presentation of sheer beauty, some lightning turn of phrase—laughter is no mean ecstasy. Good art begins with an escape from dullness.

The aim of the present work is to instruct. Its ambition is to instruct painlessly.

There is no attempt at historical completeness. The "Grundriss von Grüber" covers somewhat the same period and falls short of completeness. It consists of 21,000 folio pages, and is, needless to say, Tedescan. To this admirable work I cheerfully recommend anyone who has a passion for completeness. Omitting though it does, many of the facts concerning mediaeval literature, it yet contains references to some hundreds of other works wherein the curiosity of the earnest may in some measure be slaked.

As to my fitness or unfitness to attempt this treatise: G. H. Putman tells us that, in the early regulations of the faculty of the University of Paris, this oath is prescribed for professors: "I swear to read and to finish reading within the time set by the statutes, the books and parts of books assigned for my lectures."[2] This law I have, contrary to the custom of literary historians, complied with. My multitudinous mistakes and inaccuracies are mostly my own.

The book treats only of such mediaeval works as still possess an interest other than archaeological for the contemporary reader who is not a specialist. My criticism has consisted in selection rather than in presentation of opinion. Certain portions of the book are in the strictest sense original research. Throughout the book all critical statements are based on a direct study of the texts themselves and not upon commentaries.

My thanks are due to Dr. Wm. P. Shepard of Hamilton College, whose refined and sympathetic scholarship first led me to some knowledge of French, Italian, Spanish and Provençal, and likewise to Padre Jose Maria de Elizondo, for his kindness to me when studying in Spain.

Some stigma will doubtless attach to Mr. Ernest Rhys, at whose instigation the present volume was undertaken. Guilty of collusion, he is in no way responsible for its faults.

Amplissimas ac manu quae transcripsit gratias.

POSTSCRIPT

Toutes mes choses datent de quinze ans. Je peux commencer une chose nouvelle tous les jours, mais finir . . .?
                                                    —Brancusi (in conversation.)

My first gropings toward the conclusions tabulated in the preceding notes were published in London in 1910 via the benevolence of Ernest Rhys. I have no doubt that the work cd. be greatly improved, but one kind of improvement wd. falsify at least one of the measurements, the main difference of outlook being simply that I then knew less and had more patience. At least part of the subject matter then treated will not bear my present acids, and the student wanting, and having a perfect right to know what happened in a given time and place wd. be no better off than before I made my preliminary survey.

The reader who does not want this information can regard a good deal of what follows (Prolegomena) as footnote or mere proof that I had examined a certain amount of writing before coming to my conclusions. The detached critic may, I hope, find at the end of the whole, some signs of coherence, some proof that I started with a definite intention, and that what has up to now appeared an aimless picking up of tidbits has been governed by a plan which became clearer and more definite as I proceeded.

A good deal of what immediately follows can not be taken as criticism, but simply as information for those wanting a shortish account of a period. The mode of the statement, its idiom or jargon, will have to stand as partial confession of where I was in the year 1910.

Chapter V

Psychology and Troubadours:
A Divagation from Questions of Technique[3]

Behind the narratives is a comparatively simple state of "romanticism," behind the canzos, the "love code."

One or two theories as to its inner significance may in some way promote an understanding of the period.

The "chivalric love," was, as I understand it, an art, that is to say, a religion. The writers of "trobar clus" did not seek obscurity for the sake of obscurity.

An art is vital only so long as it is interpretative, so long, that is, as it manifests something which the artist perceives at greater intensity, and more intimately, than his public. If he be the seeing man among the sightless, they will attend him only so long as his statements seem, or are proven, true. If he forsake this honor of interpreting, if he speak for the pleasure of hearing his own voice, they may listen for a while to the babble and to the sound of the painted words, but there comes, after a little, a murmur, a slight stirring, and then that condition which we see about us, disapproved as the "divorce of art and life."

The interpretive function is the highest honor of the arts, and because it is so we find that a sort of hyper-scientific precision is the touchstone and assay of the artist's power, of his honor, his authenticity. Constantly he must distinguish between the shades and the degrees of the ineffable.

If we apply this test, first, as to the interpretive intention on the part of the artist, second, as to the exactness of presentation, we shall find that the *Divina Commedia* is a single elaborated metaphor of life; it is an accumulation of fine discriminations arranged in orderly sequence. It makes no difference *in kind* whether the artist treat of heaven and hell, of paradise upon earth and of the elysian enamelled fields beneath it, or of Love appearing in an ash-grey vision, or of the seemingly slight matter of birds and branches . . . through one and the other of all these, there is to the artist a like honorable opportunity for precision, for that precision through which alone can any of these matters take on their immortality.

"Magna pars mei," says Horace, speaking of his own futurity, "that in me which is greatest shall escape dissolution": The *accurate* artist seems to leave not only his greater self, but beside it, upon the films of his art, some living print of the circumvolving man, his taste, his temper and his foible—of the things about which he felt it never worth his while to bother other people by speaking, the things he forgot for some major interest; of these, and of another class of things, things that his audience would have taken for granted; or thirdly, of things about which he had, for some reason or other, a reticence. We find these not so much in the words—which anyone may read—but in the subtle joints of the craft, in the crannies perceptible only to the craftsman.

Such is the record left us by a man whom Dante found "best verse-wright in the fostering tongue," the *lingua materna,* Provençal Langue d'Oc; and in that affectionate epithet, *materna,* we have a slight evidence of the regard in which this forgotten speech was held by the Tuscan poets, both for its sound and for its matter.

We find this poetry divided into two schools; the first school complained about the obscurities of the second—we have them always with us. They claimed, or rather jeered in Provence, remonstrated in Tuscany, wrangle today, and will wrangle tomorrow—and not without some show of reason—that poetry, especially lyric poetry, must be simple; that you must get the meaning while the man sings it. This school had, and has always, the popular ear. The other school culminated in Dante Alighieri. There is, of course, ample room for both schools. The ballad-concert ideal is correct, in its own way. A song is a thing to sing. If you approach the canzoni of the second school with this bias you will be disappointed, *not* because their sound or form is not as lyric as that of the canzoni of the first school, but because they are not always intelligible at first hearing. They are good art as the high mass is good art. The first songs are apt to weary you after you know them; they are especially tiresome if one tries to read them *after* one has read fifty others of more or less the same sort.

The second sort of canzone is a ritual. It must be conceived and approached as ritual. It has its purpose and its effect. These are different from those of simple song. They are perhaps subtler. They make their revelations to those who are already expert.

Apart from Arnaut's aesthetic merits, his position in the history of poetry, etc., his music, the fineness of his observation and of his perceptive senses, there is a problem of meaning.

The crux of the matter might seem to rest on a very narrow base; it might seem to be a matter of taste or of opinion, of scarcely more than a personal predilection to ascribe or not to ascribe to one passage in the canzon "Doutz brais e critz," a visionary significance, where, in the third stanza, he speaks of a castle, a dream-castle, or otherwise—as you like—and says of the "lady":

> She made me a shield, extending over me her fair mantle of indigo,
> so that the slanderers might not see this.

This may be merely a conceit, a light and pleasant phrase; if we found it in Herrick or Decker, or some minor Elizabethan, we might well consider it so, and pass without further ado. If one consider it as historical, the protection offered the secret might seem inadequate. I have, however, no quarrel with those who care to interpret the passage in either of these more obvious and, to me, less satisfactory ways.

We must, however, take into our account a number of related things; consider, in following the clue of a visionary interpretation, whether it will throw light upon events and problems other than our own, and weigh the chances in favor of, or against, this interpretation. Allow for climate, consider the restless sensitive temper of our jongleur, and the quality of the minds which appreciated him. Consider what poetry was to become, within less than a century, at the hands of Guinicelli, or of "il nostro Guido" in such a poem as the *ballata,* ending: "Vedrai la sua virtù nel ciel salita,"[4] and consider the whole temper of Dante's verse. In none of these things singly is there any specific *proof.* Consider the history of the time, the Albigensian Crusade, nominally against a sect tinged with Manichean heresy, and remember how Provençal song is never wholly disjunct from pagan rites of May Day. Provence was less disturbed than the rest of Europe by invasion from the North in the darker ages; if paganism survived anywhere it would have been, unofficially, in the Langue d'Oc. That the spirit was, in Provence, Hellenic is seen readily enough by anyone who will compare the *Greek Anthology* with the work of the troubadours. They have, in some way, lost the names of the gods and remembered the names of lovers. Ovid and *The Eclogues* of Virgil would seem to have been their chief documents.

The question: Did this "close ring," this aristocracy of emotion, evolve, out of its half memories of Hellenistic mysteries, a cult—a cult stricter, or more subtle, than that of the celibate ascetics, a cult for the purgation of the soul by a refinement of, and lordship over, the senses? Consider in such passages in Arnaut as, "E quel remir contral lums de la lampa," whether a sheer love of beauty and a delight in the perception of it have not replaced all heavier emotion, whether or no the thing has not become a function of the intellect.[5]

Some mystic or other speaks of the intellect as standing in the same relation to the soul as do the senses to the mind; and beyond a certain border, surely we come to this place where the ecstasy is not a whirl or a madness of the senses, but a glow arising from the exact nature of the perception. We find a similar thought in Spinoza where he says that "the intellectual love of a thing consists in the understanding of its perfections," and adds "all creatures whatsoever desire this love."

If a certain number of people in Provence developed their own unofficial mysticism, basing it for the most part on their own experience, if the servants of Amor saw visions quite as well as the servants of the Roman ecclesiastical hierarchy, if they were, moreover, troubled with no "dark night of the soul," and the kindred incommodities of ascetic yoga, this may well have caused some scandal and jealousy to the orthodox. If we find a similar mode of thought in both devotions, we find a like similarity in the secular and sacred music. "Alba" was probably sung to "Hallelujah's" melody. Many of the troubadours, in fact nearly all who knew letters or music, had been taught in the monasteries (St. Martial, St. Leonard and the other abbeys of Limoges). Visions and the doctrines of the early Fathers could not have been utterly strange to them. The rise of Mariolatry, its pagan lineage, the romance of it, find modes of expression which verge over-easily into the speech and casuistry of Our Lady of Cyprus, as we may see in Arnaut, as we see so splendidly in Guido's "Una figura della donna miae." And there is the consummation of it all in Dante's glorification of Beatrice. There is the inexplicable address to the lady in the masculine. There is the final evolution of Amor by Guido and Dante, a new and paganish god, neither Erôs nor an angel of the Talmud.

I believe in a sort of permanent basis in humanity, that is to say, I believe that Greek myth arose when someone having passed through delightful psychic experience tried to communicate it to others and found it necessary to screen himself from persecution. Speaking aesthetically, the myths are explications of mood: you may stop there, or you may probe deeper. Certain it is that these myths are only intelligible in a vivid and glittering sense to those people to whom they occur. I know, I mean, one man who understands Persephone and Demeter, and one who understands the Laurel, and another who has, I should say, met Artemis. These things are for them *real*.

Let us consider the body as pure mechanism. Our kinship to the ox we have constantly thrust upon us; but beneath this is our kinship to the vital universe, to the tree and the living rock, and, because this is less obvious—and possibly more interesting—we forget it.

We have about us the universe of fluid force, and below us the germinal universe of wood alive, of stone alive. Man is—the sensitive physical part of him—a mechanism, for the purpose of our further discussion a mechanism rather like an electric appliance, switches, wires, etc. Chemically speaking, he is *ut credo*, a few buckets of water, tied up in a complicated sort of fig-leaf. As to his consciousness, the consciousness of some seems to rest, or to have its center more properly, in what the Greek psychologists called the *phantastikon*. Their minds are, that is, circumvolved about them like soap-bubbles reflecting sundry patches of the macrocosmos. And with certain others their consciousness is "germinal." Their thoughts are in them as the thought of the tree is in the seed, or in the grass, or the grain, or the blossom. And these minds are the more poetic, and they affect mind about them, and transmute it as the seed the earth. And this latter sort of mind is close on the vital universe; and the strength of the Greek beauty rests in this, that it is ever at the interpretation of this vital universe, by its signs of gods and godly attendants and oreads.

In the Trecento the Tuscans are busy with their *phantastikon*. In Provence we may find preparation for this, or we may find faint *reliqua* of the other consciousness; though one misses the pantheon. Line after line of Arnaut will repeat from Sappho, but the whole seems curiously barren if we turn suddenly from the Greek to it.

After the Trecento we get Humanism,[6] and as the art is carried northward we have Chaucer and Shakespeare, (Jacques-père). Man is concerned with man and forgets the whole and the flowing. And we have in sequence, first the age of drama, and then the age of prose. At any rate, when we do get into contemplation of the flowing we find sex, or some correspondance to it, "positive and negative," "North and South," "sun and moon," or whatever terms of whatever cult or science you prefer to substitute.

For the particular parallel I wish to indicate, our handiest illustrations are drawn from physics: 1st, the common electric machine, the glass disc and rotary brushes; 2nd, the wireless telegraph receiver. In the first we generate a current, or if you like, split up a static condition of things and produce a tension. This is focussed on two brass knobs or "poles." These are first in contact, and after the current is generated we can gradually widen the distance between them, and a spark will leap across it, the wider the stronger, until with the ordinary sized laboratory appliance it will leap over or around a large obstacle or pierce a heavy book cover. In the telegraph we have a charged surface—produced in a cognate manner—attracting to it, or registering movements in the invisible aether.

Substituting in these equations a more complex mechanism and a possibly subtler form of energy is, or should be, simple enough. I have no dogma, but the figures may serve as an assistance to thought.

It is an ancient hypothesis that the little cosmos "corresponds" to the greater, that man has in him both "sun" and "moon." From this I should say that there are at least two paths—I do not say that they lead to the same place—the one ascetic, the other for want of a better term "chivalric." In the first the monk or whoever he may be, develops, at infinite trouble and expense, the secondary pole within himself, produces his charged surface which registers the beauties, celestial or otherwise, by "contemplation." In the second, which I must say seems more in accord with "mens sana in corpore sano" the charged surface is produced between the predominant natural poles of two human mechanisms.

Sex is, that is to say, of a double function and purpose, reproductive and educational; or, as we see in the realm of fluid force, one sort of vibration produces at different intensities, heat and light. No scientist would be so stupid as to affirm that heat produced light, and it is into a similar sort of false ratiocination that those writers fall who find the source of illumination, or of religious experience, centred solely in the philo-progenitive instinct.

The problem, in so far as it concerns Provence, is simply this: Did this "chivalric love," this exotic, take on mediumistic properties? Stimulated by the color or quality of emotion, did that "color" take on forms interpretive of the divine order? Did it lead to an "exteriorization of the sensibility," and interpretation of the cosmos by feeling?

For our basis in nature we rest on the indisputable and very scientific fact that there are in the "normal course of things" certain times, a certain sort of moment more than another, when a man feels his immortality upon him. As for the effect of this phenomenon in Provence, before coming to any judgment upon it we should consider carefully the history of the various cults or religions of orgy and of ecstasy, from the simpler Bacchanalia to the more complicated rites of Isis or Dionysus—sudden rise and equally sudden decline. The corruptions of their priesthoods follow, probably, the admission thereto of one neophyte who was not properly "sacerdos."

There are, as we see, only two kinds of religion. There is the Mosaic or Roman or British Empire type, where someone, having to keep a troublesome rabble in order, invents and scares them with a disagreeable bogie, which he calls god.

Christianity and all other forms of ecstatic religion, on the other hand, are not in inception dogma or propaganda of something called the *one truth* or the *universal truth;* they *seem* little concerned with ethics; their general object appears to be to stimulate a sort of confidence in the life-force. Their teaching is variously and constantly a sort of working hypothesis acceptable to people of a certain range of temperament—a "regola" which suits a particular constitution of nerves and intellect, and in accord with which the people of this temperament can live at greatest peace with "the order," with man and nature. The old cults were sane in their careful inquisition or novitiate, which served to determine whether the candidates were or were not of such temper and composition.

One must consider that the types which joined these cults survived, in Provence, and survive, today—priests, maenads and the rest—though there is in our society no provision for them.

I have no particular conclusion to impose upon the reader; for a due consideration of Provençal poetry in "trobar clus," I can only suggest the evidence and lines of inquiry. The Pauline position on wedlock is of importance—I do not mean its general and inimical disapproval, but its more specific utterances. Whatever one may think of the pagan survivals in Mariolatry or of the cult of virginity, it is certain that nothing exists without due cause or causes. The language of the Christian mystics concerning the "bride" and the rest of it; the ancient ideas of union with the god, or with Queen Isis—all these, as "atmospheric influences," must be weighed; together with the testimony of the arts, and their progression of content.

In Catullus' superb epithalamium "Collis O Heliconii," we find the affair is strictly on one plane; the bride is what she is in Morocco today, and the function is "normal" and eugenic. It is the sacrificial concept. Yet Catullus, recording his own emotion, could say: "More as a father than a lover." Propertius writes: "Ingenium nobis ipsa puella fecit."

Christianity had, one might say, brought in the mystic note; but this would be much too sweeping. Anatole France, in his commentary on Horace's "Tu ne quaesaris," has told us a good deal about the various Oriental cults thronging the Eternal City. At Marseille the Greek settlement was very ancient. How much of the Roman tone, or the Oriental mode, went out from Rome to the Roman country houses which were the last hold of culture, we can hardly say; and from the end of the Sixth Century until the beginning of the Twelfth there is supposed to be little available evidence. At least we are a fair distance from Catullus when we come to Peire Vidal's: "Good Lady, I think I see God when I gaze on your delicate body."

You may take this if you like *cum grano*. Vidal was confessedly erratic. Still it is an obvious change from the manner of the Roman classics, and it cannot be regarded as a particularly pious or Christian expression. If this state of mind was fostered by the writings of the early Christian Fathers, we must regard their influence as purely indirect and unintentional.

Richard St. Victor has left us one very beautiful passage on the splendors of paradise.

They are ineffable and innumerable and no man having beheld them can fittingly narrate them or even remember them exactly. Nevertheless by naming over all the most beautiful things we know we may draw back upon the mind some vestige of the heavenly splendor.

I suggest that the troubadour, either more indolent or more logical, progresses from correlating all these details for purpose of comparison, and lumps the matter. The Lady contains the catalogue, is more complete. She serves as a sort of *mantram*.

"The lover stands ever in unintermittent imagination of his lady (co-amantis)." This is clause 30 of a chivalric code in Latin, purporting to have been brought to the court of Arthur. This code is not, I should say, the code of the "trobar clus," not the esoteric rule, but such part of it as has been more generally propagated for the pleasure of Eleanor of Poictiers or Marie de Champagne.

Yet there is, in what I have called the "natural course of events," the exalted moment, the vision unsought, or at least the vision gained without machination.

Though the servants of Amor went pale and wept and suffered heat and cold, they came on nothing so apparently morbid as the "dark night." The electric current gives light where it meets resistance. I suggest that the living conditions of Provence gave the necessary restraint, produced the tension sufficient for the results, a tension unattainable under, let us say, the living conditions of imperial Rome.

So far as "morals" go, or at least a moral code in the modern sense, which might interfere in art, Arnaut can no more be accused of having one than can Ovid.[7] Yet the attitude of the Latin *doctor amoris* and that of the *gran maestro de amor* are notably different, as for instance on such a matter as delay. Ovid takes no account of the psychic function.

It is perhaps as far a cry from a belief in higher affection to a mediumistic function or cult of Amor, as is the latter from Ovid. One must consider the temper of the time, and some of the most interesting evidence as to this temper has been gathered by Remy de Gourmont, in *Le Latin Mystique*, from which:

> Qui pascis inter lilia
> Septus choreis virginum.
> Quocumque pergis virgines
> Sequntur, atque laudibus
> Post te canentes cursitant,
> Hymnosque dulces personant[8]
> Who feedest 'mid the lilies,
> Ringèd with dancing virgins
> Where'er Thou runnest, maidens
> Follow, and with praises
> Run behind Thee singing,
> Carolling their hymns.

Or:

> Nard of Columba flourisheth;
> The little gardens flame with privet;
> Stay the glad maid with flowers,
> Encompass her with apple boughs.[9]

As for the personae of the Christian cult they are indeed treated as pagan gods—Apollo with his chorus of Muses, Adonis, the yearly slain, "victima paschalis,"[10] yet in the "sequaire" of Godeschalk, a monk in the Eleventh Century, we see a new refinement, an enrichment, I think, of paganism. The god has at last succeeded in becoming human, and it is not the beauty of the god but the personality which is the goal of the love and the invocation.

> The Pharisee murmurs when the woman weeps, conscious of guilt.
> Sinner, he despises a fellow-in-sin. Thou, unacquainted with sin, hast regard for the penitent, cleansest the soiled one, loved her to make her most fair.
> She embraces the feet of the master, washes them with tears, dries them with her hair; washing and drying them she anointed them with unguent, covered them with kisses.
> These are the feasts which please thee, O Wisdom of the Father!
> Born of the Virgin, who disdained not the touch of a sinner.
> Chaste virgins, they immaculately offer unto the Lord the sacrifice of their pure bodies, choosing Christ for their deathless bridegroom.
> O happy bridals, whereto there are no stains, no heavy dolors of childbirth, no rival mistress to be feared, no nurse molestful!

Their couches, kept for Christ alone, are walled about by angels of the guard, who, with drawn swords, ward off the unclean lest any paramour defile them.

Therein Christ sleepeth with them: happy is this sleep, sweet the rest there, wherein true maid is fondled in the embraces of her heavenly spouse.

Adorned are they with fine linen, and with a robe of purple; their left hands hold lilies, their right hands roses.

On these the lamb feedeth, and with these is he refreshed; these flowers are his chosen food.

He leapeth, and boundeth and gamboleth among them.

With them doth he rest through the noon-heat.

It is upon their bosoms that he sleepeth at mid-day, placing his head between their virgin breasts.

Virgin Himself, born of a virgin mother, virginal retreats above all he seeketh and loveth.

Quiet is his sleep upon their bosoms, that no spot by any chance should soil His snowy fleece.

Give ear unto this canticle, most noble company of virgin devotees, that by it our devotion may with greater zeal prepare a temple for the Lord.

With such language in the cloisters, would it be surprising that the rebels from it, the clerks who did not take orders, should have transferred something of the manner, and something of the spirit, to the beauty of life as they found it, that souls who belonged, not in heaven but, by reason of their refinement, somewhat above the mortal turmoil, should have chosen some middle way, something short of grasping at the union with the absolute, nor yet that their cult should have been extra-marital? Arnaut was taught in cloister, Dante praises certain "prose di romanzi" and no one can say precisely whether or no they were such *prose* for music as the Latin sequence I have just quoted. Yet one would be rash to affirm that the "passada folor" which he laments[11] at almost the summit of the purifying hill, and just below the earthly paradise, was anything more than such deflection.

NOTES

1. 1910.
2. This meant from four to six books for the Doctors of Law or Medicine. Usually one professor had one book on which to lecture.
Continued A.D. 1929: This does not of necessity indicate that either I or the Doctors wholly understood the matter before us.
3. This chapter was first published in G. R. S. Mead's *The Quest,* about 1916.
4. In this *ballata,* Guido speaks of seeing issue from his lady's lips a subtle body,

from that a subtler body, from that a star, from that a voice, proclaiming the ascent of the virtu. For effect upon the air, upon the soul, etc., the "lady" in Tuscan poetry has assumed all the properties of the Alchemist's stone.

5. Let me admit at once that a recent lecture by Mr. Mead on Simon Magus has opened my mind to a number of new possibilities. There would seem to be in the legend of Simon Magus and Helen of Tyre a clearer prototype of "chivalric love" than in anything hereinafter discussed. I recognize that all this matter of mine may have to be reconstructed or at least re-oriented about that tradition. Such rearrangement would not, however, enable us to dispense with a discussion of the parallels here collected, nor would it materially affect the manner in which they are treated. (1916.)

6. The Italian, not the recent American brand.

7. Ovid, outside his poetry, perhaps, superficially had one.

8. From *Hymns to Christ*.

9. From *Ode on St. Colum*.

10. There is a magnificent thesis to be written on the role of Fortune, coming down through the Middle Ages, from pagan mythology, via Seneca, into Guido and Dante.

Boris Eikhenbaum

1886–1959

Boris Mikhailovich Eikhenbaum, literary scholar and formalist, was born on October 4/16, 1886, in the city of Krasnyi in what is now called the oblast' of Smolensk. He graduated from the University of St. Petersburg with a degree in history and philology in 1912 and joined the Society for the Study of Poetic Language (*OPOIAZ*) in 1918.

As a critic Eikhenbaum rescued Pushkin from his status as sacrosanct master in a piece that examined the poet's transition to prose; his article on Tolstoy, which he later turned into a massive life's work, cast Tolstoy's writing into an entirely new framework, rejecting the notion that his didacticism and religiosity were an aesthetic aberration and examining his diaries and letters as purely literary documents. Eikhenbaum was the first person to appreciate the shift of literary theorists in Russia from academics to journalist-critics. Because of the emphasis formalism placed on structure and mechanics, it lasted only as long as the initial anarchic years of the Revolution: as the new government gradually centralized its forces, it expected both the theory and the practice of art to join in the spirit of the time. Eikhenbaum's formalist writing, for all its brilliance, was inappropriate—as the current expression ran, it was not consonant with the epoch. He turned to editing, including the works of such writers as Ivan Turgenev and Mikhail Saltykov-Shchedrin. No full-length biographical study of him exists. The entry for him in the *Great Soviet Encyclopedia* fittingly describes the remainder of his career:

> In his later works . . . Eikhenbaum adopted a more balanced approach. He analyzed writers' works against a broad historical, social, and cultural background, employing large quantities of biographical, documentary, and archival materials. He never returned to the solitary study that characterized his early, formalist writings.

THE THEORY
OF THE FORMAL METHOD

Le pire, à mon avis, est celui qui représente la science comme faite.
A. de Condolle

The school of thought on the theory and history of literature known as the Formal method derived from efforts to secure autonomy and concreteness for the discipline of literary studies. It did not originate (as the name might suggest) out of ambition to create any particular "methodological" system. "Method" nowadays has unsuitably broadened and has come to stand for too much. It is not the methods of studying literature but rather literature as an object of study that is of prime concern to the Formalists.[1] In fact, we are not concerned with debating methodology. Our discussions have been, and can only be, about certain theoretical principles drawn from the study of the concrete material with its specific characteristics, not about one or another ready-made methodological or aesthetic system. The Formalists' writings on the theory of literature and the history of literature state these principles clearly enough. However, so many old misconceptions and so many new issues have accumulated over the past ten years that it would not be amiss now to attempt a kind of conspectus of them—as a historical summary, not as a dogmatic codification. It is vital to bring out how the work of the Formalists began, and how and in what respects it has evolved.

The factor of evolution in the history of the Formal method is extremely important. Our opponents and many of our followers overlook it. We are hedged round with eclectics and epigones who have turned the Formal method into some sort of rigid system, a "Formalism" that stands them in good stead for manufacturing terms, schemes, and classifications. This system is very handy for criticism but not at all characteristic of the Formal method. We did not, and do not, possess any such ready-made system or doctrine. In our scholarship we value theory only as a working hypothesis with the help of which facts are disclosed and take on meaning, that is, they are apprehended as immanent properties and become material for investigation. Therefore we are not concerned with definitions, for which the epigones yearn, nor do we construct general theories, which eclectics find so appealing. We establish concrete principles and adhere to them to the extent they are proved tenable by the material. If the material requires their further elaboration or alteration, we go ahead and elaborate or alter them. In this sense we are relatively detached from our own theories, as indeed a science ought to be, seeing that there is a difference between theory and convictions. There are no ready-made sciences. The vitality of a science is not measured by its establishing truths but by its overcoming errors.

The purpose of this essay is not polemical. The initial stage of learned fracases and journalistic polemics is over and done with. To the sort of "polemic" that *Pečat' i revoljucija* (1924, No. 5) saw fit to address to me, the reply now can only be new works of scholarship. My main purpose here is to demonstrate how the Formal method, as it has been gradually evolving and expanding its field of inquiry, goes well beyond what is usually called methodology and is turning into a special scientific discipline concerned with literature as a specific system of facts. Within the scope of this discipline the most diverse methods potentially can develop, provided only, at the same time, the specificity of the object of study remain the center of attention. Such in fact was the ambition of the Formalists at the very start, and that was the exact meaning of their struggle against the older traditions. The appellation "Formal method," which accrued to this school of thought and with which it is now indelibly stamped, must be understood with the qualification that it is a historical term and ought not be taken as defining the actual nature of the school. Neither "Formalism" as a theory of aesthetics nor "methodology" as a fully formulated scientific system is characteristic of us; what does characterize us is the endeavor to create an autonomous discipline of literary studies based on the specific properties of literary material. All that we require is theoretical and historical awareness of the facts of verbal art as such.

I

The representatives of the Formal method have been reproached repeatedly and from various quarters for an inexplicitness or inadequacy of basic principles—for ignoring the broad issues of aesthetics, psychology, philosophy, sociology, etc. These reproaches (aside from qualitative differences) are equally correct in the sense that they do properly grasp a feature that is characteristic of the Formalists, and not, of course, by accident: I mean, their disengagement not only from "aesthetics from above" but also from all ready-made or putatively ready-made general theories. This disengagement (especially from aesthetics) is a phenomenon more or less typical of all modern study of art. The modern study of art has put aside a number of general problems (such as the problem of beauty, the purpose of art) and has focused on the concrete problems of art science (*Kunstwissenschaft*). A fresh start has been made in advancing the question of what is to be understood by artistic "form" and its evolution, outside of any connection with the premises of general aesthetics, and this has sprung a whole series of concrete, theoretical, and historical issues. In this regard, the appearance of catchwords like Heinrich Wölfflin's *Kunstgeschichte ohne Namen* (history of art without names) and of experiments in the concrete analysis of styles and devices, such as K. Voll's "experiment in the comparative study of paintings," was very symptomatic. In Germany it was the theory and history of the fine arts—the study richest in experience and tradition—that took over the central position in art science and began exerting an influence both on the general theory of art and on individual disciplines—for instance, the study of literature.[2] In Russia, for what were clearly local historical reasons, it was literary scholarship that occupied an analogous position.

The Formal method attracted universal attention and became an issue of the day—not, of course, because of its methodological peculiarities but because of its attitude toward how to understand and study art. Formalist works put forward in no uncertain terms principles that cut athwart the seemingly hard-and-fast traditions and the "axioms" belonging not only to literary science but also to art science as a whole. Thanks to this sharp focus on principles, the distance between the particular problems of literary science and the general problems of the science of art narrowed. For all their concreteness, the concepts and principles on which the Formalists based their work naturally tended to point toward a theory of art in general. Therefore, the regeneration of poetics from a state of total disuse represented no simple matter of reestablishing particular problems but an attack on the whole domain of art science.

The situation had resulted from a whole series of historical events, the most important of which were the crisis in philosophical aesthetics and the radical change in art (in Russia a change most crucially and patently expressed in poetry). Aesthetics proved to be denuded, and art deliberately presented itself laid bare in the full primitive mode. The Formal method and Futurism proved to have a historical interconnection. But the main historical meaning of the emergence of the Formalists comprises a topic in its own right—here I must follow a different line, inasmuch as my intention is to outline the evolution of the principles and problems of the Formal method and the position of the Formal method at the present moment.

At about the time the Formalists emerged, academic scholarship—with its utter disregard of theoretical problems and its nonchalant making-do with obsolete aesthetic, psychological, and historical "axioms"—had lost the sense of its own proper object of study to such a degree that its very existence became illusory. Academic scholarship hardly needed attack. There was no call to force open the door, because, as it turned out, there was none—we discovered, instead of a fortress, a through alley. The theoretical legacy of Potebnja and Veselovskij, once handed down to their students, was left to stagnate as so much dead capital—a fortune which they were afraid to tap and so caused it to depreciate. Authority and influence gradually passed from academic scholarship to the scholarship of what might be called "the journalistic style"—works by the critics and theorists of Symbolism. In point of fact, the books and articles by Vjačeslav Ivanov, Brjusov, A. Belyj, Merežkovskij, Čukovskij, and others had far greater influence in 1907–1912 than did the scholarly research and dissertations of the university professors. Behind that journalistic style of scholarship, for all its subjectivity and tendentiousness, there were theoretical principles and slogans that were drawing strength from the new movements in art and from the propaganda on their behalf. It was only to be expected that books like Andrej Belyj's *Symbolism* (1910) would mean incomparably more to the younger generation than gratuitous monographs written by literary historians devoid of any scientific verve, any standpoint on things.

That is why, when the time came for the historical confrontation between the two generations (a confrontation this time highly charged with fundamental issues), it was not academic scholarship that set the terms but rather a journalistic scholarship comprised of Symbolist theories and the methods of impressionistic criticism. We engaged in battle with the Symbolists in order to wrest poetics from their hands and, once having divested poetics of any ties with subjective, aesthetic, or philosophical theories, to redirect it to the route of a scientific investigation of facts. Having ourselves been educated on Symbolist works, we had the advantage of being able to see their mistakes all the more clearly. The revolt of the Futurists (Xlebnikov, Kručenyx, Majakovskij) against the poetic system of Symbolism, a revolt that had taken definite shape at about that time, lent support to the Formalists and imbued their struggle with an even greater relevance.

The basic motto uniting the original group of Formalists was the emancipation of the poetic word from philosophical and religious biases to which the Symbolists had increasingly fallen prey. Dissension among the theorists of Symbolism (1910–1911) and the appearance of the Acmeists prepared the ground for an all-out revolt. All compromises had to be cast aside. History demanded from us a genuine revolutionary élan—categorical theses, pitiless irony, a pugnacious refusal to come to terms on any basis whatsoever. In this state of affairs it was vital to counter the subjective-aesthetic principles that had served the Symbolists as inspiration with propaganda for an objective-scientific attitude toward facts. That is the source of the new spirit of scientific positivism that characterizes the Formalists: the rejection of philosophical premises, psychological or aesthetic interpretations, and so forth. The break with philosophical aesthetics and ideological theories of art was dictated by the very state of affairs. It was time to turn to the facts and, eschewing general systems and problems, to start from the center—from where the facts of art confront us. Art had to be approached at close range, and science had to be made concrete.

II

The organization of the Formal method was governed by the principle that the study of literature should be made specific and concrete. All efforts were directed toward terminating the earlier state of affairs, in which literature, as A. Veselovskij observed, was *res nullius*. That was what made the Formalists so intolerant of other "methods" and of eclectics. In rejecting these "other" methods, the Formalists actually were rejecting (and still reject) not methods but the gratuitous mixing of different scientific disciplines and different scientific problems. Their basic point was, and still is, that the object of literary science, as literary science, ought to be the investigation of the specific properties of literary material, of the properties that distinguish such material from material of any other kind, notwithstanding the fact that its secondary and oblique features make that material properly and legitimately exploitable, as auxiliary material, by other disciplines. The point was consummately formulated by Roman Jakobson:

   The object of study in literary science is not literature but "literariness," that is, what makes a given work a *literary* work. Meanwhile, the situation has been that historians of literature act like nothing so much as policemen, who, out to arrest a certain culprit, take into custody (just in case) everything and everyone they find at the scene as well as any passers-by for good measure. The historians of literature have helped themselves to everything—environment, psychology, politics, philosophy. Instead of a science of literature, they have worked up a concoction of homemade disciplines. They seem to have forgotten that those subjects pertain to their own fields of study—to the history of philosophy, the history of culture, psychology, and so on, and that those fields of study certainly may utilize literary monuments as documents of a defective and second-class variety among other materials.[3]

   To establish this principle of specificity without resorting to speculative aesthetics required the juxtaposing of the literary order of facts with another such order. For this purpose one order had to be selected from among existent orders, which, while contiguous with the literary order, would contrast with it in terms of functions. It was just such a methodological procedure that produced the opposition between "poetic" language and "practical" language. This opposition was set forth in the first *Opojaz* publications (L. Jakubinskij articles), and it served as the activating principle for the Formalists' treatment of the fundamental problems of poetics. Thus, instead of an orientation toward a history of culture or of social life, toward psychology, or aesthetics, and so on, as had been customary for literary scholars, the Formalists came up with their own characteristic orientation toward linguistics, a discipline contiguous with poetics in regard to the material under investigation, but one approaching that material from a different angle and with different kinds of problems to solve. The linguists in their turn took an interest in the Formal method, inasmuch as the facts of poetic language, brought to light by its juxtaposition with practical language, might be regarded in the purely linguistic sphere of problems as facts of language in general. What came about was something analogous to the relationship of mutual utilization and delimitation, such as exists, for instance, between physics and chemistry. Against this background, the issues once raised by Potebnja and accepted on faith by his disciples revived and took on new meaning.
   The comparison of poetic language with practical language was made in general terms by Lev Jakubinskij in his first article, "On Sounds in Verse Language."[4] The formulation of the difference between the two language systems ran as follows:

   The phenomena of language ought to be classified according to the purpose for which the speaker uses his language resources in any given instance. If the speaker uses them for the purely practical purpose of communication, then we are dealing with the system of *practical language* (discursive thought), in which language resources (sounds, morphological segments, and so forth) have no autonomous value and are merely a *means* of communication. But it is possible to conceive and in fact to find language systems in which the practical aim retreats to the background (it does not necessarily disappear altogether), and language resources acquire autonomous value.

It was important to establish this difference not only as a foundation for building a poetics but also in order to grasp the meaning of the Futurists' trend toward a "transrational language" (*zaumnyj jazyk*) as the utmost baring of autonomous value, a phenomenon already observable in some aspects in children's language, in the glossolalia of religious sectarians, and so forth. The transrational experiments of the Futurists acquired considerable significance in principle as demonstration against the tendency of Symbolism to balk at going beyond the sound "orchestration" accompanying meaning and, as a consequence, to debase the role of sounds in verse. The issue of sounds in verse then took on particular point. Just at that juncture, the Formalists, joining forces with the Futurists, clashed with the theorists of Symbolism face to face. It was perfectly natural for the Formalists to have given battle on these grounds first: the issue of sounds had to be reexamined, above all with the aim of pitting a system of exact observations against the Symbolists' philosophical and aesthetic biases, and the pertinent scientific conclusions had to be drawn. That is what accounts for the makeup of our first volume of studies—a volume devoted entirely to the problem of sounds and of "transrational language."

Along with Jakubinskij, there was Viktor Šklovskij, who, in his article "On Poetry and Transrational Language,"[5] used a large variety of examples to demonstrate that "words are a human need even apart from meaning." Transrational quality was found to be a widespread fact of language and a phenomenon characteristic of poetry: "A poet doesn't set out to make a transrational utterance; transrational quality is usually hidden under the guise of some sort of content, often deceptive or illusory in nature—the sort of thing that makes poets admit that they themselves don't understand what their own poems are about." Šklovskij's article shifted the central question from the level of pure sound (acoustics in which connections between sound and the object or emotion depicted are apt to be posited and given impressionistic interpretations) to the level of articulation, the implementation of sound: "Beyond doubt, the articulatory aspect is a vital component in the enjoyment of a referenceless transrational utterance. It may very well be that a large part of the pleasure poetry gives us stems from its articulatory aspect—from a special dance of the organs of speech." The question of how to regard transrational language thus acquired the significance of a serious scientific problem, the illumination of which might elucidate many facts of verse speech in general. Šklovskij did in fact formulate the general issue:

> If we stipulate that a word in order to be a word must designate a concept and must in all circumstances be meaningful, then, of course, transrational language goes out of the picture as something external

with regard to language. However, it is not all that goes out of the picture: the facts that have been cited make one wonder whether the words in a speech that is not only unmarked as transrational but is simply poetic do always have meaning, or, whether this impression is a false one and a consequence of our inattentiveness.

The natural conclusion from all these observations and principles was that poetic language is not just a language of "images," and that sounds in verse are not at all mere elements of external euphony serving only to "accompany" meaning, but that they do have autonomous value. The stage was set for a reexamination of Potebnja's general theory with its basic assertion that poetry is "thinking in images." This conception, which was the one accepted by the theorists of Symbolism, made it requisite to regard the sounds of verse as the "expression" of something standing behind a poem and to interpret them either as onomatopoeia or as "painting with sounds." Andrej Belyj's studies are especially illustrative of this. Belyj found in two lines of Puškin the complete "picture in sounds" of champagne being poured from a bottle into a glass and in Blok's repetition of cluster *rdt* the "tragedy of turning sober."[6] Such attempts, verging on parody, to "explain" alliterations were bound to provoke on our part energetic opposition in terms of basic theory and our endeavors to demonstrate concretely that sounds in verse exist outside any connection with imagery and have an independent speech function.

L. Jakubinskij's articles linguistically substantiated the autonomous value of sounds in verse. Osip Brik's article "Sound Repetitions"[7] brought actual material to the fore (excerpts from Puškin and Lermontov) and arranged it in various typological classes. After disputing the popular notion of poetic language as the language of "images," Brik came to the following conclusion:

> However the interrelationship of sound and image may be regarded, one thing is certain: sounds and sound harmonies are not merely a euphonic extra but are the result of an autonomous poetic endeavor. The orchestration of poetic speech is not fully accounted for by a repertoire of overt euphonic devices, but represents in its entirety the complex product of the interaction of the general laws of euphony. Rhythm, alliteration, and so forth are only the obvious manifestation of particular instances of basic euphonic laws.

In contrast to Belyj's works, Brik's article contained no interpretations of what particular cases of alliteration were supposed to mean; the article limited itself to the supposition that repetition in verse is analogous to tautology in folklore, that is, that repetition in these instances plays some aesthetic role in its own right. "It is likely that we are dealing here with various manifestations of the same general poetic principle—the principle of simple combination, the material being either the sounds of the words, or their meaning, or both." This sort of predication of one device applied to a wide range of material was very characteristic of the early period of the Formalists' work. After Brik's article, the issue of sounds in verse lost its special point and assumed its place within the general system of the problems of poetics.

III

The Formalists had begun their work with the most militant and crucial issue of the time—the sounds of verse. Behind that particular question of poetics were theses of a more general nature, and these were indeed bound to emerge. The distinction between the poetic and the practical language systems, which had shaped the work of the Formalists from the very start, was bound to make its mark on the formulation of a whole series of basic questions. The conception of poetry as "thinking in images" and the equation "poetry = imagery" derived from it were blatantly out of keeping with the facts observed and in contradiction to the general principles the facts suggested. Rhythm, sounds, syntax—all these things from that point of view were secondary matters not necessarily characteristic of poetry, and they had to drop out of the system. The Symbolists, who had adopted Potebnja's general theory because it substantiated the predominance of the image symbol, were unable to overcome its much acclaimed correlative, "the harmony of form and content," despite its being blatantly contradictory to their own predilection for formal experimentations and despite its adulterating that predilection with "aestheticism." In departing from Potebnja's point of view, the Formalists simultaneously freed themselves from the traditional correlation of "form-content" and from the conception of form as an outer cover or as a vessel into which a liquid (the content) is poured. The facts testified that the specificity of art is expressed not in the elements that go to make up a work but in *the special way they are used*. By the same token, the concept of "form" took on a different meaning; it no longer had to be paired with any other concept, it no longer needed correlation.

In 1914, before the *Opojaz* alliance and during the days of the Futurists' public demonstrations, Šklovskij published a pamphlet, *The Resurrection of the Word*.[8] Relying in part on Potebnja and Veselovskij (the question of imagery had then not yet acquired crucial meaning), he advanced the principle of the palpableness (*oščutimost*) of form as the specific criterion of perception in art:

> We do not experience the familiar, we do not see it, we recognize it. We do not see the walls of our rooms. We find it very difficult to catch mistakes when reading proof (especially if it is in a language we are very used to), the reason being that we cannot force ourselves to see, to read, and not just "recognize," a familiar word. If it is a definition of "poetic" perception or of "artistic" perception in general we are after, then we must surely hit upon this definition: "artistic" perception is a perception that entails awareness of form (perhaps not only form, but invariably form).

It should be evident that *perception* figures here not as a simple psychological concept (the perception of individual human beings) but as an element of art in itself, since it is impossible for art to exist without being perceived. A concept of form in a new meaning had now come into play—not just the outer covering but the whole entity, something concrete and dynamic, substantive in itself, and unqualified by any correlation. This signalized a decisive departure from the principles of Symbolism, which had held that something already "substantive" was supposed to emanate "through form." It also meant that "aestheticism"—a delectation with certain elements of form consciously divorced from "content"—had likewise been overcome.

This, however, did not yet constitute an adequate basis for concrete work. To supplement the points established by the recognition of a difference between poetic language and practical language and by the recognition that the specificity of art is expressed in a special usage of material, the principle of the palpableness of form had to be made concrete enough to foster the analysis of form itself—form understood as content. It had to be shown that the palpableness of form results from special artistic devices acting on perceivers so as to force them to experience form. Šklovskij's "Art as Device,"[9] a kind of manifesto of the Formal method, set the stage for the concrete analysis of form. Here the removal from Potebnja and Potebnjaism and by the same token from the principles of Symbolism was made perfectly explicit. The article opens with objections to Potebnja's basic stand on imagery and on the relationship of the image with what it is meant to explain. Šklovskij points out among other things that images are almost always static:

The more light you shed on a literary period, the more you become convinced that the images you had considered to be the creation of a certain particular poet had been borrowed by him from other poets, virtually unchanged. All that the work of poetic schools amounts to is the acquisition and demonstration of new devices for deploying and elaborating verbal materials; in particular, it amounts much more to deploying images than creating them. Images are handed down; and poetry involves far more reminiscence of images than thinking in them. In any case, imagistic thinking is not that factor whose change constitutes the essence of the momentum of poetry.

Further on, the difference between the poetic and the prosaic image is pointed out. The poetic image is defined as one of the means of poetic language—a device equal in the task it fulfills to other devices of poetic language: parallelism (simple and negative), comparison, repetition, symmetry, hyperbole, etc. The concept of the image was relegated to a position within the general system of poetic devices, and so it had lost its overriding importance for theory. Concomitantly, the principle of artistic economy, a principle deeply embedded in the theory of art, had been refuted. Šklovskij countered by advancing the device of "making it strange" (ostranenie) and the device of impeded form, "which augments the difficulty and the duration of perception, since the process of perception in art is an end in itself and is supposed to be prolonged." Art is conceived as a way of breaking down automatism in perception, and the aim of the image is held to be, not making a meaning more accessible for our comprehension, but bringing about a special perception of a thing, bringing about the "seeing," and not just the "recognizing," of it. Hence the usual connection between the image and the device of "making strange."

The break with Potebnjaism was definitively formulated in Šklovskij's "Potebnja."[10] He repeats once again that the use of images and symbols does not constitute the distinguishing feature of poetic language as against prosaic (practical) language:

> Poetic language is distinguished from prosaic language by the palpableness of its construction. The palpableness may be brought about by the acoustical aspect or the articulatory aspect or the semasiological aspect. Sometimes what is palpable is not the structure of the words but the use of words in a construction, their arrangement. One of the means of creating a palpable construction, the very fabric of which is experienced, is the poetic image, but it is only one of the means.... If scientific poetics is to be brought about, it must start with the factual assertion, founded on massive evidence, that there are such things as "poetic" and "prosaic" languages, each with their different laws, and it must proceed from an analysis of those differences.

These articles may be considered the summation of the initial period in the Formalists' work. The main accomplishment of that period consisted in establishing a number of theoretical principles to serve as working hypotheses for a further concrete investigation of facts; it also surmounted popularly held theories derived from Potebnjaism. As is evident from the articles cited, the basic efforts of the Formalists were directed neither toward the study of so-called "form" nor toward the construction of a special "method," but toward substantiating the claim that verbal art must be studied in its specific features, that it is essential for that purpose to take the different functions of poetic and practical languages as the starting point. As for "form," all that concerned the Formalists was to shift the meaning of that badly confused term in such a way as to obviate its persistent association with the concept of "content," a term even more badly confused than form and totally unscientific. It was important to do away with the traditional correlation and by so doing to enrich the concept of form with new meanings. As matters further evolved, it was the concept of "device" that had a far greater significance, because it stemmed directly from the recognition of the difference between poetic and practical languages.

IV

The preliminary stage of the theoretical work had been passed. The general theories likely to aid in orienting ourselves within the context of the facts had been mapped out. Now we needed to come closer to the material and to make the problems involved concrete. At the center of things stood the issues of theoretical poetics, of which our early work had provided only a general outline. We had now to go beyond the issue of sounds in verse—the significance of which had actually been a matter of illustrating the general proposition of the difference between the poetic and the practical languages— and to take up the general theory of verse. We had to move from general considerations of the device to the study of plot, and so on. Side by side with the Potebnja question, there emerged the question of what to do about Veselovskij's ideas and his theory of plots.

Naturally enough, the Formalists were using literary works at this point only as material for testing and corroborating theoretical theses, to the exclusion of tradition, evolution, and so forth. It was vital to attain the widest possible purview of the material, to establish sui generis "laws," and to carry out a preliminary survey of the facts. Thus the Formalists kept clear of resorting to abstract premises, and on the positive side they managed to master the material without floundering among details.

Šklovskij's work on the theory of plot and the theory of the novel was particularly significant during this period. Using a wide variety of materials— fairy tales, oriental tales, Cervantes's *Don Quixote,* Tolstoj, Sterne's *Tristram Shandy,* and other material—Šklovskij demonstrated the existence of special devices of "plot formation" (*sjužetosloženie*) and their connection with the general devices of style. Leaving the details aside (their treatment properly belongs to specialized studies, and not in a general essay on the Formal method), I shall focus only on those points with a theoretical bearing exclusive of the problem of plot as such, which left their mark on the further evolution of the Formal method.

A whole series of such points are contained in the first of these works by Šklovskij, "The Connection of Devices of Plot Formation with General Devices of Style."[11] First, the very assertion of the actuality of special devices of plot formation—an assertion copiously illustrated with examples—altered the traditional notion of plot as a set of motifs and redirected it from the provenance of thematic concepts to that of compositional concepts.

Thus the concept of plot (*sjužet*) *acquired a new meaning which did not coincide with that of story (fabula),* and plot formation itself assumed its natural place in the sphere of formal study as a specific property of literary works. The concept of form became enriched with new features and at the same time as it gradually relinquished its previous abstractness, it relinquished its significance as a crucial polemical issue as well. It was becoming clear that for us the concept of form was beginning gradually to coincide with the concept of literature as such—that is, the concept of literary fact. Furthermore, the postulation of an analogy between devices of plot formation and devices of style held promise of major theoretical importance. The typically epic serial construction (*stupenčatoe postroenie*) could be grouped together with sound repetition, tautology, tautological parallelism, other kinds of repetitions, etc., as the general principle of verbal art's being structured step by step, with progress arrested.

Thus Roland's three attempts to break his sword against a rock (*Song of Roland*) and similar triple repetitions common in folktale plots are brought into conjunction as things of the same order as Gogol''s use of synonyms, or such

verbal constructs as *kudy-mudy, pljuški-mljuški* [cf. similar English redupli-
cations like "even-steven," "actor-schmacter," and so on.] "All these instances
of slowed-down serial construction are usually not classed together, as the
attempt is made to provide each with a separate explanation." What is clearly
at stake here is the endeavor to predicate a unity of device over a diversity of
material. And that was the point at which a characteristic conflict with
Veselovskij occurred, seeing that Veselovskij had been in the habit of resorting
in such instances to a historical-genetic, not a theoretical, hypothesis, in
attempting to explain epic repetitions by the mechanics of the original
performance (amoebaean song). That kind of explanation, even if correct
in genetic terms, does not elucidate the phenomenon in question as literary
fact. Šklovskij did not reject the overall interrelationship between literature
and communal culture which Veselovskij and other representatives of the
ethnographic school had used to explain the properties of folktale motifs and
plots; all he did was deny its capacity to explain those proportion as literary fact.
The genetic approach can elucidate only origin and nothing more, while for
poetics the elucidation of literary function is vital. Precisely what the genetic
point of view fails to reckon with is the device as a special kind of utilization of
material; it fails to reckon with the selection of material from communal
culture, its transformation, its constructional role; it fails, finally, to reckon
with the fact that a detail of communal culture may disappear, and yet its
literary function remains; it remains not as a mere relic but as a literary device,
retaining its own meaning, even if totally unrelated to communal culture.
Typically enough, Veselovskij lapses into contradiction with himself when he
calls the adventure series of the Greek (Hellenistic) novel a purely stylistic
device.

Veselovskij's "ethnographism" met with natural opposition on the Formalists' part, because it ignored the specificity of the literary device and supplanted a theoretical and evolutionary point of view with a genetic one.[12] It was
only to be expected that the Formalists would be unable to agree with
Veselovskij whenever he had had his say about general questions of literary
evolution. The clash with the Potebnja doctrine had resulted in a clarification
of the basic problems of theoretical poetics; the clash with the general outlook
of Veselovskij and his followers could be expected to result in a definition of the
Formalists' views on literary evolution and, by extension, their views on
constructing a history of literature.

And, indeed, the process found its start in this very same article by
Šklovskij. Confronted with Veselovskij's formula—a formula based on the
same, broadly understood ethnographic principles—that "new form comes
about in order to express new content," Šklovskij advanced a different point of
view:

> A work of art is perceived against the background of, and by way of
> association with, other works of art. The form of a work of art is
> determined by its relationship with other forms existing prior to it. . . .
> Creation as a parallel with and contrast to some model is a description

applicable not just to parody but to any work of art in general. New form comes about not in order to express new content but in order to replace an old form that has already lost its artistic viability.

In support of his thesis, Šklovskij brings to bear B. Christiansen's point about special "differential impressions" or "impressions of divergencies," making it the basis for the dynamism characteristic of art—a dynamism expressed in incessant violations of the canon being established. At the end of the article, he quotes Brunetière's statement declaring that "chief among all influences operative in the history of literature is the influence of *work on work*," and that "one ought not multiply causes uselessly or, on the pretext that literature is an expression of society, confuse the history of literature with the history of manners and morals. They are two completely different things."

Thus, Šklovskij's article mapped the way out of the sphere of theoretical poetics into the history of literature. The original concept of form took on the added complexity of new features of evolutionary dynamism, of incessant change. The transition to the history of literature had come about, not by way of simply expanding the range of topics for investigation, but as the result of an evolution in the concept of form. It was now evident that a literary work is not perceived in isolation—its form produces an impression against the background of other works, and not on its own. This meant that the Formalists had made a decisive move beyond the "formalism" conceived as a process of manufacturing schemes and classifications (the common notion of the Formal method held by ill-informed critics), which is so eagerly utilized by certain scholastics who always welcome any dogma with joy. This scholastic "formalism" has no connection, either historically or in principle, with the work of *Opojaz*—quite to the contrary of our being apologists for it, we are its most irreconcilable and convinced foes.

V

Before I turn to the Formalists' endeavors in literary history, I want to bring to a conclusion my survey of the theoretical principles and problems contained in the *Opojaz* works of the earliest period. In that article by Šklovskij already discussed, there is another concept that played a major role in the subsequent study of the novel: the concept of "motivation" (*motivirovka*). The determination of various devices of plot formation (serial construction, parallelism, framing, concatenation, and others) established the distinction between the elements of a work's construction and the elements comprising the material it uses (the story stuff, the choice of motifs, of protagonists, of themes, etc.). This distinction was then stressed especially heavily, because the main task was to establish the unity of any chosen structural device within the greatest possible diversity of material. Older scholarship had operated exclusively with material conceived as the "content" and had relegated everything else to "outer form," which it regarded a matter of interest only to fanciers of form, or even as a matter of no interest at all. That is the derivation of the naive and touching "aestheticism," by which our older critics and historians of literature discovered the "neglect of form" in Tjutčev's poetry and simply "poor form" in writers like Nekrasov or Dostoevskij.

What saved the situation was the fact that form was forgiven these writers out of deference to the profundity of their ideas or attitudes. It was only natural that the Formalists, during their years of struggle and polemics against traditions of that sort, should have directed all their efforts toward promoting the significance of structural devices and subordinating everything else as *motivation*. In discussing the Formal method and its evolution, it is essential always to keep in mind that a great many of the principles advanced by the Formalists during those years of intense struggle with their opponents had value not only as scientific principles but also as slogans—slogans spiked with paradoxes in the interest of propaganda and opposition. To fail to take that fact into account and to treat the *Opojaz* works of 1916–1921 as works of an academic character is to ignore history.

The concept of motivation enabled the Formalists to approach literary works (in particular, novels and short stories) at even closer range and to observe the details of their construction. And that is just what Šklovskij did in his next two studies, *Plot Unfolding* and *Sterne's* Tristram Shandy *and the Theory of the Novel*.[13] In both of these works he scrutinized the relationship between device and motivation, using Cervantes's *Don Quixote* and Sterne's *Tristram Shandy* as material for a study of the construction of story and novel outside the context of literary historical problems. *Don Quixote* is viewed as a point of transition from story collections (like the *Decameron*) to the single-hero novel, structured on the device of concatenation, with a journey serving as motivation.

That *Don Quixote* was the novel singled out for special attention had to do with the fact that device and motivation are not so integrated in it as to produce a fully motivated novel with all parts fused together. The material is often merely interpolated and not infused; the devices of plot formation and the techniques of manipulating material to further the plot stand out sharply, whereas the later development of novel construction goes "the way of ever more tightly wedging fragments of material into the very body of the novel." In the course of analyzing "how *Don Quixote* is made," Šklovskij, among other things, points out the hero's pliability and infers that this very "type" of hero came about "under the impact of devising the construction of the novel." Thus, the predominance of the construction, of the plot over material, was stressed.

The most suitable material for illustrating theoretical problems of this sort is, understandably enough, art which is not fully motivated or which deliberately tears away motivation and bares its construction. The very existence of works with an intentionally bared construction necessarily stands these problems in good stead as confirmation of the importance of their treatment and the real fact of their pertinence. Moreover, it is precisely the light shed by these problems and principles that elucidates the works themselves. And that was exactly the case with Sterne's *Tristram Shandy*. Thanks to Šklovskij's study, this novel not only contributed illustrations for theoretical postulations but also acquired a new meaning of its own so that it attracted fresh attention. Against the background of a new-found interest in its construction, Sterne's novel became a piece of contemporary writing, and Sterne became a topic of discussion for people who, until then, had seen nothing in his novel except tedious chatter or curios, or who had viewed it from the angle of its much-made-of "sentimentalism," a "sentimentalism" for which Sterne was as little responsible as Gogol' was for "realism."

Observing in Sterne a deliberate baring of constructional devices, Šklovskij argues that the very design of construction is emphasized in Sterne's novel: Sterne's awareness of form, brought out by way of his violation of form, is what in fact constitutes the content of the novel. At the end of his study, Šklovskij formulates the distinction between plot *(sjužet)* and story-stuff *(fabula)*:

> The concept of *plot* is too often confused with the depiction of events—with what I tentatively propose terming "story-stuff." The story-stuff actually is only material for filling in the plot. Therefore, the plot of *Evgenij Onegin* is not the hero's romance with Tat'jana but the plot-processing of this story-stuff worked out by introducing intermittent digressions. . . . The forms of art are to be explained by their artistic immanence, not by real-life motivation. When an artist holds back the action of a novel, not by employing intruders, for example, but simply by transposing the order of the parts, he makes us aware of the aesthetic laws underlying both devices of composition.

It was in connection with the construction of the short story that my article "How Gogol''s 'Overcoat' Is Made"[14] was written. The article couples the problem of plot with the problem of *skaz*, that is, the problem of a construction based on a narrator's manner of narrating. I tried to show that Gogol''s text "is composed of animated locutions and verbalized emotions," that "words and sentences were chosen and linked together in Gogol' on the principle of expressive *skaz*, in which a special role belongs to articulation, miming, sound gestures, etc." From that point of view the composition of *The Overcoat* proved on analysis to be built on a successive alternation of comic *skaz* (with its anecdotes, play on words, etc.) and sentimental-melodramatic declamation, thus imparting to the story the character of a grotesque. In this connection, the ending of *The Overcoat* was interpreted as an apotheosis of the grotesque—something like the mute scene in *The Inspector General*. Traditional arguments about Gogol''s "romanticism" or "realism" proved to be unnecessary and irrelevant.

The problem of the study of prose fiction was therefore moved off dead center. A distinction had been established between the concept of plot, as that of construction, and the concept of story-stuff, as that of material; the typical devices of plot formation had been clarified thanks to which the stage was now set for work on the history and theory of the novel; concomitantly, *skaz* had been advanced as the constructional principle of the plotless story. These studies exercised an influence detectable in a whole series of investigations produced in later years by persons not directly connected with *Opojaz*.

VI

As the theoretical problems broadened and deepened, a natural division of specialization set in—one all the more reasonable since *Opojaz* had added to its membership persons previously unaffiliated with it or only then beginning their work. The basic dividing line ran between prose fiction and verse. Contrary to the Symbolists, who were then attempting to liquidate, both in theory and practice, the boundaries between poetry and prose fiction and were using all their ingenuity to educe, for this purpose, meter from prose, the Formalists advocated a clear-cut discrimination between these two kinds of verbal art.

The preceding section of this essay has shown how intensive the Formalists' work was in the study of prose fiction. We were the pioneers in that field, not counting certain Western works which coincided with ours in individual details of concrete observation (e.g., Wilhelm Dibelius's *Englische Romankunst,* 1910) but were far removed from our theoretical problems and principles. We felt ourselves almost completely detached from tradition in our work on prose fiction.

Things were somewhat different in the case of poetry. Vast numbers of works by Western and Russian theorists, the Symbolists' practical and theoretical experiments, debates over the concepts of rhythm and meter, and the whole corpus of specialized literature to which those debates gave rise between 1910 and 1917, and finally, the appearance of the Futurists' new verse forms—all this did not so much facilitate as complicate the study of verse and even the formulation of the problems involved. Instead of addressing themselves to the basic issues, many investigators devoted their efforts to special problems in metrics or to the task of sorting out the systems and views already amassed. Meanwhile, no theory of verse, in the broad sense of the word, was to be had; there was no theoretical illumination of the problem of verse rhythm or of the connection between rhythm and syntax or of sounds in verse (the Formalists had only identified a certain linguistic groundwork), or of verse vocabulary and semantics, and so on. In other words, the problem of verse, as such, remained essentially up in the air. An approach was needed which would steer away from particular problems of metrics and would engage verse from some more fundamental point of view. What was needed, first of all, was a restatement of the problem of rhythm in such a way that the problem would not hinge on metrics and would encompass the more substantive aspects of verse language.

In this chapter, as in the preceding one, I shall limit my topic, focusing on the problem of verse only to the extent that its elaboration led to new theoretical views of verbal art or of verse speech. The start was made by Osip Brik's "On Rhythmic-Syntactic Figures."[15] Brik's report demonstrated the actual existence in verse of constant syntactic formations inseparably bound with rhythm. Therefore the concept of rhythm relinquished its abstract character and touched on the very fabric of verse—*the phrase unit*. Metrics retreated to the background, retaining a significance as the rudiments, the alphabet, of verse. This step was as important for the study of verse as the coupling of plot with construction had been for the study of prose fiction. The discovery of rhythmic-syntactic figures conclusively discredited the notion that rhythm is an external increment, something confined to the surface of speech. The theory of verse was led down a line of inquiry which treated rhythm as the structural base from which all elements of verse—nonacoustical as well as acoustical—derived definition. The stage was set for a more sophisticated theory of verse under which metrics would have to occupy the position of propaedeutics. The Symbolists and the theorists of the Belyj school, despite all their efforts, had failed to come up with this line of inquiry precisely because the issues of metrics as such persisted as their focal point.

However, Brik's work only hinted at the possibility of this new line of inquiry. His report, as was also true of his first article, "Sound Repetitions," went no further than bringing out examples and ordering them in groups. One could proceed from Brik's work either in the direction of new problems or (equally as well) in the direction of simple classification and cataloging, or the systematization of material, something which had no essential connection with the Formal method at all. The latter is exactly the type of work to which V. Žirmunskij's book *Composition of Lyric Verse*[16] belongs. Not sharing *Opojaz*'s theoretical principles, Žirmunskij found the Formal method of interest only as one of a set of possible scientific rubrics—as the technique of breaking material down into various groupings under various labels. With such a conception of the Formal method, nothing else could have been expected of him than what he in fact produced.

His procedure is to take some egregious feature as the criterion and to sort out the material in groups from that standpoint. Hence, the invariable classificatory and handbook character of all Žirmunskij's theoretical writings. Work of this type had no fundamental meaning in the overall evolution of the Formal method; it only marked a tendency (evidently a bit of historical inevitability) to add an academic aura to the Formal method. It is not surprising, therefore, that Žirmunskij, as things developed, entirely withdrew from *Opojaz,* with whose principles he has repeatedly disagreed in his later works (see especially his preface to the translation of O. Walzel's *Problem of Form in Poetry,* 1923).

There was a certain connection between Brik's work on rhythmic-syntactic figures and my book *Verse Melodics,*[17] a study which had been shaped by an interest in the sound aspect of verse and in that respect was connected with a whole series of Western works (Sievers, Saran, and others). I started from the position that, since stylistic differentiation was usually based on vocabulary, "we thereby sidestep verse as such and really deal with poetic language in general. . . . It is essential to find something connected with the verse *phrase unit* that, at the same time, would not lead us away from verse as such—something located on the border between phonetics and semantics.

That 'something' is syntax." Rhythmic-syntactic phenomena in my study were examined, not in and of themselves, but in connection with the problem concerning the constructional significance of intonation in verse and speech. I thought it particularly important to emphasize the concept of the *dominant* (that which underlies the organization of any poetic style) and to discriminate between a concept of "melodics," as a system of intonation, and the concept of the general "musicality" of verse. Taking that as my starting point, I proposed distinguishing three basic styles in lyric poetry: declamatory (oratorical), *chantant (napevnyj)*, and discursive *(govornoj)*. The whole book was devoted to the study of the melodic properties of the *chantant* style, using as material lyric verse by Žukovskij, Tjutčev, Lermontov, and Fet. Avoiding hard and fast schemes, I made this point in the conclusion to my book:

> What I consider most important in scholarship is not erecting schemes but being able to see facts. Theory is essential for this, because it is precisely in the light of theory that facts become visible, that is, really become facts. Theories may perish or change, but the facts discovered and established with their help abide.

The tradition of specialized metrical studies remained in force among the theorists affiliated with Symbolism (A. Belyj, V. Brjusov, S. Bobrov, V. Čudovskij, and others), but gradually it went the way of meticulous statistical computations and lost its relevance to fundamental principles. A role of considerable importance to the problem was played by B. Tomaševskij in a series of metrical investigations ending with his textbook *Russian Versification.*[18] The net effect was the subordination of metrics (as an auxiliary discipline with a very restricted range of problems) and the advancement of the theory of verse, in its full scope, to the fore. An early article of Tomaševskij's, "Puškin's Iambic Pentameter,"[19] in which the attempt was made to go beyond metrics into language, had already evinced the ambition (which had marked the whole preceding development of the Formal method) to expand and enrich the idea of verse rhythm by connecting it with the structure of verse language. It was here that the basic charge against Belyj and his school was made: "The task that rhythm carries out is not conformity with factitious paeons but the distribution of expiratory energy over a single wave—the verse line." This ambition was again expressed with the greatest explicitness in another article by Tomaševskij, "The Problem of Verse Rhythm."[20] In this article the earlier opposition of meter and rhythm is expanded to the whole range of linguistic elements in the makeup of a verse line: alongside rhythm of the word-accent variety are placed "phrasal-intonational" rhythm and "harmonic" rhythm (alliterations and the like). Therefore, the concept of *verse* becomes the concept of a *special type of speech* which—instead of being forced into one or another metrical pattern, resisting it and producing "rhythmic deviations" (the point of view Zirmunskij adheres to in his *Introduction to Metrics*)[21]—functions wholly in the creation of a poem. According to Tomaševskij,

Verse speech is speech *organized* in its sound aspect. But inasmuch as sound aspect is a *complex* phenomenon, only some one particular element of sound is canonized. Thus in classical metrics the canonized element is the word stress, which classical metrics proceeded to subject to codification as a norm under its rules. . . . But once the authority of traditional forms is even slightly shaken, the compelling thought arises that these primary features do not exhaust the nature of verse, that verse is viable also in its secondary features of sound, that there is such a thing as a recognizable rhythm along with meter, that verse can be written with only its secondary features observed, that *speech can sound like verse even without its observing a meter.*

The importance of "rhythmic impulse," a concept which had already figured in Brik's work, is affirmed by Tomaševskij as the general rhythmic operational mode:

Rhythmic devices can participate in various degrees in the creation of a rhythmic impression of artistic value: in individual works some one device or another may predominate; some one procedure or another may be the *dominant*. Focus on one rhythmic device or another determines the character of the work's concrete rhythm, and, with this in mind, verse may be classified as tonic-metrical verse (e.g., the description of the battle in *Poltava*), intonational-melodic verse (Žukovskij's poetry), and harmonic verse (typical of Russian Symbolism in its later years).

Verse form, so understood, is not in opposition to any "content" extrinsic to it; it is not forced to fit inside this "form" but is conceived of as the genuine content of verse speech. Thus the very concept of form, as in our previous works, emerges with a new sense of sufficiency.

VII

New problems in the general theory of verse rhythm and verse language were put forward in Roman Jakobson's book *On Czech Verse*.[22] Against the theory of "the unqualified correspondence of poetry with the spirit of the language, the nonresistance of form to material," Jakobson advanced the theory of "the organized coercion of language by poetic form." A characteristic corrective entered in the discrimination between the sound system of practical language and the sound system of poetic language: it was pointed out that the dissimilation of liquids, which, according to Jakubinskij, is absent in poetic language as against practical language,[23] is actually possible in both, but in practical language it is "conditioned," whereas in poetic language it is, so to speak, "made purposeful, i.e., the two are essentially different phenomena." Moreover, Jakobson pointed out the difference in principle between emotive language and poetic language (a topic already discussed as far back as his first work, *Recent Russian Poetry*):

Poetry may employ the methods of emotive language, but only *for its own purposes*. This resemblance between the two language systems and this employment by poetic language of the means customary in emotive language often suggest an identification of poetic language with emotive language. Such an identification is fallacious, for it fails to take into account the cardinal *functional* difference between the two language systems.

In this connection, Jakobson invalidates attempts by Grammont and other investigators of verse to explain sound constructs by resorting to onomatopoeia or to emotive ties established between sounds and images or ideas: "A sound construct is not always a construct of sound imagery, and a construct of sound imagery does not always make use of the methods of emotive language." Jakobson's study may be regarded as highly characteristic of the Formal method because it constantly exceeds the limits of its special, particular topic (the prosody of Czech verse), shedding light on general questions in the theory of poetic language and theory of verse. For example, at the end a complete essay on Majakovskij, supplementing Jakobson's earlier work on Xlebnikov, is appended.

In my own study of Anna Axmatova (1923) I also made a point of reexamining the basic theoretical issues related to the theory of verse: the connection of rhythm with syntax and intonation, sounds in verse in connection with articulation, and, last, the vocabulary of verse and its semantics. Referring to a study by Jurij Tynjanov (then being written), I advanced the idea that "a word incorporated into verse is, as it were, wrenched from ordinary speech, surrounded with a new aura of meaning, and perceived against a background composed not of speech in general but precisely of speech in poetry." I also postulated that the formation of lateral meanings, disrupting the usual associations of words, is the chief property of verse semantics.

In about the same period the original connection of the Formal method with linguistics slackened considerably. The division of fields of inquiry had been worked out to such an extent that we no longer needed special support from linguistics, particularly from psychologically oriented linguistics. As a matter of fact, certain works by linguists pertaining to the study of poetic style were causing us to react with objections to fundamental terms. The appearance at the moment of Tynjanov's *The Problem of Verse Language*[24] had the effect of underscoring the difference between psychological linguistics and the study of poetic language and style. This work, with its revelation of the close connection between the meaning of words and the verse structure, gave our concept of verse rhythm a new and fresher content and applied the Formal method to a line of study which inquired not only into the acoustical and syntactic properties of verse speech but into its semantic properties as well. In his preface Tynjanov declares:

The study of *verse* has recently made great strides forward; the near future will undoubtedly see its development into an entire field, even though the drafting stage of the study may still be fresh in everybody's mind. But alongside that study there is the issue of poetic language and style. Studies in this area have been separated from the study of verse; the impression has been created that poetic language and style are unconnected with verse, have no relationship with it. The concept of "poetic language," advanced only recently, is now undergoing a crisis brought on by the extensiveness, the amorphousness, of the scope and content of the concept in its reliance on a psychological-linguistic base.

Among the general issues of poetics posed and illuminated afresh by this study, the question, how to understand "material," had a crucial significance. The accepted practice had been to oppose this concept to the concept of "form," with the result that both concepts suffered a loss of meaning in serving merely as a substitute for the old opposition of "form" versus "content." In point of fact, as already stated, the concept of form in the Formalists' usage, having accrued a sense of complete sufficiency, had merged with the idea of the work of art in its entirety. Thus it did not require any opposition other than with another category of forms of the nonartistic variety. Tynjanov points out that the material of verbal art is not uniform either in kind or in value, that "one factor may be put forward at the expense of the others, as a result of which these others are deformed and sometimes are reduced to the level of a neutral prop." The conclusion is that "the concept of material does not extend beyond form—it too is formal; its confusion with extraconstructional factors is a mistake." In this context form takes on complexity via the features of dynamism:

> The unity of a work is not a matter of a closed, symmetrical whole (*celost'*) but of an evolving, dynamic integratedness (*celostnost'*); between its elements there can be no static equal or plus signs, but there are always the dynamic signs of correlation and integration. The form of a literary work must be recognized as dynamic.

Rhythm is presented in Tynjanov's study as the basic structural factor of verse, permeating all its elements. The *unity and the compactness of the rhythmic series,* the one in direct relationship with the other, are established as the objective sign of verse rhythm. The fundamental difference between verse and prose is affirmed anew:

> An orientation in verse toward prose is an emplacement of the unity and compactness of its series in an unusual object and, therefore, does not entail effacing the essence of verse but rather puts verse in relief with new force. . . . Once incorporated into the domain of verse, any element of prose turns another, functionally projected facet of itself in the verse line and thus displays two factors at once: the structure-emphasizing factor—the factor of verse—and the factor of the deformation of an unusual object.

Further on the semantic issue is raised: "Isn't it true that in verse we have a deformed semantics, which, for that very reason, cannot be studied with speech when isolated from its structural government?" The answer to this question takes up the entire second part of Tynjanov's work, which establishes the tight relationship between the factors of rhythm and semantics. The decisive circumstance for the verbal items is their membership in rhythmic unities: "These members prove to have a stronger and closer connection than is true in ordinary speech; a *correlation by position* comes into play," one which is absent in prose.

Thus the Formalists' departure from Potebnja's theory and the conclusions associated with it received a new substantiation, and new prospects were opened for the theory of verse. Tynjanov's work showed us the possibility of encompassing new problems and also the advancing evolution. It became unmistakably clear, even to those outside *Opojaz*, that the essence of our work lay, not in erecting some rigid "Formal method," but in studying the specific properties of verbal art, and that the point was not the method but the object of study. Tynjanov again formulated this idea:

> The object of a study claiming to be the study of *art* must be to identify that specific set of things which distinguishes art from all other domains of intellectual activity, and which makes them its material or tools. Each work of art involves a complex interaction of many factors; consequently, the task to be carried out in investigation and research is the determination of the specific character of this interaction.

VIII

Above I noted that point in our development when, alongside theoretical problems, there arose, naturally enough, the issue of the movement and succession of forms, i.e., the issue of literary evolution. It arose in connection with our reexamination of Veselovskij's views on folktale motifs and devices, and the answer given then ("New form comes about not in order to express new content but in order to replace old form") derived from our new way of understanding form. Form conceived as content itself, incessantly changing shape in relation to previous models, naturally required our approaching it without abstract, hard-and-fast classificatory schemes, but instead our taking into account its concrete historical meaning and significance. A kind of duplex perspective took shape: one dimension was that of theoretical study (Sklovskij's *Plot Unfolding* or my *Verse Melodics*, for example) focused on some particular problem of theory and having the greatest possible variety of material; the other dimension was that of historical study, the study of literary evolution as such. The conjunction of these two dimensions of study, an organic consequence of the development of the Formal method, confronted us with a series of new and very complex problems, many of which have remained until now unelucidated and even partially undefined.

The fact of the matter is that the Formalists' original endeavor to pin down some particular constructional device and trace its unity through voluminous material had given way to an endeavor to qualify further the generalized idea, to grasp the concrete *function* of the device in each given instance. This concept of functional value gradually moved out to the forefront and overshadowed our original concept of the device. Such a process of making further qualifications of one's own general concepts and principles is characteristic of the entire evolution of the Formal method. We maintain no general, dogmatic positions that would bind our hands and keep us from getting at the facts. We do not vouch for the schemata we construct if other people try to apply them to facts unknown to us—the facts may require changes or elaborations or corrections in our schemata. Work on concrete material is what started us talking about function and by that very fact led us to a new level of complexity in the concept of the device. Theory itself required our branching out into history.

Here again we came into conflict with the traditions of academic scholarship and certain tendencies in literary criticism. During our student days, the academic history of literature had confined itself by and large to the biographical and psychological study of individual writers—only, needless to say, "the greats." There was not even any trace of the earlier attempts at compiling histories of Russian literature in its entirety, attempts that revealed an intention to systematize a huge quantity of historical material. Nevertheless, the tradition of such compilations (like A. N. Pypin's *History of Russian Literature*) did retain scientific authority, all the more so because the succeeding generation was reluctant to undertake such vast pursuits. Meanwhile, these compilations had relied heavily on such vague generalities as the concepts of "realism" and "romanticism" (with the added qualification that realism is better than romanticism); evolution was taken to mean a steady advancement toward perfection, like human progress (hence, from romanticism to realism); succession was understood as a decorous transfer of a legacy from father to son; literature, as such, played no role whatever—it had been supplanted by material taken from the history of social movements, from biography, and so on.

This primitive historicism, with its effect of leading away from literature, naturally provoked a reaction against any kind of historicism on the part of the Symbolist theorists and the literary critics. A whole literature of impressionistic sketches and "silhouettes" developed, and the rage set in for "modernizing" writers of the past and turning them into "eternal companions." The history of literature was implicitly (and sometimes even explicitly) declared useless.

We had to demolish those academic traditions and liquidate those tendencies in journalistic criticism. We had to pit against those forces a new concept of literary evolution and of literature itself—a concept divorced from ideas of progress and decorous succession, from the concepts of realism and romanticism, from any material extrinsic to literature as a specific order of things. As for the critics, we had to proceed by pointing out concrete historical facts, the mobility and mutability of form, the need to take into account the concrete functions of particular devices, in short, by pointing out the difference between a literary work as a definite historical fact and the free interpretation of it from the standpoint of present-day literary needs, tastes, or interests. Thus the governing spirit of our literary historical work had to be the spirit of destruction and negation—as it had been during our theoretical debut—that afterward had assumed a more moderate character once the individual problems involved had been resolved.

That explains why our first pronouncements on literary history took the form of something close to spontaneous theses exhibited in connection with some piece of concrete material. A particular issue would unexpectedly develop into a general problem—theory merged with history. Tynjanov's *Dostoevskij and Gogol'*[25] and Šklovskij's *Rozanov*[26] were two highly characteristic examples.

Tynjanov's main task was to prove that Dostoevskij's *Village of Stepančikovo* may be regarded a parody and that behind the overt features of the story there is the background of Gogol' and his *Correspondence with Friends*. In Tynjanov's hands, however, this particular issue swelled to the proportions of a whole theory of parody—parody as a device of style (parody-stylization) and as one manifestation of the dialectical change of schools having particular literary historical significance. In this connection, the question of how to understand "succession" and "tradition" emerged, and consequently the basic problems of literary evolution were raised:

> When people talk about "literary tradition" or "succession". . . they usually imagine a kind of straight line joining a younger representative of a given literary branch with an older one. As it happens, things are much more complex than that. It is not a matter of continuing on a straight line, but rather one of setting out and pushing off from a given point—a struggle. . . . Each instance of literary succession is first and foremost a struggle involving a destruction of the old unity and a new construction out of the old elements.

Our idea of literary evolution took on new complexity once the factors of struggle and periodic revolts were pointed out, and it relinquished its older meaning of a decorous progression. Dostoevskij's literary relationship with Gogol' assumed in this context the character of a complex struggle.

Running through Šklovskij's pamphlet on Rozanov was what was almost a digression from the main topic—a whole theory of literary evolution reflecting the lively discussion of that problem then taking place in the *Opojaz* circle. Šklovskij pointed out that literature moves ahead in a broken line:

> Not one but several literary schools exist during each literary epoch. They exist in literature simultaneously, but one of them forms the canonized crest. The others exist without being canonized and without resonance, as, for instance, in Puškin's time, the Deržavin tradition existed in the poetry of Kjuxelbeker and Griboedov simultaneously with the tradition of Russian vaudeville verse and a host of other

traditions, for example, the tradition of the pure adventure novel as represented by Bulgarin.

Once the older art has been canonized, new forms are created in a lower stratum, the "junior line," which

> forces its way into the position occupied by the older one, and so we get the vaudevillist Belopjatkin becoming Nekrasov (Osip Brik's study), Tolstoj, the direct heir of the eighteenth century, creating a new novel (Boris Èjxenbaum), Blok canonizing the themes and tempos of the "gypsy song" and Čexov's bringing *Budil' nik* [The Alarm Clock—the name of a Russian comic newspaper] into Russian literature. Dostoevskij raises the devices of the dime novel to the level of the literary norm. Each new school of literature is a revolution— something like the emergence of a new class. But that, of course, is only an analogy. The defeated line is not annihilated, it does not cease to exist. It only topples from the crest, drops below for a time of lying fallow, and may again rise as an ever present pretender to the throne. Moreover, in practice, things are complicated by the fact that the new hegemony is usually not a pure instance of a restoration of earlier form, but one involving the presence of features from other junior schools, even features (but now in a subordinate role) inherited from its predecessor on the throne.

A discussion of the dynamism of genres is also presented, and Rozanov's books are interpreted as the inception of a new genre, as a new type of novel, with no motivation binding its parts together: "On the level of thematics, they are characterized by the canonization of new themes; on the compositional level, by laying the device bare."

In connection with the general theory, the idea of the "dialectical self-generation of new forms" is introduced, an idea with implications both for an analogy with the development of other orders of culture and also for the substantiation of the autonomy of literary evolution. In oversimplified form, this theory was quickly embraced on all sides, and, as always happens, it took the shape of a simple and static schema of the kind criticism finds very handy. In actual fact, all we had here was a general outline of evolution outfitted with a whole set of complex qualifications. The Formalists proceeded from this general outline to a more closely argued elaboration of literary historical problems and facts, giving their original theoretical premises a new concreteness and complexity.

IX

Naturally, with our understanding of literary evolution as the dialectical change of forms, we do not resort to the material that occupied a central position in literary historical criticism of the old type. We study literary evolution to the extent that it bears a specific character, and within such limits as allow us to call it autonomous, not directly dependent on other orders of culture. In other words, we limit the factors so as not to wallow in an endless quantity of vague "connections" and "correspondences," which, in any case, cannot elucidate the evolution of literature as such. We do not incorporate into our work issues involving biography or the psychology of creativity—assuming that those problems, very serious and complex in their own right, ought to have their place in other disciplines. We are concerned with finding in evolution the features of immanent historical laws. Therefore, we leave aside whatever, from that point of view, may be said to be "fortuitous," not relevant to history. What interests us is the very process of evolution, the very *dynamics* of literary forms in so far as it may be observed in the facts of the past. The central problem of literary history for us is the problem of evolution outside individual personality—the study of literature as a *social phenomenon sui generis*. In this connection, the issue that takes on enormous importance for us is the formation and the successive change of genres, including "second-rate" and "popular" literature, insofar as that literature plays a role in the process. All that is required here is to make a distinction between that type of popular literature which prepared the ground for the formation of new genres and that type which comes about in the process of their dissolution and which may be regarded as material for the study of historical inertia.

On the other hand, it is not the past *per se,* the past as discrete historical fact, that interests us—we are not in the business of simply restoring epochs that for some reason or other appeal to us. History gives us what the contemporary situation cannot—a full measure of material. But that is precisely why we approach history with a certain supply of theoretical problems and principles suggested in part by the facts of contemporary literature. Hence, the Formalists' distinguishing characteristic of maintaining close contact with the contemporary literary scene and of making criticism approach scholarship (in contrast to the Symbolists, who made scholarship approach criticism, and to the earlier historians of literature, who for the most part kept their distance from the contemporary scene). Thus the history of literature for us is not so much a special *subject,* as against theory, but a special *method,* a special dimension of study. That is what explains the nature of our literary historical works of always having a bearing not only on historical but also on theoretical conclusions—on the posing of new theoretical problems and the verification of old ones.[27]

What remains for me now is a general summing up. The evolution of the Formal method, which I have attempted to delineate, presents a picture of the consecutive development of theoretical principles above and beyond, so to speak, the individual role of any single one of us. Indeed, *Opojaz* realized in practice a genuine type of collective endeavor. This came about, in all likelihood, for the very reason that we understood our concern from the outset to be *historical,* and not our personal concern. Herein is our major link with our age. Science itself is evolving, and we are evolving together with it. Now I shall briefly indicate the basic factors in the evolution of the Formal method over the past ten years.

1. From an initial summary opposition between poetic language and practical language, we arrived at a differentiation within the concept of practical language in terms of its functions (Jakubinskij) and at a discrimination between the methods of poetic language and the methods of emotive language (Jakobson). Associated with this evolution is our special interest in studying oratory—precisely that kind of speech, from the practical sphere, that is closest to poetic speech but differs with respect to function—and we have begun discussing the necessity of revitalizing rhetoric along with poetics. (See the articles on Lenin's language in *Lef,* No. 1(5), 1924, by Šklovskij, Èjxenbaum, Tynjanov, Jakubinskij, Kazanskij, and Tomaševskij.)

2. From the general concept of form in its new meaning, we arrived at the concept of device, and hence at the concept of function.

3. From the concept of verse rhythm in its opposition with meter, we arrived at the concept of rhythm as the structural factor of verse in its total integrity and therefore to the concept of verse as a special form of speech possessing its own special linguistic (syntactic, lexical, and semantic) qualities.

4. From the concept of plot as construction, we arrived at the concept of materials as motivation, and hence at that of material as an element participating in the construction in dependence on the character of the form-organizing *dominant*.

5. From the predication of the unity of a device over diverse material, we arrived at a differentiation within device in terms of function, and hence at the issue of the evolution of forms, that is, at the problem of literary historical study.

We are facing a whole series of new problems. The clear evidence of this fact is seen in Tynjanov's recent article "Literary Fact."[28] It poses the question of the nature of the relationship between life and literature—a problem "solved" by a great many people with all the facility of dilettantism. Examples are used in the article to show how cultural life becomes literature, and, conversely, how literature retreats into cultural life: "During the period of the dissolution of a genre, it shifts from center to periphery, and, from literary backyards and domestic life, a new phenomenon emerges to take its place."

There was good reason for my having entitled this essay "The Theory of the Formal Method" and for having produced what is evidently a sketch of its evolution. We possess no theory of such a kind as could be deployed as a rigid, ready-made system. Theory and history have merged for us, not only in what we preach, but also in what we practice. We are too well trained by history itself to imagine that we could do without history. The moment we ourselves are obliged to acknowledge that ours is a theory which is all-encompassing, able to cope with all contingencies of past and future, and therefore neither in need of nor amenable to evolution, we shall at the same time be obliged to acknowledge that the Formal method has ceased to exist and that the spirit of scientific inquiry has abandoned it. So far that has not happened.

NOTES

1. By "Formalists" I mean that group of theorists who banded together in the *Obščestvo izučenija poètičeskogo jazyka (Opojaz)* [Society for the Study of Poetic Language], and who began issuing their own publication in 1916.

2. R. Unger notes the powerful influence Wölfflin's work had on representatives of the "aesthetic" trend in contemporary German historical study, men such as O. Walzel and F. Strich. See Wölfflin's article "Moderne Strömungen in der deutschen Literaturwissenschaft," in *Die Literatur*, 2 November 1923. See also Walzel's *Gehalt und Gestalt im Kunstwerk des Dichters* (Berlin, 1923).

3. *Novejšaja russkaja poèzija. Nabrosok pervyj* [Recent Russian Poetry, Sketch 1] (Prague, 1921), p. 11.

4. "O zvukax stixotvornogo jazyka" in *Sborniki po teorii poètičeskogo jazyka, Vypusk pervyi* (Petrograd, 1916).

5. "O poèzii i zaumnom jazyke."

6. See Andrej Belyj's articles in the collection of essays, *Skify* (1017), and in *Vetv'* (1917), and my article, "O zvukax v stixe" [On Sound in Verse] (1920), reprinted in the collection of my essays, *Skvoz' literaturu* (1924).

7. "Zvukovye povtory," in *Sborniki po teorii poètičeskogo jazyka, Vypusk II* (Petrograd, 1917).

8. *Voskrešenie slova.*

9. "Iskusstvo kak priem," in *Sborniki po teorii poètičeskogo jazyka, Vypusk II*, 1917.

10. "Potebnja," in *Poètika: Sborniki po teorii poètičeskogo jazyka* (Petrograd, 1919).

11. "Svjaz' priemov sjužetosloženija s obščimi priemami stilja," in *Poètika, 1919.*

12. Somewhat later than the period now being discussed, Veselovskij's view of "syncretism" as a phenomenon belonging only to archaic poetry, engendered by the communal culture of the time, came under criticism in a work by B. Kazanskij, "Ideja istoričeskoj poètiki" [The Idea of Historical Poetics], in *Poètika I*, Leningrad, "Academia," 1926. Kazanskij affirmed the existence of syncretic tendencies, strikingly pronounced during certain periods in each of the arts and refuted the "ethnographic" point of view.

13. *Razvertyvanie sjužeta* and *Tristram Šendi Sterna i teorija romana* (published separately by Opojaz in 1921).

14. "Kak sdelana 'Šinel' Gogolja," in *Poètika*, 1919.

15. "O ritmiko-sintaktičeskix figurax" (a report delivered to Opojaz in 1920 and not only never published but even, I believe, never fully completed).

16. *Kompozicija liričeskix stixotvorenij.* Opojaz 1921.

17. *Melodika stixa.* Opojaz 1922.

18. *Russkoe stixosloženie* 1924.

19. "Pjatistopnyj jamb Puškina." First printed in 1919 and reprinted in the collection of essays *Očerki po poètike Puškina* (Berlin, 1923).

20. "Problema stixotvornogo ritma," in *Literaturnaja mysl, Vypusk II,* 1922.

21. *Vvedenie v metriku.* 1925.

22. *O češskom stixe (Sborniki po teorii poètičeskogo jazyka, Vypusk V,* 1923). [See also Brown University Slavic Reprint VI, 1969.]

23. By this time Jakubinskij himself had pointed out the excessive inclusiveness of the concept "practical language" and the necessity of breaking it down in terms of

functions (colloquial, scientific, oratorical, etc.). See his article, "O dialogičeskoj reči" [On Dialogic Speech] in the collection of essays *Russkaja reč* 1923.

24. *Problema stixotvornogo jazyka.* Academia 1924.

25. *Dostoevskij i Gogol'.* Opojaz 1921.

26. *Rozanov.* Opojaz 1921.

27. Between 1921 and 1924 a whole series of works of the type I have been talking about appeared. I shall list the main ones.

Jurij Tynjanov: "Stixovye formy Nekrasova" [Nekrasov's Verse Forms]; "Dostoevskij i Gogol'" [Dostoevskij and Gogol']; "Vopros o Tjutčeve" [The Tjutčev Question]; "Tjutčev i Gejne" [Tjutčev and Heine]; "Arxaisty i Puškin" [The Archaists and Puškin]; "Puškin i Tjutčev" [Puškin and Tjutčev]; "Oda kak deklamacionnyj žanr" [The Ode as a Declamatory Genre].

Boris Tomaševskij: *Gavrilliada* (a critical edition of Puškin's *Gavrilliada*, chapters on composition and genre): Puškin—čitatel francužskix poètov" [Puškin, Reader of the French Poets]; "Puškin" (on contemporary problems of the historical study of literature); "Puškin i Bualo" [Puškin and Boileau]; "Puškin i Lafonten" [Puškin and La Fontaine].

Boris Èjxenbaum: *Molodoj Tolstoj* [The Young Tolstoj]; *Lermontov;* "Problemy poètiki Puškina" [Problems of Puškin's Poetics]; "Put' Puškina k proze" [Puškin's Approach to Prose]; "Nekrasov."

One should add to this list historical works on literature not directly connected with Opojaz but following the same line of study. For example: V. Vinogradov: "Sjužet i kompozicija povesti Gogolja 'Nos'" [The Plot and Composition of Gogol''s Story 'Nose']; "Sjužet i arxitektonika romana Dostoevskogo *Bednye ljudi*" [The Plot and Architectonics of Dostevskij's Novel, *Poor Folk*].

The following items have to do with the poetics of the Natural School: "Gogol' i Žjul' Žanen" [Gogol' and Jules Janin]; "Gogol' i real'naja škola" [Gogol' and the Realist School]; "Ètjudy o stile Gogolja" [Studies on Gogol''s Style].

V. Žirmunskij: *Bajron i Puškin* [Byron and Puškin].

S. Baluxatyj: *Dramaturgija Čexova* [Čexov's Dramaturgy].

A. Cejtlin: "Povesti o bednom činovnike Dostoevskogo" [Dostoevskij's Tales of a Poor Clerk].

K. Simkevič: "Nekrasov i Puškin" [Nekrasov and Puškin].

Furthermore, certain members of seminars given under our direction at the university and at the Institute for the History of Arts have produced a series of works, published as the collection *Russkaja proza* [Russian Prose], Academia 1926, on Dal', Marlinskij, Senkovskij, Vjaźemskij, Vel'tman, Karamzin, on the genre of the journey, and other topics.

This is not the place to discuss these studies in any detail. I need say only that they all typically draw on "second-rate" writers (the *entourage*), meticulously elucidate traditions, follow changes in genres and styles, and so on. As part and parcel of this work, many forgotten names and facts have been made viable again, popular estimates of reputations have been proved wrong, traditional ideas have been altered, and, most importantly, the very process of evolution has gradually been made clearer. The work of studying this material has only just begun. A set of new problems lies before us: the further qualification of our theoretical and historical concepts of literature, the incorporation of new material, the postulation of new issues, and so on.

28. "Literaturnyj fakt." *Lef,* No. 2(6), 1925.

Tristan Tzara

1896–1963

Tristan Tzara, the prime mover of the "Dadaist" movement, was born in Moinesti, Rumania, on April 14, 1896. Sent to Zurich to study mathematics, he soon made common cause with many of the expatriate artists and writers residing there; the impregnable neutrality of Switzerland made it an especially attractive haven for radical intellectuals during the war years, and Tzara forged close ties with such figures as Jean Arp, Francis Picabia, Marcel Duchamp, Hugo Ball, and Richard Huelsenbeck. At the Cabaret Voltaire—where, according to pious legend, Tzara and Lenin met for games of chess—members of this group came together to exchange ideas and collaborate on various literary and dramatic projects: poetry readings, concerts of "Negro music," exhibitions of modern art— and the creation of a new literary journal, *Dada*.

"Dada," as Tzara pointed out in *A Dada Manifesto* (1918), is a meaningless term. Ostensibly a childish expression for "horse," it was chosen at random from the *Larousse* encyclopedia as an arbitrary label for a movement which aimed at the subversion of all extant social, moral, religious, philosophical, and artistic conventions. Dada spectacles were deliberately chaotic events, at which nonsensical poems were shouted derisively at audiences who, more often than not, were themselves loudly berating the poets. The first Dada play, *La Première Aventure céleste de Monsieur Antipyrine* (*The First Celestial Adventure of Mr. Fire-Extinguisher*), written and produced by Tzara in 1916, has been described as "an assault on the bastion of aesthetics." Its bizarre style—in which disparate words and syllables are joined in impossible combinations— mirrors (in literary form) what Kurt Schwitters and the other *collagists* were trying to achieve in the plastic arts, through the random juxtaposition of "found objects."

This was not a purely nihilistic approach. Tzara wanted to restore the "magic" power of words by removing them from their ordinary structures and presenting them, as it were, for the first time. The destructive force of Dada was provisional: it anticipated new creation upon old ground. Forms had to be emptied of all meaning in order that new meanings might be supplied. In *A Dada Manifesto*, Tzara wrote: "We are not sentimental. We shred the linen of clouds and prayers like a furious wind, preparing the great spectacle of disaster, fire, decomposition. . . . Let every man shout: there is a great destructive, negative work to be accomplished. Sweeping, cleaning. The cleanliness of the individual affirms itself after the state of madness, the aggressive, complete madness of a world left in the hands of bandits who vandalize and destroy centuries." There was in this approach a bitter reflection of the war, which was then accomplishing on the material plane what the Dadaists were attempting on the aesthetic.

In 1919 Tzara made his long-awaited move to Paris, where he was welcomed enthusiastically. He had for some years been in close contact with André Breton, the editor of *Littérature,* and now the two joined forces as the acknowledged leaders of Dada. Abrasive spectacles and raucous meetings were arranged, as in Zurich, but Breton soon lost patience with Tzara's increasingly violent and anarchical rhetoric, and the two gradually became more and more estranged. When Tzara refused to participate in Breton's Congress of Paris in 1922—arguing, quite consistently, that any attempt to influence social and aesthetic development through parliamentary conferences ran directly counter to the spirit of Dada—Breton denounced Tzara and the Dadaists, and proclaimed the advent of Surrealism. In 1923 Breton and a gang of Surrealists tried to disrupt the opening performance of Tzara's play, *Le Coeur à gaz* (Gas-Operated Heart), and an angry riot ensued.

Dada as a movement faded quickly thereafter, its demise made inevitable by its inherent self-destructive tendencies. Tzara himself followed Breton into Surrealism around 1930 (see his *Essay on the State of Poetry,* 1931), and became a Communist in 1936. His activity in the Resistance during World War II had a profound humanizing effect upon him, and went a long way toward removing the last vestiges of his nihilism; his later verse was quieter, gentler, almost lyrical in tone. Toward the end of his life he became weary of Surrealism, and, in an interview for *L'Express* in December 1963, accused Breton of keeping the movement alive artificially. He died two days later, on Christmas Eve.

A DADA MANIFESTO

The magic of a word—DADA—which has set the journalists at the door of an unexpected world, has not the slightest importance for us.

To proclaim a manifesto you have to want: A.B.C., thunder against 1,2,3, lose your patience and sharpen your wings to conquer and spread a's, b's, c's little and big, sign, scream, swear, arrange the prose in a form of absolute and irrefutable evidence, prove your non-plus-ultra and maintain that novelty resembles life just as the latest appearance of a whore proves the essence of God. His existence was already proved by accordions, landscapes, and gentle words.٭ * ٭ To impose your A.B.C. is a natural thing—therefore regrettable. Everyone does it in a form of crystalbluffmadonna, a monetary system, a pharmaceutical product, a bare leg beckoning to an ardent and sterile spring. The love of novelty is the agreeable cross, proves a naive Idon'tgiveadamnism, sign with no cause, fleeting and positive. But this need has aged also. By giving to art the impulse of supreme simplicity: novelty, you are human and true about being amused, impulsive and vibrant in order to crucify boredom. At the crossroads of lights, alert, attentive, on the watch for passing years, in the forest.٭ * ٭

I am writing a manifesto and I don't want anything, I say however certain things and I am on principle against manifestoes, as I am also against principles (half-pints for judging the moral value of each sentence—too easy; approximation was invested by the impressionists).٭ * ٭ I am writing this manifesto to show that you can do contrary actions together, in one single fresh breath; I am against action; for continual contradiction, for affirmation also, I am neither for nor against and I don't explain because I hate common sense.

DADA—now there's a word that sets off ideas; each bourgeois is a little playwright, inventing different dialogs, instead of setting characters suitable to the level of his intelligence, like pupae on chairs, seeking causes or purposes (according to the psychoanalytic method he practices) to cement his plot, a story which defines itself in talking.٭ * ٭ Each spectator is a plotter, if he tries to explain a word (knowledge!). From the cotton-padded refuge of serpentine complications, he has his instincts manipulated. Thence the misfortunes of conjugal life.
Explaining: Amusement of redbellies on the mills of empty skulls.

DADA MEANS NOTHING

If you find it futile and if you don't waste your time for a word that doesn't mean anything. . . . The first thought revolving in these heads is bacteriological: at least find its etymological, historical, or psychological origin. You learn from the papers that the Krou blacks call the tail of a holy cow: DADA. In a certain part of Italy, the cube and the mother: DADA. A hobby-horse, a nurse, double affirmation in Russian and in Rumanian: DADA. Certain learned journalists see in it an art for babies, other holy jesusescallinglittlechildren, a return to a dry and noisy, noisy and monotonous primitivism. You don't build a sensitivity on one word; every construction converges in a boring perfection, the stagnant idea of a gilded swamp, a relative human product. The work of art should not be beauty itself, because that is dead; neither gay nor sad, neither clear nor obscure, simply making individuals happy or sad in serving them cakes of sacred haloes or the sweatings of an arched course across the atmospheres. A work of art is never beautiful by decree, objectively, for everybody. Criticism is therefore useless, it only exists subjectively for each person and without the slightest generality. Do you think you have found the psychic basis common to all humanity? The experience of Jesus and the Bible cover under their broad and benevolent wings: excrement, animals, days. How do you mean to put order in the chaos constituting this infinite and formless variation: man? The principle: "love your neighbor" is an hypocrisy. "Know thyself" is a utopia but more acceptable because it contains nastiness within it. No pity. After the carnage we still have the hope of a purified humanity. I always speak of myself because I don't want to convince anyone, I don't have the right to drag others along in my current, I am not obliging anyone to follow me and everyone does his art in his own way, if he knows the joy ascending like arrows toward the stars, or that burrowing in the mines to the flowers of corpses and their fertile spasms. Stalactites: look for them everywhere, in the cribs pain has widened, their eyes white like angels' hares. So DADA was born of a desire for independence, of a distrust of the community. Those who belong to us keep their freedom. We don't recognize any theory. We have had enough of cubist and futurist academies: laboratories of formal ideas. Do you practice art to earn money and fondle the middle class? Rhymes ring the assonance of coins and inflection slides along the line of the tummy in profile. All the groupings of artists have ended at this bank even while they rode high along on diverse comets. A door open to the possibilities of luxuriating in cushions and food.

Here we cast anchor in rich earth.

Here we have the right to proclaim for we have known the shivers and the waking. Returning drunken with energy we stab the trident in the unsuspecting flesh. We are the flowing of maledictions in a tropical abundance of vertiginous vegetation, rubber and rain are our sweat, we bleed and burn thirst, our blood is vigor.

Cubism was born from the simple way of looking at the object: Cézanne painted a cup twenty centimeters lower than his eyes, the cubists look at it from above, others complicate its appearance by making one part perpendicular and in putting it nicely on one side. (I am not forgetting the creators, nor the great motives of the matter they make definitive.)* * * The futurist sees the same cup in movement, a succession of objects one alongside the other embellished maliciously by some lines of force. Which doesn't keep the canvas from being a good or bad painting destined to be an investment for intellectual capital. The new painter creates a world whose elements are also the means of creating it, a sober and definite work, against which there can be no argument. The new artist protests: he no longer paints (symbolic and illusionistic reproduction) but rather creates directly in stone, wood, iron, tin, rocks, and locomotive organisms that can be turned about on any side by the limpid wind of momentary sensation.* * * Any pictorial or plastic work is useless; let it be a monster frightening to servile minds, and not sickly-sweet in order to decorate the refectories of animals dressed like men, illustrations of this sad fable of humanity.—A painting is the art of making two geometrically parallel lines meet on a canvas, in front of our eyes, in the reality of a world transposed according to new conditions and possibilities. This world is not specified or defined in the work; it belongs in its innumerable variations to the spectator. For its creator, it is without cause and without theory. *Order = disorder; I = not-I; affirmation = negation:* supreme radiations from an absolute art. Absolute in its purity of ordered cosmic chaos, eternal in the globule a second without duration, breathing, light, or control.* * * I like an old work for its novelty. Only contrast links us to the past.* * * Writers who teach morality and discuss or ameliorate the psychological basis have, in addition to a hidden desire to win, a ridiculous knowledge of life, which they have classified, divided, channeled; they insist on seeing categories dance in time to their measure. Their readers snicker and keep going: what is the use?

There is a literature which doesn't reach voracious masses. A work of creators, the result of a real need of the author, and done for himself. Knowledge of a supreme egoism, where laws fade away.* * * Each page ought to explode, either from deep and weighty seriousness, a whirlwind, dizziness, the new, or the eternal, from its crushing humor, the enthusiasm of principles or its typographical appearance. Here is a tottering world fleeing, future spouse of the bells of the infernal scale, and here on the other side: new men. Harsh, leaping, riders of hiccups. Here are a mutilated world and the literary medicine men with a passion for improvement.

I say: there is no beginning and we are not trembling, we are not sentimental. We shred the linen of clouds and prayers like a furious wind, preparing the great spectacle of disaster, fire, decomposition. Let's get ready to cast off mourning and to replace tears with mermaids stretched out from one continent to the next. Pavilions of intense joy, empty of the sadness of poison. * * * DADA is the signboard of abstraction; advertising and business are also poetic elements.

I destroy the drawers of the brain and of social institutions: demoralizing everything and hurling the celestial hand to hell, the hellish eyes to heaven, setting up once more the fecund wheel of a universal circus in the actual power and the fantasy of each individual.

Philosophy is the question: from what side to start looking at life, god, the idea, or anything else. Everything you look at is false. I don't believe the relative result to be any more important than the choice between cake and cherries after dinner. The approach of looking quickly at the other side of a thing in order to impose your opinion indirectly is called dialectic, that is, haggling over the spirit of french fries while dancing the method around. If I shout:

> IDEAL, IDEAL, IDEAL,
> KNOWLEDGE, KNOWLEDGE, KNOWLEDGE,
> BOOMBOOM, BOOMBOOM, BOOMBOOM,

I have put down rather exactly the progress, the laws, morality, and all the other lovely qualities that various very intelligent people have discussed in so many books, just in order to say finally that each man has danced anyway according to his own personal boomboom, and that he is right in his boomboom, as a satisfaction of unhealthy curiosity; private ringing for inexplicable needs; bath; monetary difficulties; stomach with repercussions in real life; authority of the mystical wand expressed as a bouquet of orchestra-ghost with mute bows, greased with potions based on animal manure. With the blue lorgnon of an angel they dug out the inside for a nickel of unanimous gratitude.* * * If they are all right and if all pills are just Pink pills, let's try for once to be wrong.* * * You think you can explain rationally, by thinking, what is written. But it's quite relative. Thought is a nice thing for philosophy but it's relative. Psychoanalysis is a dangerous sickness, lulls the antirealistic tendencies of man and codifies the bourgeoisie. There is no final Truth. Dialectic is an amusing machine which leads us

> in a banal manner
> to opinions we would have had anyway.

Do you think that by the scrupulous refinements of logic you have demonstrated truth and established the exactness of your opinions? Logic restricted by the senses is an organic sickness. Philosophers like to add to that element: the power of observation. But precisely this magnificent quality of the mind is the proof of its impotence. You observe, you look at things from one or many points of view, you choose them among the existing millions. Experience is also a result of chance and of individual faculties.* * * Science repulses me as soon as it becomes speculative-system, losing its useful character—so very useless—but at least individual. I hate complacent objectivity and harmony, that science that finds everything in order. Carry on, children, humanity. . . . Science says that we are the servants of nature: everything is in order, make love and die. Carry on children, humanity, nice bourgeois people and virgin journalists . . . * * I am against systems, the most acceptable system is the one of not having any system, on principle.* * * Making yourself complete, growing perfect in your own littleness until you have filled up the vase of your self, the courage to fight for and against thought, the mystery of bread sudden unleashing of an infernal helix into economic lilies:

DADAIST SPONTANEITY

I call Idon'tgiveadamnism the state of a life where each person keeps his own conditions, although knowing how to respect other individuals, if not defending himself, the two-step becoming a national hymn, a whatnot store, a radio playing Bach fugues, neon lights and signs for brothels, the organ diffusing carnations for God, all that together and actually replacing photography and unilateral catechism.

Active simplicity
The inability to discern degrees of brightness: licking the penumbra and floating in the great mouth full of honey and excrement. Measured by the scale of Eternity, all action is vain—(if we let thought undertake an adventure whose result would be infinitely grotesque—an important fact for the knowledge of human impotence). But if life is a bad farce, with neither goal nor initial labor pains, and because we think we should withdraw as fresh as washed chrysanthemums from the whole business, we have proclaimed as the single basis of understanding: art. It does not have the importance that we, as mercenaries of the mind, have attributed to it for centuries. Art afflicts no one and those who can get interested in it will earn the right to be caressed and the wonderful occasion to blanket the country with their conversation. Art is a private thing, the artist does it for himself; a comprehensible work is the product of a journalist, and because right now I feel like dabbing this monster in oil paints: a paper tube imitating the metal you squeeze and out come hatred, cowardice, meanness automatically. The artist, the poet are delighted with the venom of the mass concentrated into a section manager of this industry; they love to be insulted: a proof of their unchanging nature. The author and the artist praised in the papers notice how their work is understood: as the miserable lining of a cloak for public use, rags covering brutality, piss coalescing with the heat of an animal hatching the basest instincts. Flabby insipid flesh multiplying by means of typographic microbes.

We have discarded the sniveling tendency in ourselves. Every filtration of that kind is candied diarrhea. Encouraging this art means directing it. We must have strong, upright works, precise, and forever unintelligible. Logic is a complication. Logic is always false. It draws the strings of ideas, words, along their formal exterior, toward illusory extremes and centers. Its chains kill, like an enormous centipede stifling independence. Married to logic, art would live in incest, swallowing, devouring its own tail still attached, fornicating with itself and the personality would become a nightmare tarred with protestantism, a monument, a heap of heavy gray intestines.

But suppleness, enthusiasm, and even the joy of injustice, that little truth which we practice innocently and which gives us our good looks: we are delicate and our fingers are adjustable and glide like the branches of that insinuating, almost liquid plant; it gives our soul precision, the cynics say. That is a point of view too; but fortunately all flowers aren't saintly, and what is divine in us is the awakening of antihuman action. We're talking about a paper flower for the buttonhole of the gentlemen who customarily frequent the ball of masked life, kitchen of grace, white cousins supple or fat. They do business with whatever we have chosen. Contradiction and unity of polarities in one single stream can be truth. If you are going to pronounce that banality anyway, evil-smelling appendix to a libidinous morality. Morality atrophies like any scourge that intelligence produces. The rigidity of morality and logic have made us impassive in the presence of policemen—the cause of slavery—putrid rats filling middle-class stomachs and infecting the only bright and clean glass corridors which remained open to artists.

Let every man shout: there is a great destructive, negative work to be accomplished. Sweeping, cleaning. The cleanliness of the individual affirms itself after the state of madness, the aggressive, complete madness of a world left in the hands of bandits who vandalize and destroy centuries. Without goal or plan, disorganized, unconquerable folly, decomposition. Those strong in words or in strength will survive, for they are quick to defend themselves, the agility of body and feeling flames up on their faceted flesh.

Morality has determined charity and pity, two suet balls grown like elephants, like planets, that people call good. They have nothing good about them. Goodness is lucid, bright and determined, pitiless towards compromise and politics. Morality is the infusion of chocolate in the veins of all men. No supernatural force ordains such comportment, rather the monopoly of the idea sellers and the university profiteers. Sentimentality: seeing a group of men arguing and being bored, they invented the calendar and the medicine prudence. The philosophers' battle started by labeling (mercantilism, balance, meticulous and paltry measures) and it was once more understood that pity is a feeling just like diarrhea in its relation to the sickly disgust, the revolting task of corpses to compromise the sun.

I proclaim the opposition of all cosmic faculties to this gonorrhea of a putrid sun coming out of the factories of philosophic thought, the fierce battle with all the possible means of

DADAIST DISGUST

Every product of disgust capable of becoming a negation of the family is *dada;* the whole being protesting in its destructive force with clenched fists: **DADA;** knowledge of all the means rejected up to this point by the timid sex of easy compromise and sociability: DADA; abolition of logic, dance of all those impotent to create: *DADA;* of all hierarchy and social equation installed for the preservation of values by our valets: DADA; each and every object, feelings and obscurities, apparitions and the precise shock of parallel lines, can be means for the combat: DADA; abolition of memory; **DADA;** abolition of archeology:

DADA; abolition of the prophets: **DADA;** abolition of the future: DADA; an absolute indisputable belief in each god immediate product of spontaneity: **DADA;** elegant and unprejudicial leap from one harmony to the other sphere; trajectory of a word tossed like a sonorous cry of phonograph record; respecting all individualities in their momentary madness: serious, fearful, timid, ardent, vigorous, determined, enthusiastic; stripping its chapel of every useless awkward accessory; spitting out like a luminous waterfall any unpleasant or amorous thought, or coddling it—with the lively satisfaction of knowing that it doesn't matter—with the same intensity in the bush of his soul, free of insects for the aristocrats, and gilded with archangels' bodies. Freedom: **DADA DADA DADA;** shrieking of contracted colors, intertwining of contraries and of all contradictions, grotesqueries, nonsequiturs: LIFE.

A Proclamation without Pretention

Art goes to sleep for the birth of a new world
"ART"—a *parrot word*—replaced by **DADA**
PLESIAUSARUS, or handkerchief
The talent WHICH YOU CAN LEARN *makes the poet a druggist*
TODAY *criticism balances no longer launches resemblances*
Hypertrophic painters hypcrestheticized and hypnotized by the
hyancinths of muezzins of hypocritical appearance
CONSOLIDATE THE EXACT HARVEST OF CALCULATIONS
HYPERDROME OF IMMORTAL GUARANTEES. *There is no importance there*
is no transparency or apparency
MUSICIANS BREAK YOUR BLIND INSTRUMENTS on the stage
The **SYRINGE** *is only for my understanding.* **I am writing because**
it is as natural as pissing as being sick
Art needs an operation
Art is a **PRETENTION** heated in the TIMIDITY of the urinary
basin, **Hysteria** born in the **Studio**
We are seeking **upright pure sober unique** strength we are seeking
NOTHING we affirm the **VITALITY** of each instant
the anti-philosophy of **Spontaneous** acrobatics
In this moment I hate the man who whispers before intermission—
eau de cologne—bitter theater. CHEERY WIND.
IF EVERYBODY SAYS THE OPPOSITE IT IS BECAUSE THEY ARE RIGHT.
Prepare the geyser actions of our blood—submarine formation
of transchromatic airplanes, cellular metals numbered in the
leap of images
       above the regulations of the
BEAUTIFUL and its control
It is not for the runts who are still worshipping
their navel

A Note on Poetry

The poet of the last station no longer weeps in vain; lamenting would slow down his gait. Humidity of ages past. Those who feed on tears are happy and heavy; they slip them on to deceive the snakes behind the necklaces of their souls. The poet can devote himself to calisthenics. But to obtain abundance and explosion, he knows how to set hope afire TODAY. Tranquil, ardent, furious, intimate, pathetic, slow, impetuous, his desire boils for enthusiasm, that fecund form of intensity.

Knowing how to recognize and follow the traces of the strength we are waiting for, tracks which are everywhere, in an essential language of numbers, engraved on crystals, on seashells, on rail tracks, in clouds, in glass, inside snow, light, on coal, on the hand, in the radiations grouped around magnetic poles, on wings.

Persistence sharpens and shoots joy up like an arrow toward the astral bells, distillation of the waves of impassive food, creator of a new life. Streaming in all colors and bleeding among the leaves of all trees. Vigor and thirst, emotion before the formation unseen and unexplained: poetry.

Let's not look for analogies among the forms in which art finds outer shape; each has its freedom and its limits. There is no equivalent in art; each branch of the star develops independently, extends and absorbs the world appropriate to it. But the parallel sensed between the lines of a new life, free of any theory, will characterize the age.

Giving to each element its integrity, its autonomy, a necessary condition for the creation of new constellations each has its place in the group. A will to the word: a being upright, an image, a unique, fervent construction, of a dense color and intensity, communion with life.

Art is a procession of continual differences. For there is no measurable distance between the "how are you," the level where worlds are expanded, and human actions seen from this angle of submarine purity. The strength to formulate in *the instant* this varying succession is the work itself. Globe of duration, volume born under a fortuitous pressure.

The mind carries in it new rays of possibilities: centralize them, capture them on the lens which is neither physical nor defined—popularly—the soul. The ways of expressing them, transforming them: the means. Clear golden brilliance—a faster beating of spreading wings.

Without pretensions to a romantic absolute, I present some banal negations.

The poem is no longer subject, rhythm, rhyme, sonority: formal action. Projected on the commonplace, these become means whose use is neither regulated nor registered to which I assign the same importance as to the crocodile, burning ore, grass. Eye, water, scales, sun, kilometer, and everything I can conceive at one time as representing a value which can be humanized: *sensitivity*. The elements grow fond of each other when they are so tightly joined, really entwined like the hemispheres of the brain and the cabins of an ocean liner.

Rhythm is the pace of intonations you hear; there is a rhythm unseen and unheard: radiation of an interior grouping toward a constellation of order. Rhythm was until now only the beatings of a dried-up heart: tinklings in rotten and muffled wood. I don't want to treat with a rigid exclusiveness of principle a subject where only liberty matters. But the poet will be severe toward his work in order to find true necessity: from this asceticism will flower order, essential and pure. (Goodness without sentimental echo, its material side.)

To be severe and cruel, pure and honest toward your work which you prepare to place among men new organisms, creations living in bones of light and in fabulous forms of action. (REALITY.)

The rest, called *literature*, is a notebook of human imbecility to aid future professors.

The poem pushes or digs a crater, is silent, murders, or shrieks along accelerated degrees of speed. It will no longer be a product of optics, sense or intelligence, but an impression or a means of transforming the tracks left by feelings.

Simile is a literary tool which no longer satisfies us. There are ways of formulating an image or integrating it but the elements will be taken from differing and distant spheres.

Logic guides us no longer and its commerce, easy, impotent, a deceptive glimmer scattering the coins of a sterile relativism, is extinguished for us forever. Other productive forces shout their freedom, flamboyant, indefinable and gigantic, on the mountains of crystal and of prayer.

Freedom, freedom: not being a vegetarian I'm not giving any recipes.

Darkness is productive if it is a light so white and pure that our neighbors are blinded by it. From their light, ahead, begins our own. Their light is for us, in the mist, the miniscule microscopic dance of the shadowy elements in an imprecise fermentation. Isn't matter in its purity dense and sure?

Under the bark of the fallen trees, I seek the painting of things to come, strength, and in the canals perhaps life is swelling already, the darkness of iron and coal.

Leo Spitzer

1887–1960

Leo Spitzer was born in Vienna on February 7, 1887. He received a doctorate in that city in 1910 under the direction of the famous Romance philologist Wilhelm Meyer-Lübke. In an autobiographical essay Spitzer later recalled his training as admirable in its rigor but lamentably rigid: minute etymological studies pursued with complete disregard for questions of historical context or philosophical and psychological speculation. Spitzer himself would combine methodological rigor with wider interests: already, while a junior professor ostensibly working towards a post as a medievalist, he gave lectures on contemporary literature. During World War I he worked as a censor for the Austrian government on the Italian border. He taught at the University of Bonn from 1922 to 1925, and was then given a professorship at Marburg, where he would be succeeded by Erich Auerbach when he himself went on to Cologne in 1930. When the Nazis came to power, Spitzer—once more slightly in advance of Auerbach —took a position at Istanbul; however, unlike Auerbach, who would stay in Turkey until after the war, Spitzer, whose work could not continue without better facilities, accepted an offer from Johns Hopkins University in 1936; he would stay there until 1956. He died in Italy on September 16, 1960.

Spitzer's works include several series of studies in Romance philology, ranging from Provençal poetry to Diderot to the twentieth century; a polemic against the pseudo-science of the Nazi apologist and racist Houston Stewart Chamberlain, written in 1918, in which he uses philological methods to demolish the false assumptions of an ideologue; and a study of the now-forgotten, twentieth-century French writer Henri Barbusse. But Spitzer's three major works are *Stilstudien* (1928), *Linguistics and Literary History* (1948), and *Essays in Historical Semantics* (1948).

Spitzer was a great linguist who wrote on literatures in many languages—even English and American literature later on in his life. His attention to etymology was exceptional; he devoted an entire study to the word *ambiance,* and a study of the single German word *Stimmung* ("harmony") yielded an article on "Classical and Christian Ideas of World Harmony." Thus, for Spitzer, subtle textual inflections—often a single recurrent turn of phrase which would "tip him off" to underlying psychological or philosophical characteristics of his author or text—were chiefly a springboard to the most far-reaching speculations, often covering several "disciplines" at once. His fellow emigré and colleague, Auerbach, was not alone in expressing reserve at these speculations; but Spitzer, a lively polemicist, relished debates and actively sought the most sharp and surprising turns of thought in his work. His catholicity of taste extended not only to modern literature (at his death he was planning a study of the French novel of the 1950s) but also to mass culture: he wrote a long textual study of a pictorial advertisement for Sunkist Oranges explaining its content in terms of literary convention. The influence of Freud was important to Spitzer: he found the style of Diderot controlled by the rhythms of sex. In the diction of Peguy he heard traces of Bergson's metaphysics; for Claudel and Whitman he elaborated the notion of "chaotic enumeration." For all his borrowing from philosophy he refused to reduce any literary work to an illustration of an extant philosophical system: his own "method," by which he set great store, was both more empirical and flexible and also more theological. He himself described the moment of understanding a text as a flash of sudden intuitive enlightenment, a "click." Nonetheless, although his free combination of close textual reading, stylistic analysis, and speculation makes him akin to certain postwar French critics (or even, in English, William Empson), he never claimed to found a "movement" within literary studies as they did, preferring to see his own originality more modestly as a matter of style as particular as that of the texts he analyzed. His work never had the political bent of Barthes and Foucault, nor has it achieved their popularity, for his allegiance was rather to the severe discipline of philology he had learned in Vienna, and not to the public, political *engagement* of the French intellectual.

LINGUISTICS AND LITERARY HISTORY[1]

T he title of this book is meant to suggest the ultimate unity of linguistics and literary history. Since my activity, throughout my scholarly life, has been largely devoted to the rapprochement of these two disciplines, I may be forgiven if I preface my remarks with an autobiographic sketch of my first academic experiences: What I propose to do is to tell you only my own story, how I made my way through the maze of linguistics, with which I started, toward the enchanted garden of literary history—and how I discovered that there is as well a paradise in linguistics as a labyrinth in literary history; that the methods and the degree of certainty in both are basically the same; and, that if today the humanities are under attack (and, as I believe, under an unwarranted attack, since it is not the humanities themselves that are at fault but only some so-called humanists who persist in imitating an obsolete approach to the natural sciences, which have themselves evolved toward the humanities)—if, then, the humanities are under attack, it would be pointless to exempt any one of them from the verdict: if it is true that there is no value to be derived from the study of language, we cannot pretend to preserve literary history, cultural history—or history.

I have chosen the autobiographical way because my personal situation in Europe forty years ago was not, I believe, essentially different from the one with which I see the young scholar of today (and in this country) generally faced. I chose to relate to you my own experiences also because the basic approach of the individual scholar, conditioned as it is by his first experiences, by his *Erlebnis,* as the Germans say, determines his method: *Methode ist Erlebnis,* Gundolf has said. In fact, I would advise every older scholar to tell his public the basic experiences underlying his methods, his *Mein Kampf,* as it were—without dictatorial connotations, of course.

I had decided, after college had given me a solid foundation in the classical languages, to study the Romance languages and particularly French philology, because, in my native Vienna, the gay and orderly, skeptic and sentimental, Catholic and pagan Vienna of yore was filled with adoration of the French way of life. I had always been surrounded by a French atmosphere and, at that juvenile stage of experience, had acquired a picture, perhaps overgeneralized, of French literature, which seemed to me definable by an Austrianlike mixture of sensuousness and reflection, of vitality and discipline, of sentimentality and critical wit. The moment when the curtain rose on a French play given by a French troupe, and the valet, in a knowing accent of psychological alertness, with his rich, poised voice, pronounced the words "Madame est servie," was a delight to my heart.

But when I attended the classes of French linguistics of my great teacher

363

Meyer-Lübke no picture was offered us of the French people, or of the Frenchness of their language: in these classes we saw Latin *a* moving, according to relentless phonetic laws, toward French *e (pater > père);* there we saw a new system of declension spring up from nothingness, a system in which the six Latin cases came to be reduced to two, and later to one—while we learned that similar violence had been done to the other Romance languages and, in fact, to many modern languages. In all this, there were many facts and much rigor in the establishment of facts, but all was vague in regard to the general ideas underlying these facts. What was the mystery behind the refusal of Latin sounds or cases to stay put and behave themselves? We saw incessant change working in language—but why? I was a long while realizing that Meyer-Lübke was offering only the *pre*-history of French (as he established it by a comparison with the other Romance languages), not its history. And we were never allowed to contemplate a phenomenon in its quiet being, to look into its face: we always looked at its neighbors or at its predecessors—we were always looking over our shoulder. There were presented to us the relationships of phenomenon *a* and phenomenon *b;* but phenomenon *a* and phenomenon *b* did not exist in themselves, nor did the historical line *a—b*. In reference to a given French form, Meyer-Lübke would quote Old Portuguese, Modern Bergamesque and Macedorumanian, German, Celtic, and paleo-Latin forms; but where was reflected in this teaching my sensuous, witty, disciplined Frenchman, in his presumably 1000 years of existence? He was left out in the cold while we talked about his language; indeed, French was not the language of the Frenchman, but an agglomeration of unconnected, separate, anecdotic, senseless evolutions: a French historical grammar, apart from the word-material, could as well have been a Germanic or a Slav grammar: the leveling of paradigms, the phonetic evolutions occur there just as in French.

When I changed over to the classes of the equally great literary historian Philipp August Becker, that ideal Frenchman seemed to show some faint signs of life—in the spirited analyses of the events in the *Pèlerinage de Charlemagne,* or of the plot of a Molière comedy; but it was as if the treatment of the contents were only subsidiary to the really scholarly work, which consisted in fixing the dates and historical data of these works of art, in assessing the amount of autobiographical elements and written sources which the poets had supposedly incorporated into their artistic productions. Had the *Pèlerinage* to do with the Xth crusade? Which was its original dialect? Was there any epic poetry, Merovingian or other, which preceded Old French epic poetry? Had Molière put his own matrimonial disillusionment into the *École des femmes?* (While Becker did not insist on an affirmative conclusion, he considered such a question to be a part of legitimate literary criticism.) Did the medieval farce survive in the Molière comedy? The existing works of art were stepping-stones from which to proceed to other phenomena, contemporary or previous, which were in reality quite heterogeneous. It seemed indiscreet to ask what made them works of art, what was expressed in them, and why these expressions appeared in France, at that particular time. Again, it was prehistory, not history, that we were offered, and a kind of materialistic prehistory, at that. In this attitude of positivism, exterior events were taken thus seriously only to evade the more completely the real question: Why did the phenomena *Pèlerinage* and *École des femmes* happen at all? And, I must admit, in full loyalty to Meyer-Lübke, that he taught more of reality than did Becker: it was unquestionable that Latin *a* had evolved to French *e;* it was untrue that Molière's experience with the possibly faithless Madeleine Béjart had evolved to the work of art *École des femmes.* But, in both fields, that of linguistics as well as that of literary history (which were separated by an enormous gulf: Meyer-Lübke spoke only of language and Becker only of literature), a meaningless industriousness prevailed: not only was this kind of humanities not centered on a particular people in a particular time, but the subject matter itself had got lost: Man.[2] At the end of my first year of graduate studies, I had come to the conclusion, not that the science offered *ex cathedra* was worthless but that I was not fit for such studies as that of the irrational vowel *-i-* in Eastern French dialects, or of the *Subjektivismusstreit* in Molière: never would I get a Ph.D.! It was the benignity of Providence, exploiting my native Teutonic docility toward scholars who knew more than I, which kept me faithful to the study of Romance philology. By not abandoning prematurely this sham science, by seeking, instead, to appropriate it, I came to recognize its true value as well as my own possibilities of work—and to establish my life's goal. By using the tools of science offered me, I came to see under their dustiness the fingerprints of a Friedrich Diez and of the Romantics, who had created these tools; and henceforth they were not dusty any more, but ever radiant and ever new. And I had learned to handle many and manifold facts: training in handling facts, brutal facts, is perhaps the best education for a wavering, youthful mind.

And now let me take you, as I promised to do, on the path that leads from the most routinelike techniques of the linguist toward the work of the literary historian. The different fields will appear here in the ascending order, as I see them today, while the concrete examples, drawn from my own activity, will not respect the chronological order of their publication.

Meyer-Lübke, the author of the comprehensive and still final etymological dictionary of Romance languages, had taught me, among many other things, how to find etymologies; I shall now take the liberty of inflicting upon you a concrete example of this procedure—sparing you none of the petty drudgery involved. Since my coming to America, I have been curious about the etymology of two English words, characterized by the same "flavor": *conundrum* "a riddle the answer to which involves a pun; a puzzling question," and *quandary* "a puzzling situation." The NED attests *conundrum* first in 1596; early variants are *conimbrum, quonundrum, quadrundum.* The meaning is "whim" or "pun." In the seventeenth century it was known as an Oxford term: preachers were wont to use in their sermons the baroque device of puns and conundrums, e.g. "Now all House is turned into an Alehouse, and a pair of dice is made a Paradice; was it thus in the days of Noah? Ah no." This baroque technique of interlarding sermons with puns is well known from the *Kapuziner-*

Predigt, inspired by Abraham a Santa Clara, in Schiller's *Wallenstein's Lager:* "Der *Rheinstrom* ist worden zu einem *Peinstrom,*" etc.

The extraordinary instability (reflecting the playfulness of the concept involved) of the phonetic structure: *conundrum—conimbrum—quadrundrum,* points to a foreign source, to a word which must have been (playfully) adapted in various ways. Since the English variants include among them a *-b-* and a *-d-* which are not easily reducible to any one basic sound, I propose to submit a French word-family which, in its different forms, contains both *-b-* and *-d-:* the French *calembour* is exactly synonymous with *conundrum* "pun." This *calembour* is evidently related to *calembredaine* "nonsensical or odd speech," and we can assume that *calembour,* too, had originally this same general reference. This word-family goes back probably to Fr. *bourde* "tall story" to which has been added the fanciful, semipejorative prefix *cali-,* that can be found in *à califourchon* "straddling" (from Latin *quadrifurcus,* French *carrefour* "crossroads": the *qu-* of the English variants points to this Latin etymon). The French ending *-aine* of *calembredaine* developed to *-um: n* becomes *m* as in *ransom* from French *rançon; ai* becomes *o* as in *mitten* (older *mitton*) from French *mitaine.* Thus *calembourdane,* as a result of various assimilations and shortenings which I will spare you, becomes **colundrum, *columbrum* and then *conundrum, conimbrum,* etc. Unfortunately, the French word-family is attested rather late, occurring for the first time in a comic opera of Vadé in 1754. We do find, however, an *équilbourdie* "whim" as early as 1658 in the *Muse normande,* a dialectal text. The fact is that popular words of this sort have, as a rule, little chance of turning up in the (predominantly idealistic) literature of the Middle Ages; it is, therefore, a mere accident that English *conundrum* is attested in 1596 and French *calembour* only in 1757; at least, the chance appearance of *équilbourdie* in the dialectal text of 1658 gives us an earlier attestation of the French word-family. That the evidently popular medieval words emerge so late in literature is a fact explainable by the currents prevalent in literature; the linguist must take his chances with what literature offers him in the way of attestation. In view of the absolute evidence of the equation *conundrum = calembredaine* we need not be intimidated by chronological divergencies—which the older school of etymologists (as represented by the editors of the NED) seem to have overrated.

After *conundrum* had ceased to be a riddle to me, I was emboldened to ask myself whether I could not now solve the etymology of the word *quandary—* which also suggested to me a French origin. And, lo and behold: this word, of unknown origin, which is attested from about 1580 on, revealed itself etymologically identical with *conundrum!* There are English dialect forms such as *quándorum quóndorum* which serve to establish an uninterrupted chain: *calembredaine* becomes *conimbrum conundrum quonundrum quandorum* and these give us *quandary.*[3]

Now what can be the humanistic, the spiritual value of this (as it may have seemed to you) juggling with word forms? The particular etymology of *conundrum* is an inconsequential fact; that an etymology can be found by man is a miracle. An etymology introduces meaning into the meaningless: in our case, the evolution of two words in time—that is, a piece of linguistic history—has been cleared up. What seemed an agglomeration of mere sounds now appears motivated. We feel the same "inner click" accompanying our comprehension of this evolution in time as when we have grasped the meaning of a sentence or a poem—which then become more than the sum total of their single words or sounds (*poem* and *sentence* are, in fact, the classical examples given by Augustine and Bergson in order to demonstrate the nature of a stretch of *durée réelle*: the parts aggregating to a whole, time filled with contents). In the problem which we chose, two words which seemed erratic and fantastic, with no definite relationships in English, have been unified among themselves and related to a French word-family.

The existence of such a loan-word is another testimony to the well-known cultural situation obtaining when medieval England was in the sway of French influence: the English and French word-families, although attested centuries after the Middle Ages, must have belonged to one Anglo-French word-family during that period, and their previous existence is precisely proved by proving their family relationship. And it is not by chance that English borrows words for "pun" or "whim" from the witty French, who have also given *carriwitchet* "quibble" and (perhaps: see the NED) *pun* itself to English. But, since a loan-word rarely feels completely at home in its new environment, we have the manifold variations of the word, which fell apart into two word-groups (clearly separated, today, by the current linguistic feeling): *conundrum-quandary.* The instability and disunity of the word-family is symptomatic of its position in the new environment.

But the instability apparent in our English words had already been characteristic of *calembredaine—calembour,* even in the home environment: this French word-family, as we have said, was a blend of at least two word-stems. Thus we must conclude that the instability is also connected with the semantic content: a word meaning "whim, pun" easily behaves whimsically—just as, in all languages throughout the world, the words for "butterfly" present a kaleidoscopic instability. The linguist who explains such fluttery words has to juggle, because the speaking community itself (in our case, the English as well as the French) has juggled. This juggling in itself is psychologically and culturally motivated: language is not, as the behavioristic, antimentalistic, mechanistic or materialistic school of linguists, rampant in some universities, would have it: a meaningless agglomeration of corpses: dead word-material, automatic "speech habits" unleashed by a trigger motion. A certain automatism may be predicated of the use of *conundrum* and *quandary* in contemporary English, and of *calembour, calembredaine* in contemporary French (though, even today, this automatism is not absolute, since all these words have still a connotation of whimsicality or fancifulness and are, accordingly, somewhat motivated). But this is certainly not true for the history of the words: the linguistic creation is always meaningful and, yes, clear-minded: it was a feeling for the appositeness of nomenclature which prompted the communities to use, in our case, two-track words. They gave a playful expression to a playful concept, symbolizing in the word their attitude toward the concept. It was when the creative, the Renaissance, phase had passed that English let the words congeal, petrify, and split into two. This petrification is, itself, due to a decision of the community which, in eighteenth-century England, passed from the Renaissance attitude to the classicistic attitude toward language, which would replace creativity by standardization and regulation. Another cultural climate, another linguistic style. Out of the infinity of word-histories which could be imagined we have chosen only one, one which shows quite individual circumstances, such as the borrowing of a foreign word by English, the original French blend, the subsequent alterations and restrictions; every word has its own history, not to be confused with that of any other. But what repeats itself in all word-histories is the possibility of recognizing the signs of a people at work, culturally and psychologically. To speak in the language of the homeland of philology: *Wortwandel ist Kultur-wandel und Seelenwandel;* this little etymological study has been humanistic in purpose.

If we accept the equation: *conundrum* and *quandary* = *calembredaine*— how has this been found? I may say, by quite an orthodox technique which would have been approved by Meyer-Lübke—though he would not, perhaps, have stopped to draw the inferences on which I have insisted. First, by collecting the material evidence about the English words, I was led to seek a French origin. I had also observed that the great portion of the English vocabulary which is derived from French has not been given sufficient attention by etymologists; and, of course, my familiarity with the particular behavior of "butterfly words" in language was such as to encourage a relative boldness in the reconstruction of the etymon. I had first followed the inductive method—or rather a quick intuition—in order to identify *conundrum* with *calembredaine;* later, I had to proceed deductively, to verify whether my assumed etymon concorded with all the known data, whether it really explained all the semantic and phonetic variations; while following this path I was able to see that *quandary* must also be a reflection of *calembredaine.* (This to-and-fro movement is a basic requirement in all humanistic studies, as we shall see later.) For example, since the French word-family is attested later than is the English, it seemed necessary to dismiss the chronological discrepancies; fortunately—or, as I would say, providentially—the Normandian *équilbourdie* of 1658 turned up! In this kind of gentle blending together of the words, of harmonizing them and smoothing out difficulties, the linguist undoubtedly indulges in a propensity to see things as shifting and melting into each other—an attitude to which you may object: I cannot contend more than that this change was *possible* in the way I have indicated, since it contradicts no previous experience; I can say only that two unsolved problems (the one concerning the prehistory of *conundrum,* the other that of *calembredaine*) have, when brought together, shed light on each other, thereby enabling us to see the common solution. I am reminded here of the story of the Pullman porter to whom a passenger complained in the morning that he had got back one black shoe and one tan; the porter replied that, curiously enough, a similar discovery had been made by another passenger. In the field of language, the porter who has mixed up the shoes belonging together is language itself, and the linguist is the passenger who must bring together what was once a historical unit. To place two phenomena within a framework adds something to the knowledge about their common nature. There is no mathematical demonstrability in such an equation, only a feeling of inner evidence; but this feeling, with the trained linguist, is the fruit of observation combined with experience, of precision supplemented by imagination—the dosage of which cannot be fixed a priori, but only in the concrete case. There is underlying such a procedure the belief that this is the way things happened; but there is always a belief underlying the humanist's work (similarly, it cannot be demonstrated that the Romance languages form a unity going back to Vulgar Latin; this basic assumption of the student in Romance languages, first stated by Diez, cannot be proved to the disbeliever).[4] And who says belief, says suasion: I have, deliberately and tendentiously, grouped the variants of *conundrum* in the most plausible order possible for the purpose of winning your assent. Of course, there are more easily believable etymologies, reached at the cost of less stretching and bending: no one in his senses would doubt that French *père* comes from Latin *pater,* or that this, along with English *father,* goes back to an Indo-European prototype. But we must not forget that these smooth, standard equations are relatively rare—for the reason that a word such as "father" is relatively immune to cultural revolutions or, in other words, that, in regard to the "father," a continuity of feeling, stretching over more than 4000 years, exists in Indo-European civilization.

Thus our etymological study has illuminated a stretch of linguistic history, which is connected with psychology and history of civilization; it has suggested a web of interrelations between language and the soul of the speaker. This web could have been as well revealed by a study of a syntactical, a morphological evolution—even a phonetic evolution of the type *"a* becomes *e,"* wherein Meyer-Lübke had failed to see the *durée réelle,* exclusively concerned as he was with *l'heure de la montre:* his historical "clock time."

Now, since the best document of the soul of a nation is its literature, and since the latter is nothing but its language as this is written down by elect speakers, can we perhaps not hope to grasp the spirit of a nation in the language of its outstanding works of literature? Because it would have been rash to compare the whole of a national literature to the whole of a national language (as Karl Vossler has prematurely tried to do) I started, more modestly, with the question: "Can one distinguish the soul of a particular French writer in his particular language?" It is obvious that literary historians have held this conviction, since, after the inevitable quotation (or misquotation) of Buffon's saying: *"Le style c'est l'homme,"* they generally include in their monographs a chapter on the style of their author. But I had in mind the more rigorously scientific definition of an individual style, the definition of a linguist which should replace the casual, impressionistic remarks of literary critics. Stylistics, I thought, might bridge the gap between linguistics and literary history. On the other hand, I was warned by the scholastic adage: *individuum est ineffabile;*

could it be that any attempt to define the individual writer by his style is
doomed to failure? The individual stylistic deviation from the general norm
must represent a historical step taken by the writer, I argued: it must reveal a
shift of the soul of the epoch, a shift of which the writer has become conscious
and which he would translate into a necessarily new linguistic form; perhaps
it would be possible to determine the historical step, psychological as well as
linguistic? To determine the beginning of a linguistic innovation would be
easier, of course, in the case of contemporary writers, because their linguistic
basis is better known to us than is that of past writers.

In my reading of modern French novels, I had acquired the habit of
underlining expressions which struck me as aberrant from general usage, and
it often happened that the underlined passages, taken together, seemed to
offer a certain consistency. I wondered if it would not be possible to establish
a common denominator for all or most of these deviations; could not the
common spiritual etymon, the psychological root, of several individual "traits of
style" in a writer be found, just as we have found an etymon common to
various fanciful word formations?[5] I had, for example, noticed in the novel
Bubu de Montparnasse of Charles-Louis Philippe (1905), which moves in the
underworld of Parisian pimps and prostitutes, a particular use of *à cause de*,
reflecting the spoken, the unliterary language: "Les réveils de midi sont lourds
et poisseux. . . . On éprouve un sentiment de déchéance *à cause* des réveils
d'autrefois." More academic writers would have said "en se rappelant des
réveils d'autrefois . . . ," "à la suite du souvenir. . . ." This, at first glance, prosaic
and commonplace *à cause de* has nevertheless a poetic flavor, because of the
unexpected suggestion of a causality, where the average person would see only
coincidence: it is, after all, not unanimously accepted that one awakes with a
feeling of frustration from a noon siesta *because* other similar awakenings have
preceded; we have here an assumed, a poetic reality, but one expressed by a
prosaic phrase. We find this *à cause de* again in a description of a popular
celebration of the 14th of July: "[le peuple], *à cause de* l'anniversaire de sa
délivrance, laisse ses filles danser en liberté." Thus, one will not be surprised
when the author lets this phrase come from the mouth of one of his characters:
"Il y a dans mon coeur deux ou trois cent petites émotions qui brûlent *à cause
de toi*." Conventional poetry would have said "qui brûlent pour toi"; "qui
brûlent *à cause de toi*" is both less and more: more, since the lover speaks his
heart better in this sincere, though factual manner. The causal phrase, with all
its semipoetic implications, suggests rather a commonplace speaker, whose
speech and whose habits of thought the writer seems to endorse in his own
narrative.

Our observation about *à cause de* gains strength if we compare the use, in
the same novel, of other causal conjunctions, such as *parce que:* for example,
it is said of the pimp's love for his sweetheart Berthe: "[il aimait] sa volupté
particulière, quand elle appliquait son corps contre le sien. . . . Il aimait cela qui
la distinguait de toutes les femmes qu'il avait connues *parce que* c'était plus
doux, *parce que* c'était plus fin, et *parce que* c'était sa femme à lui, qu'il avait
eue vierge. Il l'aimait *parce qu'*elle était honnête et qu'elle en avait l'air, et pour

toutes les raisons qu'ont les bourgeois d'aimer leur femme." Here, the reasons why Maurice loved to embrace his sweetheart (*parce que c'était doux, fin, parce que c'était sa femme a lui*) are outspokenly classified or censored by the writer as being *bourgeois;* and yet, in Philippe's narrative, the *parce que* is used as if he considered these reasons to be objectively valid.

The same observation holds true for the causal conjunction *car:* in the following passage which describes Maurice as a being naturally loved by women: "Les femmes l'entouraient d'amour comme des oiseaux qui chantent le soleil et la force. Il était un de ceux que nul ne peut assujettir, *car* leur vie, plus forte et plus belle, comporte l'amour du danger."

Again, it can happen that a causal relationship is implied without the use of a conjunction, a relationship due to the gnomic character adherent, at least in that particular milieu, to a general statement—the truth of which is, perhaps, not so fully accepted elsewhere: "Elle l'embrassa à pleine bouche. *C'est une chose hygiénique* et bonne entre un homme et sa femme, qui vous amuse un petit quart d'heure avant de vous endormir." (Philippe could as well have written "car . . . ," "parce que c'est une chose hygiénique. . . .") Evidently this is the truth only in that particular world of sensuous realism which he is describing. At the same time, however, the writer, while half-endorsing these bourgeois platitudes of the underworld, is discreetly but surely suggesting his criticism of them.

Now I submit the hypothesis that all these expansions of causal usages in Philippe cannot be due to chance: there must be "something the matter" with his conception of causality. And now we must pass from Philippe's style to the psychological etymon, to the radix in his soul. I have called the phenomenon in question "pseudo-objective motivation": Philippe, when presenting causality as binding for his characters, seems to recognize a rather objective cogency in their sometimes awkward, sometimes platitudinous, sometimes semipoetic reasonings; his attitude shows a fatalistic, half-critical, half-understanding, humorous sympathy with the necessary errors and thwarted strivings of these underworld beings dwarfed by inexorable social forces. The pseudo-objective motivation, manifest in his style, is the clue to Philippe's *Weltanschauung;* he sees, as has also been observed by literary critics, without revolt but with deep grief and a Christian spirit of contemplativity, the world functioning wrongly with an appearance of rightness, of objective logic. The different word-usages, grouped together (just as was done with the different forms of *conundrum* and *quandary*) lead toward a psychological etymon, which is at the bottom of the linguistic as well as of the literary inspiration of Philippe.

Thus we have made the trip from language or style to the soul. And on this journey we may catch a glimpse into a historical evolution of the French soul in the twentieth century: first we are given insight into the soul of a writer who has become conscious of the fatalism weighing on the masses, then, into that of a section of the French nation itself, whose faint protest is voiced by our author. And in this procedure there is, I think, no longer the timeless, placeless philology of the older school, but an explanation of the concrete *hic et nunc* of a historical phenomenon. The to-and-fro movement we found to be basic with the humanist has been followed here, too: first we grouped together certain causal expressions, striking with Philippe, then hunted out their psychological explanation, and finally, sought to verify whether the element of "pseudo-objective motivation"[6] concorded with what we know, from other sources, about the elements of his inspiration. Again, a belief is involved—which is no less daring than is the belief that the Romance languages go back to one invisible, basic pattern manifest in them all: namely, the belief that the mind of an author is a kind of solar system into whose orbit all categories of things are attracted: language, motivation, plot, are only satellites of this mythological entity (as my antimentalistic adversaries would call it): *mens Philippina*. The linguist as well as his literary colleague must always ascend to the etymon which is behind all those particular so-called literary or stylistic devices which the literary historians are wont to list. And the individual *mens Philippina* is a reflection of the *mens Franco-gallica* of the twentieth century; its ineffability consists precisely in Philippe's anticipatory sensitivity for the spiritual needs of the nation.

Now, it is obvious that a modern writer such as Philippe, faced with the social disintegration of humanity in the twentieth century, must show more patent linguistic deviations, of which the philologist may take stock in order to build up his "psychogram" of the individual artist. But does Philippe, a stranded being broken loose from his moorings, transplanted, as it were, into a world from which he feels estranged—so that he must, perforce, indulge in arbitrary whimsicality—represent only a modern phenomenon? If we go back to writers of more remote times, must it not be that we will always find a balanced language, with no deviations from common usage?

It suffices to mention the names of such dynamic writers of older times as Dante or Quevedo or Rabelais to dispel such a notion. Whoever has thought strongly and felt strongly has innovated in his language; mental creativity immediately inscribes itself into the language, where it becomes linguistic creativity; the trite and petrified in language is never sufficient for the needs of expression felt by a strong personality. In my first publication, "Die Wortbildung als stilistisches Mittel" (a thesis written in 1910), I dealt with Rabelais' comic word-formations, a subject to which I was attracted because of certain affinities between Rabelaisian and Viennese (Nestroy!) comic writing, and which offered the opportunity of bridging the gap between linguistic and literary history. Be it said to the eternal credit of the scholarly integrity of Meyer-Lübke that he, in contrast to the antimentalists who would suppress all expressions of opposition to their theories, recommended for publication a book with an approach so aberrant from his own. In this work I sought to show, for example, that a neologism such as *pantagruélisme,* the name given by Rabelais to his stoic-epicurean philosophy ("certaine gayeté d'esprict, conficte en mépris des choses fortuites") is not only a playful outburst of a genuine gaiety, but a thrust from the realm of the real into that of the unreal and the unknown—as is true, in fact, of any nonce-word. On the one hand, a form with the suffix *-ism* evokes a school of serious philosophic thought (such as *Aristotelianism, scholasticism,* etc.); on the other, the stem, *Pantagruel,* is the name of a character created by Rabelais, the half-jocular, half-philosophical giant and patriarchal king. The coupling of the learned philosophical suffix with the fanciful name of a fanciful character amounts to positing a half-real, half-unreal entity: "the philosophy of an imaginary being." The contemporaries of Rabelais who first heard this coinage must have experienced the reactions provoked by any nonce-word: a moment of shock followed by a feeling of reassurance: to be swept toward the unknown frightens, but realization of the benignly fanciful result gives relief: laughter, our physiological reaction on such occasions, arises precisely out of a feeling of relief following upon a temporary breakdown of our assurance. Now, in a case such as that of the creation *pantagruélisme,* the designation of a hitherto unknown but, after all, innocuous philosophy, the menacing force of the neologism is relatively subdued. But what of such a list of names as that concocted by Rabelais for the benefit of his hated adversaries, the reactionaries of the Sorbonne: *sophistes, sorbillans, sorbonagres, sorbonigenes, sorbonicoles, sorboniformes, sorboniseques, niborcisans, sorbonisans, saniborsans.* Again, though differently, there is an element of realism present in these coinages: the Sorbonne is an existing reality, and the formations are explainable by well-known formative processes. The edition of Abel Lefranc, imbued with his positivistic approach, goes to the trouble of explaining each one of these formations: *sorboniforme* is after *uniforme, sorbonigene* after *homogène,* while *niborcisans, saniborsans* offer what, in the jargon of the linguists, is called a metathesis. But by explaining every coinage separately, by dissolving the forest into trees, the commentators lose sight of the whole phenomenon: they no longer see the forest—or rather the jungle which Rabelais must have had before his eyes, teeming with viperlike, hydralike, demonlike shapes. Nor is it enough to say that the scholarly Rabelais indulges in humanistic word lists with a view to enriching the vocabulary—in the spirit of an Erasmus who prescribed the principle of *copia verborum* to students of Latin—or that Rabelais' rich nature bade him make the French language rich; the aesthetics of richness is, in itself, a problem; and why should richness tend toward the frightening, the bottomless? Perhaps Rabelais' whole attitude toward language rests upon a vision of imaginary richness whose support is the bottomless. He creates word-families, representative of gruesome fantasy-beings, copulating and engendering before our eyes, which have reality only in the world of language, which are established in an intermediate world between reality and irreality, between the nowhere that frightens and the "here" that reassures. The *niborcisans* are as yet an entity vaguely connected with the *sorbonisans,* but at the same time so close to nothingness that we laugh—uneasily; it is *le comique grotesque* which skirts the abyss. And Rabelais will shape grotesque word-families (or families of word-demons) not only by altering what exists: he may leave intact the forms of his word material and create by juxtaposition: savagely piling epithet upon epithet to an ultimate effect of terror, so that, from the well known emerges the shape of the unknown—a phenomenon the more startling with the French, who are generally considered to inhabit an orderly, clearly regulated, well-policed language. Now, of a sudden, we no longer recognize this French language, which has become a chaotic word-world situated somewhere in the chill of cosmic space. Just listen to the inscription on the *abbaye de Thélème*, that Renaissance convent of his shaping, from which Rabelais excludes the hypocrites:

> *Cy n'entrez pas, hypocrites, bigots,*
> *Vieux matagotz, marmiteux, borsoufles,*
> *Torcoulx, badaux, plus que n'estoient les Gotz,*
> *Ny Ostrogotz, precurseurs des magotz,*
> *Haires, cagotz, cafars empantouflez,*
> *Gueux mitoufles, frapars escorniflez,*
> *Befflez, enflez, fagoteurs de tabus;*
> *Tirez ailleurs pour vendre vos abus.*

The prosaic commentators of the Lefranc edition would explain that this kind of rather mediocre poetry is derived from the popular genre of the *cry* (the harangue of a barker), and overloaded with devices of the *rhétoriqueur* school. But I can never read these lines without being frightened, and I am shaken in this very moment by the horror emanating from this accumulation of *-fl-* and *-got-* clusters—of sounds which, in themselves, and taken separately, are quite harmless, of words grouped together, bristling with Rabelais' hatred of hypocrisy—that greatest of all crimes against life. A *cry*, yes, but in a more extensive meaning of the word: it is the gigantic voice of Rabelais which cries to us directly across the gulf of the centuries, as shattering now as at the hour when Rabelais begot these word-monsters.

If, then, it is true that Rabelais' word-formation reflects an attitude somewhere between reality and irreality, with its shudders of horror and its comic relief, what of Lanson's famous statement on Rabelais in general, which is repeated in thousands of French schools and in most of the Lanson-imbued seminars of French throughout the world: "Jamais réalisme plus pur, plus puissant et plus triomphant ne s'est vu"? Well, it is simply wrong. I have not time to develop here the conclusions which would round out the utterly antirealistic picture of Rabelais that stands out in his work; it could be shown that the whole plot of Rabelais' epic, the fantastic voyage of fantastic people to the oracle of the priestess Bacbuc (whose ambiguous response: *"Trinc!"* is just a nowhere word) as well as the invention of detail (e.g. Panurge's speech on debtors and lenders, in which the earthy Panurge drives forward, from his astute egoistic refusal to live without debts, to a cosmic, utopian vision of a paradoxical world resting on the universal law of indebtedness)—that everything in Rabelais' work tends toward the creation of a world of irreality.

Thus, what has been disclosed by the study of Rabelais' language, the literary study would corroborate; it could not be otherwise, since language is only one outward crystallization of the "inward form," or, to use another metaphor: the life-blood of the poetic creation[7] is everywhere the same, whether we tap the organism at "language" or "ideas," at "plot" or at "composition." As regards the last, I could as well have begun with a study of

the rather loose literary composition of Rabelais' writings and only later have
gone over to his ideas, his plot, his language. Because I happened to be a
linguist it was from the linguistic angle that I started, to fight my way to his
unity. Obviously, no fellow scholar must be required to do the same. What he
must be asked to do, however, is, I believe, to work from the surface to the
"inward life-center" of the work of art: first observing details about the
superficial appearance of the particular work (and the "ideas" expressed by a
poet are, also, only one of the superficial traits in a work of art);[8] then, grouping
these details and seeking to integrate them into a creative principle which may
have been present in the soul of the artist; and, finally, making the return trip
to all the other groups of observations in order to find whether the "inward
form" one has tentatively constructed gives an account of the whole. The
scholar will surely be able to state, after three or four of these "fro voyages,"
whether he has found the life-giving center, the sun of the solar system (by
then he will know whether he is really permanently installed in the center, or
whether he finds himself in an "excentric" or peripheric position). There is no
shadow of truth in the objection raised not long ago by one of the representatives of the mechanist Yale school of linguists against the "circularity of
arguments" of the mentalists: against the "explanation of a linguistic fact by an
assumed psychological process for which the only evidence is the fact to be
explained."[9] I could immediately reply that my school is not satisfied with
psychologizing one trait but bases its assumptions on several traits carefully
grouped and integrated; one should, in fact, embrace *all* the linguistic traits
observable with a given author (I myself have tried to come as close as possible
to this requirement of completeness in my studies on Racine, Saint-Simon,
Quevedo [in *RSL*]). And the circle of which the adversary just quoted speaks
is not a vicious one; on the contrary, it is the basic operation in the humanities,
the *Zirkel im Verstehen* as Dilthey has termed the discovery, made by the
Romantic scholar and theologian Schleiermacher, that cognizance in philology
is reached not only by the gradual progression from one detail to another detail,
but by the anticipation or divination of the whole—because "the detail can be
understood only by the whole and any explanation of detail presupposes the
understanding of the whole."[10] Our to-and-fro voyage from certain outward
details to the inner center and back again to other series of details is only an
application of the principle of the "philological circle." After all, the concept of
the Romance languages as based on one Vulgar Latin substratum, and
reflected in them although identical with none—this has been reached by the
founder of Romance philology, Diez, the pupil of the Romantics, precisely by
means of this "philological circle," which allowed him to sit installed in the
center of the phenomenon "Romance Languages," whereas Raynouard, his
predecessor, by identifying one of the Romance varieties, Provençal, with
Proto-Romance, found himself in an excentric position, from which point it
was impossible to explain satisfactorily all the outward traits of Romance. To
proceed from some exterior traits of Philippe's or Rabelais' language to the soul
or mental center of Philippe and Rabelais, and back again to the rest of the
exterior traits of Philippe's and Rabelais' works of art, is the same *modus*

operandi as that which proceeds from some details of the Romance languages to a Vulgar Latin prototype and then, in reverse order, explains other details by this assumed prototype—or even, from that which infers from some of the outward, phonetic and semantic appearances of the English word *conundrum* to its medieval French soul, and back to all its phonetic and semantic traits.

To posit a soul of Rabelais which creates from the real in the direction of the unreal is, of course, not yet all that is desirable in order to understand the whole phenomenon: the Rabelaisian entity must be integrated into a greater unit and located somewhere on a historical line, as Diez, in a grandiose way, did with Romance—as we have tried to do, on a minor scale, with *calembredaine—conundrum*. Rabelais may be a solar system which, in its turn, forms part of a transcending system which embraces others as well as himself, others around, before, and after him; we must place him, as the literary historians would say, within the framework of the history of ideas, or *Geistesgeschichte*. The power of wielding the word as though it were a world of its own between reality and irreality, which exists to a unique degree with Rabelais, cannot have sprung out of nothingness, cannot have entirely ebbed after him. Before him there is, for example, Pulci, who, in his *Morgante Maggiore*, shows a predilection for word-lists, especially when he has his facetious knights indulge in name-calling. And, with Pulci, the Rabelaisian tendency to let language encroach on reality, is also to be found: when he retells, in half-facetious vein, the story immortalized by Turoldus of the battle of Roncevaux, we learn that the Saracens fell under the blows of the Christian knights in a trice: they stayed not upon the order of their dying but died at once: not tomorrow, or the day after tomorrow, nor the day after the day after tomorrow, nor the day after the day after the day after tomorrow: not *crai e poscrai, o poscrilla, o posquacchera*. In this sequel of gurgling and guttural sounds, the words *crai* and *poscrai* are genuine Italian reflections of the Latin words *cras* and *posteras;* but *poscrilla, posquacchera* are popular fantasy words.[11] The onomatopoeias with which popular language likes to juggle have here been used by a reflective poet for purposes of grotesque art: we can see here the exact point of transition of popular language into literature. Pulci believes in the ideals of Christian orthodox knighthood less full-heartedly than did Turoldus, for whom the heroic and religious values were real, and who must needs subordinate his language to the expression of these values. The word-world, admitted to a work of art by Pulci, was not yet available to Turoldus, or even to Dante (the "etymological puns" of the *Vita nuova* are quite another matter: they are only "illustrations," just as had been true of the puns of the Church Fathers).[12] The appearance of this intermediate world is conditioned by a belief in the reality of words, a belief which would have been condemned by the "realists" of the Middle Ages. The belief in such vicarious realities as words is possible only in an epoch whose belief in the *universalia realia* has been shaken. It is this phantasmagoric climate, casually evoked by Pulci, in which Rabelais will move easily and naturally, with a kind of cosmic independence. It is the belief in the autonomy of the word which made possible the whole movement of Humanism, in which so much importance was given to the word of the ancients and of the Biblical writers; it is this belief which will in part explain the extraordinary development of mathematics in the sixteenth and seventeenth centuries—i.e. of the most autonomous language that man has ever devised.

Now, who are the descendants of Rabelais? French classical literature, with its ideal of the *mot juste,* of the *mot mis à sa place,* broke away from the Renaissance tradition of the autonomy of the word. But undercurrents persisted, and I would say that Balzac, Flaubert (in his Letters), Théophile Gautier (in his *grotesqueries*), Victor Hugo (in his *William Shakespeare*), and Huysmans are, to a certain extent, descendants of Rabelais in the nineteenth century. In our own time, with Ferdinand Céline, who can build a whole book out of invectives against the Jews ("Bagatelles pour un massacre"), we may see language exceed its boundaries: this book, in the words of André Gide, is a "chevauchée de Don Quichotte en plein ciel . . ." ; "ce n'est pas la réalité que peint Céline; c'est l'hallucination que la réalité provoque." The following sample of Celinian inspiration makes a pseudo-Rabelaisian effect, and can be compared with the apocalyptic inscription over the portal of Thélème: "Penser 'sozial!' cela veut dire dans la pratique, en termes bien crus: 'penser juif! pour les juifs! par les juifs, sous les juifs!' Rien d'autre! Tout le surplus immense des mots, le vrombissant verbiage socialitico-humanitaro-scientifique, tout le cosmique carafouillage de l'impératif despotique juif n'est que l'enrobage mirageux, le charabia fatras poussif, la sauce orientale pour ces encoulés d'aryens, la fricassée terminologique pour rire, pour l'adulation des 'aveulis blancs,' ivrognes rampants, intouchables, qui s'en foutrent, à bite que veux-tu, s'en mystifient, s'en baffrent à crever."

Here, evidently, the verbal creation, itself a *vrombissant verbiage* (to use the alliterative coinage of Céline), has implications more eschatological than cosmic: the word-world is really only a world of noisy words, clanking sounds, like so many engines senselessly hammering away, covering with their noise the fear and rage of man lonely in the doomed modern world. Words and reality fall apart. This is really a *voyage au bout du monde:* not to the oracle of Bacbuc but to chaos, to the end of language as an expression of thought.

The historical line we have drawn (we may call it the evolution of an idea: the idea of "language become autonomous"), which is marked by the stages Pulci—Rabelais—Victor Hugo—Céline, is paralleled or crossed by other historical lines with other names located on the historical ladder. Victor Hugo is not Rabelais, although there may be Hugoesque traits in Rabelais, Rabelaisian traits in Hugo. We must not confuse a historical line with a solar system resting in itself: what appeared to us central in Rabelais may be peripheric in Victor Hugo, and the reverse. Every solar system, unique in itself, undefinable (*"ineffabile"*) to a certain extent, is traversed by different historical lines of "ideas," whose intersection produces the particular climate in which the great literary work matures—just as the system of a language is made up of the intersections of different historical lines of the *calembredaine—conundrum* variety.

Thus we started with a particular historical line, the etymology of a particular word-family, and found therein evidences of a change of historical climate. Then we considered the change of a whole historical climate as expressed in the innovations, linguistic and literary, of writers of two different epochs (the twentieth and the sixteenth), finally to arrive at the point of positing theoretically self-sufficient systems: the great works of art, determined by different historical developments and reflecting in all their outward details, linguistic as well as literary, their respective central "sun." It is obvious that, in this paper, I have been able to give you only scattered samples, the conclusions from which I have loaded, and perhaps overloaded, with an experience resulting from hundreds of such to-and-fro voyages—all directed by the same principles, but each one bound for an unpredictable goal. My personal way has been from the observed detail to ever broadening units which rest, to an increasing degree, on speculation. It is, I think, the philological, the inductive way, which seeks to show significance in the apparently futile, in contrast to the deductive procedure which begins with units assumed as given—and which is rather the way followed by the theologians who start from on high, to take the downward path toward the earthly maze of detail, or by the mathematicians, who treat their axioms as if these were God-given. In philology, which deals with the all-too-human, with the interrelated and the intertwined aspects of human affairs, the deductive method has its place only as a verification of the principle found by induction—which rests on observation.

But, of course, the attempt to discover significance in the detail,[13] the habit of taking a detail of language as seriously as the meaning of a work of art—or, in other words, the attitude which sees all manifestations of man as equally serious—this is an outgrowth of the preestablished firm conviction, the "axiom," of the philologian, that details are not an inchoate chance aggregation of dispersed material through which no light shines. The philologian must believe in the existence of some light from on high, of some *post nubila Phoebus*. If he did not know that at the end of his journey there would be awaiting him a life-giving draught from some *dive bouteille,* he would not have commenced it: "Tu ne me chercherais pas si tu ne m'avais pas déjà trouvé," says Pascal's God. Thus, humanistic thought, in spite of the methodological distinction just made, is not so completely divorced from that of the theologian as is generally believed; it is not by chance that the "philological circle" was discovered by a theologian, who was wont to harmonize the discordant, to retrace the beauty of God in this world. This attitude is reflected in the word coined by Schleiermacher: *Weltanschauung:*[14] "die Welt anschauen": "to see, to cognize the universe *in its sensuous detail.*" The philologian will then continue the pursuit of the microscopic because he sees therein the microcosmic; he will practice that *"Andacht zum Kleinen"* which Jacob Grimm has prescribed; he will go on filling his little cards with dates and examples, in the hope that supernal light will shine over them and bring out the clear lines of truth. The Humanist believes in the power bestowed on the human mind of investigating the human mind. When, with scholars whose goal and whose tool are thus identical, the faith in the human mind, as a tool and as a goal, is broken, this can only mean a crisis in the humanities—or, should I say, in the *Divinities*? And this is the situation today. A man without belief in the human mind is a stunted human being—how can he be a Humanist? The humanities will be restored only when the Humanists shed their agnostic attitudes, when they become human again, and share the belief of Rabelais' humanistic and religious king: "sapience n'entre point en ame malivole; et science sans conscience n'est que ruine de l'ame"—or, to go back to the Augustinian wording: "Non intratur in veritatem nisi per charitatem."[15]

In the essays to follow I have made an attempt to apply the principle of the "philological circle" to various authors of different nations and periods, applying it in varying degree and manner and in combination with other methods. But these articles are conceived not only as illustrations of my procedure, but as independent contributions to the understanding of the writers treated therein: contributions which should prove readable for any cultured person interested in the style of works of art.[16] For if my procedure should have any value, this must be revealed in the new results, the scholarly progress, attained by its means: the philological circle should not imply that one moves complacently in the circle of the already-known, in a *piétinement sur place*. Thus each single essay is intended to form a separate, independent unit: I hope that the repetitions of theoretical and historical statements which are the unavoidable consequence of this manner of presentation, will be felt by the reader rather as recurrent *leitmotifs* or *refrains* destined to emphasize a constancy and unity of approach.

Before putting to the test the method of the "philological circle" already delineated, I should like to warn the reader that he must not expect to find, in my demonstration of this method, the systematic step-by-step procedure which my own description of it may have seemed to promise.[17] For, when I spoke in terms of a series of back-and-forth movements (first the detail, then the whole, then another detail, etc.), I was using a linear and temporal figure in an attempt to describe states of apperception which, in the mind of the humanist, only too often co-exist. This gift, or vice (for it has its dangers), of seeing part and whole together, at any moment, and which, to some degree, is basic to the operation of the philological mind, is, perhaps, in my own case, developed to a particular degree, and has aroused objections from students and readers—in Germany, where the synthetic capacities of the public are, in general, superior to their analytic capacities, as well as in America where the opposite obtains. A very understanding but critical ex-student of mine, an American, once wrote me: "To establish a behavioristic technique which would reveal the application of your method is, it seems to me, beyond your possibilities. You know the principles that motivate you, rather than any 'technique' that you rigorously follow. Here, it may be a memory from boyhood, there an inspiration you got from another poem; here, there and everywhere it is an urge in you, an instinct backed up by your experience, that tells you immediately: 'this is not important; this is.' At every second you are making choices, but you hardly know that you make them: what seems right to you must be immediately right. And you can only show by doing; you see the meaning as a whole from the beginning; there are almost no steps in your mental processes; and, writing from the midst of your thoughts you take it for granted that the reader is with you and that what is self-evident to you as the next step (only, it's not the next step, even: it's already included, somehow) will also be so to him."

These words, obviously, offer a picture of the limitations of a particular individual temperament. But much of what my correspondent says is given with the operation of the circle—when this is applied, not to routine reading, on the one hand, or to the deductions of schematic linguistics on the other, but to a work of art: the solution attained by means of the circular operation cannot be subjected to a rigorous rationale because, at its most perfect, this is a negation of steps: once attained, it tends to obliterate the steps leading up to it (one may remember the lion of medieval bestiaries who, at every step forward, wiped out his footprints with his tail, In order to elude his pursuers!).

Why do I insist that it is impossible to offer the reader a step-by-step rationale to be applied to a work of art? For one reason, that the first step, on which all may hinge, can never be planned: it must already have taken place. This first step is the awareness of having been struck by a detail, followed by a conviction that this detail is connected basically with the work of art; it means that one has made an "observation,"—which is the starting point of a theory, that one has been prompted to raise a question—which must find an answer. To begin by omitting this first step must doom any attempt at interpretation—as was the case with the dissertation (mentioned in note I of my article on Diderot) devoted to the "imagery" of Diderot, in which the concept "imagery" was based on no preliminary observation but on a ready-made category applied from without to the work of art.

Unfortunately, I know of no way to guarantee either the "impression" or the conviction just described: they are the results of talent, experience, and faith. And, even then, the first step is not to be taken at our own volition: how often, with all the theoretical experience of method accumulated in me over the years, have I stared blankly, quite similar to one of my beginning students, at a page that would not yield its magic. The only way leading out of this state of unproductivity is to read and reread,[18] patiently and confidently, in an endeavor to become, as it were, soaked through and through with the atmosphere of the work. And suddenly, one word, one line, stands out, and we realize that, now, a relationship has been established between the poem and us. From this point on, I have usually found that, what with other observations adding themselves to the first, and with previous experiences of the circle intervening, and with associations given by previous education building up before me (all of this quickened, in my own case, by a quasi-metaphysical urge toward solution) it does not seem long until the characteristic "click" occurs, which is the indication that detail and whole have found a common denominator—which gives the etymology of the writing.[19] And looking back on this process (whose end, of course, marks only the conclusion of the *preliminary* stage of analysis), how can we say when exactly it began? (Even the "first step" was preconditioned.) We see, indeed, that to read is to have read, to understand is equivalent to having understood.[20]

I have just spoken of the importance of past experience in the process of understanding the work of art—but as only one of the intervening factors. For experience with the "circle" is not, itself, enough to enable one to base thereupon a program applicable to all cases. For every poem the critic needs a separate inspiration, a separate light from above (it is this constant need which makes for humility, and it is the accumulation of past enlightenments that encourages a sort of pious confidence). Indeed, a Protean mutability is required of the critic, for the device which has proved successful for one work of art cannot be applied mechanically to another: I could not expect that the "trick of the five *grands*" (which I shall apply to an ode of Claudel's) would work for the "récit de Théramène," or that proper names, which will serve as a point of departure in my article on Cervantes, would play any part in the study on Diderot. It is, indeed, most trying for the experienced teacher to have to watch a beginner re-use and consequently mis-use, a particular clue that had served the teacher when he was treating a quite different writer—as though a young actor were to use the leer of Barrymore's Richard III for his performance of Othello. The mutability required of the critic can be gained only by repeated experiences with totally different writers; the "click" will come oftener and more quickly after several experiences of "clicks" have been realized by the critic. And, even then, it is not a foregone conclusion that it will inevitably come; nor can one ever foretell just when and where it will materialize ("The Spirit bloweth . . .").

The reason that the clues to understanding cannot be mechanically transferred from one work of art to another lies in the fact of artistic expressivity itself: the artist lends to an outward phenomenon of language an inner significance (thereby merely continuing and expanding the basic fact of human language: that a meaning is quite arbitrarily—arbitrarily, at least, from the point of view of the current usage of the language—associated with an acoustic phenomenon); just *which* phenomena the literary artist will choose for the embodiment of his meaning is arbitrary from the point of view of the "user" of the work of art. To overcome the impression of an arbitrary association in the work of art, the reader must seek to place himself in the creative center of the artist himself—and re-create the artistic organism. A metaphor, an anaphora, a staccato rhythm may be found anywhere in literature; they may or may not be significant. What tells us that they are important is only the feeling, which we must have already acquired, for the whole of the particular work of art.

And the capacity for this feeling is, again, deeply anchored in the previous life and education of the critic, and not only in his scholarly education: in order to keep his soul ready for his scholarly task he must have already made choices, in ordering his life, of what I would call a moral nature; he must have chosen to cleanse his mind from distraction by the inconsequential, from the obsession of everyday small details—to keep it open to the synthetic apprehension of the "wholes" of life, to the symbolism in nature and art and language. I have sometimes wondered if my "explication de texte" in the university classroom, where I strive to create an atmosphere suitable for the appreciation of the work of art, would not have succeeded much better if that atmosphere had been present at the breakfast table of my students.

NOTES

1. Text of an address, originally entitled "Thinking in the Humanities," delivered to the Department of Modern Languages and Literatures of Princeton University, to which some notes and an epilogue have been added.

It is paradoxical that professors of literature who are too superficial to immerse themselves in a text and who are satisfied with stale phrases out of a manual, are precisely those who contend that it is superfluous to teach the aesthetic value of a text of Racine or Victor Hugo: the student will, in some way or another, come to grasp its beauty without any direction—or, if he is incapable of doing so, it is useless to talk about it. But there are hidden beauties which do not reveal themselves at the first exploratory attempts (as the apologetic theologians know); in fact, all beauty has some mysterious quality which does not appear at first glance. But there is no more reason for dodging the description of the aesthetic phenomenon than of any natural phenomenon. Those who oppose the aesthetic analysis of poetic works seem to affect at times the susceptibility of a sensitive plant: if one is to believe them, it is because they cherish so deeply the works of art, it is because they respect their chastity, that they would not deflower, by means of intellectual formulas, the virginal and ethereal quality of works of art, they would not brush off the shimmering dust from the wings of these poetic butterflies! I would maintain, on the contrary, that to formulate observations by means of words is not to cause the artistic beauty to evaporate in vain intellectualities; rather, it makes for a widening and a deepening of the aesthetic taste. Love, whether it be love for God, love for one's fellow men, or the love of art, can only gain by the effort of the human intellect to search for the reasons of its most sublime emotions, and to formulate them. It is only a frivolous love that cannot survive intellectual definition; great love prospers with understanding.

2. The presentation of so great a scholar as Meyer-Lübke from the only angle which concerns us here is necessarily one-sided; for a more complete evaluation of his scholarship, as well as for a picture of his personality, I may refer the reader to my paper, "Mes souvenirs sur Meyer-Lübke" in *Le français moderne*, vi, 213. As for Philipp August Becker, my few remarks have given no real idea of his exuberant personality—which seldom penetrated into his scholarship; his was an orgiastic nature which somehow did not fit into the traditional pattern of a scholar. A story told me by Walther von Wartburg may illustrate this: Becker, who was rather given to the worship of Bacchus-Dionysos, used to invite his colleagues at Leipzig to a certain popular inn for copious libations. One night, after many hours of merrymaking, he realized that the bourgeois patrons sitting around him were shocked by his exuberance; immediately turning to his colleagues, he remarked: "And now I want to tell you something about early Christian hymns!" For almost an hour he talked, to the delight, not only of his colleagues but also of the crowd of *Spiessbürger* who had gradually drawn closer to him,

enthralled by the eloquence of this greybeard bard who was reviving the spirit of Saint Ambrosius in a tavern.

3. These etymologies have appeared in the *Journal of English and Germanic Philology*, xLII, 405; there I suggested also the possibility of a **calembourd-on* as etymon, but today I prefer *calembredaine* to that unattested formation.

4. In fact, Ernst Lewy would destroy the unity of "Romance Languages" by placing French and Spanish, along with Basque and Irish, in an Atlantic group of languages, and Rumanian within the Balkan group (see my discussion in *Anales de l'Inst. de lingüística de Cuyo*, II). Again, there is the Russian school of "Japhetists" who believe not in "families" but in "systems" of languages, and who make bold to discover in any given language certain primeval basic "elements" of the prelogical period in human speech (see Malkiel's article in *Language*, xx, 157).

5. Perhaps the transition from a particular historical line in language, as traced by an etymology, to the self-contained system of a work of literature, may seem violent to the reader: in the first case the "etymon" is the "soul of the nation" at the moment of the creation of the word; in the second, it is the "soul of one particular author." The difference, as Professor Singleton has pointed out to me, is that between the unconscious will of the nation that creates its language, and the conscious will of one member of the nation who creates wilfully and more or less systematically. But, apart from the fact that there are rational elements in popular linguistic creations, and irrational ones in those of the creative artist—what I would point out here is the relationship, common to both, between the linguistic detail and the soul of the speaker(s), and the necessity, in both cases, of the to-and-fro philological movement.

Perhaps a better parallel to the system of a work of art would be the system of a language at a definite moment of its evolution. I attempted just such a characterization of a linguistic system in my article on Spanish in *Stilstudien*, I.

6. This study has been published in *Stilstudien*, II.

The method I have been describing in the text is, of course, one that is followed by all of us when we must interpret the correspondence of someone with whom we are not well acquainted. For several years I had been in correspondence with a German emigrant in France whom I did not know personally and whose letters had given me the impression of a rather self-centered person who craved a cozy and congenial environment. When she was finally rescued to another country, she published a book of memoirs, a copy of which was sent me. On the cover of the book I saw pictured the window of the room she had occupied in Paris; behind this window, in the foreground, was a great cat looking out upon the Cathedral of Notre Dame. A great part of the book itself was taken up with this cat, and I had not read far before I found—without great surprise—several sentences such as "blottie dans un fauteuil, j'éprouvai un tel bonheur, je me sentis si bien à mon aise sous ce soleil doux qui me faisait ronronner à la manière des chats." Evidently a catlike existence was the deep-felt aspiration of this emigrant who, in the midst of world catastrophe, had lost the feeling of protectedness and had had to seek protection in herself.

7. We could here also be reminded of Goethe's simile (in *Die Wahlverwandtschaften*, II, 2): "We have learned about a special arrangement of the English Navy: all ropes of the Royal Fleet, from the strongest to the thinnest, have a red thread woven into them in such a way that it cannot be taken out without completely raveling the rope, so that even the smallest particle is stamped as the property of the Crown. Similarly, Ottilia's diary is pervaded by a thread of affection and attachment which connects every part and characterizes the whole of it." In this passage Goethe has formulated the principle of inner cohesion as it exists in a sensitive writer. It is the

recognition of this principle which enabled Freud to apply his psychoanalytical finds to works of literature. While I do not wish to disavow the Freudian influence in my earlier attempts at explaining literary texts, my aim today is to think, not so much in terms of the all-too-human "complexes" which, in Freud's opinion, are supposed to color the writing of the great figures of literature, but of "ideological patterns," as these are present in the history of the human mind.

Mr. Kenneth Burke, in his book *Philosophy of Literary Form* (Louisiana, 1940), has worked out a methodology of what he calls the "symbolic" or "strategic" approach to poetry—an approach which comes very close to the Freudian one (and to my own, as far as it was influenced by Freud), and which consists of establishing emotional clusters. When Mr. Burke finds such clusters in Coleridge, for example, and observes their constancy in the writings of this poet, he will claim to have found a factual, observable, irrefutable basis for the analysis of the structure of the work of art in general.

What I would object to in this method is that it can, obviously, be applied only to those poets who do, in fact, reveal such associational clusters—which is to say, only to those poets who do allow their phobias and idiosyncrasies to appear in their writing. But this must exclude all writers before the eighteenth century, the period in which the theory of the "original genius" was discovered and applied. Before this period, it is very difficult to discover, in any writer, "individual" associations, that is to say, associations not prompted by a literary tradition. Dante, Shakespeare, Racine are great literary "individuals," but they did not (or could not) allow their style to be permeated by their personal phobias and idiosyncrasies (even Montaigne, when portraying himself, thought of himself as "l'homme"). When a student of mine, working on the style of Agrippa d'Aubigné, was influenced by Professor Burke's book to apply the method of "emotional clusters" to that sixteenth-century epic poet, and was able, indeed, to find a series of antithetical associations, such as "milk—poison," "mother—serpent," "nature—unnatural" used in reference to pairs represented by the Catholic Catherine de Medicis and her Protestant opponents, I had to point out to him that these particular associational patterns (which had reminded him of Joyce) were all given by classical and Scriptural tradition: D'Aubigné merely gave powerful expression to age-old ideological motifs that transcended his personal, nervous temperament: the starting point for his "mère non-mère" was, obviously, the Greek μήτηρ ἀμήτωρ. Recently, I have had occasion also to point out the same truth in regard to the sixteenth-century poet Guevara, whose style has been explained by Freudian frustration.

8. Under the noble pretext of introducing "history of ideas" into literary criticism, there have appeared in recent times, with the approval of the departments of literary history, academic theses with such titles as "Money in Seventeenth-Century French (English, Spanish etc.) Comedy," "Political Tendencies in Nineteenth-Century French (English, Spanish etc.) Literature." Thus we have come to disregard the philological character of the discipline of literary history, which is concerned with ideas couched in linguistic and literary form, not with ideas in themselves (this is the field of history of philosophy) or with ideas as informing action (this is the field of history and the social sciences). Only in the linguistico-literary field are we philologians competent qua scholars. The type of dissertations cited above reveals an unwarranted extension of the (in itself commendable) tendency toward breaking down departmental barriers, to such a degree that literary history becomes the gay sporting ground of incompetence. Students of the department of literature come to treat the complex subjects of a philosophical, political, or economic nature with the same self-assurance that once characterized those Positivists who wrote on "The Horse in Medieval Literature." But

while it is possible for the average person to know "what a horse is" (if less so what "a horse in literature" is), it is much more difficult for a student of literature to know "what money is" (and still more so what "money in literature" is). In fact, this new type of thesis is only an avatar of the old positivistic thesis; but, while the original positivism was motivated by a sincere respect for competence, the neo-positivists now would administer the death-blow to scholarly competence.

9. Cf. my article in *Modern Philological Quarterly:* "Why Does Language Change?" and the polemics resulting therefrom in *Language,* xx, 45 and 245.

10. Cf. Schleiermacher, *Sämtl. Werke,* iii, 3, p. 343. "Über den Begriff der Hermeneutik mit Bezug auf F. A. Wolfs Andeutungen und Arts Lehrbuch"—a speech delivered in 1829. Schleiermacher distinguishes between the "comparative" and the "divinatory" methods, the combination of which is necessary in "hermeneutics," and since hermeneutics falls into two parts, a "grammatical" and a "psychological" part, both methods must be used in both parts of hermeneutics. Of the two methods, it is the divinatory which requires the "Zirkelschluss." We have been dealing here with the *Zirkelschluss* in the "divination" of the psychology of authors; as for "grammatical divination," any college student who attempts to parse a Ciceronian period is constantly using it: he cannot grasp the construction except by passing continuously from the parts to the whole of the sentence and back again to its parts.

Dr. Ludwig Edelstein has called my attention to the Platonic origin of Schleiermacher's discovery: it is in *Phaedo* that Socrates states the importance of the whole for the cognition of the parts. Accordingly, it would appear that I err in adopting Schleiermacher's "theological" approach and that I am undiplomatic in asking for an approach so at variance with that which is traditional in the humanities (when Dewey reproved the Humanists for the residues of theology in their thinking, they made haste to disavow any theological preoccupation—while I take the stand of saying: "Yes, we Humanists are theologians!"); would it not, I am asked, be better to show the irrationalism inherent in any rational operation in the humanities, than to demand the overt irrationalism of religion which our secular universities must thoroughly abhor? My answer is that Socrates himself was a religious genius and that, through Plato, he is present in much of Christian thought. As concerns the necessity, for the scholar, of having recourse to religion, cf. the conclusive reasoning of Erich Frank in his book *Philosophical Understanding and Religious Truth* (1945).

The traditional view of the "viciousness" of the philological circle is unfortunately held in an otherwise brilliant attack against "the biographical fashion in literary criticism" (University of California Publications, in *Classical Philology,* xii, 288) by Professor Harold Cherniss: in his argument against the philologians of the Stefan George school who, though not dealing with the outward biography of artists, believe that the inner form of the artist's personality can be grasped in his works by a kind of intuition, Cherniss writes: "The intuition which discovers in the writings of an author the 'natural law' and 'inward form' of his personality, is proof against all objections, logical and philological; but, while one must admit that a certain native insight, call it direct intelligence or intuition as you please, is required for understanding any text, it is, all the same, a vicious circle to intuit the nature of the author's personality from his writings and then to interpret those writings in accordance with the 'inner necessity' of that intuited personality. Moreover, once the intuition of the individual critic is accepted as the ultimate basis of all interpretation, the comprehension of a literary work becomes a completely private affair, for the intuition of any one interpreter has no more objective validity than that of any other."

I believe that the word "intuition" with its deliberate implication of extraordinary mystic qualities on the part of the critic, vitiates not only the reasoning of the Stefan George school but also that of their opponents. The "circle" is vicious only when an uncontrolled intuition is allowed to exercise itself upon the literary works; the procedure from details to the inner core and back again is not in itself at all vicious; in fact, the "intelligent reading" which Professor Cherniss advocates without defining it (though he is forced to grant rather uncomfortably that it is "a certain native insight, call it direct intelligence or intuition as you please") is based precisely on that very philological circle. To understand a sentence, a work of art, or the inward form of an artistic mind involves, to an increasing degree, irrational moves—which must, also to an increasing degree, be controlled by reason.

Heidegger, in *Sein und Zeit,* I, 32 ("Verstehen und Auslegung"), shows that all "exegesis" is circular, i.e. is a catching up with the "understanding," which is nothing else than an anticipation of the whole that is "existentially" given to man: "Zuhandenes wird immer schon aus der Bewandtnisganzheit der verstanden. . . . Die Auslegung gründet jeweils in einer *Vorsicht,* die das in Vorhabe Genommene auf eine bestimmte Auslegbarkeit hin 'anschneidet.' . . . Auslegung ist nie ein voraussetzungsloses Erfassen eines Vorgegebenen. . . . Alle Auslegung, die Verständnis beistellen soll, muss schon das Auszulegende verstanden haben. . . . *Aber in diesem Zirkel ein vitiosum sehen und nach Wegen Ausschau halten, ihn zu vermeiden, ja ihn auch nur als unvermeidliche Unvollkommenheit 'empfinden,' heisst das Verstehen von Grund aus missverstehen* [the italics are the author's]. . . . Das Entscheidende ist nicht aus dem Zirkel heraus-, sondern in ihn nach der rechten Weise hineinzukommen. . . . In ihm verbirgt sich eine positive Möglichkeit ursprünglichsten Erkennens, die freilich in echter Weise nur dann ergriffen ist, wenn die Auslegung verstanden hat, dass ihre erste, ständige und letzte Aufgabe bleibt, sich jeweils Vorhabe, Vorsicht und Vorgriff nicht durch Einfälle und Volksbegriffe vorgeben zu lassen, sondern in deren Ausarbeitung aus den Sachen selbst her das wissenschaftliche Thema zu sichern. Der 'Zirkel' im Verstehen gehört zur Struktur des Sinnes, welches Phänomen in der existenzialen Verfassung des Daseins, im auslegenden Verstehen verwurzelt ist."

This "Vorsicht," this anticipation of the whole, is especially necessary for the understanding of philosophical writing. Franz Rosenzweig, "Das neue Denken" (in *Kleinere Schriften,* 1937) writes: "The first pages of philosophical books are held by the reader in special respect. . . . He thinks they [such books] ought to be 'especially logical,' and by this he means that each sentence depends on the one that precedes it, so that if the famous one stone is pulled, 'the whole tumbles.' Actually, this is nowhere less the case than in philosophical books. Here a sentence does not follow from its predecessor, but much more probably from its successor. . . . Philosophical books refuse such methodical ancien-régime strategy; they must be conquered à la Napoleon, in a bold thrust against the main body of the enemy; and after the victory at this point, the small fortresses will fall of themselves." (I owe this quotation to Kurt H. Wolf's article, "The Sociology of Knowledge" in *Philosophy of Science,* x; Wolf calls the anticipatory understanding of wholes a "central attitude": "In our everyday social interaction we constantly practice the central-attitude approach without which we could not 'know' how to behave toward other persons, or how to read a book, to see a picture, or to play or listen to a piece of music. . . .") What Heidegger, Rosenzweig, and Wolf describe is the method of the humanities which Pascal has called the "esprit de finesse" (as contrasted to the "esprit géométrique").

For the students in Romance Gröber formulated the idea of the philological circle (without mentioning the "circle" itself) in *Gröber's Grundriss* 1/3 (1888): "Absichtslose Wahrnehmung, unscheinbare Anfänge gehen dem zielbewussten Suchen, dem allseitigen Erfassen des Gegenstandes voraus. Im sprungweisen Durchmessen des Raumes hascht dann der Suchende nach dem Ziel, Mit einem Schema unfertiger Ansichten über ähnliche Gegenstände scheint er das Ganze erfassen zu können, ehe Natur und Teile gekannt sind. Der vorschnellen Meinung folgt die Einsicht des Irrtums, nur langsam der Entschluss, dem Gegenstand in kleinen und kleinsten vorsichtigen Schritten nahe zu kommen, Teil und Teilchen zu beschauen und nicht zu ruhen, bis die Überzeugung gewonnen ist, dass sie nur so und nicht anders aufgefasst werden müssen."

It is also true of the comparative linguist who establishes his "phonetic laws" on the basis of "evident etymologies," which themselves are based on those "phonetic laws," that he moves in a circle, in the words of Zupitza, *Zeitschr. f. vergl. Sprachwissenschaft*, xxxvii (1904) p. 387: "Unsere wissenschaft kommt aus einem kreislauf nicht heraus: sie geht von evidenten gleichungen aus, entnimmt diesen ihre gesetze und prüft an diesen gesetzen jene gleichungen, die ihre grundlage bilden." And even elementary language teaching must move in a circle: R. A. Hall in *Bull. of the American University Professors*, xxxi, 6, advocating the modern "direct method" as preferable to the old "reading method," writes: "When he [the student] has learnt a sufficient number of examples, the linguistic analysis becomes simply a series of obvious deductions from what he has learned; it helps him to perceive the patterns inherent in what he already knows, and tells him how far he can go in extending these patterns to new material." The inference from "patterns" is nothing but an anticipation of a whole deduced from the known examples.

11. This point has been entirely overlooked in the treatment of the passage by an antimentalist; see my article in *Italica*, xxi, 154.

12. This is not to say that the puns and repetitions used by Rabelais do not historically develop from the same devices used by the Fathers and the medieval writers. Rabelais' facetious etymology *Beauce* = "[je trouve] beau ce," and his repetition of words, such as *moine moinant de moinerie*, are scholastic devices—only that they are used by him in an antimedieval manner, informed by a worldly spirit and, most important of all, by the consciousness of the autonomy of a "word world."

13. I have often wondered how historians of literature could make such sweeping statements, as they are wont to do, on the whole of the literary work of a poet, or of a period, without descending into the detail of texts (and into the linguistic detail). Goethe speaks pertinently ("Einleitung in die Propyläen") of the "Anschauung" necessary for the concrete apperception of works of art: "Um von Kunstwerken eigentlich und mit wahrem Nutzen für sich und andere zu sprechen, sollte es freilich nur in Gegenwart derselben geschehen. Alles kommt aufs Anschauen an; es kommt darauf an, dass bei dem Worte, wodurch man ein Kunstwerk zu erläutern hofft, das Bestimmteste gedacht werde, weil sonst gar nichts gedacht wird. Daher geschieht es so oft, dass derjenige, der über Kunstwerke schreibt, bloss im Allgemeinen verweilt. . . ."

The same seems to have been felt by Santayana in regard to the field of philosophy; in *The Middle Span*, p. 155, he has the following to say about the habits of his Harvard students during the last decades of the nineteenth century: "I doubt that the texts were much studied directly in those days at Harvard. The undergraduates were thinking only of examinations and relied on summaries in the histories of philosophy and on lecture notes. . . . Philosophy can be communicated only by being evoked: the pupil's mind must be engaged dialectically in the discussion. Otherwise, all that can be taught is the literary history of philosophy, that is, the *phrases* that various philosophers have rendered famous. To conceive what those phrases meant or could mean would require a philosophical imagination in the public which cannot be demanded. All that usually exists is familiarity with current phrases, and a shock, perhaps of pleased curiosity but more often of alarm and repulsion, due to the heterodoxy of any different phrases." It is needless to add that a "literary history" which is satisfied with enumerating the "phrases" (whether famous or not) used by a writer (philosophical or otherwise), without establishing any connection between them and the mainspring of the writer's inspiration, is sham literary history.

14. According to Gundolf, in his essay on Schleiermacher. According to A. Götze, *Euphorion*, 1924, however, the word was not previously coined by him, but is a creation of his period.

15. Even with philologians (who are not by nature apt to be insensitive to literary values, as are so many of the so-called "linguists") one can discern "unhumanistic" prejudices. For example, Professor Entwistle ("Idealistic Extensions of Linguistics" in *Miscellania Fabra*, Buenos Aires, 1943) maintains that the linguistic interpretation of poetry implies the crossing of an intellectual frontier: the philologian has to deal not with "science" which treats of things that can be measured and weighed, not with "unambiguous facts" which can be tested by anyone, but with "knowledge" irreducible to "scientific" treatment—to which belongs hermeneutics, the study of the poet's meaning: this meaning cannot be treated in the "old assertive language" of the positivistic linguist, and still less can be the elusive significance of a poetic text, which transcends the poet's conscious intention. By such distinctions Professor Entwistle is perpetuating the nineteenth-century rift between positivistic science and wisdom. As concerns what Entwistle considers to be the purely scientific part of philology—such as the phonetic laws, which he ranks with the facts testable by everyone—I wonder if the formulation of a phonetic law is not as much of a speculation as is the attempt to discover the significance of a poetic passage; and is it really true that a phonetic law can be tested by anyone who has not had a preparation for this type of study? It can be done only to the same extent, I should think, which would hold true for the establishment of the meaning of a poetic passage. And as for the unconscious intentions of the poet, I simply would not advise the interpreter to concern himself with them. As a matter of fact, the example of "unconscious poetic intention" offered by Mr. Entwistle seems to me to show how little he has grasped the purpose of philological studies: of the passage from the *Aeneid* in which Aeneas sees depicted on the walls of Carthage the Trojan war and his father's deeds:

> *En Priamus! Sunt hic etiam sua praemia laudi;*
> *sunt lacrimae rerum, et mentem mortalia tangunt.*
> *Solve metus; feret haec aliquam tibi fama salutem.*

Entwistle writes: "The sense of the second last line, in its context, seems to be encouraging [he has translated it: "tears are shed for his misfortunes and his death moves men's minds to pity"]: it is better to be remembered sorrowfully than to be forgotten altogether. Yet *sunt lacrimae rerum* means something other and more moving than that. There is music and intensity in the line beyond anything Vergil may have consciously meant. . . . 'Nature's tears and the mortal sadness of mankind' has been discovered in that music by posterity, and, I think, justly so." But it can be *proved* by the philologist that Vergil *meant* (and it is only with conscious meaning that the philologian is concerned) the first, the "lesser" of the two meanings mentioned (as is indicated by the two anaphoric *sunt*'s which suggest a parallelism of arguments leading to the encouraging final line). The second meaning which has been attached to the line by posterity is an error due to its isolated consideration out of context (which led to the misinterpretation of *rerum* as "Nature" instead of "misfortunes," an error comparable to the famous misinterpretation of Buffon's "le style c'est l'homme même"—or even to many witty or punning misinterpretations of certain poetic lines (e.g. when the line of Schiller's Maid of Orleans: "Johanna geht und nimmer kehrt sie wieder" is facetiously interpreted to mean that never again will she sweep the floor). To the philologian this secondary graft or palimpsest imposed upon the original text may be historically quite interesting, but it has to be discarded from his interpretation of the given work of art. There is no music in Vergil's poetry but that which he put in it—but, by the same token, it is also necessary that this music be retained and not destroyed, as it is by such a translation as "tears are shed for *his* misfortunes and *his* death": the indefinite quality of "misfortune" and "death" should be preserved. Vergil's poetic music consists in the procedure of expanding the particular example of Priam's fate to that of man (and, similarly, *mortalia* should not be concretized to "death" but left as "the mortal fate"); it is the general gnome, so indissolubly linked by Vergil with the particular case, that posterity has arbitrarily detached (and, in addition to this antipoetic first move, has misinterpreted—this time poetically, in the manner mentioned above).

In this, as in the following studies, the reader will find me polemizing against the views of fellow scholars. I have sometimes been accused of raising up straw men just to knock them down, instead of being satisfied with offering my own picture of the phenomenon in question. My answer is that, in matters stylistic as well as in factual questions of literary history or linguistics, the *consensus omnium* is a desideratum, the only path to which is the discussion of the pros and cons of theories different from one's own, which enable us to vindicate the relative superiority of our own theory. The greater the objective certainty that a stylistic explanation can claim, the more we will have overcome that impressionism which, until recently, has seemed the only alternative to the positivistic treatment of literature.

16. The frequent occurrence, in my text, of quotations in the original foreign language (or languages) may prove a difficulty for the English reader. But since it is my purpose to take the word (and the wording) of the poets seriously, and since the convincingness and rigor of my stylistic conclusions depends entirely upon the minute linguistic detail of the original texts, it was impossible to offer translations.

17. Perhaps I should make it clear that I am using the word "method" in a manner somewhat aberrant from common American use: it is for me much more a "habitual procedure of the mind" (Lalande, *Vocabulaire de la philosophie*, s.v. *méthode* 1) than a "program regulating beforehand a series of operations . . . in view of reaching a well-defined result" (*ibid.* 2). As used by me it is nearly synonymous with *Erlebnis*, and consequently would correspond relatively to what is called in America "approach," were it not for the volitional and even "strategic" nuance, in this word, of military siege or of tracking down a quarry, by which it may be historically explained.

In this connection I may quote a passage from a letter of Descartes to Mersenne (*Oeuvres*, ed. Adam-Tannery, I, 347): "Mais ie n'ay sceu bien entendre ce que vous objectez touchant le titre [Discours de la Méthode]; car ie ne mets pas *Traité de la methode*, mais *Discours de la methode*, ce qui est le mesme que *Preface ou Advis touchant la methode*, pour monstrer que ie n'ay pas dessein de l'enseigner, mais seulement d'en parler. Car comme on peut voir de ce que i'en dis, elle consiste plus en Pratique qu'en Theorie, & ie nomme les Traitez suivans des *Essais de cette methode*, pource que ie pretens que les choses qu'ils contiennent n'ont pû estre trouvées sans elle, & qu'on peut connoistre par eux ce qu'elle vaut."

18. If I were to give one piece of advice to our students of literary history, it would be substantially the same as that which Lanson, touring the United States forty years ago, gave to the students of his time who were then, as they are now, only too eager to

rush to their big libraries to find in the many books of "secondary literature" an alibi for getting away from the "primary" texts they should study: *"Read your texts!"* My "circular method" is, in fact, nothing but an expansion of the common practice of "reading books": reading at its best requires a strange cohabitation in the human mind of two opposite capacities: contemplativity on the one hand and, on the other, a Protean mimeticism. That is to say: an undeflected patience that "stays with" a book until the forces latent in it unleash in us the recreative process.

19. Sometimes it may happen that this "etymology" leads simply to a characterization of the author that has been long accepted by literary historians (who have not needed, apparently, to follow the winding path I chose), and which can be summed up in a phrase which smacks of a college handbook. But, to make our own way to an old truth is not only to enrich our own understanding: it produces inevitably new evidence, of objective value, for this truth—which is thereby renewed. A *comédie-proverbe* of Musset is based, after all, on a commonplace saying: was it a waste of time to illustrate so wittily "il faut qu'une porte soit ouverte ou fermée"?

20. The requirement at St. John's for the Hundred Great Books is good, I believe, in so far as it may encourage the "click" to repeat itself in an accelerated manner—if, of course, it has come about in the first experiences: to have read these hundred books "without click" would be equivalent to not having read a single book.

T. S. Eliot

1888–1965

Thomas Stearns Eliot was born in St. Louis, Missouri on September 26, 1888, the son of a businessman in the rapidly industrializing town. His early education included the classics, languages, and ancient and modern history, preparing him for his later studies at Harvard in the American and European literary traditions. He was considerably influenced by his associations with George Santayana and the literary historian Irving Babbitt. The latter instructed Eliot against the individualistic philosophy of the Romantic period in favor of the more disciplined thought of classicism and tradition. Eliot also discovered Arthur Symons' *The Symbolist Movement in Literature* (1899), which directed his attention to Laforgue, Rimbaud, Verlaine, and Corbière. His studies in philosophy and literature continued at Harvard Graduate School in 1909 and at the Sorbonne in Paris in 1910, where he attended lectures by Henri Bergson. In 1911 Eliot returned to Harvard and began preparing his doctoral dissertation in philosophy on the English metaphysician F. H. Bradley. Three years later he was awarded a traveling fellowship to study Greek philosophy at Merton College, Oxford, at which time he began his long association with Ezra Pound.

Eliot's first important publication, "The Love Song of J. Alfred Prufrock," appeared in 1915 in *Poetry* at Pound's recommendation. In the same year Eliot married Vivienne Haigh-Wood, beginning an unstable marriage which ended in divorce in 1933. Before taking a position in the Foreign Department of Lloyd's Bank in 1917, Eliot earned a living by teaching and writing reviews. He also served as assistant editor to *The Egoist,* later founding his own magazine, *The Criterion,* in 1922. Eliot's role as poet-critic was further complemented by his association with the publishing firm of Faber & Faber beginning in 1925, placing him in one of the centers from which literature was judged and organized.

Following the publications of *Prufrock and Other Observations* (1917) and *Poems* (1919), *The Waste Land* appeared in 1922, having been extensively edited by Pound. *The Waste Land* illustrated Eliot's idea of "historical sense," discussed in his early essay "Tradition and the Individual Talent" (1919), by which a writer must combine the temporality of his own generation with the timelessness of his literary tradition. The poem's radically innovative form presented the reader with a poetic entity of images and expressions with which to apprehend and experience the dissociated world to which it referred. "The Hollow Men" (1925) framed accusations of bitterness and degeneration within the irony of ritual. Eliot's early interest in the Jacobean form of verse drama led him to experiment with the dramatic poetry of *Sweeney Agonistes* (1926), *The Rock* (1934), and *Murder in the Cathedral* (1935).

In 1927 Eliot converted to the Anglican Church and became a British subject. Religion offered a discipline by which to achieve some measure of understanding and peace through a cycle of suffering, despair, and renewal of will. Among the poems which address these possibilities are *Ash-Wednesday* (1930) and *Four Quartets* (1943). The latter examines man's relation to the cyclical process of time and the universe: "In my end is my beginning."

Eliot's extensive study of philosophy shaped his literary criticism as decisively as his poetry. His first collection of essays, *The Sacred Wood* (1920), included "Tradition and the Individual Talent." This essay contains Eliot's "impersonal theory of poetry" whereby poetry is not required to be aware of its influences and exists independently of them and its author, whereas criticism must have an end and must serve to analyze by intelligence and not by emotions. The role of the critic must never be creative or serve to highlight the critic rather than the poetry. Eliot acknowledged the idealism of such a definition and also asserted that a poet's criticism must be assessed in relation to his poetry. In his late essay "To Criticize the Critic" (1961) Eliot acknowledged the personal element in his criticism: "my best essays being, in my opinion, those concerned with writers who had influenced me in my poetry." Eliot saw the history of criticism as a continual readaptation of each particular age with the eternal and the permanent.

Eliot's own division of his literary criticism differentiates between the "essays of generalization" and "those of appreciation of individual authors." The former include "The Function of Criticism" (1923) and *The Use of Poetry and the Use of Criticism* (1933); the latter, appreciations of Pound, Joyce, Dante, Baudelaire, Pascal, Yeats, Milton, and Virgil. Eliot's philosophy of social criticism is represented in such essays as "The Idea of a Christian Society" (1939) and *Notes toward a Definition of Culture* (1949).

Eliot's last publications were *The Cocktail Party* (1950), *The Confidential Clerk* (1956), and *The Elder Statesman* (1959). He married his assistant, Valerie Fletcher, in 1957, with whom he remained until his death on January 4, 1965. His honors include the Order of Merit awarded by George VI, the 1948 Nobel Prize, and a memorial at Poets' Corner in Westminster Abbey.

TRADITION AND
THE INDIVIDUAL TALENT

In English writing we seldom speak of tradition, though we occasionally apply its name in deploring its absence. We cannot refer to "the tradition" or to "a tradition"; at most, we employ the adjective in saying that the poetry of So-and-so is "traditional" or even "too traditional." Seldom, perhaps, does the word appear except in a phrase of censure. If otherwise, it is vaguely approbative, with the implication, as to the work approved, of some pleasing archaeological reconstruction. You can hardly make the word agreeable to English ears without this comfortable reference to the reassuring science of archaeology.

Certainly the word is not likely to appear in our appreciations of living or dead writers. Every nation, every race, has not only its own creative, but its own critical turn of mind; and is even more oblivious of the shortcomings and limitations of its critical habits than of those of its creative genius. We know, or think we know, from the enormous mass of critical writing that has appeared in the French language the critical method or habit of the French; we only conclude (we are such unconscious people) that the French are "more critical" than we, and sometimes even plume ourselves a little with the fact, as if the French were the less spontaneous. Perhaps they are; but we might remind ourselves that criticism is as inevitable as breathing, and that we should be none the worse for articulating what passes in our minds when we read a book and feel an emotion about it, for criticizing our own minds in their work of criticism. One of the facts that might come to light in this process is our tendency to insist, when we praise a poet, upon those aspects of his work in which he least resembles any one else. In these aspects or parts of his work we pretend to find what is individual, what is the peculiar essence of the man. We dwell with satisfaction upon the poet's difference from his predecessors, especially his immediate predecessors; we endeavour to find something that can be isolated in order to be enjoyed. Whereas if we approach a poet without this prejudice we shall often find that not only the best, but the most individual parts of his work may be those in which the dead poets, his ancestors, assert their immortality most vigorously. And I do not mean the impressionable period of adolescence, but the period of full maturity.

Yet if the only form of tradition, of handing down, consisted in following the ways of the immediate generation before us in a blind or timid adherence to its successes, "tradition" should positively be discouraged. We have seen many such simple currents soon lost in the sand; and novelty is better than repetition. Tradition is a matter of much wider significance. It cannot be inherited, and if you want it you must obtain it by great labour. It involves, in the first place, the historical sense, which we may call nearly indispensable to any one who would continue to be a poet beyond his twenty-fifth year; and the historical sense involves a perception, not only of the pastness of the past, but of its presence; the historical sense compels a man to write not merely with his own generation in his bones, but with a feeling that the whole of the literature of Europe from Homer and within it the whole of the literature of his own country has a simultaneous existence and composes a simultaneous order. This historical sense, which is a sense of the timeless as well as of the temporal and of the timeless and of the temporal together, is what makes a writer traditional. And it is at the same time what makes a writer most acutely conscious of his place in time, of his own contemporaneity.

No poet, no artist of any art, has his complete meaning alone. His significance, his appreciation is the appreciation of his relation to the dead poets and artists. You cannot value him alone; you must set him, for contrast and comparison, among the dead. I mean this as a principle of aesthetic, not merely historical, criticism. The necessity that he shall conform, that he shall cohere, is not onesided; what happens when a new work of art is created is something that happens simultaneously to all the works of art which preceded it. The existing monuments form an ideal order among themselves, which is modified by the introduction of the new (the really new) work of art among them. The existing order is complete before the new work arrives; for order to persist after the supervention of novelty, the *whole* existing order must be, if ever so slightly, altered; and so the relations, proportions, values of each work of art toward the whole are readjusted; and this is conformity between the old and the new. Whoever has approved this idea of order, of the form of European, of English literature will not find it preposterous that the past should be altered by the present as much as the present is directed by the past. And the poet who is aware of this will be aware of great difficulties and responsibilities.

In a peculiar sense he will be aware also that he must inevitably be judged by the standards of the past. I say judged, not amputated, by them; not judged to be as good as, or worse or better than, the dead; and certainly not judged by the canons of dead critics. It is a judgment, a comparison, in which two things are measured by each other. To conform merely would be for the new work not really to conform at all; it would not be new, and would therefore not be a work of art. And we do not quite say that the new is more valuable because it fits in; but its fitting in is a test of its value—a test, it is true, which can only be slowly and cautiously applied, for we are none of us infallible judges of conformity. We say: it appears to conform, and is perhaps individual, or it appears individual, and many conform; but we are hardly likely to find that it is one and not the other.

To proceed to a more intelligible exposition of the relation of the poet to the past: he can neither take the past as a lump, an indiscriminate bolus, nor can he form himself wholly on one or two private admirations, nor can he form himself wholly upon one preferred period. The first course is inadmissible, the second is an important experience of youth, and the third is a pleasant and highly desirable supplement. The poet must be very conscious of the main current, which does not at all flow invariably through the most distinguished reputations. He must be quite aware of the obvious fact that art never improves, but that the material of art is never quite the same. He must be aware that the mind of Europe—the mind of his own country—a mind which he learns in time to be much more important than his own private mind—is a mind which changes, and that this change is a development which abandons nothing *en route*, which does not superannuate either Shakespeare, or Homer, or the rock drawing of the Magdalenian draughtsmen. That this development, refinement perhaps, complication certainly, is not, from the point of view of the artist, any improvement. Perhaps not even an improvement from the point of view of the psychologist or not to the extent which we imagine; perhaps only in the end based upon a complication in economics and machinery. But the difference between the present and the past is that the conscious present is an awareness of the past in a way and to an extent which the past's awareness of itself cannot show.

Some one said: "The dead writers are remote from us because we *know* so much more than they did." Precisely, and they are that which we know.

I am alive to a usual objection to what is clearly part of my programme for the *métier* of poetry. The objection is that the doctrine requires a ridiculous amount of erudition (pedantry), a claim which can be rejected by appeal to the lives of poets in any pantheon. It will even be affirmed that much learning deadens or perverts poetic sensibility. While, however, we persist in believing that a poet ought to know as much as will not encroach upon his necessary receptivity and necessary laziness, it is not desirable to confine knowledge to whatever can be put into a useful shape for examinations, drawing-rooms, or the still more pretentious modes of publicity. Some can absorb knowledge, the more tardy must sweat for it. Shakespeare acquired more essential history from Plutarch than most men could from the whole British Museum. What is to be insisted upon is that the poet must develop or procure the consciousness of the past and that he should continue to develop this consciousness throughout his career.

What happens is a continual surrender of himself as he is at the moment to something which is more valuable. The progress of an artist is a continual self-sacrifice, a continual extinction of personality.

There remains to define this process of depersonalization and its relation to the sense of tradition. It is in this depersonalization that art may be said to approach the condition of science. I, therefore, invite you to consider, as a suggestive analogy, the action which takes place when a bit of finely filiated platinum is introduced into a chamber containing oxygen and sulphur dioxide.

II

Honest criticism and sensitive appreciation are directed not upon the poet but upon the poetry. If we attend to the confused cries of the newspaper critics and the *susurrus* of popular repetition that follows, we shall hear the names of poets in great numbers; if we seek not Blue-book knowledge but the enjoyment of poetry, and ask for a poem, we shall seldom find it. I have tried to point out the importance of the relation of the poem to other poems by other authors, and suggested the conception of poetry as a living whole of all the poetry that has ever been written. The other aspect of this Impersonal theory of poetry is the relation of the poem to its author. And I hinted, by an analogy, that the mind of the mature poet differs from that of the immature one not precisely in any valuation of "personality," not being necessarily more interesting, or having "more to say," but rather by being a more finely perfected medium in which special, or very varied, feelings are at liberty to enter into new combinations.

The analogy was that of the catalyst. When the two gases previously mentioned are mixed in the presence of a filament of platinum, they form sulphurous acid. This combination takes place only if the platinum is present; nevertheless the newly formed acid contains no trace of platinum, and the platinum itself is apparently unaffected; has remained inert, neutral, and unchanged. The mind of the poet is the shred of platinum. It may partly or exclusively operate upon the experience of the man himself; but, the more perfect the artist, the more completely separate in him will be the man who suffers and the mind which creates; the more perfectly will the mind digest and transmute the passions which are its material.

The experience, you will notice, the elements which enter the presence of the transforming catalyst, are of two kinds: emotions and feelings. The effect of a work of art upon the person who enjoys it is an experience different in kind from any experience not of art. It may be formed out of one emotion, or may be a combination of several; and various feelings, inhering for the writer in particular words or phrases or images, may be added to compose the final result. Or great poetry may be made without the direct use of any emotion whatever: composed out of feelings solely. Canto XV of the *Inferno* (Brunetto Latini) is a working up of the emotion evident in the situation; but the effect, though single as that of any work of art, is obtained by considerable complexity of detail. The last quatrain gives an image, a feeling attaching to an image, which "came," which did not develop simply out of what precedes, but which was probably in suspension in the poet's mind until the proper combination arrived for it to add itself to. The poet's mind is in fact a receptacle for seizing and storing up numberless feelings, phrases, images, which remain there until all the particles which can unite to form a new compound are present together.

If you compare several representative passages of the greatest poetry you see how great is the variety of types of combination, and also how completely any semi-ethical criterion of "sublimity" misses the mark. For it is not the "greatness," the intensity, of the emotions, the components, but the intensity of the artistic process, the pressure, so to speak, under which the fusion takes place, that counts. The episode of Paolo and Francesca employs a definite emotion, but the intensity of the poetry is something quite different from whatever intensity in the supposed experience it may give the impression of. It is no more intense, furthermore, than Canto XXVI, the voyage of Ulysses, which has not the direct dependence upon an emotion. Great variety is possible in the process of transmutation of emotion: the murder of Agamemnon, or the agony of Othello, gives an artistic effect apparently closer to a possible original than the scenes from Dante. In the *Agamemnon,* the artistic emotion approximates to the emotion of an actual spectator; in *Othello* to the emotion of the protagonist himself. But the difference between art and the event is always absolute; the combination which is the murder of Agamemnon is probably as complex as that which is the voyage of Ulysses. In either case there has been a fusion of elements. The ode of Keats contains a number of feelings which have nothing particular to do with the nightingale, but which the nightingale, partly, perhaps, because of its attractive name, and partly because of its reputation, served to bring together.

The point of view which I am struggling to attack is perhaps related to the metaphysical theory of the substantial unity of the soul: for my meaning is, that the poet has, not a "personality" to express, but a particular medium, which is only a medium and not a personality, in which impressions and experiences combine in peculiar and unexpected ways. Impressions and experiences which are important for the man may take no place in the poetry, and those which become important in the poetry may play quite a negligible part in the man, the personality.

I will quote a passage which is unfamiliar enough to be regarded with fresh attention in the light—or darkness—of these observations:

> And now methinks I could e'en chide myself
> For doating on her beauty, though her death
> Shall be revenged after no common action.
> Does the silkworm expend her yellow labours
> For thee? For thee does she undo herself?
> Are lordships sold to maintain ladyships
> For the poor benefit of a bewildering minute?
> Why does yon fellow falsify highways,
> And put his life between the judge's lips,
> To refine such a thing—keeps horse and men
> To beat their valours for her? . . .

In this passage (as is evident if it is taken in its context) there is a combination of positive and negative emotions: an intensely strong attraction toward beauty and an equally intense fascination by the ugliness which is contrasted with it and which destroys it. This balance of contrasted emotion is in the dramatic situation to which the speech is pertinent, but that situation alone is inadequate to it. This is, so to speak, the structural emotion, provided by the drama. But the whole effect, the dominant tone, is due to the fact that a number of floating feelings, having an affinity to this emotion by no means superficially evident, have combined with it to give us a new art emotion.

It is not in his personal emotions, the emotions provoked by particular events in his life, that the poet is in any way remarkable or interesting. His particular emotions may be simple, or crude, or flat. The emotion in his poetry will be a very complex thing, but not with the complexity of the emotions of people who have very complex or unusual emotions in life. One error, in fact, of eccentricity in poetry is to seek for new human emotions to express; and in this search for novelty in the wrong place it discovers the perverse. The business of the poet is not to find new emotions, but to use the ordinary ones and, in working them up into poetry, to express feelings which are not in actual emotions at all. And emotions which he has never experienced will serve his turn as well as those familiar to him. Consequently, we must believe that "emotion recollected in tranquillity" is an inexact formula. For it is neither emotion, nor recollection, nor, without distortion of meaning, tranquillity. It is a concentration, and a new thing resulting from the concentration, of a very great number of experiences which to the practical and active person would not seem to be experiences at all; it is a concentration which does not happen consciously or of deliberation. These experiences are not "recollected," and they finally unite in an atmosphere which is "tranquil" only in that it is a passive attending upon the event. Of course this is not quite the whole story. There is a great deal, in the writing of poetry, which must be conscious and deliberate. In fact, the bad poet is usually unconscious where he ought to be conscious, and conscious where he ought to be unconscious. Both errors tend to make him "personal." Poetry is not a turning loose of emotion, but an escape from emotion; it is not the expression of personality, but an escape from personality. But, of course, only those who have personality and emotions know what it means to want to escape from these things.

III

ὁ δὲ νοῦς ἴσως θειότερόν τι χαὶ ἀπαθές ἐστιν.

This essay proposes to halt at the frontier of metaphysics or mysticism, and confine itself to such practical conclusions as can be applied by the responsible person interested in poetry. To divert interest from the poet to the poetry is a laudible aim: for it would conduce to a juster estimation of actual poetry, good and bad. There are many people who appreciate the expression of sincere emotion in verse, and there is a smaller number of people who can appreciate technical excellence. But very few know when there is an expression of *significant* emotion, emotion which has its life in the poem and not in the history of the poet. The emotion of art is impersonal. And the poet cannot reach this impersonality without surrendering himself wholly to the work to be done. And he is not likely to know what is to be done unless he lives in what is not merely the present, but the present moment of the past, unless he is conscious, not of what is dead, but of what is already living.

THE FUNCTION OF CRITICISM

W riting several years ago on the subject of the relation of the new to the old in art, I formulated a view to which I still adhere, in sentences which I take the liberty of quoting, because the present paper is an application of the principles they express:

"The existing monuments form an ideal order among themselves, which is modified by the introduction of the new (the really new) work of art among them. The existing order is complete before the new work arrives; for order to persist after the supervention of novelty, the *whole* existing order must be, if ever so slightly, altered; and so the relations, proportions, values of each work of art toward the whole are readjusted; and this is conformity between the old and the new. Whoever has approved this idea of order, of the form of European, of English literature, will not find it preposterous that the past should be altered by the present as much as the present is directed by the past."

I was dealing then with the artist, and the sense of tradition which, it seemed to me, the artist should have; but it was generally a problem of order; and the function of criticism seems to be essentially a problem of order too. I thought of literature then, as I think of it now, of the literature of the world, of the literature of Europe, of the literature of a single country, not as a collection of the writings of individuals, but as "organic wholes," as systems in relation to which, and only in relation to which, individual works of literary art, and the works of individual artists, have their significance. There is accordingly something outside of the artist to which he owes allegiance, a devotion to which he must surrender and sacrifice himself in order to earn and to obtain his unique position. A common inheritance and a common cause unite artists consciously or unconsciously: it must be admitted that the union is mostly unconscious. Between the true artists of any time there is, I believe, an unconscious community. And, as our instincts of tidiness imperatively command us not to leave to the haphazard of unconsciousness what we can attempt to do consciously, we are forced to conclude that what happens unconsciously we could bring about, and form into a purpose, if we made a conscious attempt. The second-rate artist, of course, cannot afford to surrender himself to any common action; for his chief task is the assertion of all the trifling differences which are his distinction: only the man who has so much to give that he can forget himself in his work can afford to collaborate, to exchange, to contribute.

If such views are held about art, it follows that *a fortiori* whoever holds them must hold similar views about criticism. When I say criticism, I mean of course in this place the commentation and exposition of works of art by means of written words; for of the general use of the word "criticism" to mean such writings, as Matthew Arnold uses it in his essay, I shall presently make several qualifications. No exponent of criticism (in this limited sense) has, I presume, ever made the preposterous assumption that criticism is an autotelic activity. I do not deny that art may be affirmed to serve ends beyond itself; but art is not required to be aware of these ends, and indeed performs its function, whatever that may be, according to various theories of value, much better by indifference to them. Criticism, on the other hand, must always profess an end in view, which, roughly speaking, appears to be the elucidation of works of art and the correction of taste. The critic's task, therefore, appears to be quite clearly cut out for him; and it ought to be comparatively easy to decide whether he performs it satisfactorily, and in general, what kinds of criticism are useful and what are otiose. But on giving the matter a little attention, we perceive that criticism, far from being a simple and orderly field of beneficent activity, from which impostors can be readily ejected, is no better than a Sunday park of contending and contentious orators, who have not even arrived at the articulation of their differences. Here, one would suppose, was a place for quiet co-operative labour. The critic, one would suppose, if he is to justify his existence, should endeavour to discipline his personal prejudices and cranks— tares to which we are all subject—and compose his differences with as many of his fellows as possible, in the common pursuit of true judgment. When we find that quite the contrary prevails, we begin to suspect that the critic owes his livelihood to the violence and extremity of his opposition to other critics, or else to some trifling oddities of his own with which he contrives to season the opinions which men already hold, and which out of vanity or sloth they prefer to maintain. We are tempted to expel the lot.

Immediately after such an eviction, or as soon as relief has abated our rage, we are compelled to admit that there remain certain books, certain essays, certain sentences, certain men, who have been "useful" to us. And our next step is to attempt to classify these, and find out whether we establish any principles for deciding what kinds of book should be preserved, and what aims and methods of criticism should be followed.

II

The view of the relation of the work of art to art, of the work of literature to literature, of "criticism" to criticism, which I have outlined above, seemed to me natural and self-evident. I owe to Mr. Middleton Murry my perception of the contentious character of the problem; or rather, my perception that there is a definite and final choice involved. To Mr. Murry I feel an increasing debt of gratitude. Most of our critics are occupied in labour of obnubilation; in reconciling, in hushing up, in patting down, in squeezing in, in glozing over, in concocting pleasant sedatives, in pretending that the only difference between themselves and others is that they are nice men and the others of very doubtful repute. Mr. Murry is not one of these. He is aware that there are definite positions to be taken, and that now and then one must actually reject something and select something else. He is not the anonymous writer who in a literery paper several years ago asserted that Romanticism and Classicism are much the same thing, and that the true Classical Age in France was the

Age which produced the Gothic cathedrals and—Jeanne d'Arc. With Mr. Murry's formulation of Classicism and Romanticism I cannot agree; the difference seems to me rather the difference between the complete and the fragmentary, the adult and the immature, the orderly and the chaotic. But what Mr. Murry does show is that there are at least two attitudes toward literature and toward everything, and that you cannot hold both. And the attitude which he professes appears to imply that the other has no standing in England whatever. For it is made a national, a racial issue.

Mr. Murry makes his issue perfectly clear. "Catholicism," he says, "stands for the principle of unquestioned spiritual authority outside the individual; that is also the principle of Classicism in literature." Within the orbit within which Mr. Murry's discussion moves, this seems to me an unimpeachable definition, though it is of course not all that there is to be said about either Catholicism or Classicism. Those of us who find ourselves supporting what Mr. Murry calls Classicism believe that men cannot get on without giving allegiance to something outside themselves. I am aware that "outside" and "inside" are terms which provide unlimited opportunity for quibbling, and that no psychologist would tolerate a discussion which shuffled such base coinage; but I will presume that Mr. Murry and myself can agree that for our purpose these counters are adequate, and concur in disregarding the admonitions of our psychological friends. If you find that you have to imagine it as outside, then it is outside. If, then, a man's interest is political, he must, I presume, profess an allegiance to principles, or to a form of government, or to a monarch; and if he is interested in religion, and has one, to a Church; and if he happens to be interested in literature, he must acknowledge, it seems to me, just that sort of allegiance which I endeavoured to put forth in the preceding section. There is, nevertheless, an alternative, which Mr. Murry has expressed. "The English writer, the English divine, the English statesman, inherit no rules from their forebears; they inherit only this: a sense that in the last resort they must depend upon the inner voice." This statement does, I admit, appear to cover certain cases; it throws a flood of light upon Mr. Lloyd George. But why "*in the last resort*"? Do they, then, avoid the dictates of the inner voice up to the last extremity? My belief is that those who possess this inner voice are ready enough to hearken to it, and will hear no other. The inner voice, in fact, sounds remarkably like an old principle which has been formulated by an elder critic in the now familiar phrase of "doing as one likes." The possessors of the inner voice ride ten in a compartment to a football match at Swansea, listening to the inner voice, which breathes the eternal message of vanity, fear, and lust.

Mr. Murry will say, with some show of justice, that this is a wilful misrepresentation. He says: "If they (the English writer, divine, statesman) dig *deep enough* in their pursuit of self-knowledge—a piece of mining done not with the intellect alone, but with the whole man—they will come upon a self that is universal"—an exercise far beyond the strength of our football enthusiasts. It is an exercise, however, which I believe was of enough interest to Catholicism for several handbooks to be written on its practice. But the Catholic practitioners were, I believe, with the possible exception of certain heretics, not palpitating Narcissi; the Catholic did not believe that God and himself were identical. "The man who truly interrogates himself will ulti- mately hear the voice of God," Mr. Murry says. In theory, this leads to a form of pantheism which I maintain is not European—just as Mr. Murry maintains that "Classicism" is not English. For its practical results, one may refer to the verses of *Hudibras*.

I did not realise that Mr. Murry was the spokesman for a considerable sect, until I read in the editorial columns of a dignified daily that "magnificent as the representatives of the classical genius have been in England, they are not the sole expressions of the English character, which remains at bottom obstinately 'humorous' and nonconformist." This writer is moderate in using the qualifi- cation *sole,* and brutally frank in attributing this "humorousness" to "the unreclaimed Teutonic element in us." But it strikes me that Mr. Murry, and this other voice, are either too obstinate or too tolerant. The question is, the first question, *not* what comes natural or what comes *easy* to us, but what is right? Either one attitude is better than the other, or else it is indifferent. But how can such a choice be indifferent? Surely the reference to racial origins, or the mere statement that the French are thus, and the English otherwise, is not expected to settle the question: which, of two antithetical views, is *right*? And I cannot understand why the opposition between Classicism and Romanticism should be profound enough in Latin countries (Mr. Murry says it is) and yet of no significance among ourselves. For if the French are *naturally* classical, why should there be any "opposition" in France, any more than there is here? And if Classicism is not natural to them, but something acquired, why not acquire it here? Were the French in the year 1600 classical, and the English in the same year romantic? A more important difference, to my mind, is that the French in the year 1600 *had already a more mature prose*.

III

This discussion may seem to have led us a long way from the subject of this paper. But it was worth my while to follow Mr. Murry's comparison of Outside Authority with the Inner Voice. For to those who obey the inner voice (perhaps "obey" is not the word) nothing that I can say about criticism will have the slightest value. For they will not be interested in the attempt to find any common principles for the pursuit of criticism. Why have principles, when one has the inner voice? If I like a thing, that is all I want; and if enough of us, shouting all together, like it, that should be all that *you* (who don't like it) ought to want. The law of art, said Mr. Clutton Brock, is all case law. And we can not only like whatever we like to like but we can like it for any reason we choose. We are not, in fact, concerned with literary *perfection* at all—the search for perfection is a sign of pettiness, for it shows that the writer has admitted the existence of an unquestioned spiritual authority outside himself, to which he has attempted to *conform*. We are not in fact interested in art. We will not worship Baal. "The principle of classical leadership is that obeisance is made to the office or to the tradition, never to the man." And we want, not principles, but men.

Thus speaks the Inner Voice. It is a voice to which, for convenience, we may give a name: and the name I suggest is Whiggery.

IV

Leaving, then, those whose calling and election are sure and returning to those who shamefully depend upon tradition and the accumulated wisdom of time, and restricting the discussion to those who sympathise with each other in this frailty, we may comment for a moment upon the use of the terms "critical" and "creative" by one whose place, on the whole, is with the weaker brethren. Matthew Arnold distinguishes far too bluntly, it seems to me, between the two activities: he overlooks the capital importance of criticism in the work of creation itself. Probably, indeed, the larger part of the labour of an author in composing his work is critical labour; the labour of sifting, combining, constructing, expunging, correcting, testing: this frightful toil is as much critical as creative. I maintain even that the criticism employed by a trained and skilled writer on his own work is the most vital, the highest kind of criticism; and (as I think I have said before) that some creative writers are superior to others solely because their critical faculty is superior. There is a tendency, and I think it is a whiggery tendency, to decry this critical toil of the artist; to propound the thesis that the great artist is an unconscious artist, unconsciously inscribing on his banner the words Muddle Through. Those of us who are Inner Deaf Mutes are, however, sometimes compensated by a humble conscience, which, though without oracular expertness, counsels us to do the best we can, reminds us that our compositions ought to be as free from defects as possible (to atone for their lack of inspiration), and, in short, makes us waste a good deal of time. We are aware, too, that the critical discrimination which comes so hardly to us has in more fortunate men flashed in the very heat of creation; and we do not assume that because works have been composed without apparent critical labour, no critical labour has been done. We do not know what previous labours have prepared, or what goes on, in the way of criticism, all the time in the minds of the creators.

But this affirmation recoils upon us. If so large a part of creation is really criticism, is not a large part of what is called "critical writing" really creative? If so, is there not creative criticism in the ordinary sense? The answer seems to be, that there is no equation. I have assumed as axiomatic that a creation, a work of art, is autotelic; and that criticism, by definition, is *about* something other than itself. Hence you cannot fuse creation with criticism as you can fuse criticism with creation. The critical activity finds its highest, its true fulfilment in a kind of union with creation in the labour of the artist.

But no writer is completely self-sufficient, and many creative writers have a critical activity which is not all discharged into their work. Some seem to require to keep their critical powers in condition for the real work by exercising them miscellaneously; others, on completing a work, need to continue the critical activity by commenting on it. There is no general rule. And as men can learn from each other, so some of these treatises have been useful to other writers. And some of them have been useful to those who were not writers.

At one time I was inclined to take the extreme position that the *only* critics worth reading were the critics who practised, and practised well, the art of which they wrote. But I had to stretch this frame to make some important inclusions; and I have since been in search of a formula which should cover everything I wished to include, even if it included more than I wanted. And the most important qualification which I have been able to find, which accounts for the peculiar importance of the criticism of practitioners, is that a critic must have a very highly developed sense of fact. This is by no means a trifling or frequent gift. And it is not one which easily wins popular commendations. The sense of fact is something very slow to develop, and its complete development means perhaps the very pinnacle of civilisation. For there are so many spheres of fact to be mastered, and our outermost sphere of fact, of knowledge, of control, will be ringed with narcotic fancies in the sphere beyond. To the member of the Browning Study Circle, the discussion of poets about poetry may seem arid, technical, and limited. It is merely that the practitioners have clarified and reduced to a state of fact all the feelings that the member can only enjoy in the most nebulous form; the dry technique implies, for those who have mastered it, all that the member thrills to; only that has been made into something precise, tractable, under control. That, at all events, is one reason for the value of the practitioner's criticism—he is dealing with his facts, and he can help us to do the same.

And at every level of criticism I find the same necessity regnant. There is a large part of critical writing which consists in "interpreting" an author, a work. This is not on the level of the Study Circle either; it occasionally happens that one person obtains an understanding of another, or a creative writer, which he can partially communicate, and which we feel to be true and illuminating. It is difficult to confirm the "interpretation" by external evidence. To any one who is skilled in fact on this level there will be evidence enough. But who is to prove his own skill? And for every success in this type of writing there are thousands of impostures. Instead of insight, you get a fiction. Your test is to apply it again and again to the original, with your view of the original to guide you. But there is no one to guarantee your competence, and once again we find ourselves in a dilemma.

We must ourselves decide what is useful to us and what is not; and it is quite likely that we are not competent to decide. But it is fairly certain that "interpretation" (I am not touching upon the acrostic element in literature) is only legitimate when it is not interpretation at all, but merely putting the reader in possession of facts which he would otherwise have missed. I have had some experience of Extension lecturing, and I have found only two ways of leading any pupils to like anything with the right liking: to present them with a selection of the simpler kind of facts about a work—its conditions, its setting, its genesis—or else to spring the work on them in such a way that they were not prepared to be prejudiced against it. There were many facts to help them with Elizabethan drama: the poems of T. E. Hulme only needed to be read aloud to have immediate effect.

Comparison and analysis, I have said before, and Remy de Gourmont has said before me (a real master of fact—sometimes, I am afraid, when he moved outside of literature, a master illusionist of fact), are the chief tools of the critic. It is obvious indeed that they *are* tools, to be handled with care, and not employed in an inquiry into the number of times giraffes are mentioned in the English novel. They are not used with conspicuous success by many contemporary writers. You must know what to compare and what to analyse. The late Professor Ker had skill in the use of these tools. Comparison and analysis need only the cadavers on the table; but interpretation is always producing parts of the body from its pockets, and fixing them in place. And any book, any essay, any note in *Notes and Queries*, which produces a fact even of the lowest order about a work of art is a better piece of work than nine-tenths of the most pretentious critical journalism, in journals or in books. We assume, of course, that we are masters and not servants of facts, and that we know that the discovery of Shakespeare's laundry bills would not be of much use to us; but we must always reserve final judgment as to the futility of the research which has discovered them, in the possibility that some genius will appear who will know of a use to which to put them. Scholarship, even in its humblest forms, has its rights; we assume that we know how to use it, and how to neglect it. Of course the multiplication of critical books and essays may create, and I have seen it create, a vicious taste for reading about works of art instead of reading the works themselves, it may supply opinion instead of educating taste. But *fact* cannot corrupt taste; it can at worst gratify one taste—a taste for history, let us say, or antiquities, or biography—under the illusion that it is assisting another. The real corrupters are those who supply opinion or fancy; and Goethe and Coleridge are not guiltless—for what is Coleridge's *Hamlet:* is it an honest inquiry as far as the data permit, or is it an attempt to present Coleridge in an attractive costume?

We have not succeeded in finding such a test as any one can apply; we have been forced to allow ingress to innumerable dull and tedious books; but we have, I think, found a test which, for those who are able to apply it, will dispose of the really vicious ones. And with this test we may return to the preliminary statement of the polity of literature and of criticism. For the kinds of critical work which we have admitted, there is the possibility of co-operative activity, with the further possibility of arriving at something outside of ourselves, which may provisionally be called truth. But if any one complains that I have not defined truth, or fact, or reality, I can only say apologetically that it was no part of my purpose to do so, but only to find a scheme into which, whatever they are, they will fit, if they exist.

THE METAPHYSICAL POETS

By collecting these poems [*Metaphysical Lyrics and Poems of the Seventeenth Century: Donne to Butler.* Selected and edited, with an Essay, by Herbert J. C. Grierson (Oxford: Clarendon Press. London: Milford)] from the work of a generation more often named than read, and more often read than profitably studied, Professor Grierson has rendered a service of some importance. Certainly the reader will meet with many poems already preserved in other anthologies, at the same time that he discovers poems such as those of Aurelian Townshend or Lord Herbert of Cherbury here included. But the function of such an anthology as this is neither that of Professor Saintsbury's admirable edition of Caroline poets nor that of the *Oxford Book of English Verse*. Mr. Grierson's book is in itself a piece of criticism and a provocation of criticism; and we think that he was right in including so many poems of Donne, elsewhere (though not in many editions) accessible, as documents in the case of "metaphysical poetry." The phrase has long done duty as a term of abuse or as the label of a quaint and pleasant taste. The question is to what extent the so-called metaphysicals formed a school (in our own time we should say a "movement"), and how far this so-called school or movement is a digression from the main current.

Not only is it extremely difficult to define metaphysical poetry, but difficult to decide what poets practise it and in which of their verses. The poetry of Donne (to whom Marvell and Bishop King are sometimes nearer than any of the other authors) is late Elizabethan, its feeling often very close to that of Chapman. The "courtly" poetry is derivative from Jonson, who borrowed liberally from the Latin; it expires in the next century with the sentiment and witticism of Prior. There is finally the devotional verse of Herbert, Vaughan, and Crashaw (echoed long after by Christina Rossetti and Francis Thompson); Crashaw, sometimes more profound and less sectarian than the others, has a quality which returns through the Elizabethan period to the early Italians. It is difficult to find any precise use of metaphor, simile, or other conceit, which is common to all the poets and at the same time important enough as an element of style to isolate these poets as a group. Donne, and often Cowley, employ a device which is sometimes considered characteristically "metaphysical"; the elaboration (contrasted with the condensation) of a figure of speech to the farthest stage to which ingenuity can carry it. Thus Cowley develops the commonplace comparison of the world to a chess-board through long stanzas ("To Destiny"), and Donne, with more grace, in "A Valediction," the comparison of two lovers to a pair of compasses. But elsewhere we find, instead of the mere explication of the content of a comparison, a development by rapid association of thought which requires considerable agility on the part of the reader.

> On a round ball
> A workman that hath copies by, can lay
> An Europe, Afrique, and an Asia,
> And quickly make that, which was nothing, All,
> So doth each teare,
> Which thee doth weare,
> A globe, yea, world by that impression grow,
> Till thy tears mixt with mine doe overflow
> This world, by waters sent from thee, my heaven dissolved so.

Here we find at least two connexions which are not implicit in the first figure, but are forced upon it by the poet: from the geographer's globe to the tear, and the tear to the deluge. On the other hand, some of Donne's most successful and characteristic effects are secured by brief words and sudden contrasts:

> A bracelet of bright hair about the bone,

where the most powerful effect is produced by the sudden contrast of associations of "bright hair" and of "bone." This telescoping of images and multiplied associations is characteristic of the phrase of some of the dramatists of the period which Donne knew: not to mention Shakespeare, it is frequent in Middleton, Webster, and Tourneur, and is one of the sources of the vitality of their language.

Johnson, who employed the term "metaphysical poets," apparently having Donne, Cleveland, and Cowley chiefly in mind, remarks of them that "the most heterogeneous ideas are yoked by violence together." The force of this impeachment lies in the failure of the conjunction, the fact that often the ideas are yoked but not united; and if we are to judge of styles of poetry by their abuse, enough examples may be found in Cleveland to justify Johnson's condemnation. But a degree of heterogeneity of material compelled into unity by the operation of the poet's mind is omnipresent in poetry. We need not select for illustration such a line as:

> Notre âme est un trois-mâts cherchant son Icarie;

We may find it in some of the best lines of Johnson himself (*The Vanity of Human Wishes*):

> His fate was destined to a barren strand,
> A petty fortress, and a dubious hand;
> He left a name at which the world grew pale,
> To point a moral, or adorn a tale.

where the effect is due to a contrast of ideas, different in degree but the same in principle, as that which Johnson mildly reprehended. And in one of the finest poems of the age (a poem which could not have been written in any other age), the *Exequy* of Bishop King, the extended comparison is used with perfect success: the idea and the simile become one, in the passage in which the Bishop illustrates his impatience to see his dead wife, under the figure of a journey:

> Stay for me there; I will not faile
> To meet thee in that hollow Vale.
> And think not much of my delay;
> I am already on the way,
> And follow thee with all the speed
> Desire can make, or sorrows breed.
> Each minute is a short degree,
> And ev'ry houre a step towards thee.
> At night when I betake to rest,
> Next morn I rise nearer my West
> Of life, almost by eight houres sail,
> Than when sleep breath'd his drowsy gale. . . .
> But heark! My Pulse, like a soft Drum
> Beats my approach, tells *Thee* I come;
> And slow howere my marches be,
> I shall at last sit down by *Thee*.

(In the last few lines there is that effect of terror which is several times attained by one of Bishop King's admirers, Edgar Poe.) Again, we may justly take these quatrains from Lord Herbert's Ode, stanzas which would, we think, be immediately pronounced to be of the metaphysical school:

> So when from hence we shall be gone,
>   And be no more, nor you, nor I,
>   As one another's mystery,
> Each shall be both, yet both but one.
> This said, in her up-lifted face,
>   Her eyes, which did that beauty crown,
>   Were like two starrs, that having faln down,
> Look up again to find their place:
> While such a moveless silent peace
>   Did seize on their becalmed sense,
>   One would have thought some influence
> Their ravished spirits did possess.

There is nothing in these lines (with the possible exception of the stars, a simile not at once grasped, but lovely and justified) which fits Johnson's general observations on the metaphysical poets in his essay on Cowley. A good deal resides in the richness of association which is at the same time borrowed from and given to the word "becalmed"; but the meaning is clear, the language simple and elegant. It is to be observed that the language of these poets is as a rule simple and pure; in the verse of George Herbert this simplicity is carried as far as it can go—a simplicity emulated without success by numerous modern poets. The *structure* of the sentences, on the other hand, is sometimes far from simple, but this is not a vice; it is a fidelity to thought and feeling. The effect, at its best, is far less artificial than that of an ode by Gray. And as this fidelity induces variety of thought and feeling, so it induces variety of music. We doubt whether, in the eighteenth century, could be found two poems in nominally the same metre, so dissimilar as Marvell's "Coy Mistress" and Crashaw's "Saint Teresa"; the one producing an effect of great speed by the use of short syllables, and the other an ecclesiastical solemnity by the use of long ones:

> Love, thou art absolute sole lord
> Of life and death.

If so shrewd and sensitive (though so limited) a critic as Johnson failed to define metaphysical poetry by its faults, it is worth while to inquire whether we may not have more success by adopting the opposite method: by assuming that the poets of the seventeenth century (up to the Revolution) were the direct and normal development of the precedent age; and, without prejudicing their case by the adjective "metaphysical," consider whether their virtue was not something permanently valuable, which subsequently disappeared, but ought not to have disappeared. Johnson has hit, perhaps by accident, on one of their peculiarities, when he observes that "their attempts were always analytic"; he would not agree that, after the dissociation, they put the material together again in a new unity.

It is certain that the dramatic verse of the later Elizabethan and early Jacobean poets expresses a degree of development of sensibility which is not found in any of the prose, good as it often is. If we except Marlowe, a man of prodigious intelligence, these dramatists were directly or indirectly (it is at least a tenable theory) affected by Montaigne. Even if we except also Jonson and Chapman, these two were notably erudite, and were notably men who incorporated their erudition into their sensibility: their mode of feeling was directly and freshly altered by their reading and thought. In Chapman especially there is a direct sensuous apprehension of thought, or a recreation of thought into feeling, which is exactly what we find in Donne:

> in this one thing, all the discipline
> Of manners and of manhood is contained;
> A man to join himself with th' Universe
> In his main sway, and make in all things fit
> One with that All, and go on, round as it;
> Not plucking from the whole his wretched part,
> And into straits, or into nought revert,
> Wishing the complete Universe might be
> Subject to such a rag of it as he;
> But to consider great Necessity.

We compare this with some modern passage:

No, when the fight begins within himself,
A man's worth something. God stoops o'er his head,
Satan looks up between his feet—both tug—
He's left, himself, i' the middle; the soul wakes
And grows. Prolong that battle through his life!

It is perhaps somewhat less fair, though very tempting (as both poets are concerned with the perpetuation of love by offspring), to compare with the stanzas already quoted from Lord Herbert's Ode the following from Tennyson:

One walked between his wife and child,
With measured footfall firm and mild,
And now and then he gravely smiled.
  The prudent partner of his blood
  Leaned on him, faithful, gentle, good,
  Wearing the rose of womanhood.
And in their double love secure,
The little maiden walked demure,
Pacing with downward eyelids pure.
These three made unity so sweet,
My frozen heart began to beat,
Remembering its ancient heat.

The difference is not a simple difference of degree between poets. It is something which had happened to the mind of England between the time of Donne or Lord Herbert of Cherbury and the time of Tennyson and Browning; it is the difference between the intellectual poet and the reflective poet. Tennyson and Browning are poets, and they think; but they do not feel their thought as immediately as the odour of a rose. A thought to Donne was an experience; it modified his sensibility. When a poet's mind is perfectly equipped for its work, it is constantly amalgamating disparate experience; the ordinary man's experience is chaotic, irregular, fragmentary. The latter falls in love, or reads Spinoza, and these two experiences have nothing to do with each other, or with the noise of the typewriter or the smell of cooking; in the mind of the poet these experiences are always forming new wholes.

We may express the difference by the following theory: The poets of the seventeenth century, the successors of the dramatists of the sixteenth, possessed a mechanism of sensibility which could devour any kind of experience. They are simple, artificial, difficult, or fantastic, as their predecessors were; no less nor more than Dante, Guido Cavalcanti, Guinizelli, or Cino. In the seventeenth century a dissociation of sensibility set in, from which we have never recovered; and this dissociation, as is natural, was aggravated by the influence of the two most powerful poets of the century, Milton and Dryden. Each of these men performed certain poetic functions so magnificently well that the magnitude of the effect concealed the absence of others. The language went on and in some respects improved; the best verse of Collins, Gray, Johnson, and even Goldsmith satisfies some of our fastidious demands better than that of Donne or Marvell or King. But while the language became more refined, the feeling became more crude. The feeling, the sensibility, expressed in the *Country Churchyard* (to say nothing of Tennyson and Browning) is cruder than that in the "Coy Mistress."

The second effect of the influence of Milton and Dryden followed from the first, and was therefore slow in manifestation. The sentimental age began early in the eighteenth century, and continued. The poets revolted against the ratiocinative, the descriptive; they thought and felt by fits, unbalanced; they reflected. In one or two passages of Shelley's *Triumph of Life,* in the second *Hyperion,* there are traces of a struggle toward unification of sensibility. But Keats and Shelley died, and Tennyson and Browning ruminated.

After this brief exposition of a theory—too brief, perhaps, to carry conviction—we may ask, what would have been the fate of the "metaphysical" had the current of poetry descended in a direct line from them, as it descended in a direct line to them? They would not, certainly, be classified as metaphysical. The possible interests of a poet are unlimited; the more intelligent he is the better; the more intelligent he is the more likely that he will have interests: our only condition is that he turn them into poetry, and not merely meditate on them poetically. A philosophical theory which has entered into poetry is established, for its truth or falsity in the one sense ceases to matter, and its truth in another sense is proved. The poets in question have, like other poets, various faults. But they were, at best, engaged in the task of trying to find the verbal equivalent for states of mind and feeling. And this means both that they are more mature, and that they wear better, than later poets of certainly not less literary ability.

It is not a permanent necessity that poets should be interested in philosophy, or in any other subject. We can only say that it appears likely that poets in our civilization, as it exists at present, must be *difficult.* Our civilization comprehends great variety and complexity, and this variety and complexity, playing upon a refined sensibility, must produce various and complex results. The poet must become more and more comprehensive, more allusive, more indirect, in order to force, to dislocate if necessary, language into his meaning. (A brilliant and extreme statement of this view, with which it is not requisite to associate oneself, is that of M. Jean Epstein, *La Poésie d'aujourd-hui.*) Hence we get something which looks very much like the conceit—we get, in fact, a method curiously similar to that of the "metaphysical poets," similar also in its use of obscure words and of simple phrasing.

> *O géraniums diaphanes, guerroyeurs sortilèges,*
> *Sacrilèges monomanes!*
> *Emballages, dévergondages, douches! O pressoirs*
> *Des vendanges des grands soirs!*
> *Layettes aux abois,*
> *Thyrses au fond des bois!*
> *Transfusions, représailles,*

> *Relevailles, compresses at l'éternal potion,*
> *Angélus! n'en pouvoir plus*
> *De débâcles nuptiales! de débâcles nuptiales!*

The same poet could write also simply:

> *Elle est bien loin, elle pleure,*
> *Le grand vent se lamente aussi . . .*

Jules Laforgue, and Tristan Corbière in many of his poems, are nearer to the "school of Donne" than any modern English poet. But poets more classical than they have the same essential quality of transmuting ideas into sensations, of transforming an observation into a state of mind.

> *Pour l'enfant, amoureux de cartes et d'estampes,*
> *L'univers est égal à son vaste appétit.*
> *Ah, que le monde est grand à la clarté des lampes!*
> *Aux yeux du souvenir que le monde est petit!*

In French literature the great master of the seventeenth century—Racine—and the great master of the nineteenth—Baudelaire—are in some ways more like each other than they are like any one else. The greatest two masters of diction are also the greatest two psychologists, the most curious explorers of the soul. It is interesting to speculate whether it is not a misfortune that two of the greatest masters of diction in our language, Milton and Dryden, triumph with a dazzling disregard of the soul. If we continued to produce Miltons and Drydens it might not so much matter, but as things are it is a pity that English poetry has remained so incomplete. Those who object to the "artificiality" of Milton or Dryden sometimes tell us to "look into our hearts and write." But that is not looking deep enough; Racine or Donne looked into a good deal more than the heart. One must look into the cerebral cortex, the nervous system, and the digestive tracts.

May we not conclude, then, that Donne, Crashaw, Vaughan, Herbert and Lord Herbert, Marvell, King, Cowley at his best, are in the direct current of English poetry, and that their faults should be reprimanded by this standard rather than coddled by antiquarian affection? They have been enough praised in terms which are implicit limitations because they are "metaphysical" or "witty," "quaint" or "obscure," though at their best they have not these attributes more than other serious poets. On the other hand, we must not reject the criticism of Johnson (a dangerous person to disagree with) without having mastered it, without having assimilated the Johnsonian canons of taste. In reading the celebrated passage in his essay on Cowley we must remember that by wit he clearly means something more serious than we usually mean today; in his criticism of their versification we must remember in what a narrow discipline he was trained, but also how well trained; we must remember that Johnson tortures chiefly the chief offenders, Cowley and

Cleveland. It would be a fruitful work, and one requiring a substantial book, to break up the classification of Johnson (for there has been none since) and exhibit these poets in all their difference of kind and of degree, from the massive music of Donne to the faint, pleasing tinkle of Aurelian Townshend— whose "Dialogue between a Pilgrim and Time" is one of the few regrettable omissions from the excellent anthology of Professor Grierson.

BAUDELAIRE

Anything like a just appreciation of Baudelaire has been slow to arrive in England, and still is defective or partial even in France. There are, I think, special reasons for the difficulty in estimating his worth and finding his place. For one thing, Baudelaire was in some ways far in advance of the point of view of his own time, and yet was very much of it, very largely partook of its limited merits, faults, and fashions. For one thing, he had a great part in forming a generation of poets after him; and in England he had what is in a way the misfortune to be first and extravagantly advertised by Swinburne, and taken up by the followers of Swinburne. He was universal, and at the same time confined by a fashion which he himself did most to create. To dissociate the permanent from the temporary, to distinguish the man from his influence, and finally to detach him from the associations of those English poets who first admired him, is no small task. His comprehensiveness itself makes difficulty, for it tempts the partisan critic, even now, to adopt Baudelaire as the patron of his own beliefs.

It is the purpose of this essay to affirm the importance of Baudelaire's prose works, a purpose justified by the translation of one of those works which is indispensable for any student of his poetry.[1] This is to see Baudelaire as something more than the author of the *Fleurs du mal,* and consequently to revise somewhat our estimate of that book. Baudelaire came into vogue at a time when "Art for Art's sake" was a dogma. The care which he took over his poems, and the fact that contrary to the fluency of his time, both in France and England he restricted himself to this one volume, encouraged the opinion that Baudelaire was an artist exclusively for art's sake. The doctrine does not, of course, really apply to anybody; no one applied it less than Pater, who spent many years, not so much in illustrating it, as in expounding it as a *theory of life,* which is not the same thing at all. But it was a doctrine which did affect criticism and appreciation, and which did obstruct a proper judgment of Baudelaire. He is in fact a greater man than was imagined, though perhaps not such a perfect poet.

Baudelaire has, I believe, been called a fragmentary Dante, for what that description is worth. It is true that many people who enjoy Dante enjoy Baudelaire; but the differences are as important as the similarities. Baudelaire's inferno is very different in quality and significance from that of Dante. Truer, I think, would be the description of Baudelaire as a later and more limited Goethe. As we begin to see him now, he represents his own age in somewhat the same way as that in which Goethe represents an earlier age. As a critic of the present generation, Mr. Peter Quennell has recently said in his book, *Baudelaire and the Symbolists:*

He had enjoyed a *sense of his own age,* had recognized its pattern while the pattern was yet incomplete, and—because it is only our misapprehension of the present which prevents our looking into the immediate future, our ignorance of today and of its real as apart from its spurious tendencies and requirements—had anticipated many problems, both on the aesthetic and on the moral plane, in which the fate of modern poetry is still concerned.

Now the man who has this sense of his age is hard to analyse. He is exposed to its follies as well as sensitive to its inventions; and in Baudelaire, as well as in Goethe, is some of the outmoded nonsense of his time. The parallel between the German poet who has always been the symbol of perfect "health" in every sense, as well as of universal curiosity, and the French poet who has been the symbol of morbidity in mind and concentrated interests in work, may seem paradoxical. But after this lapse of time the difference between "health" and "morbidity" in the two men becomes more negligible; there is something artificial and even priggish about Goethe's healthiness, as there is about Baudelaire's unhealthiness; we have passed beyond both fashions, of health or malady, and they are both merely men with restless, critical, curious minds and the "sense of the age"; both men who understood and foresaw a great deal. Goethe, it is true, was interested in many subjects which Baudelaire left alone; but by Baudelaire's time it was no longer necessary for a man to embrace such varied interests in order to have the sense of the age; and in retrospect some of Goethe's studies seem to us (not altogether justly) to have been merely dilettante hobbies. The most of Baudelaire's prose writings (with the exception of the translations from Poe, which are of less interest to an English reader) are as important as the most of Goethe. They throw light on the *Fleurs du mal* certainly, but they also expand immensely our appreciation of their author.

It was once the mode to take Baudelaire's Satanism seriously, as it is now the tendency to present Baudelaire as a serious and Catholic Christian. Especially as a prelude to the *Journaux intimes* this diversity of opinion needs some discussion. I think that the latter view—that Baudelaire is essentially Christian—is nearer the truth than the former, but it needs considerable reservation. When Baudelaire's Satanism is dissociated from its less creditable paraphernalia, it amounts to a dim intuition of a part, but a very important part, of Christianity. Satanism itself, so far as not merely an affectation, was an attempt to get into Christianity by the back door. Genuine blasphemy, genuine in spirit and not purely verbal, is the product of partial belief, and is as impossible to the complete atheist as to the perfect Christian. It is a way of affirming belief. This state of partial belief is manifest throughout the *Journaux intimes*. What is significant about Baudelaire is his theological innocence. He is discovering Christianity for himself; he is not assuming it as a fashion or weighting social or political reasons, or any other accidents. He is beginning, in a way, at the beginning; and being a discoverer, is not altogether certain what he is exploring and to what it leads; he might almost be said to be making again, as one man, the effort of scores of generations. His Christianity is rudimentary or embryonic; at best, he has the excesses of a Tertullian (and even Tertullian is not considered wholly orthodox and well balanced). His

business was not to practise Christianity, but—what was much more important for his time—to assert its *necessity*.

Baudelaire's morbidity of temperament cannot, of course, be ignored: and
no one who has looked at the work of Crépet or the recent small biographical
study of François Porché can forget it. We should be misguided if we treated
it as an unfortunate ailment which can be discounted or to attempt to detach
the sound from the unsound in his work. Without the morbidity none of his work
would be possible or significant; his weaknesses can be composed into a larger
whole of strength, and this is implied in my assertion that neither the health
of Goethe nor the malady of Baudelaire matters in itself: it is what both men
made of their endowments that matters. To the eye of the world, and quite
properly for all questions of private life, Baudelaire was thoroughly perverse and
insufferable: a man with a talent for ingratitude and unsociability, intolerably
irritable, and with a mulish determination to make the worst of everything; if
he had money, to squander it; if he had friends, to alienate them; if he had any
good fortune, to disdain it. He had the pride of the man who feels in himself great
weakness and great strength. Having great genius, he had neither the patience
nor the inclination, had he had the power, to overcome his weakness; on the
contrary, he exploited it for theoretical purposes. The morality of such a course
may be a matter for endless dispute; for Baudelaire, it was the way to liberate
his mind and give us the legacy and lesson that he has left.

He was one of those who have great strength, but strength merely to
suffer. He could not escape suffering and could not transcend it, so he
attracted pain to himself. But what he could do, with that immense passive
strength and sensibilities which no pain could impair, was to study his
suffering. And in this limitation he is wholly unlike Dante, not even like any
character in Dante's Hell. But, on the other hand, such suffering as
Baudelaire's implies the possibility of a positive state of beatitude. Indeed, in
his way of suffering is already a kind of presence of the supernatural and of the
superhuman. He rejects always the purely natural and the purely human; in
other words, he is neither "naturalist" nor "humanist." Either because he
cannot adjust himself to the actual world he has to reject it in favour of Heaven
and Hell, or because he has the perception of Heaven and Hell he rejects the
present world: both ways of putting it are tenable. There is in his statements
a good deal of romantic detritus; *ses ailes de géant l'empêchent de marcher*, he
says of the Poet and of the Albatross, but not convincingly; but there is also
truth about himself and about the world. His *ennui* may of course be
explained, as everything can be explained in psychological or pathological
terms; but it is also, from the opposite point of view, a true form of *acedia,*
arising from the unsuccessful struggle towards the spiritual life.

II

From the poems alone, I venture to think, we are not likely to grasp what
seems to me the true sense and significance of Baudelaire's mind. Their
excellence of form, their perfection of phrasing, and their superficial coher-

ence, may give them the appearance of presenting a definite and final state of mind. In reality, they seem to me to have the external but not the internal form of classic art. One might even hazard the conjecture that the care for perfection of form, among some of the romantic poets of the nineteenth century, was an effort to support, or to conceal from view, an inner disorder. Now the true claim of Baudelaire as an artist is not that he found a superficial form, but that he was searching for a form of life. In minor form he never indeed equalled Théophile Gautier, to whom he significantly dedicated his poems: in the best of the slight verse of Gautier there is a satisfaction, a balance of inwards and form, which we do not find in Baudelaire. He had a greater technical ability than Gautier, and yet the content of feeling is constantly bursting the receptacle. His apparatus, by which I do not mean his command of words and rhythms, but his stock of imagery (and every poet's stock of imagery is circumscribed somewhere), is not wholly perdurable or adequate. His prostitutes, mulattoes, Jewesses, serpents, cats, corpses, form a machinery which has not worn very well; his Poet, or his Don Juan, has a romantic ancestry which is too clearly traceable. Compare with the costumery of Baudelaire the stock of imagery of the *Vita Nuova,* or of Cavalcanti, and you find Baudelaire's does not everywhere wear as well as that of several centuries earlier; compare him with Dante or Shakespeare, for what such a comparison is worth, and he is found not only a much smaller poet, but one in whose work much more that is perishable has entered.

To say this is only to say that Baudelaire belongs to a definite place in time. Inevitably the offspring of romanticism, and by his nature the first counter-romantic in poetry, he could, like any one else, only work with the materials which were there. It must not be forgotten that a poet in a romantic age cannot be a "classical" poet except in tendency. If he is sincere, he must express with individual differences the general state of mind—not as a *duty,* but simply because he cannot help participating in it. For such poets, we may expect often to get much help from reading their prose works and even notes and diaries; help in deciphering the discrepancies between head and heart, means and end, material and ideals.

What preserves Baudelaire's poetry from the fate of most French poetry of the nineteenth century up to his time, and has made him, as M. Valéry has said in a recent introduction to the *Fleurs du mal,* the one modern French poet to be widely read abroad, is not quite easy to conclude. It is partly that technical mastery which can hardly be overpraised, and which has made his verse an inexhaustible study for later poets, not only in his own language. When we read

> *Maint joyau dort enseveli*
> *Dans les ténèbres et l'oubli,*
> *Bien loin des pioches et des sondes;*
> *Mainte fleur épanche à regret*
> *Son parfum doux comme un secret*
> *Dans les solitudes profondes,*

we might for a moment think it a more lucid bit of Mallarmé; and so original is the arrangement of words that we might easily overlook its borrowing from Gray's *Elegy*. When we read

> *Valse mélancolique et langoureux vertige!*

we are already in the Paris of Laforgue. Baudelaire gave to French poets as generously as he borrowed from English and American poets. The renovation of the versification of Racine has been mentioned often enough; quite genuine, but might be overemphasized, as it sometimes comes near to being a trick. But even without this, Baudelaire's variety and resourcefulness would still be immense.

Furthermore, besides the stock of images which he used that seems already second-hand, he gave new possibilities to poetry in a new stock of imagery of contemporary life.

> . . . *Au cœur d'un vieux faubourg, labyrinthe fangeux*
> *Ou l'humanité grouille en ferments orageux,*
> *On voit un vieux chiffonnier qui vient, hochant le tête*
> *Buttant, et se cognant aux murs comme un poète.*

This introduces something new, and something universal in modern life. (The last line quoted, which in ironic terseness anticipates Corbière, might be contrasted with the whole poem *Bénédiction* which begins the volume.) It is not merely in the use of imagery of common life, not merely in the use of imagery of the sordid life of a great metropolis, but in the elevation of such imagery to the *first intensity*—presenting it as it is, and yet making it represent something much more than itself—that Baudelaire has created a mode of release and expression for other men.

This invention of language, at a moment when French poetry in particular was famishing for such invention, is enough to make of Baudelaire a great poet, a great landmark in poetry. Baudelaire is indeed the greatest exemplar in *modern* poetry in any language, for his verse and langauge is the nearest thing to a complete renovation that we have experienced. But his renovation of an attitude towards life is no less radical and no less important. In his verse, he is now less a model to be imitated or a source to be drained than a reminder of the duty, the consecrated task, of sincerity. From a fundamental sincerity he could not deviate. The superficies of sincerity (as I think has not always been remarked) is not always there. As I have suggested, many of his poems are insufficiently removed from their romantic origins, from Byronic paternity and Satanic fraternity. The "satanism" of the Black Mass was very much in the air; in exhibiting it Baudelaire is the voice of his time; but I would observe that in Baudelaire, as in no one else, it is redeemed by *meaning something else*. He uses the same paraphernalia, but cannot limit its symbolism even to all that of which he is conscious. Compare him with Huysmans in *À Rebours, En Route*, and *Là-bas*. Huysmans, who is a first-rate realist of his time, only succeeds in making his diabolism interesting when he treats it externally, when he is merely describing a manifestation of his period (if such it was). His own interest in such matters is, like his interest in Christianity, a petty affair. Huysmans merely provides a document. Baudelaire would not even provide that, if he had been really absorbed in that ridiculous hocus-pocus. But actually Baudelaire is concerned, not with demons, black masses, and romantic blasphemy, but with the real problem of good and evil. It is hardly more than an accident of time that he uses the current imagery and vocabulary of blasphemy. In the middle nineteenth century, the age which (at its best) Goethe had prefigured, an age of bustle, programmes, platforms, scientific progress, humanitarianism and revolutions which improved nothing, an age of progressive degradation, Baudelaire perceived that what really matters is Sin and Redemption. It is a proof of his honesty that he went as far as he could honestly go and no further. To a mind observant of the post-Voltaire France (*Voltaire . . . le prédicateur des concierges*), a mind which saw the world of *Napoléon le petit* more lucidly than did that of Victor Hugo, a mind which at the same time had no affinity for the *Saint-Sulpicerie* of the day, the recognition of the reality of Sin is a New Life; and the possibility of damnation is so immense a relief in a world of electoral reform, plebiscites, sex reform and dress reform, that damnation itself is an immediate form of salvation—of salvation from the ennui of modern life, because it at last gives some significance to living. It is this, I believe, that Baudelaire is trying to express; and it is this which separates him from the modernist Protestantism of Byron and Shelley. It is apparently Sin in the Swinburnian sense, but really Sin in the permanent Christian sense, that occupies the mind of Baudelaire.

Yet, as I said, the sense of Evil implies the sense of good. Here too, as Baudelaire apparently confuses, and perhaps did confuse, Evil with its theatrical representations, Baudelaire is not always certain in his notion of the Good. The romantic idea of Love is never quite exorcised, but never quite surrendered to. In "Le Balcon," which M. Valéry considers, and I think rightly, one of Baudelaire's most beautiful poems, there is all the romantic idea, but something more: the reaching out towards something which cannot be had *in*, but which may be had partly *through*, personal relations. Indeed, in much romantic poetry the sadness is due to the exploitation of the fact that no human relations are adequate to human desires, but also to the disbelief in any further object for human desires than that which, being human, fails to satisfy them. One of the unhappy necessities of human existence is that we have to "find things out for ourselves." If it were not so, the statement of Dante would have, at least for poets, have done once for all. Baudelaire has all the romantic sorrow, but invents a new kind of romantic nostalgia, a derivative of his nostalgia being the *poésie des dé parts*, the *poésie des salles d'attente*. In a beautiful paragraph of the volume in question, "Mon Cœur mis à nu," he imagines the vessels lying in habour as saying: *Quand partons-nous vers le bonheur?* and his minor successor Laforgue exclaims: *Comme ils sont beaux, les trains manqués*. The poetry of flight—which, in contemporary France, owes a great debt to the poems of the A. O. Barnabooth of Valery Larbaud—is, in its origin in this paragraph of Baudelaire, a dim recognition of the direction of beatitude.

But in the adjustment of the natural to the spiritual, of the bestial to the human and the human to the supernatural, Baudelaire is a bungler compared with Dante; the best that can be said, and that is a very great deal, is that what he knew he found out for himself. In his book, the *Journaux intimes*, and especially in "Mon Cœur mis à nu," he has a great deal to say of the love of man and woman. One aphorism which has been especially noticed is the following: *la volupté unique et suprême de l'amour gît dans la certitude de faire le mal.* This means, I think, that Baudelaire has perceived that what distinguishes the relations of man and woman from the copulation of beasts is the knowledge of Good and Evil (of *moral* Good and Evil which are not natural Good and Bad or puritan Right and Wrong). Having an imperfect, vague romantic conception of Good, he was at least able to understand that the sexual act as evil is more dignified, less boring, than as the natural, "lifegiving," cheery automatism of the modern world. For Baudelaire, sexual operation is at least something not analogous to Kruschen Salts.

So far as we are human, what we do must be either evil or good;[2] so far as we do evil or good, we are human; and it is better, in a paradoxical way, to do evil than to do nothing: at least, we exist. It is true to say that the glory of man is his capacity for salvation; it is also true to say that his glory is his capacity for damnation. The worst that can be said of most of our malefactors, from statesmen to thieves, is that they are not men enough to be damned. Baudelaire was man enough for damnation: whether he *is* damned is, of course, another question, and we are not prevented from praying for his repose. In all his humiliating traffic with other beings, he walked secure in this high vocation, that he was capable of a damnation denied to the politicans and the newspaper editors of Paris.

III

Baudelaire's notion of beatitude certainly tended to the wishy-washy; and even in one of the most beautiful of his poems, "L'Invitation au voyage," he hardly exceeds the *poésie des départs*. And because his vision is here so restricted, there is for him a gap between human love and divine love. His human love is definite and positive, his divine love vague and uncertain: hence his insistence upon the evil of love, hence his constant vituperations of the female. In this there is no need to pry for psychopathological causes, which would be irrelevant at best; for his attitude towards women is consistent with the point of view which he had reached. Had he been a woman he would, no doubt, have held the same views about men. He has arrived at the perception that a woman must be to some extent a symbol; he did not arrive at the point of harmonising his experience with his ideal needs. The complement, and the correction to the *Journaux intimes*, so far as they deal with the relations of man and woman, is the *Vita Nuova*, and the *Divine Comedy*. But—I cannot assert it too strongly—Baudelaire's view of life, such as it is, is objectively apprehensible, that is to say, his idiosyncrasies can partly explain his view of life, but they cannot explain it away. And this view of life is one which has grandeur and which exhibits heroism; it was an evangel to his time and to ours. *La vraie civilisation*, he wrote, *n'est pas dans le gaz, ni dans la vapeur, ni dans les tables tournantes. Elle est dans la diminution des traces du péché originel*. It is not quite clear exactly what *diminution* here implies, but the tendency of his thought is clear, and the message is still accepted by but few. More than half a century later T. E. Hulme left behind him a paragraph which Baudelaire would have approved:

"In the light of these absolute values, man himself is judged to be essentially limited and imperfect. He is endowed with Original Sin. While he can occasionally accomplish acts which partake of perfection, he can never himself *be* perfect. Certain secondary results in regard to ordinary human action in society follow from this. A man is essentially bad, he can only accomplish anything of value by discipline—ethical and political. Order is thus not merely negative, but creative and liberating. Institutions are necessary."

NOTES

1. *Intimes*, translated by Christopher Isherwood, and published by the Blackamore Press.

2. "Know ye not, that to whom ye yield yourselves servants to obey, his servants ye are to whom ye obey: whether of sin unto death, or of obedience unto righteousness?"—Romans vi. 16.

To Criticize the Critic[1]

Of what use, or uses, is literary criticism, is a question worth asking again and again, even if we find no answer satisfactory. Criticism may be, what F. H. Bradley said of metaphysics, 'the finding of bad reasons for what we believe upon instinct, but to find these reasons is no less an instinct.' But as I propose to talk about my own criticsm my choice of subject needs to be further defended. In casting an eye over my own literary criticism of the last forty-odd years, I hope that I may be able to draw some conclusions, some plausible generalizations of wider validity, or—what is still more worth while—stimulate other minds to do so; also I hope I may provoke other critics to make similar confessions. My justification must be that there is no other critic, living or dead, about whose work I am so well informed as I am about my own. I know more about the genesis of my essays and reviews than about those of any other critic; I know the chronology, the circumstances under which each essay was written and the motive for writing it, and about all those changes of attitude, taste, interest and belief which the years bring to pass. For the work of those masters of English criticism whom I regard with most reverence such full information is not available to me. I am thinking especially of Samuel Johnson and of Coleridge, and not ignoring Dryden or Arnold. But at this point I should distinguish between the several types of literary critic, in order to remind you that generalizations drawn from the study of the work of a critic of one type may not be applicable to that of others.

First of all among those types of critics other than mine, I should put down the Professional Critic—the writer whose literary criticism is his chief, perhaps his only title to fame. This critic might also be called the Super-Reviewer, for he has often been the official critic for some magazine or newspaper, and the occasion for each of his contributions the publication of some new book. The exemplar of this kind of criticism is of course the French critic Sainte-Beuve, who was the author of two important books, *Port-Royal* and *Chateaubriand et ses amis*, but the bulk of whose work consists of volume after volume of collected essays which had previously appeared week by week in the *feuilleton* of a newspaper. The Profesional Critic may be, as Sainte-Beuve certainly was, a *failed* creative writer; and in the case of Sainte-Beuve it is certainly worth while to look at his poems, if one can come by them, as an aid to understanding why he wrote better about authors of the past than about his contemporaries. The Professional Critic however is not *necessarily* a failed poet, dramatist or novelist: so far as I know, my old friend in America, Paul Elmer More, whose Shelburne Essays have something of the monumental appearance of the *Causeries du lundi*, attempted no creative writing. Another old friend of mine who was a Professional Critic, of both books and theatre, Desmond MacCarthy, confined his literary activity to his weekly article or review and employed his leisure in delightful conversation instead of devoting it to the books he never wrote. And Edmund Gosse—a different case again: for it is not his industry as a critic, but one book of autobiography which is already a classic—*Father and Son*—that will perpetuate his name.

Second, I name the Critic with Gusto. This critic is not called to the seat of judgment; he is rather the advocate of the authors whose work he expounds, authors who are sometimes the forgotten or unduly despised. He calls our attention to such writers, helps us to see merit which we had overlooked and to find charm where we had expected only boredom. Of such was George Saintsbury, an erudite and genial man with an insatiable appetite for the second-rate, and a flair for discovering the excellence which is often to be found in the second-rate. Who but Saintsbury, in writing a book on the French Novel, would give far more pages to Paul de Kock than to Flaubert? There was also my old friend Charles Whibley: for example, read him on Sir Thomas Urquhart or on Petronius. There was also Quiller-Couch, who must have taught many of those who attended his lectures at Cambridge, to find fresh sources of delight in English literature.

Third, the Academic and the Theoretical. I mention these two together, as they can overlap; but this category is perhaps too comprehensive, since it ranges from the purely scholarly, like W. P. Ker, who could illuminate an author of one age or language by an unexpected parallel with some author of another age or another language, to the philosophical critic, such as I. A. Richards and his disciple the philosophical critic William Empson. Mr. Richards and Mr. Empson are also poets, but I do not regard their work as a by-product of their poetry. And where are we to place other contemporaries, such as L. C. Knights or Wilson Knight, except as men who have combined teaching with original critical work? And another critic of importance, Dr. F. R. Leavis, who may be called the Critic as Moralist? The critic who is also tenant of an academic post is likely to have made a special study of one period or one author but to call him a specialist Critic would seem a kind of abridgment of his right to examine whatever literature he pleases.

And finally we come to the critic whose criticism may be said to be a by-product of his creative activity. Particularly, the critic who is also a poet. Shall we say, the poet who has written some literary criticism? The condition of entrance into this category is that the candidate should be known primarily for his poetry, but that his criticism should be distinguished for its own sake, and not merely for any light it may throw upon its author's verse. And here I put Samuel Johnson, and Coleridge; and Dryden and Racine in their prefaces; and Matthew Arnold with reservations; and it is into this company that I must shyly intrude. I hope you need by now no further assurance that it was not laziness that impelled me to turn to my own writings for my material. It most certainly was not vanity: for when I first applied myself to the required reading for this address, it was so long since I had read many of my essays that I approached them with apprehension rather than with hopeful expectations.

I am happy to say that I did not find quite so much to be ashamed of as I had feared. There are, to be sure, statements with which I no longer agree; there are views which I maintain with less firmness of conviction than when

I first expressed them, or which I maintain only with important reservations; there are statements the meaning of which I no longer understand. There may be areas in which my knowledge has increased; there are areas in which my knowledge has evaporated. On re-reading my essay on Pascal, for instance, I was astonished at the extent of the information I seem to have possessed when I wrote it. And there are some matters in which I have simply lost interest, so that, if asked whether I still hold the same belief, I could only say 'I don't know' or 'I don't care'. There are errors of judgment, and, what I regret more, there are errors of tone: the occasional note of arrogance, of vehemence, of cocksureness or rudeness, the braggadocio of the mild-mannered man safely entrenched behind his typewriter. Yet I must acknowledge my relationship to the man who made those statements, and in spite of all these exceptions, I continue to identify myself with the author.

Even in saying that, however, I think of a qualification. I find myself constantly irritated by having my words, perhaps written thirty or forty years ago, quoted as if I had uttered them yesterday. One very intelligent expositor of my work, who regarded it, furthermore, with a very favourable eye, discussed my critical writings some years ago as if I had, at the outset of my career as a literary critic, sketched out the design for a massive critical structure, and spent the rest of my life filling in the details. When I publish a collection of essays, or whenever I allow an essay to be re-published elsewhere, I make a point of indicating the original date of publication, as a reminder to the reader of the distance of time that separates the author when he wrote it from the author as he is today. But rare is the writer who, quoting me, says 'this is what Mr. Eliot thought (or felt) in 1933' (or whatever the date was). Every writer is accustomed to seeing his words quoted out of context, in such a way as to put an unintended construction upon them, by not over-scrupulous controversialists. But the quotation of pronouncements of many years ago, as if they had been made yesterday, is still more frequent, because it is most often wholly without malice. I will give one instance of a statement which has continued to dog its author long after it has ceased, in his opinon, to be a satisfactory statement of his beliefs. It is a sentence from the preface to a small collection of essays entitled *For Lancelot Andrewes,* to the effect that I was a classicist in literature, a royalist in politics, and an Anglo-Catholic in religion. I ought to have foreseen that so quotable a sentence would follow me through life as Shelley tells us his thoughts followed him:

> And his own thoughts, along that rugged way,
> Pursued, like raging hounds, their father and their prey.

The sentence in question was provoked by a personal experience. My old teacher and master, Irving Babbitt, to whom I owe so much, stopped in London on his way back to Harvard from Paris, where he had been lecturing, and he and Mrs. Babbitt dined with me. I had not seen Babbitt for some years, and I felt obliged to acquaint him with a fact as yet unknown to my small circle of readers (for this was I think in the year 1927) that I had recently been baptized and confirmed into the Church of England. I knew that it would come as a shock to him to learn that any disciple of his had so turned his coat, though he had already had what must have been a much greater shock when his close friend and ally Paul Elmer More defected from Humanism to Christianity. But all Babbitt said was: 'I think you should come out into the open.' I may have been a little nettled by this remark; the quotable sentence turned up in the preface to the book of essays I had in preparation, swung into orbit, and has been circling my little world ever since. Well, my religious beliefs are unchanged, and I am strongly in favour of the maintenance of the monarchy in all countries which have a monarchy; as for Classicism and Romanticism, I find that the terms have no longer the importance to me that they once had. But even if my statement of belief needed no qualification at all after the passage of the years, I should not be inclined to express it in quite this way.

So far as I can judge, from references, quotations and reprints in anthologies, it is my earlier essays which have made the deeper impression. I attribute this to two causes. The first is the dogmatism of youth. When we are young we see issues sharply defined: as we age we tend to make more reservations, to qualify our positive assertions, to introduce more parentheses. We see objections to our own views, we regard the enemy with greater tolerance and even sometimes with sympathy. When we are young, we are confident in our opinions, sure that we possess the whole truth; we are enthusiastic, or indignant. And readers, even mature readers, are attracted to a writer who is quite sure of himself. The second reason for the enduring popularity of some of my early criticism is less easily apprehended, especially by readers of a younger generation. It is that in my earlier criticism, both in my general affirmations about poetry and in writing about authors who had influenced me, I was implicitly defending the sort of poetry that I and my friends wrote. This gave my essays a kind of urgency, the warmth of appeal of the advocate, which my later, more detached and I hope more judicial essays cannot claim. I was in reaction, not only against Georgian poetry, but against Georgian criticism; I was writing in a context which the reader of today has either forgotten, or has never experienced.

In a lecture on Johnson's *Lives of the Poets*, published in one of my collections of essays and addresses,[2] I made the point that in appraising the judgments of any critic of a past age, one needed to seem him in the context of that age, to try to place oneself at his point of view. This is a difficult effort for the imagination; one, indeed, in which we cannot hope for more than partial success. We cannot discount the influence upon our formation of the creative writing and the critical writing of the intervening generations, or the inevitable modifications of taste, or our greater knowledge and understanding of the literature preceding that of the age which we are trying to understand. Yet merely to make that effort of imagination, and to have these difficulties in mind, is worth our while. In reviewing my own early criticism, I am struck by the degree to which it was conditioned by the state of literature at the time at which it was written, as well as by the stage of maturity at which I had arrived, by the influences to which I had been exposed, and by the occasion of each essay. I cannot myself bring to mind all these circumstances, reconstruct all the conditions under which I wrote: how much less can any future critic of my work have knowledge of them, or, if he has knowledge have understanding, or if he has both knowledge and understanding, find my essays of the same interest that they had for those who read them sympathetically when they first appeared? No literary criticism can for a future generation excite more than curiosity, unless it continues to be of use in itself to future generations, to have intrinsic value out of its historical context. But if any part of it does have this timeless value, then we shall appreciate that value all the more precisely if we also attempt to put ourselves at the point of view of the writer and his first readers. To study the criticism of Johnson or of Coleridge in this way is undoubtedly rewarding.

I can divide my own critical writing roughly into three periods. There was first the period of *The Egoist,* that remarkably bi-weekly edited and published by Miss Harriet Weaver. Richard Aldington had been sub editor, and when he was called up for military service in the First World War Ezra Pound nominated me to Miss Weaver to fill his place. In *The Egoist* appeared an essay called 'Tradition and the Individual Talent', which still enjoys immense popularity among those editors who prepare anthological text-books for American college students. There were then two influences which are not so incongruous as might at first sight appear: that of Irving Babbitt and that of Ezra Pound. The influence of Pound at that time may be detected in references to Remy de Gourmont, in my papers on Henry James, an author whom Pound much admired, but for whom my own enthusiasm has somewhat flagged, and sundry allusions to authors, such as Gavin Douglas, whose work I hardly knew. The influence of Babbitt (with an infusion later of T. E. Hulme and of the more literary essays of Charles Maurras) is apparent in my recurrent theme of Classicism versus Romanticism. In my second period, after 1918, when *The Egoist* had come to an end, I was writing essays and reviews for two editors in whom I was fortunate, for they both gave me always the right books to review: Middleton Murry in the short-lived *Athenaeum,* and Bruce Richmond in *The Times Literary Supplement.* Most of my contributions remain buried in the files of these two papers, but the best, and they are among the best of my essays, are reprinted in my collections. My third period has been, for one reason or another, one of public lectures and addresses rather than of articles and reviews.

And here I wish to draw what seems to me an important line of demarcation between the essays of generalization (such as 'Tradition and the Individual Talent') and appreciations of individual authors. It is those in the latter category which seem to me to have the best chance of retaining some value for future readers: and I wonder whether this assertion does not itself imply a generalization applicable to other critics of my type. But I must draw a distinction here too. Several years ago my New York publishers brought out a paper-back selection of my essays on Elizabethan and Jacobean drama. I made the selection myself, and wrote a preface explaining my choice. I found that the essays with which I was still pleased were those on the contemporaries of Shakespeare, not those on Shakespeare himself. It was from these minor dramatists that I, in my own poetic formation, had learned my lessons; it was by them, and not by Shakespeare, that my imagination had been stimulated, my sense of rhythm trained, and my emotions fed. I had read them at the age at which they were best suited to my temperament and stage of development, and had read them with passionate delight long before I had any thought, or any opportunity of writing about them. At the period in which the stirrings of desire to write verse were becoming insistent, these were the men whom I took as my tutors. Just as the modern poet who influenced me was not Baudelaire but Jules Laforgue, so the dramatic poets were Marlowe and Webster and Tourneur and Middleton and Ford, not Shakespeare. A poet of the supreme greatness of Shakespeare can hardly influence, he can only be imitated: and the difference between influence and imitation is that influence can fecundate, whereas imitation—especially unconscious imitation—can only sterilize. (But when I came to attempt one brief imitation of Dante I was fifty-five years old and knew exactly what I was doing.) Besides, imitation of a writer in a foreign language can often be profitable—because we cannot succeed.

So much for those of my essays in literary criticism which I think have the best chance of survival, in the sense that they are those which have, I believe, the best chance of giving pleasure, and possibly enlarging the understanding, on the part of future readers, of the authors criticized. Now what of the generalizations, and the phrases which have flourished, such as 'dissociation of sensibility' and 'objective correlative'? I think also of an article on 'the function of criticism' written for *The Criterion*. I am not sure, at this distance of time, how valid are the two phrases I have just cited: I am always at a loss what to say, when earnest scholars, or schoolchildren, write to ask me for an explanation. The term 'objective correlative' occurs in an essay on 'Hamlet and His Problems' in which I was perhaps not altogether guiltless of trailing my coat: I was at that time hand-in-glove with that gallant controversialist, J. M. Robertson, in his critical studies of Tudor and Stuart drama. But whatever the future of these phrases, and even if I am unable to defend them now with any forensic plausibility, I think they have been useful in their time. They have been accepted, they have been rejected, they may soon go out of fashion completely: but they have served their turn as stimuli to the critical thinking of others. And literary criticism, as I hinted at the beginning, is an instinctive activity of the civilized mind. But I prophesy that if my phrases are given consideration, a century hence, it will be only in their historical context, by scholars interested in the mind of my generation.

What I wish to suggest, however, is that these phrases may be accounted for as being conceptual symbols for emotional preferences. Thus, the emphasis on tradition came about, I believe, as a result of my reaction against the poetry, in the English language, of the nineteenth and early twentieth centuries, and my passion for the poetry, both dramatic and lyric, of the late sixteenth and early seventeenth centuries. The 'objective correlative' in the essay on Hamlet may stand for my bias towards the more mature plays of Shakespeare—*Timon, Antony and Cleopatra, Coriolanus* notably—and towards those late plays of

Shakespeare about which Mr. Wilson Knight has written illuminatingly. And the 'dissociation of sensibility' may represent my devotion to Donne and the metaphysical poets, and my reaction against Milton.

It seems to me, in fact, that these concepts, these generalizations, had their origin in my sensibility. They arise from my feeling of kinship with one poet or with one kind of poetry rather than another. I ought not to claim that what I am now saying holds good of other types of critic than mine, or even of other critics of the type to which I myself belong—that is, of poets who have also written critical essays. But about any writer in the field of aesthetics I always incline to ask: 'what literary works, paintings, sculpture, architecture and music does this theorist really enjoy?' We can, of course—and this is a danger to which the philosophical critic of art may be exposed—adopt a theory and then persuade ourselves that we like the works of art that fit into that theory. But I am sure that my own theorizing has been epiphenomenal of my tastes, and that in so far as it is valid, it springs from direct experience of those authors who have profoundly influenced my own writing. I am aware, of course, that my 'objective correlative' and my 'dissociation of sensibility' must be attacked or defended on their own level of abstraction, and that I have done no more than indicate what I believe to have been their genesis. I am also aware that in accounting for them in this way I am now making a generalization about my generalizations. But I am certain of one thing: that I have written best about writers who have influenced my own poetry. And I say 'writers' and not only 'poets', because I include F. H. Bradley, whose works— I might say whose personality as manifested in his works—affected me profoundly; and Bishop Lancelot Andrewes, from one of whose sermons on the Nativity I lifted several lines of my *Journey of the Magi* and of whose prose there may be a faint reflection in the sermon in *Murder in the Cathedral*. I include, in fact, any writers whether of verse or prose, whose style has strongly affected my own. I have hope that such essays of mine on individual writers who have influenced me, may retain some value even for a future generation which will reject or ridicule my theories. I spent three years, when young, in the study of philosophy. What remains to me of these studies? The style of three philosophers: Bradley's English, Spinoza's Latin and Plato's Greek.

It is in relation to essays on individual poets that I come to consider the question: how far can the critic alter public taste for one or another poet or one or another period of literature of the past? Have I myself, for example, been to any degree responsible for arousing interest and promoting appreciation of the early dramatists or of the metaphysical poets? I should say, hardly at all—as critic. We must distinguish of course between *taste* and *fashion*. Fashion, the love of change for its own sake, the desire for something new, is very transient; *taste* is something that springs from a deeper source. In a language in which great poetry has been written for many generations, as it has in ours, each generation will vary in its preferences among the classics of that language. Some writers of the past will respond to the taste of the living generations more nearly than others; some periods of the past may have closer affinity to our own age than others. To a young reader, or a critic of crude taste, the authors whom his generation favours may seem to be better than those fancied by the previous generation; the more conscious critic may recognize that they are simply more congenial, but not necessarily of greater merit. It is one function of the critic to assist the literate public of his day to recognize its affinity with one poet, or with one type of poetry, or one age of poetry, rather than with another.

The critic, however, cannot create a taste. I have sometimes been credited with starting the vogue for Donne and other metaphysical poets, as well as for the minor Elizabethan and Jacobean dramatists. But I did not discover any of these poets. Coleridge, and Browning in turn, admired Donne; and as for the early dramatists, there is Lamb, and the enthusiastic tributes of Swinburne are by no means without critical merit. In our own time, John Donne has lacked no publicity: Gosse's *Life and Letters,* in two volumes, appeared in 1899. I remember being introduced to Donne's poetry when I was a Freshman at Harvard by Professor Briggs, an ardent admirer; Grierson's edition of the Poems, in two volumes, was published in 1912; and it was Grierson's *Metaphysical Poetry,* sent me to review, that gave me my first occasion to write about Donne. I think that if I wrote well about the metaphysical poets, it was because they were poets who had inspired me. And if I can be said to have had any influence whatever in promoting a wider interest in them, it was simply because no previous poet who had praised these poets had been so deeply influenced by them as I had been. As the taste for my own poetry spread, so did the taste for the poets to whom I owed the greatest debt and about whom I had written. Their poetry, and mine, were congenial to that age. I sometimes wonder whether that age is not coming to an end.

It is true that I owed, and have always acknowledged, an equally great debt to certain French poets of the late nineteenth century, about whom I have never written. I have written about Baudelaire, but nothing about Jules Laforgue, to whom I owe more than to any one poet in any language, or about Tristan Corbière, to whom I owe something also. The reason, I believe, is that no one commissioned me to do so. For these early essays were all written for money, which I needed, and the occasion was always a new book about an author, a new edition of his works, or an anniversary.

The question of the extent to which a critic may influence the taste of his time I have answered, speaking for myself alone, by saying that I do not believe that my own criticism has had, or could have had, any influence whatever apart from my own poems. Let me turn now to the question: how far, and in what ways do the critic's own tastes and views alter in the course of his lifetime? To what extent do such changes indicate greater maturity, when do they indicate decay, and when must we consider them merely as changes— neither for better nor for worse? For myself, again, I find that my opinion of poets whose work influenced me in my formative stage remains unchanged, and I abate nothing of the praise I have given them. True, they do not now give me that intense excitement and sense of enlargement and liberation which comes from a discovery which is also a discovery of oneself: but that is an experience which can only happen once. And indeed it is to other poets than these that I am likely to turn now for pure delight. I turn more often the pages of Mallarmé than those of Laforgue, those of George Herbert than those of Donne, of Shakespeare than of his contemporaries and epigoni. This does not necessarily involve a judgment of relative greatness: it is merely that what has best responded to my need in middle and later age is different from the nourishment I needed in my youth. So great is Shakespeare, however, that a lifetime is hardly enough for growing up to appreciate him. There is one poet, however, who impressed me profoundly when I was twenty-two and with only a rudimentary acquaintance with his language started to puzzle out his lines, one poet who remains the comfort and amazement of my age, although my knowledge of his language remains rudimentary. I was never more than an inferior classical scholar: the poet I speak of is Dante. In my youth, I think that Dante's astonishing economy and directness of language—his arrow that goes unerringly to the centre of the target—provided for me a wholesome corrective to the extravagances of the Elizabethan, Jacobean and Caroline authors in whom I also delighted.

Perhaps what I want to say now is true of all literary criticism. I am sure that it is true of mine, that it is at its best when I have been writing of authors whom I have wholeheartedly admired. And my next best are of authors whom I greatly admire, but only with qualifications with which other critics may disagree. I do not ask to be reassured about my essays on minor Elizabethan dramatists, but am always interested to hear what other critics of poetry think, for instance, about what I have written on Tennyson or Byron. As for criticism of negligible authors, it can hardly be of permanent interest, because people will cease to be interested in the writers criticized. And censure of a great writer—or a writer whose works have had the test of time—is likely to be influenced by other than literary considerations. The personality of Milton, as well as some of his politics and theology, was obviously antipathetic to Samuel Johnson, as it is to me. (But when I wrote my first essay on Milton, I was considering his poetry as poetry and in relation to what I conceived to be the needs of my own time; and when I wrote my second essay on Milton I did not intend it to be, what Desmond MacCarthy and others took it to be, a recantation of my earlier opinion, but a development in view of the fact that there was no longer any likelihood of his being imitated, and that therefore he could profitably be studied. This reference to Milton is parenthetical.) I do not regret what I have written about Milton: but when an author's mind is so antipathetic to my own as was that of Thomas Hardy, I wonder whether it might not have been better never to have written about him at all.

Perhaps my judgment is less assured about writers who are contemporary or nearly so, than about writers of the past. Yet my valuation of the work of those poets contemporary with me, and of those poets younger than myself with whom I feel an affinity, remains unchanged. There is however one contemporary figure about whom my mind will, I fear, always waver between dislike, exasperation, boredom and admiration. That is D. H. Lawrence.

My opinions of D. H. Lawrence seem to form a tissue of praise and execration. The more vehement of my ejaculations of dislike are preserved, like flies in amber, or like wasps in honey, by the diligence of Dr. Leavis; but between two passages which he quotes, one published in 1927 and the other in 1933, I find that in 1931 I was wagging my finger rather pompously at the bishops who had assembled at the Lambeth Conference, and reproaching them for 'missing an opportunity for dissociating themselves from the condemnation of two very serious and improving writers'—namely, Mr. James Joyce and Mr. D. H. Lawrence. I cannot account for such apparent contradictions. Last year, in the *Lady Chatterley* case, I expressed my readiness to appear as a witness for the defence. Perhaps the counsel for the defence were well advised not to put me into the witness box, as it might have been rather difficult to make my views clear to a jury by that form of inquisition, and a really wily prosecutor might have tied me up in knots. I felt then, as I feel now, that the prosecution of such a book—a book of most serious and highly moral *intention*—was a deplorable blunder, the consequences of which would be most unfortunate whatever the verdict, and give the book a kind of vogue which would have been abhorrent to the author. But my antipathy to the author remains, on the ground of what seems to me egotism, a strain of cruelty, and a failing in common with Thomas Hardy—the lack of a sense of humour.

My particular reason for referring to my response to the work of Lawrence is that it is well to remind ourselves, in discussing the subject of literary criticism, that we cannot escape personal bias, and that there are other standards besides that of 'literary merit', which cannot be excluded. It was noticeable, in the Chatterley case, that some witnesses for the defence defended the book for the moral intentions of the author rather than on the ground of its being important as a work of literature.

In most of what I have been saying today, however, I have endeavoured to confine myself to that part of my own critical prose which is most nearly definable as '*literary* criticism'. May I sum up the conclusions to which I have come, after re-reading all of my writing which can be covered by that designation? I have found that my best work falls within rather narrow limits, my best essays being, in my opinion, those concerned with writers who had influenced me in my poetry; naturally the majority of these writers were poets. And it is that part of my criticism concerned with writers towards whom I felt gratitude and whom I could praise wholeheartedly, which is the part in which I continue to feel most confidence as the years pass. And as for the phrases of generalization which have been so often quoted, I am convinced that their force comes from the fact that they are attempts to summarize, in conceptual form, direct and intense experience of the poetry that I have found most congenial.

It is risky, and perhaps presumptuous, for me to generalize from my own experience, even about critics of my own type—that is, writers who are primarily creative but reflect upon their own vocation and upon the work of other practitioners. I am, I admit, much more interested in what other poets have written about poetry than in what critics who are not poets have said about it. I have suggested also that it is impossible to fence off *literary* criticism from criticism on other grounds, and that moral, religious and social judgments cannot be wholly excluded. That they can, and that literary merit can be estimated in complete isolation, is the illusion of those who believe that literary merit alone can justify the publication of a book which could otherwise be condemned on moral grounds. But the nearest we get to pure literary criticism is the criticism of artists writing about their own art; and for this I turn to Johnson, and Wordsworth and Coleridge. (Paul Valéry's is a special case.) In other types of criticism, the historian, the philosopher, the moralist, the sociologist, the grammarian may play a large part; but in so far as literary criticism is purely literary, I believe that the criticism of artists writing about their own art is of greater intensity, and carries more authority, though the area of the artist's competence may be much narrower. I feel that I myself have spoken with authority (if the phrase itself does not suggest arrogance) only about those authors—poets and a very few prose writers—who have influenced me; that on poets who have not influenced me I still deserve serious consideration; and that on authors whose work I dislike my views may—to say the least—be highly disputable. And I should remind you again, in closing, that I have directed attention on my literary criticism *qua* literary, and that a study in respect of my religious, social, political or moral beliefs, and of that large part of my prose writing which is directly concerned with these beliefs would be quite another exercise in self-examination. But I hope that what I have said today may suggest reasons why, as the critic grows older, his critical writings may be less fired by enthusiasm, but informed by wider interest and, one hopes, by greater wisdom and humility.

NOTES

1. The sixth Convocation Lecture delivered at the University of Leeds in July 1961.
2. *On Poetry and Poets* (Faber & Faber, 1957).

Walter Benjamin

1892–1940

Walter Benjamin was born into an upper-middle-class German-Jewish family in Berlin on July 15, 1892. He was educated at a progressive grade school and an elite experimental preparatory school in Toringia, and in 1912 he went to the University of Freiburg. There he came under the influence of neo-Kantians, and as a leader of the "free students" in the German youth movement he gave speeches advocating education reform from a rigorously Kantian standpoint. With the outbreak of World War I, however, Benjamin broke with what he saw as the callow nationalism of the youth movement, and successfully faked sciatica and neuralgia in order to avoid being drafted to fight in a war to which he was morally opposed. Like Kafka and Karl Kraus, both of whom he later wrote about, and Gershom Scholem, who became his lifelong friend, Benjamin despised the spiritual aridity of bourgeois Germany and sought alternatives in religion, philosophy, radical politics, and the study of literature.

In 1917 Benjamin married and moved to Bern, Switzerland. His only son, Stefan, was born in 1918. Living in seclusion with his family except for occasional visits from Scholem (in whom he saw the living spirit of authentic Judaism), Benjamin continued his studies and completed his dissertation on "The Concept of Art Criticism in the German Romantic Movement." Around 1920 inflation forced him to leave Switzerland and to return with his wife and son to his parents' home in Berlin—a difficult arrangement for everyone involved. Partially in order to placate his father, Benjamin began working at this time on a *Habilitationschrift*—a book-length treatise that would earn him a place in the German academic establishment. Conceived in Benjamin's defiantly idiosyncratic way as a mosaic of quotations to which the interpolating text was secondary, and prefaced by an "episto-critical prologue" which, Benjamin suggested, only someone who had read the Kabbalah could understand, *The Origin of the German Tragic Drama* seems to have baffled its adjudicating readers and in 1925 it was rejected (it was later published in 1928).

Without a place in the academic world, uncomfortable with the current literary "scene," and in a stage of intellectual transition from metaphysical to Marxist categories of thinking, Benjamin took up a nomadic lifestyle as an itinerant man of letters. Hounded by domestic and economic difficulties, he spent much of the next fifteen years wandering through various European cities, especially Paris, collecting books and writing and translating on commission from small literary journals. It was during these travels that Benjamin developed his characteristic mode of observation—that of "the flâneur." Taking seriously the Surrealists' advice to "walk the streets," Benjamin believed that the elusive essence of history itself could be discovered there; some of his most noted writing describes the shifting physiognomies of modern cities and the work of their poets—Kafka, Baudelaire, Proust, and Brecht.

In 1931 Benjamin had taken his own apartment in Berlin, but with the Nazi seizure of power in 1933 it became impossible for him to remain in Germany. He spent the remainder of the 1930s largely in Paris, still writing extensively and scrupulously avoiding the attention of the French police. Friendship with Brecht and the personal experience of economic hardship had deepened his Marxist convictions, and in 1932 he established a relationship with Theodor Adorno's and Max Horkheimer's Institute for Social Research. Despite serious reservations about Benjamin's undialectical use of Marxist categories and his tendency to mix materialist and theological frames of reference, the Institute provided him with a monthly stipend through these difficult years. He remained in France until the crisis of 1940, when he was detained attempting to leave via the Spanish border. Mistakenly believing that he would be deported to a concentration camp in the morning, he committed suicide by ingesting cyanide on September 27, 1940.

When all the literary fragments that Benjamin had left scattered in his wake were gathered together in the 1950s, what emerged was a remarkable literary achievement. In his early work he adumbrated a theory of language that still stands as an alternative to both bourgeois signification and pure mysticism. In his work on the German tragic drama, he initiated epistemological inquiries into questions of representation, allegory, and symbolism that have since been developed by Paul de Man and his students. The essays in literary criticism of the 1930s established the style for the Marxist aesthetic criticism subsequently developed by Theodor Adorno and the Frankfurt school. He wrote the first major critical essays on Brecht, Kafka, Karl Kraus, and the French Surrealists. He translated and wrote major studies of Proust, Baudelaire, and Goethe. He speculated on the metaphysics of translation, and he anticipated modern semiotics by "reading" several European cities as many-layered texts.

"The Storyteller" and "The Work of Art in the Age of Mechanical Reproduction" were both written in 1936, at the height of Benjamin's Marxist period. Both essays are primarily meditations on the way the actual material conditions in which a work of art is experienced affect the nature of work itself. In these later Marxist works, Benjamin clearly experienced a turn toward materialism, departing from his earlier religious mode of thinking. But he continued to believe that the split was not irreparable. His last work, *Theses on the Philosophy of History,* was a vigorous effort to integrate the competing strains of his thought.

THE STORYTELLER

Reflections on the Works of Nikolai Leskov

I

Familiar though his name may be to us, the storyteller in his living immediacy is by no means a present force. He has already become something remote from us and something that is getting even more distant. To present someone like Leskov as a storyteller does not mean bringing him closer to us but, rather, increasing our distance from him. Viewed from a certain distance, the great, simple outlines which define the storyteller stand out in him, or rather, they become visible in him, just as in a rock a human head or an animal's body may appear to an observer at the proper distance and angle of vision. This distance and this angle of vision are prescribed for us by an experience which we may have almost every day. It teaches us that the art of storytelling is coming to an end. Less and less frequently do we encounter people with the ability to tell a tale properly. More and more often there is embarrassment all around when the wish to hear a story is expressed. It is as if something that seemed inalienable to us, the securest among our possessions, were taken from us: the ability to exchange experiences.

One reason for this phenomenon is obvious: experience has fallen in value. And it looks as if it is continuing to fall into bottomlessness. Every glance at a newspaper demonstrates that it has reached a new low, that our picture, not only of the external world but of the moral world as well, overnight has undergone changes which were never thought possible. With the [First] World War a process began to become apparent which has not halted since then. Was it not noticeable at the end of the war that men returned from the battlefield grown silent—not richer, but poorer in communicable experience? What ten years later was poured out in the flood of war books was anything but experience that goes from mouth to mouth. And there was nothing remarkable about that. For never has experience been contradicted more thoroughly than strategic experience by tactical warfare, economic experience by inflation, bodily experience by mechanical warfare, moral experience by those in power. A generation that had gone to school on a horse-drawn streetcar now stood under the open sky in a countryside in which nothing remained unchanged but the clouds, and beneath these clouds, in a field of force of destructive torrents and explosions, was the tiny, fragile human body.

II

Experience which is passed on from mouth to mouth is the source from which all storytellers have drawn. And among those who have written down the tales, it is the great ones whose written version differs least from the speech of the many nameless storytellers. Incidentally, among the last named there are two groups which, to be sure, overlap in many ways. And the figure of the storyteller gets its full corporeality only for the one who can picture them both. "When someone goes on a trip, he has something to tell about," goes the German saying, and people imagine the storyteller as someone who has come from afar. But they enjoy no less listening to the man who has stayed at home, making an honest living, and who knows the local tales and traditions. If one wants to picture these two groups through their archaic representatives, one is embodied in the resident tiller of the soil, and the other in the trading seaman. Indeed, each sphere of life has, as it were, produced its own tribe of storytellers. Each of these tribes preserves some of its characteristics centuries later. Thus, among nineteenth-century German storytellers, writers like Hebel and Gotthelf stem from the first tribe, writers like Sealsfield and Gerstäcker from the second. With these tribes, however, as stated above, it is only a matter of basic types. The actual extension of the realm of storytelling in its full historical breadth is inconceivable without the most intimate interpenetration of these two archaic types. Such an interpenetration was achieved particularly by the Middle Ages in their trade structure. The resident master craftsman and the traveling journeymen worked together in the same rooms; and every master had been a traveling journeyman before he settled down in his home town or somewhere else. If peasants and seamen were past masters of storytelling, the artisan class was its university. In it was combined the lore of faraway places, such as a much-traveled man brings home, with the lore of the past, as it best reveals itself to natives of a place.

III

Leskov was at home in distant places as well as distant times. He was a member of the Greek Orthodox Church, a man with genuine religious interests. But he was a no less sincere opponent of ecclesiastic bureaucracy. Since he was not able to get along any better with secular officialdom, the official positions he held were not of long duration. Of all his posts, the one he held for a long time as Russian representative of a big English firm was presumably the most useful one for his writing. For this firm he traveled through Russia, and these trips advanced his worldly wisdom as much as they did his knowledge of conditions in Russia. In this way he had an opportunity of becoming acquainted with the organization of the sects in the country. This left its mark on his works of fiction. In the Russian legends Leskov saw allies in his fight against Orthodox bureaucracy. There are a number of his legendary tales whose focus is a righteous man, seldom an ascetic, usually a simple, active man who becomes a saint apparently in the most natural way in the world. Mystical exaltation is not Leskov's forte. Even though he occasionally liked to indulge in the miraculous, even in piousness he prefers to stick with a sturdy nature. He sees the prototype in the man who finds his way about the world without getting too deeply involved with it.

He displayed a corresponding attitude in worldly matters. It is in keeping with this that he began to write late, at the age of twenty-nine. That was after his commercial travels. His first printed work was entitled "Why Are Books Expensive in Kiev?" A number of other writings about the working class, alcoholism, police doctors, and unemployed salesmen are precursors of his works of fiction.

IV

An orientation toward practical interests is characteristic of many born storytellers. More pronouncedly than in Leskov this trait can be recognized, for example, in Gotthelf, who gave his peasants agricultural advice; it is found in Nodier, who concerned himself with the perils of gas light; and Hebel, who slipped bits of scientific instruction for his readers into his *Schatzkästlein*, is in this line as well. All this points to the nature of every real story. It contains, openly or covertly, something useful. The usefulness may, in one case, consist in a moral; in another, in some practical advice; in a third, in a proverb or maxim. In every case the storyteller is a man who has counsel for his readers. But if today "having counsel" is beginning to have an old-fashioned ring, this is because the communicability of experience is decreasing. In consequence we have no counsel either for ourselves or for others. After all, counsel is less an answer to a question than a proposal concerning the continuation of a story which is just unfolding. To seek this counsel one would first have to be able to tell the story. (Quite apart from the fact that a man is receptive to counsel only to the extent that he allows his situation to speak.) Counsel woven into the fabric of real life is wisdom. The art of storytelling is reaching its end because the epic side of truth, wisdom, is dying out. This, however, is a process that has been going on for a long time. And nothing would be more fatuous than to want to see in it merely a "symptom of decay," let alone a "modern" symptom. It is, rather, only a concomitant symptom of the secular productive forces of history, a concomitant that has quite gradually removed narrative from the realm of living speech and at the same time is making it possible to see a new beauty in what is vanishing.

V

The earliest symptom of a process whose end is the decline of storytelling is the rise of the novel at the beginning of modern times. What distinguishes the novel from the story (and from the epic in the narrower sense) is its essential dependence on the book. The dissemination of the novel became possible only with the invention of printing. What can be handed on orally, the wealth of the epic, is of a different kind from what constitutes the stock in trade of the novel. What differentiates the novel from all other forms of prose literature—the fairy tale, the legend, even the novella—is that it neither comes from oral tradition nor goes into it. This distinguishes it from storytelling in particular. The storyteller takes what he tells from experience—his own or that reported by others. And he in turn makes it the experience of those who are listening to his tale. The novelist has isolated himself. The birthplace of the novel is the solitary individual, who is no longer able to express himself by giving examples of his most important concerns, is himself uncounseled, and cannot counsel others. To write a novel means to carry the incommensurable to extremes in the representation of human life. In the midst of life's fullness, and through the representation of this fullness, the novel gives evidence of the profound perplexity of the living. Even the first great book of the genre, *Don Quixote,* teaches how the spiritual greatness, the boldness, the helpfulness of one of the noblest of men, Don Quixote, are completely devoid of counsel and do not contain the slightest scintilla of wisdom. If now and then, in the course of the centuries, efforts have been made—most effectively, perhaps, in *Wilhelm Meisters Wanderjahre*—to implant instruction in the novel, these attempts have always amounted to a modification of the novel form. The *Bildungsroman,* on the other hand, does not deviate in any way from the basic structure of the novel. By integrating the social process with the development of a person, it bestows the most frangible justification on the order determining it. The legitimacy it provides stands in direct opposition to reality. Particularly in the *Bildungsroman,* it is this inadequacy that is actualized.

VI

One must imagine the transformation of epic forms occurring in rhythms comparable to those of the change that has come over the earth's surface in the course of thousands of centuries. Hardly any other forms of human communication have taken shape more slowly, been lost more slowly. It took the novel, whose beginnings go back to antiquity, hundreds of years before it encountered in the evolving middle class those elements which were favorable to its flowering. With the appearance of these elements, storytelling began quite slowly to recede into the archaic; in many ways, it is true, it took hold of the new material, but it was not really determined by it. On the other hand, we recognize that with the full control of the middle class, which has the press as one of its most important instruments in fully developed capitalism, there emerges a form of communication which, no matter how far back its origin may lie, never before influenced the epic form in a decisive way. But now it does exert such an influence. And it turns out that it confronts storytelling as no less of a stranger than did the novel, but in a more menacing way, and that it also brings about a crisis in the novel. This new form of communication is information.

Villemessant, the founder of *Le Figaro,* characterized the nature of information in a famous formulation. "To my readers," he used to say, "an attic fire in the Latin Quarter is more important than a revolution in Madrid." This makes strikingly clear that it is no longer intelligence coming from afar, but the information which supplies a handle for what is nearest that gets the readiest hearing. The intelligence that came from afar—whether the spatial kind from foreign countries or the temporal kind of tradition—possessed an authority which gave it validity, even when it was not subject to verification. Information, however, lays claim to prompt verifiability. The prime requirement is that it appear "understandable in itself." Often it is no more exact than the intelligence of earlier centuries was. But while the latter was inclined to borrow from the miraculous, it is indispensable for information to sound plausible. Because of this it proves incompatible with the spirit of storytelling. If the art of storytelling has become rare, the dissemination of information has had a decisive share in this state of affairs.

Every morning brings us the news of the globe, and yet we are poor in noteworthy stories. This is because no event any longer comes to us without already being shot through with explanation. In other words, by now almost nothing that happens benefits storytelling; almost everything benefits information. Actually, it is half the art of storytelling to keep a story free from explanation as one reproduces it. Leskov is a master at this (compare pieces like "The Deception" and "The White Eagle"). The most extraordinary things, marvelous things, are related with the greatest accuracy, but the psychological connection of the events is not forced on the reader. It is left up to him to interpret things the way he understands them, and thus the narrative achieves an amplitude that information lacks.

VII

Leskov was grounded in the classics. The first storyteller of the Greeks was Herodotus. In the fourteenth chapter of the third book of his *Histories* there is a story from which much can be learned. It deals with Psammenitus.

When the Egyptian king Psammenitus had been beaten and captured by the Persian king Cambyses, Cambyses was bent on humbling his prisoner. He gave orders to place Psammenitus on the road along which the Persian triumphal procession was to pass. And he further arranged that the prisoner should see his daughter pass by as a maid going to the well with her pitcher. While all the Egyptians were lamenting and bewailing this spectacle, Psammenitus stood alone, mute and motionless, his eyes fixed on the ground; and when presently he saw his son, who was being taken along in the procession to be executed, he likewise remained unmoved. But when afterwards he recognized one of his servants, an old, impoverished man, in the ranks of the prisoners, he beat his fists against his head and gave all the signs of deepest mourning.

From this story it may be seen what the nature of true storytelling is. The value of information does not survive the moment in which it was new. It lives only at that moment; it has to surrender to it completely and explain itself to it without losing any time. A story is different. It does not expend itself. It preserves and concentrates its strength and is capable of releasing it even after a long time. Thus Montaigne referred to this Egyptian king and asked himself why he mourned only when he caught sight of his servant. Montaigne answers: "Since he was already overfull of grief, it took only the smallest increase for it to burst through its dams." Thus Montaigne. But one could also say: The king is not moved by the fate of those of royal blood, for it is his own fate. Or: We are moved by much on the stage that does not move us in real life; to the king, this servant is only an actor. Or: Great grief is pent up and breaks forth only with relaxation. Seeing this servant was the relaxation. Herodotus offers no explanations. His report is the driest. That is why this story from ancient Egypt is still capable after thousands of years of arousing astonishment and thoughtfulness. It resembles the seeds of grain which have lain for centuries in the chambers of the pyramids shut up air-tight and have retained their germinative power to this day.

VIII

There is nothing that commends a story to memory more effectively than that chaste compactness which precludes psychological analysis. And the more natural the process by which the storyteller forgoes psychological shading, the greater becomes the story's claim to a place in the memory of the listener, the more completely is it integrated into his own experience, the greater will be his inclination to repeat it to someone else someday, sooner or later. This process of assimilation, which takes place in depth, requires a state of relaxation which is becoming rarer and rarer. If sleep is the apogee of physical relaxation, boredom is the apogee of mental relaxation. Boredom is the dream bird that hatches the egg of experience. A rustling in the leaves drives him away. His nesting places—the activities that are intimately associated with boredom—are already extinct in the cities and are declining in the country as well. With this the gift for listening is lost and the community of listeners disappears. For storytelling is always the art of repeating stories, and this art is lost when the stories are no longer retained. It is lost because there is no more weaving and spinning to go on while they are being listened to. The more self-forgetful the listener is, the more deeply is what he listens to impressed upon his memory. When the rhythm of work has seized him, he listens to the tales in such a way that the gift of retelling them comes to him all by itself. This, then, is the nature of the web in which the gift of storytelling is cradled. This is how today it is becoming unraveled at all its ends after being woven thousands of years ago in the ambience of the oldest forms of craftsmanship.

IX

The storytelling that thrives for a long time in the milieu of work—the rural, the maritime, and the urban—is itself an artisan form of communication, as it were. It does not aim to convey the pure essence of the thing, like information or a report. It sinks the thing into the life of the storyteller, in order to bring it out of him again. Thus traces of the storyteller cling to the story the way the handprints of the potter cling to the clay vessel. Storytellers tend to begin their story with a presentation of the circumstances in which they themselves have learned what is to follow, unless they simply pass it off as their own experience. Leskov begins his "Deception" with the description of a

train trip on which he supposedly heard from a fellow passenger the events
which he then goes on to relate; or he thinks of Dostoevsky's funeral, where he
sets his acquaintance with the heroine of his story "À Propos of the Kreutzer
Sonata"; or he evokes a gathering of a reading circle in which we are told the
events that he reproduces for us in his "Interesting Men." Thus his tracks are
frequently evident in his narratives, if not as those of the one who experienced
it, then as those of the one who reports it.

This craftsmanship, storytelling, was actually regarded as a craft by
Leskov himself. "Writing," he says in one of his letters, "is to me no liberal art,
but a craft." It cannot come as a surprise that he felt bonds with craftsmanship,
but faced industrial technology as a stranger. Tolstoy, who must have
understood this, occasionally touches this nerve of Leskov's storytelling talent
when he calls him the first man "who pointed out the inadequacy of economic
progress. . . . It is strange that Dostoevsky is so widely read. . . . But I simply
cannot comprehend why Leskov is not read. He is a truthful writer." In his
artful and high-spirited story "The Steel Flea," which is midway between
legend and farce, Leskov glorifies native craftsmanship through the silver-
smiths of Tula. Their masterpiece, the steel flea, is seen by Peter the Great and
convinces him that the Russians need not be ashamed before the English.

The intellectual picture of the atmosphere of craftsmanship from which
the storyteller comes has perhaps never been sketched in such a significant
way as by Paul Valéry. "He speaks of the perfect things in nature, flawless
pearls, full-bodied, matured wines, truly developed creatures, and calls them
'the precious product of a long chain of causes similar to one another.'" The
accumulation of such causes has its temporal limit only at perfection. "This
patient process of Nature," Valéry continues, "was once imitated by men.
Miniatures, ivory carvings, elaborated to the point of greatest perfection, stones
that are perfect in polish and engraving, lacquer work or paintings in which a
series of thin, transparent layers are placed one on top of the other—all these
products of sustained, sacrificing effort are vanishing, and the time is past in
which time did not matter. Modern man no longer works at what cannot be
abbreviated."

In point of fact, he has succeeded in abbreviating even storytelling. We
have witnessed the evolution of the "short story," which has removed itself
from oral tradition and no longer permits that slow piling one on top of the
other of thin, transparent layers which constitutes the most appropriate picture
of the way in which the perfect narrative is revealed through the layers of a
variety of retellings.

X

Valéry concludes his observations with this sentence: "It is almost as if the
decline of the idea of eternity coincided with the increasing aversion to
sustained effort." The idea of eternity has ever had its strongest source in
death. If this idea declines, so we reason, the face of death must have changed.
It turns out that this change is identical with the one that has diminished the

communicability of experience to the same extent as the art of storytelling has declined.

It has been observable for a number of centuries how in the general consciousness the thought of death has declined in omnipresence and vividness. In its last stages this process is accelerated. And in the course of the nineteenth century bourgeois society has, by means of hygienic and social, private and public institutions, realized a secondary effect which may have been its subconscious main purpose: to make it possible for people to avoid the sight of the dying. Dying was once a public process in the life of the individual and a most exemplary one; think of the medieval pictures in which the deathbed has turned into a throne toward which the people press through the wide-open doors of the death house. In the course of modern times dying has been pushed further and further out of the perceptual world of the living. There used to be no house, hardly a room, in which someone had not once died. (The Middle Ages also felt spatially what makes that inscription on a sun dial of Ibiza, *Ultima multis* [the last day for many], significant as the temper of the times.) Today people live in rooms that have never been touched by death, dry dwellers of eternity, and when their end approaches they are stowed away in sanatoria or hospitals by their heirs. It is, however, characteristic that not only a man's knowledge or wisdom, but above all his real life—and this is the stuff that stories are made of—first assumes transmissible form at the moment of his death. Just as a sequence of images is set in motion inside a man as his life comes to an end—unfolding the views of himself under which he has encountered himself without being aware of it—suddenly in his expressions and looks the unforgettable emerges and imparts to everything that concerned him that authority which even the poorest wretch in dying possesses for the living around him. This authority is at the very source of the story.

XI

Death is the sanction of everything that the storyteller can tell. He has borrowed his authority from death. In other words, it is natural history to which his stories refer back. This is expressed in exemplary form in one of the most beautiful stories we have by the incomparable Johann Peter Hebel. It is found in the *Schatzkästlein des rheinischen Hausfreundes,* is entitled "Unexpected Reunion," and begins with the betrothal of a young lad who works in the mines of Falun. On the eve of his wedding he dies a miner's death at the bottom of his tunnel. His bride keeps faith with him after his death, and she lives long enough to become a wizened old woman; one day a body is brought up from the abandoned tunnel which, saturated with iron vitriol, has escaped decay, and she recognizes her betrothed. After this reunion she too is called away by death. When Hebel, in the course of this story, was confronted with the necessity of making this long period of years graphic, he did so in the following sentences: "In the meantime the city of Lisbon was destroyed by an earthquake, and the Seven Years' War came and went, and Emperor Francis I died, and the Jesuit Order was abolished, and Poland was partitioned, and Empress Maria Theresa died, and Struensee was executed. America became independent, and the united French and Spanish forces were unable to capture Gibraltar. The Turks locked up General Stein in the Veteraner Cave in Hungary, and Emperor Joseph died also. King Gustavus of Sweden conquered Russian Finland, and the French Revolution and the long war began, and Emperor Leopold II went to his grave too. Napoleon captured Prussia, and the English bombarded Copenhagen, and the peasants sowed and harvested. The millers ground, the smiths hammered, and the miners dug for veins of ore in their underground workshops. But when in 1809 the miners at Falun . . ."

Never has a storyteller embedded his report deeper in natural history than Hebel manages to do in this chronology. Read it carefully. Death appears in it with the same regularity as the Reaper does in the processions that pass around the cathedral clock at noon.

XII

Any examination of a given epic form is concerned with the relationship of this form to historiography. In fact, one may go even further and raise the question whether historiography does not constitute the common ground of all forms of the epic. Then written history would be in the same relationship to the epic forms as white light is to the colors of the spectrum. However this may be, among all forms of the epic there is not one whose incidence in the pure, colorless light of written history is more certain than the chronicle. And in the broad spectrum of the chronicle the ways in which a story can be told are graduated like shadings of one and the same color. The chronicler is the history-teller. If we think back to the passage from Hebel, which has the tone of a chronicle throughout, it will take no effort to gauge the difference between the writer of history, the historian, and the teller of it, the chronicler. The historian is bound to explain in one way or another the happenings with which he deals; under no circumstances can he content himself with displaying them as models of the course of the world. But this is precisely what the chronicler does, especially in his classical representatives, the chroniclers of the Middle Ages, the precursors of the historians of today. By basing their historical tales on a divine plan of salvation—an inscrutable one—they have from the very start lifted the burden of demonstrable explanation from their own shoulders. Its place is taken by interpretation, which is not concerned with an accurate concatenation of definite events, but with the way these are embedded in the great inscrutable course of the world.

Whether this course is eschatologically determined or is a natural one makes no difference. In the storyteller the chronicler is preserved in changed form, secularized, as it were. Leskov is among those whose work displays this with particular clarity. Both the chronicler with his eschatological orientation and the storyteller with his profane outlook are so represented in his works that in a number of his stories it can hardly be decided whether the web in which they appear is the golden fabric of a religious view of the course of things, or the multicolored fabric of a worldly view.

Consider the story "The Alexandrite," which transports the reader into "that old time when the stones in the womb of the earth and the planets at celestial heights were still concerned with the fate of men, and not today when both in the heavens and beneath the earth everything has grown indifferent to the fates of the sons of men and no voice speaks to them from anywhere, let alone does their bidding. None of the undiscovered planets play any part in horoscopes any more, and there are a lot of new stones, all measured and weighed and examined for their specific weight and their density, but they no longer proclaim anything to us, nor do they bring us any benefit. Their time for speaking with men is past."

As is evident, it is hardly possible unambiguously to characterize the course of the world that is illustrated in this story of Leskov's. Is it determined eschatologically or naturalistically? The only certain thing is that in its very nature it is by definition outside all real historical categories. Leskov tells us that the epoch in which man could believe himself to be in harmony with nature has expired. Schiller called this epoch in the history of the world the period of naïve poetry. The storyteller keeps faith with it, and his eyes do not stray from that dial in front of which there moves the procession of creatures of which, depending on circumstances, Death is either the leader or the last wretched straggler.

XIII

It has seldom been realized that the listener's naïve relationship to the storyteller is controlled by his interest in retaining what he is told. The cardinal point for the unaffected listener is to assure himself of the possibility of reproducing the story. Memory is the epic faculty *par excellence*. Only by virtue of a comprehensive memory can epic writing absorb the course of events on the one hand and, with the passing of these, make its peace with the power of death on the other. It is not surprising that to a simple man of the people, such as Leskov once invented, the Czar, the head of the sphere in which his stories take place, has the most encyclopedic memory at his command. "Our Emperor," he says, "and his entire family have indeed a most astonishing memory."

Mnemosyne, the rememberer, was the Muse of the epic art among the Greeks. This name takes the observer back to a parting of the ways in world history. For if the record kept by memory—historiography—constitutes the creative matrix of the various epic forms (as great prose is the creative matrix of the various metrical forms), its oldest form, the epic, by virtue of being a kind of common denominator includes the story and the novel. When in the course of centuries the novel began to emerge from the womb of the epic, it turned out that in the novel the element of the epic mind that is derived from the Muse—that is, memory—manifests itself in a form quite different from the way it manifests itself in the story.

Memory creates the chain of tradition which passes a happening on from generation to generation. It is the Muse-derived element of the epic art in a broader sense and encompasses its varieties. In the first place among these is the one practiced by the storyteller. It starts the web which all stories together form in the end. One ties on to the next, as the great storytellers, particularly the Oriental ones, have always readily shown. In each of them there is a Scheherazade who thinks of a fresh story whenever her tale comes to a stop. This is epic remembrance and the Muse-inspired element of the narrative. But this should be set against another principle, also a Muse-derived element in a narrower sense, which as an element of the novel in its earliest form—that is, in the epic—lies concealed, still undifferentiated from the similarly derived element of the story. It can, at any rate, occasionally be divined in the epics, particularly at moments of solemnity in the Homeric epics, as in the invocations to the Muse at their beginning. What announces itself in these passages is the perpetuating remembrance of the novelist as contrasted with the short-lived reminiscences of the storyteller. The first is dedicated to *one* hero, *one* odyssey, *one* battle; the second, to *many* diffuse occurrences. It is, in other words, *remembrance* which, as the Muse-derived element of the novel, is added to reminiscence, the corresponding element of the story, the unity of their origin in memory having disappeared with the decline of the epic.

XIV

"No one," Pascal once said, "dies so poor that he does not leave something behind." Surely it is the same with memories too—although these do not always find an heir. The novelist takes charge of this bequest, and seldom without profound melancholy. For what Arnold Bennett says about a dead woman in one of his novels—that she had had almost nothing in the way of real life—is usually true of the sum total of the estate which the novelist administers. Regarding this aspect of the matter we owe the most important elucidation to Georg Lukács, who sees in the novel "the form of transcendental homelessness." According to Lukács, the novel is at the same time the only art form which includes time among its constitutive principles.

"Time," he says in his *Theory of the Novel*, "can become constitutive only when connection with the transcendental home has been lost. Only in the novel are meaning and life, and thus the essential and the temporal, separated; one can almost say that the whole inner action of a novel is nothing else but a struggle against the power of time. . . . And from this . . . arise the genuinely epic experiences of time: hope and memory. . . . Only in the novel . . . does there occur a creative memory which transfixes the object and transforms it. . . . The duality of inwardness and outside world can here be overcome for the subject 'only' when he sees the . . . unity of his entire life . . . out of the past life-stream which is compressed in memory. . . . The insight which grasps this unity . . . becomes the divinatory-intuitive grasping of the unattained and therefore inexpressible meaning of life."

The "meaning of life" is really the center about which the novel moves.

But the quest for it is no more than the initial expression of perplexity with which its reader sees himself living this written life. Here "meaning of life"— there "moral of the story": with these slogans novel and story confront each other, and from them the totally different historical co-ordinates of these art forms may be discerned. If *Don Quixote* is the earliest perfect specimen of the novel, its latest exemplar is perhaps the *Éducation sentimentale*.

In the final words of the last-named novel, the meaning which the bourgeois age found in its behavior at the beginning of its decline has settled like sediment in the cup of life. Frédéric and Deslauriers, the boyhood friends, think back to their youthful friendship. This little incident then occurred: one day they showed up in the bordello of their home town, stealthily and timidly, doing nothing but presenting the *patronne* with a bouquet of flowers which they had picked in their own gardens. "This story was still discussed three years later. And now they told it to each other in detail, each supplementing the recollection of the other. 'That may have been,' said Frédéric when they had finished, 'the finest thing in our lives.' 'Yes, you may be right,' said Deslauriers, 'that was perhaps the finest thing in our lives.'"

With such an insight the novel reaches an end which is more proper to it, in a stricter sense, than to any story. Actually there is no story for which the question as to how it continued would not be legitimate. The novelist, on the other hand, cannot hope to take the smallest step beyond that limit at which he invites the reader to a divinatory realization of the meaning of life by writing "Finis."

XV

A man listening to a story is in the company of the storyteller; even a man reading one shares this companionship. The reader of a novel, however, is isolated, more so than any other reader. (For even the reader of a poem is ready to utter the words, for the benefit of the listener.) In this solitude of his, the reader of a novel seizes upon his material more jealously than anyone else. He is ready to make it completely his own, to devour it, as it were. Indeed, he destroys, he swallows up the material as the fire devours logs in the fireplace. The suspense which permeates the novel is very much like the draft which stimulates the flame in the fireplace and enlivens its play.

It is a dry material on which the burning interest of the reader feeds. "A man who dies at the age of thirty-five," said Moritz Heimann once, "is at every point of his life a man who dies at the age of thirty-five." Nothing is more dubious than this sentence—but for the sole reason that the tense is wrong. A man—so says the truth that was meant here—who died at thirty-five will appear to *remembrance* at every point in his life as a man who dies at the age of thirty-five. In other words, the statement that makes no sense for real life becomes indisputable for remembered life. The nature of the character in a novel cannot be presented any better than is done in this statement, which says that the "meaning" of his life is revealed only in his death. But the reader of a novel actually does look for human beings from whom he derives the "meaning of life." Therefore he must, no matter what, know in advance that he will share their experience of death: if need be their figurative death—the end of the novel—but preferably their actual one. How do the characters make him understand that death is already waiting for them—a very definite death and at a very definite place? That is the question which feeds the reader's consuming interest in the events of the novel.

The novel is significant, therefore, not because it presents someone else's fate to us, perhaps didactically, but because this stranger's fate by virtue of the flame which consumes it yields us the warmth which we never draw from our own fate. What draws the reader to the novel is the hope of warming his shivering life with a death he reads about.

XVI

"Leskov," writes Gorky, "is the writer most deeply rooted in the people and is completely untouched by any foreign influences." A great storyteller will always be rooted in the people, primarily in a milieu of craftsmen. But just as this includes the rural, the maritime, and the urban elements in the many stages of their economic and technical development, there are many grada-tions in the concepts in which their store of experience comes down to us. (To say nothing of the by no means insignificant share which traders had in the art of storytelling; their task was less to increase its didactic content than to refine the tricks with which the attention of the listener was captured. They have left deep traces in the narrative cycle of *The Arabian Nights*.) In short, despite the primary role which storytelling plays in the household of humanity, the concepts through which the yield of the stories may be garnered are manifold. What may most readily be put in religious terms in Leskov seems almost automatically to fall into place in the pedagogical perspectives of the Enlight-enment in Hebel, appears as hermetic tradition in Poe, finds a last refuge in Kipling in the life of British seamen and colonial soldiers. All great storytellers have in common the freedom with which they move up and down the rungs of their experience as on a ladder. A ladder extending downward to the interior of the earth and disappearing into the clouds is the image for a collective experience to which even the deepest shock of every individual experience, death, constitutes no impediment or barrier.

"And they lived happily ever after," says the fairy tale. The fairy tale, which to this day is the first tutor of children because it was once the first tutor of mankind, secretly lives on in the story. The first true storyteller is, and will continue to be, the teller of fairy tales. Whenever good counsel was at a premium, the fairy tale had it, and where the need was greatest, its aid was nearest. This need was the need created by the myth. The fairy tale tells us of the earliest arrangements that mankind made to shake off the nightmare which the myth had placed upon its chest. In the figure of the fool it shows us how mankind "acts dumb" toward the myth; in the figure of the youngest brother it shows us how one's chances increase as the mythical primitive times are left behind; in the figure of the man who sets out to learn what fear is it shows us that the things we are afraid of can be seen through; in the figure of the wiseacre it shows us that the questions posed by the myth are simple-minded, like the riddle of the Sphinx; in the shape of the animals which come to the aid of the child in the fairy tale it shows that nature not only is subservient to the myth, but much prefers to be aligned with man. The wisest thing—so the fairy tale taught mankind in olden times, and teaches children to this day—is to meet the forces of the mythical world with cunning and with high spirits. (This is how the fairy tale polarizes *Mut*, courage, dividing it dialectically into *Untermut*, that is, cunning, and *Übermut*, high spirits.) The liberating magic which the fairy tale has at its disposal does not bring nature into play in a mythical way, but points to its complicity with liberated man. A mature man feels this complicity only occasionally, that is, when he is happy; but the child first meets it in fairy tales, and it makes him happy.

XVII

Few storytellers have displayed so profound a kinship with the spirit of the fairy tale as did Leskov. This involves tendencies that were promoted by the dogmas of the Greek Orthodox Church. As is well known, Origen's speculation about *apokatastasis*—the entry of all souls into Paradise—which was rejected by the Roman Church plays a significant part in these dogmas. Leskov was very much influenced by Origen and planned to translate his work *On First Principles*. In keeping with Russian folk belief he interpreted the Resurrection less as a transfiguration than as a disenchantment, in a sense akin to the fairy tale. Such an interpretation of Origen is at the bottom of "The Enchanted Pilgrim." In this, as in many other tales by Leskov, a hybrid between fairy tale and legend is involved, not unlike that hybrid which Ernst Bloch mentions in a connection in which he utilizes our distinction between myth and fairy tale in his fashion.

"A hybrid between fairy tale and legend," he says, "contains figuratively mythical elements, mythical elements whose effect is certainly captivating and static, and yet not outside man. In the legend there are Taoist figures, especially very old ones, which are 'mythical' in this sense. For instance, the couple Philemon and Baucis: magically escaped though in natural repose. And surely there is a similar relationship between fairy tale and legend in the Taoist climate of Gotthelf, which, to be sure, is on a much lower level. At certain points it divorces the legend from the locality of the spell, rescues the flame of life, the specifically human flame of life, calmly burning, within as without."

"Magically escaped" are the beings that lead the procession of Leskov's creations: the righteous ones. Pavlin, Figura, the toupee artiste, the bear keeper, the helpful sentry—all of them embodiments of wisdom, kindness, comfort the world, crowd about the storyteller. They are unmistakably suf-fused with the *imago* of his mother.

This is how Leskov describes her: "She was so thoroughly good that she was not capable of harming any man, nor even an animal. She ate neither meat nor fish, because she had such pity for living creatures. Sometimes my father used to reproach her with this. But she answered: 'I have raised the little animals myself, they are like my children to me. I can't eat my own children, can I?' She would not eat meat at a neighbor's house either. 'I have seen them alive,' she would say; 'they are my acquaintances. I can't eat my acquaintances, can I?'"

The righteous man is the advocate for created things and at the same time he is their highest embodiment. In Leskov he has a maternal touch which is occasionally intensified into the mythical (and thus, to be sure, endangers the purity of the fairy tale). Typical of this is the protagonist of his story "Kotin the Provider and Platonida." This figure, a peasant named Pisonski, is a hermaphrodite. For twelve years his mother raised him as a girl. His male and female organs mature simultaneously, and his bisexuality "becomes the symbol of God incarnate."

In Leskov's view, the pinnacle of creation has been attained with this, and at the same time he presumably sees it as a bridge established between this world and the other. For these earthily powerful, maternal male figures which again and again claim Leskov's skill as a storyteller have been removed from obedience to the sexual drive in the bloom of their strength. They do not, however, really embody an ascetic ideal; rather, the continence of these righteous men has so little privative character that it becomes the elemental counterpoise to uncontrolled lust which the storyteller has personified in *Lady Macbeth of Mzensk*. If the range between a Pavlin and this merchant's wife covers the breadth of the world of created beings, in the hierarchy of his characters Leskov has no less plumbed its depth.

XVIII

The hierarchy of the world of created things, which has its apex in the righteous man, reaches down into the abyss of the inanimate by many gradations. In this connection one particular has to be noted. This whole created world speaks not so much with the human voice as with what could be called "the voice of Nature" in the title of one of Leskov's most significant stories.

This story deals with the petty official Philip Philipovich who leaves no stone unturned to get the chance to have as his house guest a field marshal passing through his little town. He manages to do so. The guest, who is at first surprised at the clerk's urgent invitation, gradually comes to believe that he recognizes in him someone he must have met previously. But who is he? He cannot remember. The strange thing is that the host, for his part, is not willing to reveal his identity. Instead, he puts off the high personage from day to day, saying that the "voice of Nature" will not fail to speak distinctly to him one day. This goes on until finally the guest, shortly before continuing on his journey, must grant the host's public request to let the "voice of Nature" resound. Thereupon the host's wife withdraws. She "returned with a big, brightly polished, copper hunting horn which she gave to her husband. He took the horn, put it to his lips, and was at the same instant as though transformed. Hardly had he inflated his cheeks and produced a tone as powerful as the rolling of thunder when the field marshal cried: 'Stop, I've got it now, brother. This makes me recognize you at once! You are the bugler from the regiment of jaegers, and because you were so honest I sent you to keep an eye on a crooked supplies supervisor.' 'That's it, Your Excellency,' answered the host. 'I didn't want to remind you of this myself, but wanted to let the voice of Nature speak.'"

The way the profundity of this story is hidden beneath its silliness conveys an idea of Leskov's magnificent humor. This humor is confirmed in the same story in an even more cryptic way. We have heard that because of his honesty the official was assigned to watch a crooked supplies supervisor. This is what we are told at the end, in the recognition scene. At the very beginning of the story, however, we learn the following about the host: "All the inhabitants of the town were acquainted with the man, and they knew that he did not hold a high office, for he was neither a state official nor a military man, but a little supervisor at the tiny supply depot, where together with the rats he chewed on the state rusks and boot soles, and in the course of time had chewed himself together a nice little frame house." It is evident that this story reflects the traditional sympathy which storytellers have for rascals and crooks. All the literature of farce bears witness to it. Nor is it denied on the heights of art; of all Hebel's characters, the Brassenheim Miller, Tinder Frieder, and Red Dieter have been his most faithful companions. And yet for Hebel, too, the righteous man has the main role in the *theatrum mundi*. But because no one is actually up to this role, it keeps changing hands. Now it is the tramp, now the haggling Jewish peddler, now the man of limited intelligence who steps in to play this part. In every single case it is a guest performance, a moral improvisation. Hebel is a casuist. He will not for anything take a stand with any principle, but he does not reject it either, for any principle can at some time become the instrument of the righteous man. Compare this with Leskov's attitude. "I realize," he writes in his story "À Propos of the Kreutzer Sonata," "that my thinking is based much more on a practical view of life than on abstract philosophy or lofty morality; but I am nevertheless used to thinking the way I do." To be sure, the moral catastrophes that appear in Leskov's world are to the moral incidents in Hebel's world as the great, silent flowing of the Volga is to the babbling, rushing little millstream. Among Leskov's historical tales there are several in which passions are at work as destructively as the wrath of Achilles or the hatred of Hagen. It is astonishing how fearfully the world can darken for this author and with what majesty evil can raise its scepter. Leskov has evidently known moods—and this is probably one of the few characteristics he shares with Dostoevsky—in which he was close to antinomian ethics. The elemental natures in his *Tales from Olden Times* go to the limit in their ruthless passion. But it is precisely the mystics who have been inclined to see this limit as the point at which utter depravity turns into saintliness.

XIX

The lower Leskov descends on the scale of created things the more obviously does his way of viewing things approach the mystical. Actually, as will be shown, there is much evidence that in this, too, a characteristic is revealed which is inherent in the nature of the storyteller. To be sure, only a few have ventured into the depths of inanimate nature, and in modern narrative literature there is not much in which the voice of the anonymous storyteller, who was prior to all literature, resounds so clearly as it does in Leskov's story "The Alexandrite." It deals with a semi-precious stone, the chrysoberyl. The mineral is the lowest stratum of created things. For the storyteller, however, it is directly joined to the highest. To him it is granted to see in this chrysoberyl a natural prophecy of petrified, lifeless nature concerning the historical world in which he himself lives. This world is the world of Alexander II. The storyteller—or rather, the man to whom he attributes his own knowledge—is a gem engraver named Wenzel who has achieved the greatest conceivable skill in his art. One can juxtapose him with the silver-smiths of Tula and say that—in the spirit of Leskov—the perfect artisan has access to the innermost chamber of the realm of created things. He is an incarnation of the devout. We are told of this gem cutter: "He suddenly squeezed my hand on which was the ring with the alexandrite, which is known to sparkle red in artificial light, and cried: 'Look, here it is, the prophetic Russian stone! O crafty Siberian. It was always green as hope and only toward evening was it suffused with blood. It was that way from the beginning of the world, but it concealed itself for a long time, lay hidden in the earth, and permitted itself to be found only on the day when Czar Alexander was declared of age, when a great sorcerer had come to Siberia to find the stone, a magician. . . .' 'What nonsense are you talking,' I interrupted him; 'this stone wasn't found by a magician at all, it was a scholar named Nordenskjöld!' 'A magician! I tell you, a magician!' screamed Wenzel in a loud voice. 'Just look; what a stone! A green morning is in it and a bloody evening . . . This is fate, the fate of noble Czar Alexander!' With these words old Wenzel turned to the wall, propped his head on his elbows, and . . . began to sob."

One can hardly come any closer to the meaning of this significant story than by some words which Paul Valéry wrote in a very remote context. "Artistic observation," he says in reflections on a woman artist whose work consisted in the silk embroidery of figures, "can attain an almost mystical depth. The objects on which it falls lose their names. Light and shade form very particular systems, present very individual questions which depend upon no knowledge and are derived from no practice, but get their existence and value exclusively from a certain accord of the soul, the eye, and the hand of someone who was born to perceive them and evoke them in his own inner self."

With these words, soul, eye, and hand are brought into connection. Interacting with one another, they determine a practice. We are no longer familiar with this practice. The role of the hand in production has become more modest, and the place it filled in storytelling lies waste. (After all, storytelling, in its sensory aspect, is by no means a job for the voice alone. Rather, in genuine storytelling the hand plays a part which supports what is expressed in a hundred ways with its gestures trained by work.) That old co-ordination of the soul, the eye, and the hand which emerges in Valéry's words is that of the artisan which we encounter wherever the art of storytelling is at home. In fact, one can go on and ask oneself whether the relationship of the storyteller to his material, human life, is not in itself a craftsman's relationship, whether it is not his very task to fashion the raw material of experience, his own and that of others, in a solid, useful, and unique way. It is a kind of procedure which may perhaps most adequately be exemplified by the proverb if one thinks of it as an ideogram of a story. A proverb, one might say, is a ruin which stands on the site of an old story and in which a moral twines about a happening like ivy around a wall.

Seen in this way, the storyteller joins the ranks of the teachers and sages. He has counsel—not for a few situations, as the proverb does, but for many, like the sage. For it is granted to him to reach back to a whole lifetime (a life, incidentally, that comprises not only his own experience but no little of the experience of others; what the storyteller knows from hearsay is added to his own). His gift is the ability to relate his life; his distinction, to be able to tell his entire life. The storyteller: he is the man who could let the wick of his life be consumed completely by the gentle flame of his story. This is the basis of the incomparable aura about the storyteller, in Leskov as in Hauff, in Poe as in Stevenson. The storyteller is the figure in which the righteous man encounters himself.

THE WORK OF ART IN THE AGE OF MECHANICAL REPRODUCTION

Our fine arts were developed, their types and uses were established, in times very different from the present, by men whose power of action upon things was insignificant in comparison with ours. But the amazing growth of our techniques, the adaptability and precision they have attained, the ideas and habits they are creating, make it a certainty that profound changes are impending in the ancient craft of the Beautiful. In all the arts there is a physical component which can no longer be considered or treated as it used to be, which cannot remain unaffected by our modern knowledge and power. For the last twenty years neither matter nor space nor time has been what it was from time immemorial. We must expect great innovations to transform the entire technique of the arts, thereby affecting artistic invention itself and perhaps even bringing about an amazing change in our very notion of art.[1]

—Paul Valéry, *Pièces sur l'art,*
"La Conquète de l'ubiquité," Paris.

PREFACE

When Marx undertook his critique of the capitalistic mode of production, this mode was in its infancy. Marx directed his efforts in such a way as to give them prognostic value. He went back to the basic conditions underlying capitalistic production and through his presentation showed what could be expected of capitalism in the future. The result was that one could expect it not only to exploit the proletariat with increasing intensity, but ultimately to create conditions which would make it possible to abolish capitalism itself.

The transformation of the superstructure, which takes place far more slowly than that of the substructure, has taken more than half a century to manifest in all areas of culture the change in the conditions of production. Only today can it be indicated what form this has taken. Certain prognostic requirements should be met by these statements. However, theses about the art of the proletariat after its assumption of power or about the art of a classless society would have less bearing on these demands than theses about the developmental tendencies of art under present conditions of production. Their dialectic is no less noticeable in the superstructure than in the economy. It would therefore be wrong to underestimate the value of such theses as a weapon. They brush aside a number of outmoded concepts, such as creativity and genius, eternal value and mystery—concepts whose uncontrolled (and at present almost uncontrollable) application would lead to a processing of data in the Fascist sense. The concepts which are introduced into the theory of art in what follows differ from the more familiar terms in that they are completely useless for the purposes of Fascism. They are, on the other hand, useful for the formulation of revolutionary demands in the politics of art.

I

In principle a work of art has always been reproducible. Man-made artifacts could always be imitated by men. Replicas were made by pupils in practice of their craft, by masters for diffusing their works, and, finally, by third parties in the pursuit of gain. Mechanical reproduction of a work of art, however, represents something new. Historically, it advanced intermittently and in leaps at long intervals, but with accelerated intensity. The Greeks knew only two procedures of technically reproducing works of art: founding and stamping. Bronzes, terra cottas, and coins were the only art works which they could produce in quantity. All others were unique and could not be mechanically reproduced. With the woodcut graphic art became mechanically reproducible for the first time, long before script became reproducible by print. The enormous changes which printing, the mechanical reproduction of writing, has brought about in literature are a familiar story. However, within the phenomenon which we are here examining from the perspective of world history, print is merely a special, though particularly important, case. During the Middle Ages engraving and etching were added to the woodcut; at the beginning of the nineteenth century lithography made its appearance.

With lithography the technique of reproduction reached an essentially new stage. This much more direct process was distinguished by the tracing of the design on a stone rather than its incision on a block of wood or its etching on a copperplate and permitted graphic art for the first time to put its products on the market, not only in large numbers as hitherto, but also in daily changing forms. Lithography enabled graphic art to illustrate everyday life, and it began to keep pace with printing. But only a few decades after its invention, lithography was surpassed by photography. For the first time in the process of pictorial reproduction, photography freed the hand of the most important artistic functions which henceforth devolved only upon the eye looking into a lens. Since the eye perceives more swiftly than the hand can draw, the process of pictorial reproduction was accelerated so enormously that it could keep pace with speech. A film operator shooting a scene in the studio captures the images at the speed of an actor's speech. Just as lithography virtually implied the illustrated newspaper, so did photography foreshadow the sound film. The technical reproduction of sound was tackled at the end of the last century. These convergent endeavors made predictable a situation which Paul Valéry pointed up in this sentence: "Just as water, gas, and electricity are brought into our houses from far off to satisfy our needs in response to a minimal effort, so we shall be supplied with visual or auditory images, which will appear and disappear at a simple movement of the hand, hardly more than a sign" (*op. cit.*,

p. 226). Around 1900 technical reproduction had reached a standard that not only permitted it to reproduce all transmitted works of art and thus to cause the most profound change in their impact upon the public; it also had captured a place of its own among the artistic processes. For the study of this standard nothing is more revealing than the nature of the repercussions that these two different manifestations—the reproduction of works of art and the art of the film—have had on art in its traditional form.

II

Even the most perfect reproduction of a work of art is lacking in one element: its presence in time and space, its unique existence at the place where it happens to be. This unique existence of the work of art determined the history to which it was subject throughout the time of its existence. This includes the changes which it may have suffered in physical condition over the years as well as the various changes in its ownership.[2] The traces of the first can be revealed only by chemical or physical analyses which it is impossible to perform on a reproduction; changes of ownership are subject to a tradition which must be traced from the situation of the original.

The presence of the original is the prerequisite to the concept of authenticity. Chemical analyses of the patina of a bronze can help to establish this, as does the proof that a given manuscript of the Middle Ages stems from an archive of the fifteenth century. The whole sphere of authenticity is outside technical—and, of course, not only technical—reproducibility.[3] Confronted with its manual reproduction, which was usually branded as a forgery, the original preserved all its authority; not so *vis à vis* technical reproduction. The reason is twofold. First, process reproduction is more independent of the original than manual reproduction. For example, in photography, process reproduction can bring out those aspects of the original that are unattainable to the naked eye yet accessible to the lens, which is adjustable and chooses its angle at will. And photographic reproduction, with the aid of certain processes, such as enlargement or slow motion, can capture images which escape natural vision. Secondly, technical reproduction can put the copy of the original into situations which would be out of reach for the original itself. Above all, it enables the original to meet the beholder halfway, be it in the form of a photograph or a phonograph record. The cathedral leaves its locale to be received in the studio of a lover of art; the choral production, performed in an auditorium or in the open air, resounds in the drawing room.

The situations into which the product of mechanical reproduction can be brought may not touch the actual work of art, yet the quality of its presence is always depreciated. This holds not only for the art work but also, for instance, for a landscape which passes in review before the spectator in a movie. In the case of the art object, a most sensitive nucleus—namely, its authenticity—is interfered with whereas no natural object is vulnerable on that score. The authenticity of a thing is the essence of all that is transmissible from its beginning, ranging from its substantive duration to its testimony to the history which it has experienced. Since the historical testimony rests on the authenticity, the former, too, is jeopardized by reproduction when substantive duration ceases to matter. And what is really jeopardized when the historical testimony is affected is the authority of the object.[4]

One might subsume the eliminated element in the term "aura" and go on to say: that which withers in the age of mechanical reproduction is the aura of the work of art. This is a symptomatic process whose significance points beyond the realm of art. One might generalize by saying: the technique of reproduction detaches the reproduced object from the domain of tradition. By making many reproductions it substitutes a plurality of copies for a unique existence. And in permitting the reproduction to meet the beholder or listener in his own particular situation, it reactivates the object reproduced. These two processes lead to a tremendous shattering of tradition which is the obverse of the contemporary crisis and renewal of mankind. Both processes are intimately connected with the contemporary mass movements. Their most powerful agent is the film. Its social significance, particularly in its most positive form, is inconceivable without its destructive, cathartic aspect, that is, the liquidation of the traditional value of the cultural heritage. This phenomenon is most palpable in the great historical films. It extends to ever new positions. In 1927 Abel Gance exclaimed enthusiastically: "Shakespeare, Rembrandt, Beethoven will make films . . . all legends, all mythologies and all myths, all founders of religion, and the very religions . . . await their exposed resurrection, and the heroes crowd each other at the gate."[5] Presumably without intending it, he issued an invitation to a far-reaching liquidation.

III

During long periods of history, the mode of human sense perception changes with humanity's entire mode of existence. The manner in which human sense perception is organized, the medium in which it is accomplished, is determined not only by nature but by historical circumstances as well. The fifth century, with its great shifts of population, saw the birth of the late Roman art industry and the Vienna Genesis, and there developed not only an art different from that of antiquity but also a new kind of perception. The scholars of the Viennese school, Riegl and Wickhoff, who resisted the weight of classical tradition under which these later art forms had been buried, were the first to draw conclusions from them concerning the organization of perception at the time. However far-reaching their insight, these scholars limited themselves to showing the significant, formal hallmark which characterized perception in late Roman times. They did not attempt—and, perhaps, saw no way—to show the social transformations expressed by these changes of perception. The conditions for an analogous insight are more favorable in the present. And if changes in the medium of contemporary perception can be comprehended as decay of the aura, it is possible to show its social causes.

The concept of aura which was proposed above with reference to historical objects may usefully be illustrated with reference to the aura of natural ones.

We define the aura of the latter as the unique phenomenon of a distance, however close it may be. If, while resting on a summer afternoon, you follow with your eyes a mountain range on the horizon or a branch which casts its shadow over you, you experience the aura of those mountains, of that branch. This image makes it easy to comprehend the social bases of the contemporary decay of the aura. It rests on two circumstances, both of which are related to the increasing significance of the masses in contemporary life. Namely, the desire of contemporary masses to bring things "closer" spatially and humanly, which is just as ardent as their bent toward overcoming the uniqueness of every reality by accepting its reproduction.[6] Every day the urge grows stronger to get hold of an object at very close range by way of its likeness, its reproduction. Unmistakably, reproduction as offered by picture magazines and newsreels differs from the image seen by the unarmed eye. Uniqueness and permanence are as closely linked in the latter as are transitoriness and reproducibility in the former. To pry an object from its shell, to destroy its aura, is the mark of a perception whose "sense of the universal equality of things" has increased to such a degree that it extracts it even from a unique object by means of reproduction. Thus is manifested in the field of perception what in the theoretical sphere is noticeable in the increasing importance of statistics. The adjustment of reality to the masses and of the masses to reality is a process of unlimited scope, as much for thinking as for perception.

IV

The uniqueness of a work of art is inseparable from its being imbedded in the fabric of tradition. This tradition itself is thoroughly alive and extremely changeable. An ancient statue of Venus, for example, stood in a different traditional context with the Greeks, who made it an object of veneration, than with the clerics of the Middle Ages, who viewed it as an ominous idol. Both of them, however, were equally confronted with its uniqueness, that is, its aura. Originally the contextual integration of art in tradition found its expression in the cult. We know that the earliest art works originated in the service of a ritual—first the magical, then the religious kind. It is significant that the existence of the work of art with reference to its aura is never entirely separated from its ritual function.[7] In other words, the unique value of the "authentic" work of art has its basis in ritual; the location of its original use value. This ritualistic basis, however remote, is still recognizable as secularized ritual even in the most profane forms of the cult of beauty.[8] The secular cult of beauty, developed during the Renaissance and prevailing for three centuries, clearly showed that ritualistic basis in its decline and the first deep crisis which befell it. With the advent of the first truly revolutionary means of reproduction, photography, simultaneously with the rise of socialism, art sensed the approaching crisis which has become evident a century later. At the time, art reacted with the doctrine of *l'art pour l'art,* that is, with a theology of art. This gave rise to what might be called a negative theology in the form of the idea of "pure" art, which not only denied any social function of art but also any categorizing by subject matter. (In poetry, Mallarmé was the first to take this position.)

An analysis of art in the age of mechanical reproduction must do justice to these relationships, for they lead us to an all-important insight: for the first time in world history, mechanical reproduction emancipates the work of art from its parasitical dependence on ritual. To an ever greater degree the work of art reproduced becomes the work of art designed for reproducibility.[9] From a photographic negative, for example, one can make any number of prints; to ask for the "authentic" print makes no sense. But the instant the criterion of authenticity ceases to be applicable to artistic production, the total function of art is reversed. Instead of being based on ritual, it begins to be based on another practice—politics.

V

Works of art are received and valued on different planes. Two polar types stand out: with one, the accent is on the cult value; with the other, on the exhibition value of the work.[10] Artistic production begins with ceremonial objects destined to serve in a cult. One may assume that what mattered was their existence, not their being on view. The elk portrayed by the man of the Stone Age on the walls of his cave was an instrument of magic. He did expose it to his fellow men, but in the main it was meant for the spirits. Today the cult value would seem to demand that the work of art remain hidden. Certain statues of gods are accessible only to the priest in the cella; certain Madonnas remain covered nearly all year round; certain sculptures on medieval cathedrals are invisible to the spectator on ground level. With the emancipation of the various art practices from ritual go increasing opportunities for the exhibition of their products. It is easier to exhibit a portrait bust that can be sent here and there than to exhibit the statue of a divinity that has its fixed place in the interior of a temple. The same holds for the painting as against the mosaic or fresco that preceded it. And even though the public presentability of a mass originally may have been just as great as that of a symphony, the latter originated at the moment when its public presentability promised to surpass that of the mass.

With the different methods of technical reproduction of a work of art, its fitness for exhibition increased to such an extent that the quantitative shift between its two poles turned into a qualitative transformation of its nature. This is comparable to the situation of the work of art in prehistoric times when, by the absolute emphasis on its cult value, it was, first and foremost, an instrument of magic. Only later did it come to be recognized as a work of art. In the same way today, by the absolute emphasis on its exhibition value the work of art becomes a creation with entirely new functions, among which the one we are conscious of, the artistic function, later may be recognized as incidental.[11] This much is certain: today photography and the film are the most serviceable exemplifications of this new function.

VI

In photography, exhibition value begins to displace cult value all along the line. But cult value does not give way without resistance. It retires into an ultimate retrenchment: the human countenance. It is no accident that the portrait was the focal point of early photography. The cult of remembrance of loved ones, absent or dead, offers a last refuge for the cult value of the picture. For the last time the aura emanates from the early photographs in the fleeting expression of a human face. This is what constitutes their melancholy, incomparable beauty. But as man withdraws from the photographic image, the exhibition value for the first time shows its superiority to the ritual value. To have pinpointed this new stage constitutes the incomparable significance of Atget, who, around 1900, took photographs of deserted Paris streets. It has quite justly been said of him that he photographed them like scenes of crime. The scene of a crime, too, is deserted; it is photographed for the purpose of establishing evidence. With Atget, photographs become standard evidence for historical occurrences, and acquire a hidden political significance. They demand a specific kind of approach; free-floating contemplation is not appropriate to them. They stir the viewer; he feels challenged by them in a new way. At the same time picture magazines begin to put up signposts for him, right ones or wrong ones, no matter. For the first time, captions have become obligatory. And it is clear that they have an altogether different character than the title of a painting. The directives which the captions give to those looking at pictures in illustrated magazines soon become even more explicit and more imperative in the film where the meaning of each single picture appears to be prescribed by the sequence of all preceding ones.

VII

The nineteenth-century dispute as to the artistic value of painting versus photography today seems devious and confused. This does not diminish its importance, however; if anything, it underlines it. The dispute was in fact the symptom of a historical transformation the universal impact of which was not realized by either of the rivals. When the age of mechanical reproduction separated art from its basis in cult, the semblance of its autonomy disappeared forever. The resulting change in the function of art transcended the perspective of the century; for a long time it even escaped that of the twentieth century, which experienced the development of the film.

Earlier much futile thought had been devoted to the question of whether photography is an art. The primary question—whether the very invention of photography had not transformed the entire nature of art—was not raised. Soon the film theoreticians asked the same ill-considered question with regard to the film. But the difficulties which photography caused traditional aesthetics were mere child's play as compared to those raised by the film. Whence the insensitive and forced character of early theories of the film. Abel Gance, for instance, compares the film with hieroglyphs: "Here, by a remarkable regres-

sion, we have come back to the level of expression of the Egyptians. . . .
Pictorial language has not yet matured because our eyes have not yet adjusted
to it. There is as yet insufficient respect for, insufficient cult of, what it
expresses."[12] Or, in the words of Séverin-Mars: "What art has been granted a
dream more poetical and more real at the same time! Approached in this
fashion the film might represent an incomparable means of expression. Only
the most high-minded persons, in the most perfect and mysterious moments of
their lives, should be allowed to enter its ambience."[13] Alexandre Arnoux
concludes his fantasy about the silent film with the question: "Do not all the
bold descriptions we have given amount to the definition of prayer?"[14] It is
instructive to note how their desire to class the film among the "arts" forces
these theoreticians to read ritual elements into it—with a striking lack of
discretion. Yet when these speculations were published, films like *L'Opinion
publique* and *The Gold Rush* had already appeared. This, however, did not keep
Abel Gance from adducing hieroglyphs for purposes of comparison, nor
Séverin-Mars from speaking of the film as one might speak of paintings by Fra
Angelico. Characteristically, even today ultrareactionary authors give the film
a similar contextual significance—if not an outright sacred one, then at least
a supernatural one. Commenting on Max Reinhardt's film version of *A
Midsummer Night's Dream,* Werfel states that undoubtedly it was the sterile
copying of the exterior world with its streets, interiors, railroad stations,
restaurants, motorcars, and beaches which until now had obstructed the
elevation of the film to the realm of art. "The film has not yet realized its true
meaning, its real possibilities . . . these consist in its unique faculty to express
by natural means and with incomparable persuasiveness all that is fairylike,
marvelous, supernatural."[15]

VIII

The artistic performance of a stage actor is definitely presented to the
public by the actor in person; that of the screen actor, however, is presented by
a camera, with a twofold consequence. The camera that presents the performance of the film actor to the public need not respect the performance as an
integral whole. Guided by the cameraman, the camera continually changes its
position with respect to the performance. The sequence of positional views
which the editor composes from the material supplied him constitutes the
completed film. It comprises certain factors of movement which are in reality
those of the camera, not to mention special camera angles, close-ups, etc.
Hence, the performance of the actor is subjected to a series of optical tests.
This is the first consequence of the fact that the actor's performance is
presented by means of a camera. Also, the film actor lacks the opportunity of
the stage actor to adjust to the audience during his performance, since he does
not present his performance to the audience in person. This permits the
audience to take the position of a critic, without experiencing any personal
contact with the actor. The audience's identification with the actor is really an
identification with the camera. Consequently the audience takes the position

of the camera; its approach is that of testing.[16] This is not the approach to which cult values may be exposed.

IX

For the film, what matters primarily is that the actor represents himself to the public before the camera, rather than representing someone else. One of the first to sense the actor's metamorphosis by this form of testing was Pirandello. Though his remarks on the subject in his novel *Si Gira* were limited to the negative aspects of the question and to the silent film only, this hardly impairs their validity. For in this respect, the sound film did not change anything essential. What matters is that the part is acted not for an audience but for a mechanical contrivance—in the case of the sound film, for two of them. "The film actor," wrote Pirandello, "feels as if in exile—exiled not only from the stage but also from himself. With a vague sense of discomfort he feels inexplicable emptiness: his body loses its corporeality, it evaporates, it is deprived of reality, life, voice, and the noises caused by his moving about, in order to be changed into a mute image, flickering an instant on the screen, then vanishing into silence. . . . The projector will play with his shadow before the public, and he himself must be content to play before the camera."[17] This situation might also be characterized as follows: for the first time—and this is the effect of the film—man has to operate with his whole living person, yet forgoing its aura. For aura is tied to his presence; there can be no replica of it. The aura which, on the stage, emanates from Macbeth, cannot be separated for the spectators from that of the actor. However, the singularity of the shot in the studio is that the camera is substituted for the public. Consequently, the aura that envelops the actor vanishes, and with it the aura of the figure he portrays.

It is not surprising that it should be a dramatist such as Pirandello who, in characterizing the film, inadvertently touches on the very crisis in which we see the theater. Any thorough study proves that there is indeed no greater contrast than that of the stage play to a work of art that is completely subject to or, like the film, founded in, mechanical reproduction. Experts have long recognized that in the film "the greatest effects are almost always obtained by 'acting' as little as possible. . . ." In 1932 Rudolf Arnheim saw "the latest trend . . . in treating the actor as a stage prop chosen for its characteristics and . . . inserted at the proper place."[18] With this idea something else is closely connected. The stage actor identifies himself with the character of his role. The film actor very often is denied this opportunity. His creation is by no means all of a piece; it is composed of many separate performances. Besides certain fortuitous considerations, such as cost of studio, availability of fellow players, décor, etc., there are elementary necessities of equipment that split the actor's work into a series of mountable episodes. In particular, lighting and its installation require the presentation of an event that, on the screen, unfolds as a rapid and unified scene, in a sequence of separate shootings which may take hours at the studio; not to mention more obvious montage. Thus a jump from the window can be shot in the studio as a jump from a scaffold, and the ensuing flight, if need be, can be shot weeks later when outdoor scenes are taken. Far more paradoxical cases can easily be construed. Let us assume that an actor is supposed to be startled by a knock at the door. If his reaction is not satisfactory, the director can resort to an expedient: when the actor happens to be at the studio again he has a shot fired behind him without his being forewarned of it. The frightened reaction can be shot now and be cut into the screen version. Nothing more strikingly shows that art has left the realm of the "beautiful semblance" which, so far, had been taken to be the only sphere where art could thrive.

X

The feeling of strangeness that overcomes the actor before the camera, as Pirandello describes it, is basically of the same kind as the estrangement felt before one's own image in the mirror. But now the reflected image has become separable, transportable. And where is it transported? Before the public.[19] Never for a moment does the screen actor cease to be conscious of this fact. While facing the camera he knows that ultimately he will face the public, the consumers who constitute the market. This market, where he offers not only his labor but also his whole self, his heart and soul, is beyond his reach. During the shooting he has as little contact with it as any article made in a factory. This may contribute to that oppression, that new anxiety which, according to Pirandello, grips the actor before the camera. The film responds to the shriveling of the aura with an artificial build-up of the "personality" outside the studio. The cult of the movie star, fostered by the money of the film industry, preserves not the unique aura of the person but the "spell of the personality," the phony spell of a commodity. So long as the movie-makers' capital sets the fashion, as a rule no other revolutionary merit can be accredited to today's film than the promotion of a revolutionary criticism of traditional concepts of art. We do not deny that in some cases today's films can also promote revolutionary criticism of social conditions, even of the distribution of property. However, our present study is no more specifically concerned with this than is the film production of Western Europe.

It is inherent in the technique of the film as well as that of sports that everybody who witnesses its accomplishments is somewhat of an expert. This is obvious to anyone listening to a group of newspaper boys leaning on their bicycles and discussing the outcome of a bicycle race. It is not for nothing that newspaper publishers arrange races for their delivery boys. These arouse great interest among the participants, for the victor has an opportunity to rise from delivery boy to professional racer. Similarly, the newsreel offers everyone the opportunity to rise from passer-by to movie extra. In this way any man might even find himself part of a work of art, as witness Vertoff's *Three Songs about Lenin* or Ivens' *Borinage*. Any man today can lay claim to being filmed. This claim can best be elucidated by a comparative look at the historical situation of contemporary literature.

For centuries a small number of writers were confronted by many thousands of readers. This changed toward the end of the last century. With the increasing extension of the press, which kept placing new political, religious, scientific, professional, and local organs before the readers, an increasing number of readers became writers—at first, occasional ones. It began with the daily press opening to its readers space for "letters to the editor." And today there is hardly a gainfully employed European who could not, in principle, find an opportunity to publish somewhere or other comments on his work, grievances, documentary reports, or that sort of thing. Thus, the distinction between author and public is about to lose its basic character. The difference becomes merely functional; it may vary from case to case. At any moment the reader is ready to turn into a writer. As expert, which he had to become willy-nilly in an extremely specialized work process, even if only in some minor respect, the reader gains access to authorship. In the Soviet Union work itself is given a voice. To present it verbally is part of a man's ability to perform the work. Literary license is now founded on polytechnic rather than specialized training and thus becomes common property.[20]

All this can easily be applied to the film, where transitions that in literature took centuries have come about in a decade. In cinematic practice, particularly in Russia, this change-over has partially become established reality. Some of the players whom we meet in Russian films are not actors in our sense but people who portray *themselves*—and primarily in their own work process. In Western Europe the capitalistic exploitation of the film denies consideration to modern man's legitimate claim to being reproduced. Under these circumstances the film industry is trying hard to spur the interest of the masses through illusion-promoting spectacles and dubious speculations.

XI

The shooting of a film, especially of a sound film, affords a spectacle unimaginable anywhere at any time before this. It presents a process in which it is impossible to assign to a spectator a viewpoint which would exclude from the actual scene such extraneous accessories as camera equipment, lighting machinery, staff assistants, etc.—unless his eye were on a line parallel with the lens. This circumstance, more than any other, renders superficial and insignificant any possible similarity between a scene in the studio and one on the stage. In the theater one is well aware of the place from which the play cannot immediately be detected as illusionary. There is no such place for the movie scene that is being shot. Its illusionary nature is that of the second degree, the result of cutting. That is to say, in the studio the mechanical equipment has penetrated so deeply into reality that its pure aspect freed from the foreign substance of equipment is the result of a special procedure, namely, the shooting by the specially adjusted camera and the mounting of the shot together with other similar ones. The equipment-free aspect of reality here has become the height of artifice; the sight of immediate reality has become an orchid in the land of technology.

Even more revealing is the comparison of these circumstances, which differ so much from those of the theater, with the situation in painting. Here the question is: How does the cameraman compare with the painter? To answer this we take recourse to an analogy with a surgical operation. The surgeon represents the polar opposite of the magician. The magician heals a sick person by the laying on of hands; the surgeon cuts into the patient's body. The magician maintains the natural distance between the patient and himself; though he reduces it very slightly by the laying on of hands, he greatly increases it by virtue of his authority. The surgeon does exactly the reverse; he greatly diminishes the distance between himself and the patient by penetrating into the patient's body, and increases it but little by the caution with which his hand moves among the organs. In short, in contrast to the magician—who is still hidden in the medical practitioner—the surgeon at the decisive moment abstains from facing the patient man to man; rather, it is through the operation that he penetrates into him.

Magician and surgeon compare to painter and cameraman. The painter maintains in his work a natural distance from reality, the cameraman penetrates deeply into its web.[21] There is a tremendous difference between the pictures they obtain. That of the painter is a total one, that of the cameraman consists of multiple fragments which are assembled under a new law. Thus, for contemporary man the representation of reality by the film is incomparably more significant than that of the painter, since it offers, precisely because of the thoroughgoing permeation of reality with mechanical equipment, an aspect of reality which is free of all equipment. And that is what one is entitled to ask from a work of art.

XII

Mechanical reproduction of art changes the reaction of the masses toward art. The reactionary attitude toward a Picasso painting changes into the progressive reaction toward a Chaplin movie. The progressive reaction is characterized by the direct, intimate fusion of visual and emotional enjoyment with the orientation of the expert. Such fusion is of great social significance. The greater the decrease in the social significance of an art form, the sharper the distinction between criticism and enjoyment by the public. The conventional is uncritically enjoyed, and the truly new is criticized with aversion. With regard to the screen, the critical and the receptive attitudes of the public coincide. The decisive reason for this is that individual reactions are predetermined by the mass audience response they are about to produce, and this is nowhere more pronounced than in the film. The moment these responses become manifest they control each other. Again, the comparison with painting is fruitful. A painting has always had an excellent chance to be viewed by one person or by a few. The simultaneous contemplation of paintings by a large public, such as developed in the nineteenth century, is an early symptom of the crisis of painting, a crisis which was by no means occasioned exclusively by photography but rather in a relatively independent manner by the appeal of art works to the masses.

Painting simply is in no position to present an object for simultaneous collective experience, as it was possible for architecture at all times, for the epic poem in the past, and for the movie today. Although this circumstance in itself should not lead one to conclusions about the social role of painting, it does constitute a serious threat as soon as painting, under special conditions and, as it were, against its nature, is confronted directly by the masses. In the churches and monasteries of the Middle Ages and at the princely courts up to the end of the eighteenth century, a collective reception of paintings did not occur simultaneously, but by graduated and hierarchized mediation. The change that has come about is an expression of the particular conflict in which painting was implicated by the mechanical reproducibility of paintings. Although paintings began to be publicly exhibited in galleries and salons, there was no way for the masses to organize and control themselves in their reception.[22] Thus the same public which responds in a progressive manner toward a grotesque film is bound to respond in a reactionary manner to surrealism.

XIII

The characteristics of the film lie not only in the manner in which man presents himself to mechanical equipment but also in the manner in which, by means of this apparatus, man can represent his environment. A glance at occupational psychology illustrates the testing capacity of the equipment. Psychoanalysis illustrates it in a different perspective. The film has enriched our field of perception with methods which can be illustrated by those of Freudian theory. Fifty years ago, a slip of the tongue passed more or less unnoticed. Only exceptionally may such a slip have revealed dimensions of depth in a conversation which had seemed to be taking its course on the surface. Since the *Psychopathology of Everyday Life* things have changed. This book isolated and made analyzable things which had heretofore floated along unnoticed in the broad stream of perception. For the entire spectrum of optical, and now also acoustical, perception the film has brought about a similar deepening of apperception. It is only an obverse of this fact that behavior items shown in a movie can be analyzed much more precisely and from more points of view than those presented on paintings or on the stage. As compared with painting, filmed behavior lends itself more readily to analysis because of its incomparably more precise statements of the situation. In comparison with the stage scene, the filmed behavior item lends itself more readily to analysis because it can be isolated more easily. This circumstance derives its chief importance from its tendency to promote the mutual penetration of art and science. Actually, of a screened behavior item which is neatly brought out in a certain situation, like a muscle of a body, it is difficult to say which is more fascinating, its artistic value or its value for science. To demonstrate the identity of the artistic and scientific uses of photography which heretofore usually were separated will be one of the revolutionary functions of the film.[23]

By close-ups of the things around us, by focusing on hidden details of familiar objects, by exploring commonplace milieus under the ingenious guidance of the camera, the film, on the one hand, extends our comprehension of the necessities which rule our lives; on the other hand, it manages to assure us of an immense and unexpected field of action. Our taverns and our metropolitan streets, our offices and furnished rooms, our railroad stations and our factories appeared to have us locked up hopelessly. Then came the film and burst this prison-world asunder by the dynamite of the tenth of a second, so that now, in the midst of its far-flung ruins and debris, we calmly and adventurously go traveling. With the close-up, space expands; with slow motion, movement is extended. The enlargement of a snapshot does not simply render more precise what in any case was visible, though unclear: it reveals entirely new structural formations of the subject. So, too, slow motion not only presents familiar qualities of movement but reveals in them entirely unknown ones "which, far from looking like retarded rapid movements, give the effect of singularly gliding, floating, supernatural motions."[24] Evidently a different nature opens itself to the camera than opens to the naked eye—if only because an unconsciously penetrated space is substituted for a space consciously explored by man. Even if one has a general knowledge of the way people walk, one knows nothing of a person's posture during the fractional second of a stride. The act of reaching for a lighter or a spoon is familiar routine, yet we hardly know what really goes on between hand and metal, not to mention how this fluctuates with our moods. Here the camera intervenes with the resources of its lowerings and liftings, its interruptions and isolations, its extensions and accelerations, its enlargements and reductions. The camera introduces us to unconscious optics as does psychoanalysis to unconscious impulses.

XIV

One of the foremost tasks of art has always been the creation of a demand which could be fully satisfied only later.[25] The history of every art form shows critical epochs in which a certain art form aspires to effects which could be fully obtained only with a changed technical standard, that is to say, in a new art form. The extravagances and crudities of art which thus appear, particularly in the so-called decadent epochs, actually arise from the nucleus of its richest historical energies. In recent years, such barbarisms were abundant in Dadaism. It is only now that its impulse becomes discernible: Dadaism attempted to create by pictorial—and literary—means the effects which the public today seeks in the film.

Every fundamentally new, pioneering creation of demands will carry beyond its goal. Dadaism did so to the extent that it sacrificed the market values which are so characteristic of the film in favor of higher ambitions—though of course it was not conscious of such intentions as here described. The

Dadaists attached much less importance to the sales value of their work than to its uselessness for contemplative immersion. The studied degradation of their material was not the least of their means to achieve this uselessness. Their poems are "word salad" containing obscenities and every imaginable waste product of language. The same is true of their paintings, on which they mounted buttons and tickets. What they intended and achieved was a relentless destruction of the aura of their creations, which they branded as reproductions with the very means of production. Before a painting of Arp's or a poem by August Stramm it is impossible to take time for contemplation and evaluation as one would before a canvas of Derain's or a poem by Rilke. In the decline of middle-class society, contemplation became a school for asocial behavior; it was countered by distraction as a variant of social conduct.[26] Dadaistic activities actually assured a rather vehement distraction by making works of art the center of scandal. One requirement was foremost: to outrage the public.

From an alluring appearance or persuasive structure of sound the work of art of the Dadaists became an instrument of ballistics. It hit the spectator like a bullet, it happened to him, thus acquiring a tactile quality. It promoted a demand for the film, the distracting element of which is also primarily tactile, being based on changes of place and focus which periodically assail the spectator. Let us compare the screen on which a film unfolds with the canvas of a painting. The painting invites the spectator to contemplation; before it the spectator can abandon himself to his associations. Before the movie frame he cannot do so. No sooner has his eye grasped a scene than it is already changed. It cannot be arrested. Duhamel, who detests the film and knows nothing of its significance, though something of its structure, notes this circumstance as follows: "I can no longer think what I want to think. My thoughts have been replaced by moving images."[27] The spectator's process of association in view of these images is indeed interrupted by their constant, sudden change. This constitutes the shock effect of the film, which, like all shocks, should be cushioned by heightened presence of mind.[28] By means of its technical structure, the film has taken the physical shock effect out of the wrappers in which Dadaism had, as it were, kept it inside the moral shock effect.[29]

XV

The mass is a matrix from which all traditional behavior toward works of art issues today in a new form. Quantity has been transmuted into quality. The greatly increased mass of participants has produced a change in the mode of participation. The fact that the new mode of participation first appeared in a disreputable form must not confuse the spectator. Yet some people have launched spirited attacks against precisely this superficial aspect. Among these, Duhamel has expressed himself in the most radical manner. What he objects to most is the kind of participation which the movie elicits from the masses. Duhamel calls the movie "a pastime for helots, a diversion for uneducated, wretched, worn-out creatures who are consumed by their worries . . . , a spectacle which requires no concentration and presupposes no intelligence . . . , which kindles no light in the heart and awakens no hope other than the ridiculous one of someday becoming a 'star' in Los Angeles."[30] Clearly, this is at bottom the same ancient lament that the masses seek distraction whereas art demands concentration from the spectator. That is a commonplace. The question remains whether it provides a platform for the analysis of the film. A closer look is needed here. Distraction and concentration form polar opposites which may be stated as follows: A man who concentrates before a work of art is absorbed by it. He enters into this work of art the way legend tells of the Chinese painter when he viewed his finished painting. In contrast, the distracted mass absorbs the work of art. This is most obvious with regard to buildings. Architecture has always represented the prototype of a work of art the reception of which is consummated by a collectivity in a state of distraction. The laws of its reception are most instructive.

Buildings have been man's companions since primeval times. Many art forms have developed and perished. Tragedy begins with the Greeks, is extinguished with them, and after centuries its "rules" only are revived. The epic poem, which had its origin in the youth of nations, expires in Europe at the end of the Renaissance. Panel painting is a creation of the Middle Ages, and nothing guarantees its uninterrupted existence. But the human need for shelter is lasting. Architecture has never been idle. Its history is more ancient than that of any other art, and its claim to being a living force has significance in every attempt to comprehend the relationship of the masses to art. Buildings are appropriated in a twofold manner: by use and by perception—or rather, by touch and sight. Such appropriation cannot be understood in terms of the attentive concentration of a tourist before a famous building. On the tactile side there is no counterpart to contemplation on the optical side. Tactile appropriation is accomplished not so much by attention as by habit. As regards architecture, habit determines to a large extent even optical reception. The latter, too, occurs much less through rapt attention than by noticing the object in incidental fashion. This mode of appropriation, developed with reference to architecture, in certain circumstances acquires canonical value. For the tasks which face the human apparatus of perception at the turning points of history cannot be solved by optical means, that is, by contemplation, alone. They are mastered gradually by habit, under the guidance of tactile appropriation.

The distracted person, too, can form habits. More, the ability to master certain tasks in a state of distraction proves that their solution has become a matter of habit. Distraction as provided by art presents a covert control of the extent to which new tasks have become soluble by apperception. Since, moreover, individuals are tempted to avoid such tasks, art will tackle the most difficult and most important ones where it is able to mobilize the masses. Today it does so in the film. Reception in a state of distraction, which is increasing noticeably in all fields of art and is symptomatic of profound changes in apperception, finds in the film its true means of exercise. The film with its shock effect meets this mode of reception halfway. The film makes the cult value recede into the background not only by putting the public in the position of the critic, but also by the fact that at the movies this position requires no attention. The public is an examiner, but an absent-minded one.

EPILOGUE

The growing proletarianization of modern man and the increasing formation of masses are two aspects of the same process. Fascism attempts to organize the newly created proletarian masses without affecting the property structure which the masses strive to eliminate. Fascism sees its salvation in giving these masses not their right, but instead a chance to express themselves.[31] The masses have a right to change property relations; Fascism seeks to give them an expression while preserving property. The logical result of Fascism is the introduction of aesthetics into political life. The violation of the masses, whom Fascism, with its *Führer* cult, forces to their knees, has its counterpart in the violation of an apparatus which is pressed into the production of ritual values.

All efforts to render politics aesthetic culminate in one thing: war. War and war only can set a goal for mass movements on the largest scale while respecting the traditional property system. This is the political formula for the situation. The technological formula may be stated as follows: Only war makes it possible to mobilize all of today's technical resources while maintaining the property system. It goes without saying that the Fascist apotheosis of war does not employ such arguments. Still, Marinetti says in his manifesto on the Ethiopian colonial war: "For twenty-seven years we Futurists have rebelled against the branding of war as antiaesthetic. . . . Accordingly we state: . . . War is beautiful because it establishes man's dominion over the subjugated machinery by means of gas masks, terrifying megaphones, flame throwers, and small tanks. War is beautiful because it initiates the dreamt-of metalization of the human body. War is beautiful because it enriches a flowering meadow with the fiery orchids of machine guns. War is beautiful because it combines the gunfire, the cannonades, the cease-fire, the scents, and the stench of putrefaction into a symphony. War is beautiful because it creates new architecture, like that of the big tanks, the geometrical formation flights, the smoke spirals from burning villages, and many others. . . . Poets and artists of Futurism! . . . remember these principles of an aesthetics of war so that your struggle for a new literature and a new graphic art . . . may be illumined by them!"

This manifesto has the virtue of clarity. Its formulations deserve to be accepted by dialecticians. To the latter, the aesthetics of today's war appears as follows: If the natural utilization of productive forces is impeded by the property system, the increase in technical devices, in speed, and in the sources of energy will press for an unnatural utilization, and this is found in war. The destructiveness of war furnishes proof that society has not been mature enough to incorporate technology as its organ, that technology has not been sufficiently developed to cope with the elemental forces of society. The horrible features of imperialistic warfare are attributable to the discrepancy between the tremendous means of production and their inadequate utilization in the process of production—in other words, to unemployment and the lack of markets. Imperialistic war is a rebellion of technology which collects, in the form of "human material," the claims to which society has denied its natural material. Instead of draining rivers, society directs a human stream into a bed of trenches; instead of dropping seeds from airplanes, it drops incendiary bombs over cities; and through gas warfare the aura is abolished in a new way.

"*Fiat ars—pereat mundus*," says Fascism, and, as Marinetti admits, expects war to supply the artistic gratification of a sense perception that has been changed by technology. This is evidently the consummation of "*l'art pour l'art*." Mankind, which in Homer's time was an object of contemplation for the Olympian gods, now is one for itself. Its self-alienation has reached such a degree that it can experience its own destruction as an aesthetic pleasure of the first order. This is the situation of politics which Fascism is rendering aesthetic. Communism responds by politicizing art.

NOTES

1. Quoted from Paul Valéry, *Aesthetics*, "The Conquest of Ubiquity," translated by Ralph Manheim, p. 225. Pantheon Books, Bollingen Series, New York, 1964.

2. Of course, the history of a work of art encompasses more than this. The history of the "Mona Lisa," for instance, encompasses the kind and number of its copies made in the 17th, 18th, and 19th centuries.

3. Precisely because authenticity is not reproducible, the intensive penetration of certain (mechanical) processes of reproduction was instrumental in differentiating and grading authenticity. To develop such differentiations was an important function of the trade in works of art. The invention of the woodcut may be said to have struck at the root of the quality of authenticity even before its late flowering. To be sure, at the time of its origin a medieval picture of the Madonna could not yet be said to be "authentic." It became "authentic" only during the succeeding centuries and perhaps most strikingly so during the last one.

4. The poorest provincial staging of *Faust* is superior to a Faust film in that, ideally, it competes with the first performance at Weimar. Before the screen it is unprofitable to remember traditional contents which might come to mind before the stage—for instance, that Goethe's friend Johann Heinrich Merck is hidden in Mephisto, and the like.

5. Abel Gance, "Le Temps de l'image est venu," *L'Art cinématographique*, Vol. 2, pp. 94f, Paris, 1927.

6. To satisfy the human interest of the masses may mean to have one's social function removed from the field of vision. Nothing guarantees that a portraitist of today, when painting a famous surgeon at the breakfast table in the midst of his family, depicts his social function more precisely than a painter of the 17th century who portrayed his medical doctors as representing this profession, like Rembrandt in his "Anatomy Lesson."

7. The definition of the aura as a "unique phenomenon of a distance however close it may be" represents nothing but the formulation of the cult value of the work of art in categories of space and time perception. Distance is the opposite of closeness. The essentially distant object is the unapproachable one. Unapproachability is indeed a major quality of the cult image. True to its nature, it remains "distant, however close it may be." The closeness which one may gain from its subject matter does not impair the distance which it retains in its appearance.

8. To the extent to which the cult value of the painting is secularized the ideas of its fundamental uniqueness lose distinctness. In the imagination of the beholder the uniqueness of the phenomena which hold sway in the cult image is more and more displaced by the empirical uniqueness of the creator or of his creative achievement. To be sure, never completely so; the concept of authenticity always transcends mere genuineness. (This is particularly apparent in the collector who always retains some traces of the fetishist and who, by owning the work of art, shares in its ritual power.) Nevertheless, the function of the concept of authenticity remains determinate in the evaluation of art; with the secularization of art, authenticity displaces the cult value of the work.

9. In the case of films, mechanical reproduction is not, as with literature and painting, an external condition for mass distribution. Mechanical reproduction is inherent in the very technique of film production. This technique not only permits in the most direct way but virtually causes mass distribution. It enforces distribution because the production of a film is so expensive that an individual who, for instance, might afford to buy a painting no longer can afford to buy a film. In 1927 it was calculated that a major film, in order to pay its way, had to reach an audience of nine million. With the sound film, to be sure, a setback in its international distribution occurred at first: audiences became limited by language barriers. This coincided with the Fascist emphasis on national interests. It is more important to focus on this connection with Fascism than on this setback, which was soon minimized by synchronization. The simultaneity of both phenomena is attributable to the depression. The same disturbances which, on a larger scale, led to an attempt to maintain the existing property structure by sheer force led the endangered film capital to speed up the development of the sound film. The introduction of the sound film brought about a temporary relief, not only because it again brought the masses into the theaters but also because it merged new capital from the electrical industry with that of the film industry. Thus, viewed from the outside, the sound film promoted national interests, but seen from the inside it helped to internationalize film production even more than previously.

10. This polarity cannot come into its own in the aesthetics of Idealism. Its idea of beauty comprises these polar opposites without differentiating between them and consequently excludes their polarity. Yet in Hegel this polarity announces itself as clearly as possible within the limits of Idealism. We quote from his *Philosophy of History*:

> Images were known of old. Piety at an early time required them for worship, but it could do without *beautiful* images. These might even be disturbing. In every beautiful painting there is also something nonspiritual, merely external, but its spirit speaks to man through its beauty. Worshipping, conversely, is concerned with the work as an object, for it is but a spiritless stupor of the soul. . . . Fine art has arisen . . . in the church . . . , although it has already gone beyond its principle as art.

Likewise, the following passage from *The Philosophy of Fine Art* indicates that Hegel sensed a problem here.

> We are beyond the stage of reverence for works of art as divine and objects deserving our worship. The impression they produce is one of a more reflective kind, and the emotions they arouse require a higher test. . . . — G. W. F. Hegel, *The Philosophy of Fine Art,* trans., with notes, by F. P. B. Osmaston, Vol. I, p. 12, London, 1920.

The transition from the first kind of artistic reception to the second characterizes the history of artistic reception in general. Apart from that, a certain oscillation between these two polar modes of reception can be demonstrated for each work of art. Take the Sistine Madonna. Since Hubert Grimme's research it has been known that the Madonna originally was painted for the purpose of exhibition. Grimme's research was inspired by the question: What is the purpose of the molding in the foreground of the painting which the two cupids lean upon? How, Grimme asked further, did Raphael come to furnish the sky with two draperies? Research proved that the Madonna had been commissioned for the public lying-in-state of Pope Sixtus. The Popes lay in state in a certain side chapel of St. Peter's. On that occasion Raphael's picture had been fastened in a nichelike background of the chapel, supported by the coffin. In this picture Raphael portrays the Madonna approaching the papal coffin in clouds from the background of the niche, which was demarcated by green drapes. At the obsequies of Sixtus a pre-eminent exhibition value of Raphael's picture was taken advantage of. Some time later it was placed on the high altar in the church of the Black Friars at Piacenza. The reason for this exile is to be found in the Roman rites which forbid the use of paintings exhibited at obsequies as cult objects on the high altar. This regulation devalued Raphael's picture to some degree. In order to obtain an adequate price nevertheless, the Papal See resolved to add to the bargain the tacit toleration of the picture above the high altar. To avoid attention the picture was given to the monks of the far-off provincial town.

11. Bertolt Brecht, on a different level, engaged in analogous reflections: "If the concept of 'work of art' can no longer be applied to the thing that emerges once the work is transformed into a commodity, we have to eliminate this concept with cautious care but without fear, lest we liquidate the function of the very thing as well. For it has to go through this phase without mental reservation, and not as noncommittal deviation from the straight path; rather, what happens here with the work of art will change it fundamentally and erase its past to such an extent that should the old concept be taken up again—and it will, why not?—it will no longer stir any memory of the thing it once designated."

12. Abel Gance, op. cit., pp. 100–1.

13. Séverin-Mars, quoted by Abel Gance, op. cit., p. 100.

14. Alexandre Arnoux, *Cinéma pris,* 1929, p. 28.

15. Franz Werfel, "Ein Sommernachtstraum, Ein Film von Shakespeare und Reinhardt," *Neues Wiener Journal,* cited in *Lu* 15, November, 1935.

16. "The film . . . provides—or could provide—useful insight into the details of human actions. . . . Character is never used as a source of motivation; the inner life of the persons never supplies the principal cause of the plot and seldom is its main result." (Bertolt Brecht, *Versuche,* "Der Dreigroschenprozess," p. 268.) The expansion of the field of the testable which mechanical equipment brings about for the actor corresponds to the extraordinary expansion of the field of the testable brought about for the individual through economic conditions. Thus, vocational aptitude tests become

constantly more important. What matters in these tests are segmental performances of the individual. The film shot and the vocational aptitude test are taken before a committee of experts. The camera director in the studio occupies a place identical with that of the examiner during aptitude tests.

17. Luigi Pirandello, *Si Gira,* quoted by Léon Pierre-Quint, "Signification du cinéma," *L'Art cinématographique,* op. cit., pp. 14–15.

18. Rudolf Arnheim, *Film als Kunst,* Berlin, 1932, pp. 176f. In this context certain seemingly unimportant details in which the film director deviates from stage practices gain in interest. Such is the attempt to let the actor play without make-up, as made among others by Dreyer in his *Jeanne d'Arc.* Dreyer spent months seeking the forty actors who constitute the Inquisitors' tribunal. The search for these actors resembled that for stage properties that are hard to come by. Dreyer made every effort to avoid resemblances of age, build, and physiognomy. If the actor thus becomes a stage property, this latter, on the other hand, frequently functions as actor. At least it is not unusual for the film to assign a role to the stage property. Instead of choosing at random from a great wealth of examples, let us concentrate on a particularly convincing one. A clock that is working will always be a disturbance on the stage. There it cannot be permitted its function of measuring time. Even in a naturalistic play, astronomical time would clash with theatrical time. Under these circumstances it is highly revealing that the film can, whenever appropriate, use time as measured by a clock. From this more than from many other touches it may clearly be recognized that under certain circumstances each and every prop in a film may assume important functions. From here it is but one step to Pudovkin's statement that "the playing of an actor which is connected with an object and is built around it . . . is always one of the strongest methods of cinematic construction." (W. Pudovkin, *Filmregie und Filmmanuskript,* Berlin, 1928, p. 126.) The film is the first art form capable of demonstrating how matter plays tricks on man. Hence, films can be an excellent means of materialistic representation.

19. The change noted here in the method of exhibition caused by mechanical reproduction applies to politics as well. The present crisis of the bourgeois democracies comprises a crisis of the conditions which determine the public presentation of the rulers. Democracies exhibit a member of government directly and personally before the nation's representatives. Parliament is his public. Since the innovations of camera and recording equipment make it possible for the orator to become audible and visible to an unlimited number of persons, the presentation of the man of politics before camera and recording equipment becomes paramount. Parliaments, as much as theaters, are deserted. Radio and film not only affect the function of the professional actor but likewise the function of those who also exhibit themselves before this mechanical equipment, those who govern. Though their tasks may be different, the change affects equally the actor and the ruler. The trend is toward establishing controllable and transferrable skills under certain social conditions. This results in a new selection, a selection before the equipment from which the star and the dictator emerge victorious.

20. The privileged character of the respective techniques is lost. Aldous Huxley writes:

> Advances in technology have led . . . to vulgarity. . . . Process reproduction and the rotary press have made possible the indefinite multiplication of writing and pictures. Universal education and relatively high wages have created an enormous public who know how to read and can afford to buy reading and pictorial matter. A great industry has been called into existence in order to

supply these commodities. Now, artistic talent is a very rare phenomenon; whence it follows . . . that, at every epoch and in all countries, most art has been bad. But the proportion of trash in the total artistic output is greater now than at any other period. That it must be so is a matter of simple arithmetic. The population of Western Europe has a little more than doubled during the last century. But the amount of reading—and seeing—matter has increased, I should imagine, at least twenty and possibly fifty or even a hundred times. If there were n men of talent in a population of x millions, there will presumably be 2n men of talent among 2x millions. The situation may be summed up thus. For every page of print and pictures published a century ago, twenty or perhaps even a hundred pages are published today. But for every man of talent then living, there are now only two men of talent. It may be of course that, thanks to universal education, many potential talents which in the past would have been stillborn are now enabled to realize themselves. Let us assume, then, that there are now three or even four men of talent to every one of earlier times. It still remains true to say that the consumption of reading—and seeing—matter has far outstripped the natural production of gifted writers and draughtsmen. It is the same with hearing-matter. Prosperity, the gramophone and the radio have created an audience of hearers who consume an amount of hearing-matter that has increased out of all proportion to the increase of population and the consequent natural increase of talented musicians. It follows from all this that in all the arts the output of trash is both absolutely and relatively greater than it was in the past; and that it must remain greater for just so long as the world continues to consume the present inordinate quantities of reading-matter, seeing-matter, and hearing-matter.— Aldous Huxley, *Beyond the Mexique Bay: A Traveller's Journal,* London, 1949, pp. 274 ff. First published in 1934.

This mode of observation is obviously not progressive.

21. The boldness of the cameraman is indeed comparable to that of the surgeon. Luc Durtain lists among specific technical sleights of hand those "which are required in surgery in the case of certain difficult operations. I choose as an example a case from oto-rhinolaryngology; . . . the so-called endonasal perspective procedure; or I refer to the acrobatic tricks of larynx surgery which have to be performed following the reversed picture in the laryngoscope. I might also speak of ear surgery which suggests the precision work of watchmakers. What range of the most subtle muscular acrobatics is required from the man who wants to repair or save the human body! We have only to think of the couching of a cataract where there is virtually a debate of steel with nearly fluid tissue, or of the major abdominal operations (laparotomy)."—Luc Durtain, op. cit.

22. This mode of observation may seem crude, but as the great theoretician Leonardo has shown, crude modes of observation may at times be usefully adduced. Leonardo compares painting and music as follows: "Painting is superior to music because, unlike unfortunate music, it does not have to die as soon as it is born. . . . Music which is consumed in the very act of its birth is inferior to painting which the use of varnish has rendered eternal." (Trattato I, 29.)

23. Renaissance painting offers a revealing analogy to this situation. The incomparable development of this art and its significance rested not least on the integration of a number of new sciences, or at least of new scientific data. Renaissance painting made use of anatomy and perspective, of mathematics, meteorology, and chromatology. Valéry writes: "What could be further from us than the strange claim of a Leonardo to

whom painting was a supreme goal and the ultimate demonstration of knowledge? Leonardo was convinced that painting demanded universal knowledge, and he did not even shrink from a theoretical analysis which to us is stunning because of its very depth and precision. . . ." —Paul Valéry, *Pièces sur l'art,* "Autour de Corot," Paris, p. 191.

24. Rudolf Arnheim, loc. cit., p. 138.

25. "The work of art," says André Breton, "is valuable only in so far as it is vibrated by the reflexes of the future." Indeed, every developed art form intersects three lines of development. Technology works toward a certain form of art. Before the advent of the film there were photo booklets with pictures which flitted by the onlooker upon pressure of the thumb, thus portraying a boxing bout or a tennis match. Then there were the slot machines in bazaars; their picture sequences were produced by the turning of a crank.

Secondly, the traditional art forms in certain phases of their development strenuously work toward effects which later are effortlessly attained by the new ones. Before the rise of the movie the Dadaists' performances tried to create an audience reaction which Chaplin later evoked in a more natural way.

Thirdly, unspectacular social changes often promote a change in receptivity which will benefit the new art form. Before the movie had begun to create its public, pictures that were no longer immobile captivated an assembled audience in the so-called *Kaiserpanorama*. Here the public assembled before a screen into which stereoscopes were mounted, one to each beholder. By a mechanical process individual pictures appeared briefly before the stereoscopes, then made way for others. Edison still had to use similar devices in presenting the first movie strip before the film screen and projection were known. This strip was presented to a small public which stared into the apparatus in which the succession of pictures was reeling off. Incidentally, the institution of the *Kaiserpanorama* shows very clearly a dialectic of the development. Shortly before the movie turned the reception of pictures into a collective one, the individual viewing of pictures in these swiftly outmoded establishments came into play once more with an intensity comparable to that of the ancient priest beholding the statue of a divinity in the cella.

26. The theological archetype of this contemplation is the awareness of being alone with one's God. Such awareness, in the heyday of the bourgeoisie, went to strengthen the freedom to shake off clerical tutelage. During the decline of the bourgeoisie this awareness had to take into account the hidden tendency to withdraw from public affairs those forces which the individual draws upon in his communion with God.

27. Georges Duhamel, *Scènes de la vie future,* Paris, 1930, p. 52.

28. The film is the art form that is in keeping with the increased threat to his life which modern man has to face. Man's need to expose himself to shock effects is his adjustment to the dangers threatening him. The film corresponds to profound changes in the apperceptive apparatus—changes that are experienced on an individual scale by the man in the street in big-city traffic, on a historical scale by every present-day citizen.

29. As for Dadaism, insights important for Cubism and Futurism are to be gained from the movie. Both appear as deficient attempts of art to accommodate the pervasion of reality by the apparatus. In contrast to the film, these schools did not try to use the apparatus as such for the artistic presentation of reality, but aimed at some sort of alloy in the joint presentation of reality and apparatus. In Cubism, the premonition that this apparatus will be structurally based on optics plays a dominant part; in Futurism, it is the premonition of the effects of this apparatus which are brought out by the rapid sequence of the film strip.

30. Duhamel, op. cit., p. 58.

31. One technical feature is significant here, especially with regard to newsreels, the propagandist importance of which can hardly be overestimated. Mass reproduction is aided especially by the reproduction of masses. In big parades and monster rallies, in sports events, and in war, all of which nowadays are captured by camera and sound recording, the masses are brought face to face with themselves. This process, whose significance need not be stressed, is intimately connected with the development of the techniques of reproduction and photography. Mass movements are usually discerned more clearly by a camera than by the naked eye. A bird's-eye view best captures gatherings of hundreds of thousands. And even though such a view may be as accessible to the human eye as it is to the camera, the image received by the eye cannot be enlarged the way a negative is enlarged. This means that mass movements, including war, constitute a form of human behavior which particularly favors mechanical equipment.

Erich Auerbach

1892–1957

Erich Auerbach was born in Berlin on November 9, 1892. He began his academic career with a law degree from the University of Heidelberg in 1913; after military service during World War I he changed professions, obtaining a Ph.D. in Romance philology from the University of Greifswald in 1921. He was married in 1923 and had one son. From 1923 to 1929 he was a librarian at the Prussian State Library in Berlin, after which he received an appointment to a chair of Romance philology at the University of Marburg (where at that time Martin Heidegger was teaching). In 1935 he was dismissed from his post under the Nazi laws respecting "racial purity"; a year later he left Germany for good to take a post at the Turkish state university in Istanbul. It was there, during the isolation of the war years, that he wrote his most famous work, *Mimesis* (1946), soon recognized as a work not only indispensable to scholars but also of interest to non-academic readers; one of the book's first and most ardent admirers was W. H. Auden. In 1947 Auerbach emigrated to the United States, becoming a naturalized citizen in 1953. He spent 1948–49 at Pennsylvania State University and the next year at the Institute for Advanced Studies in Princeton; in 1950 he joined the faculty of Yale University, where he would remain as Sterling Professor of Romance Philology until his death on October 13, 1957. Other works include *Dante, Poet of the Secular* (1929), an early study of Dante's "mixed style" and the dialogue between realism, history, and theology that Auerbach perceived at the center of Dante's work; "Figura" (1939), an investigation of medieval typology and the view of history it implies; *Neue Dantestudien* (1944), reprinted in English in the posthumous *Scenes from the Drama of European Literature* (1959); and his most complex and difficult work, the posthumous *Literary Language and Its Public in Latin Late Antiquity and in the Middle Ages* (1965).

Auerbach was, to borrow Hannah Arendt's phrase, a "man in dark times"; the bitter experience of exile and war gave a sober and fundamentally pessimistic tone to his work, as he was himself acutely aware that he was performing a salvage operation, an attempt to rescue what he felt valid in European literature from the catastrophe around him. Even in his later years, in relative ease in America, his last works have, as Geoffrey Green has written, "a spectral tonality, an intimation that the world would soon end." This sense gives his work both its peculiar intensity and also its undeniable conservatism: although *Mimesis* ends with a discussion of Virginia Woolf and the "fragmentation of the exterior action" in modern fiction, the larger design of the book, its attempt to impose one intelligible order on the entirety of Western literature from Homer and the Bible onward, is more conservative than experimental. Auerbach's desire always to "write history," that is, to see literature in the light of larger historical contexts and movements, has often been contrasted with the immanent form criticism of his fellow emigré Leo Spitzer, who opposed the explanation of texts through "history of ideas" with his own minutely specific and subtle linguistic interpretations. The notion of "represented reality" governing the immense history of literature which is *Mimesis* depends entirely upon Auerbach's belief in the unity of Western experience, which artistic technique only passively reflects. There is thus no place in Auerbach's universe for the radical subjectivity and artifice, the claim to absolute aesthetic autonomy, of modernist formal experiments, which seek in new techniques an escape from and criticism of actual conditions instead of their "representation." Auerbach's notion of the motive forces of the history he wrote was similarly un-technical, even idealistic: what defined history for him was not primarily economic or social forces, although these are not excluded from his view; decisive are rather the "changes in human self-understanding." This has been compared with the art historian Heinrich Wölfflin's idea of the "history of vision." Both notions originate in a peculiarly German idea of *Geistesgeschichte* (literally "history of the spirit"), a "discipline" invented largely by the early twentieth-century idealist philosopher Wilhelm Dilthey, whose "philosophy of life" sought to explain the totality of historical experience through reference to the activity of the Spirit. This influence was modified in Auerbach's work by that of Vico; and his own philological acumen and historicist's skepticism of total models constantly kept the inheritance of Dilthey in check. The tension between his broader synthesizing notions of the "European experience" and his careful attention to individual texts informs the whole of Auerbach's work.

Scenes from the Drama of European Literature

FIGURA

I. From Terence to Quintilian

Originally *figura,* from the same stem as *fingere, figulus, fictor,* and *effigies,* meant "plastic form." Its earliest occurrence is in Terence, who in *Eunuchus* (317) says that a young girl has a *nova figura oris* ("unaccustomed form of face"). The following fragment of Pacuvius (270-1, in Ribbeck, *Scaen. Roman. Poesis Fragm.,* I, 110) probably dates from about the same period:

> *Barbaricam pestem subinis nostris optulit*
> *Nova figura factam . . .* [1]

> (To our spears she presented an outlandish plague
> Fashioned in unaccustomed shape.)

The word was probably unknown to Plautus; he twice uses *fictura* (*Trinummus,* 365; *Miles Gloriosus,* 1189); but both times in a sense closer to the activity of forming than to its result; in later authors *fictura* becomes very rare.[2] The mention of *fictura* calls our attention to a peculiarity of *figura:* it is derived directly from the stem and not, like *natura* and other words of like ending, from the supine (Ernout-Meillet, *Dictionnaire étymologique de la langue latine,* 346). An attempt has been made (Stolz-Schmalz, *Lat. Gramm.,* 5th edition, 219) to explain this as an assimilation to *effigies:* in any case this peculiar formation expresses something living and dynamic, incomplete and playful, and it is equally certain that the word had a graceful sound which fascinated many poets. Perhaps it is no more than an accident that in our two oldest examples *figura* occurs in combination with *nova;* but even if accidental, it is significant, for the notion of the new manifestation, the changing aspect, of the permanent runs through the whole history of the word.

This history begins for us with the Hellenization of Roman education in the last century B.C. Three authors played a decisive part in its beginnings: Varro, Lucretius, and Cicero. Of course we can no longer tell exactly what they may have taken over from earlier material that has been lost; but the contributions of Lucretius and Cicero are so distinctive and original that one cannot but credit them with a considerable part in the creation of its meaning.

Varro shows the least originality of the three. If in his writings *figura* sometimes means "outward appearance" or even "outline"[3] and is thus beginning to move away from its earliest signification, the narrower concept of plastic form, this seems to have been the result of a general linguistic process, the causes of which we shall discuss further on. In Varro this development is not even very pronounced. He was an etymologist, well aware of the origin of the word (*fictor cum dicit fingo figuram imponit* ["The image-maker (*fictor*), when he says *fingo* (I shape), puts a *figura* on the thing"]: *De Lingua Latina*, 6, 78), and thus when he uses the word in connection with living creatures and objects, there is usually a connotation of plastic form. How strong this connotation still was in his time is sometimes hard to decide: for example, when he says that in buying slaves one should consider not only the *figura* but also the qualities—in horses the age, in cocks the breeding value, in apples the aroma (ibid., 9, 35); or when he says that a star has changed its *colorem*, *magnitudinem, figuram, cursum* (quoted in Augustine, *De Civitate Dei,* 21, 8); or when, in *De Lingua Latina* (5, 117) he compares forked palisade poles with the *figura* of the Latin letter V. The word becomes quite unplastic when he begins to talk of word forms. We have, as he says in *De Lingua Latina* (9, 21), taken over new forms of vessels from the Greeks; why do people struggle against new word forms, *formae vocabulorum*, as though they were poisonous? *Et tantum inter duos sensus interesse volunt, ut oculis semper aliquas figuras supellectilis novas conquirant, contra auris expertes velint esse?* ("And do they think there is so much difference between the two senses, that they are always looking for new shapes of furniture for their eyes, but yet wish their ears to avoid such things?"). Here we are not far from the idea that figures exist also for the sense of hearing; and it should also be borne in mind that Varro, like all Latin authors who were not specialists in philosophy endowed with an exact terminology, used *figura* and *forma* interchangeably, in the general sense of form. Strictly speaking, *forma* meant "mold," French *"moule,"* and was related to *figura* as the hollow form to the plastic shape that issues from it; but in Varro we seldom find a trace of this distinction, though perhaps we have an exception in the fragment cited in Gellius (III, 10, 7): *semen genitale fit ad capiendam figuram idoneum* ("the life-bearing seed is rendered fit to take on a shape").

As we have intimated, the actual innovation or break with the original meaning, which we first find in Varro, occurs in the field of grammar. It is in Varro that we first find *figura* used in the sense of grammatical, inflected, or derived form. In Varro *figura multitudinis* means the form of the plural. *Alia nomina quinque habent figuras* (9, 52) means: Some nouns have five case forms. This usage became widespread (cf. *Thesaurus Linguae Latinae*, VI, s.v. *figura*, part 1, III A, 2a, col. 730 and 2e, col. 734); *forma* was also much used in the same sense, beginning in Varro's time, but *figura* seems to have been more popular and frequent with the Latin grammarians. How is it possible that both words, but particularly *figura,* the form of which was a clear reminder of its origin, should so quickly have taken on a purely abstract meaning? It happened through the Hellenization of Roman education. Greek, with its incomparably richer scientific and rhetorical vocabulary, had a great many words for the concept of form: *morphē, eidos, schēma, typos, plasis,* to mention only the most important. In the philosophical and rhetorical elaboration of the language of Plato and Aristotle, a special sphere was assigned to each of these words; a clear dividing line was drawn particularly between *morphē* and *eidos* on the one hand and *schēma* on the other: *morphē* and *eidos* were the form or idea which "informs" matter; *schēma* is the purely perceptual shape; the classical example of this is Aristotle's *Metaphysics*, VII, 3, 1029a, in which he discusses *ousia* (essence); here *morphē* is defined as *schēma tēs ideas*, the ideal form; thus Aristotle employs *schēma* in a purely perceptual sense to designate one of the qualitative categories, and he also uses it in the combinations with *megethos, kinēsis,* and *chrōma* that we have already encountered in Varro. It was only natural that *forma* should come to be used in Latin for *morphē* and *eidos,* since it originally conveyed the notion of model; sometimes we also find *exemplar;* for *schēma* on the other hand *figura* was usually employed. But since in the learned Greek terminology—in grammar, rhetoric, logic, mathematics, astronomy—*schēma* was widely used in the sense of "outward shape," *figura* was always used for this purpose in Latin. Thus side by side with the original plastic signification and overshadowing it, there appeared a far more general concept of grammatical, rhetorical, logical, mathematical—and later even of musical and choreographic—form. To be sure, the original plastic sense was not entirely lost, for *typos,* "imprint," and *plasis, plasma,* "plastic form," were often rendered by *figura* as the radical *fig-* suggested. From the meaning of *typos* developed the use of *figura* as "imprint of the seal," a metaphor with a venerable history running from Aristotle (*De Memoria et Reminiscentia,* 450a, 31: *hē kinēsis ensēmainetai hoion typon tina tou aisthēmatos* ["the movement implies some impression of the thing sensed"], through Augustine (*Epist.,* 162, 4 [*Patrologia Latina,* XXXIII, col. 706], and Isidore (*Differentiae,* 1, 528 [*Patrologia Latina,* LXXXIII, col. 63]), to Dante (*come figura in cera si suggella* ["as a seal is stamped in wax"], *Purg.,* 10, 45, or *Par.,* 27, 52).[4] However, it was not only the plastic sense of *typos,* but also its inclination toward the universal, lawful, and exemplary (cf. the combination with *nomikōs,* Aristotle, *Politics,* II, 7, 1341b, 31) that exerted an influence on *figura,* and this in turn helped to efface the already faint dividing line with *forma.* The connection with words such as *plasis* increased the tendency of *figura*—which was probably present from the very beginning but developed only slowly—to expand in the direction of "statue," "image," "portrait," to impinge on the domain of *statua* and even of *imago, effigies, species, simulacrum.* Thus, though we may say in general that in Latin usage *figura* takes the place of *schēma,* this does not exhaust the force of the word, the *potestas verbi: figura* is broader, sometimes more plastic, in any case more dynamic and radiant than *schēma.* To be sure, *schēma* itself in Greek is more dynamic than the word as we use it; in Aristotle, for example, mimic gestures, especially of actors, are called *schēmata;* the meaning of dynamic form is by no means foreign to *schēma;* but *figura* developed this element of movement and transformation much further.[5]

Lucretius uses *figura* in the Greek philosophical sense, but in an extremely individual, free, and significant way. He starts with the general concept of "figure," which occurs in every possible shading from the plastic figure shaped by man (*manibus tractata figura*, 4, 230) to the purely geometric outline (2, 778; 4, 503); he transposes the term from the plastic and visual to the auditory sphere, when (in 4, 556) he speaks of the *figura verborum* ("the figure of words").[6] The important transition from the form to its imitation, from model to copy, may best be noted in the passage dealing with the resemblance of children to their parents, the mixture of seeds, and heredity; with children who are *utriusque figurae* ("of both *figurae*"), resembling both father and mother, and who often reflect *proavorum figuras* ("the *figurae* of their ancestors"), and so on: *inde Venus varias producit sorte figuras* ("thence Venus brought forth diverse *figurae* in turn") (4, 1223). Here we see that only *figura* could serve for this play on model and copy; *forma* and *imago* are too solidly anchored in one or the other of the two meanings; *figura* is more concrete and dynamic than *forma*. Here, of course, as in connection with later poets, we should not forget what a fine last foot for a hexameter is provided by *figura* in all its inflectional forms.[7] A special variant of the meaning "copy" occurs in Lucretius' doctrine of the structures that peel off things like membranes and float round in the air, his Democritean doctrine of the "film images" (Diels), or *eidola*, which he takes in a materialistic sense. These he calls *simulacra, imagines, effigies,* and sometimes *figurae;* and consequently it is in Lucretius that we first find the word employed in the sense of "dream image," "figment of fancy," "ghost."

These variants had great vitality, and were to enjoy a significant career; "model," "copy," "figment," "dream image"—all these meanings clung to *figura*. But it was in still another sphere that Lucretius developed his most ingenious use of the word. As we know, he professed the cosmogony of Democritus and Epicurus, according to which the world is built up of atoms. He calls the atoms *primordia, principia, corpuscula, elementa, semina,* and in a very general sense, he also called them *corpora, quorum concursus motus ordo positura figura*[8] (1, 685, and 2, 1021) ("bodies whose combination, motion, order, position, *figura*") brings forth the things of the world. But though small, the atoms are material and formed: they have infinitely diverse shapes; and so it comes about that he often calls them "forms," *figurae,* and that conversely one may often translate *figurae,* as Diels has done, by "atoms."[9] The numerous atoms are in constant motion; they move about in the void, combine and repel one another: a dance of figures. This use of the word does not seem to have gone beyond Lucretius; the *Thesaurus* cites only one other example of it in Claudian (*Rufinum* 1, 17), at the end of the fourth century. In this small sphere, Lucretius' most original creation was without influence; but there is no doubt that of all the authors I have studied in connection with *figura,* it was Lucretius who made the most brilliant, though not the most historically important contribution.

In Cicero's frequent and extremely flexible use of the word, every variation of the concept of form that could possibly have been suggested by his political, publicistic, juridical, and philosophical activity, seems to be represented; and his use of the word reveals his lovable, volatile, and vacillating nature. Often he applies it to man, sometimes in tones of pathos. In *Pro S. Roscio* (63), he writes: *portentum atque monstrum certissimum est, esse aliquem humana specie et figura, qui tantum immanitate bestias vicerit, ut . . .* ("it is unquestionably an unnatural and monstrous thing, that a being in human form and *figura* should exist so far surpassing the wild beasts in savagery that . . ."). And in *Pro Q. Roscio* (20) *tacita corporis figura* ("the silent *figura* of a body") is the silent mien whose mere appearance betrays the scoundrel. The limbs and inner organs, animals, utensils, stars, in short all perceptible things have *figura*, and so do the gods and the universe as a whole. The sense of "appearance" and even "semblance" contained in the Greek *schēma* emerges clearly when he says that the tyrant has only *figura hominis* ("the semblance of a man") and that immaterial conceptions of God are without *figura* and *sensus* ("appearance and perception"). Clear distinctions between *figura* and *forma* are rare (e.g., *De Natura Deorum* I, 90; cf. note 7 above), and neither is confined to the realm of the visual; Cicero speaks of *figura vocis* ("of the voice"), *figura negotii* ("types of occupation"), and quite frequently of *figurae dicendi* ("figures of speech"). Of course geometric and stereometric forms also possess a *figura*. However, *figura* in the sense of copy or image is scarcely developed in Cicero. In *De Natura Deorum* (I, 71), to be sure, it is said that Cotta, one of the participants in the dialogue, might more readily understand the words *quasi corpus* ("a semblance of body") of the gods, *si in cereis fingeretur aut fictilibus figuris* ("if it were waxen images or clay figures"), and in *De Divinatione* (1, 23) he speaks of the *figura* of a rock which is not unlike a little Pan. But this does not suffice, for the *figura* of which he is speaking is that of the clay or stone, not of what is represented.[10] Cicero uses the word *imagines* for the *schēmata* of Democritus and Lucretius, which emanate from the body (*a corporibus enim solidis et a certis figuris vult fluere imagines Democritus* ["Democritus would have it that phantoms emanate from solid bodies and from actual *figurae*"] *De Divinatione*, 2, 137),[11] and in Cicero the images of the gods are usually called *signa*, never *figurae*. As an example we may cite the malicious joke against Verres (2, 2, 89): Verres planned to steal a precious statue of a god in a Sicilian city, but fell in love with his landlord's wife: *contemnere etiam signum illud Himerae jam videbatur quod eum multo magis figura et lineamenta hospitae delectabant* ("he seemed now even to despise that statue of Himera, so much more did the *figura* and features of his hostess delight him").[12] There is no sign of any such bold innovations as in Lucretius. Cicero's contribution consisted mainly in introducing the word in the sense of perceptible form to the educated language. He used it chiefly in his philosophical and rhetorical works, most frequently in his essay on the nature of the gods. In these works he tried to devise what today we should call an all-embracing concept of form. It is not only because of his well-known preoccupation with well-rounded oratorical periods that he seldom contents himself with *figura* alone, but usually piles up several related words with a view to expressing a whole: *forma et figura, conformatio quaedam et figura totius oris et corporis, habitus et figura, humana species et figura, vis et figura* ("form and *figura*," "a certain arrangement and *figura* of the whole face and body," "appearance and *figura*," "the human appearance and *figura*," "force and *figura*"), and many more of the same kind. His striving for a comprehensive view of the phenomenal world is unmistakable, and he may have communicated some of it to the Roman reader. But he lacked the right kind of talent and his eclectic attitude made it impossible for him to work out and formulate a compelling idea of form; his concept remained hazy. We must content ourselves with the richness and balance of his words. What is more important for the subsequent development of *figura* is something else: it is in Cicero and the author of the *Ad Herennium* that it occurs for the first time as a technical term in rhetoric, rendering the *schēmata* or *charaktēres lexeōs*, the three levels of style, which in *Ad Herennium* (4, 8, 11) are designated as *figura gravis*, *mediocris*, and *extenuata* ("the grand, the middle, the simple *figura*"), and in *De oratore* (3, 199, and 212) as *plena*, *mediocris*, and *tenuis* ("full, middle, plain"). However, Cicero (as Emil Vetter, author of the article *"Figura"* in *Thesaurus Linguae Latinae* expressly notes [VI, part 1, col. 731, ll. 80 f.]) does not yet use the word as a technical term for the ornamental circumlocutions that we call "figures of speech." Though he knows them and describes them at length, he does not like later writers call them *figurae*, but—again pleonastically—*formae et lumina orationis* ("forms and ornaments of speech"). He does employ the turn *figura dicendi*, or more frequently *forma et figura dicendi*, not in a strict technical sense but simply to denote a mode of eloquence, either in a general sense when he wishes to say that there are innumerable kinds of eloquence (*De Oratore*, 3, 34) or individually when he says that Curio *suam quandam expressit quasi formam figuramque dicendi* ("has expressed as it were his own special pattern and figure of oratory," ibid., 2, 98). The students at the schools of rhetoric, where Cicero's treatises on eloquence soon became a canon, became accustomed to this combination.

Thus by the end of the republican era, *figura* was firmly ingrained in the language of philosophy and cultivated discourse, and during the first century of the Empire its possibilities continued to develop. As one may well imagine, it is the poets who were most interested in the shades of meaning between model and copy, in changing form and the deceptive likenesses that walk in dreams. Catullus (*Attis*, 62) has the characteristic passage: *Quod enim genus figurae est ego quod non obierim?* ("for what kind of *figura* is there that I had not?") Propertius[13] writes: (3, 24, 5) *mixtam te varia laudavi saepe figura* ("I often praised the blending of thy varied *figura*") or (4, 2, 21) *opportuna meast cunctis natura figuris* ("my nature finds every *figura* suitable"). And speaking, in the magnificent conclusion of his *Panegyricus ad Messalam*, of death's power to change the forms of man, he employs the words *mutata figura* ("changed *figura*"); and Virgil (*Aeneid*, 10, 641) in describing the phantom of Aeneas that appears to Turnus, writes *morte obita qualis fama est volitare figuras* ("*figurae* such as, they say, flit about after death"). But the richest source for *figura* in the sense of changing form is of course Ovid. To be sure, he uses *forma* freely in the same sense when the metre calls for a dissyllabic word; but most often he employs *figura*. He has an impressive store of combinations at his command: *figuram mutare, variare, vertere, retinere, inducere, sumere, deponere, perdere.* The following little collection may give an idea of the countless ways in which he employs the word:

> . . . tellus . . . partimque figuras / rettulit antiquas   (*Metamorphoses*, I, 436);
> . . . *se mentitis superos celasse figuris*   (ibid., 5, 326);
> *sunt quibus in plures ius est transire figuras*   (ibid., 8, 730);
> . . . *artificem simulatoremque figurae / Morphea*   (ibid., 11, 634);
> *ex aliis alias reparat natura figuras*   (ibid., 15, 253);
> *animam . . . in varias doceo migrare figuras*   (ibid., 15, 172);
> *lympha figuras / datque capitque novas*   (ibid., 15, 308).

(the earth . . . in part restored the ancient shapes; the gods hid themselves in lying shapes; there are some who have power to take on many shapes; Morpheus, the skillful artificer and imitator of [man's] shape; nature builds up forms from other forms; I teach that the soul . . . passes through various forms; water gives and receives new forms).

There is also a fine example of the imprint of the seal:

> *Utque novis facilis signatur cera figuris*
> *Nec manet ut fuerat nec formas servat easdem,*
> *Sed tamen ipsa eadem est . . .*   (ibid., 15, 169 ff.).

(And as the soft wax is stamped with new *figurae*, and does not remain as it was nor retain the same forms, though it remains itself the same . . .)

In addition, *figura* already appears quite plainly in Ovid as "copy," as for example, in *Fasti* (9, 278): *globus immensi parva figura poli* ("a globe, a small figure of the vast vault of heaven"), or in *Heroides* (14, 97) and *Ex Ponto* (2, 8, 64); in the sense of "letter" which had already been given it by Varro, *ducere consuescat multas manus una figuras* (*Ars Amatoria*, 3, 493) ("let one hand be accustomed to tracing many figures"); finally, as "position" in love play: *Venerem iungunt per mille figuras* ("They embrace in a thousand *figurae*") (*Ars*, 2, 679). Throughout Ovid *figura* is mobile, changeable, multiform, and deceptive. The word is also used skillfully by Manilius, author of the *Astronomica*, who apart from the meanings already mentioned, employs it (as well as *signum* and *forma*) in the sense of "constellation." It occurs in the sense of dream figment in Lucan and Statius.

In Vitruvius the architect we find something very different both from these meanings and from those that we shall find in the rhetoricians. In his writings *figura* is architectural and plastic form, or in any case the reproduction of such form, the architect's plan; here there is no trace of deception or transformation; in his language *figurata similitudine* (7, 5, 1) does not mean "by dissimulation," but "by creating a likeness." Often *figura* means "ground plan" (*modice picta operis futuri figura,* slightly tinted, a plan of the future work 1, 2, 2), and *universae figurae species* or *summa figuratio,* signifies the general form of a building or a man (he often compares the two from the standpoint of symmetry). Despite his occasional mathematical use of the word, *figura* (as well as *fingere*) has a definitely plastic significance for him and for other technical writers of the period; thus in Festus (98), *crustulum cymbi figura*[14] ("a little cake shaped like a boat") in Celsus, *venter reddit mollia, figurata* (2, 5, 5) ("the belly gives forth soft, formed notions"), in Columella, *ficos comprimunt in figuram stellarum flioscularumque* (12, 15, 5) ("they press figs into the shape of stars and little flowers"). Even in this detail Pliny the Elder, who belonged to a different social and cultural class, is a far richer source; in his work every shading of the concepts of form and species is represented. The transition from form to portrait is clearly discernible in the memorable beginning of his thirty-fifth book, in which he deplores the decline of portrait painting: *Imaginum quidem pictura, qua maxime similes in aevum propagantur figurae* . . . ("The painting of portraits, whereby extremely lifelike *figurae* were transmitted down through the ages"); and somewhat later, when he speaks of the books illustrated with portraits, a technique invented by Varro: *imaginum amorem flagrasse quondam testes sunt . . . et Marcus Varro . . . insertis . . . septingentorum illustrium . . . imaginibus: non passus intercidere figuras, aut vetustatem aevi contra homines valere, inventor muneris etiam diis invidiosi, quando immortalitatem non solum dedit, verum etiam in omnes terras misit, ut praesentes esse ubique credi possent.* ("That there was a keen passion for portraits in olden days . . . is shown by . . . Marcus Varro . . . who inserted in his works portraits of 700 famous people: not allowing their likenesses to disappear or the passing of time to prevail against men, and thus being the inventor of a benefit which even the gods might envy, for he not only bestowed immortality but also sent it all over the world, that those concerned might be felt to be present everywhere.")

The juridical literature of the first century has a few passages in which *figura* means "empty outward form" or "semblance." In *Digest*, 28, 5, 70, we find: *non solum figuras sed vim quoque condicionis continere* (Proculus) and in *Digest*, 50, 16, 116: *Mihi Labeo videtur verborum figuram sequi, Proculus mentem* (Javolenus). ("It seems to me that Labes followed the *figura* of the words, but Proculus their intention.")

But from the standpoint of its future destinies the most important thing that happened to *figura* in the first century was the refinement of the concept of the rhetorical figure. The result has come down to us in the ninth book of Quintilian. The idea is older, it is Greek; and as we have seen above, it had already been expressed in Latin by Cicero; but Cicero did not yet use the word *figura,* and moreover the technique of the figure of speech seems to have been very much refined after his time in the course of endless discussions on rhetorical questions. When the word was first used in this sense cannot be exactly determined; probably soon after Cicero, as may be presumed from the title of a book (*De Figuris Sententiarum*, by Annaeus Cornutus) mentioned in Gellius (9, 10, 5), and from the remarks and allusions of both Senecas[15] and of Pliny the Younger. The development was only natural, since the Greek term was *schēma*. In general we must assume that the technical use of the word had developed earlier and more richly than can be demonstrated by the sources that have come down to us; that, for example, the figures of the syllogism (the *schēmata syllogismou* originated with Aristotle himself) must have been mentioned much earlier in Latin than in Boethius or the pseudo-Augustinian *Book of Categories*.

In the last section of the eighth book and in the ninth book of the *Institutio Oratoria*, Quintilian gives a detailed account of the theory of tropes and figures. This disquisition, which seems to represent a comprehensive critique of former opinions and works, became the fundamental work on the subject, and all later efforts were based on it. Quintilian distinguishes tropes from figures; trope is the more restricted concept, referring to the use of words and phrases in a sense other than literal; figure, on the other hand, is a form of discourse which deviates from the normal and most obvious usage. The aim of a figure is not, as in all tropes, to substitute words for other words; figures can be formed from words used in their proper meaning and order. Basically all discourse is a forming, a figure, but the word is employed only for formations that are particularly developed in a poetic or rhetorical sense. Thus he distinguishes between simple (*carens figuris, aschēmatistos* ["lacking in figures"]) and figurative (*figuratus, eschēmatismenos*) modes of speech. The distinction between trope and figure proves to be difficult. Quintilian himself often hesitates before classifying a turn of speech as one or the other; in later usage *figura* is generally regarded as the higher concept, including trope, so that any unliteral or indirect form of expression is said to be as figurative. As tropes Quintilian names and describes metaphor, synecdoche (*mucronem pro gladio; puppim pro navi* ("blade for sword; prow for ship")), metonymy (Mars for war; Virgil for Virgil's works), antonomasia (Pelides for Achilles), and many more; he divides figures into those involving content and those involving words (*figurae sententiarum* and *verborum*). As *figurae sententiarum* he lists: the rhetorical question which the orator himself answers; the various ways of anticipating objections (prolepsis); the affectation of drawing judges or audience into one's confidence; prosopopoeia, in which one puts words into the mouths of other persons, such as one's adversary, or of personifications, such as the fatherland; the solemn apostrophe; the embroidering of a narrative with concrete detail, *evidentia* or *illustratio;* the various forms of irony; aposiopesis or *obticentia* or *interruptio,* in which one "swallows" part of the phrase; affected repentance over something one has said; and so on; but the figure which was then regarded as the most important and seemed before all others to merit the name of figure was the hidden allusion in its diverse forms. Roman orators had developed a refined technique of expressing or insinuating something without saying it, in most cases of course something which for political or tactical reasons, or simply for the sake of effect, had best remain secret or at least unspoken. Quintilian speaks of the importance attached to training in this technique in the schools of rhetoric, and tells us how speakers would invent special cases, *controversiae figuratae,* in order to perfect and distinguish themselves in it. As "word figures" he finally mentions intentional solecisms, rhetorical repetitions, antitheses, phonetic resemblances, omissions of a word, asyndeton, climax, etc.

His exposition of tropes and figures, of which we have given only the barest essentials, is accompanied by an abundance of examples and detailed studies of the different forms and the distinctions between them; it takes up a large part of his eighth and ninth books. The system that he set forth was a very elaborate one; yet it seems likely that for a rhetorician Quintilian was relatively free in his thinking and as disinclined to excessive hairsplitting as the spirit of the times permitted. The art of the hinting, insinuating, obscuring circumlocution, calculated to ornament a statement or to make it more forceful or mordant, had achieved a versatility and perfection that strike us as strange if not absurd. These turns of speech were called *figurae*. The Middle Ages and the Renaissance, as we know, still attached a good deal of importance to the science of figures of speech. For the theorists of style of the twelfth and thirteenth century the *Ad Herennium*[16] was the main source of wisdom.

So much for the history of the word *figura* in pagan antiquity; a few grammatical, rhetorical, and logical extensions follow automatically from the meanings already stated, and some have been mentioned by other writers.[17,18] But the meaning which the Church Fathers gave the word on the basis of the development described in the previous pages was of the greatest historical importance.

II. Figura *in the*
Phenomenal Prophecy of the Church Fathers

The strangely new meaning of *figura* in the Christian world is first to be found in Tertullian, who uses it very frequently. In order to clarify its meaning we shall discuss a few passages. In his polemic *Adversus Marcionem* (3, 16) Tertullian speaks of Oshea, son of Nun, whom Moses (according to Num. 13:16) named Jehoshua (Joshua):

> . . . *et incipit vocari Jesus. . . . Hanc prius dicimus figuram futurorum fuisse. Nam quia Jesus Christus secundum populum, quod sumus nos, nati in saeculi desertis, introducturus erat in terram promissionis, melle et lacte manantem, id est vitae aeternae possessionem, qua nihil dulcius; idque non per Moysen, id est, non per legis disciplinam, sed per Jesum, id est per evangelii gratiam provenire habebat* (Vulgar Latin form for "was to happen"), *circumcisis nobis petrina acie, id est Christi praeceptis; Petra enim Christus; ideo is vir, qui in huius sacramenti imagines parabatur, etiam nominis dominici inauguratus est figura, Jesus cognominatus.*

(For the first time he is called Jesus. . . . This, then, we first observe, was a figure of things to come. For inasmuch as Jesus Christ was to introduce a new people, that is to say us, who are born in the wilderness of this world, into the promised land flowing with milk and honey, that is to say, into the possession of eternal life, than which

nothing is sweeter; and that, too, was not to come about through
Moses, that is to say, through the discipline of the Law, but through
Jesus, that is, through the grace of the gospel, our circumcision being
performed by a knife of stone, that is to say, by Christ's precepts—for
Christ is a rock; therefore that great man, who was prepared as a type
of this sacrament, was even consecrated in figure with the Lord's
name, and was called Jesus.)

Here the naming of Joshua-Jesus is treated as a prophetic event foreshadowing things to come.[19] Just as Joshua and not Moses led the people of Israel
into the promised land of Palestine, so the grace of Jesus, and not the Jewish
law, leads the "second people" into the promised land of eternal beatitude. The
man who appeared as the prophetic annunciation of this still hidden mystery,
qui in huius sacramenti imagines parabatur, was introduced under the *figura*
of the divine name. Thus the naming of Joshua-Jesus is a phenomenal
prophecy or prefiguration of the future Saviour; *figura* is something real and
historical which announces something else that is also real and historical. The
relation between the two events is revealed by an accord or similarity. Thus, for
example, Tertullian says in *Adversus Marcionem* (5, 7): *Quare Pascha
Christus, si non Pascha figura Christi per similitudinem sanguinis salutaris
et pecoris Christi?* ("How is Christ the Passover, except inasmuch as the
Passover is a figure of Christ through the likeness of the saving blood and of
the flock of Christ?") Often vague similarities in the structure of events or in
their attendant circumstances suffice to make the *figura* recognizable; to find
it, one had to be determined to interpret in a certain way. As for example, when
(ibid., 3, 17, or *Adv. Iudaeos,* 14) the two sacrificial goats of Lev. 16: 7 ff. are
interpreted as figures of the first and second coming of Christ; or when, as in
De Anima, 43 (cf. also *De Monogamia,* 5) Eve, as *figura Ecclesiae,* is developed
from Adam as *figura Christi: Si enim Adam de Christo figuram dabat, somnus
Adae mors erat Christi dormituri in mortem, ut de iniuria* (wound) *perinde
lateris eius vera mater viventium figuraretur ecclesia.*[20] ("For if Adam
provided a *figura* of Christ, the sleep of Adam was the death of Christ who was
to sleep in death, that precisely by the wound in his side should be figured the
Church, the mother of all living.")
We shall speak later on of how the desire to interpret in this way arose. At
all events the aim of this sort of interpretation was to show that the persons and
events of the Old Testament were prefigurations of the New Testament and its
history of salvation. Here it should be noted that Tertullian expressly denied
that the literal and historical validity of the Old Testament was diminished by
the figural interpretation. He was definitely hostile to spiritualism and refused
to consider the Old Testament as mere allegory; according to him, it had real,
literal meaning throughout, and even where there was figural prophecy, the
figure had just as much historical reality as what it prophesied. The prophetic
figure, he believed, is a concrete historical fact, and it is fulfilled by concrete
historical facts. For this Tertullian uses the term *figuram implere* (*Adversus
Marcionem,* 4, 40: *figuram sanguinis sui salutaris implere* ["to fulfill the

figure of his saving blood"]) or *confirmare* (*De Fuga in Persecutione,* XI: *Christo confirmante figuras suas* ["Christ confirming his figures"]). From now on we shall refer to the two events as figure and fulfillment.

Tertullian was a staunch realist, as we know in other connections. For him the *figura,* in the simple sense of "form," is a part of the substance, and in *Adversus Marcionem* (5, 20) he equates it with the flesh. Just above (4, 40), he had spoken of bread in the Eucharist:

> *Corpus illum suum fecit "Hoc est corpus meum" dicendo, "id est, figura corporis mei." Figura autem non fuisset, nisi veritatis esset corpus. Ceterum vacua res, quod est phantasma, figuram capere non posset. Aut si propterea panem corpus sibi finxit, quia corporis carebat veritate, ergo panem debuit tradere pro nobis. Faciebat ad vanitatem Marcionis, ut panis crucifigeretur. Cur autem panem corpus suum appellat, et non magis peponem, quem Marcion cordis loco habuit? Non intelligens veterem fuisse istam figuram corporis Christi, dicentis per Ieremiam* [11:19]: *Adversus me cogitaverunt cogitatum dicentes, Venite, coniiciamus lignum in panem eius, scilicet crucem in corpus eius.*

> (He made it his own body, saying, "This is my body, that is, the figure of my body." For there could not have been a figure unless there were a true body. An empty thing, that is, a phantom, could not take on a figure. If, therefore, he pretended the bread to be his body, because he lacked the reality of a body, then he must have given bread for us. It would suit Marcion's fantastic claim that the bread should be crucified. But why does he call his body bread and not rather a melon, such as Marcion must have had in place of a heart? He did not understand how ancient was that figure of the body of Christ, who said through Jer. (11:19): They have devised devices against me, saying, Come, let us put wood upon his bread, which means, of course, the cross upon his body.)

These powerful sentences—in the following the wine, *figura sanguinis* ("figure of the blood") is represented no less forcefully as *probatio carnis* ("a proof of the flesh")[21]—show clearly how concretely both terms were intended in Tertullian's figural interpretation; in every case the only spiritual factor is the understanding, *intellectus spiritualis,* which recognizes the figure in the fulfillment. The Prophets, he says in *De Resurrectione Carnis* (19 ff.), did not speak only in images; for if they had, we should be unable to recognize the images; a great deal should be taken quite literally, as also in the New Testament: *nec omnia umbrae, sed et corpora; ut in ipsum quoque Dominum insigniora quaeque luce clarius praedicantur; nam et virgo concepit in utero, non figurate; et peperit Emanuelem nobiscum Jesum Christum, non oblique.* ("And not all are shadows, but there are bodies also; so that we have prophecies even about the Lord himself, which are clearer than the day. For it was not figuratively that the Virgin conceived in her womb; and not by a metaphor that she gave birth to Emmanuel, God with us, Christ Jesus.") And he resolutely attacks those who twist the clearly proclaimed resurrection of the dead into an "imaginary meaning" (*in imaginariam significationem distorquent*). There are many passages of this kind, in which he combats the spiritualizing tendencies of contemporary groups. His realism stands out still more clearly in the relation between figure and fulfillment, for sometimes the one and sometimes the other seems to possess a higher degree of historical concreteness. In *Adversus Marcionem* (4, 40), for example (*an ipse erat, qui . . . tamquam ovis coram tendente sic os non aperturus, figuram sanguinis sui salutaris implere concupiscebat?* ["was it not that he, who . . . as a sheep before her shearers, was not to open his mouth, desired so ardently to fulfill the figure of his saving blood?"]), the figure of the servant of God as a lamb seems to be a mere simile; in another passage the Law as a whole is juxtaposed to Christ as its fulfillment (ibid., 5, 19: *de umbra transfertur ad corpus, id est, de figuris ad veritatem* ["It is transferred from the shadow to the substance, that is, from figures to the reality"]). It might seem that in the first case the simile and in the second case the abstraction give the figure a lesser force of reality. But there is no lack of examples in which the figure has the greater concreteness. In *De Baptismo* (5), where the pool of Bethesda appears as a figure of the baptism, we find the sentence: *figura ista medicinae corporalis spiritalem medicinam canebat, ea forma qua semper carnalia in figuram spiritalium antecedunt.* ("This figure of bodily healing told of a spiritual healing, according to the rule by which carnal things come first as a figure of spiritual things.") But the one and the other, the pool of Bethesda and the baptism, are concretely real, and all that is spiritual about them is the interpretation or effect; for the baptism too, as Tertullian himself hastens to add (ibid., 7), is a carnal action: *sic et in nobis carnaliter currit unctio, sed spiritaliter proficit; quomodo et ipsius baptismi carnalis actus, quod in aqua mergimur, spiritalis effectus, quod delictis liberamur.* ("Thus with us also the unction runs down carnally, but its profit is spiritual; in the same way as the act of baptism is carnal, in that we are plunged in water, but its effects are spiritual, namely that we are freed from transgression.") These examples give us the feeling that even in the first two cases Tertullian had in mind not only a metaphorical but also a real lamb, and not only the law in the abstract but also the era of the law as a historical era.

And sometimes two statements are related to one another as figure and fulfillment, as in *De Fuga in Persecutione*, 11: *certe quidem bonus pastor animam pro pecoribus ponit; ut Moyses, non Domino adhuc Christo revelato, etiam in se figurato, ait: Si perdis hunc populum, inquit, et me pariter cum eo disperde* [Exod. 32:32]. *Ceterum, Christo confirmante figuras suas, malus pastor est . . .* [John 10:12]. ("Assuredly a good shepherd lays down his life for his sheep, even as Moses said, when the Lord Christ had not yet been revealed, but was shadowed forth in himself: If you destroy this people, said he, destroy me also along with them [Exod. 32:32]. And Christ himself, confirming these figures, says: But the evil shepherd, etc. [John 10:12].") But both statements are historical events, and moreover it is not so much the statements as Moses and Christ themselves who are related as figure and fulfillment.[22] The fulfillment is often designated as *veritas,* as in an example above, and the figure correspondingly as *umbra* or *imago;* but both shadow and truth are abstract only in reference to the meaning first concealed, then revealed; they are concrete in reference to the things or persons which appear as vehicles of the meaning. Moses is no less historical and real because he is an *umbra* or *figura* of Christ, and Christ, the fulfillment, is no abstract idea, but also a historical reality. Real historical figures are to be interpreted spiritually (*spiritaliter interpretari*), but the interpretation points to a carnal, hence historical fulfillment (*carnaliter adimpleri: De Resurrectione,* 20)—for the truth has become history or flesh.

From the fourth century on, the usage of the word *figura* and the method of interpretation connected with it are fully developed in nearly all the Latin Church writers.[23] Sometimes to be sure—a practice that later became general—common allegory was also termed *figura;* in *Divinae Institutiones* (2, 10) Lactantius interprets south and north as *figurae vitae et mortis* ("figures of life and death"), day and night as true and false faith; yet the Christian notion of prefiguration and fulfillment immediately enters in: *etiam in hoc praescius futurorum Deus fecit, ut ex iis, et verae religionis, et falsarum superstitionum imago quaedam ostenderetur* ("and here also, in his foreknowledge of the future, God caused that an image, as it were, should be displayed in these things both of true religion and of false superstitions"). And thus *figura* often appears in the sense of "deeper meaning in reference to future things": the sufferings of Jesus *non fuerunt inania, sed habuerunt figuram et significationem* ("were not vain but had figure and significance") and he speaks in this connection of divine works in general *quorum vis et potentia valebat quidem in praesens, sed declarabat aliquid in futurum* ("whose force and power were of avail indeed in the present time, but also foreshowed something in the future"). This conception also dominates his eschatology which, following a speculation then widespread, interpreted the six days of Creation as six millennia, which were then almost at an end; the millennial kingdom was imminent (ibid., 7, 14): *saepe diximus, minora et exigua magnorum figuras et praemonstrationes esse; ut hunc diem nostrum qui ortu solis occasuque finitur, diei magni speciem gerere, quem circuitus annorum mille determinat. Eodem modo figuratio terreni hominis caelestis populi praeferebat in posterum fictionem.*[24] ("We have frequently said that small and trivial things are figures and foreshadowings of great things; thus, this day of ours, which is bounded by sunrise and sunset, bears the likeness of that great day which is circumscribed by the passing of a thousand years. In the same way the *figuratio* of man on earth carried with it a parable of the heavenly people yet to be.")

In most authors of the same period the figural interpretation and its most familiar examples are current coin,[25] as are the opposition between *figura* and *veritas.* But sometimes we encounter a more spiritualist, allegorical, and ethical mode of interpretation—as in Origen's Bible commentaries. In one passage, dealing with the sacrifice of Isaac—in other respects this is one of the most famous examples of the realistic type of figural interpretation—Rufinus, the Latin translator of Origen (*Patrologia Graeca*, 12, 209; the Greek original has been lost) has the following: *Sicut in Domino corporeum nihil est, etiam tu in his omnibus corporeum nihil sentias: sed in spiritu generes etiam tu filium Isaac, cum habere coeperis fructum spiritus, gaudium, pacem.* ("As there is no bodily element in the Lord, so do you also see nothing corporal in all these things; but you also may bear your son Isaac in the spirit, when you begin to possess the fruit of the spirit, joy, and peace.") Origen, to be sure, is far from being as abstractly allegorical as, for example, Philo; in his writings, the events of the Old Testament seem alive, with a direct bearing on the reader and his real life; yet in his fine explanation of the three-day journey in Exodus, for example (loc. cit., pp. 313 ff.), mystical and moral considerations seem definitely to overshadow the strictly historical element.[26] The difference between Tertullian's more historical and realistic interpretation and Origen's ethical, allegorical approach reflects a current conflict, known to us from other early Christian sources: one party strove to transform the events of the New and still more of the Old Testament into purely spiritual happenings, to "spirit away" their historical character—the other wished to preserve the full histo-ricity of the Scriptures along with the deeper meaning. In the West the latter tendency was victorious, although the spiritualists always maintained a certain influence, as may be seen from the progress of the doctrine of the different meanings of Scripture; for while the adherents of this doctrine recognize the literal or historical sense, they sever its connection with the equally real prefiguration by setting up other, purely abstract interpretations beside or in place of the prefigural interpretation. St. Augustine played a leading part in the compromise between the two doctrines. On the whole he favored a living, figural interpretation, for his thinking was far too concrete and historical to content itself with pure abstract allegory.

The whole classical tradition was very much alive in St. Augustine, and of this his use of the word *figura* is one more indication. In his writings we find it expressing the general notion of form in all its traditional variants, static and dynamic, outline and body; it is applied to the world, to nature as a whole, and to the particular object; along with *forma, color*, and so on, it stands for the outward appearance (*Epist.*, 120, 10, or 146, 3); or it may signify the variable aspect over against the imperishable essence. It is in this last sense that he interprets I Cor. 7:31: *Peracto quippe iudicio tunc esse desinet hoc coelum et haec terra, quando incipiet esse coelum novum et terra nova. Mutatione namque rerum non omni modo interitu transibit hic mundus. Unde et apostolus dicit: praeterit enim figura huius mundi, volo vos sine sollicitudine esse. Figura enim praeterit, non natura (De Civitate Dei*, 20, 14). ("When the judgment shall be finished, then this heaven and this earth shall cease to be, and a new heaven and a new earth shall begin. But this world will not be utterly consumed; it will only undergo a change; and therefore the Apostle says: The fashion [*figura*] of this world passeth away, and I would have you to be without care. The fashion [*figura*] goes away, not the nature.") [Trans. John Healey, Everyman edition. London, 1950, Vol. II, p. 289.] *Figura* appears also as idol, as dream figure or vision, as mathematical form; scarcely one of the many known variants is missing. But by far the most often it appears in the sense of prefiguration. Augustine explicitly adopted the figural interpretation of the Old Testament and emphatically recommended its use in sermons and missions (e.g., *De Catechizandis Rudibus*, III, 6), and developed on the method. Its whole repertory of interpretations passes us by in his work: Noah's ark is *praefiguratio ecclesiae* ("a prefiguration of the Church,") (*De Civitate Dei* 15, 27); in several different ways Moses is *figura Christi* (e.g., *De Civitate Dei*, 10, 8, or 18, 11); Aaron's *sacerdotium* is *umbra et figura aeterni sacerdotii* ("shadow and figure of the eternal priesthood") (ibid., 17, 6); Hagar, the slave woman, is a *figura* of the Old Testament, of the *terrena Jerusalem* ("earthly Jerusalem"), and Sarah of the New Testament, of the *superna Jerusalem civitas Dei* ("the heavenly Jerusalem, the city of God") (ibid., 16, 31; 17, 3; *Expos. ad Galatas,* 40); Jacob and Esau *figuram praebuerunt duorum populorum in Christianis et Iudeis* ("prefigured the two peoples of Jews and Christians") (*De Civitate Dei,* 16, 42); the king of Judaea *(Christi) figuram prophetica unctione gestabant* (ibid., 17, 4) ("by being anointed by the prophets bore a prefiguration of the Christ."). These are only a few examples; the whole Old Testament, or at least its important figures and events, are all interpreted figurally; even where hidden meanings are found, as for example in Hannah's prayer of thanksgiving (I Sam. 2:1–10) in *De Civ.,* 17, 4, the interpretation is not only allegorical but figural as well; Hannah's song of praise over the birth of her son Samuel is explained as a figure for the transformation of the old earthly kingdom and priesthood into the new heavenly kingdom and priesthood; she herself becomes a *figura ecclesiae.*

Augustine emphatically rejected the purely allegorical interpretation of the Holy Scriptures and dismissed the notion that the Old Testament was a kind of hermetic book that became intelligible only if one discarded the literal historical meaning and the vulgar interpretation. He held that every believer could gradually penetrate its sublime content. In *De Trinitate* (11, 2) he writes: . . . *sancta scriptura parvulis congruens nullius generis rerum verba vitavit, ex quibus quasi gradatim ad divina atque sublimia noster intellectus velut nutritus assurgeret* ("the Holy Scriptures, as is fitting for little ones, did not shun any kind of verbal expression through which our understanding might be nourished and rise step by step to divine and sublime things"). And again, referring more plainly to the problem of figures: *Ante omnia, fratres, hoc in nomine Domini et admonemus, et praecipimus, ut quando auditis exponi sacramentum scripturae narrantis quae gesta sunt, prius illud quod lectum est credatis sic gestum, quomodo lectum est; ne substrato fundamento rei gestae, quasi in aere quaeratis aedificare* (*Serm.,* 2, 6)[27] ("Before all things, brethren, we admonish and command you in the name of the Lord, that when you hear an exposition of the mystery of the Scriptures telling of things that took place, you believe what is read to have actually taken place as the reading narrates; lest, undermining the foundation of actuality, you seek as it were to build in the air"). He took the view—which had long ago become part of the tradition—that the Old Testament was pure phenomenal prophecy, and he laid more stress than others on certain passages in the Pauline epistles of which we shall have more to say later on. The observances of the law *quas tamquam umbras futuri saeculi nunc respuunt Christiani, id tenentes, quod per illas umbras figurate promittebatur* ("which Christians now cast aside as mere shadows of the age to come, possessing as they do that which was promised in a figure by those shadows") and the sacraments *quae habuerunt promissivas figuras* ("which served as figures of promise"), are the letter of Scripture, precisely in the sense that their undoubted carnal and historical reality has, no less historically, been revealed and spiritually interpreted by the Christian fulfillment—and as we shall soon see, replaced by a new, more complete, and clearer promise. Consequently a Christian should hold *non ad legem operum, ex qua nemo iustificatur, sed ad legem fidei, ex qua iustus vivit* (*De Spiritu et Littera*, XIV, 23) ("not the works of the law, by which no man is justified, but to the law of faith, by which the just man lives"). The Jews of the Old Testament, *quando adhuc sacrificium verum, quod fideles norunt, in figuris praenuntiabatur, celebrabant figuram futurae rei; multi scientes, sed plures ignorantes* (*Enarr. in Psalm.*, 39, 12) ("when they still foretold in figures that true sacrifice which the faithful know, were celebrating figures of a reality to come in the future; for they knew many things, but were ignorant of even more"); while the latter-day Jews, and here he strikes a theme which was to run through all subsequent polemics against the Jews,[28] refused in their obdurate blindness to recognize this: *Non enim frustra Dominus ait Judaeis: si crederetis Moysi, crederetis et mihi; de me enim ille scripsit* (*Joan.*, 5, 46); *carnaliter quippe accipiendo legem, et eius promissa terrena rerum coelestium figuras esse nescientes* (*De Civ.*, 20, 28) ("For the Lord spoke not idly ... when He told the Jews, saying: 'Had ye believed Moses, you would have believed Me, for he wrote of Me.' For these men accepted the law in a carnal sense and did not understand its earthly promises as types [*figuras*] of heavenly things.") But the "heavenly" fulfillment is not complete, and consequently, as in certain earlier writers but more definitely in Augustine, the confrontation of the two poles, figure and fulfillment, is sometimes replaced by a development in three stages: the Law or history of the Jews as a prophetic *figura* for the appearance of Christ; the incarnation as fulfillment of this *figura* and at the same time as a new promise of the end of the world and the Last Judgment; and finally, the future occurrence of these events as ultimate fulfillment. In *Serm.*, 4, 8, we read: *Vetus enim Testamentum est promissio figurata, novum Testamentum est promissio spiritualiter intellecta* ("The Old Testament is a promise in figure, the New is a promise understood after the spirit"), and still more clearly in *Contra Faustinum*, 4, 2: *Temporalium quidem rerum promissiones Testamento Veteri contineri, et ideo Vetus Testamentum appellari nemo nostrum ambigit; et quod aeternae vitae promissio regnumque coelorum ad Novum pertinet Testamentum: sed in illis temporalibus figuras fuisse futurorum quae implerentur in nobis, in quos finis saeculorum obvenit, non suspicio mea, sed apostolicus intellectus est, dicente Paulo, cum de talibus loqueretur: Haec omnia . . .* ("For we are all aware that the Old Testament contains promises of temporal things, and that is why it is called the Old

Testament; and that the promise of eternal life and the kingdom of heaven belongs to the New Testament: but that in these temporal figures there was the promise of future things, which were to be fulfilled in us, on whom the ends of the world are come, is no fantasy of mine, but the interpretation of the apostles, as Paul says, speaking of these matters: For all these things. . . .") And at this point Augustine quotes I Cor. 10:6 and 11. Although here the ultimate fulfillment is regarded as imminent, it is clear that Augustine has in mind two promises, one concealed and seemingly temporal in the Old Testament, the other clearly expressed and supratemporal in the Gospel. This gives the doctrine of the fourfold meaning of Scripture a far more realistic, historical, and concrete character, for three of the four meanings become concrete, historical, and interrelated, while only one remains purely ethical and allegorical—as Augustine explains in *De Genesi ad Litteram,* 1, 1: *In libris autem omnibus sanctis intueri oportet, quae ibi aeterna intimentur* ("In all the holy books those things are to be looked for which are indicated as having to do with eternity")—end of the world and eternal life, analogical interpretation; *quae futura praenuntientur* ("which foretell future events")—figural meaning in the strict sense, in the Old Testament the prefigurations of the coming of Christ; *quae agenda praecipiantur vel moneantur* ("which command or advise what we are to do")—ethical meaning.

Even though Augustine rejects abstract allegorical spiritualism and develops his whole interpretation of the Old Testament from the concrete historical reality, he nevertheless has an idealism which removes the concrete event, completely preserved as it is, from time and transposes it into a perspective of eternity. Such ideas were implicit in the notion of the incarnation of the Word; the figural interpretation of history paved the way for them, and they made their appearance at an early day. When Tertullian, for example, says (*Adversus Marcionem,* 3, 5) that in Isa. 50:6 *dorsum meum posui in flagella* (Vulgate, *corpus meum dedi percutientibus*) ("I gave my back to the smiters"), the future is represented figurally by past events, he adds that for God there is no *differentia temporis* ("difference of time"). But none among Augustine's precursors or contemporaries seems to have developed this idea so profoundly and completely as Augustine himself. Time and again he stresses the opposition which Tertullian felt only because of the perfect tense employed in the narrative; for example, in *De Civ.,* 17, 8: *Scriptura sancta etiam de rebus gestis prophetans quodammodo in eo figuram delineat futurorum* ("the Holy Scripture, even when prophesying of things that are already done, outlines in a certain manner a figure of future things"); or in reference to a discrepancy between Psalm 113, *In exitu,* and the corresponding narrative in Exodus (*Enarr. in Psalm.,* 113, 1): *ne arbitremini nobis narrari praeterita, sed potius futura praedici . . . ut id, quod in fine saeculorum manifestandum reservabatur, figuris rerum atque verborum praecurrentibus nuntiaretur* ("Do not look upon as telling of the past, but rather as foretelling the future . . . that what was reserved to be made manifest at the end of the ages should be announced in material and verbal figures to those who came before"). Perhaps Augustine's view of the eternal character of the figures is best appreciated in a passage that does not refer expressly to figural interpretation: *Quid enim est praescientia, nisi scientia futurorum? Quid actem futurum est Deo qui omnia supergreditur tempora? Si enim scientia Dei res ipsas habet, non sunt ei futurae, sed praesentes; ac per hoc non jam praescientia, sed tantum scientia dici potest* (*De Div. Quaest. ad Simplicianum*, II, qu. 2, n. 2) ("For what is foreknowledge but knowledge of the future? But what is future to God who transcends all time? If God's knowledge contains these things, they are not future to Him but present; therefore it can be termed not foreknowledge, but simply knowledge").

The figural interpretation was of great practical use for the mission of the fourth and following centuries; it was constantly employed in sermons and religious instruction, often, to be sure, mixed with purely allegorical and ethical interpretations. The *Formulae Spiritalis Intelligentiae*[29] of Bishop Eucherius of Lyons (early fifth century), educated at Lerins, is a textbook of figural and ethical interpretation; from the sixth century we have the *Instituta Regularia Divinae Legis* of Junilius, *Quaestor sacri palatii* (*Patrologia Latina*, Vol. 68, cols. 15 ff.), which is a translation of a Greek work influenced by the Antioch school; in its first chapter we find the following doctrine: *Veteris Testamenti intentio est Novum figuris praenuntiationibusque monstrare; Novi autem ad aeternae beatitudinis gloriam humanas mentes accendere* ("The intention of the Old Testament is to point to the New by figures and prophecies; that of the New is to kindle the minds of men to the glory of eternal beatitude"). A practical example of how the figural interpretation was used in the instruction of new converts is provided by the explanation of the paschal sacrifice in the second Sermon of Bishop Gaudentius of Brescia (*Patrologia Latina*, 20, col. 855), who gives us a perhaps unconscious expression of figural perspective when he says that the *figura* (preceding in time) is not *veritas*, but *imitatio veritatis*. We find a good many strange and farfetched figural interpretations, often mixed with purely abstract, ethical allegory. But the basic view that the Old Testament, both as a whole and in its most important details, is a concrete historical prefiguration of the Gospel, became a firmly rooted tradition.

Now let us return to our semantic investigation and ask how the Church Fathers arrived at the new sense of *figura*. The earliest works of Christian literature were written in Greek, and the word most often used in them for "prefiguration"—in the *Epistle of Barnabas* for example—is *typos*. This leads to the presumption—which may have come to the reader in connection with some of our quotations, the passages from Lactantius, for example—that *figura* passed directly from its general meaning of "formation" or "form" to its new signification; and indeed the usage of the oldest ecclesiastical writers makes this seem likely. When they write that persons or events of the Old Testament *figuram Christi (ecclesiae, baptismi, etc.) gerunt* or *gestant* ("provide a *figura* of Christ, the Church, baptism, etc."), that the Jewish people in all things *figuram nostram portat* ("bears our *figura*"), that the Holy Scripture *figuram delineat futurorum* ("delineates the *figura* of things to come"), *figura* in these sentences can simply be translated as "form." But then the idea of the *schēma* as molded by pre-Christian poetry and oratory—the rhetorical image or circumlocution that conceals, transforms, and even deceives—enters in. The opposition between *figura* and *veritas,* the interpretation *(exponere)* and unveiling *(aperire, revelare)*[30] of figures, the equation of *figura* with *umbra,* of *sub figura* with *sub umbra* (e.g., *ciborum,* ["of foodstuffs"], or in a more general sense, *legis* ["of the law"], the notion of a *figura* under which something other, future, true, lies concealed)—all this shows that the old sense of rhetorical image had survived, though it had moved from the purely nominalistic world of the schools of oratory and of Ovid's half playful myths into a realm both real and spiritual, hence authentic, significant, and existential. The distinction between figures of word and figures of substance that we find in Quintilian is resumed in the distinction between *figura verborum* and *figurae rerum,* word and prophetic events or phenomenal prophecies.

On this new basis the word has vastly extended its range of signification. We find *figura* as "deeper meaning," as for example in Sedulius *(ista res habet egregiam figuram, Carm. Pasch.,* 5, 384 f. ["this event has an extraordinary *figura*"]) and in Lactantius; as "deception" or "deceptive form" (Filastrius 61, *Liber de Haeresibus, Patrologia Latina,* Vol. 12, col. 1176) *(sub figura confessionis christianae)* ["under the *figura* of the Christian faith"] meaning "alleging to be Christians"), or Sulpicius Severus, *De Vita Beati Martini,* 21, 1 *(Pastrologia Latina,* Vol. 20, col. 172), who says that the Devil *sive [se] in diversas figuras spiritalis nequitiae transtulisset* ("transformed himself into various *figurae* of spiritual wickedness"), or Leo the Great, *Epist.,* 98, 3 *(Patrologia Latina,* 54, 955): *lupum pastorali pelle nudantes, qua prius quoque figura tantummodo convincebatur obtectus* ("stripping the wolf of his sheep's clothing, wherewith formerly in a figure he was shown to be concealed"); as an "empty" or "deceptive manner of speaking" or "evasion" *(per tot figuras ludimur,* Prudentius, *Peristephanon,* 2, 315 ["we are made sport of by all these *figurae*"]), or Rufinus, *Apologia adversus Hieronymus,* 2, 22: *qualibus (Ambrosium) figuris laceret* ("figures with which he mangled Ambrose"); or simply as "discourse" or "word" *(te . . . incauta violare figura* ["I feared to hurt thee with an incautious figure"] Paulinus of Nola, *Carmina,* 11, 12); and finally in variations of the new meaning which scarcely permit of an appropriate translation: in the poetic *De Actibus Apostolorum* of the sixth-century subdeacon Arator *(Patrologia Latina,* 68, cols. 83 ff.) we find the verses: *tamen illa figura, qua sine nulla vetus* (i.e., *Veteris Testamenti) subsistit littera, demum hac melius novitate manet* (Bk. 2, el. 361–3) ("but that figure, without which not a letter of the Old Testament exists, now at length endures to better purpose in the New"); and from just about the same time, a passage in the writings of Bishop Avitus of Vienne *(Poema,* 5, 1. 284, *MG Auct. Ant.,* VI, 2)[31] in which he speaks of the Last Judgment; just as God in killing the first-born in Egypt spared the houses daubed with blood, so may He recognize and spare the faithful by the sign of the Eucharist: *Tu cognosce tuam salvanda in plebe figuram* ("recognize thine own figure in the people that are to be saved").

Beside the opposition between *figura* and fulfillment or truth, there

appears another, between *figura* and *historia; historia* or *littera* is the literal
sense or the event related; *figura* is the same literal meaning or event in
reference to the fulfillment cloaked in it, and this fulfillment itself is *veritas,* so
that *figura* becomes a middle term between *littera-historia* and *veritas.* In this
connection *figura* is roughly equivalent to *spiritus* or *intellectus spiritalis,*
sometimes replaced by *figuralitas,* as in the following passage from the
Continentia Vergiliana of Fulgentius (90, 1): *sub figuralitate historiae
plenum hominis monstravimus statum* ("we have shown the whole state of
mankind under the figure of history"). Of course *figura* and *historia* may often
be used interchangeably (*ab historia in mysterium surgere* ["to rise from
historia to mystery"]), says Gregory the Great (*Ezech.,* 1, 6, 3) and further on
both *historiare* and *figurare* mean "to represent in images," "to illustrate," the
first however only in the literal sense, the second also in the sense of "to
interpret allegorically."[32]

    Figura is not the only Latin word used for historic prefiguration; often we
find the Greek terms *allegoria* and still more frequently *typus; allegoria*
generally refers to any deeper meaning and not only to phenomenal prophecy,
but the boundary is fluid, for *figura* and *figuraliter* often extend beyond figural
prophecy. Tertullian uses *allegoria* almost synonymously with *figura,* though
much less frequently, and in Arnobius (*Adversus Nationes* 5, 32; *Patrologia
Latina,* Vol. 53, col. 1147) we find *historia* opposed to *allegoria; allegoria* also
benefited by the authority of Gal. 4:24. But *allegoria* could not be used
synonymously with *figura* in all contexts, for it did not have the same
implication of "form"; one could not write that *Adam est allegoria Christi.* As
for *typus,* the only reason why it fell behind *figura* is that it was a foreign word.
But this consideration was far from negligible, for in anyone who spoke Latin
(or later a Romance language), *figura* more or less consciously evoked all the
notions involved in its history, while *typus* remained an imported, lifeless sign.
As for the Latin words which were, or at least could be employed for
prefiguration in place of *figura,* they are as follows: *ambages, effigies,
exemplum, imago, similitudo, species,* and *umbra. Ambages* was dropped as too
pejorative; *effigies* in the sense of "copy" was too narrow, and even in
comparison with *imago,* seems to have developed little power of expansion; the
others cut across the meaning of "figural prophecy" in various ways, but do not
fully satisfy it. They are all used occasionally, the most frequent being *imago*
and *umbra. Imagines,* absolute and without a genitive, was employed for the
statues of ancestors in Roman houses; in Christian usage they became the
pictures and statues of the saints, so that the meaning developed in a different
direction; nevertheless, according to the Vulgate, man was made *ad imaginem
Dei* ("in the image of God"), and consequently *imago* long competed with
figura, though only in passages where the context made the meaning "image"
identical with "prefiguration." *Umbra* was supported chiefly by a few passages
in the Pauline Epistles (Col. 2:17; Heb. 8:5 and 10:1); it occurs frequently, but
more as a metaphoric turn for *figura* than as a direct designation. In any event,
none of these words combined the elements of the concept so fully as *figura:*
the creative, formative principle, change amid the enduring essence, the

shades of meaning between copy and archetype. Hence it is not surprising that *figura* should have been most often and most widely used for this purpose.

III. Origin and Analysis of Figural Interpretation

In the last section we involuntarily digressed several times from our purely semantic discussion, because the idea which the word expresses in the Church Fathers is itself in need of explanation. It thus becomes necessary to investigate the origins of this idea in greater detail, to distinguish it from related ideas, and to examine its historical destinies and influence.

The Church Fathers often justify the figural interpretation on the basis of certain passages in early Christian writings, mostly from the Pauline Epistles.[33] The most important of these is I Cor. 10:6 and 11, where the Jews in the desert are termed *typoi hēmōn* ("figures of ourselves"), and where it is written that *tauta de typikōs synebainen ekeinois* ("these things befell them as figures"). Another passage often adduced is Gal. 4:21–31, where Paul explains to the freshly baptized Galatians, who, still under the influence of Judaism, wished to be circumcised, the difference between law and grace, the old and the new covenant, servitude and freedom, by the example of Hagar-Ishmael and Sarah-Isaac, linking the narrative in Genesis with Is. 54:1 and interpreting it in terms of figural prophecy. Still others are Col. 2:16 f., saying that the Jewish dietary laws and holidays are only the shadow of things to come, whereas the body is Christ; Rom. 5:12 ff. and I Cor. 15:21, where Adam appears as the *typos* of the future Christ, and grace is opposed to the law; II Cor. 3:14, which speaks of the veil *(kalymnos)* that covers the Scripture when the Jews read it; and finally Heb. 9:11 ff., where the sacrifice of Christ's blood is represented as the fulfillment of the high priest's sacrifice in the Old Testament.

Certain passages in Acts (e.g., 8:32) show that figural interpretation played an important part in the Christian mission from the very start. It seems only natural that the new Judaeo-Christians should have looked for prefigurations and confirmations of Jesus in the Old Testament and incorporated the interpretations thus arrived at into the tradition; particularly since the notion was current among them that the Messiah would be a second Moses, that his redemption would be a second exodus from Egypt in which the miracles of the first would be repeated.[34] This would require no further explanation. But an examination of the above-cited passages, particularly if they are considered in connection with Paul's preaching as a whole, shows that in him these Jewish conceptions were combined with a pronounced hostility to the ideas of the Judaeo-Christians, and that it is this attitude which gives them their special significance. Those passages in the Pauline Epistles which contain figural interpretations were almost all written in the course of Paul's bitter struggle in behalf of his mission among the Gentiles; many are answers to the attacks and persecutions of the Judaeo-Christians; nearly all are intended to strip the Old

Testament of its normative character and show that it is merely a shadow of things to come. His whole figural interpretation was subordinated to the basic Pauline theme of grace versus law, faith versus works: the old law is annulled; it is shadow and *typos;* observance of it has become useless and even harmful since Christ made his sacrifice; a Christian is justified not by works in observance of the law, but by faith; and in its Jewish and Judaistic legal sense the Old Testament is the letter that kills, while the new Christians are servants of the new covenant, of the spirit that gives life. This was Paul's doctrine, and the former Pharisee and disciple of Gamaliel looked eagerly in the Old Testament for passages in support of it. As a whole it ceased for him to be a book of the law and history of Israel and became from beginning to end a promise and prefiguration of Christ, in which there is no definitive, but only a prophetic meaning which has now been fulfilled, in which everything is written "for our sakes" (I Cor. 9:10, cf. Rom. 15:4) and in which precisely the most important and sacred events, sacraments and laws are provisional forms and figurations of Christ and the Gospel: *etenim Pascha nostrum immolatus est Christi* (I Cor. 5:7) ("for even Christ our passover is sacrificed for us").[35]

In this way his thinking, which eminently combined practical politics with creative poetic faith, transformed the Jewish conception of Moses risen again in the Messiah into a system of figural prophecy, in which the risen one both fulfills and annuls the work of his precursor. What the Old Testament thereby lost as a book of national history, it gained in concrete dramatic actuality. Paul devised no systematic interpretation of the Old Testament, but the few passages about the Exodus, about Adam and Christ, Hagar and Sarah, etc., show sufficiently what his intention was. The Old Testament controversies of the ensuing period kept his conception and interpretation alive; true, the influence of the Judaeo-Christians with their fidelity to the law soon diminished, but a new opposition came from those who wished either to exclude the Old Testament altogether or to interpret it only abstractly and allegorically— whereby Christianity would necessarily have lost its conception of a providential history, its intrinsic concreteness, and with these no doubt some of its immense persuasive power. In the struggle against those who despised the Old Testament and tried to despoil it of its meaning, the figural method again proved its worth.

In this connection we should bear in mind another factor which became important as Christianity spread through the countries of the western and northern Mediterranean. As we have seen, the figural interpretation changed the Old Testament from a book of laws and a history of the people of Israel into a series of figures of Christ and the Redemption, such as we find later in the procession of prophets in the medieval theater and in the cyclic representations of medieval sculpture. In this form and in this context, from which Jewish history and national character had vanished, the Celtic and Germanic peoples, for example, could accept the Old Testament; it was a part of the universal religion of salvation and a necessary component of the equally magnificent and universal vision of history that was conveyed to them along with this religion. In its original form, as law book and history of so foreign and remote a nation, it would have been beyond their reach. This of course was a later insight, far from the thoughts of the first preachers to the Gentiles and of the Church Fathers. The problem did not arise in the early period, for the first pagan converts lived among the Jews of the Diaspora, and what with the important influence of the Jews and the receptivity of the Hellenistic world of that time to religious experience, they had long been familiar with Jewish history and religion. But the fact that we can only discern it in retrospect does not make this consideration any less important. It was not until very late, probably not until after the Reformation, that Europeans began to regard the Old Testament as Jewish history and Jewish law; it first came to the newly converted peoples as *figura rerum* or phenomenal prophecy, as a prefiguration of Christ, so giving them a basic conception of history, which derived its compelling force from its inseparable bond with the faith, and which for almost a thousand years remained the only accepted view of history. Consequently the attitude embodied in the figural interpretation became one of the essential elements of the Christian picture of reality, history, and the concrete world in general. This consideration leads us to the second of the tasks we set ourselves at the beginning of this chapter, namely to define figural interpretation more sharply and to distinguish it from other, related forms of interpretation.

Figural interpretation establishes a connection between two events or persons, the first of which signifies not only itself but also the second, while the second encompasses or fulfills the first. The two poles of the figure are separate in time, but both, being real events or figures, are within time, within the stream of historical life. Only the understanding of the two persons or events is a spiritual act, but this spiritual act deals with concrete events whether past, present, or future, and not with concepts or abstractions; these are quite secondary, since promise and fulfillment are real historical events, which have either happened in the incarnation of the Word, or will happen in the second coming. Of course purely spiritual elements enter into the conceptions of the ultimate fulfillment, since "my kingdom is not of this world"; yet it will be a real kingdom, not an immaterial abstraction; only the *figura,* not the *natura* of this world will pass away (see above p. 513), and the flesh will rise again. Since in figural interpretation one thing stands for another, since one thing represents and signifies the other, figural interpretation is "allegorical" in the widest sense. But it differs from most of the allegorical forms known to us by the historicity both of the sign and what it signifies. Most of the allegories we find in literature or art represent a virtue (e.g., wisdom), or a passion (jealousy), an institution (justice), or at most a very general synthesis of historical phenomena (peace, the fatherland)—never a definite event in its full historicity. Such are the allegories of late antiquity and the Middle Ages, extending roughly from the *Psychomachia*[36] of Prudentius to Alain de Lille and the *Roman de la rose*. We find something very similar (or diametrically opposite if one prefers) in the allegorical interpretations of historical events,[37] which were usually interpreted as obscure illustrations of philosophical doctrines. In biblical exegesis this allegorical method long competed with the figural interpretation; it was the method of Philo[38] and the catechetical school of Alexandria, which was under his influence. It was rooted in a much older tradition. Various philosophical schools had long interpreted the Greek myths, particularly Homer and Hesiod, as veiled expositions of their own physico-cosmological system. And various later influences, no longer purely rationalistic but more mystical and religious, were also at work. All the numerous sects and occult doctrines of late antiquity cultivated the allegorical interpretation of myths, signs, and texts, and in their interpretations the physical and cosmological aspect gradually gave way to the ethical and mystical. Philo himself, who in keeping with the Jewish tradition constructed his philosophy as a commentary on Scripture, interpreted the various events of the Bible as phases in the development of the soul and its relation to the intelligible world; in the destinies of Israel as a whole and of the protagonists of Jewish history, he saw an allegory of the movement of the sinful soul in need of salvation, its fall, hope, and ultimate redemption. This clearly spiritual and extrahistorical form of interpretation enjoyed great influence in late antiquity, in part because it was merely the most respectable manifestation of an immense spiritualist movement centered in Alexandria; not only texts and events, but also natural phenomena, stars, animals, stones, were stripped of their concrete reality and interpreted allegorically or on occasion somewhat figurally. The spiritualist-ethical-allegorical method was taken up by the catechetical school of Alexandria and found its outstanding Christian exponent in Origen. As we know, it continued into the Middle Ages side by side with the figural method. But despite the existence of numerous hybrid forms, it is very different from figural interpretation. It too transforms the Old Testament; in it too the law and history of Israel lose their national and popular character; but these are replaced by a mystical or ethical system, and the text loses far more of its concrete history than in the figural system. This type of exegesis long maintained its position; in the doctrine of the fourfold meaning of Scripture, it wholly determined one of the four meanings, the ethical, and partly accounted for another, the analogical. And yet I believe, though I can offer no strict proof of it, that independently, that is to say, without the support of the figural method, it would have had little influence on the freshly converted peoples. There is something scholarly, indirect, even abstruse about it, except on the rare occasions when a gifted mystic breathes force into it. By its origin and nature, it was limited to a relatively small circle of intellectuals and initiates; they alone could find pleasure and nourishment in it. Figural phenomenal prophecy, however, had grown out of a definite historical situation, the Christian break with Judaism and the Christian mission among the Gentiles; it had a historical function. Its integral, firmly teleological view of history and the providential order of the world gave it the power to capture the imagination and innermost feeling of the convert nations. By its success it paved the way for less concrete schools of allegorism, such as that of the Alexandrians. But although this and other spiritualistic methods of interpretation may be older than the figural method of the apostles and Chruch Fathers, they are unmistakably late forms, while the figural interpretation with its living historicity, though scarcely primitive or archaic, was assuredly a fresh beginning and rebirth of man's creative powers.

Aside from the allegorical form we have just been discussing there are still other ways of representing one thing by another that may be compared with figural prophecy: namely the so-called symbolic or mythical forms, which are often regarded as characteristic of primitive cultures, and which in any case are often found in them; so much material concerning these forms has been brought to light in recent years, and the process of sifting and explaining this material is so far from complete that we can speak of them only with caution. These forms were first recognized and described by Vico. Their characteristic feature is that the thing represented must always be something very important and holy for those concerned, something affecting their whole life and thinking, and that this something is not only expressed or imitated in the sign or symbol, but considered to be itself present and contained in it. Thus the symbol itself can act and be acted upon in its place; to act upon the symbol is conceived as tantamount to acting on the thing symbolized, and consequently magical powers are imputed to the symbol. Such symbolic or mythical forms still existed in the Mediterranean countries in late antiquity, but for the most part they had lost their magical force and had paled to allegory; very much as vestiges of them, the symbols of justice in heraldry and national emblems, for example, have lived on in our modern cultures, though on the other hand, as we may observe, both in late antiquity and in modern times, new ideas of universal appeal never cease to create symbols which act as magical realities. These symbolic or mythical forms have certain points of contact with the figural interpretation; both aspire to interpret and order life as a whole; both are conceivable only in religious or related spheres. But the differences are self-evident. The symbol must possess magic power, not the *figura;* the *figura,* on the other hand, must always be historical, but not the symbol. Of course Christianity has no lack of magic symbols; but the *figura* as such is not one of them.[39] What actually makes the two forms completely different is that figural prophecy relates to an interpretation of history—indeed it is by nature a textual interpretation—while the symbol is a direct interpretation of life and originally no doubt for the most part, of nature. Thus figural interpretation is a product of late cultures, far more indirect, complex, and charged with history than the symbol or myth. Indeed, seen from this point of view, it has something vastly old about it: a great culture had to reach its culmination and indeed to show signs of old age, before an interpretive tradition could produce something on the order of figural prophecy.

These two comparisons, with allegory on the one hand and with the symbolical, mythical forms on the other, disclose figural prophecy in a twofold light: youthful and newborn as a purposive, creative, concrete interpretation of universal history; infinitely old as the late interpretation of a venerable text, charged with history, that had grown for hundreds of years. Its youthful vitality gave it the almost unequalled persuasive power with which it captivated not only the late cultures of the Mediterranean, but also the relatively youthful peoples of the West and North; what was old in it gave the thinking of those peoples and their understanding of history a peculiarly puzzling quality, which we shall now attempt to elucidate. Figural prophecy implies the interpretation of one worldly event through another; the first signifies the second, the second fulfills the first. Both remain historical events; yet both, looked at in this way, have something provisional and incomplete about them; they point to one another and both point to something in the future, something still to come, which will be the actual, real, and definitive event. This is true not only of Old Testament prefiguration, which points forward to the incarnation and the proclamation of the gospel, but also of these latter events, for they too are not the ultimate fulfillment, but themselves a promise of the end of time and the true kingdom of God. Thus history, with all its concrete force, remains forever a figure, cloaked and needful of interpretation. In this light the history of no epoch ever has the practical self-sufficiency which, from the standpoint both of primitive man and of modern science, resides in the accomplished fact; all history, rather, remains open and questionable, points to something still concealed, and the tentativeness of events in the figural interpretation is fundamentally different from the tentativeness of events in the modern view of historical development. In the modern view, the provisional event is treated as a step in an unbroken horizontal process; in the figural system the interpretation is always sought from above; events are considered not in their unbroken relation to one another, but torn apart, individually, each in relation to something other that is promised and not yet present. Whereas in the modern view the event is always self-sufficient and secure, while the interpretation is fundamentally incomplete, in the figural interpretation the fact is subordinated to an interpretation which is fully secured to begin with: the event is enacted according to an ideal model which is a prototype situated in the future and thus far only promised. This model situated in the future and imitated in the figures (one is reminded of the term *imitatio veritatis* ["imitation of the truth"], above) recalls Platonistic notions. It carries us still further. For every future model, though incomplete as history, is already fulfilled in God and has existed from all eternity in His providence. The figures in which He cloaked it, and the incarnation in which He revealed its meaning, are therefore prophecies of something that has always been, but which will remain veiled for men until the day when they behold the Saviour *revelata facie,* with the senses as well as in spirit. Thus the figures are not only tentative; they are also the tentative form of something eternal and timeless; they point not only to the concrete future, but also to something that always has been and always will be; they point to something which is in need of interpretation, which will indeed be fulfilled in the concrete future, but which is at all times present, fulfilled in God's providence, which knows no difference of time. This eternal thing is already figured in them, and thus they are both tentative fragmentary reality, and veiled eternal reality. This becomes eminently clear in the sacrament of the sacrifice, the Last Supper, the *pascha nostrum,* which is *figura Christi.*[40]

This sacrament, which is figure as well as symbol, and which has long existed historically—namely, since it was first established in the old covenant—gives us the purest picture of the concretely present, the veiled and tentative, the eternal and supratemporal elements contained in the figures.

IV. Figural Art in the Middle Ages

The figural interpretation, or to put it more completely, the figural view of history was widespread and deeply influential up to the Middle Ages, and beyond. This has not escaped the attention of scholars. Not only theological works on the history of hermeneutics but also studies on the history of art and literature have met with figural conceptions on their way, and dealt with them. This is particularly true of the history of art in connection with medieval iconography, and of the history of literature in connection with the religious theater of the Middle Ages. But the special nature of the problem does not seem to have been recognized; the figural or typological or phenomenal structure is not sharply distinguished from other, allegorical or symbolical, forms. A beginning is to be found in T. C. Goode's instructive dissertation on Gonzalo de Berceo's *El Sacrificio de la misa* (Washington, 1933); although he does not go into fundamental questions, II. Pflaum shows a clear understanding of the situation in his *Die religiose Disputation in der europäischen Dichtung des Mittelalters* (Geneva-Florence, 1935). Recently (in *Romania*, LXIII) his sound understanding of the word *figure* enabled him to give a correct interpretation of some Old French verses that had been misunderstood by the editor and to restore the text. Perhaps other examples have escaped me,[41] but I do not think that there is any systematic treatment of the subject. Yet such an investigation strikes me as indispensable for an understanding of the mixture of spirituality and sense of reality which characterizes the European Middle Ages and which seems so baffling to us.[42] In most European countries figural interpretation was active up to the eighteenth century; we find traces of it not only in Bossuet as might be expected, but many years later in the religious authors whom Groethuysen quotes in *Les Origines de la France bourgeoise*.[43] A clear knowledge of its character and how it differed from related but differently structured forms would generally sharpen and deepen our understanding of the documents of late antiquity and the Middle Ages, and solve a good many puzzles. Might the themes that recur so frequently on early Christian sarcophagi and in the catacombs not be figures of the Resurrection? Or to cite an example from Mâle's great work, might not the legend of Maria Aegyptiaca, the representations of which in the Toulouse Museum he describes (op. cit., p. 240 ff.), be a figure of the people of Israel going out of Egypt, hence to be interpreted exactly as the Psalm *In exitu Israel de Aegypto* was generally interpreted in the Middle Ages?

But individual interpretations do not exhaust the importance of the figural method. No student of the Middle Ages can fail to see how it provides the medieval interpretation of history with its general foundation and often enters into the medieval view of everyday reality. The analogism that reaches into every sphere of medieval thought is closely bound up with the figural structure; in the interpretation of the Trinity that extends roughly from Augustine's *De Trinitate* to St. Thomas, I, q. 45, art. 7, man himself, as the image of God, takes on the character of a *figura Trinitatis*. It is not quite clear to me how far aesthetic ideas were determined by figural conceptions—to what extent the work of art was viewed as the *figura* of a still unattainable fulfillment in reality. The question of the imitation of nature in art aroused little theoretical interest in the Middle Ages; but all the more attention was accorded to the notion that the artist, as a kind of figure for God the Creator, realized an archetype that was alive in his spirit.[44] These, as we see, are ideas of Neoplatonic origin. But the question remains: to what extent were this archetype and the work of art produced from it regarded as figures for a reality and truth fulfilled in God? I have found no conclusive answer in the texts available to me here and the most important works of the specialized literature are lacking. But I should like to quote a few passages which happen to be at hand, and which point somewhat in the direction I have in mind. In an article on the representation of musical tones in the capitals of the Abbey of Cluny (*Deutsche Vierteljahrsschrift,* 7, p. 264) L. Schrade quotes an explanation of the word *imitari* by Remigius of Auxerre: *scilicet persequi, quia veram musicam non potest humana musica imitari* ("that is, to follow after, for the music of man cannot imitate the true music"). This is probably based on the notion that the artist's work is an imitation or at least a shadowy figuration of a true and likewise sensuous reality (the music of the heavenly choirs). In the *Purgatorio* Dante praises the works of art created by God himself, representing examples of virtues and vices, for their perfectly fulfilled sensuous truth, beside which human art and even nature pales (*Purg.,* 10 and 12); his invocation to Apollo (*Par.,* 1) includes the lines:

> *O divina virtù, se mi ti presti*
> *tanto che l'ombra del beato regno*
> *segnata nel mio capo io manifesti*

(O divine Virtue, if thou dost so far lend thyself to me, that I make manifest the shadow of the blessed realm imprinted on my brain.) Temple Classics ed., p. 5.

Here his poetry is characterized as an *umbra* of truth, engraved in his mind, and his theory of inspiration is sometimes expressed in statements that may be explained along the same lines. But these are only suggestions; an investigation purporting to explain the relation between Neoplatonic and figural elements in medieval aesthetics would require broader foundations. Still, the present remarks suffice, I believe, to show the need for distinguishing the figural structure from the other forms of imagery. We may say roughly that the figural method in Europe goes back to Christian influences, while the allegorical method derives from ancient pagan sources, and also that the one is applied primarily to Christian, the other to ancient material. Nor shall we be going too far afield in terming the figural view the predominantly Christian-medieval one, while the allegorical view, modeled on pagan or not inwardly Christianized authors of late antiquity, tends to appear where ancient, pagan, or strongly secular influences are dominant. But such observations are too general and imprecise, for the many phenomena that reflect an intermingling of different cultures over a thousand years do not admit of such simple classifications. At a very early date profane and pagan material was also interpreted figurally; Gregory of Tours, for example, uses the legend of the Seven Sleepers as a figure for the Resurrection; the waking of Lazarus from the dead and Jonah's rescue from the belly of the whale were also commonly interpreted in this sense. In the high Middle Ages, the Sybils, Virgil, the characters of the *Aeneid,* and even those of the Breton legend cycle (e.g., Galahad in the quest for the Holy Grail) were drawn into the figural interpretation, and moreover there were all sorts of mixtures between figural, allegoric, and symbolic forms. All these forms, applied to classical as well as Christian material, occur in the work which concludes and sums up the culture of the Middle Ages: the *Divine Comedy.* But I shall now attempt to show that basically it is the figural forms which predominate and determine the whole structure of the poem.

At the foot of the mountain of Purgatory, Dante and Virgil meet a man of venerable mien, whose countenance is illumined by four stars signifying the four cardinal virtues. He inquires sternly into the legitimacy of their journey and from Virgil's respectful reply—after he has told Dante to kneel before this man—we learn that it is Cato of Utica. For after explaining his divine mission, Virgil continues as follows (*Purg.,* 1, 70–5):

> *Or ti piaccia gradir la sua ventuta.*
> *libertà va cercando, che è si cara,*
> *come sa chi per lei vita rifiuta.*
> *Tu il sai, chè non ti fu per lei amara*
> *in Utica la morte, ove lasciasti*
> *la vesta che al gran dì sarà sì chiara.*

(Now may it please thee to be gracious unto his coming: he seeketh freedom, which is so precious, as he knows who giveth up life for her.

Thou knowest it; since for her sake death was not bitter to thee in Utica, where thou leftest the raiment which at the great day shall be so bright.)

                                                    Temple Classics ed., p. 7.

Virgil goes on, asking Cato to favor him for the sake of the memory of Marcia, his former wife. This plea Cato rejects with undiminished severity; but if such is the desire of the *donna del ciel* (Beatrice), that suffices; and he orders that before his ascent Dante's face be cleansed of the stains of Hell and that he be girded with reeds. Cato appears again at the end of the second canto, where he sternly rebukes the souls just arrived at the foot of the mountain, who are listening in self-forgetfulness to Casella's song, and reminds them to get on with their journey.

It is Cato of Utica whom God has here appointed guardian at the foot of Purgatory: a pagan, an enemy of Caesar, and a suicide. This is startling, and the very first commentators, such as Benvenuto of Imola, expressed their bewilderment. Dante mentions only a very few pagans who were freed from Hell by Christ; and among them we find an enemy of Caesar, whose associates, Caesar's murderers, are with Judas in the jaws of Lucifer, who as a suicide seems no less guilty than those others "who have done themselves violence" and who for the same sin are suffering the most frightful torments in the seventh circle of Hell. The riddle is solved by the words of Virgil, who says that Dante is seeking freedom, which is so precious as you yourself know who have despised life for its sake. The story of Cato is removed from its earthly and political context, just as the stories of Isaac, Jacob, etc., were removed from theirs by the patristic exegetes of the Old Testament, and made into a *figura futurorum*. Cato is a *figura,* or rather the earthly Cato, who renounced his life for freedom, was a *figura,* and the Cato who appears here in the *Purgatorio* is the revealed or fulfilled figure, the truth of that figural event. The political and earthly freedom for which he died was only an *umbra futurorum:* a prefiguration of the Christian freedom whose guardian he is here appointed, and for the sake of which he here again opposes all earthly temptation; the Christian freedom from all evil impulses, which leads to true domination of self, the freedom for the acquisition of which Dante is girded with the rushes of humility, until, on the summit of the mountain, he actually achieves it and is crowned by Virgil as lord over himself. Cato's voluntary choice of death rather than political servitude is here introduced as a *figura* for the eternal freedom of the children of God, in behalf of which all earthly things are to be despised, for the liberation of the soul from the servitude of sin. Dante's choice of Cato for this role is explained by the position "above the parties" that Cato occupies according to the Roman authors, who held him up as a model of virtue, justice, piety, and love of freedom. Dante found him praised equally in Cicero, Virgil, Lucan, Seneca, and Valerius Maximus; particularly Virgil's *secretosque pios his dantem iura Catonem* (*Aeneid,* 8, 670) ("the righteous in a place apart, with Cato their lawgiver"), coming as it did from a poet of the Empire, must have made a great impression on him. His admiration for Cato may be judged from several passages in the *Convivio,* and in his *De Monarchia* (2, 5) he has a quotation from Cicero[45] saying that Cato's voluntary death should be judged in a special light and connecting it with the examples of Roman political virtue to which Dante attached so much importance; in this passage Dante tries to show that Roman rule was legitimized by Roman virtue; that it fostered the justice and freedom of all mankind. The chapter contains this sentence: *Romanum imperium de fonte nascitur pietatis* ("the Roman Empire springs from the fount of justice").[46]

Dante believed in a predetermined concordance between the Christian story of salvation and the Roman secular monarchy; thus it is not surprising that he should apply the figural interpretation to a pagan Roman—in general he draws his symbols, allegories, and figures from both worlds without distinction. Beyond any doubt Cato is a *figura;* not an allegory like the characters from the *Roman de la rose,* but a figure that has become the truth. The *Comedy* is a vision which regards and proclaims the figural truth as already fulfilled, and what constitutes its distinctive character is precisely that, fully in the spirit of figural interpretation, it attaches the truth perceived in the vision to historical, earthly events. The character of Cato as a severe, righteous, and pious man, who in a significant moment in his own destiny and in the providential history of the world sets freedom above life, is preserved in its full historical and personal force; it does not become an allegory for freedom; no, Cato of Utica stands there as a unique individual, just as Dante saw him; but he is lifted out of the tentative earthly state in which he regarded political freedom as the highest good (just as the Jews singled out strict observance of the Law), and transposed into a state of definitive fulfillment, concerned no longer with the earthly works of civic virtue or the law, but with the *ben dell'intelletto,* the highest good, the freedom of the immortal soul in the sight of God.

Let us attempt the same demonstration in a somewhat more difficult case. Virgil has been taken by almost all commentators as an allegory for reason—the human, natural reason which leads to the right earthly order, that is, in Dante's view, the secular monarchy. The older commentators had no objection to a purely allegorical interpretation, for they did not, as we do today, feel that allegory was incompatible with authentic poetry. Many modern critics have argued against this idea, stressing the poetic, human, personal quality of Dante's Virgil; still, they have been unable either to deny that he "means something" or to find a satisfactory relation between this meaning and the human reality. Recently (and not only in connection with Virgil) a number of writers (L. Valli and Mandonnet, for example) have gone back to the purely allegorical or symbolic aspect and attempted to reject the historical reality as "positivistic" or "romantic." But actually there is no choice between historical and hidden meaning; both are present. The figural structure preserves the historical event while interpreting it as revelation; and must preserve it in order to interpret it.

In Dante's eyes the historical Virgil is both poet and guide. He is a poet and a guide because in the righteous Aeneas' journey to the underworld he prophesies and glorifies universal peace under the Roman Empire, the political order which Dante regards as exemplary, as the *terrena Jerusalem;*[47] and because in his poem the founding of Rome, predestined seat of the secular and spiritual power, is celebrated in the light of its future mission. Above all he is poet and guide because all the great poets who came after him have been inflamed and inspired by his work; Dante not only states this for himself, but brings in a second poet, Statius, to proclaim the same thing most emphatically: in the meeting with Sordello and perhaps also in the highly controversial verse about Guido Cavalcanti (*Inf.,* 10, 63) the same theme is sounded. In addition, Virgil is a guide because, beyond his temporal prophecy, he also—in the Fourth Eclogue—proclaimed the eternal transcendent order, the appearance of Christ which would usher in the renewal of the temporal world without, to be sure, suspecting the significance of his own words, but nevertheless in such a way that posterity might derive inspiration from his light. Virgil the poet was a guide because he had described the realm of the dead—thus he knew the way thither. But also as a Roman and a man, he was destined to be a guide, for not only was he a master of eloquent discourse and lofty wisdom but also possessed the qualities that fit a man for guidance and leadership, the qualities that characterize his hero Aeneas and Rome in general: *iustitia* and *pietas*. For Dante the historical Virgil embodied this fullness of earthly perfection and was therefore capable of guiding him to the very threshold of insight into the divine and eternal perfection; the historic Virgil was for him a *figura* of the poet-prophet-guide, now fulfilled in the other world. The historical Virgil is "fulfilled" by the dweller in limbo, the companion of the great poets of antiquity, who at the wish of Beatrice undertakes to guide Dante. As a Roman and poet Virgil had sent Aeneas down to the underworld in search of divine counsel to learn the destiny of the Roman world; and now Virgil is summoned by the heavenly powers to exercise a no less important guidance; for there is no doubt that Dante saw himself in a mission no less important than that of Aeneas: elected to divulge to a world out of joint the right order, which is revealed to him upon his way. Virgil is elected to point out and interpret for him the true earthly order, whose laws are carried out and whose essence is fulfilled in the other world, and at the same time to direct him toward its goal, the heavenly community of the blessed, which he has presaged in his poetry—yet not into the heart of the kingdom of God, for the meaning of his presage was not revealed to him during his earthly lifetime, and without such illumination he has died an unbeliever. Thus God does not wish Dante to enter His kingdom with Virgil's help; Virgil can lead him only to the threshold of the kingdom, only as far as the limit which his noble and righteous poetry was able to discern. "Thou first," says Statius to Virgil, "didst send me towards Parnassus to drink in its caves, and then didst light me on to God. Thou didst like one who goes by night, and carries the light behind him, and profits not himself, but maketh persons wise that follow him. . . . Through thee I was a poet, through thee a Christian."[48] And just as the earthly Virgil led Statius to salvation, so now, as a fulfilled figure, he leads Dante: for Dante too has received from him the lofty style of poetry, through him he is saved from eternal damnation and set on the way of salvation; and just as he once illumined Statius, without himself seeing the light that he bore and proclaimed, so now he leads Dante to the threshold of the light, which he knows of but may not himself behold.

Thus Virgil is not an allegory of an attribute, virtue, capacity, power, or historical institution. He is neither reason nor poetry nor the Empire. He is Virgil himself. Yet he is not himself in the same way as the historical characters whom later poets have set out to portray in all their historical involvement, as for example, Shakespeare's Caesar or Schiller's Wallenstein. These poets disclose their historical characters in the thick of their earthly existence; they bring an important epoch to life before our eyes, and look for the meaning of the epoch itself. For Dante the meaning of every life has its place in the providential history of the world, the general lines of which are laid down in the Revelation which has been given to every Christian, and which is interpreted for him in the vision of the *Comedy*. Thus Virgil in the *Divine Comedy* is the historical Virgil himself, but then again he is not; for the historical Virgil is only a *figura* of the fulfilled truth that the poem reveals, and this fulfillment is more real, more significant than the *figura*. With Dante, unlike modern poets, the more fully the figure is interpreted and the more closely it is integrated with the eternal plan of salvation, the more real it becomes. And for him, unlike the ancient poets of the underworld, who represented earthly life as real and the life after death as shadow, for him the other world is the true reality, while this world is only *umbra futurorum*—though indeed the *umbra* is the prefiguration of the transcendent reality and must recur fully in it.

For what has been said here of Cato and Virgil applies to the *Comedy* as a whole. It is wholly based on a figural conception. In my study of Dante as a poet of the earthly world (1929) I attempted to show that in the *Comedy* Dante undertook "to conceive the whole earthly historical world . . . as already subjected to God's final judgment and thus put in its proper place as decreed by the divine judgment, to represent it as a world already judged . . . in so doing, he does not destroy or weaken the earthly nature of his characters, but captures the fullest intensity of their individual earthly-historical being and identifies it with the ultimate state of things" (p. 108). At that time I lacked a solid historical grounding for this view, which is already to be found in Hegel and which is the basis of my interpretation of the *Divine Comedy;* it is suggested rather than formulated in the introductory chapters of the book. I believe that I have now found this historical grounding; it is precisely the figural interpretation of reality which, though in constant conflict with purely spiritualist and Neoplatonic tendencies, was the dominant view in the European Middle Ages: the idea that earthly life is thoroughly real, with the reality of the flesh into which the Logos entered, but that with all its reality it is only *umbra* and *figura* of the authentic, future, ultimate truth, the real reality that will unveil and preserve the *figura*. In this way the individual earthly event is not regarded as a definitive self-sufficient reality, nor as a link in a chain of development in which single events or combinations of events perpetually give rise to new events, but viewed primarily in immediate vertical connection with a divine order which encompasses it, which on some future day will itself be concrete reality; so that the earthly event is a prophecy or *figura* of a part of a wholly divine reality that will be enacted in the future. But this reality is not only future; it is always present in the eye of God and in the other world, which is to say that in transcendence the revealed and true reality is present at all times, or timelessly. Dante's work is an attempt to give a poetic and at the same time systematic picture of the world in this light. Divine grace comes to the help of a man menaced by earthly confusion and ruin—this is the framework of the vision. From early youth he had been favored by special grace, because he was destined for a special task; at an early age he had been privileged to see revelation incarnated in a living being, Beatrice—and here as so often figural structure and Neoplatonism are intertwined. In her lifetime she had, though covertly, favored him with a salutation of her eyes and mouth; and in dying she had distinguished him in an unspoken mysterious way.[49] When he strays from the right path, the departed Beatrice, who for him was revelation incarnate, finds the only possible salvation for him; indirectly she is his guide and in Paradise directly; it is she who shows him the unveiled order, the truth of the earthly figures. What he sees and learns in the three realms is true, concrete reality, in which the earthly *figura* is contained and interpreted; by seeing the fulfilled truth while still alive, he himself is saved, while at the same time he is enabled to tell the world what he has seen and guide it to the right path.

Insight into the figural character of the *Comedy* does not offer a universal method by which to interpret every controversial passage; but we can derive certain principles of interpretation from it. We may be certain that every historical or mythical character occurring in the poem can only mean something closely connected with what Dante knew of his historical or mythical existence, and that the relation is one of fulfillment and figure; we must always be careful not to deny their earthly historical existence altogether, not to confine ourselves to an abstract, allegorical interpretation. This applies particularly to Beatrice. The romantic realism of the nineteenth century overemphasized the human Beatrice, tending to make the *Vita Nova* a kind of sentimental novel. Since then a reaction has set in; the new tendency is to do away with her entirely, to dissolve her in an assortment of increasingly subtle theological concepts. But actually there is no reality in such a choice. For Dante the literal meaning or historical reality of a figure stands in no contradiction to its profounder meaning, but precisely "figures" it; the historical reality is not annulled, but confirmed and fulfilled by the deeper meaning. The Beatrice of the *Vita Nova* is an earthly person; she really appeared to Dante, she really saluted him, really withheld her salutation later on, mocked him, mourned for a dead friend and for her father, and really died. Of course this reality can only be the reality of Dante's experience—for a poet forms and transforms the events of his life in his consciousness, and we can take account only of what lived in his consciousness and not of the outward reality. It should also be borne in mind that from the first day of her appearance the earthly Beatrice was for Dante a miracle sent from Heaven, an incarnation of divine truth. Thus the reality of her earthly person is not, as in the case of Virgil or Cato, derived from the facts of a historic tradition, but from Dante's own experience: this experience showed him the earthly Beatrice as a miracle.[50] But an incarnation, a miracle are real happenings; miracles happen on earth, and incarnation is flesh. The strangeness of the medieval view of reality has prevented modern scholars from distinguishing between figuration and allegory and led them for the most part to perceive only the latter.[51] Even so acute a theological critic as Mandonnet (op. cit., pp. 218–19) considers only two possibilities: either Beatrice is a mere allegory (and this is his opinion) or she is *la petite Bice Portinari,* a notion that he ridicules. Quite aside from the misunderstanding of poetic reality that such a judgment shows, it is surprising to find so deep a chasm between reality and meaning. Is the *terrena Jerusalem* without historical reality because it is a *figura aeternae Jerusalem?*

In the *Vita Nova,* then, Beatrice is a living woman from the reality of Dante's experience—and in the *Comedy* she is no *intellectus separatus,* no angel, but a blessed human being who will rise again in the flesh at the Last Judgment. Actually there is no dogmatic concept that would wholly describe her; certain events in the *Vita Nova* would not fit into any allegory, and in regard to the *Comedy* there is the additional problem of drawing an exact distinction between her and various other persons of the *Paradiso*, such as the Apostle-Examiners and St. Bernard. Nor can the special character of her relation to Dante be fully understood in this way. Most of the older commentators interpreted Beatrice as theology; more recent ones have sought subtler formulations; but this has led to exaggeration and mistakes: even Mandonnet, who applies to Beatrice the extremely broad notion of *ordre surnaturel*, derived from the contrast with Virgil, comes up with hairsplitting subdivisions, makes mistakes,[52] and forces his concepts. The role that Dante attributes to her is perfectly clear from her actions and the epithets attached to her. She is a figuration or incarnation of revelation (*Inf.*, 2, 76): *sola per cui l'umana spezie eccede ogni contento da quel ciel, che ha minor li cerchi sui* ("through whom alone mankind excels all that is contained within the heaven which has the smallest circles"); (*Purg.*, 6, 45): *che lume fia tra il vero e l'intelletto* ("who shall be a light between truth and intellect") which, out of love (*Inf.*, 2, 72), divine grace sends to man for his salvation, and which guides him to the *visio Dei*. Mandonnet forgets to say that she is precisely an incarnation of divine revelation and not revelation pure and simple, although he quotes the pertinent passages from the *Vita Nova* and from St. Thomas, and the above-mentioned invocation, *O Donna di virtù, sola per cui, etc.* One cannot address the "supernatural order" as such, one can only address its incarnate revelation, that part of the divine plan of salvation which precisely is the miracle whereby men are raised above other earthly creatures. Beatrice is incarnation, she is *figura* or *idolo Christi* (her eyes reflect her twofold nature, *Purg.*, 31, 126) and thus she is not exhausted by such explanations; her relation to Dante cannot fully be explained by dogmatic considerations. Our remarks are intended only to show that theological interpretation, while always useful and even indispensable, does not compel us to abandon the historical reality of Beatrice—on the contrary.

With this we close for the present our study of *figura*. Our purpose was to show how on the basis of its semantic development a word may grow into a historical situation and give rise to structures that will be effective for many centuries. The historical situation that drove St. Paul to preach among the Gentiles developed figural interpretation and prepared it for the influence it was to exert in late antiquity and the Middle Ages.

NOTES

1. As P. Friedlaender informs me, the *barbarica pestis* is probably the sting of a ray, by which Odysseus was mortally wounded; *subinis* is uncertain. [As is my translation of it. TRANS.]

2. In late antiquity (Chalcidius, Isidore) and in the Middle Ages it reappears in a play on words with *pictura*. Cf. E. R. Curtius in *Zeitschrift für romanische Philologie*, 58 (1938), 45.

3. Many later definitions take this direction. Cf. *Thesaurus Linguae Latinae*, VI, part 1, col. 722, 1. 54.

4. In Aristotle (and in Plato) *typōi* means "in general," "in broad outlines," "as a rule." His phrase *pachulōs kai typōi* (*Nichomachean Ethics*, 1094b, 20), or *kath' holou lechthen kai typōi* was handed down by way of Irenaeus (2, 76) and Boethius (*Topicorum Aristoteles Interpretatio*, 1, 1 [*Patrologia Latina*, LXIV, col. 911]) to the French and Italian, cf. Godefroy, s.v. *figural: Il convient que la manière de procéder en ceste œuvre soit grosse et figurele*. Or s.v. *figuralment: Car la manière de produyre/ Ne se peut monstrer ne deduyre/ Par effect, si non seulement/ Grossement et figuraulment* (Greban). In Italian the understanding for the combination *sommariamente e figuralmente* seems to have been lost at an early date; cf. the examples in Tommaseo-Bellini, *Dizionario della lingua italiana* (1869), II, part I, p. 789, s.v. *figura* 18.

5. *Schēma* has meanings that do not occur or that did not persist in *figura*, as, for example, the meaning of "constitution."

6. Cf. also the shaping of tones in 2, 412–13: *per chordas organici quae/ mobilibus digitis expergefacta figurant* ("which harpers with nimble fingers arouse and shape on the strings").

7. Accordingly, *forma* usually appears where two syllables are needed. Even in Lucretius the relation between the two words is rather loose and vacillating. There are passages, however, particularly in Lucretius, where the two concepts are sharply distinguished; as when he speaks of the primal elements:

> *quare . . . necessest*
> *natura quoniam constant neque facta manu sunt*
> *unius ad certam formam primordia rerum*
> *dissimili inter se quadam volitare figura.*
>
> (2, 377–80)

(And so it must be that the first beginning of things, existing as they do by nature and not being hand-made after the definite form of one single pattern, must some of them have different shapes as they fly about.)

Like the *formai servare figuram* of 4, 69, this clearly expresses the well-known relation between *morphē* and *schēma*, which Ernout-Meillet, loc. cit. suggests with *la configuration du moule*. Cf. Cicero, *De Natura Deorum*, I, 90.

8. The last three words (as Munro has pointed out) reflect the formula of Democritus and Leucippus: *rysmos, tropē, diathigē* (Cf. Diels, *Fragmente der Vorsokratiker*, 2, 4th edition, p. 22). Aristotle employs *schēma* in explaining *rysmos* (*Metaphysics*, 985b, 16 and 1042b, 11; *Physics*, 188a, 24). Lucretius translated the term by *figura*.

9. A few passages: 2, 385, 514, 679, 682; 3, 190, 246; 6, 770.

10. The transition from "*figura* of the material" to "*figura* of the reproduced object" was effected only very gradually, first in the poets. Cf. (aside from Lucretius) Catullus, 64, 50, and 64, 265; Propertius, 2, 6, 33. In Velleius Paterculus, 1, 11, 4, *Expressa similitudine figurarum* means "portraitlike."

11. Cf. also *Ad Familiares*, 15, 16. On the other hand, Quintilian, 10, 2, 15: *illas Epicuri figuras . . .* ("those *figurae* of Epicurus").

12. Later *figura* becomes quite frequent in the sense of "divine image"—and, in the Christian authors, of "idol"—or of the image on a coin.

13. In Propertius and also in Ovid, *figurae* ("forms") at times means "kind," "manner," as opposed to "class," "sort"; this is the same evolution as *species-espèce*.

14. In connection with pastry, cf. also Martial, 14, 222, 1; Festus, 129, *ficta quaedam ex farina in hominum figuras* ("things made of dough in the shapes of men"); and Petronius, 33, 6, *ova ex farina figurata* ("eggs fashioned of meal"). The pastry-cook was often regarded and employed as a sculptor and decorator, an attitude revived by later periods, particularly the Renaissance, and the baroque and rococo periods; Cf. Goethe, *Wilhelm Meister's Lehrjahre*, Book 3, Chapter 7, and Creizenach's note on this passage in the Jubiläumsausgabe, Vol. 17, p. 344.

15. In *Epist.*, 65, 7, Seneca has a passage significant in another connection, where *figura* stands for archetype, idea, *forma*, but in the Neoplatonic sense of the inner model of the forms in the mind of the artist. In this passage he also makes the comparison, which later became so frequent, between the artist and the Creator: the sculptor, says Seneca, can find the model (*exemplar*) of his work in himself or outside; it can be provided him by his eyes or his mind; and God has within him all the *exemplaria* of things: *plenus his figuris est quas Plato ideas appellat immortales* ("He is full of those figures that Plato calls immortal ideas"). Cf. Dürer: "For a good painter is inwardly full of figures (*voller Figur*); cf. E. Panofsky, *Idea* (1924), p. 70.

16. See Faral, *Les Arts poétiques du 12ème et du 13ème siècle* (Paris, 1924), pp. 48 ff. and 99 ff.

17. A noteworthy variant occurs in Ammianus Marcellinus, who uses the word for the topography of battlefields. Cf. *Thesaurus Linguae Latinae,* VI, part 1, 726, 37 ff.

18. In Sedulius, *Carmen Paschale*, 5, 101–2, there is a passage in which *figura* can hardly mean anything other than "face," as in modern French:

> *Namque per hos colaphos caput est sanabile nostrum;*
> *Haec sputa per Dominum nostram lavere figuram.*

(For our head can be healed by these blows. This spittle has washed our face in the Lord's person.)

Since the poet had spoken previously of *spuere in faciem* ("spitting in the face") and *colaphis pulsare caput* ("plying the head with blows"), the meaning of "face" cannot be doubted; still, it is possible that Sedulius was led to choose the more general *figura* by the need for a trisyllable with a long middle syllable with which to conclude the line. In any event it is the only certain ancient example known to us of Latin *figura* for "face." Jeanneret's presumption, in *La Langue des tablettes d'exécration latines* (Neuchâtel, 1918), p. 108, that *figura* in the Minturnian tablet of execration means "face," is certainly unfounded, if only because of the juxtaposition with *membra* and *colorem*, which is very frequent. In the sense of "form" it belongs to the general attributes (or parts) of the body, with which the curse begins: then follow the special attributes. Jeanneret's contention is also rejected by Wartburg in FEW, *ad v. figura*, 9. The question remains unsettled in regard to a fragment of Laberius: *figura humana inimico (nimio) ardore ignescitur*, Ribbeck, 2, p. 343.

19. In the Septuagint Joshua is already called Jesus, which is a contraction of Joshua. Cf. the illustrations of the Vatican Scroll of Joshua, which is thought to be a sixth-century copy of a fourth-century original. The only part of it now available to me is a page in K. Pfister's *Mittelaterlicher Buchmalerei* (Munich, 1922), representing the setting up of the twelve stones (Josh. 4:20–1); in text and inscription Joshua is called *Iēsous ho tou Nauē* ("Jesus [the son] of Nave"), bears a halo, and is plainly intended to suggest Christ. Later allusions to the "figure" of Joshua are frequent; cf. Hildebert of Tours, *Sermones de Diversis*, XXIII, *Patrologia Latina*, Vol. 171, cols. 842 ff.

20. *Figuraretur* means here at once "would be formed" and "would be figured," the latter by blood and water, the Lord's Supper and baptism. The juxtaposition of the two wounds in the side long remained an important theme. Cf. Burdach, *Vorspiel,* I, 1 (1925), pp. 162 and 212; Dante, *Par.,* 13, 37 ff.

21. *Ita et nunc sanguinem suum in vino consecravit qui tunc vinum in sanguine figuravit* ("so now also he consecrated his blood in wine who then had figured wine in blood").

22. Moses is in general a figuration of Christ, e.g., in the crossing of the Red Sea or the transformation of the bitter water into sweet water for baptism. But this does not prevent him, in the first example, from figuring the law in contradiction to his figuration of Christ.

23. Cf. Hilary of Poitiers, *Tractatus Mysteriorum,* 1 (*Corp. Vind.,* Vol. 65, p. 3), quoted in Labriolle, *History and Literature of Christianity* (London and New York, 1924), p. 243.

24. Cf. Hilarian, *De Cursu Temporum, Patrologia Latina,* 13, col. 173, 2: *sabbati aeterni imaginem et figuram tenet sabbatus temporalis* ("the temporal sabbath is an image and figure of the eternal sabbath").

25. How deeply ingrained the habit of interpretation had become in this world may be seen from the half jesting interpretation of gifts in the correspondence of St. Jerome (Letter 44, *Selected Letters of St. Jerome,* M. F. A. Wright [London and New York, 1933], pp. 176–7).

26. St. Jerome attacks Origen for this, saying that he is *allegoricus semper interpres et historiae fugiens veritatem . . . nos simplicem et veram sequamur historiam ne quibusdam nubibus atque praestigiis involvamur* (Jeremiam 27, 3, 4; *Patrologia Latina,* 24, col. 849) ("always an allegorical exegete, shunning historical truth . . . as for us, let us simply follow the true history and not involve ourselves in phantasms and charlatanism"). On the relation of the Alexandrians, particularly Origen, to figural interpretation, cf. A. Freiherr von Ungern-Sternberg, *Der traditionelle Alttestamentl. Schriftbeweis . . .* (Halle, 1913), pp. 154 ff. On p. 160 he says of Origen: "He did not live in the biblical realism of scriptural proof."

27. Cf. also *De Civ.,* 15, 27; ibid., 20, 21 (*Ad Isaiam,* 65, 17ff.).

28. A. Rüstow calls my attention to the following stanza in a Shrovetide play by Hans Folz (about 1500):

> *Hör Jud, so merk dir und verstee*
> *Dass alle Geschicht der alten Ee*
> *Und aller Propheten Red gemein*
> *Ein Figur der neuen Ee ist allein.*

(Hear, Jew, take note and understand that the whole history of the old covenant and all the sayings of the Prophets are only a figure for the new covenant.)

29. *Corp. Vind.,* Vol. 31, cf. Labriolle, op. cit., p. 424.

30. In addition, of course, we find *claudere* ("to close, conceal"), in recollection of Isa. 22:22 and Rev. 3:7. Cf. at a later day Peter Lombard, *Commentarium* in *Ps.,* 146, 6 (*Patrologia Latina,* Vol. 191, col. 1276): *clausa Dei* "what God has concealed by obscurity of expression," and *prov. clus.*

31. Quoted according to *Patrologia Latina,* 59, col. 360.

32. Cf. Du Cange and Dante, *Purg.,* 10, 73, and 12, 22; Alain de Lille, *De Planctu Naturae, Patrologia Latina,* 210, 438; many passages might be found. Amyot says in

Thém., 52: *La parole de l'homme ressemble proprement à une tapisserie historiée et figurée* ("the speech of man truly resembles a figured and storied tapestry").

33. Suggestions of figural prophecy are not entirely lacking in the Synoptic Gospels; as for example when Jesus likens himself to Jonah, Matt. 12:39 ff., Luke 11:29 ff. In St. John one might mention 5:46. But next to the passages in the Epistles, these are no more than feeble intimations.

34. This was pointed out to me by R. Bultmann; the specialized literature is not available to me at the moment. Cf. among other passages Deut. 18:15; John 1:45; 6:14; 6:26 ff.; Acts 3:22 f.

35. Sedulius, *Eleg.*, 1, 87: *Pellitur umbra die, Christo veniente figura* ("The shadow is dispelled by the day, the figure by Christ's coming").

36. Though Prudentius does not seem to recognize figural interpretation, examples of it occur in his *Dittochaeon* (see Prudentius, ed. H. J. Thomson, 2 vols. [London and Cambridge (Mass.), 1949–53], Vol. 2, pp. 346 ff.).

37. This includes legendary and mythical as well as strictly historical events. Whether the material to be interpreted is really historical or only passes as such is immaterial for our purpose.

38. Cf. Emile Bréhier, *Les Idées philosophiques de Philon d'Alexandrie*, 2d. ed. (Paris, 1925), pp. 35 ff.

39. There are many intermediate forms combining figure and symbol; above all the Eucharist in which Christ is felt to be concretely present, and the cross as tree of life, *arbor vitae crucifixae*, which played a significant role extending roughly from the fourth-century poem *De Cruce*, cf. Labriolle, op. cit., p. 318, to the "spiritual" Franciscan Ubertino de Casale or Dante and beyond.

40. In the prayer corresponding to the *Quam oblationem* of the present-day Roman mass, the book *De Sacramentis* (fourth century) has the following text: *Fac nobis hanc oblationem ascriptam, ratam, rationabilem, acceptabilem, quod figura est corporis et sanguinis Christi. Qui pridie . . .* ("Make for us this offering consecrated, approved, reasonable, and acceptable, which is a figure of the body and blood of Christ. Who on the day before he suffered . . ."). See Dom F. Cabrol in *Liturgia: Encyclopédie populaire des connaissances liturgiques*, ed. R. Aigrain (Paris, 1930), p. 543. Cf. also a much later text, the *Rhythmus ad Sanctam Eucharistiam* (thirteenth century):

> *Adoro te devote, latens deitas*
> *Quae sub his figuris vere latitas*

(Humbly I adore thee, hidden Deity
which beneath these figures art concealed from me)

and later:

> *Jesu quem velatum nunc adspicio,*
> *Oro fiat illud quod tam sitio,*
> *Ut te revelata cernens facie*
> *Visu sim beatus tuae gloriae.*

(Jesus whom thus veiled I must see below,
When shall that be given which I long for so,
That at last beholding thy uncovered face,
Thou shalt satisfy me with thy fullest grace?)
(Trans. J. M. Neale, *Collected Hymns*
[London, 1914], p. 63.)

41. Many allusions may be found in Gilson, *Les Idées et les lettres,* esp. pp. 68 ff. and 155 ff. In his article, "Le Moyen Âge et l'histoire" (in *L'Esprit de la philosophie médiévale,* Paris, 1932) he refers to the figural element in the medieval philosophy of history, but with no great emphasis, since his main concern was to uncover the medieval roots of modern conceptions. Cf. also, for the German religious drama, T. Weber, *Die Praefigurationen in geistlichen Drama Deutschlands,* Marburg Dissertation 1909, and L. Wolff, "Die Verschmelzung des Dargestellten mit der Gegenwartswirklichkeit im deutschen geistlichen Drama des Mittelalters," *Deutsche Vierteljahrsschrift für Literaturwissenschaft und Geistesgeschichte,* 7, p. 267 ff. On figural elements in the portrayal of Charlemagne in the *Chanson de Roland,* cf. A. Pauphilet's well-known article in *Romania,* LIX, esp. pp. 183 ff.

42. Of course there are numerous analyses of the fourfold meaning of Scripture, but they do not bring out what strikes me as indispensable. It is natural that medieval theology, while distinctly differentiating the various forms of allegory (e.g., Petrus Comestor in the prologue to his *Historia Scholastica*), should attribute no fundamental importance, but only a kind of technical interest to these distinctions. But even so outstanding a modern theologian as the Dominican Père Mandonnet, who gives an outline of the history of symbolism in his *Dante le Théologien* (Paris, 1935, pp. 163 ff.), regards the knowledge of these differentiations as a mere technical instrument for the understanding of texts, and takes no account of the different conceptions of reality involved.

43. By that time of course the foundations of figural interpretation had already been destroyed; even many ecclesiastics no longer understood it. As Emile Mâle tells us (*L'Art religieux du 12ème siècle en France,* 3d ed., 1928, p. 391) Montfaucon interpreted the rows of Old Testament figures at the sides of certain church porches as Merovingian kings. In a letter from Leibniz to Burnett (1696, Gerhardt edition, III, 306) we find the following: "M. Mercurius van Helmont believed that the soul of Jesus Christ was that of Adam and that the new Adam repairing what the first had ruined was the same personage paying his old debt. I think one does well to spare oneself the trouble of refuting such ideas."

44. In speaking of the architect, St. Thomas says *quasi idea* (*Quodlibetales,* IV, 1, 1). Cf. Panofsky, *Idea* (Leipzig, 1924), p. 20 ff. and note, p. 85; cf. also the quotation from Seneca in our note 15.

45. See Zingarelli, *Dante,* 3d ed., 1931, pp. 1029 ff., and the literature cited in the note.

46. Cf. J. Balogh in *Deutsches Dante-Jahrbuch,* 10, 1928, p. 202.

47. Accordingly Dante, *Purg.,* 32, 102, describes *quelle Roma onde Cristo è Romano* ("that Rome whereof Christ is a Roman") as the fulfilled kingdom of God.

48. *Purg.,* 22, 69–73, Temple Classics ed. The fact that in the Middle Ages Virgil often appears among the prophets of Christ has been several times discussed in detail since Comparetti. A certain amount of new material is to be found in the festival volume, *Virgilio nel medio evo,* of the *Studi medievali* (N.S.V., 1932); I should like to make special mention of K. Strecker's *Iam nova progenies caelo dimittitur alto,* p. 167, where a bibliography and some material on figural structure in general may be found; further E. Mâle, *Virgile dans l'art du moyen âge,* p. 325, particularly plate 1; and Luigi Suttina, *L'effigie di Virgilio nella Cattedrale di Zamorra,* p. 342.

49. The words *mi converrebbe essere laudatore di me medesimo* ("it would behove me to be a praiser of myself"), *Vita Nova,* (Temple Classics ed., p. 109) 29, are an allusion to II Cor. 12:1. Cf. Grandgent in *Romania,* 31, 14, and Scherillo's commentary.

50. This is indicated by the title of the book, by his first designation of her as *la*

gloriosa donna de la mia mente ("the glorious lady of my mind"), by the name-mysticism, the trinitarian significance of the number nine, by the effects emanating from her, etc., etc. Sometimes she appears as a *figura Christi;* one need only consider the interpretation of her appearance behind Monna Vanna (24); the events accompanying the vision of her death (23); eclipse, earthquake, the hosannas of the angels; and the effect of her appearance in *Purg.,* 30. Cf. Galahad in the "Queste del Saint Graal," Gilson, *Les Idées et les lettres,* p. 71.

51. To avoid misunderstandings it should be mentioned here that Dante and his contemporaries termed the figural meaning "allegory," while they referred to what is here called allegory as "ethical" or "tropological" meaning. The reader will surely understand why in this historical study we have stuck to the terminology created and favored by the Church Fathers.

52. He denies that she ever smiles in spite of *Purg.,* 31, 133 ff., and 32, beginning. His remarks on Beatrice may be found in op. cit., pp. 212 ff.

I. A. Richards

1893–1979

Ivor Armstrong Richards was born in Sandbach, Cheshire, on February 26, 1893. The son of a Welsh engineer, Richards was educated at Clifton College in Bristol. He survived several childhood attacks of tuberculosis and attended Magdalene College, Cambridge. He read moral sciences and later natural sciences, graduating with a B.A. in 1914 and an M.A. in 1918. In his college years Richards absorbed both the utilitarianism of Jeremy Bentham and the idealism of Kant and Hegel. Kant's aesthetics laid the foundation for those of Richards, whose romantic conception of art's function in morality and the enlargement of consciousness also parallels his mentor Coleridge, later the subject of a book-length study, *Coleridge on Imagination* (1935). From 1922 to 1929 Richards lectured at Cambridge and published three important works of criticism, *The Meaning of Meaning* (a pioneering study of semantics written with C. K. Ogden and published in 1923), *Principles of Literary Criticism* (1924), and *Practical Criticism* (1929). With these volumes Richards became the acknowledged founder of the New Criticism, influencing such critics as F. R. Leavis, Kenneth Burke, and William Empson. *Practical Criticism,* in which a set of unattributed poems was given for review to a group of university students whose responses were then analyzed by Richards, reveals his commitment to neurological and psychological terminology; in it he coined such phrases as "stock response," "pseudo-statement," "disguised imperatives," "private poem," and "storehouse of recorded values." As a scientist Richards was interested primarily in stimuli and response.

Richards married Dorothy Pilley in 1926 and traveled to China in 1929 to work as a language trainer. Using C. K. Ogden's model for an international language, Richards taught Basic English, a modified system of communication based on only 850 words. After teaching in Beijing and serving as Director of the Orthological Institute of China, Richards took a teaching post at Harvard in 1939. There he wrote the main texts of the Basic English movement: *Basic English and Its Uses* (1943) and *Learning Basic English* (1945). In 1942 he translated Plato's *Republic* into Basic English. Richards was an active professor at Harvard until 1963, and devoted much of his time to the writing of poetry. His first volume appeared in 1958 under the title *Goodbye Earth and Other Poems.* Many of his poems deal with old age and with his favorite pastime, mountaineering. Richards published three more collections of poetry, including *New and Selected Poems* (1978), as well as three verse plays.

Richards' poetry was generally well received, and he won the King's Medal for poetry and the Russell Loines Award for poetry from the National Institute of Arts and Letters. An honorary fellow of Magdalene College, he was awarded honorary degrees by Harvard and Cambridge. In 1964 he was made a Companion of Honour and spent his last years in England. In the final year of his life he returned to China and taught classes to university students. Falling ill there, Richards came back to Cambridge, where he died on September 7, 1979.

PRACTICAL CRITICISM

Chapter I

The Four Kinds of Meaning

From whence it happens, that they which trust to books, do as they that cast up many little summs into a greater, without considering whether those little summes were rightly cast up or not; and at last finding the errour visible, and not mistrusting their first grounds, know not which way to cleere themselves; but spend time in fluttering over their bookes; as birds that entring by the chimney, and finding themselves inclosed in a chamber, flutter at the false light of a glasse window, for want of wit to consider which way they came in.

Leviathan.

After so much documentation the reader will be in a mood to welcome an attempt to point some morals, to set up some guiding threads by which the labyrinth we have perambulated may be made less bewildering. Otherwise we might be left with a mere defeatist acquiescence in *quot homines tot sententiæ* as the sovereign critical principle, a hundred verdicts from a hundred readers as the sole fruit of our endeavours—a result at the very opposite pole from my hope and intention. But before it can be pointed, the moral has first to be disengaged, and the guiding threads cannot be set up without some preliminary engineering. The analyses and distinctions that follow are only those that are indispensable if the conclusions to which they lead are to be understood with reasonable precision or recommended with confidence.

The proper procedure will be to inquire more closely—now that the material has passed before us—into the ten difficulties listed towards the end of Part I, taking them one by one in the order there adopted. Reasons for this order will make themselves plain as we proceed, for these difficulties depend one upon another like a cluster of monkeys. Yet in spite of this complicated interdependence it is not very difficult to see where we must begin. The *original* difficulty of all reading, the problem of *making out the meaning,* is our obvious starting-point. The answers to those apparently simple questions: 'What is a meaning?' 'What are we doing when we endeavour to make it out?' '*What* is it we are making out?' are the master-keys to all the problems of criticism. If we can make use of them the locked chambers and corridors of the theory of poetry open to us, and a new and impressive order, is discovered even in the most erratic twists of the protocols. Doubtless there are some who, by a natural dispensation, acquire the 'Open Sesame'! to poetry without labour, but, for the rest of us, certain general reflections we are not often encouraged to undertake can spare us time and fruitless trouble.

The all-important fact for the study of literature—or any other mode of communication—is that there are several kinds of meaning. Whether we know and intend it or not, we are all jugglers when we converse, keeping the billiard-balls in the air while we balance the cue on our nose. Whether we are active, as in speech or writing, or passive,[1] as readers or listeners, the Total Meaning we are engaged with is, almost always, a blend, a combination of several contributory meanings of different types. Language—and pre-eminently language as it is used in poetry—has not one but several tasks to perform simultaneously, and we shall misconceive most of the difficulties of criticism unless we understand this point and take note of the differences between these functions. For our purposes here a division into four types of function, four kinds of meaning, will suffice.

It is plain that most human utterances and nearly all articulate speech can be profitably regarded from four points of view. Four aspects can be easily distinguished. Let us call them *Sense, Feeling, Tone,* and *Intention.*

1. Sense. We speak *to say something,* and when we listen we expect something to be said. We use words to direct our hearers' attention upon some state of affairs, to present to them some items for consideration and to excite in them some thoughts about these items.

2. Feeling.[2] But we also, as a rule, have some feelings *about these items,* about the state of affairs we are referring to. We have an attitude towards it, some special direction, bias, or accentuation of interest towards it, some personal flavour or colouring of feeling; and we use language to *express* these feelings, this nuance of interest. Equally, when we listen we pick it up, rightly or wrongly; it seems inextricably part of what we receive; and this whether the speaker be conscious himself of his feelings towards what he is talking about or not. I am, of course, here describing the normal situation, my reader will be able without difficulty to think of exceptional cases (mathematics, for example) where no feeling enters.

3. Tone. Furthermore, the speaker has ordinarily *an attitude to his listener.* He chooses or arranges his words differently as his audience varies, in automatic or deliberate *recognition of his relation to them.* The tone of his utterance reflects his awareness of this relation, his sense of how he stands towards those he is addressing. Again the exceptional case of dissimulation, or instances in which the speaker unwittingly reveals an attitude he is not consciously desirous of expressing, will come to mind.

4. Intention. Finally, apart from what he says (Sense), his attitude to what he is talking about (Feeling), and his attitude to his listener (Tone), there is the speaker's intention, his aim, *conscious or unconscious,* the effect he is endeavouring to promote. Ordinarily he speaks for a purpose, and his purpose modifies his speech. The understanding of it is part of the whole business of apprehending his meaning. Unless we know what he is trying to do, we can hardly estimate the measure of his success. Yet the number of readers who omit such considerations might make a faint-hearted writer despair. Sometimes, of course, he will purpose no more than to state his thoughts (1), or to express his feelings about what he is thinking of, e.g. Hurrah! Damn! (2), or to express his attitude to his listener (3). With this last case we pass into the realm of endearments and abuse.

Frequently his intention operates through and satisfies itself in a combination of the other functions. Yet it has effects not reducible to their effects. It may govern the stress laid upon points in an argument for example, shape the arrangement, and even call attention to itself in such phrases as 'for contrast's sake' or 'lest it be supposed'. It controls the 'plot' in the largest sense of the word, and is at work whenever the author is 'hiding his hand'. And it has especial importance in dramatic and semi-dramatic literature. Thus the influence of his intention upon the language he uses is additional to, and separable from, the other three influences, and its effects can profitably be considered apart.

We shall find in the protocols instances, in plenty, of failure on the part of one or other of these functions. Sometimes all four fail together; a reader garbles the sense, distorts the feeling, mistakes the tone and disregards the intention; and often a partial collapse of one function entails aberrations in the others. The possibilities of human misunderstanding make up indeed a formidable subject for study, but something more can be done to elucidate it than has yet been attempted. Whatever else we may do by the light of nature it would be folly to maintain that we should read by it. But before turning back to scrutinise our protocols some further explanation of these functions will be in place.

If we survey our uses of language as a whole, it is clear that, at times, now one now another of the functions may become predominant. It will make the possible situations clearer if we briefly review certain typical forms of composition. A man writing a scientific treatise, for example, will put the *Sense* of what he has to say first, he will subordinate his *Feelings* about his subject or about other views upon it and be careful not to let them interfere to distort his argument or to suggest bias. His *Tone* will be settled for him by academic convention; he will, if he is wise, indicate respect for his readers and a moderate anxiety to be understood accurately and to win acceptance for his remarks. It will be well if his *Intention,* as it shows itself in the work, be on the whole confined to the clearest and most adequate statement of what he has to say (Function 1, Sense). But, if the circumstances warrant it, further relevant aims—an intention to reorientate opinion, to direct attention to new aspects, or to encourage or discourage certain methods of work or ways of approach—are obviously fitting. Irrelevant aims—the acceptance of the work as a thesis for a Ph.D., for example,—come in a different category.

Consider now a writer engaged upon popularising some of the results and hypotheses of science. The principles governing his language are not nearly so simple, for the furtherance of his intention will properly and inevitably interfere with the other functions.

In the first place, precise and adequate statement of the sense may have to be sacrificed, to some degree, in the interests of general intelligibility. Simplifications and distortions may be necessary if the reader is to 'follow'. Secondly, a much more lively exhibition of feelings on the part of the author towards his subject-matter is usually appropriate and desirable, in order to awaken and encourage the reader's interest. Thirdly, more variety of tone will be called for; jokes and humorous illustrations, for example, are admissible, and perhaps a certain amount of cajolery. With this increased liberty, tact, the subjective counterpart of tone, will be urgently required. A human relation between the expert and his lay audience must be created, and the task, as many specialists have discovered, is not easy. These other functions will interfere still more with strict accuracy of statement; and if the subject has a 'tendency', if political, ethical or theological implications are at all prominent, the intention of the work will have further opportunities to intervene.

This leads us to the obvious instance of political speeches. What rank and precedence shall we assign to the four language functions if we analyse public utterances made in the midst of a General Election? Function 4, the further-ance of intentions (of all grades of worthiness) is unmistakably predominant. Its instruments are Function 2, the expression of feelings about causes, policies, leaders and opponents, and Function 3, the establishment of favour-able relations with the audience ('the great heart of the people'). Recognising this, ought we to be pained or surprised that Function 1, the presentation of facts (or of objects of thought to be regarded as facts are regarded), is equally subordinated?[3] But further consideration of this situation would lead us into a topic that must be examined later, that of Sincerity, a word with several important meanings. (See Chapter VII.)

In conversation, perhaps, we get the clearest examples of these shifts of function, the normal verbal apparatus of one function being taken over by another. Intention, we have seen, may completely subjugate the others; so, on occasion, may Feeling or Tone express themselves through Sense, translating themselves into explicit statements about feelings and attitudes towards things and people—statements sometimes belied by their very form and manner. Diplomatic formulæ are often good examples, together with much of the social language (Malinowski's 'phatic communion'), the 'Thank you so very much'es, and 'Pleased to meet you's, that help us to live amicably with one another.

Under this head, too, may be put the psychological analyses, the intro-spective expatiations that have recently flourished so much in fiction as well as in sophisticated conversation. Does it indicate a confusion or a tenuousness in our feelings that we should now find ourselves so ready to make statements about them, to translate them into disquisitions, instead of expressing them in more direct and natural ways? Or is this phenomenon simply another result of the increased study of psychology? It would be rash to decide as yet. Certainly some psychologists lay themselves open to a charge of emptiness, of having so dealt with themselves that they have little left within them to talk about. 'Putting it into words,' if the words are those of a psychological textbook, is a process which may well be damaging to the feelings. I shall be lucky if my reader does not murmur *de te fabula* at this point.

But Feeling (and sometimes Tone) may take charge of and operate through Sense in another fashion, one more constantly relevant in poetry. (If indeed the shift just dealt with above might not be better described as Sense interfering with and dominating Feeling and Tone.)

When this happens, the statements which appear in the poetry are there for the sake of their effects upon feelings, not for their own sake. Hence to challenge their truth or to question whether they deserve serious attention *as statements claiming truth,* is to mistake their function. The point is that many, if not most, of the statements in poetry are there *as a means* to the manipulation[4] and expression of feelings and attitudes, not as contributions to any body of doctrine of any type whatever. With narrative poetry there is little danger of any mistake arising, but with 'philosophical' or meditative poetry there is great danger of a confusion which may have two sets of consequences.

On the one hand there are very many people who, if they read any poetry at all, try to take all its statements seriously—and find them silly. 'My soul is a ship in full sail,' for example, seems to them a very profitless kind of contribution to psychology. This may seem an absurd mistake but, alas! it is none the less common. On the other hand there are those who succeed too well, who swallow 'Beauty is truth, truth beauty. . .', as the quintessence of an æsthetic philosophy, not as the expression of a certain blend of feelings, and proceed into a complete stalemate of muddle-mindedness as a result of their linguistic naïvety. It is easy to see what those in the first group miss; the losses of the second group, though the accountancy is more complicated, are equally lamentable.

A temptation to discuss here some further intricacies of this shift of function must be resisted. An overflow into Appendix A, which may serve as a kind of technical workshop for those who agree with me that the matter is important enough to be examined *with pains,* will be the best solution. I am anxious to illustrate these distinctions from the protocols before tedium too heavily assails us. It will be enough here to note that this subjugation of statement to emotive purposes has innumerable modes. A poet may distort his statements; he may make statements which have logically nothing to do with the subject under treatment; he may, by metaphor and otherwise, present objects for thought which are logically quite irrelevant; he may perpetrate logical nonsense, be as trivial or as silly, logically, as it is possible to be; all in the interests of the other functions of his language—to express feeling or adjust tone or further his other intentions. If his success in these other aims justify him, no reader (of the kind at least to take his meaning as it should be taken) can validly say anything against him.

But these indirect devices for expressing feeling through logical irrelevance and nonsense, through statements not to be taken strictly, literally or seriously, though pre-eminently apparent in poetry, are not peculiar to it. A great part of what passes for criticism comes under this head. It is much harder to obtain statements about poetry, than expressions of feelings towards it and towards the author. Very many apparent statements turn out on examination to be only these disguised forms, indirect expressions, of Feeling, Tone and Intention. Dr Bradley's remark that *Poetry is a spirit,* and Dr Mackail's that it is *a continuous substance or energy whose progress is immortal* are eminent examples that I have made use of elsewhere, so curious that I need no apology for referring to them again. Remembering them, we may be more ready to apply to the protocols every instrument of interpretation we possess. May we avoid if possible in our own reading of the protocols those errors of misunderstanding which we are about to watch being committed towards the poems.

Chapter IV

Poetic Form

Beauty and melody have not the arithmetical password, and so are barred out. This teaches us that what exact science looks for is not entities of some particular category, but entities with a metrical aspect. . . . It would be no use for beauty, say, to fake up a few numerical attributes in the hope of thereby gaining admission into the portals of science and carrying on an æsthetic crusade within. It would find that the numerical aspects were duly admitted, but æsthetic significance of them left outside.

A. S. EDDINGTON, *The Nature of the Physical World.*

That the art of responding to the form of poetry is not less difficult than the art of grasping its content—its sense and feeling—will be evident to anyone who has glanced through Part II. And since half perhaps of the feeling that poetry carries comes through its form (and through the interaction of form and content) the need for better educational methods, here also, will be admitted. The condition of blank incapacity displayed in 1·161, 3·15, 3·51, in half the comments on *Poem VI*, in 10·61, 11·41, 12·52 and 13·61, to mention but a few salient examples; the desperate efforts to apply the fruits of the traditional classical training shown in 3·44, 6·33, 12·51 and 13·62; and the occurrence of such divergences as those between 1·14 and 1·141, 2·2 and 2·61, 4·27 and 4·31, or 9·3 and 9·31, all tell the same story. A large proportion of even a picked public neither understand the kind of importance that attaches to the movement of words in verse, nor have any just ideas of how to seize this movement or judge it.

It may be objected that just ideas upon a point admittedly so difficult as the nature of rhythm are not easy to attain, that what matters is sensitiveness, and that this is a special endowment. But, once again, too many young children show an aptitude for the reading of poetry and a capacity to seize its rhythm, for us to admit that so many adults need be so obtuse. Mistaken ideas, and crude unconsidered assumptions certainly play their part. It may be that the best way to learn how verse should be spoken is to listen to a good speaker; but a few reasonable ideas upon the matter can certainly assist, and without them we remain unnecessarily at the mercy of any authoritative mangler of verses we may encounter.

Let us begin with the assumption that the protocols show to be most damaging, the notion that *regularity* is the merit of verse. (13·62 and 3·44 will make the force of this notion clear to us). It derives very largely from the cruder by-products of Classical Education. Unless very well taught, Latin verse composition is a bad instrument by which to train a mind in the appreciation of rhythm. A few very brilliant or very rebellious boys escape, but the rest receive the impression (often indelible) that good verses are simply those that fit a certain framework of rules, and that this framework is the measure of their rhythmical virtue. Applied to English verse the notion meets with a check in the fact that no set of rules has been found (or, at least, agreed upon), but the efforts of the rival schools of prosodists seem all directed towards establishing some set of rules, and the general impression that metrical excellence lies in regularity is encouraged, and readers who have not heard of more refined ideas naturally retain this simple notion. 'Irregular', as we know from other contexts, is a word that carries several shades of disapprobation.

But the patent fact that the best verses are frequently irregular, that almost as often as not they fail to conform, however many 'licences', 'substitutions' and 'equivalences' are introduced into the rules of scansion to bring them into line, has forced upon many prosodists an improved idea of metre. Instead of strict conformity with a pattern, an arrangement of departures from and returns to the pattern has come to be regarded as the secret of poetic rhythm. The ear, it has been thought, grows tired of strict regularity but delights in recognising behind the variations the standard that still governs them.

This conception, though an improvement, is still too superficial. I have put it in a language which reveals its weakness, for the apprehension of poetic rhythm is only partly an affair of the ear. The defect of the view is that it regards poetic rhythm as a character of the sound of the words apart from their effects in the mind of the reader. The rhythm is supposed to belong to them and to be the cause of these effects. But the difference between good rhythm and bad is not simply a difference between certain sequences of sounds; it goes deeper, and to understand it we have to take note of the meanings of the words as well.

This point, which is of some practical importance, appears clearly if we imagine ourselves reciting verses into the ear of an instrument designed to record (by curves drawn on squared paper) all the physical characters of the sequences of sounds emitted, their strength, pitch, durations, and any other features we choose to examine. (This is not a fantastic suggestion, for such instruments can be arranged and begin to be part of the furniture of good phonetic laboratories.) The shape of our curves will give us a transcription of all the physical rhythms[5] of the verses. Now the view objected to would lead us to conclude that verses which are good poetry would show *some* peculiarity[6] in their curves, that verses which are bad poetry could not show. Put in this manner, it will be agreed, I hope, that the conclusion is most unplausible. But if we say, as many have said, that poetic rhythm is a quality of the sound, the sensuous form, of words, there is no means of escaping it.

Yet it is perfectly true that many great passages of poetry do *seem to possess,* merely as sounds, a peculiar undeniable virtue. And it is sometimes suggested that a sensitive listener, knowing no Italian, who listens to Dante, well read, would be able to distinguish the verses of the *Divina Comedia* from those of some skilful but negligible imitator. Their superiority in sound, it is said, would reveal them. The experiment might be interesting, but it has an obvious flaw which makes it inconclusive. The reader must be presumed to understand what he is reading, and it is likely that what the sensitive listener would really discern would be signs, in the reader's voice and manner, of the differences due to this understanding. For whether a speaker is really interested or not in what he is saying, and in what fashion, is a point we can be quick to detect.

How, then, are we to explain this apparent superiority in the sound of good poetry if we admit that on the recording drum its curves might be indistinguishable from those of rubbish. The answer is that the rhythm which we admire, which we seem to detect actually *in* the sounds, and which we seem to respond to, is something which we only *ascribe* to them and is, actually, a rhythm of the mental activity through which we apprehend not only the sound of the words but their sense and feeling. The mysterious glory which seems to inhere in the sound of certain lines is a projection[7] of the thought and emotion they evoke, and the peculiar satisfaction they seem to give *to the ear* is a reflection of the adjustment *of our feelings* which has been momentarily achieved. Those who find this a hard saying may be invited to consider anew the reception of *Poem IV.*

Such an explanation has this incidental advantage, that it accounts for the passionate admiration sometimes accorded to stray lines that seem of a mediocre manufacture. The reader (1·31) who compares the exhortations in *Poem I* to 'wonderful music' serves us excellently as an example (1·145, 1·21 and 1·3 may also be re-examined). The phenomenon is paralleled in all human affairs into which feeling enters, and this is no occasion to expatiate upon it.

But the theory of poetic rhythm as something 'projected', *ascribed* to verses rather than inherent in them, must not lead us to *under*-estimate the part played by the actual sounds. They are a very important contributing factor though they do not carry the whole responsibility for the rhythm. They are the skeleton upon which the reader casts flesh and clothing. And if the skeleton is too much out of joint, or if it is the skeleton of a whippet, when sense and feeling demand that of a cat, no goodwill on the part of the reader and no depth of realisation of sense and feeling will overcome the disability. To see this we have only to change the rhythm of any convenient passage of good verse, while preserving its vocabulary and, so far as possible, its syntax.

> Whether nobler it is in the mind to suffer
> The arrows and slings of Fortune outrageous.

The effect is that of comic-opera patter. The sense fights in vain to master the form, and its failure gives it an inevitable air of frivolity.

Metrical form, therefore, that is to say the rhythm inherent in the
sequence of the actual sounds in verse, the rhythm that appears in the records
of the kymograph, is very important. It can easily make what might be a good
poem into a bad one. But it cannot be judged apart from the sense and feeling
of the words out of which it is composed nor apart from the precise order in
which that whole of sense and feeling builds itself up. The movement or plot
of the word-by-word development of the poem, as a structure of the intellect
and emotions, is always, in good poetry, in the closest possible relation to the
movement of the metre, not only giving it its tempo, but even distorting it—
sometimes violently. Readers who take up a poem as though it were a bicycle,
spot its metre, and pedal off on it regardless of where it is going, will naturally,
if it is a good poem, get into trouble. For only a due awareness of its sense and
feeling will bring its departures from the pattern metre into a coherent,
satisfying whole.

The notion that verses must conform to metrical patterns was described
earlier in this chapter as the most damaging enemy to good reading. It is a
double-edged notion, blindly destructive on both sides. It leads, on the one
hand, to mechanical reading, to a 'cruel forcing' (3·44) of syllables into a mould
which they were never meant to fit, and to a ruthless lopping away of vocables
(cf. 8·44, 12·51, 13·62), treatment that is fatal to the movement of the verse.
On the other hand it leads to bitter complaints against irregularity and a refusal
to enter into poems which do not accord smoothly with the chosen pattern
(8·43).

Against these unnecessary mistakes it cannot be too much insisted that
there is no obligation upon verses to conform to any standard. The pattern is
only a convenience, though an invaluable one; it indicates the *general*
movement of the rhythm; it gives a model, a central line, from which variations
in the movement take their direction and gain an added significance; it gives
both poet and reader a firm support, a fixed point of orientation in the
indefinitely vast world of possible rhythms; it has other virtues of a psychological order; but it has no compulsory powers, and there is no good reason
whatever to accord it them.

After the conformity notion, its close cousin, the notion that poetic rhythm
is independent of sense, is the most hurtful. It is easy, however, to show how
much the rhythm we *ascribe* to words (and even their inherent rhythm as
sounds) is influenced by our apprehension of their meanings. Prepare a few
phrases with their sounds and inherent rhythms as closely alike as possible but
with different meanings. Then compare for example:—

Deep into a gloomy grot

with

Peep into a roomy cot.

The ascribed rhythm, the movement of the words, trivial though it be in both
cases, is different, though almost every prosodist would have to scan them in

the same fashion, and the kymograph would, I think, for most readers, show few important differences.[8]

Going a step further, if the meaning of the words is irrelevant to the form of the verse, and if this independent form possesses æsthetic virtue, as not a few have maintained (3·6 will do as a specimen), it should be possible to take some recognised masterpiece of poetic rhythm and compose, with nonsense syllables, a double or dummy which at least comes recognisably near to possessing the same virtue.

> J. Drootan-Sussting Benn
> Mill-down Leduren N.
>   Telamba-taras oderwainto weiring
> Awersey zet bidreen
> Ownd istellester sween
>   Lithabian tweet ablissood owdswown stiering
> Apleven aswetsen sestinal
> Yintomen I adaits afurf I gallas Ball.

If the reader has any difficulty in scanning these verses, reference to Milton, 'On the Morning of Christ's Nativity', xv, will prove of assistance, and the attempt to divine the movement of the original before looking it up will at least show how much the sense, syntax, and feeling of verse may serve as an introduction to its form. But the illustration will also support a subtler argument against anyone who affirms that the mere sound of verse has *independently* any considerable æsthetic virtue. For he will *either* have to say that this verse is valuable (when he may be implored to take up his pen at once and enrich the world with many more such verses, for nothing could be easier), *or* he will have to say that it is the differences *in sound* between this purified dummy and the original which deprive the dummy of poetic merit. In which case he will have to account for the curious fact that just those transformations which redeem it as sound, should also give it the sense and feeling we find in Milton. A staggering coincidence, unless the meaning were highly relevant to the effect of the form.

Such arguments (which might be elaborated) do not tend to diminish the power of the sound (the inherent rhythm) *when it works in conjunction with sense and feeling*. The reception of *Poem VI* (and especially 6·32, 6·33) proves both the subtlety and the importance of this collaboration. The twofold contrasts of 4·23 and 4·24 and 4·25 also admirably display the point. The mistake of neglecting sound altogether must rank next after the Regularity and Independence myths as a source of bad reading. In fact the close co-operation of the form with the meaning—modifying it and being modified by it in ways that though subtle are, in general, perfectly intelligible—is the chief secret of Style in poetry. But so much mystery and obscurity has been raised around this relation by talk about the *identity* of Form and Content, or about the extirpation of the Matter in the Form, that we are in danger of forgetting how natural and inevitable their co-operation must be.

By bad reading I suggest that we should mean not so much reading that would offend our susceptibilities if we were listening,[9] as reading that prevents the reader himself from entering into the poem. The sounds most people make when they read aloud probably seem very different to their audience and to them. The phenomena of 'projection' are noticeable here. We invest our rendering with the qualities we wish it to have—unless some critical eye is cocked upon us—and two readings of the same poem that sound very different may not, to the readers themselves, be after all so unlike. The rhythms they *ascribe* to the poem may be more similar than the rhythms they actually succeed in giving it. Thus though private reading aloud is much to be recommended[10] as an aid in working out the form of a poem, it is doubtful whether public-reading (in the classroom for example) should be encouraged. Nothing more easily defeats the whole aim of poetry than to hear it incompetently mouthed or to struggle oneself to read out a poem in public before it has given up most of its secrets. For to read poetry well is extremely difficult. One piece of advice which has proved its usefulness may perhaps be offered: to remember that we are more likely to read too fast than to read too slow. Certainly, if the rhythm of a poem is not yet clear to us, a *very slow* private reading gives a better chance for the necessary interaction of form and meaning to develop than any number of rapid perusals. This simple neurological fact, if it could be generally recognised and respected, would probably more than anything else help to make poetry understood.

Chapter VI

Sentimentality and Inhibition

May the tears of sympathy crystallise as they fall and be worn as pearls in the bosom of our affections.
                        Nineteenth Century Commercial Travellers' Toast.

Among the politer terms of abuse there are few so effective as 'sentimental'. Not very long ago the word 'silly' was fairly useful for this purpose. The most intelligent would wince, the less intelligent would become angry, and the stupid would grow indignant if they, or views dear to their hearts, were so described—the three shades of feeling corresponding perhaps to a suspicion, a fear, and an absolute certainty as to there *not* being something in it. But since Bergsonism began its insidious dry-rot-like invasion of contemporary intellectualism the word 'silly' has lost some of its sting. Nowadays the accusation of sentimentality is more annoying than any slur cast upon our capacity as thinkers, for our moral capital is invested in our feelings rather than in our thoughts.

The very fact that it is so annoying suggests that 'sentimental'—though often it *may* mean something precise and capable of definition—may be also, like an insulting gesture, the vehicle of another kind of utterance; that it is sometimes not so much the instrument of a statement as an expression of contempt. Such an expression cannot, of course, be defined as though it were a scientific term. Given the occasion and the speakers we can describe the feelings the word excites and the attitudes from which it springs. But there we have to leave the matter. And 'sentimental rubbish' is doubtless more often than not a mere phrase of abuse. Compare the phrase 'damn nonsense'. The logician or the expert in definitions would waste his time trying to assign a precise scope to the adjective in either case.

But 'sentimental' may be more than a piece of abuse, an emotive gesture. It may be a description, may stand for a vague idea, or for any one of several precise ideas; and two of these are extremely important. So important that there is no need to be surprised if 'sentimental' is one of the most overworked words in the whole vocabulary of literary criticism. Its frequency, its twofold use, as an insult and as a description, its fogginess in the second capacity and its social significance in the first are all sufficiently evidenced in the protocols. *Poems IV* and *VIII* and, to a lesser degree, *Poems II* and *XIII* provide us with our most instructive examples. But before examining these in detail we must attempt some definitions and elucidations.

Setting aside the abusive use of 'sentimental' as a mere gesture indicating little more than dislike, let us reflect first upon the vaguer senses of the word. We often use it to say only that there is something wrong in the feelings involved by the thing, whatever it is, which we call sentimental. And we do not attempt to specify what is wrong. Using a vague thought like this has been happily compared by Bertrand Russell to aiming at a target with a lump of putty. The putty spreads out, and we have a good chance of bespattering the bull's-eye with some of it. But it will spread over the rings too. A precise thought is more like a bullet. We can perhaps hit with it just what we want to hit and nothing else, but we are much more likely to miss altogether. Vague thoughts are best sometimes; they economise labour and are easier to follow, they have their obvious uses in poetry; but for this purpose we need more precise ones.

The first of these is easy to state. A person may be said to be sentimental when his emotions are too easily stirred, too light on the trigger. As we all know to our cost the trigger adjustment for the feelings varies with all manner of odd circumstances. Drugs, the weather, 'the brave music of a *distant* drum', fatigue, illness—these and many other extraneous factors can make our emotions too facile. The lover of the bottle in his maudlin stage is a famous sentimentalist. Certain rhythms—as in the case of the brass band above mentioned—and sounds of a certain quality, perhaps through their associa-tions—the trumpet and the nightingale, for example—all these readily facili-tate emotional orgies. So do certain conditions of mass suggestion. Reunions, processions; we often have to blush for our sentimentality when we escape from the crowd. Most remarkable of all, perhaps, are some effects of illness. I reluctantly recall that the last time I had influenza a very stupid novel filled my eyes with tears again and again until I could not see the pages. Influenza is thought by many to be a disorder of the autonomic nervous system, and if this be so, there would be nothing surprising in this effect. All our emotional susceptibilities may be more or less affected, but the results are most marked with those which we can luxuriate in, those which do not obviously endanger our self-esteem.

This last factor is one in which individuals vary amazingly. Some people regard indulgence in the soft and tender emotions as always creditable, and they wallow in them so greedily that one is forced to regard them as emotionally starved. Others are apt to think about these emotions as Alexander Bain, the once celebrated author of *The Emotions and the Will,* thought about kissing (he called it osculation). "The occasion", he said, "should be adequate and the actuality rare".

But what is this adequate occasion and what makes it adequate?

Postponing consideration of this awkward problem, let us first trace these differences in emotional susceptibility, in the touchiness of the feelings, a little further. They are very noticeable as between infancy, maturity, and old age. The child often appears singularly unfeeling, so does the over-experienced adult.

> No more, no more, O never more on me
>   The freshness of the heart will fall like dew,
> Which out of all the lovely things we see
>   Extracts emotions beautiful and new—

as Byron wrote. The point expressed in the last word will also have to be considered later. In between the infant and the adult come the adolescents, who, as is well known, are regarded both by their juniors and their seniors as sentimentalists *in excelsis*. The girl of twelve is apt to think her seventeen-year-old sister very 'sloppy'. As we shall see, there may be several reasons for this phenomenon. In old age, sometimes, but not always, a return of heightened emotional susceptibility takes place. 'Sentimental' here applies to persons. It means that they are too susceptible, the flood-gates of their emotions too easily raised.

This then gives us a precise, though very general, sense for 'sentimental', a *quantitative* sense. A response is sentimental if it is too great for the occasion. We cannot, obviously, judge that any response is sentimental in this sense unless we take careful account of the situation.

Another sense, of which this is not true, is that in which 'sentimental' is equivalent to 'crude'. A crude emotion, as opposed to a refined emotion, can be set off by all manner of situations, whereas a refined emotion is one that can only be aroused by a narrow range of situations. Refined emotions are like sensitive instruments; they reflect slight changes in the situations which call them forth. The distinction is parallel in several ways to the distinction made above between vague and precise thoughts. Though refined responses are capable of much more appropriateness than crude ones, they are much more likely to go astray, as super-subtle folk often show us. On the other hand, though crude emotions are less likely to go altogether wrong, they are less likely to go entirely right, if we judge them by high standards of rightness. Neither crudeness nor refinement need imply anything about the intensity of the emotion—they are *qualitative* not quantitative characters. A crude emotion need not be intense, nor a refined one feeble. It is true, however, that the most violent emotions are usually crude. Terror and rage, as we all know, are apt, once they are aroused, to spread and apply themselves to anything. And while intensity is under discussion one further point may be noted. Violence of emotion, though much popular criticism seems to assume so, does not necessarily imply value. Poems which are very 'moving' may be negligible or bad. It is the quality rather than the violence which matters. As Wordsworth wrote,

> The Gods approve
> The depth, and not the tumult, of the soul.

We may suspect that to-day the demand for violence reflects some poverty, through inhibition, in the everyday emotional life. In Elizabethan times a perhaps not analogous demand could not, however, admit of this explanation.

One more sense of 'sentimental' requires definition before we can turn to consider when accusations of sentimentality are justified and when they are not. This sense derives from the psychologists' use of the word 'sentiment'. A sentiment in his terminology is not an experience in the way that an emotion, a pain, the sight of something, an image, and a thought, are experiences. It is not a momentary thing but a more or less permanent arrangement in the mind: a group of tendencies towards certain thoughts and emotions organised around a central object. Love, for example, is a sentiment, if by love we mean, not a particular experience lasting certain minutes or hours, but a set of tendencies to behave in certain ways, to think certain thoughts, to feel certain emotions, in connection with a person. Sentiments can be very complex; love includes a tendency to feel resentful towards anyone who annoys the loved person, and so on. A sentiment, in brief, is a persisting, organised system of dispositions.

Sentiments, in this sense, are formed in us through our past experience in connection with the central object. They are the result of our past interest in the object. For this reason they are apt to persist even when our present interest in the object is changed. For example, a schoolmaster that we discover in later life to have been always a quite unimportant and negligible person may still retain something of his power to overawe us. Again the object itself may change, yet our sentiment towards it—not as it was but as it is—may so much remain the same that it becomes inappropriate. For example, we may go on living in a certain house although increase in motor traffic has made life there almost insupportable. Conversely, though the object is just what it was, our sentiment towards it may completely change—through a strange and little understood influence from other sentiments of later growth. The best example is the pathetic and terrible change that can too often be observed in the sentiments entertained towards the War by men who suffered from it and hated it to the extremist degree while it was raging. After only ten years they sometimes seem to feel that after all it was 'not so bad', and a Brigadier-General recently told a gathering of Comrades of the Great War that they 'must agree that it was the happiest time of their lives'. A familiar parallel example is the illusion so many middle-aged men entertain that they enjoyed their school-days, when in fact they were then acutely wretched.

I shall use these two forms of distortion to define a third sense of 'sentimental' as follows: A response is sentimental when, either through the over-persistence of tendencies or through the interaction of sentiments, it is inappropriate to the situation that calls it forth. It becomes inappropriate, as a rule, either by confining itself to one aspect only of the many that the situation can present, or by substituting for it a factitious, illusory situation that may, in extreme cases, have hardly anything in common with it. We can study these extreme cases in dreams and in asylums.

Let us now apply these three definitions to some of the accusations of sentimentality contained in the protocols. With the first two senses however—the quantitative sense and the crudeness sense—an obvious ambiguity remains that must first be disposed of. When we apply the word to a human product, a poem for example, we may mean either of two things which we hardly ever distinguish, or we may mean both. If we would more often distinguish them we should avoid many mistakes and some needless injustice.

We may mean—to take Sense One—that the poem was the product of a mind which was too easily stirred to emotion, that it came about through facile feelings, that the *author* was himself sentimental. Or we may mean that *we* should be too easily moved, we should ourselves be sentimental, if we allowed our own emotions a vigorous outing. Sometimes doubtless, both these assertions are true, but often we are only entitled to make the second. (Compare what has been said about sincerity in connection with *Poem VII* and *Poem VIII*.)

Now let us consider *Poem IV* with this distinction in mind. We must, of course, not read the verses as a piece of imaginative sociology such as Zola dreamed of. It is not an attempt by a novelist to render *realistically* the stock thoughts and feelings and the diction of a girl without poetic ability, expressing herself in verse. (But cf. 4·1, 4·3.) We have to take it, in the usual way that lyrical, emotional verse is taken, as a semi-dramatic utterance not *inviting* ironical contemplation—to be judged on its merits as poetry.

This problem of approach is especially relevant here. 'Sentimentality recollected in very sentimental tranquillity' (4·1), with the rest of the protocol as a gloss, seems to accuse the author (perhaps identified, improperly, with the heroine of the poem) of over-production of emotion (Sense One) and suggests further a cause for this excess:[11] namely, preoccupation with the emotion for its own sake rather than with the situation occasioning it. New emotions—as Byron hints in the verse quoted above—easily divert attention to themselves. Very few people, for example, fall in love for the first time without becoming enthralled by their emotions merely as a novel experience. They become absorbed in them often to the exclusion of genuine interest in the loved object. Similarly those who are discovering for the first time that poetry can cause them emotion do often, for this very reason, pay little attention to the poetry. Writers too, who find that they can imagine feelings and express them in words, may readily become fascinated by this occupation, as a kind of game, and lose sight of the real sanctions of the feelings in experience. We may easily work the feelings up for their own sake, forgetting intermittently what the feelings are like in our eagerness to hang them on to the forms of expression which occur to us. Seeing a chance to make a violent emotional effect, we forget whether this is the effect we desire.

Both the accusation and the suggestion as to the source of the excess feeling seem justified here. The antitheses, so much praised (4·22, 4·24) and so much disliked (4·23, 4·31), the rhymes, and the mechanical structure, do seem to indicate that facilities and conveniences of expression have led feeling, rather than that feeling has dictated expression. As to the excess of feeling over its justification in the actual situation presented by the poem, we must beware of a misconception which though obviously a mistake is none the less insidious.

If we separate out the subject or theme of the poem, *A girl bewailing her lost or absent lover,* and take this, abstractly, as the situation, we may think that it sounds sufficient to justify any extremity of sympathetic emotion. But this abstracted theme is nothing in itself, and might be the basis of any one of as many different developments as there are kinds of girls. It cannot in itself be an excuse for any emotion. If the mere fact that some girl somewhere is thus lamenting were an occasion for emotion, into what convulsions ought not the evening paper to throw us nightly? This is obvious, but there is reason to think that very many people are ready to react emotionally to a 'pathetic' situation merely at this level of abstractness, provided it is put before them in some kind of metre; and, if so, such reactions are certainly 'sentimental' in the sense of excessive.

The situation evidently has to be something more concrete. It is the poet's business to present it—not necessarily apart from his presentation of the emotion. He will usually be presenting both together through the same words. Here, since the girl is speaking herself, every word, every cadence, every movement and transition of thought and feeling is part of the situation.

This being so, we may ask two questions. Is the situation so given concrete enough, near enough to us, and coherent enough to justify the vigorous emotional response invited from us? And is it, in its concreteness, nearness and coherence so far as they go, of the kind to which *this* response is appropriate? (I am not saying that nearness, concreteness and coherence are required in all poetry—this would be an illegitimate technical presupposition. But I am saying that if certain effects are aimed at, certain methods are thereby prescribed.)

On the first question 4·23, 4·25 and 4·31 forcibly present the adverse opinion, though as we have seen in Chapter IV we must be careful in applying the rhythm test. (4·25 seems, however, here to be justified in the rhythm he ascribes to the verses.) These writers, in contrast to 4·11, 4·24 or 4·52, seem to be responding to the situation as actually presented by the poet—not to situations they have imagined for him or to the 'trappings and catchwords of romance' in which he has decked out the verses. These decorations by their conventional quality raise all the problems reviewed in the last chapter. That they were the source of the poem's great popularity is not to be doubted. Equally evident is the great danger of snobbery whenever such questions arise. That a metaphor is conventional and familiar is not, of course, *in itself* sufficient ground for objection, though it is often enough the whole explanation of the complaint. Similarly, if the situation and emotion were ordinary, simple and familiar (as 4·3 suggests), that in itself would be no bar to merit, provided the emotion were properly *founded in* the situation. (Compare Gray's *Elegy*.) To suppose otherwise would be a very stupid kind of emotional snobbery. Or if lack of skill in the author were the cause of the conventional metaphors, that again would be no ground for indignation. But if the borrowed, second-hand, quality of the expression

> In slavish habit, ill-fitted weeds
> Oreworn and soild

reflects, not merely neediness or carelessness, but a similar second-hand, reach-me-down, quality in the thing expressed, then the vigour of some of the rejections is excused.

These reflections apply to the concreteness and nearness we are looking for in the poem. Conventional metaphors tend to fail in both characters, a tendency not avoided here. But they apply still more to the coherence that is required. Borrowed decorations—and here is the gravest objection to their use—are almost always irrelevant. The various items do not hang together, and their combined effect, if any, is likely to be crude in the sense discussed above. Here, for example, the sunshine and dog-roses of verse three have somehow to adjust themselves to the winter and the wailing of the wind in verse two, and the idly circulating 'wind of the years', which has possibly blown in from the pages of Swinburne,[12] has to 'whisper' above this wailing. (Such incoherences are characteristic of conventional verse; only a very intent concentration of the poet's imaginative faculties can prevent them. In themselves they *need* not be destructive, but they are a very useful corroboration if we suspect on other grounds that the central impulse of a poem is weak.) By the time these incoherent items have pooled their effects the response can hardly here be anything but crude—an undirected, objectless feeling of pathos that will attach itself to anything that will give it an excuse—to the caravan bells of Hassan (4·52), for example.

The emotion, in fact, which this poem can excite (and on which its popularity depends) is easily enjoyed for its own sake, regardless of its object or prompting situation. Most people will not find it difficult, if they so desire, to sit down by the fireside and concoct a precisely similar emotion without the assistance of any poem whatever—merely by saying Oh! to themselves in various tones of sadness, regret and tremulous hope. It is an emotion that we tend, if we indulge it at all, to luxuriate in, as 4·1 remarks. Hence the power of these verses to divide readers sharply into two camps.

Passing now to *Poem VIII*, accusations of sentimentality in the first and third of our senses appear most instructively. The charge of excessive emotional response, too light a trigger adjustment for the feelings, is coupled with the suggestions that the poet is 'revelling in emotion for its own sake' (8·1), 'positively wallowing in a warm bath of soapy sentiment' (8·12), that he 'seems to love feeling sobby' (8·41), and that he is 'trying to get effects the whole time' (8·44)—as explanations of this excess of feeling. As a rule the complainants demonstrate satisfactorily that they have mistaken the situation to which the emotion is a response. It is music in general for 8·12, 'the poet's miseries' for 8·11, his 'pure, spotless childhood' and his present state as a 'world-worn wretch' for 8·41. And as a result of these mistakes the characters of the emotions these writers attributed to the poem are equally irrelevant. The moral again is that before we can decide whether a poem is or is not sentimental in this sense we must be sure that we know both what the presented situation is and what response is invited. Only the very closest reading will tell us enough about either to make judgment worth while.

The charge of sentimentality in our third sense raises a more complicated issue, for the poem is itself clearly a study of a border-line case, and, if not read more carefully than, for example, by 8·3, or 8·31, is likely to be disastrous in its emotional effects. There is, it is true, a 'mawkish sentiment with which we so often think of childhood'; and 'one's loose emotion' does as easily attach itself to 'old Sunday evenings at home', 'the cosy parlour' and 'the vista of years' as to 'the chimney-nook' or 'the wind of the years'. But the danger, 'the appalling risk' (8·5) of arousing only these emotions need not frighten the poet away from such topics if he can give enough nearness, concreteness and coherence[13] to the situation to support and *control* the response that ensues. Or if he can build these dangerous elements into a whole response which completes and frees them. For what is bad in these sentimental responses is their confinement to one stereotyped, unrepresentative aspect of the prompting situation.

This brings us to the subject of inhibitions. Most, if not all, sentimental fixations and distortions of feeling are the result of inhibitions, and often when we discuss sentimentality we are looking at the wrong side of the picture. If a man can only think of his childhood as a lost heaven it is probably because he is afraid to think of its other aspects. And those who contrive to look back to the War as 'a good time,' are probably busy dodging certain other memories. The mind is curiously quantitative in some of its operations; undue curtailment in one direction seems to imply excess in an opposite direction. Inhibition, in due place and degree, is, of course, a necessity for mental activity—quite as much a necessity as exercise. It was Bergson, I think, who once described Time as resistance—the resistance namely against everything happening at once! Without inhibition everything in the mind *would* happen at once, which is tantamount to saying that nothing would happen or that Chaos would return. All order and proportion is the result of inhibition, we cannot indulge one mental activity without inhibiting others. Therefore the opinion sometimes emitted that all inhibition (or repression) is bad, is at the least an overstatement. What is unfortunate is the permanent curtailment of our possibilities as human beings, the blanking out, through repeated and maintained inhibition, of aspects of experience that our mental health requires us sometimes to envisage.

As a rule the source of such inhibitions is some painfulness attaching to the aspect of life that we refuse to contemplate. The sentimental response steps in to replace this aspect by some other aspect more pleasant to contemplate or by some factitious object which flatters the contemplator. There are innumerable cross-currents of motive here which may conceal from us what we are doing. The man who, in reaction to the commoner naïve forms of sentimentality, prides himself upon his hard-headedness and hard-heartedness, his hard-boiledness generally, and seeks out or invents aspects with a bitter or squalid character, for no better reason than this, is only displaying a more sophisticated form of sentimentality. Fashion, of course, is responsible for many of these secondary twists. Indeed the control of Society over our sentiments, over our publicly avowable sentiments, is remarkably efficient. Compare, for example, the attitudes to tears (especially to masculine tears) approved by the eighteenth and twentieth centuries. Very little reflection and inquiry will show conclusively that the eighteenth century in regarding a profuse discharge of the lachrymal glands as a proper and almost necessary accompaniment of tender and sorrowful emotion was much more representative of humanity in all ages than are our contemporary wooden-eyed stoics. The current attitude naturally appeared in the protocols (8·52, 8·6, 8·61). Even *Poem VIII* itself shows it, for an eighteenth-century writer would have felt no need to fight against such an emotion.

A widespread general inhibition of all the simpler expansive developments of emotion (not only of its expression) has to be recognised among our educated population. It is a new condition not easily paralleled in history, and though it is propagated through social convention its deeper causes are not easy to divine. To put it down, as many have done, to the excesses of the Victorians, is only to show an ignorance of the generations that preceded them. Possibly it is due to the increasing indefiniteness of our beliefs and disbeliefs, to the blurring of the moral background of our lives, but such speculations would take us too far.

Whatever its cause, the fact that so many readers are afraid of free expansive emotion, even when the situation warrants it, is important. It leads them, as *Poem VIII* showed, to suspect and avoid situations that may awaken strong and simple feeling. It produces shallowness and trivial complexity in their response. And it leaves those 'sentimental' over-growths that escape the taboo too free a field for their semi-surreptitious existence. The only safe cure for a mawkish attachment to an illusory childhood heaven, for example, is to take the distorted sentiment and work it into close and living relation with some scene concretely and truthfully realised, which may act as a standard of reality and awaken the dream-infected object of the sentiment into actuality. This is the treatment by expansion, and *Poem VIII* may stand as an example of how it may be done. The other, more practised, form of treatment which we apply to sentimentalists—treatment through sneers, through 'realism', through caustics, the attempt by various means not to enlarge the canalised response, but to destroy it or dry it up—is ineffective, and may lead only to increased impoverishment. For the curse of sentimentality in the third sense is not that its victims have too much feeling at their disposal, but that they have too little, that they see life in too specialised a fashion and respond to it too narrowly. The sentimentalist, in brief, is not distributing his interest widely enough, and is distributing it in too few forms.

Chapter VII

Doctrine in Poetry

Logic is the ethics of thinking, in the sense in which ethics is the bringing to bear of self-control, for the purpose of realising our desires.

CHARLES SAUNDERS PEIRCE.

With most of our critical difficulties what we have had to explain is how mistakes come to be so frequent. But here we are in the opposite case, we have to explain how they come to be so rare. For it would seem evident that poetry which has been built upon firm and definite beliefs about the world, *The Divine Comedy* or *Paradise Lost,* or Donne's *Divine Poems*, or Shelley's *Prometheus Unbound,* or Hardy's *The Dynasts*, must appear differently to readers who do and readers who do not hold similar beliefs. Yet in fact most readers, and nearly all good readers, are very little disturbed by even a direct opposition between their own beliefs and the beliefs of the poet. Lucretius and Virgil, Euripides and Aeschylus, we currently assume, are equally accessible, given the necessary scholarship, to a Roman Catholic, to a Buddhist and to a confirmed sceptic. Equally accessible in the sense that these different readers, after due study, may respond in the same way to the poetry and arrive at similar judgments about it. And when they differ, their divergencies will commonly not be a result of their different positions with regard to the doctrines[14] of the authors, but are more likely to derive from other causes—in their temperaments and personal experience.

I have instanced religious poetry because the beliefs there concerned have the widest implications, and are the most seriously entertained of any. But the same problem arises with nearly all poetry; with mythology very evidently; with such supernatural machinery as appears in *The Rime of the Ancient Mariner:*

> The horned Moon, with one bright star
> Within the nether tip,

with Blake's manifestoes; but equally, though less obtrusively, with every passage which seems to make a statement, or depend upon an assumption, that a reader may dissent from, without thereby giving proof of mental derangement.

It is essential to recognise that the problem[15] is the same whether the possible stumbling-block, the point of dissent, be trivial or important. When the point is trivial, we easily satisfy ourselves with an explanation in terms of 'poetic fictions'. When it is a matter of no consequence whether we assent or dissent, the theory that these disputable statements, so constantly presented to us in poetry, are merely *assumptions* introduced for poetic purposes, seems an adequate explanation. And when the statements, for example, Homer's account of 'the monkey-shines of the Olympian troupe', are frankly incredible, if paraded solemnly before the bar of reasoned judgment, the same explanation applies. But as the assumptions grow more plausible, and as the consequences for our view of the world grow important, the matter seems less simple. Until, in the end, with Donne's Sonnet (*Poem III*), for example, it becomes very difficult not to think that *actual belief* in the doctrine that appears in the poem is required for its full and perfect imaginative realisation. The mere assumption of Donne's theology, as a poetic fiction, may seem insufficient in view of the intensity of the feeling which is supported and conveyed to us by its means. It is at least certain, as the protocols show (3·15, 5·42, 5·37, 5·38, 7·21), that many who try to read religious poetry find themselves strongly invited to the beliefs presented, and that doctrinal dissent is a very serious obstacle to their reading. Conversely, many successful but dissenting readers find themselves in a mental attitude towards the doctrine which, if it is not belief, closely resembles belief.

Yet if we suppose that, beyond this mere 'poetic' assumption, a definite state of belief in this particular doctrine of the Resurrection of the Body is required for a full reading of Donne's poem, great difficulties at once arise. We shall have to suppose that readers who hold different beliefs incompatible with this particular doctrine must either not be able to read the poem, or must temporarily while reading it abandon their own beliefs and adopt Donne's. Both suppositions *seem* contrary to the facts, though these are matters upon which certainty is hazardous. We shall do better, however, to examine the 'poetic fiction', or assumption, theory more closely and see whether when fully stated it is capable of meeting the complaint of inadequacy noticed above.

In the first place the very word 'assumption' is unsuitable here. Ordinarily an assumption is a proposition, an object of thought, entertained intellectually in order to trace its logical consequences as a hypothesis. But here we are concerned very little with logical consequences and almost exclusively with emotional consequences. In the effect of the thought upon our feelings and attitudes, all its importance, for poetry, lies. But there are clearly two ways in which we may entertain an assumption: intellectually, that is in a context of other thoughts ready to support, contradict, or establish other logical relations with it; and emotionally, in a context of sentiments, feelings, desires and attitudes ready to group themselves around it. Behind the intellectual assumption stands the desire for logical consistency and order in the receptive side of the mind. But behind the emotional assumption stands the desire or need for order of the whole outgoing emotional side of the personality, the side that is turned towards action.

Corresponding to this distinction there are two forms of belief and similarly two forms of disbelief. Intellectual belief more resembles a weighting of an idea than anything else, a loading[16] which makes other, less heavily weighted, ideas, adjust themselves to it rather than *vice versa*. The loading may be legitimate; the quantity of evidence, its immediacy, the extent and complexity of the supporting systems of ideas are obvious forms of legitimate loading: or it may be illegitimate; our liking for the idea, its brilliance, the trouble that changing it may involve, emotional satisfactions from it, are illegitimate—*from the standpoint of intellectual belief* be it understood. The whole use of intellectual belief is to bring *all* our ideas into as perfect an ordered system as possible. We disbelieve only because we believe something else that is incompatible, as Spinoza long ago pointed out. Similarly, we perhaps only believe because it is necessary to disbelieve whatever is logically contradictory to our belief. *Neither belief nor disbelief arises,* in this intellectual sense, *unless the logical context of our ideas is in question.* Apart from these logical connections the idea is neither believed nor disbelieved, nor doubted nor questioned; it is just present. Most of the ideas of the child, of primitive man, of the peasant, of the non-intellectual world and of most poetry are in this happy condition of real intellectual disconnection.

Emotional belief is a very different matter. In primitive man, as innumerable observers have remarked, any idea which opens a ready outlet to emotion or points to a line of action in conformity with custom is quickly believed. We remain much more primitive in this phase of our behaviour than in intellectual matters. Given a need[17] (whether conscious *as a desire* or not), any idea which can be taken as a step on the way to its fulfilment is accepted, unless some other need equally active at the moment bars it out. This acceptance, this use of the idea—by our interests, desires, feelings, attitudes, tendencies to action and what not—is emotional belief. So far as the idea is useful to them it is believed, and the sense of attachment, of adhesion, of conviction, which we feel, and to which we give the name of belief, is the result of this implication of the idea in our activities.

Most beliefs, of course, that have any strength or persistence are mixtures of intellectual and emotional belief. A purely intellectual belief need have little strength, no quality of conviction about it, for unless the idea is very original and contrary to received ideas, it needs little loading to hold its own. When we find a modern physicist, for example, passionately attached to a particular theory, we may suspect illegitimate loading, his reputation is perhaps involved in its acceptance. Conversely, a very strong emotional belief may have little persistence. Last night's revelation grows dim amid this morning's affairs, for the need which gave it such glamorous reality was only a need of the moment. Of this kind are most of the revelations received from poetry and music. But though the sense of revelation has faded, we should not suppose that the shaping influence of such experiences must be lost. The mind has found through them a pattern of response which may remain, and it is this pattern rather than the revelation which is important.

The great difference between these two kinds of belief, as I have defined them, appears most plainly if we consider what *justification* amounts to for each. Whether an intellectual belief is justified is entirely a matter of its logical place in the largest, most completely ordered, system of ideas we can attain to. Now the central, most stable, mass of our ideas has already an order and arrangement fixed for it by the facts of Nature. We must bring our ideas of these facts into correspondence with them or we promptly perish. And this order among the everyday facts of our surroundings determines the arrangement of yet another system of our ideas: namely, physical theory. These ideas are thereby weighted beyond the power of irreconcilable ideas to disturb them. Anyone who understands them cannot help believing in them, and disbelieving *intellectually* in irreconcilable ideas, provided that he brings them close enough together to perceive their irreconcilability. There are obviously countless ideas in poetry which, if put into this logical context, must be disbelieved at once.

But this intellectual disbelief does not imply that emotional belief in the same idea is either impossible or even difficult—much less that it is undesirable. For an emotional belief is not justified through any logical relations between its idea and other ideas. Its only justification is its success in meeting our needs—due regard being paid to the relative claims of our many needs one against another. It is a matter, to put it simply, of the *prudence* (in view of *all* the needs of our being) of the kind of emotional activities the belief subserves. The desirability or undesirability of an emotional belief has nothing to do with its intellectual status, provided it is kept from interfering with the intellectual system. And poetry is an extraordinarily successful device for preventing these interferences from arising.

Coleridge, when he remarked that 'a willing suspension of disbelief' accompanied much poetry, was noting an important fact, but not quite in the happiest terms, for we are neither aware of a disbelief nor voluntarily suspending it in these cases. It is better to say that the question of belief or disbelief, in the intellectual sense, never arises when we are reading well. If unfortunately it does arise, either through the poet's fault or our own, we have for the moment ceased to be reading poetry and have become astronomers, or theologians, or moralists, persons engaged in quite a different type of activity.

But a possible misconception must be noted here. The intellectual exploration of the *internal* coherence of the poem, and the intellectual examination of the relations of its ideas to other ideas of ordinary experience which are *emotionally* relevant to it, are not only permissible but necessary in the reading of much poetry, as we saw in connection with the seaharp in *Poem IX*, and in connection with the sentimentality and stock-response problems of

Poems IV, VIII and *XIII.* But this restricted intellectual inquiry is a different thing from the all-embracing attempt to systematise our ideas which alone brings up the problem of intellectual belief.

We can now turn back to *Poem III,* to the point from which this long analysis started. There are many readers who feel a difficulty in giving to Donne's theology just that kind of acceptance, *and no more,* that they give to Coleridge's 'star within the nether tip'. They feel an invitation to accord to the poem that belief in its ideas which we can hardly help supposing to have been, in Donne's mind, a powerful influence over its shaping. These readers may, perhaps, be content if we insist that the fullest possible *emotional* belief is fitting and desirable. At the same time there are many who are unable to accord *intellectual* belief to these particular theological tenets. Such readers may feel that a threatened liberty is not thereby denied them. The fact that Donne probably gave both forms of belief to these ideas need not, I think, prevent a good reader from giving the fullest emotional belief while withholding intellectual belief, or rather while not allowing the question of intellectual belief to arise. The evidence is fragmentary upon the point, largely because it has been so strangely little discussed. But the very fact that the need to discuss it has not insistently arisen—seeing how many people from how many different intellectual positions have been able to agree about the value of such doctrinal poems—points strongly in this direction. The absence of intellectual belief need not cripple emotional belief, though evidently enough in some persons it may. But the habit of attaching emotional belief only to intellectually certified ideas is strong in some people; it is encouraged by some forms of education; it is perhaps becoming, through the increased prestige of science, more common.[18] For those whom it conquers it means 'Good-bye to poetry'.

For the difficulty crops up, as I have insisted, over all poetry that departs, for its own purposes, from the most ordinary universal facts of common experience or from the most necessary deductions of scientific theory. It waylays the strict rationalist with Blake's 'Sunflower', Wordsworth's 'River Duddon', and Shelley's 'Cloud', no less than with their more transcendental utterances. Shakespeare's Lark is as shocking as his Phœnix. Even so honest a man as Gray attributes very disputable motives to his Owl. As for Dryden's 'new-kindled star', the last verse of Keats' 'Ode to Melancholy', or Landor's 'Rose Aylmer'—it is very clear where we should be with them if we could not give emotional assent apart from intellectual conviction. The slightest poetry may present the problem as clearly (though not so acutely) as the greatest. And the fact that we solve it, in practice, without the least difficulty in minor cases shows, I think, that even in the major instances of philosophic and religious issues the same solution is applicable. But the temptation to confuse the two forms of belief is there greater.

For in these cases an appearance of incompleteness or insincerity may attach to emotional acceptance divorced from intellectual assent.[19] That this is simply a mistake due to a double-meaning of 'belief' has been my contention. To 'pretend to believe' what we 'don't really believe' would certainly be insincerity, if the two kinds of believing were one and the same; but if they are not, the confusion is merely another example of the prodigious power of words over our lives. And this will be the best place to take up the uncomfortable problem of 'sincerity', a word much used in criticism, but not often with any precise definition of its meaning.

The ideas, vague and precise, for which 'sincere' stands must have been constantly in the reader's mind during our discussion both of Stock Responses and of Sentimentality. We can set aside at once the ordinary 'business' sense in which a man is insincere when he deliberately attempts to deceive, and sincere when his statements and acts are governed by 'the best of his knowledge and belief'. And we can deal briefly with another sense, already touched upon in connection with *Poem VII*, in which a man is insincere when 'he kids *himself*', when he mistakes his own motives and so professes feelings which are different from those that are in fact actuating him. Two subtle points, however, must be noted before we set this sense aside. The feelings need not be stated or even openly expressed; it is enough if they are hinted to us. And they need not be actual personal 'real, live feelings'; they may be imagined feelings. All that is required for this kind of insincerity is a discrepancy between the poem's claim upon our response and its *shaping* impulses in the poet's mind. But only the shaping impulses are relevant. A good poem can perfectly well be written for money or from pique or ambition, provided these initial external motives do not interfere with its growth. Interferences of all kinds—notably the desire to make the poem 'original', 'striking', or 'poetic'—are, of course, the usual cause of insincerity in this sense. A sense which ought not, it may be remarked, to impute blame to the author, unless we are willing to agree that all men who are not good poets are therefore blameworthy in a high degree.

These subtleties were necessary to escape the conclusion that irony, for example—where the feeling really present is often the exact contrary to that overtly professed—is as insincere as simple readers often suppose it must be.

A more troublesome problem is raised if we ask whether an emotion, by itself and apart from its expression, can be sincere or insincere. We often speak as if this were so (witness 4·2, 4·23 and 8·51), and though sometimes no doubt this is only an effective way of saying that we approve (or disapprove) of the emotion, there are senses in which a fact about the emotion, not about our feelings about it, is meant. Sincere emotions, we say, are genuine or authentic, as opposed to spurious emotions, and the several senses which we may imply thereby are worth examining. We may mean that the emotion is genuine in the sense that every product of a perfect mind would be genuine. It would result only from the prompting situation *plus* all the relevant experience of that mind, and be free from impurities and from all interferences, from impulses that had in any way got out of place and become disordered. Since such minds are nowhere obtainable in this obstructive world, such a sense is useful only as an ideal standard by which to measure degrees of relative insincerity. 'There is not a just man on earth that doeth good and sinneth not'. Some great poetry, we might say, represents the closest approach to sincerity that can be found. And for extreme degrees of insincerity we should look in asylums. Possibly however, the perfect mind, if it ever appeared among us, might be put there too.

But this is plainly not a sense of sincerity which we often use, it is not what people ordinarily mean. For we would agree that stupid people can be very sincere, though their minds may be very much in a muddle, and we might even suggest that they are more likely to be sincere than the clever. Simplicity, we may think, has something to do with sincerity, for there is a sense in which 'genuine' is opposed to 'sophisticated'. The sincere feeling, it may be suggested, is one which has been left in its natural state, not worked over and complicated by reflection. Thus strong spontaneous feelings would be more likely to be sincere than feelings that have run the gauntlet of self-criticism, and a dog, for example, might be regarded as a more sincere animal than any man.

This is certainly a sense which is frequent, though whether we should praise emotions that are sincere in this sense as much as most people do, is extremely doubtful. It is partly an echo of Rousseau's romantic fiction, the 'Natural Man'. Admiration for the 'spontaneous' and 'natural' tends to select favourable examples and turns a very blind eye to the less attractive phenomena. Moreover, many emotions which look simple and natural are nothing of the kind, they result from cultivated self-control, so consummate as to seem instantaneous. These cases, and an attractive but limited virtue in some children's behaviour, explain, I believe, the popularity of sincerity in this sense. So used, the word is of little service in criticism, for this kind of sincerity in poetry must necessarily be rare.

It will be worth while hunting a little longer for a satisfactory sense of 'sincerity'. Whatever it is, it is the quality we most insistently require in poetry. It is also the quality we most need as critics. And, perhaps, in the proportion that we possess it we shall acknowledge that it is not a quality that we can take for granted in ourselves as our inalienable birthright. It fluctuates with our state of health, with the quality of our recent companions, with our responsibility and our nearness to the object, with a score of conditions that are not easy to take account of. We can *feel* very sincere when, in fact, as others can see clearly, there is no sincerity in us. Bogus forms of the virtue waylay us— confident inner assurances and invasive rootless convictions. And when we doubt our own sincerity and ask ourselves, 'Do I *really* think so; do I really feel so?' an honest answer is not easily come by. A direct effort to be sincere, like other effects to will ourselves into action, more often than not frustrates its intention. For all these reasons any light that can be gained upon the nature of sincerity, upon possible tests for it and means for inducing and promoting it, is extremely serviceable to the critic.

The most stimulating discussion of this topic is to be found in the *Chung Yung*[20] (The Doctrine of the Mean, or Equilibrium and Harmony), the treatise that embodies the most interesting and the most puzzling part of the teachings of Confucius. A more distinct (and distinguished) word than 'stimulating' would be in place to describe this treatise, were the invigorating effect of a careful reading easier to define. Sincerity—the object of some idea that seems to lie in the territory that 'sincerity' covers—appears there as the beginning and end of personal character, the secret of the good life, the only means to good government, the means to give full development to our own natures, to give full development to the nature of others, and very much more. This virtue is as mysterious as it is powerful; and, where so many great sinologues and Chinese scholars have confessed themselves baffled, it would be absurd for one who knows no Chinese to suggest interpretations. But some speculations generated by a reading of translations may round off this chapter.

The following extracts from the *Chung Yung* seem the most relevant to our discussion.

'Sincerity is the way of Heaven. The attainment of sincerity is the way of men. He who possesses sincerity, is he who, without an effort, hits what is right, and apprehends, without the exercise of thought; he is the sage who naturally and easily embodies the right way. He who attains to sincerity, is he who chooses what is good, and firmly holds it fast' (Legge, XX, 18). 'Sincerity is that whereby self-completion is effected, and its way is that by which man must direct himself' (Legge, XXV, 1). 'In self-completion the superior man completes other men and things also . . . and this is the way by which a union is effected of the external and the internal' (XXV, 3). 'In the Book of Poetry, it is said, "In hewing an axe-handle, in hewing an axe-handle, the pattern is not far off". We grasp one axe-handle to hew the other, and yet, if we look askance from the one to the other, we may consider them as apart' (XIII, 2). 'There is a way to the attainment of sincerity in one's self; if a man does not understand what is good, he will not attain sincerity in himself' (XX, 17). 'When we have intelligence resulting from sincerity, this condition is to be ascribed to nature; when we have sincerity resulting from intelligence, this condition is to be ascribed to instruction. But given the sincerity, there shall be the intelligence, given the intelligence there shall be the sincerity' (XXI). How far apart any detailed precise exposition in English, or in any modern Western language, must be from the form of thought of the original, is shown if we compare a more literal version of this last passage: 'Being true begets light, we call that nature. Light leads to being true, we call that teaching. What is true grows light; what is light grows true' (Lyall and King Chien-Kün, p. 16).

Meditating upon this chain of pronouncements we can perhaps construct (or discover) another sense of sincerity. One important enough to justify the stress so often laid upon this quality by critics, yet not compelling us to require an impossible perfection or inviting us to sentimental (Sense 3) indiscriminate over-admiration of the ebullitions of infants. And it may be possible, by apprehending this sense more clearly, to see what general conditions will encourage sincerity and what steps may be suggested to promote this mysterious but necessary virtue in the critic.

We may take self-completion as our starting-point. The completed mind would be that perfect mind we envisaged above, in which no disorder, no mutual frustration of impulses remained. Let us suppose that in the irremediable default of this perfection, default due to man's innate constitution and to the accidents to which he is exposed, there exists *a tendency towards increased order,*[21] a tendency which takes effect unless baffled by physical interferences (disease) or by fixations of habit that prevent us from continuing to learn by experience, or by ideas too invested with emotion for other ideas that disturb them to be formed, or by too lax and volatile a bond between our interests (a frivolousness that is perhaps due to the draining off of energy elsewhere) so that no formations firm enough to build upon result.

There is much to be said in favour of such a supposition. This tendency would be a need, in the sense defined above in this chapter—deriving in fact from *the* fundamental imbalance[22] to which biological development may be supposed to be due. This development with man (and his animal neighbours) seems to be predominantly in the direction of greater complexity and finer differentiation of responses. And it is easy to conceive the organism as relieving, through this differentiation, the strain put upon it by life in a partly uncongenial environment. It is but a step further to conceive it as also tending to relieve internal strains due to these developments imposed from without. And a reordering of its impulses so as to reduce their interferences with one another to a minimum would be the most successful—and the 'natural'—direction which this tendency would take.

Such a re-ordering would be a partial self-completion, temporary and provisional upon the external world remaining for the individual much what it had been in the past. And by such self-completion the superior man *would* 'effect a union of the external and the internal'. Being more at one within itself the mind thereby becomes more appropriately responsive to the outer world. I am not suggesting that this is what Confucius meant. For him 'to complete other men and things too', is possibly the prerogative of the force of example, other men merely imitating the conduct of the sage. But he *may* have meant that freedom calls out freedom; that those who are 'most themselves' cause others about them to become also 'more themselves'; which would, perhaps, be a more sagacious observation. Perhaps, too, 'the union of the external and the internal' meant for him something different from the accordance of our thoughts and feelings with reality. But certainly, for us, this accordance is one of the fruits of sincerity.

This tendency towards a more perfect order, as it takes effect, 'enables us, without effort, to hit what is right, and, without the exercise of thought, to apprehend'. The 'exercise of thought' here must be understood as that process of deliberately setting aside inappropriate ideas and feelings, which, in default of a sufficient inner order—a sufficient sincerity—is still very necessary. Confucius has enough to say elsewhere in the *Chung Yung* (Ch. XX, 20) of the need for unremitting research and reflection *before* sincerity is attained to clear himself from any charge of recommending 'intuition' as an *alternative* to investigation. 'Intuition' is the prerogative only of those who have attained to sincerity. It is only the superior man who 'naturally and easily embodies the right way'. And the superior man will know when his sincerity is insufficient and take ceaseless steps to remedy it. 'If another man (more sincere) succeed by one effort, *he* will use a hundred efforts. If another man succeed by ten efforts, he will use a thousand' (*Chung Yung*, XX, 20). It is the sincerity to which the superior man has already attained which enables him to know when it is insufficient; if it does not yet enable him to embody the right way, it at least enables him to refrain from embodying the wrong, as those who trust intuition too soon are likely to do. Indeed, looking back over the history of thought, we might say, 'are certain to do', so heavy are the probabilities against the success of guess-work.

Sincerity, then, in this sense, is obedience to that tendency which 'seeks' a more perfect order within the mind. When the tendency is frustrated (e.g., by fatigue or by an idea or feeling that has lost its link with experience, or has become fixed beyond the possibility of change) we have insincerity. When confusion reigns and we are unable to decide what we think or feel (to be distinguished sharply from the case when *decided* thoughts or feelings are present, but we are unable to define or express them) we need be neither sincere nor insincere. We are in a transitional stage which may result in either. Most good critics will confess to themselves that this is the state in which a first reading of any poem of an unfamiliar type leaves them. They know that more study is needed if they are to achieve a genuine response, and they know this in virtue of the sincerity they have already attained. It follows that people with clear definite ideas and feelings, with a high degree of practical efficiency, may be insincere in this sense. Other kinds of sincerity, fidelity to convictions for example, will not save them, and indeed it may well be this fidelity which is thwarting the life of the spirit (*Chung Yung,* XXIV) in them.

Any response (however mistaken from other points of view) which embodies the present activity of this tendency to inner adjustment will be sincere, and any response that conflicts with it or inhibits it will be insincere. Thus to be sincere is to act, feel and think in accordance with 'one's true nature', and to be insincere is to act, feel or think in a contrary manner. But the sense to be given to 'one's true nature' is, as we have seen, a matter largely conjectural. To define it more exactly would perhaps be tedious and, for our purposes here, needless. In practice we often seem to grasp it very clearly; and all that I have attempted here is to sketch the state of affairs which we then seem to grasp. 'What heaven has conferred is man's Nature; an accordance with this is the Path' (*Chung Yung,* I). Sometimes we can be certain that we have left it.[23]

On the ways in which sincerity may be increased and extended Confucius is very definite. If we seek a standard for a new response whose sincerity may be in doubt, we shall find it, he says, in the very responses which make the new one possible. The pattern for the new axe-handle is already in our hand, though its very nearness, our firm possession of it, may hide it from us. We need, of course, a founded assurance of the sincerity of these instrumental responses themselves, and this we can gain by comparison. What is meant by 'making the thoughts sincere' is the allowing no self-deception, '*as when we hate a bad smell,* and as when we love what is beautiful' (*The Great Learning,* VI, i). When we hate a bad smell we can have no doubt that our response is sincere. We can all, at least, find *some* responses beyond suspicion. These are our standard. By studying our sincerity in the fields in which we are fully competent we can extend it into the fields in which our ability is still feeling its way. This seems to be the meaning of 'choosing what is good and firmly holding fast to it,' where 'good' stands not for our Western ethical notion so much as for the fit and proper, sane and healthy. The man who does not 'hate a bad smell' 'does not understand what is good'; having no basis or standards, 'he will not attain to sincerity'.

Together with these, the simplest most definite responses, there may be suggested also, as standards for sincerity, the responses we make to the most baffling objects that can be presented to our consciousness. Something like a technique or ritual for heightening sincerity might well be worked out. When our response to a poem after our best efforts remains uncertain, when we are unsure whether the feelings it excites come from a deep source in our experience, whether our liking or disliking is genuine, is *ours,* or an accident of fashion, a response to surface detail or to essentials, we may perhaps help ourselves by considering it in a frame of feelings whose sincerity is beyond our questioning. Such are the feelings that may be aroused by contemplation of the following:

i.   Man's loneliness (the isolation of the human situation).
ii. The facts of birth, and of death, in their inexplicable oddity.
iii. The inconceivable immensity of the Universe.
iv. Man's place in the perspective of time.
v.   The enormity of his ignorance.

Taking these not as targets for doctrine, but as the most incomprehensible and inexhaustible objects for meditation, while their reverberation lasts pass the poem through the mind, silently reciting it as slowly as it allows. Whether what it can stir in us is important or not to us will, perhaps, show itself then. Many religious exercises and some of the practices of divination and magic may be thought to be directed in part towards a similar quest for sanction, to be rituals designed to provide standards of sincerity.

NOTES

1. Relatively, or technically, 'passive' only; a fact that our protocols will help us not to forget. The reception (or interpretation) of a meaning is an activity, which may go astray; in fact, there is always some degree of loss and distortion in transmission.

2. Under 'Feeling' I group for convenience the whole conative-affective aspect of life—emotions, emotional attitudes, the will, desire, pleasure-unpleasure, and the rest. 'Feeling' is shorthand for any or all of this.

3. The ticklish point is, of course, the implication that the speaker believes in the 'facts'—not only as powerful arguments but *as facts*. 'Belief' here has to do with Function 2, and, as such examples suggest, is also a word with several senses, at least as many as attach to the somewhat analogous word 'love'. Some separation and

ventilation of them, beyond that attempted in Ch. VII below, is very desirable, and I hope to explore this subject in a future work.

4. I am not assuming that the poet is conscious of any distinction between his means and his ends.

5. I use the word 'rhythm' here in the very wide sense of a repetitive configuration, i.e., a group of groups such that the several constituent groups are similar to one another, though not necessarily exactly similar. Elsewhere (in *Principles of Literary Criticism*, Ch. XVII) I have used the word in a quite different sense, namely, for that dependence of part upon part within a whole which derives from expectation and foresight. This last is not, perhaps, the most natural use of the word, but this dependence is, I think, what many people who discuss, for example, the rhythm of prose, rhythm in pictures, or rhythm in golf, have in mind; if so, the use is justified. The sense here used, on the other hand, allows us to speak of the movements of the planets as being rhythmical apart from any mind which observes them.

6. Not, of course, a simple, direct similarity of rhythm; but some order or regularity, some relevant peculiar property.

7. Projected in the sense that our pleasure is projected when we describe someone as 'pleasant' (to be distinguished from 'pleasing') or ugly (to be distinguished from 'causing a loathing'). A clear indication that this projection occurs in apprehending rhythm is the fact that we can give several alternative rhythms to a simple series of stimuli, such as a metronome-beat or the ticking of a clock. Many other facts of experiment and observation might be brought to support this conclusion.

8. I am aware that all such experiments are invalidated by the fact that *some* difference in vowel and consonantal sounds is introduced, and so the balance of the inherent rhythm is to some degree disturbed, but though not persuasive, these experiments seem to me instructive.

9. Very unfortunately most of the gramophone records yet available must be described as exceedingly bad in both senses. They would justify in a sensitive child a permanent aversion from poetry. And less sensitive children may pick up habits of 'sentimentalisation', 'emotionality' and exaggeration, very difficult to cure. Some of Mr Drinkwater's records, however, point in a better direction and deserve honourable mention.

10. Partly because movements of the organs of speech (with muscular and tactile images of them) enter into the ascribed *sound* of words almost as much as auditory sensations and images themselves.

11. Not, of course, an excess in the feeling ascribed to the girl, but an excess of the author's sympathetic emotion or of our sympathetic emotion.

12. It may also be suggested that the phrase 'life lies dead' is possibly an echo of Swinburne's 'A Forsaken Garden'.

13. I am not recommending nearness, concreteness and coherence as specifics for the avoidance of sentimentality. All depends upon what it is that is brought near, what is concrete and what coheres.

14. I am not accusing these authors of doctrinal poetry in the narrow sense of verse whose sole object is to teach. But that a body of doctrine is presented by each of these poets, even by Virgil, can hardly escape any reader's notice.

15. A supplementary and fuller discussion of this whole matter will be found in *Principles of Literary Criticism*, Ch. XXXII–XXXV, where difficulties, which here must be passed by, are treated in detail.

16. To introspection this loading seems like a feeling of trust—or trustworthiness. We 'side' with the belief intellectually, and though traditionally belief has been

discussed along with judgment it is, as William James pointed out, more allied to choice.

17. I use 'need' here to stand for an imbalance mental or physical, a tendency, given suitable conditions, for a movement towards an end-state of equilibrium. A swinging pendulum might thus be said to be actuated by a need to come to rest, and to constantly overdo its movements towards that end. We are much more like pendulums than we think, though, of course, our imbalances are infinitely more intricate.

18. I have discussed this danger at length in *Science and Poetry*. There is reason to think that poetry has often arisen through fusion (or confusion) between the two forms of belief, the boundary between what is intellectually certified and what is not being much less sharply defined in former centuries and *defined in another manner*. The standard of *verification* used in science to-day is comparatively a new thing. As the scientific view of the world (including our own nature) develops, we shall probably be forced into making a division between fact and fiction that, unless we can meet it with a twofold theory of belief on the lines suggested above, would be fatal not only to poetry but to all our finer, more spiritual, responses. That is the problem.

19. The most important example of this divorce that history provides is in the attitude of Confucius towards ancestor-worship. Here are the remarks of his chief English translator, James Legge, upon the matter. 'It will not be supposed that I wish to advocate or defend the practice of sacrificing to the dead. My object has been to point out how Confucius recognised it, without acknowledging the faith from which it must have originated, and how he enforced it as a matter of form or ceremony. It thus connects itself with the most serious charge that can be brought against him—the charge of insincerity', *The Chinese Classics*, Vol. 1, Prolegomena, Ch. V, p. 100. How far Legge was qualified to expound the Confucian doctrine of sincerity may perhaps be divined from this passage.

20. As might be expected, no translation that entirely commends itself is available. Those to whom Legge's edition of *The Chinese Classics*, Vol. 1, is not available, may consult the translation by L. A. Lyall and King Chien Kün, *The Chung Yung or The Centre, the Common* (Longmans), very literal, but perhaps slightly too much tinctured with a Y.M.C.A. flavour. Here what is translated by others 'sincerity' or 'singleness' is rendered by 'to be true' and 'being true'.

21. I have in several other places made prolonged and determined efforts to indicate the types of mental order I have in mind (*The Foundations of Æsthetics*, § XIV; *Principles of Literary Criticism*, Ch. XXII; *Science and Poetry*, § II), but without escaping certain large misunderstandings that I had hoped to have guarded myself against. Thus Mr Eliot, reviewing *Science and Poetry* in *The Dial*, describes my ideal order as 'Efficiency, a perfectly-working mental Roneo Steel Cabinet System', and Mr Read performing a similar service for *Principles* in *The Criterion*, seemed to understand that where I spoke of 'the organisation of impulses' I meant that kind of deliberate planning and arrangement which the controllers of a good railway or large shop must carry out. But 'organisation' for me stood for that kind of interdependence of parts which we allude to when we speak of living things as 'organisms'; and the 'order' which I make out to be so important is not tidiness. The distinguished names cited in this foot-note will protect the reader from a sense that these explanations are insulting to his intelligence. A good idea of some of the possibilities of order and disorder in the mind may be gained from Pavlov's *Conditioned Reflexes*.

22. Whether we can profitably posit a primal imbalance in certain forms of matter for which the appearance of living substances and their development in increasingly complex forms right up to Shakespeare would be, as it were, the swings of the

pendulum 'attempting' to come to rest again, is a speculation that has perhaps only an amusement value. The great difficulty would be to get round the separation of the reproductive functions, but that is a difficulty for any cosmologist.

23. But see *Chung Yung,* I, 2. 'The path may not be left for an instant. If it could be left, it would not be the path.' Possibly we can escape this difficulty by admitting that all mental activities are, to some degree, the operation of the tendency we have been speaking of. Thus all are the Path. But the Path can be obstructed, and may have loops. 'The regulation of (what keeps trim) the path is instruction' (*Chung Yung,* I, 1).

Victor Shklovsky

1893–1984

Victor Borisovich Shklovsky, one of the founders and theorists of the Formalist method in literary analysis, was born on January 12/24, 1893. He studied philology at the University of St. Petersburg, where he became close to the Futurist group. His first published work was an inflammatory brochure called *The Resurrection of the Word* (1914), in which the student called for learning the principles of literature by turning to their foundation—the written word itself. With its appearance, a group of other young philologists, including Boris Eikhenbaum, Osip Brik, Roman Jakobson, Yuri Tynianov, Lev Iakubinskii, and Evgenii Polianov, grouped themselves around him to form *OPOIAZ,* or the Society for the Study of Poetic Language, which became the center of Russian Formalism for the length of its existence.

The main target of the Formalists was the Symbolist generation that had preceded them. Reacting against intuitionism, biographic impressionism, and cultural-historical approaches that ignored the particular features of art, the Formalists attempted to rescue the work of art by examining it on its own terms, according to its own laws and languages. To transcend the perceived dualism of form and content, the Formalists proposed a new relationship of the elements of an artwork: material (something prior to the artist) and form (the way the material is arranged in the work). Where the previous scholarly approach to literature had reduced form to a matter of style or randomly chosen elements, Shklovsky, Eikhenbaum, and the rest of the Formalists broadened the notion of form to include the presentation of the artistic material as a whole.

Throughout the late teens and twenties Shklovsky articulated the Formalist approach for a virtually inexhaustible range of topics. He was the link between Futurism and Formalism; his essay on "Poetry and Trans-Sense Language" was the first systematic examination of the idea that poetry rested not on the meaning of the words or images it contained but on the rhythms and sound of the words themselves. Against Alexander Veselovsky's earlier formula that a new form appears in order to express a new content, Shklovsky measured a work of art exclusively in terms of its predecessors, so that "a new form appears not in order to express a new content but in order to replace an old form which has already lost its artistry." In his preface to *On the Theory of Prose* (1925), a collection of his most important work, Shklovsky summed up his approach with a topical metaphor. "Within the theory of literature," he wrote, "I work with investigating its inner laws. If one should draw an analogy with a factory, I am interested not in the state of the world cotton market, not in the politics of trusts, but only in the types of the yarn and in the means of weaving them. This is why the entire book is dedicated wholly to the question of changes in literary forms."

Examining works of art—specifically works of literature—from their formal and structural aspects was a much-needed corrective to the prevailing emphasis on subjective aesthetic and philosophical-religious theories. Formalism cut through the cloudy aspects of Symbolism, restoring the primacy of the word as such. It also broke the traditional scholarly approach of concentrating on the meaning of a work, considering form either a matter for specialists alone or simply uninteresting. As a result, instead of the critical and scholarly emphasis on psychology, aesthetics, or cultural history, the methods of the *OPOIAZ* Formalists often approached those of linguists in their neutrality toward the quality of the work in question—hence their attention to Sherlock Holmes and O. Henry as well as *Tristram Shandy* and Nikolai Gogol. To Shklovsky and the rest of the Formalists, literature was a unique social phenomenon, and they were interested in second-rate or "mass" literature insofar as it affected the evolutionary process of art: as individual historical facts in themselves, these works did not matter in the least.

Throughout the 1920s the Soviet government attacked the Formalists for their perceived hostility to proletarian literature, and Shklovsky gradually shifted his emphasis to fiction and film criticism. The former include the autobiographical *Sentimental Journey* (1923), *Zoo: Letters Not about Love; or, The Third Heloise* (1923), and *Hamburg Account* (1928). His definitive break with Formalism came with his article, "Monument to a Scholarly Error" (1930), when he began to treat literature from a broad sociohistorical viewpoint. From then on, Shklovsky worked on the historical relations between literature and society, concentrating on the Russian classics. Works from this period include *Artistic Prose* (1959), *Stories about Prose* (1966), and *The Bowstring: On the Division of the Similar* (1970). He also continued to write film theory and biographies of major Soviet film directors, including Sergei Eisenstein, L. V. Kuleshov, A. P. Dovzhenko, and Dziga Vertov. Shklovsky was awarded the Order of the Red Banner of Labor. He died at the age of ninety-one in December 1984.

On "Tristram Shandy"

In this essay I do not propose to analyze Laurence Sterne's novel, but rather to illustrate general laws of plot. Formalistically, Sterne was an extreme revolutionary; it was characteristic of him to "lay bare" his technique. The artistic form is presented simply as such, without any kind of motivation. The difference between a novel by Sterne and the ordinary kind of novel is exactly that between ordinary poetry with its phonetic instrumentation and the poetry of the Futurists, written in obscure language. Yet nothing much is written about Sterne any more; or, if it is, it consists only of a few banalities.

The first impression upon taking up Sterne's *Tristram Shandy* and beginning to read it is one of chaos. The action is continually interrupted; the author repeatedly goes backward or leaps forward; whole ten-page passages are filled with whimsical discussions about fortifications or about the influence of a person's nose or name on his character. Such digressions are unrelated to the basic narrative.

Although the beginning of the book has the tone of an autobiography, it drifts into a description of the hero's ancestors. In fact, the hero's birth is long delayed by the irrelevant material squeezed into the novel. The description of a single day takes up much of the book; I quote Sterne himself:

> I will not finish that sentence till I have made an observation upon the strange state of affairs between the reader and myself, just as things stand at present—an observation never applicable before to any one biographical writer since the creation of the world, but to myself—and I believe will never hold good to any other, until its final destruction—and therefore, for the very novelty of it alone, it must be worth your worships attending to.
>
> I am this month one whole year older than I was this time twelvemonth; and having got, as you perceive, almost into the middle of my fourth volume—and no farther than to my first day's life—'tis demonstrative that I have three hundred and sixty-four days more life to write just now, than when I first set out; so that instead of advancing, as a common writer, in my work with what I have been doing at it—on the contrary, I am just thrown so many volumes back—[pp. 285–286].

But when you begin to examine the structure of the book, you see first of all that the disorder is intentional and, in this case, poetic. It is strictly regulated, like a picture by Picasso. Everything in the book is displaced; everything is transposed. The dedication occurs on page 15, contrary to the three basic requirements of content, form, and place. Nor is the Preface in its usual position. It takes up approximately a quire, not at the beginning of the book but rather in Volume III, Chapter 20, pages 192 through 203. Sterne justifies the Preface in this way: "All my heroes are off my hands;—'tis the first time I have had a moment to spare,—and I'll make use of it, and write my preface" (p. 192). The Preface contains, of course, as many entanglements as ingenuity permits. But the most radical of the displacements is the transposition of entire chapters (Chapters 18 and 19 of Volume IX are placed after Chapter 25). Sterne justifies the transposition so: "All I wish is, that it may be a lesson to the world, *'to let people tell their stories their own way'*" (p. 633).

But this transposition of chapters reveals another of Sterne's basic techniques—that of impeding the flow of the action. In the beginning, Sterne introduces an anecdote about an act of sexual intercourse interrupted by a woman's question (p. 5). Here is how the anecdote is brought in. Tristram Shandy's mother sleeps with his father only on the first Sunday of each month and on precisely that evening Mr. Shandy winds the clock in order to get both of these domestic duties "out of the way at one time, and be no more plagued and pester'd with them the rest of the month" (p. 8). As a result, an unavoidable association has formed in his wife's mind, so that she "could never hear the said clock wound up,—but the thoughts of some other things unavoidably popp'd into her head,—& *vice versa*" (p. 9). Here is the exact question with which Tristram's mother interrupted the activity of his father: "*Pray, my dear,* . . . *have you not forgot to wind up the clock?*" (p. 5).

This anecdote is introduced into the work first by a general comment upon the inattentiveness of the parents (pp. 4–5), then by the mother's question, the context of which we do not yet know. At first we think she had merely interrupted the father's conversation. Sterne plays with our error:

> *Good G——!* cried my father, making an exclamation, but taking care to moderate his voice at the same time,—*Did ever woman, since the creation of the world, interrupt a man with such a silly question?* Pray, what was your father saying?—Nothing [p. 5].

Then his remarks about the homunculus (fetus) are spiced with anecdotal references to its right to legal defense (pp. 5–6). Only on pages 8 through 9 do we get an explanation of this whole passage and a description of the odd punctiliousness of the father in his family affairs.

Thus, from the very beginning, we find displacement of time in *Tristram Shandy*. The causes follow the consequences, and the author himself prepares the groundwork for erroneous assumptions. This is one of Sterne's characteristic techniques. The quibbling about the coitus motif itself, related to a definite day and referring back to what has already happened in the novel, reappears from time to time and ties together the various sections of this masterfully constructed and unusually complicated work.

If we visualize the digressions schematically, they will appear as cones representing an event, with the apex representing the causes. In an ordinary novel such a cone is joined to the main story line at its apex; in *Tristram Shandy* the base of the cone is joined to the main story line, so that all at once we fall into a swarm of allusions.

As we know, this same technique occurs in one of Andrey Bely's last novels, *Kotik Latayev;* it is motivated by the fact that the novel shows the formation of a world from chaos. Out of the swarming mass appears an established order, with layers of puns on the names of the substances in the order stratifying and giving form to the mass.

Such time shifts occur often enough in the poetics of the novel. Consider, for example, the time shift in [Turgenev's] *A Nest of Gentlefolk* (the shift is motivated by Lavertsky's reminiscence) or in [Goncharov's] "The Dream of Oblomov." In Gogol's *Dead Souls* no reasons are given for the time shifts (back to Chichikov's childhood and Tentetnikov's upbringing). Sterne, however, spread the technique throughout the entire work.

Exposition, preparation for a new character, always occurs after we have paused in perplexity over a strange word or an exclamation from that character. Here we have the exposure of the technique. In *Tales of Belkin*—in "The Shot," for example—Pushkin made extensive use of time shifts. In "The Shot" we first see Silvio practicing his marksmanship; next we hear Silvio's story about the unfinished duel; then we meet the Count, Silvio's enemy, and learn the outcome of the story. The parts are in a II–I–III order, and we see a reason for the shift; Sterne, however, simply lays bare the technique.

As I have said already, Sterne thought such [aesthetic] motivation an end in itself. He wrote:

> What I have to inform you, comes, I own, a little out of its due course;—for it should have been told a hundred and fifty pages ago, but that I foresaw then 'twould come in pat hereafter, and be of more advantage here than elsewhere [p. 144].

Sterne even lays bare the technique of combining separate story lines to make up the novel. In general, he accentuates the very structure of the novel. By violating the form, he forces us to attend to it; and, for him, this awareness of the form through its violation constitutes the content of the novel.

In my little book on *Don Quixote*, I have already noted several conventional methods of splicing story lines to form a novel. Sterne used still other methods or, using an old one, did not hide its conventionality but rather thrust it out protrudingly and toyed with it. In an ordinary novel digressions are cut off by a return to the main story. If there are two, or only a few, story lines in the novel, their fragments alternate with one another—as in *Don Quixote,* where the scenes showing the adventures of the knight in the court of the Duke alternate with scenes depicting the governorship of Sancho Panza. Zielinski notes something entirely different in Homer. Homer never shows two simultaneous actions. If by force of circumstances they ever had to be simultaneous, they were reported as happening in sequence. Only the activity of one character and the "standing pat" (that is, the inactivity) of another can occur simultaneously. Sterne allowed actions to occur simultaneously, and he even parodied the development of the story line and the instrusions of the new material into it.

The description of Tristram Shandy's birth is the subject of the story line developed in the first part. The topic covers 203 pages, which nevertheless contain almost nothing about the actual birth of Tristram Shandy. For the most part, they deal with the conversation between the hero's father and his uncle Toby. Here is how the development takes place:

> —I wonder what's all that noise, and running backwards and forwards for, above stairs, quoth my father, addressing himself, after an hour and a half's silence, to my uncle *Toby*,—who you must know, was sitting on the opposite side of the fire, smoking his social pipe all the time, in mute contemplation of a new pair of black-plush-breeches which he had got on;—What can they be doing brother? quoth my father,—we can scarce hear ourselves talk.
>
> I think, replied my uncle *Toby*, taking his pipe from his mouth, and striking the head of it two or three times upon the nail of his left thumb, as he began his sentence,—I think, says he:—But to enter rightly into my uncle *Toby's* sentiments upon this matter, you must be made to enter first a little into his character, the out-lines of which I shall just give you, and then the dialogue between him and my father will go on as well again [p. 63].

Then begins a discussion of inconstancy so whimsical that it would have to be quoted to be communicated properly. On page 65 Sterne remembers, "But I forget my uncle *Toby*, whom all this while we have left knocking the ashes out of his tobacco pipe." Then begins a sketch of Uncle Toby into which the story of Aunt Dinah is inserted. On page 72, Sterne remembers: "I was just going, for example, to have given you the great out-lines of my uncle *Toby's* most whimsical character;—when my aunt *Dinah* and the coachman came a-cross us, and led us a vagary. . . ." Unfortunately, I cannot include everything Sterne has written, so I shall continue with a large omission:

> from the beginning of this, you see, I have constructed the main work and the adventitious parts of it with such intersections, and have so complicated and involved the digressive and progressive movements, one wheel within another, that the whole machine, in general, has been kept a-going;—and, what's more, it shall be kept a-going these forty years, if it pleases the fountain of health to bless me so long with life and good spirits [pp. 73–74].

So ends Chapter 22; Chapter 23 continues: "I have a strong propensity in me to begin this chapter very nonsensically, and I will not balk my fancy.—Accordingly I set off thus." And new digressions are in store for us. On page 77 there is a further reminder: "If I was not morally sure that the reader must be out of all patience for my uncle *Toby's* character, . . ." and further down the page we find a description of Uncle Toby's "Hobby-Horse," his mania. It seems that Uncle Toby, wounded in the groin at the siege of Namur, was drawn into the erection of toy fortifications. Finally, on page 99, Uncle Toby can finish the activity he began on page 63:

> I think, replied my uncle *Toby,*—taking, as I told you, his pipe from his mouth, and striking the ashes out of it as he began his sentence;—I think, replied he,—it would not be amiss, brother, if we rung the bell.

Sterne repeatedly resorts to this technique; and, as we see from his facetious reminders about Uncle Toby, not only is he fully aware of the exaggerations in his use of it, but he even enjoys playing around with it.

This manner of development, as I have already noted, is the characteristic pattern of Sterne's work. For example, on page 144, uncle Toby says, "I wish, . . . you had seen what prodigious armies we had in *Flanders.*" Further on, the material about the mania of Tristram's father begins to develop. In fact, Tristram's father has attached to himself the following manias: on the harmful influence of the pressure brought to bear on the head of an infant when a woman experiences labor pains (pp. 149–154), on the influence of a man's name upon his character (a motif developed in great detail), and on the influence of the size of a man's nose on his potential greatness (this motif is developed in an unusually ostentatious way, approximately from page 217, when, after a short break, curious stories about noseology begin to develop). The Tale of Slawkenbergius is especially remarkable; Tristram's father knows ten decades of ten tales each, all with stories about Slawkenbergius. The development of the noseology ends on page 272.

Mr. Shandy's other manias also play a part in this particular development—that is, Sterne sidetracks our attention to talk about them.

The main story resumes on page 157:

> —"*I wish,* Dr. *Slop,*" quoth my uncle *Toby* (repeating his wish for Dr. *Slop* a second time, and with a degree of more zeal and earnestness in his manner of wishing, than he had wished it at first)—"*I wish,* Dr. *Slop,*" quoth my uncle *Toby,* "*you had seen what prodigious armies we had in Flanders.*"

Once again the expansion of the material interrupts. And on page 163: "What prodigious armies you had in *Flanders!*" In Sterne, conscious exaggeration of the expansion frequently occurs without the use of a transitional sentence.

> The moment my father got up into his chamber, he threw himself prostrate across his bed in the wildest disorder imaginable, but at the same time, in the most lamentable attitude of a man borne down with sorrows, that ever the eye of pity dropp'd a tear for [pp. 215–216].

An exact description of his posture follows; such descriptions are very characteristic of Sterne:

> The palm of his right hand, as he fell upon the bed, receiving his forehead, and covering the greatest part of both his eyes, gently sunk down with his head (his elbow giving way backwards) till his nose

touch'd the quilt;—his left arm hung insensible over the side of the bed, his knuckles reclining upon the handle of the chamber pot, which peep'd out beyond the valance,—his right leg (his left being drawn up towards his body) hung half over the side of the bed, the edge of it pressing upon his shin-bone.

Mr. Shandy's despondency is brought on by the fact that the bridge of his son's nose had been crushed by the obstetrical tongs during delivery and, as I have already said, an entire literary cycle on noses follows. On page 273 we finally return to the man we left lying on the bed:

My father lay stretched across the bed as still as if the hand of death had pushed him down, for a full hour and a half, before he began to play upon the floor with the toe of that foot which hung over the bed-side.

I cannot help saying a few words in general about the postures we find in Sterne. The first to introduce the description of postures into the novel, he always portrayed them strangely—or, more exactly, he defamiliarized them. I shall cite an example: "Brother *Toby*, replied my father, taking his wig from off his head with his right hand, and with his *left* pulling a striped *India* handkerchief from his right coat pocket, . . ." (p. 158). I go directly to page 159:

It was not an easy matter in any king's reign, (unless you were as lean a subject as myself) to have forced your hand diagonally, quite across your whole body, so as to gain the bottom of your opposite coat-pocket.

The method of portraying postures passed from Sterne to Leo Tolstoy, who used it more flexibly and with psychological motivation.

I now return to Sterne's technique of plot development with several examples which clearly establish the fact that awareness of form constitutes the subject matter of the novel.

What a chapter of chances, said my father, turning himself about upon the first landing, as he and my uncle *Toby* were going down stairs—what a long chapter of chances do the events of this world lay open to us! [p. 279].

(Then follows a discussion containing an erotic element which I shall say more about later.)

Is it not a shame to make two chapters of what passed in going down one pair of stairs? for we are got no farther yet than to the first landing, and there are fifteen more steps down to the bottom; and for aught I know, as my father and my uncle *Toby* are in a talking humour, there may be as many chapters as steps [p. 281].

Sterne devotes all of this chapter to a discussion of chapters.

The next chapter begins: "We shall bring all things to rights, said my father, setting his foot upon the first step from the landing—" (p. 283). And the next: "And how does your mistress? cried my father, taking the same step over again from the landing, . . ." (p. 284). And the next:

> Holla!—you chairman!—here's sixpence—do step into that book-seller's shop, and call me a *day-tall* critick. I am very willing to give any one of 'em a crown to help me with his tackling, to get my father and my uncle *Toby* off the stairs, and to put them to bed. . . .
>
> I am this month one whole year older than I was this time twelve-month; and having got, as you perceive, almost into the middle of my fourth volume—and no farther than to my first day's life—'tis demonstrative that I have three hundred and sixty-four days more to write just now, than when I first set out; so that instead of advancing, as a common writer, in my work with what I have been doing at it—on the contrary, I am just thrown so many volumes back—[pp. 285–286].

The conventionality of this organization of the form is reminiscent of those octaves and sonnets filled with the description of how they were composed.

Here is one last example of such expansion in Sterne:

> My mother was going very gingerly in the dark along the passage which led to the parlour, as my uncle *Toby* pronounced the word *wife*.—'Tis a shrill, penetrating sound of itself, and *Obadiah* had helped it by leaving the door a little a-jar, so that my mother heard enough of it, to imagine herself the subject of the conversation: so laying the edge of her finger across her two lips—holding in her breath, and bending her head a little downwards, with a twist of her neck—(not towards the door, but from it, by which means her ear was brought to the chink)—she listened with all her powers:—the listening slave, with the Goddess of Silence at his back, could not have given a finer thought for an intaglio.
>
> In this attitude I am determined to let her stand for five minutes: till I bring up the affairs of the kitchen (as *Rapin* does those of the church) to the same period [pp. 357–358].

And on page 367: "I am a *Turk* if I had not as much forgot my mother, as if Nature had plaistered me up, and set me down naked upon the banks of the river Nile, . . ." But there is another digression even after this reminder. The reminder is necessary merely to renew our awareness of the "forgotten mother" in order to prevent the impression of the expansion from fading.

At last, on page 370, the mother shifts her position: "Then, cried my mother, opening the door, . . ."

In this case Sterne expands the material by including a second parallel story; in such cases in novels, ordinary time is usually thought to be suspended, or at least not considered, as opposed to showing the passage of time by explicit appeals to our reason. Shakespeare used his interpolated scenes to suspend time—that is, to divert attention from the normal flow of time; and even if the entire inserted dialogue (invariably with new characters) continued only a few minutes, Shakespeare felt it permissible to carry on the action as if hours or even a whole night had gone by. (We assume that curtains were not lowered, for it is very likely that curtains were not used in the Shakespearean theater because of the projecting stage.) Sterne, by repeatedly mentioning and reminding us of the fact that the mother has been standing in a stooped position for the whole time, forces us to notice his handling of it.

It is interesting, in a general way, to study the role time plays in Sterne's works. "Literary time" is clearly arbitrary; its laws do not coincide with the laws of ordinary time. If one studies, for example, the numerous tales and events concentrated in *Don Quixote,* he will see that the beginning of day and the beginning of night play no compositional role in the sequence of events—that, in general, the slow, lingering passage of the day does not exist. L'Abbé Prévost narrates *Manon Lescaut* in precisely the same way. Chevalier des Grieux tells the whole first part (seven folios) without a break; then, after a slight respite, continues for another seven folios. Such a conversation would have lasted sixteen hours, even under conditions allowing for rapid speech.

I have already spoken of the arbitrariness of time on the stage. But Sterne conceived of and used the arbitrariness of "literary time" as material for a game, as in Volume II, Chapter 8:

> It is about an hour and a half's tolerable good reading since my uncle *Toby* rung the bell, when *Obadiah* was order'd to saddle a horse, and go for Dr. *Slop* the man-midwife;—so that no one can say, with reason, that I have not allowed *Obadiah* time enough, poetically speaking, and considering the emergency too, both to go and come;—tho', morally and truly speaking, the man, perhaps, has scarce had time to get on his boots.
>
> If the hypercritic will go upon this; and is resolved after all to take a pendulum, and measure the true distance betwixt the ringing of the bell, and the rap at the door;—and, after finding it to be no more than two minutes, thirteen seconds, and three fifths,—should take upon him to insult over me for such a breach in unity, or rather probability, of time;—I would remind him, that the idea of duration and of its simple modes, is got merely from the train and succession of our ideas,—and is the true scholastic pendulum,—and by which, as a scholar, I will be tried in this matter,—adjuring and detesting the jurisdiction of all other pendulums whatever.
>
> I would, therefore, desire him to consider that it is but poor eight miles from *Shandy-Hall* to Dr. *Slop,* the man mid-wife's house;—and that whilst *Obadiah* has been going those said miles and back, I have brought my uncle *Toby* from *Namur,* quite across all *Flanders,* into *England:*—That I have him ill upon my hands near four years;—and have since travelled him and Corporal *Trim,* in a chariot and four, a journey of near two hundred miles down into *Yorkshire;*—all which

put together, must have prepared the reader's imagination for the entrance of Dr. *Slop* upon the stage,—as much, at least (I hope) as a dance, a song, or a concerto between the acts.

If my hypercritic is intractable, alledging, that two minutes and thirteen seconds are no more than two minutes and thirteen seconds,—when I have said all I can about them;—and that this plea, tho' it might save me dramatically, will damn me biographically, rendering my book, from this very moment, a profess'd Romance, which, before was a book apocryphal:—If I am thus pressed—I then put an end to the whole objection and controversy about it all at once,—by acquainting him, that *Obadiah* had not got above three-score yards from the stable-yard before he met with Dr. *Slop;* . . . [pp. 103–104].

Sterne took the device of the "discovered manuscript" almost unchanged from among the old literary devices. Thus we find Yorick's sermon in the novel. But, of course, the reading of this discovered manuscript does not of itself represent a long digression from the novel, for the sermon is repeatedly interrupted, chiefly by emotional ejaculations. The course of the sermon occupies pages 125 through 140, but it is greatly expanded by insertions of the usual Sternean kind.

The reading of the sermon begins with a description of Corporal Trim's posture, depicted in Sterne's usual purposely awkward way:

He stood before them with his body swayed, and bent forward just so far, as to make an angle of 85 degrees and a half upon the plain of the horizon;—which sound orators, to whom I address this, know very well, to be the true persuasive angle of incidence [p. 122].

And so it continues to:

He stood,—for I repeat it, to take the picture of him in at one view, with his body sway'd, and somewhat bent forwards,—his right-leg firm under him, sustaining seven-eighths of his whole weight,—the foot of his left-leg, the defect of which was no disadvantage to his attitude, advanced a little,—not laterally, nor forwards, but in a line betwixt them; . . . .

And so on. The entire description continues for more than a page. The sermon itself is interrupted by a story about Corporal Trim's brother. Then come the theological protests of a Roman Catholic (pp. 125, 126, 128, 129, etc.) and Uncle Toby's remarks on fortifications (pp. 133, 134, etc.). Thus while following the course of the manuscript, Sterne also integrates it into the novel to a far greater degree than does Cervantes.

Sterne made the "discovered manuscript" a favorite technique in his *Sentimental Journey*. He finds, as he sets out to do, a manuscript by Rabelais; but, as is quite typical of Sterne, he interrupts the manuscript with a discussion about wrapping merchandise. (Sterne has made the unfinished tale acceptable in both its motivated and unmotivated forms.) The interruption of the introduced manuscript is motivated by the fact that its conclusion has been lost. On the other hand, nothing motivates the conclusion of *Tristram Shandy,* which ends with a simple cutting off of the narrative:

> L—d! said my mother, what is all this story about?—
> A cock and a bull, said *Yorick*—and one of the best of its kind, I ever heard.

The END of the NINTH VOLUME.

So also ends *Sentimental Journey:* "So that when I stretch'd out my hand, I caught hold of the Fille de Chambre's—" and it ends there.

This, of course, is a specific stylistic device based upon a variety of things. Sterne worked against a background of the adventure novel with its extraordinarily strict forms and with its formal rule to end with a wedding in the offing. In Sterne's novels the usual forms are changed and violated; it is not surprising that he handled the conclusions of his novels in the same way. We seem to stumble upon them, as if we found a trap door on a staircase where we had expected a landing. Gogol's "Ivan Fyodorovich Shponka and His Aunt" is a short story concluded in the same way; but the conclusion is motivated, for the end of the manuscript was "lost" while baking pies (Sterne wraps currant jam in his). The notes comprising E. T. A. Hoffmann's *Kater Murr* depend upon the same technique, with the nonexistent conclusion motivated by complicated time shifts and parallelism (justified by the fact that the pages are not in order).

Sterne introduces the story of Le Fever in his usual way: During a conversation about the choice of a tutor for Tristram, at the time of Tristram's birth, Uncle Toby suggests the son of poor Le Fever, and the story immediately begins, narrated not by Toby but by Tristram Shandy himself:

> Then, brother *Shandy,* answered my uncle *Toby,* raising himself off the chair, and laying down his pipe to take hold of my father's other hand,—I humbly beg I may recommend poor *Le Fever's* son to you;— a tear of joy of the first water sparkled in my uncle *Toby's* eye,—and another, the fellow to it, in the corporal's, as the proposition was made;—you will see why when you read *Le Fever's* story:—fool that I was! nor can I recollect, (nor perhaps you) without turning back to the place, what it was that hindered me from letting the corporal tell it in his own words;—but the occasion is lost,—I must tell it now in my own [pp. 415–416].

The story about Le Fever, which runs from page 416 to page 432, then begins.

A separate cycle of stories (pp. 479–538) describes Tristram's travels. Sterne later developed this episode, step by step and motif by motif, into his *Sentimental Journey.* Sterne also inserts a story about the Abbess of Andoüillets into the account of Tristram's journey (pp. 504–510).

All of this diverse material, which is augmented by extensive excerpts from the works of various pedants, would undoubtedly tear the novel to bits were it not drawn together by crisscrossing motifs. A stated motif is never fully developed, never actually realized, but is only recalled from time to time; its fulfillment is continually put off to a more and more remote time. Yet its very presence in all the dimensions of the novel ties the episodes together.

There are several such motifs, one of them concerning knots. Here is how it appears—Dr. Slop's bag of obstetrical instruments is tied up in several knots:

> 'Tis God's mercy, quoth he [Dr. Slop], (to himself) that Mrs. *Shandy* has had so bad a time of it,—else she might have been brought to bed seven times told, before one half of these knots could have got untied [p. 167].

In the next chapter, same page:

> In the case of *knots,*—by which, in the first place, I would not be understood to mean slip-knots,—because in the course of my life and opinions,—my opinions concerning them will come in more properly when I mention. . . .

And so on. Then begins a discussion about knots, hitches, fastenings, bows, and so on endlessly. Meanwhile, Dr. Slop gets a little knife and cuts the knots, but accidentally wounds his hand. Then he begins to swear, but the elder Shandy "with Cervantes-like seriousness" suggests he not swear in vain, but rather curse in accordance with the rules of art and, in lieu of a handbook, hands him the formula of excommunication from the Roman Catholic church. Slop takes it and reads; the formula occupies two pages. The curious thing here is the motivation Sterne uses to develop the material. Usually such material has to do with medieval scholarship, which by Sterne's time was already considered laughable (just as, in stories about foreigners, it is thought funny when they pronounce words according to their own dialectical peculiarities). These medieval materials are usually introduced into the story merely as manias of Tristram's father. In this case, however, the motivation is more complicated. The material about baptizing a child prior to its birth and the droll argument of the lawyers about whether a mother is her son's relative is quite removed from Sterne's usual characterization of father *Shandy.*

On page 363 the knots motif appears again, with the chambermaid motif. Sterne suggests that instead of devoting a chapter to those subjects, he would rather substitute one on chambermaids, green gowns, and old hats. But the unsettled account of the knots and packages is not forgotten and comes up again near the very end on page 617 as a promise to write a special chapter about knots.

The references to Jenny are another motif which runs through the novel. Jenny first appears in this way:

> it is no more than a week from this very day, in which I am now writing this book for the edification of the world,—which is *March 9, 1759,—* that my dear, dear *Jenny* observing I look'd a little grave, as she stood cheapening a silk of five-and-twenty shillings a yard,—told the

mercer, she was sorry she had given him so much trouble;—and immediately went and bought herself a yard-wide stuff of ten-pence a yard [p. 44].

On pages 48 and 49 Sterne plays with the reader's curiosity concerning the kind of relationship that exists between Jenny and the narrator.

I own the tender appellation of my dear, dear *Jenny,*—with some other strokes of conjugal knowledge, interspersed here and there, might, naturally enough, have misled the most candid judge in the world into such a determination against me.—All I plead for, in this case, Madam, is strict justice, and that you do so much of it, to me as well as to yourself,—as not to prejudge or receive such an impression of me, till you have better evidence, than I am positive, at present, can be produced against me:—Not that I can be so vain or unreasonable, Madam, as to desire you should therefore think, that my dear, dear *Jenny* is my kept mistress;—no,—that would be flattering my character in the other extream, and giving it an air of freedom, which, perhaps, it has no kind of right to. All I contend for, is the utter impossibility for some volumes, that you, or the most penetrating spirit upon earth, should know how this matter really stands.—It is not impossible, but that my dear, dear *Jenny!* tender as the appellation is, may be my child.—Consider,—I was born in the year eighteen.—Nor is there any thing unnatural or extravagant in the supposition, that my dear *Jenny* may be my friend.—Friend!—My friend. Surely, Madam, a friendship between the two sexes may subsist, and be supported without—Fy! Mr. *Shandy:*—Without anything, Madam, but that tender and delicious sentiment, which ever mixes in friendship, where there is a difference of sex.

The Jenny motif appears again on page 337:

I shall never get all through in five minutes, that I fear—and the thing I *hope* is, that your worships and reverences are not offended— if you are, depend upon't I'll give you something, my good gentry, next year, to be offended at—that's my dear *Jenny's* way—but who my *Jenny* is—and which is the right and which the wrong end of a woman, is the thing to be *concealed*—it will be told you the next chapter but one, to my chapter of button-holes,—and not one chapter before.

And on page 493: "I love the Pythagoreans (much more than ever I dare tell my dear *Jenny*)." There are other references to Jenny on pages 550 and 610 through 611. This last (I have let several pass) has a sentimentality seldom equalled in Sterne:

I will not argue the matter: Time wastes too fast: every letter I trace tells me with what rapidity Life follows my pen; the days and hours of it, more precious, my dear *Jenny*! than the rubies about thy neck, are flying over our heads like light clouds of a windy day, never to return more—every thing presses on—whilst thou art twisting that lock,—see! it grows grey; and every time I kiss thy hand to bid adieu, and every absence which follows it, are preludes to that eternal separation which we are shortly to make.—

—Heaven have mercy upon us both!

CHAP. IX.

Now, for what the world thinks of that ejaculation—I would not give a groat.

and so ends Chapter 9.

A few words about sentimentality in general are appropriate here. Sentimentality cannot serve as the mainstay of art, since art has no mainstay. The presentation of things from "a sentimental point of view" is a special method of presentation, like the presentation of them from the point of view of a horse (as in Tolstoy's "Kholstomer") or of a giant (as in Swift's *Gulliver's Travels*).

Art is essentially trans-emotional, as in stories told of persons rolled into the sea in a barrel spiked inside like an iron maiden. In the Russian version of "Tom Thumb" children will not permit the omission even of the detail of the cannibal cutting off the heads of his daughters, not because children are cruel, but because the detail is part of the legend. Professor Anichkov's *Ceremonial Songs of Spring* includes vernal dancing songs which deal with ugly, quarrelsome husbands; maggots; and death. Although these are unpleasant, they are part of the songs. Gore in art is not necessarily gory; it rhymes with *amor*—it is either the substance of the tonal structure or material for the construction of figures of speech.

Art, then, is unsympathetic—or beyond sympathy—except where the feeling of compassion is evoked as material for the artistic structure. In discussing such emotion we have to examine it from the point of view of the composition itself, in exactly the same way that a mechanic must examine a driving belt to understand the details of a machine; he certainly would not study the driving belt as if he were a vegetarian.

Of course, even Sterne is beyond sympathy, as I shall show. The elder Shandy's son Bobby died at his home the very moment the father was deciding whether to use money, which he had acquired accidentally, either for sending his son abroad or for improving his estate:

my uncle *Toby* hummed over the letter.

___ ___ ___ ___ ___ ___ ___ ___
___ ___ ___ ___ ___ ___ ___ ___
___ ___ ___ ___ ___ ___ ___ —he's

gone! said my uncle *Toby*.—Where—Who? cried my father.—My nephew, said my uncle *Toby*.—What—without leave—without money—without governor? cried my father in amazement. No:—he is dead, my dear brother, quoth my uncle *Toby* [p. 350].

Sterne here has used death to put his characters at "cross-purposes," a common literary device using two persons talking about two different things and thinking they are talking about one and the same thing. Gogol uses the device in *The Inspector General,* in the first conversation between the Mayor and Khlestakov:

MAYOR:
Pardon me—
KH.:
Not at all.
MAYOR:
As Chief Magistrate of this town, my duty is to see that neither transients nor people of standing are oppressed. . . .
KH.:
(first stammering a bit, then towards the end speaking quite loudly) What can be done? . . . It's not my fault. . . . Really, I shall pay. . . . They're sending me some money from home. (Bobchinsky stares in at the door.) He is far more to blame than I; the beef he serves me is as tough as a board and the devil knows what he puts in his soups—I just had to throw some out the window. He starves me for days. And such odd tea! it smells like fish, not tea. Why should I? . . . It's unheard of!
MAYOR:
(taken aback) Forgive me, really, I'm not to blame. The beef I inspect at the markets is always good; it's brought in by reliable merchants, sober, well-behaved people. I wouldn't know where his comes from. But if things are not just as they should be, then . . . let me suggest that you accompany me to other quarters.
KH.:
No, I'd rather not. I know those "other quarters"—the jail. And just what kind of authority do you have? . . . How dare you? I . . . I work at Petersburg! (Acting boldly) I . . . I . . . I . . .
MAYOR:
(aside) Oh! Good Lord, how angry he is. He knows everything; those damned shopkeepers have told him everything.
KH.:
(blustering) Even if you come here with all your men, I won't go. I'll go directly to the Prime Minister! (Pounding the table) Who do you think you are? Who?
MAYOR:
(Standing at attention, his whole body trembling) Please, don't ruin me. My wife! My little children! Don't set misfortune on a man!
KH.:
No, I don't want to. But still! What's that to me? I should go to prison just because you have a wife and children—that's lovely! (Bobchinsky, peeking through the door and thoroughly frightened, hides.) No. Thanks a lot, but I will not.

MAYOR:

(trembling) It's my inexperience, honest to God, my inexperience. The shortage of funds . . . judge for yourself—my official salary won't keep me in tea and sugar. And if I have taken anything, they were the smallest trifles. Something for the table, enough cloth for a suit. About that corporal's widow who runs a shop and whom I'm said to have flogged—that is slander, by God, slander. It's from people who think evil of me, people ready to take my life.

KH.:

So what? They are nothing to me. (Thoughtfully.) Yet I don't know why you talk of those who wish you ill and of some corporal's widow or other. A corporal's wife is something quite different. But you dare not flog me. We're a long way from that. But still. . . . Look at what we have here! I'll pay the bill, but I don't have the cash yet. That's why I'm stuck here, because I don't have a kopeck.

The same talking at cross-purposes occurs in Greboyedov's *Wit Works Woe:*

ZAGORETSKY:

On Chatsky's score this outcry has arisen.

COUNTESS GRANDMOTHER:

Chatsky was escorted out to prison?

ZAGORETSKY:

Was clubbed in the Carpathians, went muzzy from the wound.

COUNTESS GRANDMOTHER:

Has clubbed with the Freemasons and Musselman Mahound?

We find the same technique with the same motivation (deafness) in Russian folk drama, but it arises from a series of puns because of the folk drama's usually loose plot. [A long quotation from the most popular of Russian folk dramas, *Czar Maximilian,* has been omitted here; it consists of one long misunderstanding based upon a series of puns.] These punning misunderstandings are typical of folk drama. Sometimes the device supplants the plot structure itself and leaves the drama without a trace of plot. Roman Jakobson and Peter Bogatyrev analyze the technique in their work on Russian folk themes.

But Sterne's own puns on death do not astonish us as much as the puns made by the father. For Sterne, the death of Bobby Shandy is chiefly motivation for expansion of the material: "Will your worships give me leave to squeeze in a story between these two pages?" (p. 351). And he inserts a fragment from the letter of consolation from Servius Sulpicius Rufus to Cicero. The introduction of this fragment is motivated by what Father Shandy has himself uttered. Later a collection of classical anecdotes about the disdain of death begins. Curiously, Sterne himself tells of Father Shandy's eloquence:

My father was as proud of his eloquence as Marcus Tullius Cicero could be for his life, and for aught I am convinced of to the contrary at present, with as much reason: it was indeed his strength—and his weakness too.—His strength—for he was by nature eloquent,—and his weakness—for he was hourly a dupe to it; and provided an occasion in life would but permit him to shew his talents, or say either a wise thing, a witty, or a shrewd one—(bating the case of a systematick misfortune)—he had all he wanted.—A blessing which tied up my father's tongue, and a misfortune which set it loose with good grace, were pretty equal: sometimes, indeed, the misfortune was the better of the two; for instance, where the pleasure of the harangue was as *ten,* and the pain of the misfortune but as *five*—my father gained half in half, and consequently was as well again off, as it never had befallen him [p. 352].

Here Sterne shows with unusual clarity the difference between the "happiness" and "unhappiness" of life taken as an everyday occurrence and as material for art.

Later the mother has to learn about the death of her son. Sterne handles it by having her overhear the news at the door; then he takes it into his head to build a simultaneous action in the kitchen. As I have already pointed out, he plays around with the action while the poor mother is left standing in an uncomfortable pose. At this time, a conversation about the son's death is going on in the study. The thread of conversation has already passed from a discussion of death in general, through a discussion about voyages and the general diffusion of ancient learning (p. 369), and moved on to Socrates' oration before his judges:

though my mother was a woman of no deep reading, yet the abstract of *Socrates'* oration, which my father was giving my uncle *Toby,* was not altogether new to her.—She listened to it with composed intelligence, and would have done so to the end of the chapter, had not my father plunged (which he had no occasion to have done) into that part of the pleading where the great philosopher reckons up his connections, his alliances, and children; but renounces a security to be so won by working upon the passions of his judges.—"I have friends—I have relations,—I have three desolate children,"—says *Socrates.*—

—Then, cried my mother, opening the door,—you have one more, Mr. *Shandy,* than I know of.

By heaven! I have one less,—said my father, getting up and walking out of the room [p. 370].

Erotic defamiliarization, which is generally presented euphemistically (with genteel wording), is a very important part of Sterne's expansion of the material. I have already treated the basis of this phenomenon in "Art as Technique." In Sterne we find a remarkable diversity of methods of erotic defamiliarization; they are quite numerous, and I shall cite several. I shall begin with one dealing with the recognition of characters:

I am not ignorant that the *Italians* pretend to a mathematical exactness in their designations of one particular sort of character among them, from the *forte* or *piano* of a certain wind instrument they use,—which they say is infallible.—I dare not mention the name of the instrument in this place;—'tis sufficient we have it amongst us,—but never think of making a drawing by it;—this is aenigmatical, and intended to be so, at least, *ad populum:*—And therefore I beg, Madam, when you come here, that you read on as fast as you can, and never stop to make any inquiry about it [pp. 75–76].

Or here is another:

Now whether it was physically impossible, with half a dozen hands all thrust into the napkin at a time—but that some one chestnut, of more life and rotundity than the rest, must be put in motion—it so fell out, however, that one was actually sent rolling off the table; and as *Phutatorius* sat straddling under—it fell perpendicularly into that particular aperture of *Phutatorius's* breeches, for which, to the shame and indelicacy of our language be it spoke, there is no chaste word throughout all *Johnson's* dictionary—let it suffice to say—it was that particular aperture, which in all good societies, the laws of decorum do strictly require, like the temple of *Janus* (in peace at least) to be universally shut up [p. 320].

Two further episodes in *Tristram Shandy* are especially typical of Sterne's game of erotic defamiliarization. The two are similar, although one is simply an episode, while the other expands into one of those plots that continually interrupts the others and even becomes one of the major plot strands in the novel. The more important of these is Uncle Toby's wound, a severe wound in the groin. A widow courting him and waiting to marry him does not know whether or not he is castrated and at the same time hesitates to ask. This situation greatly slows the progress of the novel. Sterne comments upon it:

There is not a greater difference between a single-horse chair and madam *Pompadour's vis-à-vis*, than betwixt a single amour, and an amour thus nobly doubled, and going upon all fours, prancing throughout a grand drama [p. 209].

Hints and allusions repeatedly interrupt the novel. Approximately in Volume VI, Chapter 34, the hints begin to thicken, even though the introductory motif of the journey intrudes. In Volume VII, Chapter 43, Sterne refers to the newly introduced material as if this vein were exhausted:

I danced it along through *Narbonne, Carcasson,* and *Castle Naudairy,* till at last I danced myself into *Perdrillo's* pavillion, where pulling a paper of black lines, that I might go on straight forwards, without digressions of parenthesis, in my uncle *Toby's* amours—[p. 538].

Thus the wound in the groin and the impossibility of the woman's asking about it in detail is introduced into the romance of Uncle Toby and the widow Wadman as a delaying action. I shall show in several supporting quotations how Sterne impedes the action.

After a solemn promise to continue the story of Toby's amorous adventures without digression, Sterne then delays the action with digressions on digressions tied together by the repetition of such phrases as, "It is with love as with Cuckoldom" (pp. 540, 542). Then come the love metaphors: love is an old hat; love is a pie. The story proceeds with the attacks of the widow Wadman on Uncle Toby, but their description is again interrupted by a long "importunate story," narrated by Trim—"The Story of the King of Bohemia and his seven castles" (pp. 560–569). This story is like the one Sancho Panza tells his master on the night of the adventure with the fulling mill, when he had tied Rosinante's legs. Uncle Toby repeatedly interrupts with remarks on the nature of military techniques and on the style; I have already analyzed the method in *Don Quixote*. Like any "importunate tale," it is based upon the recognition of the stalling tactics. It must be interrupted by a listener. In some cases its function is to hold the flow of the novel in check. Later, Trim abandons his telling of the story of the King of Bohemia and takes up the story of his own love (pp. 568–575); and at last the widow Wadman reappears on the scene. Here the motif of the wound also reappears:

> I am terribly afraid, said widow *Wadman,* in case I should marry him, *Bridget*—that the poor captain will not enjoy his health, with the monstrous wound upon his groin—
> It may not, Madam, be so very large, replied *Bridget,* as you think—and I believe besides, added she—that 'tis dried up—
> —I would like to know—merely for his sake said Mrs. *Wadman*—
> —We'll know the long and the broad of it, in ten days—answered Mrs. *Bridget,* for whilst the captain is paying his addresses to you—I'm confident Mr. Trim will be for making love to me—and I'll let him as much as he will—added *Bridget*—to get it all out of him—[pp. 581–582].

In Volume VIII, Chapter 31, the new material is introduced in the form of a metaphor of the kind frequently found in Sterne. He brings into play the lexically accepted metaphor "hobby-horse" in the sense of a whim and refers it to a real horse, then introduces the "ass" (part of the body) figure of speech. (Perhaps the origin of this metaphor is found in St. Francis of Assisi's phrase about his own body, "My brother ass.") This figure of speech is also developed, and a "situation based on a misconception" is built from it.

The father asks Uncle Toby about his "ass," and the latter thinks this is a euphemistic name for the back part of his anatomy (pp. 583–584). [Shklovsky, apparently misled by the Russian, misinterprets the wordplay here as euphemistic.] A detail of the further development is interesting—Father Shandy's speech to Uncle Toby is nothing other than a parody of the speech of Don

Quixote to Sancho Panza about the governorship. I shall not show parallel extracts from both speeches here, especially since the widow Wadman awaits us. Uncle Toby and Trim are going to her, along with Mr. Shandy and his wife, who glance behind them and talk about the coming marriage.

The motif of the impotent husband who has his wife only on the first Sunday of each month crops up again here; the motif had been stated at the very beginning of the novel.

> Unless she should happen to have a child—said my mother—
> But she must persuade my brother *Toby* first to get her one—
> —To be sure, Mr. *Shandy,* quoth my mother.
> —Though if it comes to persuasion—said my father—Lord have mercy upon them.
> Amen: said my mother, *piano.*
> Amen: cried my father, *fortissimè.*
> Amen: said my mother again—but with such a sighing cadence of personal pity at the end of it, as discomfited every fibre about my father—he instantly took out his almanack; but before he could untie it, *Yorick's* congregation coming out of church, became a full answer to one half of his business with it—and my mother telling him it was a sacrament day—left him as little in doubt, as to the other part—He put his almanack into his pocket.
> The first Lord of the Treasury thinking of *ways and means,* could not have returned home, with a more embarrassed look [pp. 613–614].

I let myself quote this passage at length because I want to show how the material Sterne introduces comes not merely from the outside, but rather belongs to one of the threads which tie up all the compositional strands of the novel. Again, as the digressions along the other strands progress, the knot motif reappears (p. 617). At last the wound motif returns, presented, as is typical of Sterne, from the middle:

> —You shall see the very place, Madam; said my uncle *Toby*.
> Mrs. *Wadman* blush'd—look'd towards the door—turn'd pale—blush'd slightly again—recovered her natural colour—blush'd worse than ever; which for the sake of the unlearned reader, I translate thus—

> > "*L—d! I cannot look at it—*
> > *What would the world say if I look'd at it?*

I should drop down, if I look'd at it—
I wish I could look at it—
There can be no sin in looking at it.
—I will look at it" [p. 623].

But a new development occurs. Uncle Toby thinks the widow is interested in the geographical locality where he was wounded, not in the actual place of the wound on his body. As a result, not even the reader understands the dialogue. The whole movement of the plot is affected here; it is slowed down.

Trim brings a map of Namur (Uncle Toby was wounded at Namur) to the disappointed widow, and once more the play on Uncle Toby's wound is permitted to continue. Sterne repeatedly inserts it into the digressions (pages 625–629). And then comes the famous transposition of time; the previously bypassed Chapters 18 and 19 appear after Chapter 25. The scene resumes with Chapter 26:

It was just as natural for Mrs. *Wadman,* whose first husband was all his time afflicted with a Sciatica, to wish to know how far from the hip to the groin; and how far she was likely to suffer more or less in her feelings, in the one case than in the other.

She accordingly read *Drake's* anatomy from one end to the other. She had peeped into *Wharton* on the brain, and had borrowed[1] *Graaf* upon the bones and muscles; but could make nothing of it. . . .

To clear up all, she had twice asked Doctor *Slop,* "if poor captain *Shandy* was ever likely to recover of his wound—?"

—He is recovered, Doctor *Slop* would say—

What! quite?

—Quite: madam—

But what do you mean by a recovery? Mrs. *Wadman* would say.

Doctor *Slop* was the worst man alive at definitions [pp. 636–637].

Mrs. Wadman interrogates Captain Shandy himself about the wound:

"—Was it without remission?—

"—Was it more tolerable in bed?

"—Could he lie on both sides alike with it?

"—Was he able to mount a horse? [p. 637]

And so on. The business is finally settled when Trim speaks about Captain Shandy's wound with Bridget, the widow's maid:

and in this cursed trench, Mrs. *Bridget,* quoth the Corporal, taking her by the hand, did he receive the wound which crush'd him so miserable *here*—In pronouncing which he slightly press'd the back of her hand towards the part he felt for—and let it fall.

We thought, Mr. *Trim,* it had been more in the middle—said Mrs. *Bridget*—

That would have undone us for ever—said the Corporal.

—And left my poor mistress undone too—said *Bridget*. . . .

Come—come—said Bridget—holding the palm of her left-hand parallel to the plane of the horizon, and sliding the fingers of the other over it, in a way which could not have been done, had there been the least wart or protuberance—'Tis every syllable of it false, cried the Corporal, before she had half finished the sentence—[p. 639].

It is interesting to compare the symbolism of the hand motions with the erotic euphemism in the same novel.

A small preliminary observation. For the dramatis personae in the novel as well as for Sterne himself, the technique of decorous conversation becomes material for art in the sense that it is a method of defamiliarization. It is curious that this manual symbolism occurs in particularly masculine and "obscene" anecdotal folklore where we know the only rule of decency is the desire to speak as lewdly as possible. There too we find euphemistic material—in particular manual symbolism; once again it is a technique of defamiliarization.

Let us turn to Sterne and a simple instance of erotic defamiliarization; again I have to quote almost an entire chapter, fortunately a short one:

—'Twas nothing,—I did not lose two drops of blood by it—'twas not worth calling in a surgeon, had he lived next door to us. . . . The chamber-maid had left no ******* *** under the bed:—Cannot you contrive, master, quoth *Susannah*, lifting up the sash with one hand, as she spoke, and helping me up into the window seat with the other,—cannot you manage, my dear, for a single time to **** *** ** *** ******?

I was five years old.—*Susannah* did not consider that nothing was well hung in our family,—so slap came the sash down like lightening upon us;—Nothing is left,—cried *Susannah*,—nothing is left—for me, but to run my country—[p. 376].

She flees to the home of Uncle Toby, who takes the blame in this case since his servant Trim had removed the hook-leads from the window sash for casting toy cannons.

Again, this is Sterne's usual technique: He gives the results before he gives the causes. In this case the cause is given on pages 377–378. Trim tells the story of the accident, with the aid of hand gestures:

Trim, by the help of his forefinger, laid flat upon the table, and the edge of his hand striking a-cross it at right angles, made a shift to tell his story so, that priests and virgins might have listened to it;—and the story being told,—the dialogue went on as follows [p. 379].

Later, with digressions, discussions of digressions, etc., Sterne expands an episode about the rumors which spread among the people concerning what had happened.

It is interesting that Father Shandy, having learned what happened, runs to his son—with a book—and begins a talk about the general subject of

circumcisions; it is also interesting that at this point Sterne parodies the
motivation of interjected parts:

> —was *Obadiah* enabled to give him a particular account of it, just as
> it had happened.—I thought as much, said my father, tucking up his
> night-gown;—and so walked up stairs.
> One would imagine from this—(though for my own part I somewhat
> question it)—that my father before that time, had actually wrote that
> remarkable chapter in the *Tristrapædia,* which to me is the most
> original and entertaining one in the whole book;—and that is the
> *chapter upon sash-windows,* with a bitter *Philippick* at the end of it,
> upon the forgetfulness of chamber-maids.—I have but two reasons for
> thinking otherwise.
> First, had the matter been taken into consideration, before the event
> happened, my father certainly would have nailed up the sash-window
> for good an' all;—which, considering with what difficulty he composed
> books,—he might have done with ten times less trouble, than he could
> have wrote the chapter: this argument I foresee holds good against his
> writing the chapter, even after the event; but 'tis obviated under the
> second reason, which I have the honour to offer to the world in support
> of my opinion, that my father did not write the chapter upon
> sash-windows and chamber-pots, at the time supposed,—and it is this.
> —That, in order to render the *Tristrapædia* complete,—I wrote the
> chapter myself [pp. 383–384].

I have not even the slightest wish to follow Sterne's novel to the end
because that is not what interests me; I am interested, rather, in the theory of
the plot. I shall now remark on the abundance of quotations. It certainly would
have been possible to have made fuller use of the material introduced in each
quotation because almost no technique is represented anywhere in its pure
form; but such an approach would have transformed my work into something
like an interlinear translation with grammatical remarks. I would have
forgotten the material and so exhausted it that I would have deprived the
reader of the possibility of understanding it.

In order to follow the course of the novel in my analysis, I have had to
show the whole of its "inconsistency." The unusualness of the general plan
and the order of the novel, even of the frequently extraordinary handling of the
most ordinary elements, is what is characteristic here.

By way of a conclusion and as a demonstration of Sterne's awareness of
his work and his exaggerated violations of the usual plot structure, I introduce
his very own graphs of the flow of the story of *Tristram Shandy:*

> I am now beginning to get fairly into my work; and by the help of a
> vegitable diet, with a few of the cold seeds, I make no doubt but I shall
> be able to go on with my uncle *Toby's* story, and my own, in a tolerable
> straight line. Now,

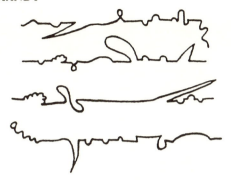

These were the four lines I moved in through my first, second, third, and fourth volumes.—In the fifth volume I have been very good,—the precise line I have described in it being this:

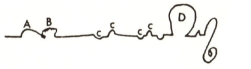

[p. 474]

By which it appears, that except at the curve, marked A. where I took a trip to *Navarre*,—and the indented curve B. which is the short airing when I was there with the Lady *Baussiere* and her page,—I have not taken the least frisk of a digression, till *John de la Casse's* devils led me the round you see marked D.—for as for *c c c c c* they are nothing but parentheses, and the common *ins* and *outs* incident to the lives of the greatest ministers of state; and when compared with what men have done,—or with my own transgressions at the letters A B D—they vanish into nothing [pp. 473–474].

Sterne's diagrams are approximately accurate, but they do not call attention to the crosscurrent of motifs.

The idea of *plot* is too often confused with the description of events—with what I propose provisionally to call the *story*. The story is, in fact, only material for plot formulation. The plot of *Evgeny Onegin* is, therefore, not the romance of the hero with Tatyana, but the fashioning of the subject of this story as produced by the introduction of interrupting digressions. One sharp-witted artist (Vladimir Miklashevsky) proposed to illustrate *Evgeny Onegin* mainly through the digressions (the "small feet," for example); considering it as a composition of motifs, such a treatment would be proper.

The forms of art are explainable by the laws of art; they are not justified by their realism. Slowing the action of a novel is not accomplished by introducing rivals, for example, but by simply *transposing* parts. In so doing the artist makes us aware of the aesthetic laws which underlie both the transposition and the slowing down of the action.

The assertion that *Tristram Shandy* is not a novel is common; for persons who make that statement, opera alone is music—a symphony is chaos.

Tristram Shandy is the most typical novel in world literature.

NOTE

1. This must be a mistake in Mr. *Shandy;* for *Graaf* wrote upon the pancreatick juice, and the parts of generation. *Sterne's note.*

André Breton

1896–1966

André Breton was born on February 18, 1896, at Tinchebray; his family moved to Paris shortly thereafter. There he wrote his first poems, very much in imitation of Stéphane Mallarmé, and made the friendship of his first mentor, Paul Valéry, who was then himself still somewhat a follower of Mallarmé. As a medical student in 1915, Breton was called up for military service; there he met the cynical nihilist Jacques Vaché, who practiced in his own life the absurdity he had encountered in the works of poet Alfred Jarry (who later committed suicide), along with Guillaume Apollinaire, whose new "Cubist" poetry led Breton away from Symbolism. The discovery of Lautréamont (*Les Chants de Maldoror,* 1868), together with readings of Rimbaud, was an integral element in forming Breton's technique in his first published collection, *Mont de piété* (1919). (One of the poems is a collage of phrases from newspaper advertisements.) In this same crucial year of 1919 Breton made his first experiments in what he called automatic writing, together with Philippe Soupault, whom (with Paul Éluard and Louis Aragon) he had met during the war; the texts would be published as *Les Champs magnétiques* (1920). Breton's relationship with Tristan Tzara, who had in 1918 published his *Dada Manifesto,* began the same year; and when the latter moved to Paris in 1920, he, Breton, and the painter Francis Picabia organized a series of theatrical presentations designed specifically to produce the noisy scandals they unleashed.

By 1921 Breton was irritated by the childishness of Tzara: the former wanted to give the spontaneous revolt of Dada a firm theoretical basis, and his readings of Freud together with his background in philosophy (he was rare among the French in knowing German, and had read Hegel) gave him the tools to elaborate a methodological and speculative foundation for what became Surrealism. The theoretical earnest with which Surrealism was formulated places it on an entirely different level from that of Dadaism's facile nose-thumbing, and a break between Breton and Tzara was not long in coming. Breton was showing his instinct for absolute intellectual domination and the ability to break violently with onetime friends over matters of intransigent principle. He was always to be at the head of an ever-changing group engaged in varying collective demonstrations or even collaborative writing practices, such as *Les Champs magnétiques*. Central to Surrealism was Lautréamont's idea that "poetry must be made by all, and not by one person": this entailed a rejection of Romanticism's glorification of individual "genius," as well as of all "psychological depth" (as in nineteenth-century novelistic "characters") in favor of an impersonal and clinically defined poetic technique aimed at the greatest possible freedom from the illusions of rational will and personal identity. Its experimental nature involves a rejection of the closed work of art (as fetish object or "eternal monument") in favor of open-ended fragments meant to demonstrate a poetic and experiential technique as important as the finished "work" itself. This conception was first stated and practiced in the poetry collection, *Clair de terre* (1923), and in the first *Manifesto of Surrealism* (1924), signed by many painters as well as writers; among the signatories of the various manifestos and proclamations of the movement were writers Paul Éluard, Louis Aragon, Antonin Artaud, Georges Bataille, and painters Picasso, Dali, Max Ernst, and André Masson.

Breton's reading of Leon Trotsky from 1925 led him to join the French Communist party in 1927, but the reactionary artistic taste of the party forced him to leave; in 1932 he broke with Aragon, who remained loyal to the party's pro-Stalin stance. By 1935–36, during the Stalinist "purges," Breton was becoming openly anti-Stalinist, leading him into a temporary alliance with Bataille; Breton visited Trotsky in Mexico in 1938, and the two collaborated on a tract entitled *For an Independent Revolutionary Art*.

In 1940, after the French defeat, Breton went to Marseille, then via Martinique to New York in 1941. There Breton founded the journal *VVV*, organized a Surrealist gallery with Marcel Duchamp (the effects of which were to be felt in the work of the New York Abstract Expressionist painters such as Jackson Pollock), and met Elisa, his second wife; their meeting and voyage to Canada in 1944 is the subject of Breton's third prose work, *Arcane 17*. While in Arizona on an Indian reservation in 1945, Breton wrote his last major poem, *Ode to Charles Fourier*, concerning the French social philosopher who designed and created utopian communities for dwelling and working. In the poem (not a product of automatic writing) is Breton's final resolution of his long struggle with official Marxism in favor of Fourier's utopia.

After his return to Paris in 1946 Breton wrote little poetry; although Surrealism was to be eclipsed first by Sartre's "littérature engagée" and then by the New Novel, Breton continued his political activities, opposing the French-Algerian War and the Soviet suppression of the 1956 Hungarian revolt. He contributed to various journals and participated in painters' expositions, showing an exceptional understanding of modern painting. He died in Paris on September 28, 1966.

THE MANIFESTO OF SURREALISM

So strong is the belief in life, in what is most fragile in life—*real* life, I mean—that in the end this belief is lost. Man, that inveterate dreamer, daily more discontent with his destiny, has trouble assessing the objects he has been led to use, objects that his nonchalance has brought his way, or that he has earned through his own efforts, almost always through his own efforts, for he has agreed to work, at least he has not refused to try his luck (or what he calls his luck!). At this point he feels extremely modest: he knows what women he has had, what silly affairs he has been involved in; he is unimpressed by his wealth or poverty, in this respect he is still a newborn babe and, as for the approval of his conscience, I confess that he does very nicely without it. If he still retains a certain lucidity, all he can do is turn back toward his childhood which, however his guides and mentors may have botched it, still strikes him as somehow charming. There, the absence of any known restrictions allows him the perspective of several lives lived at once; this illusion becomes firmly rooted within him; now he is only interested in the fleeting, the extreme facility of everything. Children set off each day without a worry in the world. Everything is near at hand, the worst material conditions are fine. The woods are white or black, one will never sleep.

But it is true that we would not dare venture so far, it is not merely a question of distance. Threat is piled upon threat, one yields, abandons a portion of the terrain to be conquered. This imagination which knows no bounds is henceforth allowed to be exercised only in strict accordance with the laws of an arbitrary utility; it is incapable of assuming this inferior role for very long and, in the vicinity of the twentieth year, generally prefers to abandon man to his lusterless fate.

Though he may later try to pull himself together upon occasion, having felt that he is losing by slow degrees all reason for living, incapable as he has become of being able to rise to some exceptional situation such as love, he will hardly succeed. This is because he henceforth belongs body and soul to an imperative practical necessity which demands his constant attention. None of his gestures will be expansive, none of his ideas generous or far-reaching. In his mind's eye, events real or imagined will be seen only as they relate to a welter of similar events, events in which he has not participated, *abortive* events. What am I saying: he will judge them in relationship to one of these events whose consequences are more reassuring than the others. On no account will he view them as his salvation.

Beloved imagination, what I most like in you is your unsparing quality.

The mere word "freedom" is the only one that still excites me. I deem it capable of indefinitely sustaining the old human fanaticism. It doubtless satisfies my only legitimate aspiration. Among all the many misfortunes to which we are heir, it is only fair to admit that we are allowed the greatest degree of freedom of thought. It is up to us not to misuse it. To reduce the imagination to a state of slavery—even though it would mean the elimination of what is commonly called happiness—is to betray all sense of absolute justice within oneself. Imagination alone offers me some intimation of what *can be,* and this is enough to remove to some slight degree the terrible injunction; enough, too, to allow me to devote myself to it without fear of making a mistake (as though it were possible to make a bigger mistake). Where does it begin to turn bad, and where does the mind's stability cease? For the mind, is the possibility of erring not rather the contingency of good?

There remains madness, "the madness that one locks up," as it has aptly been described. That madness or another. . . . We all know, in fact, that the insane owe their incarceration to a tiny number of legally reprehensible acts and that, were it not for these acts their freedom (or what we see as their freedom) would not be threatened. I am willing to admit that they are, to some degree, victims of their imagination, in that it induces them not to pay attention to certain rules—outside of which the species feels itself threatened—which we are all supposed to know and respect. But their profound indifference to the way in which we judge them, and even to the various punishments meted out to them, allows us to suppose that they derive a great deal of comfort and consolation from their imagination, that they enjoy their madness sufficiently to endure the thought that its validity does not extend beyond themselves. And, indeed, hallucinations, illusions, etc., are not a source of trifling pleasure. The best controlled sensuality partakes of it, and I know that there are many evenings when I would gladly tame that pretty hand which, during the last pages of Taine's *L'Intelligence,* indulges in some curious misdeeds. I could spend my whole life prying loose the secrets of the insane. These people are honest to a fault, and their naiveté has no peer but my own. Christopher Columbus should have set out to discover America with a boatload of madmen. And note how this madness has taken shape, and endured.

It is not the fear of madness which will oblige us to leave the flag of imagination furled.

The case against the realistic attitude demands to be examined, following the case against the materialistic attitude. The latter, more poetic in fact than the former, admittedly implies on the part of man a kind of monstrous pride which, admittedly, is monstrous, but not a new and more complete decay. It should above all be viewed as a welcome reaction against certain ridiculous tendencies of spiritualism. Finally, it is not incompatible with a certain nobility of thought.

By contrast, the realistic attitude, inspired by positivism, from Saint Thomas Aquinas to Anatole France, clearly seems to me to be hostile to any intellectual or moral advancement. I loathe it, for it is made up of mediocrity, hate, and dull conceit. It is this attitude which today gives birth to these ridiculous books, these insulting plays. It constantly feeds on and derives strength from the newspapers and stultifies both science and art by assiduously flattering the lowest of tastes; clarity bordering on stupidity, a dog's life. The activity of the best minds feels the effects of it; the law of the lowest common denominator finally prevails upon them as it does upon the others. An amusing result of this state of affairs, in literature for example, is the generous supply of novels. Each person adds his personal little "observation" to the whole. As a cleansing antidote to all this, M. Paul Valéry recently suggested that an anthology be compiled in which the largest possible number of opening passages from novels be offered; the resulting insanity, he predicted, would be a source of considerable edification. The most famous authors would be included. Such a thought reflects great credit on Paul Valéry who, some time ago, speaking of novels, assured me that, so far as he was concerned, he would continue to refrain from writing: "The Marquise went out at five." But has he kept his word?

If the purely informative style, of which the sentence just quoted is a prime example, is virtually the rule rather than the exception in the novel form, it is because, in all fairness, the author's ambition is severely circumscribed. The circumstantial, needlessly specific nature of each of their notations leads me to believe that they are perpetrating a joke at my expense. I am spared not even one of the character's slightest vacillations: will he be fairhaired? what will his name be? will we first meet him during the summer? So many questions resolved once and for all, as chance directs; the only discretionary power left me is to close the book, which I am careful to do somewhere in the vicinity of the first page. And the descriptions! There is nothing to which their vacuity can be compared; they are nothing but so many superimposed images taken from some stock catalogue, which the author utilizes more and more whenever he chooses; he seizes the opportunity to slip me his postcards, he tries to make me agree with him about the clichés:

> The small room into which the young man was shown was covered with yellow wallpaper: there were geraniums in the windows, which were covered with muslin curtains; the setting sun cast a harsh light over the entire setting. . . . There was nothing special about the room. The furniture, of yellow wood, was all very old. A sofa with a tall back turned down, an oval table opposite the sofa, a dressing table and a mirror set against the pierglass, some chairs along the walls, two or three etchings of no value portraying some German girls with birds in their hands—such were the furnishings.[1]

I am in no mood to admit that the mind is interested in occupying itself with such matters, even fleetingly. It may be argued that this school-boy description has its place, and that at this juncture of the book the author has his reasons for burdening me. Nevertheless he is wasting his time, for I refuse to go into his room. Others' laziness or fatigue does not interest me. I have too unstable a notion of the continuity of life to equate or compare my moments of depression or weakness with my best moments. When one ceases to feel, I am of the opinion one should keep quiet. And I would like it understood that I am not accusing or condemning lack of originality *as such*. I am only saying that I do not take particular note of the empty moments of my life, that it may be unworthy for any man to crystallize those which seem to him to be so. I shall, with your permission, *ignore* the description of that room, and many more like it.

Not so fast, there; I'm getting into the area of psychology, a subject about which I shall be careful not to joke.

The author attacks a character and, this being settled upon, parades his hero to and fro across the world. No matter what happens, this hero, whose actions and reactions are admirably predictable, is compelled not to thwart or upset—even though he looks as though he is—the calculations of which he is the object. The currents of life can appear to lift him up, roll him over, cast him down, he will still belong to this *readymade* human type. A simple game of chess which doesn't interest me in the least—man, whoever he may be, being for me a mediocre opponent. What I cannot bear are those wretched discussions relative to such and such a move, since winning or losing is not in question. And if the game is not worth the candle, if objective reason does a frightful job—as indeed it does—of serving him who calls upon it, is it not fitting and proper to avoid all contact with these categories? "Diversity is so vast that every different tone of voice, every step, cough, every wipe of the nose, every sneeze. . . ."[2] If in a cluster of grapes there are no two alike, why do you want me to describe this grape by the other, by all the others, why do you want me to make a palatable grape? Our brains are dulled by the incurable mania of wanting to make the unknown known, classifiable. The desire for analysis wins out over the sentiments.[3] The result is statements of undue length whose persuasive power is attributable solely to their strangeness and which impress the reader only by the abstract quality of their vocabulary, which moreover is ill-defined. If the general ideas that philosophy has thus far come up with as topics of discussion revealed by their very nature their definitive incursion into a broader or more general area, I would be the first to greet the news with joy. But up till now it has been nothing but idle repartee; the flashes of wit and other niceties vie in concealing from us the true thought in search of itself, instead of concentrating on obtaining successes. It seems to me that every act is its own justification, at least for the person who has been capable of committing it, that it is endowed with a radiant power which the slightest gloss is certain to diminish. Because of this gloss, it even in a sense ceases to happen. It gains nothing to be thus distinguished. Stendhal's heroes are subject to the comments and appraisals—appraisals which are more or less successful—made by that author, which add not one whit to their glory. Where we really find them again is at the point at which Stendhal has lost them.

We are still living under the reign of logic: this, of course, is what I have been driving at. But in this day and age logical methods are applicable only to solving problems of secondary interest. The absolute rationalism that is still in vogue allows us to consider only facts relating directly to our experience. Logical ends, on the contrary, escape us. It is pointless to add that experience itself has found itself increasingly circumscribed. It paces back and forth in a cage from which it is more and more difficult to make it emerge. It too leans for support on what is most immediately expedient, and it is protected by the sentinels of common sense. Under the pretense of civilization and progress, we have managed to banish from the mind everything that may rightly or wrongly be termed superstition, or fancy; forbidden is any kind of search for truth which is not in conformance with accepted practices. It was, apparently, by pure chance that a part of our mental world which we pretended not to be concerned with any longer—and, in my opinion by far the most important part—has been brought back to light. For this we must give thanks to the discoveries of Sigmund Freud. On the basis of these discoveries a current of opinion is finally forming by means of which the human explorer will be able to carry his investigations much further, authorized as he will henceforth be not to confine himself solely to the most summary realities. The imagination is perhaps on the point of reasserting itself, of reclaiming its rights. If the depths of our mind contain within it strange forces capable of augmenting those on the surface, or of waging a victorious battle against them, there is every reason to seize them—first to seize them, then, if need be, to submit them to the control of our reason. The analysts themselves have everything to gain by it. But it is worth noting that no means has been designated a priori for carrying out this undertaking, that until further notice it can be construed to be the province of poets as well as scholars, and that its success is not dependent upon the more or less capricious paths that will be followed.

Freud very rightly brought his critical faculties to bear upon the dream. It is, in fact, inadmissible that this considerable portion of psychic activity (since, at least from man's birth until his death, thought offers no solution of continuity, the sum of the moments of dream, from the point of view of time, and taking into consideration only the time of pure dreaming, that is the dreams of sleep, is not inferior to the sum of the moments of reality, or, to be more precisely limiting, the moments of waking) has still today been so grossly neglected. I have always been amazed at the way an ordinary observer lends so much more credence and attaches so much more importance to waking events than to those occurring in dreams. It is because man, when he ceases to sleep, is above all the plaything of his memory, and in its normal state memory takes pleasure in weakly retracing for him the circumstances of the dream, in stripping it of any real importance, and in dismissing the only *determinant* from the point where he thinks he has left it a few hours before: this firm hope, this concern. He is under the impression of continuing something that is worthwhile. Thus the dream finds itself reduced to a mere parenthesis, as is the night. And, like the night, dreams generally contribute little to furthering our understanding. This curious state of affairs seems to me to call for certain reflections:

1) Within the limits where they operate (or are thought to operate) dreams give every evidence of being continuous and show signs of organization.

Memory alone arrogates to itself the right to excerpt from dreams, to ignore the transitions, and to depict for us rather a series of dreams than the *dream itself.* By the same token, at any given moment we have only a distinct notion of realities, the coordination of which is a question of will.[4] What is worth noting is that nothing allows us to presuppose a greater dissipation of the elements of which the dream is constituted. I am sorry to have to speak about it according to a formula which in principle excludes the dream. When will we have sleeping logicians, sleeping philosophers? I would like to sleep, in order to surrender myself to the dreamers, the way I surrender myself to those who read me with eyes wide open; in order to stop imposing, in this realm, the conscious rhythm of my thought. Perhaps my dream last night follows that of the night before, and will be continued the next night, with an exemplary strictness. *It's quite possible,* as the saying goes. And since it has not been proved in the slightest that, in doing so, the "reality" with which I am kept busy continues to exist in the state of dream, that it does not sink back down into the immemorial, why should I not grant to dreams what I occasionally refuse reality, that is, this value of certainty in itself which, in its own time, is not open to my repudiation? Why should I not expect from the sign of the dream more than I expect from a degree of consciousness which is daily more acute? Can't the dream also be used in solving the fundamental questions of life? Are these questions the same in one case as in the other and, in the dream, do these questions already exist? Is the dream any less restrictive or punitive than the rest? I am growing old and, more than that reality to which I believe I subject myself, it is perhaps the dream, the difference with which I treat the dream, which makes me grow old.

2) Let me come back again to the waking state. I have no choice but to consider it a phenomenon of interference. Not only does the mind display, in this state, a strange tendency to lose its bearings (as evidenced by the slips and mistakes the secrets of which are just beginning to be revealed to us), but, what is more, it does not appear that, when the mind is functioning normally, it really responds to anything but the suggestions which come to it from the depths of that dark night to which I commend it. However conditioned it may be, its balance is relative. It scarcely dares express itself and, if it does, it confines itself to verifying that such and such an idea, or such and such a woman, has made an impression on it. What impression it would be hard pressed to say, by which it reveals the degree of its subjectivity, and nothing more. This idea, this woman, disturb it, they tend to make it less severe. What they do is isolate the mind for a second from its solvent and spirit it to heaven, as the beautiful precipitate it can be, that it is. When all else fails, it then calls upon chance, a divinity even more obscure than the others to whom it ascribes all its aberrations. Who can say to me that the angle by which that idea which affects it is offered, that what it likes in the eye of that woman is not precisely what links it to its dream, binds it to those fundamental facts which, through its own fault, it has lost? And if things were different, what might it be capable of? I would like to provide it with the key to this corridor.

3) The mind of the man who dreams is fully satisfied by what happens to him. The agonizing question of possibility is no longer pertinent. Kill, fly faster, love to your heart's content. And if you should die, are you not certain of reawaking among the dead? Let yourself be carried along, events will not tolerate your interference. You are nameless. The ease of everything is priceless.

What reason, I ask, a reason so much vaster than the other, makes dreams seem so natural and allows me to welcome unreservedly a welter of episodes so strange that they would confound me now as I write? And yet I can believe my eyes, my ears; this great day has arrived, this beast has spoken.

If man's awaking is harder, if it breaks the spell too abruptly, it is because he has been led to make for himself too impoverished a notion of atonement.

4) From the moment when it is subjected to a methodical examination, when, by means yet to be determined, we succeed in recording the contents of dreams in their entirety (and that presupposes a discipline of memory spanning generations; but let us nonetheless begin by noting the most salient facts), when its graph will expand with unparalleled volume and regularity, we may hope that the mysteries which really are not will give way to the great Mystery. I believe in the future resolution of these two states, dream and reality, which are seemingly so contradictory, into a kind of absolute reality, a *surreality,* if one may so speak. It is in quest of this surreality that I am going, certain not to find it but too unmindful of my death not to calculate to some slight degree the joys of its possession.

A story is told according to which Saint-Pol-Roux, in times gone by, used to have a notice posted on the door of his manor house in Camaret, every evening before he went to sleep, which read: THE POET IS WORKING.

A great deal more could be said, but in passing I merely wanted to touch upon a subject which in itself would require a very long and much more detailed discussion; I shall come back to it. At this juncture, my intention was merely to mark a point by noting the *hate of the marvelous* which rages in certain men, this absurdity beneath which they try to bury it. Let us not mince words: the marvelous is always beautiful, anything marvelous is beautiful, in fact only the marvelous is beautiful.

In the realm of literature, only the marvelous is capable of fecundating works which belong to an inferior category such as the novel, and generally speaking, anything that involves storytelling. Lewis' *The Monk* is an admirable proof of this. It is infused throughout with the presence of the marvelous. Long before the author has freed his main characters from all temporal constraints, one feels them ready to act with an unprecedented pride. This passion for eternity with which they are constantly stirred lends an unforgettable intensity to their torments, and to mine. I mean that this book, from beginning to end, and in the purest way imaginable, exercises an exalting effect only upon that part of the mind which aspires to leave the earth and that, stripped of an insignificant part of its plot, which belongs to the period in which it was written, it constitutes a paragon of precision and innocent grandeur.[5] It seems to me none better has been done, and that the character of Mathilda in particular is the most moving creation that one can credit to this *figurative* fashion in literature. She is less a character than a continual temptation. And if a character is not a temptation, what is he? An extreme temptation, she. In *The Monk,* the "nothing is impossible for him who dares try" gives it its full, convincing measure. Ghosts play a logical role in the book, since the critical mind does not seize them in order to dispute them. Ambrosio's punishment is likewise treated in a legitimate manner, since it is finally accepted by the critical faculty as a natural denouement.

It may seem arbitrary on my part, when discussing the marvelous, to choose this model, from which both the Nordic literatures and Oriental literatures have borrowed time and time again, not to mention the religious literatures of every country. This is because most of the examples which these literatures could have furnished me with are tainted by puerility, for the simple reason that they are addressed to children. At an early age children are weaned on the marvelous, and later on they fail to retain a sufficient virginity of mind to thoroughly enjoy fairy tales. No matter how charming they may be, a grown man would think he were reverting to childhood by nourishing himself on fairy tales, and I am the first to admit that all such tales are not suitable for him. The fabric of adorable improbabilities must be made a trifle more subtle the older we grow, and we are still at the stage of waiting for this kind of spider. . . . But the faculties do not change radically. Fear, the attraction of the unusual, chance, the taste for things extravagant are all devices which we can always call upon without fear of deception. There are fairy tales to be written for adults, fairy tales still almost blue.

The marvelous is not the same in every period of history: it partakes in some obscure way of a sort of general revelation only the fragments of which come down to us: they are the romantic *ruins,* the modern *mannequin,* or any other symbol capable of affecting the human sensibility for a period of time. In these areas which make us smile, there is still portrayed the incurable human rest-lessness, and this is why I take them into consideration and why I judge them inseparable from certain productions of genius which are, more than the others, painfully afflicted by them. They are Villon's gibbets, Racine's Greeks, Baudelaire's couches. They coincide with an eclipse of the taste I am made to endure, I whose notion of taste is the image of a big spot. Amid the bad taste of my time I strive to go further than anyone else. It would have been I, had I lived in 1820, I "the bleeding nun," I who would not have spared this cunning and banal "let us conceal" whereof the parodical Cuisin speaks, it would have been I, I who would have reveled in the enormous metaphors, as he says, all phases of the "silver disk." For today I think of a *castle,* half of which is not necessarily in ruins; this castle belongs to me, I picture it in a rustic setting, not far from Paris. The outbuildings are too numerous to mention, and, as for the interior, it has been frightfully restored, in such a manner as to leave nothing to be desired from the viewpoint of comfort. Automobiles are parked before the door, concealed by the shade of the trees. A few of my friends are living here as permanent guests: there is Louis Aragon leaving; he only has time enough to say hello; Philippe Soupault gets up with the stars, and Paul Eluard, our great Eluard, has not yet come home. There are Robert Desnos and Roger Vitrac out on the grounds poring over an ancient edict on dueling; Georges Auric, Jean Paulhan; Max Morise, who rows so well, and Benjamin Péret, busy with his equations with birds; and Joseph Delteil; and Jean Carrive; and Georges Limbour, and Georges Limbours (there is a whole hedge of Georges Limbours); and Marcel Noll; there is T. Fraenkel waving to us from his captive balloon, Georges Malkine, Antonin Artaud, Francis Gérard, Pierre Naville, J.-A. Boiffard, and after them Jacques Baron and his brother, handsome and cordial, and so many others besides, and gorgeous women, I might add. Nothing is too good for these young men, their wishes are, as to wealth, so many commands. Francis Picabia comes to pay us a call, and last week, in the hall of mirrors, we received a certain Marcel Duchamp whom we had not hitherto known. Picasso goes hunting in the neighborhood. The spirit of *demoralization* has elected domicile in the castle, and it is with it we have to deal every time it is a question of contact with our fellowmen, but the doors are always open, and one does not begin by "thanking" everyone, you know. Moreover, the solitude is vast, we don't often run into one another. And anyway, isn't what matters that we be the masters of ourselves, the masters of women, and of love too?

I shall be proved guilty of poetic dishonesty: everyone will go parading about saying that I live on the rue Fontaine[6] and that he will have none of the water that flows therefrom. To be sure! But is he certain that this castle into which I cordially invite him is an image? What if this castle really existed! My guests are there to prove it does; their whim is the luminous road that leads to it. We really live by our fantasies when we *give free rein to them*. And how could what one might do bother the other, there, safely sheltered from the sentimental pursuit and at the trysting place of opportunities?

Man proposes and disposes. He and he alone can determine whether he is completely master of himself, that is, whether he maintains the body of his desires, daily more formidable, in a state of anarchy. Poetry teaches him to. It bears within itself the perfect compensation for the miseries we endure. It can also be an organizer, if ever, as the result of a less intimate disappointment, we contemplate taking it seriously. The time is coming when it decrees the end of money and by itself will break the bread of heaven for the earth! There will still be gatherings on the public squares, and *movements* you never dared hope participate in. Farewell to absurd choices, the dreams of dark abyss, rivalries, the prolonged patience, the flight of the seasons, the artificial order of ideas, the ramp of danger, time for everything! May you only take the trouble to *practice* poetry. Is it not incumbent upon us, who are already living off it, to try and impose what we hold to be our case for further inquiry?

It matters not whether there is a certain disproportion between this defense and the illustration that will follow it. It was a question of going back to the sources of poetic imagination and, what is more, of remaining there. Not that I pretend to have done so. It requires a great deal of fortitude to try to set up one's abode in these distant regions where everything seems at first to be so awkward and difficult, all the more so if one wants to try to take someone there. Besides, one is never sure of really being there. If one is going to all that trouble, one might just as well stop off somewhere else. Be that as it may, the fact is that the way to these regions is clearly marked, and that to attain the true goal is now merely a matter of the travelers' ability to endure.

We are all more or less aware of the road traveled. I was careful to relate, in the course of a study of the case of Robert Desnos entitled ENTRÉE DES MÉDIUMS,[7] that I had been led to "concentrate my attention on the more or less partial sentences which, when one is quite alone and on the verge of falling asleep, become perceptible for the mind without its being possible to discover what provoked them." I had then just attempted the poetic adventure with the minimum of risks, that is, my aspirations were the same as they are today but I trusted in the slowness of formulation to keep me from useless contacts, contacts of which I completely disapproved. This attitude involved a modesty of thought certain vestiges of which I still retain. At the end of my life, I shall doubtless manage to speak with great effort the way people speak, to apologize for my voice and my few remaining gestures. The virtue of the spoken word (and the written word all the more so) seemed to me to derive from the faculty of foreshortening in a striking manner the exposition (since there was exposition) of a small number of facts, poetic or other, of which I made myself the substance. I had come to the conclusion that Rimbaud had not proceeded any differently. I was composing, with a concern for variety that deserved better, the final poems of *Mont de piété,* that is, I managed to extract from the blank lines of this book an incredible advantage. These lines were the closed eye to the operations of thought that I believed I was obliged to keep hidden from the reader. It was not deceit on my part, but my love of shocking the reader. I had the illusion of a possible complicity, which I had more and more difficulty giving up. I had begun to cherish words excessively for the space they allow around them, for their tangencies with countless other words that I did not utter. The poem "Black Forest" derives precisely from this state of mind. It took me six months to write it, and you may take my word for it that I did not rest a single day. But this stemmed from the opinion I had of myself in those days, which was high, please don't judge me too harshly. I enjoy these stupid confessions. At that point cubist pseudo-poetry was trying to get a foothold, but it had emerged defenseless from Picasso's brain, and I was thought to be as dull as dishwater (and still am). I had a sneaking suspicion, moreover, that from the viewpoint of poetry I was off on the wrong road, but I hedged my bet as best I could, defying lyricism with salvos of definitions and formulas (the Dada phenomena were waiting in the wings, ready to come on stage) and pretending to search for an application of poetry to advertising (I went so far as to claim that the world would end, not with a good book but with a beautiful advertisement for heaven or for hell).

In those days, a man at least as boring as I, Pierre Reverdy, was writing:

The image is a pure creation of the mind.

It cannot be born from a comparison but from a juxtaposition of two more or less distant realities.

The more the relationship between the two juxtaposed realities is distant and true, the stronger the image will be—the greater its emotional power and poetic reality . . .[8]

These words, however sibylline for the uninitiated, were extremely revealing, and I pondered them for a long time. But the image eluded me. Reverdy's aesthetic, a completely a posteriori aesthetic, led me to mistake the effects for the causes. It was in the midst of all this that I renounced irrevocably my point of view.

One evening, therefore, before I fell asleep, I perceived, so clearly articulated that it was impossible to change a word, but nonetheless removed from the sound of any voice, a rather strange phrase which came to me without any apparent relationship to the events in which, my consciousness agrees, I was then involved, a phrase which seemed to me insistent, a phrase, if I may be so bold, *which was knocking at the window*. I took cursory note of it and prepared to move on when its organic character caught my attention. Actually, this phrase astonished me: unfortunately I cannot remember it exactly, but it was something like: "There is a man cut in two by the window," but there could be no question of ambiguity, accompanied as it was by the faint visual image[9] of a man walking cut half way up by a window perpendicular to the axis of his body. Beyond the slightest shadow of a doubt, what I saw was the simple reconstruction in space of a man leaning out a window. But this window having shifted with the man, I realized that I was dealing with an image of a fairly rare sort, and all I could think of was to incorporate it into my material for poetic construction. No sooner had I granted it this capacity than it was in fact succeeded by a whole series of phrases, with only brief pauses between them, which surprised me only slightly less and left me with the impression of their being so gratuitous that the control I had then exercised upon myself seemed to me illusory and all I could think of was putting an end to the interminable quarrel raging within me.[10]

Completely occupied as I still was with Freud at that time, and familiar as I was with his methods of examination which I had had some slight occasion to use on some patients during the war, I resolved to obtain from myself what we were trying to obtain from them, namely, a monologue spoken as rapidly as possible without any intervention on the part of the critical faculties, a monologue consequently unencumbered by the slightest inhibition and which was, as closely as possible, akin to *spoken thought*. It had seemed to me, and still does— the way in which the phrase about the man cut in two had come to me is an indication of it—that the speed of thought is no greater than the speed of speech, and that thought does not necessarily defy language, nor even the fast-moving pen. It was in this frame of mind that Philippe Soupault—to whom I had confided these initial conclusions—and I decided to blacken some paper, with a praiseworthy disdain for what might result from a literary point of view. The ease of execution did the rest. By the end of the first day we were able to read to ourselves some fifty or so pages obtained in this manner, and begin to compare our results. All in all, Soupault's pages and mine proved to be remarkably similar: the same overconstruction, shortcomings of a similar nature, but also, on both our parts, the illusion of an extraordinary verve, a great deal of emotion, a considerable choice of images of a quality such that we would not have been capable of preparing a single one in longhand, a very special picturesque quality and, here and there, a strong comical effect. The only difference between our two texts seemed to me to derive essentially from our respective tempers, Soupault's being less static than mine, and, if he does not mind my offering this one slight criticism, from the fact that he had made the error of putting a few words by way of titles at the top of certain pages, I suppose in a spirit of mystification. On the other hand, I must give credit where credit is due and say that he constantly and vigorously opposed any effort to retouch or correct, however slightly, any passage of this kind which seemed to me unfortunate. In this he was, to be sure, absolutely right.[11] It is, in fact, difficult to appreciate fairly the various elements present; one may even go so far as to say that it is impossible to appreciate them at a first reading. To you who write, these elements are, on the surface, *as strange to you as they are to anyone else,* and naturally you are wary of them. Poetically speaking, what strikes you about them above all is their *extreme degree of immediate absurdity,* the quality of this absurdity, upon closer scrutiny, being to give way to everything admissible, everything legitimate in the world: the disclosure of a certain number of properties and of facts no less objective, in the final analysis, than the others.

In homage to Guillaume Apollinaire, who had just died and who, on several occasions, seemed to us to have followed a discipline of this kind, without however having sacrificed to it any mediocre literary means, Soupault and I baptized the new mode of pure expression which we had at our disposal and which we wished to pass on to our friends, by the name of SURREALISM. I believe that there is no point today in dwelling any further on this word and that the meaning we gave it initially has generally prevailed over its Apollinarian sense. To be even fairer, we could probably have taken over the word SUPERNATURALISM employed by Gérard de Nerval in his dedication to the *Filles de feu.*[12] It appears, in fact, that Nerval possessed to a tee the spirit with which we claim a kinship, Apollinaire having possessed, on the contrary, naught but *the letter,* still imperfect, of Surrealism, having shown himself powerless to give a valid theoretical idea of it. Here are two passages by Nerval which seem to me to be extremely significant in this respect:

> I am going to explain to you, my dear Dumas, the phenomenon of which you have spoken a short while ago. There are, as you know,

certain storytellers who cannot invent without identifying with the characters their imagination has dreamt up. You may recall how convincingly our old friend Nodier used to tell how it had been his misfortune during the Revolution to be guillotined; one became so completely convinced of what he was saying that one began to wonder how he had managed to have his head glued back on.

. . . And since you have been indiscreet enough to quote one of the sonnets composed in this SUPERNATURALISTIC dream-state, as the Germans would call it, you will have to hear them all. You will find them at the end of the volume. They are hardly any more obscure than Hegel's metaphysics or Swedenborg's MEMORABILIA, and would lose their charm if they were explained, if such were possible; at least admit the worth of the expression. . . .[13]

Those who might dispute our right to employ the term SURREALISM in the very special sense that we understand it are being extremely dishonest, for there can be no doubt that this word had no currency before we came along. Therefore, I am defining it once and for all:

SURREALISM, *n*. Psychic automatism in its pure state, by which one proposes to express—verbally, by means of the written word, or in any other manner—the actual functioning of thought. Dictated by thought, in the absence of any control exercised by reason, exempt from any aesthetic or moral concern.

ENCYCLOPEDIA. *Philosophy*. Surrealism is based on the belief in the superior reality of certain forms of previously neglected associations, in the omnipotence of dream, in the disinterested play of thought. It tends to ruin once and for all all other psychic mechanisms and to substitute itself for them in solving all the principal problems of life. The following have performed acts of ABSOLUTE SURREALISM: Messrs. Aragon, Baron, Boiffard, Breton, Carrive, Crevel, Delteil, Desnos, Eluard, Gérard, Limbour, Malkine, Morise, Naville, Noll, Péret, Picon, Soupault, Vitrac.

They seem to be, up to the present time, the only ones, and there would be no ambiguity about it were it not for the case of Isidore Ducasse, about whom I lack information. And, of course, if one is to judge them only superficially by their results, a good number of poets could pass for Surrealists, beginning with Dante and, in his finer moments, Shakespeare. *In the course of the various attempts I have made to reduce what is, by breach of trust, called genius, I have found nothing which in the final analysis can be attributed to any other method than that.*

Young's *Nights* are Surrealist from one end to the other; unfortunately it is a priest who is speaking, a bad priest no doubt, but a priest nonetheless.

Swift is Surrealist in malice,
Sade is Surrealist in sadism.
Chateaubriand is Surrealist in exoticism.
Constant is Surrealist in politics.
Hugo is Surrealist when he isn't stupid.
Desbordes-Valmore is Surrealist in love.
Bertrand is Surrealist in the past.
Rabbe is Surrealist in death.
Poe is Surrealist in adventure.
Baudelaire is Surrealist in morality.
Rimbaud is Surrealist in the way he lived, and elsewhere.
Mallarmé is Surrealist when he is confiding.
Jarry is Surrealist in absinthe.
Nouveau is Surrealist in the kiss.
Saint-Pol-Roux is Surrealist in his use of symbols.
Fargue is Surrealist in the atmosphere.
Vaché is Surrealist in me.
Reverdy is Surrealist at home.
Saint-Jean-Perse is Surrealist at a distance.
Roussel is Surrealist as a storyteller.
Etc.

I would like to stress this point: they are not always Surrealists, in that I discern in each of them a certain number of preconceived ideas to which—very naively!—they hold. They hold to them because they had not *heard the Surrealist voice,* the one that continues to preach on the eve of death and above the storms, because they did not want to serve simply to orchestrate the marvelous score. They were instruments too full of pride, and this is why they have not always produced a harmonious sound.[14]

But we, who have made no effort whatsoever to filter, who in our works have made ourselves into simple receptacles of so many echoes, modest *recording instruments* who are not mesmerized by the drawings we are making, perhaps we serve an even nobler cause. Thus do we render with integrity the "talent" which has been lent to us. You might as well speak of the talent of this platinum ruler, this mirror, this door, and of the sky, if you like.

We do not have any talent; ask Philippe Soupault:

Anatomical products of manufacture and low-income dwellings will destroy the tallest cities.

Ask Roger Vitrac:

No sooner had I called forth the marble-admiral than he turned on his heel like a horse which rears at the sight of the North star and showed me, in the plane of his two-pointed cocked hat, a region where I was to spend my life.

Ask Paul Eluard:

This is an oft-told tale that I tell, a famous poem that I reread: I am
leaning against a wall, with my verdant ears and my lips burned to a
crisp.

Ask Max Morise:

The bear of the caves and his friend the bittern, the vol-au-vent and
his valet the wind, the Lord Chancellor with his Lady, the scarecrow
for sparrows and his accomplice the sparrow, the test tube and his
daughter the needle, this carnivore and his brother the carnival, the
sweeper and his monocle, the Mississippi and its little dog, the coral
and its jug of milk, the Miracle and its Good Lord, might just as well
go and disappear from the surface of the sea.

Ask Joseph Delteil:

Alas! I believe in the virtue of birds. And a feather is all it takes to
make me die laughing.

Ask Louis Aragon:

During a short break in the party, as the players were gathering
around a bowl of flaming punch, I asked the tree if it still had its red
ribbon.

And ask me, who was unable to keep myself from writing the serpentine,
distracting lines of this preface.

Ask Robert Desnos, he who, more than any of us, has perhaps got closest
to the Surrealist truth, he who, in his still unpublished works[15] and in the
course of the numerous experiments he has been a party to, has fully justified
the hope I placed in Surrealism and leads me to believe that a great deal more
will still come of it. Desnos *speaks Surrealist* at will. His extraordinary agility
in orally following his thought is worth as much to us as any number of
splendid speeches which are lost, Desnos having better things to do than
record them. He reads himself like an open book, and does nothing to retain
the pages, which fly away in the windy wake of his life.

SECRETS OF
THE MAGICAL SURREALIST ART

Written Surrealist Composition
Or First and Last Draft

After you have settled yourself in a place as favorable as possible to the
concentration of your mind upon itself, have writing materials brought to you.
Put yourself in as passive, or receptive, a state of mind as you can. Forget about
your genius, your talents, and the talents of everyone else. Keep reminding

yourself that literature is one of the saddest roads that leads to everything. Write quickly, without any preconceived subject, fast enough so that you will not remember what you're writing and be tempted to reread what you have written. The first sentence will come spontaneously, so compelling is the truth that with every passing second there is a sentence unknown to our consciousness which is only crying out to be heard. It is somewhat of a problem to form an opinion about the next sentence; it doubtless partakes both of our conscious activity and of the other, if one agrees that the fact of having written the first entails a minimum of perception. This should be of no importance to you, however; to a large extent, this is what is most interesting and intriguing about the Surrealist game. The fact still remains that punctuation no doubt resists the absolute continuity of the flow with which we are concerned, although it may seem as necessary as the arrangement of knots in a vibrating cord. Go on as long as you like. Put your trust in the inexhaustible nature of the murmur. If silence threatens to settle in if you should ever happen to make a mistake— a mistake, perhaps due to carelessness—break off without hesitation with an overly clear line. Following a word the origin of which seems suspicious to you, place any letter whatsoever, the letter "l" for example, always the letter "l," and bring the arbitrary back by making this letter the first of the following word.

How Not to Be Bored
Any Longer When With Others

This is very difficult. Don't be at home for anyone, and occasionally, when no one has forced his way in, interrupting you in the midst of your Surrealist activity, and you, crossing your arms, say: "It doesn't matter, there are doubtless better things to do or not do. Interest in life is indefensible. Simplicity, what is going on inside me, is still tiresome to me!" or any other revolting banality.

To Make Speeches

Just prior to the elections, in the first country which deems it worthwhile to proceed in this kind of public expression of opinion, have yourself put on the ballot. Each of us has within himself the potential of an orator: multicolored loin cloths, glass trinkets of words. Through Surrealism he will take despair unawares in its poverty. One night, on a stage, he will, by himself, carve up the eternal heaven, that *Peau de l'ours*. He will promise so much that any promises he keeps will be a source of wonder and dismay. In answer to the claims of an entire people he will give a partial and ludicrous vote. He will make the bitterest enemies partake of a secret desire which will blow up the countries. And in this he will succeed simply by allowing himself to be moved by the immense word which dissolves into pity and revolves in hate. Incapable of failure, he will play on the velvet of all failures. He will be truly elected, and women will love him with an all-consuming passion.

To Write False Novels

Whoever you may be, if the spirit moves you burn a few laurel leaves and, without wishing to tend this meager fire, you will begin to write a novel. Surrealism will allow you to: all you have to do is set the needle marked "fair" at "action," and the rest will follow naturally. Here are some characters rather different in appearance; their names in your handwriting are a question of capital letters, and they will conduct themselves with the same ease with respect to active verbs as does the impersonal pronoun "it" with respect to words such as "is raining," "is," "must," etc. They will command them, so to speak, and wherever observation, reflection, and the faculty of generalization prove to be of no help to you, you may rest assured that they will credit you with a thousand intentions you never had. Thus endowed with a tiny number of physical and moral characteristics, these beings who in truth owe you so little will thereafter deviate not one iota from a certain line of conduct about which you need not concern yourself any further. Out of this will result a plot more or less clever in appearance, justifying point by point this moving or comforting denouement about which you couldn't care less. Your false novel will simulate to a marvelous degree a real novel; you will be rich, and everyone will agree that "you've really got a lot of guts," since it's also in this region that this something is located.

Of course, by an analogous method, and provided you ignore what you are reviewing, you can successfully devote yourself to false literary criticism.

How to Catch the Eye of a Woman You Pass in the Street

Against Death

Surrealism will usher you into death, which is a secret society. It will glove your hand, burying therein the profound M with which the word Memory begins. Do not forget to make proper arrangements for your last will and testament: speaking personally, I ask that I be taken to the cemetery in a moving van. May my friends destroy every last copy of the printing of the *Speech concerning the Modicum of Reality*.

Language has been given to man so that he may make Surrealist use of it. To the extent that he is required to make himself understood, he manages more or less to express himself, and by so doing to fulfill certain functions culled from among the most vulgar. Speaking, reading a letter, present no real problem for him, provided that, in so doing, he does not set himself a goal above the mean, that is, provided he confines himself to carrying on a conversation (for the pleasure of conversing) with someone. He is not worried about the words that are going to come, nor about the sentence which will follow after the sentence he is just completing. To a very simple question, he will be capable of making a lightning-like reply. In the absence of minor tics acquired through contact with others, he can without any ado offer an opinion on a limited number of subjects; for that he does not need to "count up to ten" before speaking or to formulate anything whatever ahead of time. Who has been able to convince him that this faculty of the first draft will only do him a disservice when he makes up his mind to establish more delicate relationships? There is no subject about which he should refuse to talk, to write about prolifically. All that results from listening to oneself, from reading what one has written, is the suspension of the occult, that admirable help. I am in no hurry to understand myself (basta! I shall always understand myself). If such and such a sentence of mine turns out to be somewhat disappointing, at least momentarily, I place my trust in the following sentence to redeem its sins: I carefully refrain from starting it over again or polishing it. The only thing that might prove fatal to me would be the slightest loss of impetus. Words, groups of words *which follow one another,* manifest among themselves the greatest solidarity. It is not up to me to favor one group over the other. It is up to a miraculous equivalent to intervene—and intervene it does.

Not only does this unrestricted language, which I am trying to render forever valid, which seems to me to adapt itself to all of life's circumstances, not only does this language not deprive me of any of my means, on the contrary it lends me an extraordinary lucidity, and it does so in an area where I least expected it. I shall even go so far as to maintain that it instructs me and, indeed, I have had occasion to use *surreally* words whose meaning I have forgotten. I was subsequently able to verify that the way in which I had used them corresponded perfectly with their definition. This would lead one to believe that we do not "learn," that all we ever do is "relearn." There are felicitous turns of speech that I have thus familiarized myself with. And I am not talking about the *poetic consciousness of objects* which I have been able to acquire only after a spiritual contact with them repeated a thousand times over.

The forms of Surrealist language adapt themselves best to dialogue. Here, two thoughts confront each other; while one is being delivered, the other is busy with it; but how is it busy with it? To assume that it incorporates it within itself would be tantamount to admitting that there is a time during which it is possible for it to live completely off that other thought, which is highly unlikely. And, in fact, the attention it pays is completely exterior; it has only time enough to approve or reject—generally reject—with all the consideration of which man is capable. This mode of language, moreover, does not allow the heart of the matter to be plumbed. My attention, prey to an entreaty which it cannot in all decency reject, treats the opposing thought as an enemy; in ordinary conversation, it "takes it up" almost always on the words, the figures of speech, it employs; it puts me in a position to turn it to good advantage in my reply by distorting them. This is true to such a degree that in certain pathological states of mind, where the sensorial disorders occupy the patient's complete attention, he limits himself, while continuing to answer the questions, to seizing the last word spoken in his presence or the last portion of the Surrealist sentence some trace of which he finds in his mind.

> Q. "How old are you?" A. "You." (*Echolalia.*)
> Q. "What is your name?" A. "Forty-five houses." (*Ganser syndrome, or beside-the-point replies.*)

There is no conversation in which some trace of this disorder does not occur. The effort to be social which dictates it and the considerable practice we have at it are the only things which enable us to conceal it temporarily. It is also the great weakness of the book that it is in constant conflict with its best, by which I mean the most demanding, readers. In the very short dialogue that I concocted above between the doctor and the madman, it was in fact the madman who got the better of the exchange. Because, through his replies, he obtrudes upon the attention of the doctor examining him—and because he is not the person asking the questions. Does this mean that his thought at this point is the stronger? Perhaps. He is free not to care any longer about his age or name.

Poetic Surrealism, which is the subject of this study, has focused its efforts up to this point on reestablishing dialogue in its absolute truth, by freeing both interlocutors from any obligations of politeness. Each of them simply pursues his soliloquy without trying to derive any special dialectical pleasure from it and without trying to impose anything whatsoever upon his neighbor. The remarks exchanged are not, as is generally the case, meant to develop some thesis, however unimportant it may be; they are as disaffected as possible. As for the reply that they elicit, it is, in principle, totally indifferent to the personal pride of the person speaking. The words, the images are only so many springboards for the mind of the listener. In *Les Champs magnétiques,* the first purely Surrealist work, this is the way in which the pages grouped together under the title *Barrières* must be conceived of—pages wherein Soupault and I show ourselves to be impartial interlocutors.

Surrealism does not allow those who devote themselves to it to forsake it whenever they like. There is every reason to believe that it acts on the mind very much as drugs do; like drugs, it creates a certain state of need and can push man to frightful revolts. It also is, if you like, an artificial paradise, and the taste one has for it derives from Baudelaire's criticism for the same reason as the others. Thus the analysis of the mysterious effects and special pleasures it can produce—in many respects Surrealism occurs as a *new vice* which does not necessarily seem to be restricted to the happy few; like hashish, it has the ability to satisfy all manner of tastes—such an analysis has to be included in the present study.

1. It is true of Surrealist images as it is of opium images that man does not evoke them; rather they "come to him spontaneously, despotically. He cannot chase them away; for the will is powerless now and no longer controls the faculties."[16] It remains to be seen whether images have ever been "evoked." If

one accepts, as I do, Reverdy's definition it does not seem possible to bring together, voluntarily, what he calls "two distant realities." The juxtaposition is made or not made, and that is the long and the short of it. Personally, I absolutely refuse to believe that, in Reverdy's work, images such as

> In the brook, there is a song that flows

or:

> Day unfolded like a white tablecloth

or:

> The world goes back into a sack

reveal the slightest degree of premeditation. In my opinion, it is erroneous to claim that "the mind has grasped the relationship" of two realities in the presence of each other. First of all, it has seized nothing consciously. It is, as it were, from the fortuitous juxtaposition of the two terms that a particular light has sprung, *the light of the image,* to which we are infinitely sensitive. The value of the image depends upon the beauty of the spark obtained; it is, consequently, a function of the difference of potential between the two conductors. When the difference exists only slightly, as in a comparison,[17] the spark is lacking. Now, it is not within man's power, so far as I can tell, to effect the juxtaposition of two realities so far apart. The principle of the association of ideas, such as we conceive of it, militates against it. Or else we would have to revert to an elliptical art, which Reverdy deplores as much as I. We are therefore obliged to admit that the two terms of the image are not deduced one from the other by the mind for the specific purpose of producing the spark, that they are the simultaneous products of the activity I call Surrealist, reason's role being limited to taking note of, and appreciating, the luminous phenomenon.

And just as the length of the spark increases to the extent that it occurs in rarefied gases, the Surrealist atmosphere created by automatic writing, which I have wanted to put within the reach of everyone, is especially conducive to the production of the most beautiful images. One can even go so far as to say that in this dizzying race the images appear like the only guideposts of the mind. By slow degrees the mind becomes convinced of the supreme reality of these images. At first limiting itself to submitting to them, it soon realizes that they flatter its reason, and increase its knowledge accordingly. The mind becomes aware of the limitless expanses wherein its desires are made manifest, where the pros and cons are constantly consumed, where its obscurity does not betray it. It goes forward, borne by these images which enrapture it, which scarcely leave it any time to blow upon the fire in its fingers. This is the most beautiful night of all, the *lightning-filled night:* day, compared to it, is night.

The countless kinds of Surrealist images would require a classification which I do not intend to make today. To group them according to their particular affinities would lead me far afield; what I basically want to mention is their common virtue. For me, their greatest virtue, I must confess, is the one that is arbitrary to the highest degree, the one that takes the longest time to translate into practical language, either because it contains an immense amount of seeming contradiction or because one of its terms is strangely concealed; or because, presenting itself as something sensational, it seems to end weakly (because it suddenly closes the angle of its compass), or because it derives from itself a ridiculous *formal* justification, or because it is of a hallucinatory kind, or because it very naturally gives to the abstract the mask of the concrete, or the opposite, or because it implies the negation of some elementary physical property, or because it provokes laughter. Here, in order, are a few examples of it:

The ruby of champagne.

(LAUTRÉAMONT)

Beautiful as the law of arrested development of the breast in adults, whose propensity to growth is not in proportion to the quantity of molecules that their organism assimilates.

(LAUTRÉAMONT)

A church stood dazzling as a bell.

(PHILIPPE SOUPAULT)

In Rrose Sélavy's sleep there is a dwarf issued from a well who comes to eat her bread at night.

(ROBERT DESNOS)

On the bridge the dew with the head of a tabby cat lulls itself to sleep.

(ANDRÉ BRETON)

A little to the left, in my firmament foretold, I see—but it's doubtless but a mist of blood and murder—the gleaming glass of liberty's disturbances.

(LOUIS ARAGON)

In the forest aflame
The lions were fresh.
(ROBERT VITRAC)

The color of a woman's stockings is not necessarily in the likeness of her eyes, which led a philosopher who it is pointless to mention, to say: "Cephalopods have more reasons to hate progress than do quadrupeds."

(MAX MORISE)

1st. Whether we like it or not, there is enough there to satisfy several demands of the mind. All these images seem to attest to the fact that the mind is ripe for something more than the benign joys it allows itself in general. This is the only way it has of turning to its own advantage the ideal quantity of events with which it is entrusted.[18] These images show it the extent of its ordinary dissipation and the drawbacks that it offers for it. In the final analysis, it's not such a bad thing for these images to upset the mind, for to upset the mind is to put it in the wrong. The sentences I quote make ample provision for this. But the mind which relishes them draws therefrom the conviction that it is on the *right track;* on its own, the mind is incapable of finding itself guilty of cavil; it has nothing to fear, since, moreover, it attempts to embrace everything.

2nd. The mind which plunges into Surrealism relives with glowing excitement the best part of its childhood. For such a mind, it is similar to the certainty with which a person who is drowning reviews once more, in the space of less than a second, all the insurmountable moments of his life. Some may say to me that the parallel is not very encouraging. But I have no intention of encouraging those who tell me that. From childhood memories, and from a few others, there emanates a sentiment of being unintegrated, and then later of *having gone astray,* which I hold to be the most fertile that exists. It is perhaps childhood that comes closest to one's "real life"; childhood beyond which man has at his disposal, aside from his laissez-passer, only a few complimentary tickets; childhood where everything nevertheless conspires to bring about the effective, risk-free possession of oneself. Thanks to Surrealism, it seems that opportunity knocks a second time. It is as though we were still running toward our salvation, or our perdition. In the shadow we again see a precious terror. Thank God, it's still only Purgatory. With a shudder, we cross what the occultists call *dangerous territory.* In my wake I raise up monsters that are lying in wait; they are not yet too ill-disposed toward me, and I am not lost, since I fear them. Here are "the elephants with the heads of women and the flying lions" which used to make Soupault and me tremble in our boots to meet, here is the "soluble fish" which still frightens me slightly. SOLUBLE FISH, am I not the soluble fish, I was born under the sign of Pisces, and man is soluble in his thought! The flora and fauna of Surrealism are inadmissible.

3rd. I do not believe in the establishment of a conventional Surrealist pattern any time in the near future. The characteristics common to all the texts of this kind, including those I have just cited and many others which alone could offer us a logical analysis and a careful grammatical analysis, do not preclude a certain evolution of Surrealist prose in time. Coming on the heels of a large number of essays I have written in this vein over the past five years, most of which I am indulgent enough to think are extremely disordered, the short anecdotes which comprise the balance of this volume offer me a glaring proof of what I am saying. I do not judge them to be any more worthless, because of that, in portraying for the reader the benefits which the Surrealist contribution is liable to make to his consciousness.

Surrealist methods would, moreover, demand to be heard. Everything is valid when it comes to obtaining the desired suddenness from certain associations. The pieces of paper that Picasso and Braque insert into their work have the same value as the introduction of a platitude into a literary analysis of the most rigorous sort. It is even permissible to entitle POEM what we get from the most random assemblage possible (observe, if you will, the syntax) of headlines and scraps of headlines cut out of the newspapers:

POEM

A burst of laughter
of sapphire in the island of Ceylon

The most beautiful straws
HAVE A FADED COLOR
UNDER THE LOCKS

on an isolated farm
FROM DAY TO DAY
the pleasant
grows worse

A carriage road
takes you to the edge of the unknown

coffee
preaches for its saint
THE DAILY ARTISAN OF YOUR BEAUTY
MADAM,

a pair
of silk stockings
is not

A leap into space
A STAG

Love above all
Everything could be worked out so well
PARIS IS A BIG VILLAGE

Watch out for
the fire that covers
THE PRAYER
of fair weather

Know that
The ultraviolet rays
have finished their task
short and sweet

THE FIRST WHITE PAPER
OF CHANCE
Red will be

The wandering singer
WHERE IS HE?
in memory
in his house
AT THE SUITORS' BALL

I do
as I dance
What people did, what they're going to do

And we could offer many many more examples. The theater, philosophy, science, criticism would all succeed in finding their bearings there. I hasten to add that future Surrealist techniques do not interest me.

Far more serious, in my opinion[19]—I have intimated it often enough—are the applications of Surrealism to action. To be sure, I do not believe in the prophetic nature of the Surrealist word. "It is the oracle, the things I say."[20] Yes, *as much as I like,* but what of the oracle itself?[21] Men's piety does not fool me. The Surrealist voice that shook Cumae, Dodona, and Delphi is nothing more than the voice which dictates my less irascible speeches to me. My *time* must not be its time, why should this voice help me resolve the childish problem of my destiny? I pretend, unfortunately, to act in a world where, in order to take into account its suggestions, I would be obliged to resort to two kinds of interpreters, one to translate its judgments for me, the other, impossible to find, to transmit to my fellow men whatever sense I could make out of them. This world, in which I endure what I endure (don't go see) this modern world, I mean, what the devil do you want me to do with it? Perhaps the Surrealist voice will be stilled, I have given up trying to keep track of those who have disappeared. I shall no longer enter into, however briefly, the marvelous detailed description of my years and my days. I shall be like Nijinski who was taken last year to the Russian ballet and did not realize what spectacle it was he was seeing. I shall be alone, very alone within myself, indifferent to all the world's ballets. What I have done, what I have left undone, I give it to you.

And ever since I have had a great desire to show forbearance to scientific musing, however unbecoming, in the final analysis, from every point of view. Radios? Fine. Syphilis? If you like. Photography? I don't see any reason why not. The cinema? Three cheers for darkened rooms. War? Gave us a good laugh. The telephone? Hello. Youth? Charming white hair. Try to make me say thank you: "Thank you." Thank you. If the common man has a high opinion of things which properly speaking belong to the realm of the laboratory, it is because such research has resulted in the manufacture of a machine or the discovery of some serum which the man in the street views as affecting him directly. He is quite sure that they have been trying to improve his lot. I am not quite sure to what extent scholars are motivated by humanitarian aims, but it does not seem to me that this factor constitutes a very marked degree of goodness. I am, of course, referring to true scholars and not to the vulgarizers and popularizers of all sorts who take out patents. In this realm as in any other, I believe in the pure Surrealist joy of the man who, forewarned that all others before him have failed, refuses to admit defeat, sets off from whatever point he chooses, along any other path save a reasonable one, and arrives wherever he can. Such and such an image, by which he deems it opportune to indicate his progress and which may result, perhaps, in his receiving public acclaim, is to me, I must confess, a matter of complete indifference. Nor is the material with which he must perforce encumber himself; his glass tubes or my metallic feathers . . . As for his method, I am willing to give it as much credit as I do mine. I have seen the inventor of the cutaneous plantar reflex at work; he manipulated his subjects without respite, it was much more than an "examination" he was employing; *it was obvious that he was following no set plan.* Here and there he formulated a remark, distantly, without nonetheless setting down his needle, while his hammer was never still. He left to others the futile task of curing patients. He was wholly consumed by and devoted to that sacred fever.

Surrealism, such as I conceive of it, asserts our complete *nonconformism* clearly enough so that there can be no question of translating it, at the trial of the real world, as evidence for the defense. It could, on the contrary, only serve to justify the complete state of distraction which we hope to achieve here below. Kant's absentmindedness regarding women, Pasteur's absentmindedness about "grapes," Curie's absentmindedness with respect to vehicles, are in this regard profoundly symptomatic. This world is only very relatively in tune with thought, and incidents of this kind are only the most obvious episodes of a war in which I am proud to be participating. Surrealism is the "invisible ray" which will one day enable us to win out over our opponents. "You are no longer trembling, carcass." This summer the roses are blue; the wood is of glass. The earth, draped in its verdant cloak, makes as little impression upon me as a ghost. It is living and ceasing to live that are imaginary solutions. Existence is elsewhere.

NOTES

1. Dostoevski, *Crime and Punishment.*
2. Pascal.
3. Barrès, *Proust.*
4. Account must be taken of the *depth* of the dream. For the most part I retain only what I can glean from its most superficial layers. What I most enjoy contemplating about a dream is everything that sinks back below the surface in a waking state, everything I have forgotten about my activities in the course of the preceding day, dark foliage, stupid branches. In "reality," likewise, I prefer to *fall.*
5. What is admirable about the fantastic is that there is no longer anything fantastic: there is only the real.
6. Breton's pun eludes translation: Fontaine = Fountain.—Tr.
7. See *Les Pas perdus,* published by N. R. F.
8. *Nord-Sud,* March 1918.
9. Were I a painter, this visual depiction would doubtless have become more important for me than the other. It was most certainly my previous predispositions which decided the matter. Since that day, I have had occasion to concentrate my attention voluntarily on similar apparitions, and I know that they are fully as clear as auditory phenomena. With a pencil and white sheet of paper to hand, I could easily trace their outlines. Here again it is not a matter of drawing, *but simply of tracing.* I could thus depict a tree, a wave, a musical instrument, all manner of things of which

I am presently incapable of providing even the roughest sketch. I would plunge into it, convinced that I would find my way again, in a maze of lines which at first glance would seem to be going nowhere. And, upon opening my eyes, I would get the very strong impression of something "never seen." The proof of what I am saying has been provided many times by Robert Desnos: to be convinced, one has only to leaf through the pages of issue number 36 of *Feuilles libres* which contains several of his drawings (*Romeo and Juliet, A Man Died This Morning,* etc.) which were taken by this magazine as the drawings of a madman and published as such.

10. Knut Hamsun ascribes this sort of revelation to which I had been subjected as deriving from *hunger,* and he may not be wrong. (The fact is I did not eat every day during that period of my life). Most certainly the manifestations that he describes in these terms are clearly the same:

"The following day I awoke at an early hour. It was still dark. My eyes had been open for a long time when I heard the clock in the apartment above strike five. I wanted to go back to sleep, but I couldn't; I was wide awake and a thousand thoughts were crowding through my mind.

"Suddenly a few good fragments came to mind, quite suitable to be used in a rough draft, or serialized; all of a sudden I found, quite by chance, beautiful phrases, phrases such as I had never written. I repeated them to myself slowly, word by word; they were excellent. And there were still more coming. I got up and picked up a pencil and some paper that were on a table behind my bed. It was as though some vein had burst within me, one word followed another, found its proper place, adapted itself to the situation, scene piled upon scene, the action unfolded, one retort after another welled up in my mind, I was enjoying myself immensely. Thoughts came to me so rapidly and continued to flow so abundantly that I lost a whole host of delicate details, because my pencil could not keep up with them, and yet I went as fast as I could, my hand in constant motion, I did not lose a minute. The sentences continued to well up within me, I was pregnant with my subject."

Apollinaire asserted that de Chirico's first paintings were done under the influence of cenesthesic disorders (migraines, colics, etc.).

11. I believe more and more in the infallibility of my thought with respect to myself, and this is too fair. Nonetheless, with this *thought-writing,* where one is at the mercy of the first outside distraction, "ebullutions" can occur. It would be inexcusable for us to pretend otherwise. By definition, thought is strong, and incapable of catching itself in error. The blame for these obvious weaknesses must be placed on suggestions that come to it from without.

12. And also by Thomas Carlyle in *Sartor Resartus* ([Book III] Chapter VIII, "Natural Supernaturalism"), 1833–34.

13. See also *L'Idéoréalisme* by Saint-Pol-Roux.

14. I could say the same of a number of philosophers and painters, including, among these latter, Uccello, from painters of the past, and, in the modern era, Seurat, Gustave Moreau, Matisse (in "La Musique," for example), Derain, Picasso (by far the most pure), Braque, Duchamp, Picabia, de Chirico (so admirable for so long), Klee, Man Ray, Max Ernst, and, one so close to us, André Masson.

15. NOUVELLES HÉBRIDES, DÉSORDRE FORMEL., DEUIL POUR DEUIL.

16. Baudelaire.

17. Compare the image in the work of Jules Renard.

18. Let us not forget that, according to Novalis' formula, "there are series of events which run parallel to real events. Men and circumstances generally modify the ideal train of circumstances, so that it seems imperfect; and their consequences are also

equally imperfect. Thus it was with the Reformation; instead of Protestantism, we got Lutheranism."

19. Whatever reservations I may be allowed to make concerning responsibility in general and the medico-legal considerations which determine an individual's degree of responsibility—complete responsibility, irresponsibility, limited responsibility (sic)—however difficult it may be for me to accept the principle of any kind of responsibility, I would like to know how the first punishable offenses, the Surrealist character of which will be clearly apparent, will be *judged*. Will the accused be acquitted, or will he merely be given the benefit of the doubt because of extenuating circumstances? It's a shame that the violation of the laws governing the Press is today scarcely repressed, for if it were not we would soon see a trial of this sort: the accused has published a book which is an outrage to public decency. Several of his "most respected and honorable" fellow citizens have lodged a complaint against him, and he is also charged with slander and libel. There are also all sorts of other charges against him, such as insulting and defaming the army, inciting to murder, rape, etc. The accused, moreover, wastes no time in agreeing with the accusers in "stigmatizing" most of the ideas expressed. His only defense is claiming that he does not consider himself to be the author of his book, said book being no more and no less than a Surrealist concoction which precludes any question of merit or lack of merit on the part of the person who signs it; further, that all he has done is copy a document without offering any opinion thereon, and that he is at least as foreign to the accused text as is the presiding judge himself.

What is true for the publication of a book will also hold true for a whole host of other acts as soon as Surrealist methods begin to enjoy widespread favor. When that happens, a new morality must be substituted for the prevailing morality, the source of all our trials and tribulations.

20. Rimbaud.

21. Still, STILL. . . . We must absolutely get to the bottom of this. Today, June 8, 1924, about one o'clock, the voice whispered to me: "Béthune, Béthune." What did it mean? I have never been to Béthune, and have only the vaguest notion as to where it is located on the map of France. Béthune evokes nothing for me, not even a scene from *The Three Musketeers*. I should have left for Béthune, where perhaps there was something awaiting me; that would have been too simple, really. Someone told me they had read in a book by Chesterton about a detective who, in order to find someone he is looking for in a certain city, simply scoured from roof to cellar the houses which, from the outside, seemed somehow abnormal to him, were it only in some slight detail. This system is as good as any other.

Similarly, in 1919, Soupault went into any number of impossible buildings to ask the concierge whether Philippe Soupault did in fact live there. He would not have been surprised, I suspect, by an affirmative reply. He would have gone and knocked on his door.

Bertolt Brecht

1898–1956

Eugen Bertolt Friedrich Brecht was born the son of a wealthy industrialist in Augsberg on February 10, 1898. He studied medicine in Munich from 1917 to 1921, serving briefly in an army hospital during 1918. In 1918 he also wrote his first play, *Baal;* its protagonist—of the same name—gives an indication of the crudeness with which Brecht himself was endowed and which he would set up as a positive model in his later work.

After the war Brecht lived alternately in Augsberg and Munich, where he wrote further plays, including *In the Thicket of the Cities* (1922), *Spartakus* (alternately titled *Drums in the Night* [1922]), and an adaptation of Marlowe's *Life of Edward the Second* (1924). His work at this time shows the influence of the Munich comedian Karl Valentin, along with that of the plays of Frank Wedekind. His mother's death in 1920 left him free to settle in Munich, where in 1922 he married his first wife (a daughter would be born less than a year later). With the production of *A Man Is a Man* (1924–25), the first period of Brecht's work is ended; the play follows the methodical "conversion" of an Ordinary Man into a caricatured soldier, and the transformation takes place largely through an externalized exchange of appearances, of masks: because Galy Gay is dressed as a soldier, and his external circumstances altered, he becomes a different "person." The extreme cynicism of Brecht's early period, characterized by hopelessly lonely vagabonds like Baal, was beginning to yield to the inherent social criticism of the idea that man is "an ensemble of social relationships."

Brecht had begun studying Marxism in 1924; his occupation with study did not prevent him from producing, in 1928, his own adaptation of John Gay's *The Beggar's Opera,* which he titled *The Threepenny Opera.* Lotte Lenya, wife of Kurt Weill (composer of the opera's score), was the leading lady, and the success of the production gave Brecht an international reputation.

From this period also date *Happy End* and *The Rise and Fall of the City of Mahagonny* (1930). These works display a mixture of cabaret parody and didactic moralizing that have made them Brecht's most popular plays. Shortly thereafter he wrote several *Lehr-stücke* ("teaching pieces"), which leave their didactic content even more bare and unconcealed; they resemble children's stories and have been used as textbooks.

The day after the burning of the Reichstag in February 1933, Brecht fled Germany with his second wife (the actress Helene Weigel, whom he had married in 1928; she was to have leading roles in many of his plays) and daughter; after stays in Prague and Zurich, they were to settle in Denmark for seven years, until the German invasion of 1940. Here, in rural isolation, Brecht was visited by Walter Benjamin, and here he wrote most of his mature work, including *The Life of Galileo* (1937–39), *The Good Woman of Setzuan* (1938–41), and *Mother Courage* (1941).

In 1940 Brecht fled to Finland, then across Siberia to Vladivostok, and thence to Santa Monica, California, where he spent the war years in failed attempts to sell scripts to Hollywood. Friendships with other German emigrés, and with Charles Chaplin, whose work he had long admired, provided some solace, as did a production of *Galileo* in New York. In 1947 he was called before the House Committee on Un-American Activities to answer for his Communist past. Brecht, who had dealt with far more sophisticated persecutors than these, managed to slip free and return to Switzerland, bringing with him the manuscript of *The Caucasian Chalk Circle* (1944; published 1949). He was determined to return to Germany, and deliberately chose East Berlin in the Soviet zone as his residence; for all that he knew of Stalinist censorship, he felt he had to commit his efforts to the experiment of a Communist society. Even though he was provided with state funds for the famous Theatre am Schiffbauerdamm, where he directed his Berliner Ensemble, he was soon bitterly contemptuous of his Marxist overlords—especially after the brutal suppression of a popular uprising in 1953 (foreshadowing that in Hungary in 1956). Theatre practice and public political involvements left him little time to write in his last years; his most important late work was the *Buckower Elegies* (1950), a collection of deceptively simple poems of unusually subdued character. He died in East Berlin on August 14, 1956.

Shouldn't We Abolish Aesthetics?

D ear Mr X,

When I invited you to look at the drama from a sociological point of view I did so because I was hoping that sociology would be the death of our existing drama. As you immediately saw, there was a simple and radical task for sociology: to prove that there was no justification for this drama's continued existence and no future for anything based (now or in the future) on the assumptions which once made drama possible. To quote a sociologist whose vocabulary I hope we both accept, there is no sociological space for it. Yours is the only branch of knowledge that enjoys sufficient freedom of thought; all the rest are too closely involved in perpetuating our period's general level of civilization.

You were immune to the usual superstition which holds that a play has undertaken to satisfy *eternal* human urges when the only eternal urge that it sets out to satisfy is the urge to see a play. You know other urges change, and you know why. As you don't feel that the disappearance of an urge means the collapse of humanity, you, the sociologist, are alone in being prepared to admit that Shakespeare's great plays, the basis of our drama, are no longer effective. These works were followed by three centuries in which the individual developed into a capitalist, and what killed them was not capitalism's conse- quences but capitalism itself. There is little point in mentioning post- Shakespearean drama, as it is invariably much feebler, and in Germany has been debauched by Latin influences. It continues to be supported just out of local patriotism.

Once we adopt the sociological point of view we realize that so far as literature is concerned we are in a bog. We may possibly be able to persuade the aesthete to admit what the sociologist believes—namely that present-day drama is no good—but we shall never deprive him of his conviction that it can be improved. (The aesthete won't hesitate to admit that he can only conceive of such an 'improvement' of the drama by using the hoary old tricks of the trade: 'better' construction in the old sense, 'better' motivation for those spectators who are used to the good old motivation, and so on.) Apparently the sociologist will only support us if we say that this kind of drama is beyond repair and beg for it to be done away with. The sociologist knows that there are circumstances where improvement no longer does any good. His scale of judgment runs not from 'good' to 'bad' but from 'correct' to 'false'. If a play is 'false' then he won't praise it on the grounds that it is 'good' (or 'beautiful'); and he alone will remain deaf to the aesthetic appeal of a 'false' production. Only he knows what is false; he does not deal in relativity; he bases himself on vital interests; he gets no fun from being able to prove everything but just wants to find out the one thing worth proving; he doesn't by any means take responsibility for everything, but only for one thing. The sociologist is the man for us.

The aesthetic point of view is ill-suited to the plays being written at present, even where it leads to favourable judgments. You can see this by looking at any move in favour of the new playwrights. Even where the critics' instincts guided them right their aesthetic vocabulary gave them very few convincing arguments for their favourable attitude, and no proper means of informing the public. What is more, the theatre, while encouraging the production of new plays, gave absolutely no practical guide. Thus in the end the new plays only served the old theatre and helped to postpone the collapse on which their own future depended. It is impossible to understand what is being written today if one ignores the present generation's active hostility towards all that preceded it, and shares the general belief that it too is merely clamouring to be let in and taken notice of. This generation doesn't want to capture the theatre, audience and all, and perform good or merely contemporary plays in the same theatre and to the same audience; nor has it any chance of doing so; it has a duty and a chance to capture the theatre for a *different* audience. The works now being written are coming more and more to lead towards that great epic theatre which corresponds to the sociological situation; neither their content nor their form can be understood except by the minority that understands this. They are not going to satisfy the old aesthetics; they are going to destroy it.

> With you in this hope,
> Brecht

A Short Organum for the Theatre

Prologue

The following sets out to define an aesthetic drawn from a particular kind of theatrical performance which has been worked out in practice over the past few decades. In the theoretical statements, excursions, technical indications occasionally published in the form of notes to the writer's plays, aesthetics have only been touched on casually and with comparative lack of interest. There you saw a particular species of theatre extending or contracting its social functions, perfecting or sifting its artistic methods and establishing or maintaining its aesthetics—if the question arose—by rejecting or converting to its own use the dominant conventions of morality or taste according to its tactical needs. This theatre justified its inclination to social commitment by pointing to the social commitment in universally accepted works of art, which only fail to strike the eye because it was the accepted commitment. As for the products of our own time, it held that their lack of any worthwhile content was a sign of decadence: it accused these entertainment emporiums of having degenerated into branches of the bourgeois narcotics business. The stage's inaccurate representations of our social life, including those classed as so-called Naturalism, led it to call for scientifically exact representations; the tasteless rehashing of empty visual or spiritual palliatives, for the noble logic of the multiplication table. The cult of beauty, conducted with hostility towards learning and contempt for the useful, was dismissed by it as itself contemptible, especially as nothing beautiful resulted. The battle was for a theatre fit for the scientific age, and where its planners found it too hard to borrow or steal from the armoury of aesthetic concepts enough weapons to defend themselves against the aesthetics of the Press they simply threatened 'to transform the means of enjoyment into an instrument of instruction, and to convert certain amusement establishments into organs of mass communication': i.e. to emigrate from the realm of the merely enjoyable. Aesthetics, that heirloom of a by now depraved and parasitic class, was in such a lamentable state that a theatre would certainly have gained both in reputation and in elbowroom if it had rechristened itself thaëter. And yet what we achieved in the way of theatre for a scientific age was not science but theatre, and the accumulated innovations worked out during the Nazi period and the war—when practical demonstration was impossible—compel some attempt to set this species of theatre in its aesthetic background, or anyhow to sketch for it the outlines of a conceivable aesthetic. To explain the theory of theatrical alienation except within an aesthetic framework would be impossibly awkward.

Today one could go so far as to compile an aesthetics of the exact sciences. Galileo spoke of the elegance of certain formulae and the point of an

617

experiment; Einstein suggests that the sense of beauty has a part to play in the making of scientific discoveries; while the atomic physicist R. Oppenheimer praises the scientific attitude, which 'has its own kind of beauty and seems to suit mankind's position on earth'.

Let us therefore cause general dismay by revoking our decision to emigrate from the realm of the merely enjoyable, and even more general dismay by announcing our decision to take up lodging there. Let us treat the theatre as a place of entertainment, as is proper in an aesthetic discussion, and try to discover which type of entertainment suits us best.

1

'Theatre' consists in this: in making live representations of reported or invented happenings between human beings and doing so with a view to entertainment. At any rate that is what we shall mean when we speak of theatre, whether old or new.

2

To extend this definition we might add happenings between humans and gods, but as we are only seeking to establish the minimum we can leave such matters aside. Even if we did accept such an extension we should still have to say that the 'theatre' set-up's broadest function was to give pleasure. It is the noblest function that we have found for 'theatre'.

3

From the first it has been the theatre's business to entertain people, as it also has of all the other arts. It is this business which always gives it its particular dignity; it needs no other passport than fun, but this it has got to have. We should not by any means be giving it a higher status if we were to turn it e.g. into a purveyor of morality; it would on the contrary run the risk of being debased, and this would occur at once if it failed to make its moral lesson enjoyable, and enjoyable to the senses at that: a principle, admittedly, by which morality can only gain. Not even instruction can be demanded of it: at any rate, no more utilitarian lesson than how to move pleasurably, whether in the physical or in the spiritual sphere. The theatre must in fact remain something entirely superfluous, though this indeed means that it is the superfluous for which we live. Nothing needs less justification than pleasure.

4

Thus what the ancients, following Aristotle, demanded of tragedy is nothing higher or lower than that it should entertain people. Theatre may be said to be derived from ritual, but that is only to say that it becomes theatre once the two have separated; what it brought over from the mysteries was not its former ritual function, but purely and simply the pleasure which accompanied this. And the catharsis of which Aristotle writes—cleansing by fear and pity, or from fear and pity—is a purification which is performed not only in a pleasurable way, but precisely for the purpose of pleasure. To ask or to accept more of the theatre is to set one's own mark too low.

5

Even when people speak of higher and lower degrees of pleasure, art stares impassively back at them; for it wishes to fly high and low and to be left in peace, so long as it can give pleasure to people.

6

Yet there are weaker (simple) and stronger (complex) pleasures which the theatre can create. The last-named, which are what we are dealing with in great drama, attain their climaxes rather as cohabitation does through love: they are more intricate, richer in communication, more contradictory and more productive of results.

7

And different periods' pleasures varied naturally according to the system under which people lived in society at the time. The Greek demos [literally: the demos of the Greek circus] ruled by tyrants had to be entertained differently from the feudal court of Louis XIV. The theatre was required to deliver different representations of men's life together: not just representations of a different life, but also representations of a different sort.

8

According to the sort of entertainment which was possible and necessary under the given conditions of men's life together the characters had to be given varying proportions, the situations to be constructed according to varying points of view. Stories have to be narrated in various ways, so that these particular Greeks may be able to amuse themselves with the inevitability of divine laws where ignorance never mitigates the punishment; these French with the graceful self-discipline demanded of the great ones of this earth by a courtly code of duty; the Englishmen of the Elizabethan age with the self-awareness of the new individual personality which was then uncontrollably bursting out.

9

And we must always remember that the pleasure given by representations of such different sorts hardly ever depended on the representation's likeness to the thing portrayed. Incorrectness, or considerable improbability even, was hardly or not at all disturbing, so long as the incorrectness had a certain consistency and the improbability remained of a constant kind. All that mattered was the illusion of compelling momentum in the story told, and this was created by all sorts of poetic and theatrical means. Even today we are happy to overlook such inaccuracies if we can get something out of the spiritual purifications of Sophocles or the sacrificial acts of Racine or the unbridled frenzies of Shakespeare, by trying to grasp the immense or splendid feelings of the principal characters in these stories.

10

For of all the many sorts of representation of happenings between humans which the theatre has made since ancient times, and which have given entertainment despite their incorrectness and improbability, there are even today an astonishing number that also give entertainment to us.

11

In establishing the extent to which we can be satisfied by representations from so many different periods—something that can hardly have been possible to the children of those vigorous periods themselves—are we not at the same time creating the suspicion that we have failed to discover the special pleasures, the proper entertainment of our own time?

12

And our enjoyment of the theatre must have become weaker than that of the ancients, even if our way of living together is still sufficiently like theirs for it to be felt at all. We grasp the old works by a comparatively new method— empathy—on which they rely little. Thus the greater part of our enjoyment is drawn from other sources than those which our predecessors were able to exploit so fully. We are left safely dependent on beauty of language, on elegance of narration, on passages which stimulate our own private imaginations: in short, on the incidentals of the old works. These are precisely the poetical and theatrical means which hide the imprecisions of the story. Our theatres no longer have either the capacity or the wish to tell these stories, even the relatively recent ones of the great Shakespeare, at all clearly: i.e. to make the connection of events credible. And according to Aristotle—and we agree there—narrative is the soul of drama. We are more and more disturbed to see how crudely and carelessly men's life together is represented, and that not only in old works but also in contemporary ones constructed according to the old recipes. Our whole way of appreciation is starting to get out of date.

13

It is the inaccurate way in which happenings between human beings are represented that restricts our pleasure in the theatre. The reason: we and our forebears have a different relationship to what is being shown.

14

For when we look about us for an entertainment whose impact is immediate, for a comprehensive and penetrating pleasure such as our theatre could give us by representations of men's life together, we have to think of ourselves as children of a scientific age. Our life as human beings in society— i.e. our life—is determined by the sciences to a quite new extent.

15

A few hundred years ago a handful of people, working in different countries but in correspondence with one another, performed certain experiments by which they hoped to wring from Nature her secrets. Members of a class of craftsmen in the already powerful cities, they transmitted their discoveries to people who made practical use of them, without expecting more from the new sciences than personal profit for themselves.

Crafts which had progressed by methods virtually unchanged during a thousand years now developed hugely; in many places, which became linked by competition, they gathered from all directions great masses of men, and these, adopting new forms of organization, started producing on a giant scale. Soon mankind was showing powers whose extent it would till that time scarcely have dared to dream of.

16

It was as if mankind for the first time now began a conscious and coordinated effort to make the planet that was its home fit to live on. Many of the earth's components, such as coal, water, oil, now became treasures. Steam was made to shift vehicles; a few small sparks and the twitching of frogs' legs revealed a natural force which produced light, carried sounds across continents, etc. In all directions man looked about himself with a new vision, to see how he could adapt to his convenience familiar but as yet unexploited objects. His surroundings changed increasingly from decade to decade, then from year to year, then almost from day to day. I who am writing this write it on a machine which at the time of my birth was unknown. I travel in the new vehicles with a rapidity that my grandfather could not imagine; in those days nothing moved so fast. And I rise in the air: a thing that my father was unable to do. With my father I already spoke across the width of a continent, but it was together with my son that I first saw the moving pictures of the explosion at Hiroshima.

17

The new sciences may have made possible this vast alteration and all-important alterability of our surroundings, yet it cannot be said that their spirit determines everything that we do. The reason why the new way of thinking and feeling has not yet penetrated the great mass of men is that the

sciences, for all their success in exploiting and dominating nature, have been
stopped by the class which they brought to power—the bourgeoisie—from
operating in another field where darkness still reigns, namely that of the
relations which people have to one another during the exploiting and dominating process. This business on which all alike depended was performed
without the new intellectual methods that made it possible ever illuminating
the mutual relationships of the people who carried it out. The new approach to
nature was not applied to society.

18

In the event people's mutual relations have become harder to disentangle
than ever before. The gigantic joint undertaking on which they are engaged
seems more and more to split them into two groups; increases in production
lead to increases in misery; only a minority gain from the exploitation of
nature, and they only do so because they exploit men. What might be progress
for all then becomes advancement for a few, and an ever-increasing part of the
productive process gets applied to creating means of destruction for mighty
wars. During these wars the mothers of every nation, with their children
pressed to them, scan the skies in horror for the deadly inventions of science.

19

The same attitude as men once showed in face of unpredictable natural
catastrophes they now adopt towards their own undertakings. The bourgeois
class, which owes to science an advancement that it was able, by ensuring that
it alone enjoyed the fruits, to convert into domination, knows very well that its
rule would come to an end if the scientific eye were turned on its own
undertakings. And so that new science which was founded about a hundred
years ago and deals with the character of human society was born in the
struggle between rulers and ruled. Since then a certain scientific spirit has
developed at the bottom, among the new class of workers whose natural
element is large-scale production; from down there the great catastrophes are
spotted as undertakings by the rulers.

20

But science and art meet on this ground, that both are there to make
men's life easier, the one setting out to maintain, the other to entertain us. In
the age to come art will create entertainment from that new productivity which
can so greatly improve our maintenance, and in itself, if only it is left
unshackled, may prove to be the greatest pleasure of them all.

21

If we want now to surrender ourselves to this great passion for producing,
what ought our representations of men's life together to look like? What is that

productive attitude in face of nature and of society which we children of a scientific age would like to take up pleasurably in our theatre?

22

The attitude is a critical one. Faced with a river, it consists in regulating the river; faced with a fruit tree, in spraying the fruit tree; faced with movement, in constructing vehicles and aeroplanes; faced with society, in turning society upside down. Our representations of human social life are designed for river-dwellers, fruit farmers, builders of vehicles and upturners of society, whom we invite into our theatres and beg not to forget their cheerful occupations while we hand the world over to their minds and hearts, for them to change as they think fit.

23

The theatre can only adopt such a free attitude if it lets itself be carried along by the strongest currents in its society and associates itself with those who are necessarily most impatient to make great alterations there. The bare wish, if nothing else, to evolve an art fit for the times must drive our theatre of the scientific age straight out into the suburbs, where it can stand as it were wide open, at the disposal of those who live hard and produce much, so that they can be fruitfully entertained there with their great problems. They may find it hard to pay for our art, and immediately to grasp the new method of entertainment, and we shall have to learn in many respects what they need and how they need it; but we can be sure of their interest. For these men who seem so far apart from natural science are only apart from it because they are being forcibly kept apart; and before they can get their hands on it they have first to develop and put into effect a new science of society; so that these are the true children of the scientific age, who alone can get the theatre moving if it is to move at all. A theatre which makes productivity its main source of entertainment has also to take it for its theme, and with greater keenness than ever now that man is everywhere hampered by men from self-production: i.e. from maintaining himself, entertaining and being entertained. The theatre has to become geared into reality if it is to be in a position to turn out effective representations of reality, and to be allowed to do so.

24

But this makes it simpler for the theatre to edge as close as possible to the apparatus of education and mass communication. For although we cannot bother it with the raw material of knowledge in all its variety, which would stop it from being enjoyable, it is still free to find enjoyment in teaching and inquiring. It constructs its workable representations of society, which are then in a position to influence society, wholly and entirely as a game: for those who are constructing society it sets out society's experiences, past and present alike, in such a manner that the audience can 'appreciate' the feelings, insights and impulses which are distilled by the wisest, most active and most passionate among us from the events of the day or the century. They must be entertained with the wisdom that comes from the solution of problems, with the anger that is a practical expression of sympathy with the underdog, with the respect due to those who respect humanity, or rather whatever is kind to humanity; in short, with whatever delights those who are producing something.

25

And this also means that the theatre can let its spectators enjoy the particular ethic of their age, which springs from productivity. A theatre which converts the critical approach—i.e. our great productive method—into pleasure finds nothing in the ethical field which it must do and a great deal that it can. Even the wholly anti-social can be a source of enjoyment to society so long as it is presented forcefully and on the grand scale. It then often proves to have considerable powers of understanding and other unusually valuable capacities, applied admittedly to a destructive end. Even the bursting flood of a vast catastrophe can be appreciated in all its majesty by society, if society knows how to master it; then we make it our own.

26

For such an operation as this we can hardly accept the theatre as we see it before us. Let us go into one of these houses and observe the effect which it has on the spectators. Looking about us, we see somewhat motionless figures in a peculiar condition: they seem strenuously to be tensing all their muscles, except where these are flabby and exhausted. They scarcely communicate with each other; their relations are those of a lot of sleepers, though of such as dream restlessly because, as is popularly said of those who have nightmares, they are lying on their backs. True, their eyes are open, but they stare rather than see, just as they listen rather than hear. They look at the stage as if in a trance: an expression which comes from the Middle Ages, the days of witches and priests. Seeing and hearing are activities, and can be pleasant ones, but these people seem relieved of activity and like men to whom something is being done. This detached state, where they seem to be given over to vague but profound sensations, grows deeper the better the work of the actors, and so we, as we do not approve of this situation, should like them to be as bad as possible.

27

As for the world portrayed there, the world from which slices are cut in order to produce these moods and movements of the emotions, its appearance is such, produced from such slight and wretched stuff as a few pieces of cardboard, a little miming, a bit of text, that one has to admire the theatre folk who, with so feeble a reflection of the real world, can move the feelings of their audience so much more strongly than does the world itself.

28

In any case we should excuse these theatre folk, for the pleasures which they sell for money and fame could not be induced by an exacter representation of the world, nor could their inexact renderings be presented in a less magical way. Their capacity to represent people can be seen at work in various instances; it is especially the rogues and the minor figures who reveal their knowledge of humanity and differ one from the other, but the central figures have to be kept general, so that it is easier for the onlooker to identify himself with them, and at all costs each trait of character must be drawn from the narrow field within which everyone can say at once: that is how it is.

For the spectator wants to be put in possession of quite definite sensations, just as a child does when it climbs on to one of the horses on a roundabout: the sensation of pride that it can ride, and has a horse; the pleasure of being carried, and whirled past other children; the adventurous daydreams in which it pursues others or is pursued, etc. In leading the child to experience all this the degree to which its wooden seat resembles a horse counts little, nor does it matter that the ride is confined to a small circle. The one important point for the spectators in these houses is that they should be able to swap a contradictory world for a consistent one, one that they scarcely know for one of which they can dream.

29

That is the sort of theatre which we face in our operations, and so far it has been fully able to transmute our optimistic friends, whom we have called the children of the scientific era, into a cowed, credulous, hypnotized mass.

30

True, for about half a century they have been able to see rather more faithful representations of human social life, as well as individual figures who were in revolt against certain social evils or even against the structure of society as a whole. They felt interested enough to put up with a temporary and exceptional restriction of language, plot and spiritual scope; for the fresh wind of the scientific spirit nearly withered the charms to which they had grown used. The sacrifice was not especially worth while. The greater subtlety of the representations subtracted from one pleasure without satisfying another. The field of human relationships came within our view, but not within our grasp. Our feelings, having been aroused in the old (magic) way, were bound themselves to remain unaltered.

31

For always and everywhere theatres were the amusement centres of a class which restricted the scientific spirit to the natural field, not daring to let it loose on the field of human relationships. The tiny proletarian section of the

public, reinforced to a negligible and uncertain extent by renegade intellectuals, likewise still needed the old kind of entertainment, as a relief from its
predetermined way of life.

32

So let us march ahead! Away with all obstacles! Since we seem to have
landed in a battle, let us fight! Have we not seen how disbelief can move
mountains? Is it not enough that we should have found that something is
being kept from us? Before one thing and another there hangs a curtain: let us
draw it up!

33

The theatre as we know it shows the structure of society (represented on
the stage) as incapable of being influenced by society (in the auditorium).
Oedipus, who offended against certain principles underlying the society of his
time, is executed: the gods see to that; they are beyond criticism. Shakespeare's great solitary figures, bearing on their breast the star of their fate,
carry through with irresistible force their futile and deadly outbursts; they
prepare their own downfall; life, not death, becomes obscene as they collapse;
the catastrophe is beyond criticism. Human sacrifices all round! Barbaric
delights! We know that the barbarians have their art. Let us create another.

34

How much longer are our souls, leaving our 'mere' bodies under cover of
the darkness, to plunge into those dreamlike figures up on the stage, there to
take part in the crescendos and climaxes which 'normal' life denies us? What
kind of release is it at the end of all these plays (which is a happy end only for
the conventions of the period—suitable measures, the restoration of order—),
when we experience the dreamlike executioner's axe which cuts short such
crescendos as so many excesses? We slink into *Oedipus;* for taboos still exist
and ignorance is no excuse before the law. Into *Othello;* for jealously still
causes us trouble and everything depends on possession. Into *Wallenstein;* for
we need to be free for the competitive struggle and to observe the rules, or it
would peter out. This deadweight of old habits is also needed for plays like
Ghosts and *The Weavers,* although there the social structure, in the shape of
a 'setting', presents itself as more open to question. The feelings, insights and
impulses of the chief characters are forced on us, and so we learn nothing
more about society than we can get from the 'setting'.

35

We need a type of theatre which not only releases the feelings, insights
and impulses possible within the particular historical field of human relations

in which the action takes place, but employs and encourages those thoughts and feelings which help transform the field itself.

36

The field has to be defined in historically relative terms. In other words we must drop our habit of taking the different social structures of past periods, then stripping them of everything that makes them different; so that they all look more or less like our own, which then acquires from this process a certain air of having been there all along, in other words of permanence pure and simple. Instead we must leave them their distinguishing marks and keep their impermanence always before our eyes, so that our own period can be seen to be impermanent too. (It is of course futile to make use of fancy colours and folklore for this, such as our theatres apply precisely in order to emphasize the similarities in human behaviour at different times. We shall indicate the theatrical methods below.)

37

If we ensure that our characters on the stage are moved by social impulses and that these differ according to the period, then we make it harder for our spectator to identify himself with them. He cannot simply feel: that's how I would act, but at most can say: if I had lived under those circumstances. And if we play works dealing with our own time as though they were historical, then perhaps the circumstances under which he himself acts will strike him as equally odd; and this is where the critical attitude begins.

38

The 'historical conditions' must of course not be imagined (nor will they be so constructed) as mysterious Powers (in the background); on the contrary, they are created and maintained by men (and will in due course be altered by them): it is the actions taking place before us that allow us to see what they are.

39

If a character responds in a manner historically in keeping with his period, and would respond otherwise in other periods, does that mean that he is not simply 'Everyman'? It is true that a man will respond differently according to his circumstances and his class; if he were living at another time, or in his youth, or on the darker side of life, he would infallibly give a different response, though one still determined by the same factors and like anyone else's response in that situation at that time. So should we not ask if there are any further differences of response? Where is the man himself, the living, unmistakeable man, who is not quite identical with those identified with him? It is clear that his stage image must bring him to light, and this will come about if this particular contradiction is recreated in the image. The image that gives historical definition will retain something of the rough sketching which indicates traces of other movements and features all around the fully-worked-out figure. Or imagine a man standing in a valley and making a speech in which he occasionally changes his views or simply utters sentences which contradict one another, so that the accompanying echo forces them into confrontation.

40

Such images certainly demand a way of acting which will leave the spectator's intellect free and highly mobile. He has again and again to make what one might call hypothetical adjustments to our structure, by mentally switching off the motive forces of our society or by substituting others for them: a process which leads real conduct to acquire an element of 'unnaturalness', thus allowing the real motive forces to be shorn of their naturalness and become capable of manipulation.

41

It is the same as when an irrigation expert looks at a river together with its former bed and various hypothetical courses which it might have followed if there had been a different tilt to the plateau or a different volume of water. And while he in his mind is looking at a new river, the socialist in his is hearing new kinds of talk from the labourers who work by it. And similarly in the theatre our spectator should find that the incidents set among such labourers are also accompanied by echoes and by traces of sketching.

42

The kind of acting which was tried out at the Schiffbauerdamm Theater in Berlin between the First and Second World Wars, with the object of producing such images, is based on the 'alienation effect' (A-effect). A representation that alienates is one which allows us to recognize its subject, but at the same time makes it seem unfamiliar. The classical and medieval theatre alienated its characters by making them wear human or animal masks; the Asiatic theatre even today uses musical and pantomimic A-effects. Such devices were certainly a barrier to empathy, and yet this technique owed more, not less, to hypnotic suggestion than do those by which empathy is achieved. The social aims of these old devices were entirely different from our own.

43

The old A-effects quite remove the object represented from the spectator's grasp, turning it into something that cannot be altered; the new are not odd in themselves, though the unscientific eye stamps anything strange as odd. The new alienations are only designed to free socially-conditioned phenomena from that stamp of familiarity which protects them against our grasp today.

44

For it seems impossible to alter what has long not been altered. We are always coming on things that are too obvious for us to bother to understand them. What men experience among themselves they think of as 'the' human experience. A child, living in a world of old men, learns how things work there. He knows the run of things before he can walk. If anyone is bold enough to want something further, he only wants to have it as an exception. Even if he realizes that the arrangements made for him by 'Providence' are only what has been provided by society he is bound to see society, that vast collection of beings like himself, as a whole that is greater than the sum of its parts and therefore not in any way to be influenced. Moreover, he would be used to things that could not be influenced; and who mistrusts what he is used to? To transform himself from general passive acceptance to a corresponding state of suspicious inquiry he would need to develop that detached eye with which the great Galileo observed a swinging chandelier. He was amazed by this pendulum motion, as if he had not expected it and could not understand its occurring, and this enabled him to come on the rules by which it was governed. Here is the outlook, disconcerting but fruitful, which the theatre must provoke with its representations of human social life. It must amaze its public, and this can be achieved by a technique of alienating the familiar.

45

This technique allows the theatre to make use in its representations of the new social scientific method known as dialectical materialism. In order to unearth society's laws of motion this method treats social situations as processes, and traces out all their inconsistencies. It regards nothing as existing except in so far as it changes, in other words is in disharmony with itself. This also goes for those human feelings, opinions and attitudes through which at any time the form of men's life together finds its expression.

46

Our own period, which is transforming nature in so many and different ways, takes pleasure in understanding things so that we can interfere. There is a great deal to man, we say; so a great deal can be made out of him. He does not have to stay the way he is now, nor does he have to be seen only as he is now, but also as he might become. We must not start with him; we must start on him. This means, however, that I must not simply set myself in his place, but must set myself facing him, to represent us all. That is why the theatre must alienate what it shows.

47

In order to produce A-effects the actor has to discard whatever means he has learnt of getting the audience to identify itself with the characters which he plays. Aiming not to put his audience into a trance, he must not go into a trance himself. His muscles must remain loose, for a turn of the head, e.g. with tautened neck muscles, will 'magically' lead the spectators' eyes and even their heads to turn with it, and this can only detract from any speculation or reaction which the gesture may bring about. His way of speaking has to be free from parsonical sing-song and from all those cadences which lull the spectator so that the sense gets lost. Even if he plays a man possessed he must not seem to be possessed himself, for how is the spectator to discover what possessed him if he does?

48

At no moment must he go so far as to be wholly transformed into the character played. The verdict: 'he didn't act Lear, he was Lear' would be an annihilating blow to him. He has just to show the character, or rather he has to do more than just get into it; this does not mean that if he is playing passionate parts he must himself remain cold. It is only that his feelings must not at bottom be those of the character, so that the audience's may not at bottom be those of the character either. The audience must have complete freedom here.

49

This principle—that the actor appears on the stage in a double role, as Laughton and as Galileo; that the showman Laughton does not disappear in the Galileo whom he is showing; from which this way of acting gets its name of 'epic'—comes to mean simply that the tangible, matter-of-fact process is no longer hidden behind a veil; that Laughton is actually there, standing on the stage and showing us what he imagines Galileo to have been. Of course the audience would not forget Laughton if he attempted the full change of personality, in that they would admire him for it; but they would in that case miss his own opinions and sensations, which would have been completely swallowed up by the character. He would have taken its opinions and sensations and made them his own, so that a single homogeneous pattern would emerge, which he would then make ours. In order to prevent this abuse the actor must also put some artistry into the act of showing. An illustration may help: we find a gesture which expresses one-half of his attitude—that of showing—if we make him smoke a cigar and then imagine him laying it down now and again in order to show us some further characteristic attitude of the figure in the play. If we then subtract any element of hurry from the image and do not read slackness into its refusal to be taut we shall have an actor who is fully capable of leaving us to our thoughts, or to his own.

50

There needs to be yet a further change in the actor's communication of these images, and it too makes the process more 'matter-on-fact'. Just as the actor no longer has to persuade the audience that it is the author's character and not himself that is standing on the stage, so also he need not pretend that the events taking place on the stage have never been rehearsed, and are now happening for the first and only time. Schiller's distinction is no longer valid: that the rhapsodist has to treat his material as wholly in the past: the mime his, as wholly here and now.[1] It should be apparent all through his performance that 'even at the start and in the middle he knows how it ends' and he must 'thus maintain a calm independence throughout'. He narrates the story of his character by vivid portrayal, always knowing more than it does and treating its 'now' and 'here' not as a pretence made possible by the rules of the game but as something to be distinguished from yesterday and some other place, so as to make visible the knotting-together of the events.

51

This matters particularly in the portrayal of large-scale events or ones where the outside world is abruptly changed, as in wars and revolutions. The spectator can then have the whole situation and the whole course of events set before him. He can for instance hear a woman speaking and imagine her speaking differently, let us say in a few weeks' time, or other women speaking differently at that moment but in another place. This would be possible if the actress were to play as though the woman had lived through the entire period and were now, out of her memory and her knowledge of what happened next, recalling those utterances of hers which were important at the time; for what is important here is what became important. To alienate an individual in this way, as being 'this particular individual' and 'this particular individual at this particular moment', is only possible if there are no illusions that the player is identical with the character and the performance with the actual event.

52

We shall find that this has meant scrapping yet another illusion: that everyone behaves like the character concerned. 'I am doing this' has become 'I did this', and now 'he did this' has got to become 'he did this, when he might have done something else'. It is too great a simplification if we make the actions fit the character and the character fit the actions: the inconsistencies which are to be found in the actions and characters of real people cannot be shown like this. The laws of motion of a society are not to be demonstrated by 'perfect examples', for 'imperfection' (inconsistency) is an essential part of motion and of the thing moved. It is only necessary—but absolutely necessary—that there should be something approaching experimental conditions, i.e. that a counter-experiment should now and then be conceivable. Altogether this is a way of treating society as if all its actions were performed as experiments.

53

Even if empathy, or self-identification with the character, can be usefully indulged in at rehearsals (something to be avoided in a performance) it has to be treated just as one of a number of methods of observation. It helps when rehearsing, for even though the contemporary theatre has applied it in an indiscriminate way it has none the less led to subtle delineation of personality. But it is the crudest form of empathy when the actor simply asks: what should I be like if this or that were to happen to me? what would it look like if I were to say this and do that?—instead of asking: have I ever heard somebody saying this and doing that? in order to piece together all sorts of elements with which to construct a new character such as would allow the story to have taken place—and a good deal else. The coherence of the character is in fact shown by the way in which its individual qualities contradict one another.

54

Observation is a major part of acting. The actor observes his fellow-men with all his nerves and muscles in an act of imitation which is at the same time a process of the mind. For pure imitation would only bring out what had been observed; and this is not enough, because the original says what it has to say with too subdued a voice. To achieve a character rather than a caricature, the actor looks at people as though they were playing him their actions, in other words as though they were advising him to give their actions careful consideration.

55

Without opinions and objectives one can represent nothing at all. Without knowledge one can show nothing; how could one know what would be worth knowing? Unless the actor is satisfied to be a parrot or a monkey he must master our period's knowledge of human social life by himself joining in the war of the classes. Some people may feel this to be degrading, because they rank art, once the money side has been settled, as one of the highest things; but mankind's highest decisions are in fact fought out on earth, not in the heavens; in the 'external' world, not inside people's heads. Nobody can stand above the warring classes, for nobody can stand above the human race. Society cannot share a common communication system so long as it is split into warring classes. Thus for art to be 'un-political' means only to ally itself with the 'ruling' group.

56

So the choice of viewpoint is also a major element of the actor's art, and it has to be decided outside the theatre. Like the transformation of nature, that of society is a liberating act; and it is the joys of liberation which the theatre of a scientific age has got to convey.

57

Let us go on to examine how, for instance, this viewpoint affects the actor's interpretation of his part. It then becomes important that he should not 'catch on' too quickly. Even if he straightway establishes the most natural cadences for his part, the least awkward way of speaking it, he still cannot regard its actual pronouncement as being ideally natural, but must think twice and take his own general opinions into account, then consider various other conceivable pronouncements; in short, take up the attitude of a man who just wonders. This is not only to prevent him from 'fixing' a particular character prematurely, so that it has to be stuffed out with afterthoughts because he has not waited to register all the other pronouncements, and especially those of the other characters; but also and principally in order to build into the character that element of 'Not—But' on which so much depends if society, in the shape of the audience, is to be able to look at what takes place in such a way as to be able to affect it. Each actor, moreover, instead of concentrating on what suits him and calling it 'human nature', must go above all for what does not suit him, is not his speciality. And along with his part he must commit to memory his first reactions, reserves, criticisms, shocks, so that they are not destroyed by being 'swallowed up' in the final version but are preserved and perceptible; for character and all must not grow on the audience so much as strike it.

58

And the learning process must be co-ordinated so that the actor learns as the other actors are learning and develops his character as they are developing theirs. For the smallest social unit is not the single person but two people. In life too we develop one another.

59

Here we can learn something from our own theatres' deplorable habit of letting the dominant actor, the star, 'come to the front' by getting all the other actors to work for him: he makes his character terrible or wise by forcing his partners to make theirs terrified or attentive. Even if only to secure this advantage for all, and thus to help the story, the actors should sometimes swap roles with their partners during rehearsal, so that the characters can get what they need from one another. But it is also good for the actors when they see their characters copied or portrayed in another form. If the part is played by somebody of the opposite sex the sex of the character will be more clearly brought out; if it is played by a comedian, whether comically or tragically, it will gain fresh aspects. By helping to develop the parts that correspond to his own, or at any rate standing in for their players, the actor strengthens the all-decisive social standpoint from which he has to present his character. The master is only the sort of master his servant lets him be, etc.

60

A mass of operations to develop the character are carried out when it is introduced among the other characters of the play, and the actor will have to memorize what he himself has anticipated in this connection from his reading of the text. But now he finds out much more about himself from the treatment which he gets at the hands of the characters in the play.

61

The realm of attitudes adopted by the characters towards one another is what we call the realm of gest. Physical attitude, tone of voice and facial expression are all determined by a social gest: the characters are cursing, flattering, instructing one another, and so on. The attitudes which people adopt towards one another include even those attitudes which would appear to be quite private, such as the utterances of physical pain in an illness, or of religious faith. These expressions of a gest are usually highly complicated and contradictory, so that they cannot be rendered by any single word and the actor must take care that in giving his image the necessary emphasis he does not lose anything, but emphasizes the entire complex.

62

The actor masters his character by paying critical attention to its manifold utterances, as also to those of his counterparts and of all the other characters involved.

63

Let us get down to the problem of gestic content by running through the opening scenes of a fairly modern play, my own *Life of Galileo*. Since we wish at the same time to find out what light the different utterances cast on one another we will assume that it is not our first introduction to the play. It begins with the man of forty-six having his morning wash, broken by occasional browsing in books and by a lesson on the solar system for Andrea Sarti, a small boy. To play this, surely you have got to know that we shall be ending with the man of seventy-eight having his supper, just after he has said good-bye for ever to the same pupil? He is then more terribly altered than this passage of time could possibly have brought about. He wolfs his food with unrestrained greed, no other idea in his head; he has rid himself of his educational mission in shameful circumstances, as though it were a burden: he, who once drank his morning milk without a care, greedy to teach the boy. But does he really drink it without care? Isn't the pleasure of drinking and washing one with the pleasure which he takes in the new ideas? Don't forget: he thinks out of self-indulgence. . . . Is that good or bad? I would advise you to represent it as good, since on this point you will find nothing in the whole play to harm society, and more especially because you yourself are, I hope, a gallant child of the scientific age. But take careful note: many horrible things will happen in this connection. The fact that the man who here acclaims the new age will be forced at the end to beg this age to disown him as contemptible, even to dispossess him; all this will be relevant. As for the lesson, you may like to decide whether the man's heart is so full that his mouth is overflowing, so that he has to talk to anybody about it, even a child, or whether the child has first to draw the knowledge out of him, by knowing him and showing interest. Again, there may be two of them who cannot restrain themselves, the one from asking, the other from giving the answer: a bond of this sort would be interesting, for one day it is going to be rudely snapped. Of course you will want the demonstration of the earth's rotation round the sun to be conducted quickly, since it is given for nothing, and now the wealthy unknown pupil appears, lending the scholar's time a monetary value. He shows no interest, but he has to be served; Galileo lacks resources, and so he will stand between the wealthy pupil and the intelligent one, and sigh as he makes his choice. There is little that he can teach his new student, so he learns from him instead; he hears of the telescope which has been invented in Holland: in his own way he gets something out of the disturbance of his morning's work. The Rector of the university arrives. Galileo's application for an increase in salary has been turned down; the university is reluctant to pay so much for the theories of physics as for those of theology; it wishes him, who after all is operating on a generally-accepted low level of scholarship, to produce something useful here and now. You will see from the way in which he offers his thesis that he is used to being refused and corrected. The Rector reminds him that the Republic guarantees freedom of research even if she doesn't pay; he replies that he cannot make much of this freedom if he lacks the leisure which good payment permits. Here you should not find his impatience too peremptory, or his poverty will not be given due weight. For shortly after that you find him having ideas which need some explanation: the prophet of a new age of scientific truth considers how he can swindle some money out of the Republic by offering her the telescope as his own invention. All he sees in the new invention, you will be surprised to hear, is a few scudi, and he examines it simply with a view to annexing it himself. But if you move on to the second scene you will find that while he is selling the invention to the Venetian Signoria with a speech that disgraces him by its falsehoods he has already almost forgotten the money, because he has realized that the instrument has not only military but astronomical significance. The article which he has been blackmailed—let us call it that—into producing proves to have great qualities for the very research which he had to break off in order to produce it. If during the ceremony, as he complacently accepts the undeserved honours paid him, he outlines to his learned friend the marvellous discoveries in view—don't overlook the theatrical way in which he does this—you will find in him a far more profound excitement than the thought of monetary gain called forth. Perhaps, looked at in this way, his charlatanry does not mean much, but it still shows how determined this man is to take the easy course, and to apply his reason in a base as well as a noble manner. A more significant test awaits him, and does not every capitulation bring the next one nearer?

64

Splitting such material into one gest after another, the actor masters his character by first mastering the 'story'. It is only after walking all round the entire episode that he can, as it were by a single leap, seize and fix his character, complete with all its individual features. Once he has done his best to let himself be amazed by the inconsistencies in its various attitudes, knowing that he will in turn have to make them amaze the audience, then the story as a whole gives him a chance to pull the inconsistencies together; for the story, being a limited episode, has a specific sense, i.e. only gratifies a specific fraction of all the interests that could arise.

65

Everything hangs on the 'story'; it is the heart of the theatrical performance. For it is what happens *between* people that provides them with all the material that they can discuss, criticize, alter. Even if the particular person represented by the actor has ultimately to fit into more than just the one episode, it is mainly because the episode will be all the more striking if it reaches fulfilment in a particular person. The 'story' is the theatre's great operation, the complete fitting together of all the gestic incidents, embracing the communications and impulses that must now go to make up the audience's entertainment.

66

Each single incident has its basic gest: *Richard Gloster courts his victim's widow. The child's true mother is found by means of a chalk circle. God has a bet with the Devil for Dr Faustus's soul. Woyzeck buys a cheap knife in order to do his wife in,* etc. The grouping of the characters on the stage and the movements of the groups must be such that the necessary beauty is attained above all by the elegance with which the material conveying that gest is set out and laid bare to the understanding of the audience.

67

As we cannot invite the audience to fling itself into the story as if it were a river and let itself be carried vaguely hither and thither, the individual episodes have to be knotted together in such a way that the knots are easily noticed. The episodes must not succeed one another indistinguishably but must give us a chance to interpose our judgment. (If it were above all the obscurity of the original interrelations that interested us, then just this circumstance would have to be sufficiently alienated.) The parts of the story have to be carefully set off one against another by giving each its own structure as a play within the play. To this end it is best to agree to use titles like those in the preceding paragraph. The titles must include the social point, saying at the same time something about the kind of portrayal wanted, i.e. should copy the tone of a chronicle or a ballad or a newspaper or a morality. For instance, a simple way of alienating something is that normally applied to customs and moral principles. A visit, the treatment of an enemy, a lovers' meeting, agreements about politics or business, can be portrayed as if they were simply illustrations of general principles valid for the place in question. Shown thus, the particular and unrepeatable incident acquires a disconcerting look, because it appears as something general, something that has become a principle. As soon as we ask whether in fact it should have become such, or what about it should have done so, we are alienating the incident. The poetic approach to history can be studied in the so-called panoramas at sideshows in fairs. As alienation likewise means a kind of fame certain incidents can just be represented as famous, as though they had for a long while been common knowledge and care must be taken not to offer the least obstacle to their further transmission. In short: there are many conceivable ways of telling a story, some of them known and some still to be discovered.

68

What needs to be alienated, and how this is to be done, depends on the exposition demanded by the entire episode; and this is where the theatre has to speak up decisively for the interests of its own time. Let us take as an example of such exposition the old play *Hamlet*. Given the dark and bloody period in which I am writing—the criminal ruling classes, the widespread doubt in the power of reason, continually being misused—I think that I can read the story thus: It is an age of warriors. Hamlet's father, king of Denmark, slew the king of Norway in a successful war of spoliation. While the latter's son Fortinbras is arming for a fresh war the Danish king is likewise slain: by his own brother. The slain king's brothers, now themselves kings, avert war by arranging that the Norwegian troops shall cross Danish soil to launch a predatory war against Poland. But at this point the young Hamlet is summoned by his warrior father's ghost to avenge the crime committed against him. After at first being reluctant to answer one bloody deed by another, and even preparing to go into exile, he meets young Fortinbras at the coast as he is marching with his troops to Poland. Overcome by this warrior-like example, he turns back and in a piece of barbaric butchery slaughters his uncle, his mother and himself, leaving Denmark to the Norwegian. These events show the young man, already somewhat stout, making the most ineffective use of the new approach to Reason which he has picked up at the university of Wittenberg. In the feudal business to which he returns it simply hampers him. Faced with irrational practices, his reason is utterly unpractical. He falls a tragic victim to the discrepancy between such reasoning and such action. This way of reading the play, which can be read in more than one way, might in my view interest our audience.

69

Whether or no literature presents them as successes, each step forward, every emancipation from nature that is scored in the field of production and leads to a transformation of society, all those explorations in some new direction which mankind has embarked on in order to improve its lot, give us a sense of confidence and triumph and lead us to take pleasure in the possibilities of change in all things. Galileo expresses this when he says: 'It is my view that the earth is most noble and wonderful, seeing the great number and variety of changes and generations which incessantly take place on it.'

70

The exposition of the story and its communication by suitable means of alienation constitute the main business of the theatre. Not everything depends on the actor, even though nothing may be done without taking him into account. The 'story' is set out, brought forward and shown by the theatre as a whole, by actors, stage designers, mask-makers, costumiers, composers and choreographers. They unite their various arts for the joint operation, without of course sacrificing their independence in the process.

71

It emphasizes the general gest of showing, which always underlies that which is being shown, when the audience is musically addressed by means of songs. Because of this the actors ought not to 'drop into' song, but should clearly mark it off from the rest of the text; and this is best reinforced by a few theatrical methods such as changing the lighting or inserting a title. For its part, the music must strongly resist the smooth incorporation which is generally expected of it and turns it into an unthinking slavery. Music does not 'accompany' except in the form of comment. It cannot simply 'express itself' by discharging the emotions with which the incidents of the play have filled it. Thus Eisler, e.g. helped admirably in the knotting of the incidents when in the carnival scene of *Galileo* he set the masked procession of the guilds to a triumphant and threatening music which showed what a revolutionary twist the lower orders had given to the scholar's astronomical theories. Similarly in *The Caucasian Chalk Circle* the singer, by using a chilly and unemotional way of singing to describe the servant-girl's rescue of the child as it is mimed on the stage, makes evident the terror of a period in which motherly instincts can become a suicidal weakness. Thus music can make its point in a number of ways and with full independence, and can react in its own manner to the subjects dealt with; at the same time it can also quite simply help to lend variety to the entertainment.

72

Just as the composer wins back his freedom by no longer having to create atmosphere so that the audience may be helped to lose itself unreservedly in the events on the stage, so also the stage designer gets considerable freedom as soon as he no longer has to give the illusion of a room or a locality when he is building his sets. It is enough for him to give hints, though these must make statements of greater historical or social interest than does the real setting. At the Jewish Theatre in Moscow *King Lear* was alienated by a structure that recalled a medieval tabernacle; Neher set *Galileo* in front of projections of maps, documents and Renaissance works of art; for *Haitang erwacht* at the Piscator-Theater Heartfield used a background of reversible flags bearing inscriptions, to mark changes in the political situation of which the persons on the stage were sometimes unaware.

73

For choreography too there are once again tasks of a realistic kind. It is a relatively recent error to suppose that it has nothing to do with the representation of 'people as they really are'. If art reflects life it does so with special mirrors. Art does not become unrealistic by changing the proportions but by changing them in such a way that if the audience took its representations as a practical guide to insights and impulses it would go astray in real life. It is of course essential that stylization should not remove the natural element but should heighten it. Anyhow, a theatre where everything depends on the gest cannot do without choreography. Elegant movement and graceful grouping, for a start, can alienate, and inventive miming greatly helps the story.

74

So let us invite all the sister arts of the drama, not in order to create an 'integrated work of art' in which they all offer themselves up and are lost, but so that together with the drama they may further the common task in their different ways; and their relations with one another consist in this: that they lead to mutual alienation.

75

And here once again let us recall that their task is to entertain the children of the scientific age, and to do so with sensuousness and humour. This is something that we Germans cannot tell ourselves too often, for with us everything easily slips into the insubstantial and unapproachable, and we begin to talk of *Weltanschauung* when the world in question has already dissolved. Even materialism is little more than an idea with us. Sexual pleasure with us turns into marital obligations, the pleasures of art subserve general culture, and by learning we mean not an enjoyable process of finding out, but the forcible shoving of our nose into something. Our activity has none of the pleasure of exploration, and if we want to make an impression we do not say how much fun we have got out of something but how much effort it has cost us.

76

One more thing: the delivery to the audience of what has been built up in the rehearsals. Here it is essential that the actual playing should be infused with the gest of handing over a finished article. What now comes before the spectator is the most frequently repeated of what has not been rejected, and so the finished representations have to be delivered with the eyes fully open, so that they may be received with the eyes open too.

77

That is to say, our representations must take second place to what is represented, men's life together in society; and the pleasure felt in their perfection must be converted into the higher pleasure felt when the rules emerging from this life in society are treated as imperfect and provisional. In this way the theatre leaves its spectators productively disposed even after the spectacle is over. Let us hope that their theatre may allow them to enjoy as entertainment that terrible and never-ending labour which should ensure their maintenance, together with the terror of their unceasing transformation. Let them here produce their own lives in the simplest way; for the simplest way of living is in art.

BIBLIOGRAPHY

GENERAL

Baldick, Chris. *The Social Mission of English Criticism 1848–1932*. Oxford: Clarendon Press, 1983.

Bowlt, John E., ed. and tr. *Russian Art of the Avant-Garde: Theory and Criticism 1902–1934*. New York: Viking Press, 1976.

Brown, Clarence Arthur, ed. *The Achievement of American Criticism*. New York: Ronald Press Co., 1954.

Eagleton, Terry. *Marxism and Literary Criticism*. London: Methuen, 1976.

Goldsmith, Arnold L. *American Literary Criticism 1905–1965*. Boston: Twayne, 1979.

Graff, Gerald. *Professing Literature: An Institutional History*. Chicago: University of Chicago Press, 1987.

Handy, William J., ed. *A Symposium on Formalist Criticism*. Austin: University of Texas Press, 1965.

Natoli, Joseph, ed. *Tracing Literary Theory*. Urbana: University of Illinois Press, 1987.

O'Connor, William Van. *An Age of Criticism 1900–1950*. Chicago: Henry Regnery Co., 1952.

Pritchard, John Paul. *Criticism in America*. Norman: University of Oklahoma Press, 1956.

Pulos, C. E. *The New Critics and the Language of Poetry*. Lincoln: University of Nebraska Press, 1958.

Siebers, Tobin. *The Ethics of Criticism*. Ithaca, NY: Cornell University Press, 1988.

Stacy, R. H. *Russian Literary Criticism: A Short History*. Syracuse: Syracuse University Press, 1974.

Stamiris, Yiannis. *Main Currents in Twentieth-Century Literary Criticism*. Troy, NY: Whitston, 1986.

Stovall, Floyd, ed. *The Development of American Literary Criticism*. Chapel Hill: University of North Carolina Press, 1955.

Watson, George. *The Literary Critics: A Study of English Descriptive Criticism*. London: Chatto & Windus, 1962.

Wellek, René. *A History of Modern Criticism 1750–1950*. New Haven: Yale University Press, 1955–86. 6 vols.

GEORGE BERNARD SHAW

Adams, Elsie B. *Bernard Shaw and the Aesthetes*. Columbus: Ohio State University Press, 1971.

Barnet, Sylvan. "Bernard Shaw on Tragedy." *PMLA* 71 (1956): 888–99.

Bentley, Eric. *Bernard Shaw*. Norfolk, CT: New Directions, 1947.

Berst, Charles A. *Bernard Shaw and the Art of Drama*. Urbana: University of Illinois Press, 1973.

Crawford, Fred D. "Bernard Shaw's Theory of Literary Art." *Journal of General Education* 34 (1982): 20–34.

Ervine, St. John. *Bernard Shaw: His Life, Work, and Friends*. London: Constable, 1956.

Fromm, Harold. *Bernard Shaw and the Theater in the Nineties: A Study of Shaw's Dramatic Criticism*. Lawrence: University of Kansas Press, 1967.

Gerould, Daniel Charles. "George Bernard Shaw's Criticism of Ibsen." *Comparative Literature* 15 (1963): 130–45.

Gibbs, A. M. *The Art and Mind of Shaw*. New York: St. Martin's Press, 1983.

Gill, Stephen. *Political Convictions of G. B. Shaw*. Cornwall, Ontario: Vesta, 1980.

Glicksberg, Charles I. "The Criticism of George Bernard Shaw." *South Atlantic Quarterly* 50 (1951): 96–108.

Greiner, Norbert. "Shaw's Aesthetics and Socialist Realism." *Shaw Review* 22 (1979): 33–45.

Hill, Eldon C. *George Bernard Shaw*. Boston: Twayne, 1978.

Holroyd, Michael, ed. *The Genius of Shaw: A Symposium*. New York: Holt, Rinehart & Winston, 1979.

Hugo, Leon. *Bernard Shaw: Playwright and Preacher*. London: Methuen, 1971.

Irvine, William. *The Universe of George Bernard Shaw*. New York: Whittlesey House, 1949.

Lutz, Jerry. *Pitchman's Melody: Shaw about "Shakespear."* Lewisburg, PA: Bucknell University Press, 1974.

Rodenbeck, John von B. "Bernard Shaw's Revolt against Rationalism." *Victorian Studies* 15 (1972): 409–37.

Rosset, B. C. *Shaw of Dublin: The Formative Years*. University Park: Pennsylvania State University Press, 1964.

Silverman, Albert H. "Bernard Shaw's Shakespeare Criticism." *PMLA* 72 (1957): 722–36.

Smith, Warren Sylvester. *Bishop of Everywhere: Bernard Shaw and the Life Force*. University Park: Pennsylvania State University Press, 1982.

Watson, Barbara Bellow. *A Shavian Guide to the Intelligent Woman*. New York: Norton, 1964.

Wisenthal, J. L. *Shaw's Sense of History*. Oxford: Clarendon Press, 1988.

SIGMUND FREUD

Bakan, David. *Sigmund Freud and the Jewish Mystical Tradition*. Princeton: Van Nostrand, 1958.

Chabot, C. Barry. *Freud on Schreber: Psychoanalytic Theory and the Critical Act*. Amherst: University of Massachusetts Press, 1982.

Clark, Ronald W. *Freud: The Man and the Cause*. New York: Random House, 1980.

Ellis, David. *Wordsworth, Freud, and the Spots of Time: Interpretation in* The Prelude. Cambridge: Cambridge University Press, 1985.

Fox, Seymour. *Freud and Education*. Springfield, IL: Thomas, 1975.

Gay, Peter. *Freud: A Life for Our Time*. New York: Norton, 1988.

George, Diana Hume. *Blake and Freud*. Ithaca, NY: Cornell University Press, 1980.

Godo, John E., and George H. Pollock, eds. *Freud, the Fusion of Science and Humanism: The Intellectual History of Psychoanalysis*. New York: International Universities Press, 1976.

Hoffman, Frederick J. *Freudianism and the Literary Mind*. Baton Rouge: Louisiana State University Press, 1945.

Horden, Peregrine, ed. *Freud and the Humanities*. New York: St. Martin's Press, 1985.

Hyman, Stanley Edgar. *The Tangled Bank: Darwin, Marx, Frazer and Freud as Imaginative Writers*. New York: Atheneum, 1962.

Jones, Ernest. *The Life and Work of Sigmund Freud*. New York: Basic Books, 1953–57. 3 vols.

Levin, Gerald. *Sigmund Freud*. Boston: Twayne, 1975.

Mahoney, Patrick. *Freud as a Writer*. New York: International Universities Press, 1982.

Marcuse, Herbert. *Eros and Civilization: A Philosophical Inquiry into Freud*. Boston: Beacon Press, 1955.

Milner, Max. *Freud et l'interpretation de la littérature*. Paris: CDU et SEDES Réunis, 1980.

Morrison, Claudia C. *Freud and the Critic: The Early Use of Depth Psychology in Literary Criticism*. Chapel Hill: University of North Carolina Press, 1968.

Orlando, Francesco. *Toward a Freudian Theory of Literature*. Tr. Charmaine Lee. Baltimore: Johns Hopkins University Press, 1978.

Rieff, Philip. *Freud: The Mind of the Moralist*. New York: Viking Press, 1959.

Spector, Jack J. *The Aesthetics of Freud: A Study of Psychoanalysis and Art*. New York: Praeger, 1973.

Trosman, Harry. *Freud and the Imaginative World*. Hillsdale, NJ: Analytic Press, 1985.

W. B. YEATS

Adams, Hazard. "Yeats, Dialectic, and Criticism." *Criticism* 10 (1968): 185–99.

Bloom, Harold. *Yeats*. New York: Oxford University Press, 1970.

Bradford, Curtis Baker. *Yeats at Work*. Carbondale: Southern Illinois University Press, 1965.

Donoghue, Denis. *Yeats*. New York: Viking Press, 1971.

Ellmann, Richard. *The Identity of Yeats*. New York: Oxford University Press, 1954.

———. *Yeats: The Man and the Masks*. New York: Dutton, 1948.

Engelberg, Edward. *The Vast Design: Patterns in W. B. Yeats's Aesthetic*. Toronto: University of Toronto Press, 1965.

Faulkner, Peter. "Yeats as Critic." *Criticism* 4 (1962): 328–39.

Hone, Joseph. *W. B. Yeats 1865–1939*. London: Macmillan, 1942.

Jaggi, Satya Dev. *Coleridge's and Yeats's Theory of Poetry*. Delhi: Cosla, 1967.

Jochum, K. P. S. *W. B. Yeats: A Classified Bibliography of Criticism*. Urbana: University of Illinois Press, 1978.

Lentricchia, Frank. *The Gaiety of Language: An Essay on the Radical Poetics of W. B. Yeats and Wallace Stevens*. Berkeley: University of California Press, 1968.

Marcus, Phillip Leduc. *Yeats and the Beginning of the Irish Renaissance*. Ithaca, NY: Cornell University Press, 1970.

North, Michael. "The Paradox of the Mausoleum: Public Monuments and the Early Aesthetics of W. B. Yeats." *Centennial Review* 26 (1982): 221–38.

O'Neill, William. "Yeats on Poetry and Politics." *Midwest Quarterly* 25 (1983): 64–73.

Peterson, Richard F. *William Butler Yeats*. Boston: Twayne, 1982.

Rajan, Balachandra. *Yeats: A Critical Introduction*. London: Hutchinson, 1965.

Sena, Vinod. "W. B. Yeats, Matthew Arnold and the Critical Imperative." *Victorian Newsletter* 56 (1979): 10–14.

Stock, Amy Geraldine. *W. B. Yeats: His Poetry and Thought*. Cambridge: Cambridge University Press, 1961.

Whitaker, Thomas Russell. *Swan and Shadow: Yeats's Dialogue with History*. Chapel Hill: University of North Carolina Press, 1964.

BENEDETTO CROCE

Brown, Merle E. *Neo-Idealistic Aesthetics: Croce-Gentile-Collingwood.* Detroit: Wayne State University Press, 1966.

Caponigri, Aloysius Robert. *History and Liberty: The Historical Writings of Benedetto Croce.* London: Routledge & Kegan Paul, 1955.

Carr, H. Wildon. *The Philosophy of Benedetto Croce: The Problem of Art and History.* London: Macmillan, 1917.

Caserta, Ernesto G. *Croce critico letterario (1882–1921).* Naples: Giannini, 1972.

De Gennaro, Angelo A. *The Philosophy of Benedetto Croce: An Introduction.* New York: Philosophical Library, 1961.

Douglas, George H. "Croce's Early Aesthetic and American Critical Theory." *Comparative Literature Studies* 7 (1970): 204–15.

Frascani, Federico. *Croce e il teatro.* Milan: Ricciardi, 1966.

Moss, M. E. *Benedetto Croce Reconsidered: Truth and Error in Theories of Art, Literature, and History.* Hanover, NH: University Press of New England, 1987.

Murray, Gilbert, et al. *Benedetto Croce: A Commemoration.* London: Istituto Italiano di Cultura, 1953.

Orsini, Gian N. G. *Benedetto Croce, Philosopher of Art and Literary Critic.* Carbondale: Southern Illinois University Press, 1961.

Palmer, L. M., and H. S. Harris, eds. *Thought, Action and Intuition: A Symposium on the Philosophy of Benedetto Croce.* Hildesheim: Georg Olms Verlag, 1975.

Puppo, Mario. *Il metodo e la critica di Benedetto Croce.* Milan: Mursia, 1964.

Roberts, David D. *Benedetto Croce and the Uses of Historicism.* Berkeley: University of California Press, 1987.

Sprigge, Cecil. *Benedetto Croce, Man and Thinker.* New Haven: Yale University Press, 1952.

Wellek, René. *Four Critics: Croce, Valéry, Lukács, and Ingarden.* Seattle: University of Washington Press, 1981.

PAUL VALÉRY

Bémol, Maurice. *La Méthode critique de Paul Valéry.* Clermont-Ferrand: G. De Bussac, 1950.

Bucher, Jean. *La Situation de Paul Valéry, critique.* Brussels: Renaissance du Livre, 1976.

Crow, Christine M. *Paul Valéry: Consciousness and Nature.* Cambridge: Cambridge University Press, 1972.

Gaède, Edouard. *Nietzsche et Valéry: Essai sur la comédie de l'esprit.* Paris: Gallimard, 1962.

Grubles, Henry. *Paul Valéry.* New York: Twayne, 1968.

Ince, W. N. *The Poetic Theory of Paul Valéry: Inspiration and Technique.* Leicester: Leicester University Press, 1961.

Laurenti, Huguette. *Paul Valéry et le théâtre.* Paris: Gallimard, 1973.

Lawler, James R. *The Poet as Analyst: Essays on Paul Valéry.* Berkeley: University of California Press, 1974.

Mackay, Agnes Ethel. *The Universal Self: A Study of Paul Valéry.* Toronto: University of Toronto Press, 1961.

Robinson, Judith. *L'Analyse de l'esprit dans les Cahiers de Valéry.* Paris: Corti, 1963.

Suckling, Norma. *Paul Valéry and the Civilized Mind*. London: Oxford University Press, 1954.

Thomson, Alastair W. *Valéry*. Edinburgh: Oliver & Boyd, 1965.

Trione, Aldo. *Valéry: Metodo e critica del fare poetico*. Naples: Guida, 1983.

Wellek, René. *Four Critics: Croce, Valéry, Lukács, and Ingarden*. Seattle: University of Washington Press, 1981.

Whiting, Charles G. *Paul Valéry*. London: Athlone Press, 1978.

WALLACE STEVENS

Beckett, Lucy. *Wallace Stevens*. Cambridge: Cambridge University Press, 1974.

Bloom, Harold. *Wallace Stevens: The Poems of Our Climate*. Ithaca, NY: Cornell University Press, 1976.

Brazeau, Peter. *Parts of a World: Wallace Stevens Remembered*. New York: Random House, 1983.

Brogan, Jacqueline Vaught. *Stevens and Simile: A Theory of Language*. Princeton: Princeton University Press, 1986.

Brown, Ashley, and Robert S. Haller, eds. *The Achievement of Wallace Stevens*. Philadelphia: Lippincott, 1962.

Burney, William. *Wallace Stevens*. New York: Twayne, 1968.

Frye, Northrop. "The Realistic Oriole: A Study of Wallace Stevens." *Hudson Review* 10 (1957): 353–70.

Heringman, Bernard. "Wallace Stevens: The Use of Poetry." *ELH* 16 (1949): 325–36.

Jarrell, Randall. "Reflections on Wallace Stevens." In *Poetry and the Age*. New York: Vintage Books, 1955, pp. 121–34.

Kermode, Frank. *Wallace Stevens*. Edinburgh: Oliver & Boyd, 1960.

Lentricchia, Frank. *The Gaiety of Language: An Essay on the Radical Poetics of W. B. Yeats and Wallace Stevens*. Berkeley: University of California Press, 1968.

Martz, Louis L. "Wallace Stevens: The World as Meditation." *Yale Review* 47 (1958): 517–36.

Morris, Adelàide Kirby. *Wallace Stevens: Imagination and Faith*. Princeton: Princeton University Press, 1974.

Morse, Samuel French. *Wallace Stevens: Poetry as Life*. New York: Pegasus, 1970.

O'Connor, William Van. *The Shaping Spirit: A Study of Wallace Stevens*. Chicago: Henry Regnery Co., 1950.

Pack, Robert. *Wallace Stevens: An Approach to His Poetry and Thought*. New Brunswick, NJ: Rutgers University Press, 1958.

Pearce, Roy Harvey. "Wallace Stevens: The Life of the Imagination." *PMLA* 66 (1951): 561–82.

Riddel, Joseph N. *The Clairvoyant Eye: The Poetry and Poetics of Wallace Stevens*. Baton Rouge: Louisiana State University Press, 1965.

Simons, Hi. "The Humanism of Wallace Stevens." *Poetry* 61 (1942): 448–52.

Stern, Herbert J. *Wallace Stevens: Art of Uncertainty*. Ann Arbor: University of Michigan Press, 1966.

Wells, Henry W. *Introduction to Wallace Stevens*. Bloomington: Indiana University Press, 1964.

VIRGINIA WOOLF

Bell, Quentin. *Virginia Woolf: A Biography*. New York: Harcourt Brace Jovanovich, 1972.

Blackstone, Bernard. *Virginia Woolf: A Commentary*. New York: Harcourt, Brace, 1949.

Daiches, David. *Virginia Woolf*. New York: New Directions, 1963.

Farwell, Marilyn R. "Virginia Woolf and Androgyny." *Contemporary Literature* 16 (1975): 433–51.

Fishman, Solomon. "Virginia Woolf on the Novel." *Sewanee Review* 51 (1943): 321–40.

Goldman, Mark. *The Reader's Art: Virginia Woolf as Literary Critic*. The Hague: Mouton, 1976.

Gorsky, Susan. *Virginia Woolf*. Boston: Twayne, 1978.

Guiguet, Jean. *Virginia Woolf and Her Works*. Tr. Jean Stewart. London: Hogarth Press, 1965.

Hill, Katherine C. "Virginia Woolf and Leslie Stephen: History and Literary Revolution." *PMLA* 96 (1981): 351–62.

Kapur, Vijay. *Virginia Woolf's Vision of Life and Her Search for Significant Form: A Study in the Shaping Vision*. Atlantic Highlands, NJ: Humanities Press, 1980.

Leavis, Q. D. "Caterpillars of the Commonwealth Unite!" *Scrutiny* 7 (1938): 203–14.

Lewis, Wyndham. "Virginia Woolf ('Mind' and 'Matter' on the Plane of a Literary Controversy)." In *Men without Art*. London: Cassell, 1934, pp. 158–71.

Love, Jean O. *Virginia Woolf: Sources of Madness and Art*. Berkeley: University of California Press, 1977.

McLaughlin, Thomas M. "Virginia Woolf's Criticism: Interpretation as Theory and as Discourse." *Southern Humanities Review* 17 (1983): 241–53.

Meisel, Perry. *The Absent Father: Virginia Woolf and Walter Pater*. New Haven: Yale University Press, 1980.

Rice, Thomas Jackson. *Virginia Woolf: A Guide to Research*. New York: Garland, 1984.

Rosenthal, Michael. *Virginia Woolf*. New York: Columbia University Press, 1979.

Sharma, Vijay L. *Virginia Woolf as Literary Critic: A Revaluation*. New Delhi: Arnold-Heinemann, 1977.

Sloman, Judith. "Virginia Woolf's Literary History: Integrating the Obscure." *Virginia Woolf Quarterly* 3 (1978): 230–40.

Steele, Elizabeth. *Virginia Woolf's Literary Sources and Allusions: A Guide to the Essays*. New York: Garland, 1983.

Wellek, René. "Virginia Woolf as Critic." *Southern Review* 13 (1977): 419–37.

T. E. HUME

Brandabur, Edward. "The Eye in the Ceiling and the Eye in the Mud: T. E. Hulme's Comedy of Perception." *Papers on Language and Literature* 9 (1973): 420–27.

Browning, W. R. F. "T. E. Hulme." *Church Quarterly Review* 145 (1947): 59–65.

Collin, W. E. "Beyond Humanism: Some Notes on T. E. Hulme." *Sewanee Review* 38 (1930): 332–39.

Csengeri, K. E. "T. E. Hulme: An Annotated Bibliography of Writings about Him." *English Literature in Transition* 29 (1986): 388–428.

Hansen, Miriam. "T. E. Hulme, Mercenary of Modernism." *ELH* 47 (1980): 355–85.

Hendry, J. F. "Hulme as Horatio." *Life and Letters* 35 (1942): 136–47.

Jones, Alun R. *The Life and Opinions of T. E. Hulme*. Boston: Beacon Press, 1960.

Kermode, Frank. "T. E. Hulme." In *Romantic Image*. London: Routledge & Kegan Paul, 1957, pp. 124–32.

Kishler, Thomas C. "Original Sin and T. E. Hulme's Aesthetics." *Journal of Aesthetic Education* 10 (1976): 99–106.

Krieger, Murray. "The Ambiguous Anti-Romanticism of T. E. Hulme." *ELH* 20 (1953): 300–314.

Nott, Kathleen. "Mr. Hulme's Sloppy Dregs." In *The Emperor's Clothes*. London: William Heinemann, 1953, pp. 72–103.

Pound, Ezra. "This Hulme Business." *Townsman* 2 (January 1939): 5.

Roberts, Michael. *T. E. Hulme*. London: Faber & Faber, 1938.

Shusterman, Richard. "Remembering Hulme: A Neglected Philospher-Critic-Poet." *Journal of the History of Ideas* 46 (1985): 559–76.

Wector, D. "Hulme and the Tragic View of Life." *Southern Review* 5 (1939): 141–52.

JOSÉ ORTEGA Y GASSET

Aguilera Cerni, Vicente. *Ortega y d'Ors en la cultura artística española*. Madrid: Ciencia Nueva, 1966.

Ayala, Francisco. "Ortega y Gasset, crítico literario." *Revista de Occidente* 140 (1974): 214–35.

Cascalès, Charles. *L'Humanisme d'Ortega y Gasset*. Paris: Presses Universitaires de France, 1957.

Diaz, Janet Winecoff. *The Major Themes of Existentialism in the Work of José Ortega y Gasset*. Chapel Hill: University of North Carolina Press, 1970.

Donoso, Anton, and Harold C. Raley. *José Ortega y Gasset: A Bibliography of Secondary Sources*. Bowling Green, OH: Philosophical Documentation Center, Bowling Green State University, 1986.

Ferrater Mora, José. *Ortega y Gasset: An Outline of His Philosophy*. New Haven: Yale University Press, 1963.

Lafuente Ferrari, Enrique. *Ortega y las artes visuales*. Madrid: Revista de Occidente, 1970.

Livingstone, Leon. "Ortega y Gasset's Philosophy of Art." *PMLA* 67 (1952): 609–54.

López Quintás, Alfonso. *El pensamiento filosófico de Ortega y Gasset: Una clave de interpretación*. Madrid: Guadarrama, 1972.

McClintock, Robert. *Man and His Circumstances: Ortega as Educator*. New York: Teachers College Press, 1971.

Marías Aguilera, Julián. *José Ortega y Gasset: Circumstance and Vocation*. Tr. Frances M. López-Morillas. Norman: University of Oklahoma Press, 1970.

Marval-McNair, Nora de, ed. *José Ortega y Gasset: Proceedings of the Espectador Universal Interdisciplinary Conference*. Westport, CT: Greenwood Press, 1987.

Morón Arroyo, Ciriaco. *El sistema de Ortega y Gasset*. Madrid: Alcalá, 1968.

Orringer, Nelson. "Ortega y Gasset's Sportive Theories of Communication." *Modern Language Notes* 85 (1970): 207–34.

Ouimette, Victor. *José Ortega y Gasset*. Boston: Twayne, 1982.

Raley, Harold C. *José Ortega y Gasset: Philosopher of European Unity*. University: University of Alabama Press, 1971.

Senabre Sempere, Ricardo. *Lengua y estilo de Ortega y Gasset*. Salamanca: Universidad de Salamanca, 1964.

Silver, Philip. *Ortega as Phenomenologist: The Genesis of* Meditations on Quixote. New York: Columbia University Press, 1978.

D. H. LAWRENCE

Arnold, Armin. *D. H. Lawrence and America*. London: Linden Press, 1958.

Bien, Peter. "The Critical Philosophy of D. H. Lawrence." *D. H. Lawrence Review* 17 (1984): 127–34.

Burns, Aidan. *Nature and Culture in D. H. Lawrence*. New York: Barnes & Noble, 1980.

Cavitch, David. *D. H. Lawrence and the New World*. New York: Oxford University Press, 1969.

Clarke, Colin. *River of Dissolution: D. H. Lawrence and English Romanticism*. New York: Barnes & Noble, 1969.

Cohen, Marvin R. "The Prophet and the Critic: A Study in Classic Lawrentian Literature." *Texas Studies in Literature and Language* 22 (1980): 1–21.

Cowan, James C. *D. H. Lawrence's American Journey: A Study in Literature and Myth*. Cleveland: Press of Case Western Reserve University, 1970.

Draper, Ronald P. *D. H. Lawrence*. New York: Twayne, 1964.

Goodheart, Eugene. *The Utopian Vision of D. H. Lawrence*. Chicago: University of Chicago Press, 1963.

Gordon, David J. *D. H. Lawrence as a Literary Critic*. New Haven: Yale University Press, 1966.

Green, Martin. "*Studies in Classic American Literature*." In *Reappraisals: Some Commonsense Readings in American Literature*. New York: Norton, 1965, pp. 231–47.

Hough, Graham. *The Dark Sun: A Study of D. H. Lawrence*. New York: Macmillan, 1957.

Journet, Debra. "D. H. Lawrence's Criticism of Modern Literature." *D. H. Lawrence Review* 17 (1984): 29–47.

Kermode, Frank. *D. H. Lawrence*. New York: Viking Press, 1973.

Klingopulos, G. D. "Lawrence's Criticism." *Essays in Criticism* 7 (1957): 294–303.

Leavis, F. R. *Thought, Words and Creativity: Art and Thought in D. H. Lawrence*. New York: Oxford University Press, 1976.

Moore, Harry T. *The Priest of Love: A Life of D. H. Lawrence*. New York: Farrar, Straus & Giroux, 1954.

Nehls, Edward, ed. *D. H. Lawrence: A Composite Biography*. Madison: University of Wisconsin Press, 1957–59. 3 vols.

Rice, Thomas Jackson. *D. H. Lawrence: A Guide to Research*. New York: Garland, 1983.

Sitesh, Aruna. *D. H. Lawrence: The Crusader as Critic*. Delhi: Macmillan, 1975.

Swigg, Richard. *Lawrence, Hardy, and American Literature*. London: Oxford University Press, 1972.

Watson, Garry. "The Real Meaning of Lawrence's Advice to the Literary Critic." *University of Toronto Quarterly* 55 (1985): 1–20.

West, Paul. "D. H. Lawrence: Mystical Critic." *Southern Review* 1 (1965): 210–28.

White, Richard L. "D. H. Lawrence as Critic: Theories of English and American Fiction." *D. H. Lawrence Review* 11 (1978): 156–74.

GEORG LUKÁCS

Arato, Andrew, and Paul Breines. *The Young Lukács and the Origins of Western Marxism*. New York: Seabury Press, 1979.

Arvon, Henri. "Bertholt [sic] Brecht and Georg Lukács." In *Marxist Aesthetics*. Tr. Helen Lane. Ithaca, NY: Cornell University Press, 1973, pp. 100–112.

Bahr, Ehrhard, and Ruth Goldschmidt Kunzer. *Georg Lukács*. New York: Ungar, 1972.

Birchall, Ian H. "Georg Lukács and the Novels of Emile Zola." In *The Sociology of Literature: Applied Studies,* ed. Diana Laurenson. Keele, Eng.: University of Keele, 1978, pp. 92–108.

Brecht, Bertolt. "Against Georg Lukács." *New Left Review* No. 84 (March–April 1974): 39–54.

de Man, Paul. "Georg Lukács's Theory of the Novel." *Modern Language Notes* 81 (1966): 527–36.

Demetz, Peter. "Georg Lukács as a Theoretician of Literature." In *Marx, Engels and the Poets: Origins of Marxist Literary Criticism.* Tr. Jeffrey L. Sammons. Chicago: University of Chicago Press, 1967, pp. 199–227.

Feenberg, Andrew. *Lukács, Marx and the Sources of Critical Theory.* Totowa, NJ: Rowman & Littlefield, 1981.

Goldmann, Lucien. "The Early Writings of Georg Lukács." *Tri-Quarterly* 9 (1967): 165–81.

Horn, András. "The Concept of *Mimesis* in Georg Lukács." *British Journal of Aesthetics* 14 (1974): 26–40.

Jameson, Fredric. "The Case for Georg Lukács." *Salmagundi* No. 13 (Summer 1970): 3–35.

Királyfalvi, Béla. *The Aesthetics of György Lukács.* Princeton: Princeton University Press, 1975.

Kurrik, Marie. "The Novel's Subjectivity: Georg Lukács's *Theory of the Novel.*" *Salmagundi* No. 28 (Winter 1975): 104–24.

Lapointe, François H. *Georg Lukács and His Critics: An International Bibliography with Annotations (1910–1982).* Westport, CT: Greenwood Press, 1983.

Lichtheim, George. *Georg Lukács.* New York: Viking Press, 1970.

Löwy, Michael. *Georg Lukács: From Romanticism to Bolshevism.* Tr. Patrick Camiller. London: New Left Books, 1979.

McInnes, Neil. "Georg Lukács." *Survey* No. 72 (Summer 1972): 122–40.

Miles, David H. "Portrait of the Marxist as a Young Hegelian: Lukács's *Theory of the Novel.*" *PMLA* 94 (1979): 22–35.

Parkinson, G. H. R. *Georg Lukács.* London: Routledge & Kegan Paul, 1977.

———, ed. *Georg Lukács: The Man, His Work, and His Ideas.* London: Weidenfeld & Nicolson, 1970.

Shor, Ira Neil. "The Novel in History: Lukács and Zola." *Clio* 2 (1972): 19–41.

Wellek, René. *Four Critics: Croce, Valéry, Lukács, and Ingarden.* Seattle: University of Washington Press, 1981.

EZRA POUND

Ackroyd, Peter. *Ezra Pound and His World.* New York: Scribner's, 1980.

Bell, Ian F. A. *Critic as Scientist: The Modernist Poetics of Ezra Pound.* London: Methuen, 1981.

Boselli, Mario. "Some Observations on the Critical Essays of Ezra Pound." In *Italian Images of Ezra Pound,* eds. Angela Jung and Guido Palandri. Taipei: Mei Ya, 1979, pp. 77–86.

Carter, Thomas H. "Ezra Pound the Critic." *Kenyon Review* 16 (1954): 490–96.

Davie, Donald. *Ezra Pound.* New York: Viking Press, 1976.
Ford, Ford Madox. "Pound and *How To Read.*" *New Review* 11 (1932): 39–45.
Fraser, G. S. *Pound.* Edinburgh: Oliver & Boyd, 1960.
Goodwin, K. L. *The Influence of Ezra Pound.* London: Oxford University Press, 1966.
Harris, Natalie Beth. "A Map of Ezra Pound's Literary Criticism." *Southern Review* 19 (1983): 548–72.
Healy, J. V. "The Pound Problem." *Poetry* 57 (1940): 200–214.
Kenner, Hugh. "Pound and the Provision of Measures." *Poetry* 83 (1953): 29–35.
Knapp, James F. *Ezra Pound.* Boston: Twayne, 1979.
Leavis, F. R. *How to Teach Reading: A Primer for Ezra Pound.* Cambridge: Heffer, 1932.
McLuhan, Marshall. "Pound's Critical Prose." In *An Examination of Ezra Pound,* ed. Peter Russell. New York: New Directions, 1950, pp. 165–71.
Palmer, Leslie H. "Matthew Arnold and Ezra Pound's *ABC of Reading.*" *Paideuma* 2 (1973): 193–98.
Stock, Noel. *The Life of Ezra Pound.* London: Routledge & Kegan Paul, 1970.
Wellek, René. "Ezra Pound's Literary Criticism." *University of Denver Quarterly* 11 (1976): 1–20.

BORIS EIKHENBAUM

Bennett, Tony. *Formalism and Marxism.* London: Methuen, 1979.
Erlich, Viktor. *Russian Formalism: History—Doctrine.* The Hague: Mouton, 1955.
Jakobson, Roman. "Boris Viktorovič Ejchenbaum." *International Journal of Slavic Linguistics and Poetics* 6 (1963): 160–67.
Medvedev, P. N., and M. M. Bakhtin. *The Formal Method in Literary Scholarship.* Tr. Albert J. White. Baltimore: Johns Hopkins University Press, 1978.
Steiner, Peter. *Russian Formalism: A Metapoetics.* Ithaca, NY: Cornell University Press, 1984.
Thompson, Ewa M. *Russian Formalism and Anglo-American New Criticism: A Comparative Study.* The Hague: Mouton, 1971.
Todorov, Tzvetan, ed. *Théorie de la littérature.* Paris: Seuil, 1966.

TRISTAN TZARA

Abastado, Claude. "Le *Manifeste Dada 1918:* Un Tourniquet." *Littérature* 39 (1980): 39–46.
Browning, Gordon Frederick. *Tristan Tzara: The Genesis of the Dada Poem; or, From Dada to Aa.* Stuttgart: Akademischer Verlag Heinz, 1979.
Caldwell, Ruth L. "From Chemical Explosion to Simple Fruits: Nature in the Poetry of Tristan Tzara." *Perspectives on Contemporary Literature* 5 (1979): 18–23.
De Pisis, Filippo. *Futurismo, dadaismo, metafisica e due carteggi con Tristan Tzara e Primo Conti.* Milan: Libri Scheiwiller, 1981.
Harwood, Lee. *Tristan Tzara: A Bibliography.* London: Aloes Books, 1974.
Ko, Won. *Buddhist Elements in Dada: A Comparison of Tristan Tzara, Takahashi Shinkichi, and Their Fellow Poets.* New York: New York University Press, 1977.
Peterson, Elmer. *Tristan Tzara: Dada and Surrational Thought.* New Brunswick, NJ: Rutgers University Press, 1971.

Russo, Adelaide M. "Picking Up the Pieces? Tzara's Explosive Text and the Surrealist Strategy." *Miorita* 9 (1985): 1–18.

Tison-Braun, Micheline. *Tristan Tzara, inventeur de l'homme nouveau*. Paris: Nizet, 1977.

LEO SPITZER

Green, Geoffrey. *Literary Criticism and the Structures of History: Erich Auerbach and Leo Spitzer*. Lincoln: University of Nebraska Press, 1982.

Krieger, Murray. "The Play and Place of Criticism." In *The Play and Place of Criticism*. Baltimore: Johns Hopkins University Press, 1967, pp. 3–16.

Leao, Angela Vaz. *Sobre a estilistica de Spitzer*. Belo Horizonte: Universidade de Minas Gerais, 1960.

Levin, Harry. "Two Romanisten in America: Spitzer and Auerbach." In *The Intellectual Migration, Europe to America 1830–1960,* eds. Donald Fleming and Bernard Bailyn. Cambridge, MA: Harvard University Press, 1969, pp. 463–84.

Morris, Wesley. "The Meeting of Opposites, II." In *Toward a New Historicism*. Princeton: Princeton University Press, 1972, pp. 167–86.

Nykl, A. R. *Speculum* 20 (1945): 252–58.

Panichas, G. A. *Modern Language Journal* 48 (1964): 464–65.

T. S. ELIOT

Ackroyd, Peter. *T. S. Eliot: A Life*. New York: Simon & Schuster, 1984.

Allan, D. Mowbray. *T. S. Eliot's Impersonal Theory of Poetry*. Lewisburg, PA: Bucknell University Press, 1973.

Austin, Allen. *T. S. Eliot: The Literary and Social Criticism*. Bloomington: Indiana University Press, 1971.

Bantock, G. H. *T. S. Eliot and Education*. New York: Random House, 1976.

Bergonzi, Bernard. *T. S. Eliot*. New York: Macmillan, 1972.

Brombert, Victor H. *The Criticism of T. S. Eliot: Problems of an "Impersonal Theory" of Poetry*. New Haven: Yale University Press, 1949.

Freed, Lewis. *T. S. Eliot: The Critic as Philosopher*. West Lafayette, IN: Purdue University Press, 1979.

Frye, Northrop. *T. S. Eliot*. Edinburgh: Oliver & Boyd, 1963.

Gray, Piers. *T. S. Eliot's Intellectual and Poetic Development 1909–1922*. Brighton: Harvester Press, 1981.

Headings, Philip R. *T. S. Eliot*. New York: Twayne, 1964.

Hyman, Stanley Edgar. "Poetry and Criticism: T. S. Eliot." *American Scholar* 30 (1961): 43–55.

Jay, Gregory S. *T. S. Eliot and the Poetics of Literary History*. Baton Rouge: Louisiana State University Press, 1983.

Kirk, Russell. *Eliot and His Age*. New York: Random House, 1971.

Kojecky, Roger. *T. S. Eliot's Social Criticism*. New York: Farrar, Straus & Giroux, 1972.

Leavis, F. R. "T. S. Eliot's Stature as a Critic: A Revaluation." *Commentary* 26 (1958): 399–410.

Lee, Brian. *Theory and Personality: The Significance of T. S. Eliot's Criticism*. Atlantic Highlands, NJ: Humanities Press, 1979.

Lobb, Edward. *T. S. Eliot and the Romantic Critical Tradition*. London: Routledge & Kegan Paul, 1981.

Lucy, Seán. *T. S. Eliot and the Idea of Tradition*. New York: Barnes & Noble, 1960.

Margolis, John D. *T. S. Eliot's Intellectual Development 1922–1939*. Chicago: University of Chicago Press, 1972.

Newton-De Molina, David, ed. *The Literary Criticism of T. S. Eliot: New Essays*. London: Athlone Press, 1977.

Noonan, James. "Poetry and Belief in the Criticism of T. S. Eliot." *Queen's Quarterly* 79 (1972): 386–96.

Praz, Mario. "T. S. Eliot as a Critic." *Sewanee Review* 74 (1966): 256–71.

Rama, Murthy. *T. S. Eliot: Critic*. Allahabad: Kitab Mahal, 1968.

Schneider, Elisabeth. *T. S. Eliot: The Pattern in the Carpet*. Berkeley: University of California Press, 1975.

Smith, Carol H. *T. S. Eliot's Dramatic Theory and Practice*. Princeton: Princeton University Press, 1963.

Smith, James. "Notes on the Criticism of T. S. Eliot." *Essays in Criticism* 22 (1972): 333–61.

Warren, Austin. "Eliot's Literary Criticism." *Sewanee Review* 74 (1966): 272–91.

Wellek, René. "The Criticism of T. S. Eliot." *Sewanee Review* 64 (1956): 398–443.

WALTER BENJAMIN

Adorno, Theodor W., et al. *Über Walter Benjamin*. Frankfurt am Main: Suhrkamp, 1968.

Arendt, Hannah. *Walter Benjamin, Bertolt Brecht: Zwei Essays*. Munich: Piper, 1971.

Buck-Morris, Susan. *The Origin of Negative Dialectics: Theodor W. Adorno, Walter Benjamin and the Frankfurt Institute*. New York: Free Press, 1977.

Bullock, Marcus Paul. *Romanticism and Marxism: The Philosophical Development of Literary Theory and Literary History in Walter Benjamin and Friedrich Schlegel*. New York: Peter Lang, 1987.

Bulthaup, Peter, ed. *Materialen zu Benjamins Thesen* Über den Begriff des Geschichte. Frankfurt am Main: Suhrkamp, 1975.

Eagleton, Terry. *Walter Benjamin; or, Towards a Revolutionary Criticism*. London: Verso, 1981.

Fuld, Werner. *Walter Benjamin: Zwischen den Stühlen: Eine Biographie*. Munich: Hanser, 1979.

Gunther, Henning. *Walter Benjamin und der humane Marxismus*. Olten: Walter-Verlag, 1974.

Hering, Christoph. *Die Reknostruktion der Revolution: Walter Benjamins messianischer Materialismus in dem Thesen* Über den Begriff der Geschichte. Frankfurt am Main: Peter Lang, 1983.

Moroncini, Bruno. *Walter Benjamin e la moralità del moderno*. Naples: Guida, 1984.

Naeher, Jurgen. *Walter Benjamins Allegorie-Begriff als Modell*. Stuttgart: Klett-Cotta, 1977.

Pasqualotto, Giangiorgio. *Avanguardia e tecnologia: Walter Benjamin, Max Bense e i problemi dell'estetica tecnologica*. Rome: Officina, 1971.

Roberts, Julian. *Walter Benjamin*. London: Macmillan, 1982.

Rutigliano, Enzo. *Lo sguardo dell'angelo su Walter Benjamin*. Bari: Dedalo Libri, 1981.

Salzinger, Helmut. *Swinging Benjamin*. Frankfurt am Main: Fischer-Taschenbuch-Verlag, 1973.

Scholem, Gershom. *Walter Benjamin: The Story of a Friendship*. Tr. Harvey Zohn. Philadelphia: Jewish Publication Society of America, 1981.

Tiedemann, Rolf. *Studien zur Philosophie Walter Benjamins*. Frankfurt am Main: Europaische Verlagsanstalt, 1965.

Unseld, Siegfried, ed. *Zur Aktualität Walter Benjamins*. Frankfurt am Main: Suhrkamp, 1972.

Wiesenthal, Lisolette. *Zur Wissenschaftstheorie Walter Benjamins*. Frankfurt am Main: Athenäum, 1973.

Witte, Bernd. *Walter Benjamin, der Intellektuelle als Kritiker*. Stuttgart: Metzler, 1976.

Wolin, Richard. *Walter Benjamin: An Aesthetic of Redemption*. New York: Columbia University Press, 1982.

ERICH AUERBACH

Bahti, Timothy. "Vico, Auerbach, and Literary History." In *Vico: Past and Present,* ed. Giorgio Tagliacozzo. Atlantic Highlands, NJ: Humanities Press, 1981, Volume 2, pp. 97–114.

Breslin, Charles. "Philosophy or Philology: Auerbach and Aesthetic Historicism." *Journal of the History of Ideas* 22 (1961): 369–81.

Ethier-Blais, Jean. "*Mimesis:* Réalisme et transcendance." *Etudes Françaises* 6 (1970): 7–24.

Evans, Arthur. "Erich Auerbach as European Critic." *Romance Philology* 25 (1971–72): 192–215.

Fleischmann, Wolfgang Bernard. "Erich Auerbach's Critical Theory and Practice: An Assessment." *Modern Language Notes* 81 (1966): 535–41.

Green, Geoffrey. *Literary Criticism and the Structures of History: Erich Auerbach and Leo Spitzer*. Lincoln: University of Nebraska Press, 1982.

Gronau, Klaus. *Literarische Form und gesellschaftliche Entwicklung: Erich Auerbachs Beitrag zur Theorie und Methodologie der Literaturgeschichte*. Konigstein: Forum Academicum, 1979.

Levin, Harry. "Two Romanisten in America: Spitzer and Auerbach." In *The Intellectual Migration, Europe and America 1930–1960,* eds. Donald Fleming and Bernard Bailyn. Cambridge, MA: Harvard University Press, 1969, pp. 463–84.

Trapp, J. B. "Erich Auerbach." *Encounter* 26 (April 1966): 79–82.

Wellek, René. "Auerbach and Vico." In *Vico: Past and Present,* ed. Giorgio Tagliacozzo. Atlantic Highlands, NJ: Humanities Press, 1981, Volume 2, pp. 85–96.

I. A. RICHARDS

Brooks, Cleanth. "I. A. Richards and *Practical Criticism*." *Sewanee Review* 89 (1981): 586–95.

Brower, Reuben; Vendler, Helen; and Hollander, John, eds. *I. A. Richards: Essays in His Honor*. New York: Oxford University Press, 1973.

Butler, Christopher. "I. A. Richards and the Fortunes of Critical Theory." *Essays in Criticism* 30 (1980): 191–204.

Cianci, Giovanni. *La critica letteraria di I. A. Richards, W. Empson, F. R. Leavis*. Bari: Adriatica, 1970.

Corts, Paul R. "I. A. Richards on Rhetoric and Criticism." *Southern Speech Journal* 36 (1970): 115–26.

Dickie, George. "I. A. Richards' Phantom Double." *British Journal of Aesthetics* 8 (1968): 54–59.

Foster, Richard. "The Romanticism of I. A. Richards." *ELH* 26 (1959): 91–101.

Glicksberg, Charles I. "I. A. Richards and the Science of Criticism." *Sewanee Review* 46 (1938): 520–33.

Graff, G. E. "The Later Richards and the New Criticism." *Criticism* 9 (1967): 229–42.

Hotopf, W. H. N. *Language, Thought and Comprehension: A Case Study of the Writings of I. A. Richards.* Bloomington: Indiana University Press, 1965.

Hunt, John Dixon. "I. A. Richards and the Advancement of Learning." *Critical Survey* 2 (1965): 84–88.

Karnani, Chetan. *Criticism, Aesthetics and Psychology: A Study of the Writings of I. A. Richards.* New Delhi: Arnold-Heinemann, 1977.

Levin, Harry. "I. A. Richards (1893–1979)." *New York Review of Books,* 6 December 1979, pp. 40–42.

McCallum, Pamela. *Literature and Method: Towards a Critique of I. A. Richards, T. S. Eliot, and F. R. Leavis.* Dublin: Gill & Macmillan, 1983.

Needham, John. *The Completest Mode: I. A. Richards and the Continuity of English Literary Criticism.* Edinburgh: Edinburgh University Press, 1982.

Rudolf, G. A. "The Aesthetic Field of I. A. Richards." *Journal of Aesthetics and Art Criticism* 14 (1956): 348–58.

Schiller, Jerome P. *I. A. Richards' Theory of Literature.* New Haven: Yale University Press, 1969.

Sibley, Francis M. "How I Read I. A. Richards." *American Scholar* 42 (1973): 318–29.

Wellek, René. "On Rereading I. A. Richards." *Southern Review* 3 (1967): 533–54.

VICTOR SHKLOVSKY

Erlich, Victor. "A Thinking Stone." *Modern Occasions,* Fall 1970, pp. 143–47.

Flaker, Aleksandar. "Shklovsky and the History of Literature: A Footnote to Erlich's *Russian Formalism.*" In *Russian Formalism: A Retrospective Glance,* eds. Robert Louis Jackson and Stephen Rudy. New Haven: Yale Center for International and Area Studies, 1985, pp. 57–67.

Harper, K. "A Russian Critic and *Tristram Shandy.*" *Modern Philology* 2 (1954): 92–99.

Hodgson, Peter. "Victor Shklovsky and the Formalist Legacy: Imitation/Stylization in Narrative Fiction." In *Russian Formalism: A Retrospective Glance,* eds. Robert Louis Jackson and Stephen Rudy. New Haven: Yale Center for International and Area Studies, 1985, pp. 195–212.

Maryamov, Yuri. "'Man's Thinking Is Bold': An Interview with Victor Shklovsky." *Soviet Literature* 9 (1985): 134–39.

Ognev, Vladimir. "Viktor Shklovskii Teaches Us to Think." *Soviet Studies in Literature* 20 (1983–84): 3–20.

Sheldon, Richard. "The Formalist Poetics of Viktor Shklovsky." *Russian Literature Triquarterly* 2 (1972): 351–71.

——. *Viktor Shklovsky: An International Bibliography of Works by and about Him.* Ann Arbor, MI: Ardis, 1977.

——. "Viktor Shklovsky and the Device of Ostensible Surrender." *Slavic Review* 34 (1975): 86–108.

Sherwood, Richard. "Viktor Shklovsky and the Development of Early Formalist Theory on Prose Literature." In *Russian Formalism*, eds. Stephen Bann and John E. Bowlt. Edinburgh: Scottish Academic Press, 1973, pp. 26–40.

Thompson, Ewa M. "Viktor Borisovich Shklovsky; or, Fish Turned Ichthyologist." *Books Abroad* 47 (1973): 79–82.

ANDRÉ BRETON

Alexandrian, Sarane. *André Breton par lui-même*. Paris: Seuil, 1971.

Audoin, Philippe. *Breton*. Paris: Gallimard, 1970.

Balakian, Anna. *André Breton: Magus of Surrealism*. New York: Oxford University Press, 1971.

Bonnet, Marguerite. *André Breton: Naissance de l'aventure surréaliste*. Paris: Corti, 1975.

Carrouges, Michel. *André Breton et les données fondamentales du surréalisme*. Paris: Gallimard, 1950.

Caws, Mary Ann. *André Breton*. New York: Twayne, 1971.

Crastre, Victor. *André Breton*. Paris: Arcanes, 1952.

Eigeldinger, Marc, ed. *André Breton: Essais et témoignages*. Neuchâtel: La Baconniere, 1949, 1970.

Fowlie, Wallace. "André Breton." In *Mid-Century French Poets*. New York: Grove Press, 1955, pp. 145–69.

Gershman, Herbert S. "Valéry and Breton." *Yale French Studies* 44 (1970): 199–207.

Lavergne, Philippe. *André Breton et le mythe*. Paris: Corti, 1985.

Legrand, Gerard. *André Breton et son temps*. Paris: Soleil Noir, 1976.

——. *Breton*. Paris: Belfond, 1977.

Lynes, Carlos. "Surrealism and the Novel: Breton's *Nadja*." *French Studies* 20 (1966): 366–87.

Matthews, J. H. *André Breton*. New York: Columbia University Press, 1967.

——. *André Breton: Sketch for an Early Portrait*. Amsterdam: J. Benjamins, 1986.

Mauriac, Claude. *André Breton: Essai*. Paris: Editions de Flore, 1949.

Michelson, Annette. "Breton's Aesthetics." *Artforum*, September 1966, pp. 72–77.

Mourier-Casile, Pascaline. *André Breton, explorateur de la Mère-Moire*. Paris: Presses Universitaires de France, 1986.

Paz, Octavio. "André Breton or the Search for the Beginning." *Studies in the Twentieth Century* 3 (1969): 41–50.

Plouvier, Paule. *Poétique de l'amour chez André Breton*. Paris: Corti, 1983.

Rosemont, Franklin. *André Breton and the First Principles of Surrealism*. London: Pluto Press, 1978.

Sheringham, Michael. *André Breton: A Bibliography*. London: Grant & Cutler, 1972.

Vielwahr, André. *Sous le signe des contradictions: André Breton de 1913 à 1924*. Paris: Nizet, 1980.

Virmaux, Alain, and Odette Virmaux. *André Breton, qui êtes-vous?* Lyon: La Manufacture, 1987.

BERTOLT BRECHT

Arendt, Hannah. *Walter Benjamin, Bertolt Brecht: Zwei Essays*. Munich: Piper, 1971.

Benjamin, Walter. *Understanding Brecht*. Tr. Anna Bostock. London: NLB, 1973.

Bentley, Eric. *The Brecht Commentaries 1943–1980*. New York: Grove Press, 1981.

Dickson, Keith A. *Towards Utopia: A Study of Brecht*. Oxford: Clarendon Press, 1978.

Esslin, Martin. *Bertolt Brecht*. New York: Columbia University Press, 1969.

––––––. *Brecht: A Choice of Evils*. London: Methuen, 1959.

Ewen, Frederic. *Bertolt Brecht: His Life, His Art, and His Times*. New York: Citadel Press, 1967.

Fuegi, John. *The Essential Brecht*. Los Angeles: Hennessey & Ingalls, 1972.

Gray, Ronald D. *Brecht*. Edinburgh: Oliver & Boyd, 1961.

Haas, Willy. *Bert Brecht*. Trs. Max Knight and Joseph Fabry. New York: Ungar, 1970.

Hayman, Ronald. *Brecht: A Biography*. New York: Oxford University Press, 1983.

Hill, Claude. *Bertolt Brecht*. New York: Twayne, 1975.

Lellis, George. *Bertolt Brecht,* Cahier du cinema *and Contemporary Film Theory*. Ann Arbor, MI: UMI Research Press, 1982.

Ley, Ralph. *Brecht as Thinker: Studies in Literary Marxism and Existentialism*. Normal, IL: Applied Literature Press, 1979.

Lyon, James K. *Bertolt Brecht in America*. Princeton: Princeton University Press, 1980.

Lyons, Charles R. *Bertolt Brecht: The Despair and the Polemic*. Carbondale: Southern Illinois University Press, 1968.

Needle, Jan, and Peter Thomas. *Brecht*. Chicago: University of Chicago Press, 1981.

Pike, David. *Lukács and Brecht*. Chapel Hill: University of North Carolina Press, 1985.

Schoeps, Karl H. *Bertolt Brecht*. New York: Ungar, 1977.

Speirs, Ronald. *Bertolt Brecht*. New York: St. Martin's Press, 1987.

Walsh, Martin. *The Brechtian Aspect of Radical Cinema*. Ed. Keith M. Griffiths. London: BFI, 1981.

Weideli, Walter. *The Art of Bertolt Brecht*. Tr. Daniel Russell. New York: New York University Press, 1963.

Willett, John. *Brecht in Context: Comparative Approaches*. London: Methuen, 1983.

ACKNOWLEDGMENTS

GEORGE BERNARD SHAW

"The Sanity of Art" is taken from *Major Critical Essays*, Volume 19 of *The Works of Bernard Shaw*, published by Constable & Co. (London), 1930. Reprinted with permission of The Society of Authors on behalf of the Bernard Shaw Estate.

SIGMUND FREUD

"The Relation of the Poet to Day-Dreaming," "The Theme of the Three Caskets," "Humour," and "Dostoevsky and Parricide" are taken from *Character and Culture*, edited by Philip Rieff, copyright © 1963 by Macmillan Publishing Co. Reprinted with permission.

W. B. YEATS

"The Philosophy of Shelley's Poetry" and "The Symbolism of Poetry" are taken from *Ideas of Good and Evil*, published by Macmillan & Co. (London and New York), 1903. "Anima Hominis" is taken from *Per Amica Silentia Lunae*, copyright © 1918 by Macmillan Publishing Co., renewed 1946 by Bertha Georgie Yeats. Reprinted with permission of Macmillan Publishing Co.

BENEDETTO CROCE

"Taste and the Reproduction of Art" is taken from *Aesthetic as Science of Expression and General Linguistics*, translated by Douglas Ainslee, published by Macmillan & Co. (London and New York), 1909. "Folk Poetry and Poets' Poetry" is taken from *Philosophy, Poetry, History: An Anthology of Essays*, edited by Cecil Sprigge, copyright © 1966 by Oxford University Press. Reprinted with permission.

PAUL VALÉRY

"Poetry and Abstract Thought" is taken from *The Art of Poetry*, translated by Denise Folliot, copyright © 1958 by the Bollingen Foundation.

WALLACE STEVENS

"The Figure of the Youth as Virile Poet" is taken from *The Necessary Angel: Essays on Reality and the Imagination*, copyright © 1944 by Wallace Stevens. Reprinted with permission of Alfred A. Knopf, Inc. "Two or Three Ideas" is taken from *Opus Posthumous*, copyright © 1957 by Elsie Stevens and Holly Stevens. Reprinted with permission of Alfred A. Knopf, Inc.

BORIS EIKHENBAUM

"The Theory of the Formal Method" is taken from *Russian Formalist Criticism: Four Essays*, translated by Lee T. Lemon and Marion J. Reis, copyright © 1965 by the University of Nebraska Press. Reprinted with permission.

TRISTAN TZARA

"A Dada Manifesto," "A Proclamation without Pretention," and "A Note on Poetry" are taken from *Tristan Tzara: Approximate Man and Other Writings*, translated by Mary Ann Caws, copyright © 1973 by Wayne State University Press. Reprinted with permission.

LEO SPITZER

"Linguistics and Literary History" is taken from *Linguistics and Literary History: Essays in Stylistics*, copyright © 1948, renewed 1976 by Princeton University Press. Reprinted with permission of Princeton University Press.

T. S. ELIOT

"Tradition and the Individual Talent," "The Function of Criticism," "The Metaphysical Poets," and "Baudelaire" are taken from *Selected Essays*, copyright © 1950 by Harcourt, Brace & Co. Reprinted with permission of Harcourt Brace Jovanovich, Inc., and Faber & Faber Ltd. "The Criticize the Critic" is taken from *To Criticize the Critic*, copyright © 1965 by Valerie Eliot. Reprinted with permission of Farrar, Straus & Giroux, Inc., and Faber & Faber Ltd.

WALTER BENJAMIN

"The Storyteller" and "The Work of Art in the Age of Mechanical Reproduction" are taken from *Illuminations*, edited by Hannah Arendt, translated by Harry Zohn, copyright © 1968 by Harcourt, Brace & World, Inc. Reprinted with permission.

ERICH AUERBACH

"Figura" is taken from *Scenes from the Drama of European Literature*, translated by Ralph Monnheim, copyright © 1959 by Meridian Books, Inc.

I. A. RICHARDS

Excerpts from *Practical Criticism*, copyright © 1929 by Kegan Paul, Trench, Trübner & Co. Reprinted with permission of Routledge & Kegan Paul and Harcourt Brace Jovanovich, Inc.

VICTOR SHKLOVSKY

"On *Tristram Shandy*" is taken from *Russian Formalist Criticism: Four Essays,* translated by Lee T. Lemon and Marion J. Reis, copyright © 1965 by the University of Nebraska Press. Reprinted with permission.

ANDRÉ BRETON

"A Manifesto of Surrealism" is taken from *Manifestoes of Surrealism,* translated by Richard Seaver and Helen R. Lore, copyright © 1962 by The University of Michigan. Reprinted with permission.

BERTOLT BRECHT

"Shouldn't We Abolish Aesthetics?" and "A Short Organum for the Theatre" are taken from *Brecht on Theatre,* translated by John Willett, copyright © 1964 by John Willett. Reprinted with permission of Hill & Wang, a division of Farrar, Straus & Giroux, Inc.